"When picking a doctor, you trust you'll find someone who will take care of you physically and mentally. In Dr. Levy I have the best of both worlds. My ability to overcome pain and injury is largely due to the care I get from Dr. Levy."

Lawrence Taylor
New York Giants

"Doc Levy is a helluva doctor and a great technician. He has great sensitivity and knows how to take care of people in a nice way. He is someone I would always go to for any kind of sports injury."

Lou Carnesecca
Former Head Coach
St. John's University and New Jersey Nets

"The first thing I did when I was coach of the Brooklyn Dodgers semi-pro football team was to hire Doc Levy. When I became the Giants director of operations, we revamped our medical staff and brought him in as the lead physician. Doc knows how and why sports injuries happen, and he certainly got the players back on the field as soon as possible without jeopardizing their health. He's a sensitive judge of a player as a person, not just a commodity."

Andy Robustelli
Former Director of Operations
New York Giants

"Doc Levy was a leader of his profession in the 1960s and 1970s and continues to be the best in his field. He was doing sports medicine when no one knew what sports medicine was. Because he has a full understanding of it, I continue to call him for private consultations."

Charlie Theokus
Athletic Director
Temple University

Sports Injury Handbook

Professional Advice for Amateur Athletes

Allan M. Levy, MD
Mark L. Fuerst

John Wiley & Sons, Inc.

New York • Chichester • Brisbane • Toronto • Singapore

Illustrations by Aher/Donnell Studios

In recognition of the importance of preserving what has been written, it is a policy of John Wiley & Sons, Inc., to have books of enduring value published in the United States printed on acid-free paper, and we exert our best efforts to that end.

This publication is designed to provide accurate and authoritative information in regard to the subject matter covered. It is sold with the understanding that the publisher and authors are not engaged in rendering medical or other professional service. If medical advice or other expert assistance is required, the services of a competent professional person should be sought.

Library of Congress Cataloging-in-Publication Data
Levy, Allan M.
    Sports injury handbook : professional advice for amateur
  athletes / by Allan M. Levy and Mark L. Fuerst.
        p.   cm.
    Includes index.
    ISBN 0-471-54737-9 (pbk. : alk. paper):
    1. Sports—Accidents and injuries—Treatment.   2. Sports—
  Accidents and injuries—Prevention.   I. Fuerst, Mark.   II. Title.
  RD97.L48 1993
  617.1'027—dc20   92–29435

Printed in the United States of America
10 9

Contents

PART THREE
What to Know from Head to Toe **47**

PART FOUR
Sport-by-Sport Injuries **133**

PART FIVE
Sports Medicine for Everyone   *249*

Foreword

Dr. Allan Levy obviously enjoys working with athletes. He has a lifetime of knowledge about treating sports injuries to pass on to all athletes, amateur and professional alike.

In my years as head coach of the New York Giants, Doc Levy was the one doctor who handled the team's medical problems on a daily basis. Over the years with the Giants, he has become an integral part of the football team and has developed an ongoing, warm relationship with the players and coaching staff.

There's always some ache or pain bothering athletes, and Doc always seems to come up with ways to get players back in action quickly. I believe that the Giants' players lose far less time to injury than other players because of his dedication and the time he and the trainers devote to them, as well as their establishment of a good conditioning program.

To reach your athletic peak and become a winner, try taking Doc Levy's expert advice.

BILL PARCELLS

Preface

Stars such as the New York Giants' Lawrence Taylor, the New York Nets' Julius "Dr. J" Erving, and the New York Yankees' Jim Bouton represent just a portion of the athletes I see and treat. The vast majority are recreational athletes.

As more and more people have fit regular exercise into their lifestyles, sports-related injuries have increased dramatically. Researchers estimate that as many as 25 million weekend jocks and joggers seek medical attention each year.

I've written this book because I believe that recreational athletes deserve the same caliber of information on the subject of treating and preventing sports injuries that professional athletes receive.

Sports injuries are a fact of life. By the very nature of contact sports, people become injured. Even in noncontact sports, the repetition of body movements leads to overuse injuries. So recreational athletes need to know how to use first aid, when to see a doctor, what their symptoms mean, what treatments will work, and how to safely recover.

Recreational athletes should also know how to prevent unnecessary injuries. Athletes who play or work out without professional instruction need tips on how to perform to win without getting hurt. Athletes who don't understand the impor-

tance of warming up and warming down should know why these are the keys to a proper workout. The tennis player, for instance, who spends three minutes rallying with his partner before the usual Sunday game and can't figure out why he tears calf muscles the first time he rushes the net needs to discover that stretching is the single most effective method of preventing an injury; he also needs to learn the best exercises for his sport. The runner who rarely worked on leg strength and stride mechanics until after she suffered an injury needs the same general conditioning and strength-training techniques that elite runners use.

Whatever your age, sport, or level of conditioning and experience, this book is for you. It puts the best, most current sports medicine knowledge at your fingertips in an easy-to-use format.

HOW TO USE THIS BOOK

In **Part One**, I take you through the essential elements of a proper workout: warmup and stretching, then either conditioning or strength training, and finally warmdown and stretching again. I also provide sound advice on what foods to eat—and when—for peak performance.

The stretching program will increase your flexibility. Flexibility is particularly important for the middle-aged athlete who tries to swing golf clubs the first nice spring weekend or who goes on a weekend ski trip after the first snowfall. Returning to action after a long layoff puts you at high risk of an injury. Overstretching a joint or muscle may result in a sprain or muscle pull, causing many miserable Mondays after weekend sports.

The strength-training program will help you build muscles throughout the body.

In **Part Two,** I focus on the most common concerns of, and fundamental precautions for, today's recreational athletes, from heart health and steroid use to on-the-spot treatment of everyday problems.

Part Three provides a complete guide to sports injuries, organized by area of the body, from head to toe. You'll learn how to recognize and treat injuries for each body part and determine when it's safe to return to action. You'll also discover how to prevent reinjury using specific exercises and protective equipment. I give practical advice, not just theoretical applications. For example, I tell when a $4 foam pad may ease a runner's foot pain as well as, if not better than, a $200 custom-made shoe insert.

I also note when an amateur's injury is different from a professional's. A weekend tennis player or a high school pitcher with a sore shoulder may have stretched out the rotator cuff muscles across the top of the shoulder, and for these athletes, simple exercises can usually reduce the stress on the shoulder joint. Only a professional tennis player or major league pitcher is likely to need surgery for a rotator cuff problem.

Anyone, however, can learn the rehabilitation techniques that the professionals use. Amateur athletes may not have four hours a day to devote to rehabilitation as pros do, but the methods are the same. It's just a matter of degree.

At the beginning of each chapter in Part Three you'll see a box of Related Sports Chapters. This allows you to cross-reference a body part injury

to a specific sport. For example, if your knee is sore, you can begin by finding the cause of the soreness and how to treat it in Chapter 11, "The Knee." Then you can consult the Related Sports Chapters box for those sports that you participate in that are particularly implicated in injuries to this body part. If you are a runner, for example, you can consult "Running, Jogging, and Track and Field" (Chapter 25), for information about how to avoid knee and other running injuries.

Next to the name of each condition in Part Three you'll find a symbol. These symbols help you understand whether you can begin to self-treat the condition or whether you must see a doctor or go for emergency treatment. The conditions are coded in the following way:

The first-aid symbol indicates that you may be able to treat the condition on your own initially with some basic first aid, though you may have to see a doctor later. For example, if you badly sprain your ankle, you should immediately get off your feet and, using first aid, ice the ankle down. But then you should have the ankle x-rayed to make sure it isn't broken.

MD This symbol means that you need to see a doctor directly for treatment. Even though the injury may seem to be minor and not that painful, such as a scratched cornea, you need to have a doctor check whether the condition is serious and needs further medical attention.

EMERGENCY This symbol indicates an emergency situation—a condition, such as a broken leg, that needs immediate medical treatment in a hospital or emergency care facility.

These symbols also appear in Parts Four and Five.

Also look for a "Prevention" section at the end of some body part chapters. These sections provide information about how to prevent certain injuries.

Part Four covers injuries on a sport-by-sport basis. Organized alphabetically by major sport, the chapters include information on more than three dozen sports. The focus is on the areas of the body most likely to be injured in each sport. If you cross-train by playing more than one sport, you can learn how to continue exercising while you are recovering from an injury. I also show you how to prevent deconditioning with the right exercises, and point out where to find related exercises and treatments in a particular body part chapter. For example, the discussion of tennis elbow in Chapter 29, "Tennis and Other Racquet Sports," refers you to Chapter 8, "The Elbow," and Chapter 9, "The Wrist and Hand," for specific exercises to strengthen the elbow, forearm, and fingers. Following the tennis elbow section is a cross-reference to the pages on which you can find a more complete description of the condition.

Perhaps most important, I end each chapter in Part Four with a "How to Improve" section. Here you'll find a compilation of inside tips on avoiding injuries and improving your performance that is not available anywhere else.

Part Five offers additional information on special concerns for the female, child, and older athlete, as well as tips on how to locate a good sports doctor (it's not easy) and what type of doctor to see for particular sports injuries.

Acknowledgments

Special thanks are in order to those people who helped make this book possible:

Bob Fiorini, an old friend and my roommate on the road in the old days of football, who put together the strength-training program.

Dr. John McNerney, who taught me most of what I know about the biomechanics of the lower part of the body and about the use of orthotics.

Merle Best, our outstanding sports nutritionist, for her major contribution to the program.

Carmine Melignano, a friend of 30 years going back to the old football days, who not only gave us office space to work in but also filmed a great many of the exercises for the illustrations.

Ronnie Barnes and Mike Ryan of the Giants training staff and John Mancuso of the Giants video staff, for filming the rest of the exercises for the illustrations.

Our agent, Faith Hamlin of Sanford J. Greenburger Associates, Inc., for guiding us through what turned out to be a six-year labor of love.

Carole Hall, Patty Aitken, Marcia Samuels, and the rest of the John Wiley staff for their tactful editing and efficient production, and Jackie Aher for her skillfully produced illustrations.

To my wife, Gail, first for putting up with the hours I spent at the desk putting this together and also for being my main source of support. Over the years I have made career decisions that moved away from the safe, financially secure path. Her unfailing answer has been, "If that's what you really want, then go for it." —*AML*

To my wife, Margie, for being there to support me through the long hours of writing and organizing and for her steadfast faith in me and my abilities as a writer. Her sundry sports-related injuries have contributed to my interest in learning about how to prevent and treat these types of conditions. —*MLF*

Exercises

Part One

Preventing Injuries

Work Out to Win

Eat to Compete

1

Work Out to Win

Whether you jog or run, play a racquet sport or football, lift weights or ski, or participate in any other fitness activity, you owe it to yourself to work out.

I understand how tempting it is to just play your sport or to rush through the time you spend preparing to play. But when you don't work out properly, you risk muscle soreness, decreased performance, and injury. Every athlete needs to work out to win.

Do you know the best way to work out for your sport? If you are engaged in any fitness activity, you probably need a workout master plan. That's what this chapter offers you. The plan can be summarized in five simple steps:

- *One:* Warm up properly.
- *Two:* Take time to stretch.
- *Three:* Include conditioning or strengthening exercises.
- *Four:* Warm down gradually.
- *Five:* Stretch again.

You may be surprised to learn how many injuries can be prevented by following these steps. Some aspects of this information may seem familiar, but as you read it carefully and begin to incorporate it into your sports and fitness activities, you'll discover the difference it makes. This information is the basis for minimizing strains, sprains, tears, and other hidden hazards.

A physically fit athlete is more likely to be a successful athlete. The goal of the workout plan is to help you become a stronger, more fit athlete so that you can reach your peak performance.

If you follow this plan during the week, you will be at your best when it comes time to play your chosen sport. In fact, you should use the plan's basic concepts before you play (warm up and stretch) as well as after you play (warm down and stretch). These are the steps that winning athletes take. They can also help you to become a winner.

STEP ONE: WARM UP PROPERLY

Warmup means warming up muscle fibers by increasing your body temperature. This leads to a wide variety of beneficial physiological changes:

- The warmer muscle fibers get, the softer and more fluid they become. They are then able to stretch more easily and to contract more rapidly. The faster a muscle contracts, the stronger it is.

- The higher the temperature of muscle cells, the faster they are able to metabolize the oxygen and fuel they need.

- As muscles warm, the response to nerve impulses quickens, causing faster contraction and, therefore, a quicker response.

- Warming joints lubricates them, allowing them to move more freely with less energy expended. This protects the joints from excessive wear.

- Warmup gradually increases the heart rate and prevents abnormal heart rhythms. Sudden strenuous exercise can cause the heart to demand more oxygen than the circulatory system can provide, resulting in a strain on the heart. Studies show that warming up may help prevent the heart attacks that result from abnormal heart rhythms.

How to Warm Up

How do you go about achieving these benefits? Before playing a sport or exercising intensively, do light calisthenics, take a brisk walk, jog lightly, ride a stationary bicycle, or do any other easy exercise gradually until you get the heart pumping and thus increase blood flow to your muscles. The goal is to raise the body's temperature by about 2° F, which leads to warm, loose muscles and joints.

How do you know when your body temperature has gone up? Luckily, most recreational athletes don't need to carry a thermometer. The body has its own natural thermometer: When you break into a sweat, your body temperature has been elevated by about 2° F.

STEP TWO: TAKE TIME TO STRETCH

Recreational athletes tend to stretch first and then begin exercising. However, cold muscles do not stretch well and can pull if overstretched.

The jogger who gets out of bed in the morning, puts on her running suit, and lies on the cold ground is not stretching muscles. She is tearing them.

The best time to stretch is after the body has been warmed up. Stretching after warmup is more likely to lengthen muscles and improve the range of motion of muscles and joints.

This also applies to aerobic exercisers. If you are a dancer, long-distance runner, or swimmer, you need to warm up slowly, stop, and stretch before getting into your strenuous aerobic activity.

Preventing Injuries

Stretching is invaluable in preventing pulled or torn muscles. In the early 1970s, the Pittsburgh Steelers were the first professional football team to have its players emulate gymnasts by stretching regularly. The thought was that gymnasts, who are superflexible, did not pull muscles often. If football players could stretch their heavy muscles, maybe they too would be less likely to pull them.

The theory proved to be correct. Lengthening muscles led to fewer muscle pulls among football players. Within two years, every team was following the Steelers' example.

Professional basketball players were slower to learn the benefits of flexibility. But now, before any game begins, both teams shoot around and then show the fans an unusual sight: two dozen tremendously tall men lying down and stretching out on the court.

How to Stretch Properly

Bouncing, or ballistic stretching, can do more damage than not stretching at all. With each bounce, muscle fibers fire and shorten the muscle—the opposite of what you are trying to do. Bouncing actually reduces flexibility.

A static stretch, holding the muscle still for 10 to 20 seconds, is much better. The muscle responds by lengthening slowly.

Each stretch should be gradual and gentle. Try to stretch in a quiet area so that you can concentrate on stretching and not be tempted to rush into action. Imagine the muscle gently stretching, the blood pulsing into the muscle, and your body becoming more flexible.

Warmup and Warmdown Stretches

The following figures show the proper way to stretch various body parts. Do these stretches for 5 to 10 minutes before and after each workout.

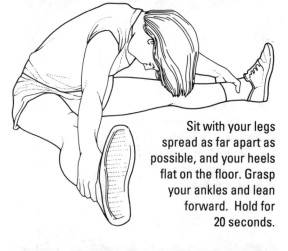

Sit with your legs spread as far apart as possible, and your heels flat on the floor. Grasp your ankles and lean forward. Hold for 20 seconds.

Forward Stretch

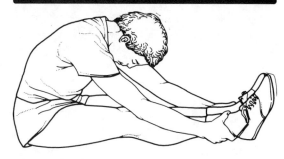

Sit with your legs together and extended straight out. Lean forward at the waist and grasp your ankles or feet. Hold for 20 seconds.

Knee Pull

Lie flat on your back and grasp one knee with interlaced fingers. Keeping your back flat, pull your knee toward your chest and hold for 20 seconds. Switch to the other knee and repeat the stretch.

Sit with your legs spread in a "V" position, heels on the floor. Lean to one side and grasp your ankle or foot. Hold for 20 seconds and then grasp the other ankle or foot for 20 more seconds.

Knee-over-Leg Stretch (Iliotibial Band Stretch)

While lying flat on your back, bend your right leg and bring it across your body to the left side. Hold the right knee down with the left hand and lean your shoulders and head back to the right. Hold for 20 seconds and then repeat on the other side.

While kneeling, lean forward with your arms stretched out in front of you until they touch the ground. your legs do not have to be totally folded underneath you. Hold for 20 seconds.

Side Stretch

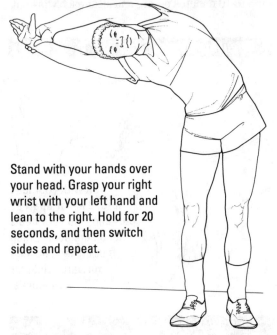

Stand with your hands over your head. Grasp your right wrist with your left hand and lean to the right. Hold for 20 seconds, and then switch sides and repeat.

Hurdler Stretch (sitting)

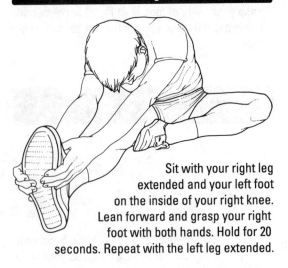

Sit with your right leg extended and your left foot on the inside of your right knee. Lean forward and grasp your right foot with both hands. Hold for 20 seconds. Repeat with the left leg extended.

Lunge Stretch

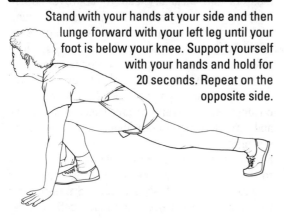

Stand with your hands at your side and then lunge forward with your left leg until your foot is below your knee. Support yourself with your hands and hold for 20 seconds. Repeat on the opposite side.

STEP THREE:
ADD CONDITIONING
OR STRENGTHENING
EXERCISES TO YOUR
ACTIVITY SCHEDULE

Once you have warmed up and stretched, you can begin your regular fitness activity. It may be your daily run, a tennis game, a roller blading session, or your weekly touch football game. Whatever it is, you will be prepared because you have warmed up and stretched. But you will be even better prepared to play if you have added conditioning or strengthening exercises to your mix of physical activities.

Remember, before you do either conditioning or strength training, you must warm up and stretch.

Gradual Conditioning:
The Walk-Jog Routine

If you have not been exercising regularly or are recovering from an injury, I recommend a grad-ual, progressive walk-jog routine after you have warmed up and stretched. Start by walking 100 paces and then jogging 100 paces, alternating this routine for 10 minutes each day. After several days of this routine, walk 10 fewer paces and jog 10 more paces. Continue to add 10 jogging paces and cut 10 walking paces every other day until you are jogging for a total of 10 minutes.

Then gradually increase your jogging speed until your heart rate is within the training range (see p. 35). Once you have achieved that, add 1 minute of jogging to your training time every other day until you have reached the 20-minute mark. Now you are training your heart to become stronger, which is called cardiovascular conditioning. You can stay at that level or increase the length of your workout gradually as you see fit.

Advanced Conditioning:
Interval Training

Once you have built up a cardiovascular base by training your heart, you can start to build speed. You do this through interval training. This consists of going hard for a short burst in the middle of a lengthy aerobic activity. For example, you might sprint during a jogging session, or if you are riding an exercise bike, pump the pedals fast for a minute or so as if you were going uphill, as some of the more sophisticated machines are programmed to do.

The following program shows you how to do interval training while running. If you are doing another type of aerobic activity, substitute short bursts (30 to 60 seconds) of intensive activity in the middle of your aerobic routine.

For joggers, I suggest you start by sprinting 50 yards after every mile you jog. Gradually increase the sprint distance to 100 yards per mile. Then increase the number of sprints—go 100 yards after every half mile. Once you feel comfortable at that level, sprint 200 yards for every half mile.

Now you are ready to take the final step. Jog one mile and then run a 200-yard sprint. Jog for 200 yards, or about 30 seconds, and then sprint another 200 yards. Continue jogging and sprinting 200 yards eight times to complete a mile. Then continue jogging to finish your workout.

This is the type of interval training the Giants players do. We have them sprint back and forth across the width of the field, resting 30 seconds between sprints. They do four sprints, each one faster than the previous one, to build up their speed.

Elite athletes often spend a full aerobic workout doing only speed work. The recreational athlete can simply put interval training in the middle of an aerobic workout and gradually increase the distance and speed. I suggest that you alternate doing long, slow aerobic workouts with interval-training aerobic workouts to build both cardiovascular conditioning and speed.

Strength Training

When Mike Gminski joined the Nets in 1979 as a skinny rookie center, he quickly learned that professional basketball is an extremely physical sport, particularly under the basket. At 6'11" and 210 pounds, Gminski found that stronger, though not necessarily taller, players were ripping rebounds out of his hands. After two frustrating years, he asked me to have Jack Spratt, the director of The Fitness and Back Institute, design an off-season strength-training program for him. Over the summer, Gminski put on 25 pounds of muscle, mostly in his upper body, and strengthened his arms and hands. He extended his career to more than a dozen years by continuing to work out with weights.

Most sports require overall strength training, but it should be adjusted to meet the specific requirements of a given sport. In football, linebackers and defensive backs, who make most of the tackles, need to improve upper-body as well as lower-body strength. Running backs and wide receivers should concentrate on lower-body strength to develop their legs. Similarly, runners, dancers, and soccer players need lower-body strength; baseball players, golfers, swimmers, and gymnasts need to work more on upper-body strength; and basketball players and wrestlers need both upper- and lower-body strength.

Tennis players require lower-body strength to develop their legs but need to pay particular attention to upper-body strength. Strengthening the shoulder helps prevent rotator cuff injuries. And if tennis players would strengthen their forearm and wrist muscles, they wouldn't get tennis elbow.

A Strength-Training Program

The following strength-training program gives you exercises for the chest, shoulders, back, legs, calves, thighs, abdominals, biceps, and triceps. Try to work different muscles on different days, and intersperse light and heavy repetitions. For example, follow a light "Day 1" program Monday and a light "Day 2" program Tuesday. Rest on Wednesday. Then on Thursday and Friday alternate heavy programs. Remember to warm up and stretch before even light repetitions, and to warm down and stretch at the end of each workout.

Start off using enough weight so that you can comfortably do 12 repetitions of an exercise on a light day. For example, if you can bench-press 80 pounds 20 times, then you need to move up to a slightly heavier weight, say 90 pounds. Once you have found the right weight to accomplish 12 repetitions of each exercise, move on to a heavy workout and use 20 percent more weight. To compensate for the greater weight, do fewer repetitions (see below).

Strength-Training Program

Exercise	Number of Sets	Number of Repetitions	
		Light Day	Heavy Day
Day 1			
Chest			
Bench press	3–4	12	6–8
Incline press	3	12	6–8
Flat fly	3	12	8–10
Shoulders			
Behind-the-neck press (Military)	3–4	12	6–8
Upright row	3	12	6–8
Lateral raise	3	12	8–10
Shoulder roll with barbell	2	12	8–10
Triceps			
Triceps extension	3–4	12	8–10
Kickback	3	12	8–10
Feet-elevated dip	3	12	8–10
Abdominals			
Decline sit-up	2–3	20	15
Standing crunch	2–3	20	15
Leg lift	2–3	20	15
Calves			
Standing raise	3	15–20	15–20
Day 2			
Legs			
Leg press	4	12	6–8
Squat	3	12	8–10
Leg extension	3	15	10
Leg curl	3	15	10
Thigh-burner	3	12–15	10–15
Back			
Wide-grip rear chin-up	3	12	8–10
Bent-over rowing	3	12	8–10
Biceps			
Arm curl (sitting)	3	12	8–10
Barbell curl	3	12	8–10
Abdominals, calves			
Same as Day 1			

Once you can very easily do 12 repetitions of an exercise on a light day, increase the amount of weight by 5 percent for both light and heavy workouts. You must be able to do 12 repetitions at the greater weight for a light workout, or else you should drop back down to the previous weight. If you follow this program regularly, each month you should be able to add about 5 percent more weight.

You will notice from the Strength-Training Program chart that exercises for both the abdominals and calves are included in each workout day. These muscles are difficult to build up and need to be exercised each day you work out. On a light day, you can do fewer abdominal exercises, but you need to work your calves virtually to exhaustion to strengthen them.

Strength-Training Exercises

Chest

Bench Press

Lie on your back on a bench with feet flat on the floor while holding a barbell at the top of your chest. Press the weight straight up, pause, and then return it back down. Barely touch your chest and start the next repetition.

Incline Press

Sit on an inclined bench and hold a barbell at chin level, palms out and elbows bent at 90°. Press the barbell overhead, pause, and then return to the starting position.

Flat Fly

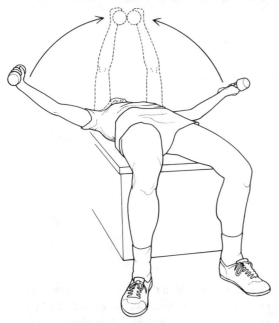

Lie on your back on a bench with feet flat on the floor while holding dumbbells out to the sides, arms bent slightly. Push the dumbbells overhead in a semicircular motion until they touch. Pause and then return to the starting position.

Shoulders

Behind-the-Neck Press (Military)

Sit holding a barbell behind your neck, with hands a few inches wider than shoulder width apart. Press the bar overhead, keeping your back straight. Pause and then lower the weight to the starting position.

Upright Row

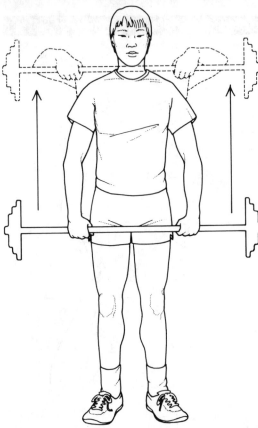

Grasp a barbell with palms down in front of you, about shoulder width apart. Bring the bar up beneath your chin, extending your elbows out to the sides. Pause and return to the starting position.

Lateral Raise

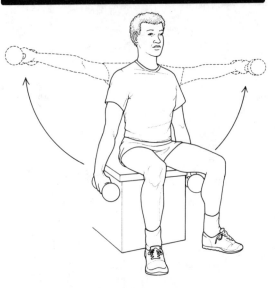

Sit on a bench with a dumbbell in each hand. With palms facing down, keep both arms straight and slowly raise them to shoulder level. Pause and then slowly lower your arms to the starting position.

Shoulder Roll with Barbell

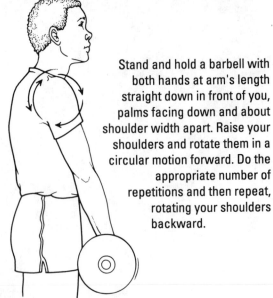

Stand and hold a barbell with both hands at arm's length straight down in front of you, palms facing down and about shoulder width apart. Raise your shoulders and rotate them in a circular motion forward. Do the appropriate number of repetitions and then repeat, rotating your shoulders backward.

Triceps

Triceps Extension

Stand holding a barbell overhead, palms facing up and elbows bent. Lower the bar behind you, keeping your upper arms stationary. Pause at the bottom and then bring the bar back up to the starting position.

Feet-Elevated Dip

Place a bench or platform about 4 feet in front of another, lower bench or platform. Put your feet up on the higher bench and support yourself with your hands at the edges of the lower bench. Starting from an arms-straight position, slowly lower yourself until your upper arms are parallel with the floor. Pause and then push back up to the starting position.

Kickback

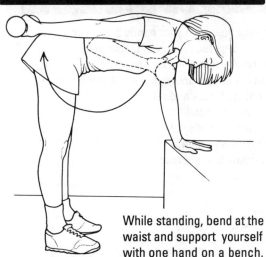

While standing, bend at the waist and support yourself with one hand on a bench. Grasp a dumbbell with the other hand and hold it with your lower arm perpendicular to the floor. Keeping your upper arm stationary, bring the weight straight back. Pause and return to the starting position.

Abdominals

Decline Sit-up

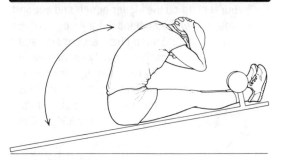

Lie on your back on an inclined board with your feet above your head and hooked under the pads. With hands behind your head and chin touching your chest, sit up until your elbows touch lightly. Lower yourself back to the starting position.

Standing Crunch

Stand with your right hand behind your head. Bring your right elbow down to meet your left knee while crunching your abdominal muscles. Pause and return to the starting position. Do the appropriate number of repetitions and then repeat with the opposite hand and knee.

Leg Lift

Sit on the floor with your hands behind you and your legs together straight out in front. Simultaneously push your body up so that your hands are supporting your weight and lift one leg straight up. Pause and return to the starting position. Do the appropriate number of repetitions and then repeat with the other leg.

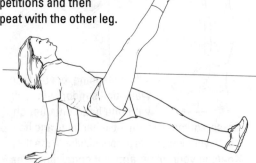

Legs

Leg Press

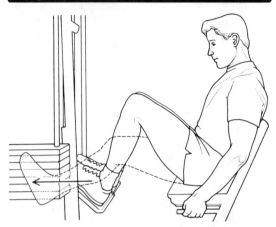

Sit on an inclined or regular leg press machine and press the weight until your legs are almost (but not quite) straight. Pause and then slowly lower the weight to the starting position.

Squat

Place a barbell on your upper back and, while standing, hold it with hands wider than shoulder width apart. Squat down until your thighs are parallel to the floor. Pause and then push back up to the starting position.

Leg Curl

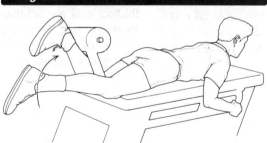

Lie face down on a bench with your head over the edge. Hold the bottom of the bench for support. Begin with your right leg straight and left leg bent at the knee, foot flexed. Lift the weight with your left thigh up as high as possible while keeping your right foot on the bench. Pause at the top and then lower your leg. Do the appropriate number of repetitions and then repeat with the other leg.

Leg Extension

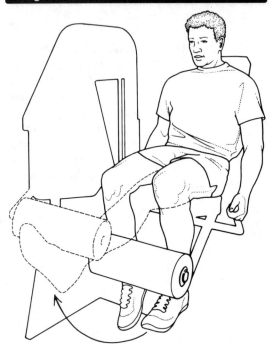

Sit on a bench or leg extension machine with your legs at a 90° angle and feet flexed (soles parallel to the floor). Hold the bottom of the bench for support and rapidly lift the weight with one leg to full extension (toes pointing up). Pause and bring your leg back down. Do the appropriate number of repetitions and then repeat with the other leg.

Thigh Burner

Stand on a step or thick telephone book with your left foot fully on the step in a 10 o'clock position and your right foot in a 2 o'clock position with the heel off the floor. Place your hands on your hips and slowly lower yourself down, keeping the right heel off the floor, until your left thigh is parallel to the floor. Almost all of your weight should be on your right thigh. Then push back up to the starting position. Do the appropriate number of repetitions and then repeat with the other leg.

Back

Wide-Grip Rear Chin-up

Bent-over Rowing

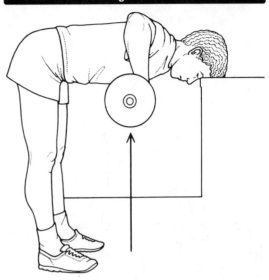

Place a barbell on the floor in front of a bench that is at waist level. Place your forehead on the bench for support, reach down, and grasp the barbell with both hands in a wide grip. Bring the barbell up until it touches your chest. Pause and then return it back down.

Biceps

Grasp a bar above your head with your grip wider than shoulder width, palms out. Bend your legs at the knees and cross your feet, and then pull yourself up until the bar touches the back of your neck. Pause and then lower yourself back down.

Arm Curl (sitting)

Sit at the end of a bench with dumbbells in both hands, palms up. Curl one dumbbell up until your forearm touches your biceps and then lower it. As you lower the dumbbell, curl the other one up. The two dumbbells should reach the starting and top positions simultaneously.

Barbell Curl

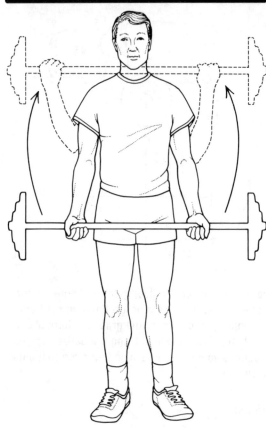

Stand and hold a barbell at arm's length with your hands shoulder width apart, palms out. Curl the bar up until it is under your chin. Pause and return to the starting position.

Calves

Standing Raise

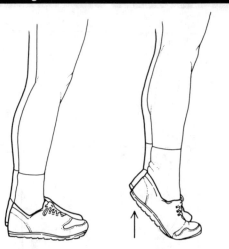

Place a barbell on top of your shoulders or position your shoulders under the bars of an upright calf machine. With only the balls of your feet on the floor or on the platform, raise up onto your toes, pause, and then return to the starting position.

Strength Training for Children

Traditionally, sports experts thought that strength training by children didn't accomplish anything. Both boys and girls supposedly lacked the boost of testosterone in their blood needed to add muscle bulk. Until a child had gone through puberty and developed secondary sexual characteristics, there was no point in strength training. Strength training was also thought to put undue stress on the growth plate in a young child's bones and stunt the child's growth. By speeding up maturation, strength training theoretically would prevent the bones from growing to their full, natural length.

Now we know that preteens, even though they lack the testosterone necessary to increase muscle bulk, can increase their strength without injuring themselves. A major study by the Sports Medicine section of the American Academy of

Orthopedic Surgeons proved that strength training does not injure the growth plate or stunt a child's growth. The American Academy of Pediatrics now accepts that children as young as 11 can begin a well-supervised weight-training program.

Unfortunately, all too frequently I see 6- and 7-year-olds being pushed into weight training by their overeager parents. Young children typically lack sufficient concentration and regimentation to do themselves much good. They often do themselves harm because they don't have the coordination to handle weights and are not mature enough to understand what they are doing or why. Any child interested in strength training needs to be closely supervised.

Starting at age 11, a child can begin lifting light weights with many repetitions in order to learn the proper techniques. More weight can be added as the child gets stronger and grows. With an adequately supervised program, there is room for great improvement in a child's strength without the threat of injury.

Strength Trainining for Women

Strength is just as important for women as for men. Girls and young women may be afraid of "bulking" up, but as long as their hormone levels and menstrual cycles are normal, their muscles will become stronger, not massively bigger, with training.

The big difference between a man's and a woman's strength is in the upper body. In fact, a woman's lower-body strength is, pound-for-pound, about the same as a man's. Women runners know that the longer the distance to be covered, the more closely they can compete with men because they don't have to propel as much weight. Currently, the top women marathoners finish about 20 minutes behind the men. As more women compete in ultramarathons of more than 100 miles, I predict that they will eventually have better times than men.

Women swimmers epitomize what strength training can do for performance. When the winning men's times in the 1956 Olympics are compared with the winning women's times recently, none of the men would have won a medal against the women. In the intervening years, improved tracks allow runners to go faster and fiberglass poles allow vaulters to go higher. But water is water, and pools haven't changed to allow swimmers to swim faster.

The main reason for the difference in the swimming times is better strength training. Girls and young women swimmers are among the leaders in strength training. Anyone who has seen a women's swim meet knows that these sleek athletes don't have bulky muscles from training with weights.

STEP FOUR: WARM DOWN GRADUALLY

I use the term "warm down" instead of "cool down" to indicate that this step is the reverse of the warmup. The body naturally cools down by itself at the end of activity. Warmdown is a 5- to 10-minute period of continued, mild activity after strenuous exercise.

A gradual warmdown allows your heart to slow down and adjust its blood flow without any pooling of blood in the muscles. Say you're a jogger who has just finished a run of several miles, and you stop suddenly. While you were running, the blood vessels to your muscles dilated to increase the blood supply of oxygen and fuel to the muscles. At the same time, your heart rate rose rapidly as the heart pumped more blood to the muscles. So the blood vessels to your legs are now wide open, and your heart is pumping blood down to your legs.

The body depends on a massaging action of contracting and relaxing muscles on the veins to return blood from the legs back up to the heart. When you suddenly stop, your heart rate remains high for a short while, and blood keeps pumping down to your legs. Without the massaging action of your leg muscles, there will be very little return flow to the heart, and large amounts of blood will pool in your legs. This may not leave enough blood to supply your brain or hard-working heart, and this can lead to fainting or even a heart attack, particularly if you are an older athlete.

But if you keep moving after running, or after any heavy exercise, the massaging action will pump blood back to the heart until your heart rate has returned to normal and your body's blood vessels have returned to normal size. Simply walking for 5 to 10 minutes is usually enough.

Warmdown also enhances the removal of lactic acid from the muscle, which reduces muscle soreness. Lactic acid builds up in muscles as a by-product of anaerobic metabolism after the body's primary energy source (glycogen) has been exhausted. Keeping the blood flowing through muscles during warm down washes lactic acid out of the muscles.

"Pumping Up"

During a strength-training workout, circulation to straining muscles increases markedly, causing the muscles to swell. This is the "pump" that weight lifters delight in, a sign that the muscles are working hard.

Strength training is basically an anaerobic exercise. If a large amount of blood pools in muscles, as it does during the "pump," then the lactic acid remains in the muscles.

The gradually decreasing exercise of the warm-down period massages out the pooled blood as the muscles contract. The blood moves back to the heart and takes the lactic acid with it. So

if you are doing an upper-body workout, use light dumbbells to keep your muscles moving as you warmdown. If you are doing a lower-body workout, simply walk around to keep the blood flowing in the muscles. If you are working the whole body, use dumbbells as you walk around.

STEP FIVE: STRETCH AGAIN

Stretching your muscles after the warmdown helps restore full range of motion and flexibility and reduces the likelihood of tearing a muscle during your next workout. A runner who warms up, stretches, goes for a four-mile run, warms down, and begins to stretch again may find that her toe-touch is 3 inches shorter than it was before her run. One good stretch for 15 to 20 seconds, and she can extend as far down as she did before.

Restretching the muscles after exercise can also prevent soreness and stiffness. Exercised muscles tend to shorten. If left that way, they will be stiff and sore the following day. Still-warm muscles can be restretched easily during warmdown to alleviate any annoying stiffness.

So after you have warmed down, go through the same stretching program you used after warming up. You will find that those 10 to 20 minutes of stretching after warmup and warmdown will go a long way toward preventing injuries, muscle soreness, and stiffness. This may be the most important time you spend during your entire workout.

2

Eat to Compete

Back in the late 1950s at Westwood High School in New Jersey, I concocted a mixture of orange juice, salt, and honey with my trainers, and we gave it to the players at halftime of football games. They loved it. The orange juice cut their thirst and replenished their potassium, the salt replaced the salt they lost in sweat, and the honey was a source of energy for the second half. If we'd only realized that we had invented Gatorade®, we'd be rich today.

Good nutrition can mean the difference between being physically fit and being physically fizzled. Eating right is imperative for championship athletes, but anyone can gain an edge by knowing the best foods to eat and when to eat them.

What makes for high-performance nutrition? Unfortunately, most dietary advice buzzed around locker rooms is exaggerated, inaccurate, or downright harmful. This chapter dispels some of these myths and offers solid principles on which to build a better, more competitive body:

- Eat a winning diet combination.
- Know what to eat and when.
- Know what to drink and when.

- Have your diet and body composition assessed.
- Gain muscle, lose excess fat.

THE WINNING DIET COMBINATION

To support training, performance, and health you should eat a balanced diet of low-fat, moderate-protein, high-carbohydrate foods and beverages; snack on high-carbohydrate, low-fat foods; and drink extra fluids.

How do you get a balanced diet? For breakfast, choose one item from each of the following categories: bread, cereal, and grains; fruits and juices; and skim or 1% milk or other low-fat dairy products. For lunch and dinner, choose one item each of bread, cereal, and grains; fruits and juices; skim milk; vegetables; fish, poultry, and lean meat; and fats and oils. For seconds and snacks, if you are still hungry or are trying to bulk up, choose from vegetables; fruits and juices; bread, cereal, and grains; or skim milk.

Within those categories, choose lower-fat items whenever possible:

- Have a slice of whole wheat bread, an English muffin, a bagel, or a nongranola cereal without nuts or seeds, such as Cheerios®, Wheaties®, or corn flakes.

- Eat fresh, whole fruits, which are better for weight loss because they contain more fiber than juices. Drink 100 percent fruit juice rather than juice drinks.

- Develop a taste for low-fat dairy products such as skim or 1% milk.

- Choose brightly colored vegetables and fresh or frozen vegetables without added fat because they have more vitamins and are more nutritious.

- Eat fish, seafood, and poultry more often than beef and other red meats. Eat lean cuts of well-trimmed meat with little marbling. Have poultry without the skin and nonbreaded and nonfried whenever possible.

- Use reduced-fat margarine, mayonnaise, and salad dressing. Use canola or olive oil and salad dressing without cream or cheese. Take in fat primarily in the form of fish, canola oil, or olive oil.

Making the change to a better diet sometimes comes as the result of pressure from other family members. Children are open to change and can provide an incentive for the rest of the family. A parent might not change the daily meals for herself or her spouse, but she often will for her child. When a child comes home and says, "Coach says I have to eat better," the parent usually becomes motivated to provide more nutritious meals. And the rest of the family ends up eating better, too.

At the professional level, where virtually all athletes are superior physically and genetically and have nearly similar abilities and training facilities, just a small change in nutrition can make a significant difference in performance. Although you may not have the physical gifts of a professional, good nutrition can help you reach your athletic potential.

Emphasize Carbohydrates

In one research study, doctors put volunteers on a normal diet composed of 50 percent carbohydrates, 34 percent fats, and 16 percent proteins. The maximum amount of time their muscles could work continuously was 114 minutes. On a noncarbohydrate diet composed of 46 percent fats and 54 percent proteins, the maximum was 57 minutes. But on a high-carbohydrate diet of 82 percent carbohydrates and 18 percent proteins, the maximum was 167 minutes, nearly three times as long as for the noncarbohydrate diet.

Thus, if you eat more carbohydrates, you will have more energy and endurance and will be able to work out longer. Endurance athletes know that a high-carbohydrate diet helps performance by storing more fuel (glycogen) in the muscle. But a high-carbohydrate diet is relevant to all sports. People in stop-and-start sports, such as tennis, after consecutive days of hard training, also deplete their muscle glycogen stores. A diet sufficiently high in carbohydrates is necessary after each day's workout to replace the glycogen used up.

Unfortunately, such a diet is not the norm among recreational athletes. Here is a typical scenario: A busy executive wakes up late and skips breakfast. She eats a small lunch and works out at the gym after work. She doesn't replace her fluids, so she is tired and doesn't eat much for dinner. After a few days of this routine, she feels "flat" because she isn't replacing her carbohydrates on a consistent basis.

A diet high in carbohydrates, moderate in proteins, and low in fats can also help keep your energy level up during a weight loss program. Carbohydrates also have a fair amount of fiber, so they fill you up with fewer calories. A lot of fatty foods contain fat and fat-soluble vitamins, but nothing else. Many foods high in carbohydrates have small amounts of protein and a number of vitamins and minerals. Sources of carbohydrates include breads, cereals, grains, and other starches such as potatoes, corn, milk, beans, peas, lentils, fruits and fruit juices, and vegetables.

Without a doubt, carbohydrates are the best foods for athletes to sustain training and competition, promote rapid recovery, and prevent staleness and fatigue.

Remember Protein

Although protein can't be metabolized for energy, it contains the building blocks for body tissue, the amino acids. In any athletic endeavor, there is a breakdown of body tissue. This is obvious for contact sports such as football, but it also occurs in nonviolent sports such as jogging. The continued use of muscle fibers breaks them down, and the body needs protein to repair them.

While children need a relatively high level of protein in their diets because they are still growing, adults need only enough protein to maintain tissue repair.

KNOW WHAT TO EAT AND WHEN

Principles of Pregame Eating

In general, you should eat at least 2 hours before working out. In advance of an upcoming game, because of the added anxiety, allow more time than you normally would before a routine workout—about 3 to $4\frac{1}{2}$ hours. Being nervous slows down digestion, and you may become more aware of stomach upset. This may be tolerable during a regular workout but could affect your game performance, when you are giving your maximum effort.

Eating foods high in fats and proteins will slow down the stomach-emptying process, so you should drop high-fat, high-protein foods from pre-event meals. Try high-carbohydrate, low-fat foods, such as breads and pasta, at least 2 hours before a workout or competition so that your stomach empties before you exercise.

Forget the candy bar before you exercise. You may think you are getting quick energy, but you

are not. Eating candy causes a sharp increase in blood sugar levels. Your body responds by releasing insulin, which burns up your blood sugar reserves and depletes your overall energy rather than supplying you with an extra boost. Some of the symptoms of low blood sugar are dizziness, inability to think clearly, shakiness or weakness, and difficulty concentrating.

Your blood sugar supply will be low if you haven't eaten for 8 hours. Eating carbohydrates can restore and maintain your blood sugar during exercise and prevent hunger and exhaustion after a workout. So you need to leave enough time so that food empties from your stomach, yet eat close enough to your workout to prevent hunger and exhaustion later on.

A Pre-Exercise Meal

A pre-exercise meal (or breakfast) for best performance contains lots of carbohydrates and little fat. The meal should include bread, cereal, grains, fruit and fruit juices, skim milk, and low-fat dairy products. An example of a good meal is a bowl of nongranola cereal (which is low in fat), skim milk, and an orange; or a piece of toast with jam, low-fat cottage cheese, and fruit juice. Remember, it should be eaten from 2 to $4\frac{1}{2}$ hours before you exercise.

Carbo Loading

One specialized method of pregame eating is "carbo loading." This is a widely misunderstood concept. First, carbo loading is valuable only before long-distance events, where you need to delay the conversion to the fat metabolism, or anaerobic energy, cycle. The process is probably of no value for any race distance less than 10 kilometers.

Second, it is valuable only for widely spaced events. It takes a full week to accomplish the loading, and there should be a prolonged recovery period afterward. Thus, a high school cross-country runner who races three miles twice a week is not a good candidate for carbo loading.

Only those who run long-distance races three to four times a year are viable candidates.

Finally, carbo loading should not be confused with eating a high-carbohydrate meal the night before a race. This is a good meal for anyone running any distance.

The technique of carbo loading begins with starving the body of carbohydrates for four days. When carbohydrate reserves are totally depleted, then large amounts of carbohydrates are consumed for three days. The result is a rebound effect that raises carbohydrate levels higher than a simple high-carbohydrate diet would.

During the first four days of carbo loading, you should work out heavily and eat foods as high in protein and as low in carbohydrates as possible. This causes total carbohydrate depletion. It also can make you depressed and irritable, so be aware that there are drawbacks. During the last three days, your diet should be all carbohydrates, and your workouts should be minimized or eliminated. This produces the desired rebound effect and should allow you to go longer without lactic acid buildup during the race.

Carbo loading should be undertaken only under a doctor's supervision. This especially applies to anyone with a medical problem. If you have any health problems, or any questions about how to carbo-load, consult a sports doctor or nutritionist.

Eating after Exercise

For meals and snacks after exercise, eat high-carbohydrate foods first, and then replenish fluids with water, electrolyte drinks, and fruit juices as well as salty and high-potassium foods such as pickles and relish.

Sodium-sensitive people need to limit their intake of salt. That's fine if you have high blood pressure, but if you're working out regularly in hot weather, don't completely eliminate salty foods. You need some extra salt to compensate for sweat losses, particularly if you do consecutive workouts, as we do during the Giants' summer training camp.

High-potassium foods such as citrus fruits, bananas, melons, and skim milk are good for athletes because they are great sources of carbohydrates and proteins, contain no fat, and provide lots of vitamins and minerals.

KNOW WHAT TO DRINK AND WHEN

Fluid intake is important because people can suffer heat problems from inadequate fluid replacement. Heat exhaustion or heat stroke can be life-threatening for both professional and amateur athletes.

There is a good way to determine your need for fluid replacement. First, weigh yourself before exercising. Then immediately after your workout, weigh yourself again. Replace each pound of weight lost with one pint (16 ounces) of water, an electrolyte replacement drink such as Gatorade, or a combination of the two. In this way you will be sure to replace lost fluids and won't get dehydrated.

Before Your Workout

If it's hot and you are doing an endurance activity, prehydrate with 16 ounces of water within 15 minutes of your workout, whether you're thirsty or not. Thirst is not a good guide for fluid replacement. The minute you're thirsty, you're already somewhat dehydrated.

During the two hours before you exercise, drink only plain, noncarbonated water. The bubbles in carbonated water just fill you up, so plain water is better. Before exercising, don't take any salt pills or drinks containing salt, such as electrolyte replacement drinks. Take no high-carbohydrate supplements, protein powders or amino acids, juices, sodas, candy, sugar, or honey.

If milk causes problems for you, do without it for the pregame meal. A large percentage of people can't drink milk but don't know it. They don't like milk, and they always seem to have a lot of gas and don't know why. These people probably have lactose intolerance, which is a problem in digesting lactose (milk sugar). Luckily, lactose-reduced products, including nonfat milk and cottage cheese, are available. Also, a product called Lactaid®, which contains the enzyme necessary for lactose digestion, can be added to foods.

During warmup, cold water is always appropriate. Cold water empties from the stomach faster than warm water. If you have stomach cramps, it's probably from taking too much water at once. If you experience cramps, try warm water or fluids with salt or sugar in them.

During Your Workout

Drink four to eight ounces of water every 15 minutes during your performance. Try this in workouts first since your stomach may not tolerate this much fluid. Besides cold water, you can drink watered-down electrolyte replacement drinks, which contain a combination of glucose and electrolytes such as sodium and potassium. Small amounts of glucose and sodium increase the speed of water absorption from the intestines. Some research indicates that you don't have to water down these drinks, but from a practical standpoint, a number of athletes can't tolerate these drinks straight and get upset stomachs. Generally, it's better to water down the drinks with one or two parts water for every part of the replacement drink. On the sidelines during Giants games you always see three bright orange Gatorade tubs. One is filled with watered-down Gatorade, and the other two contain plain water.

After Your Workout

After your workout, drink plain cold water or a watered-down electrolyte drink. Within two hours after exercise, and preferably within 15 minutes, have a high-carbohydrate drink as well. Ingesting carbohydrates within that time frame seems to accelerate the replacement of muscle glycogen reserves. Some of the drinks available are Gatorlode®, Exceed High Carb®, and Carboplex®. Regardless of what these drinks say on their labels, take them only after you have

completed exercise, not during or before. The manufacturers want you to believe that the drinks give you a jolt of energy. In reality, they will sit in your stomach during exercise, preventing fluids from passing through and, as a result, lowering your blood sugar.

Since high-carbohydrate drinks slow fluid replacement, it's best to get some fluid replacement under way first. A good rule of thumb is to take water, then an electrolyte replacement drink, and then a high-carbohydrate drink within two hours, and as close to 15 minutes as possible, after exercise.

When you rehydrate, limit caffeinated drinks such as coffee, cola, and iced tea. This can be hard to do because you're tired, and a quick shot of caffeine makes you feel better. But if you drink too much caffeine, you will urinate more and lose fluids. The same goes for alcohol, which goes through your body as if it were a leaky tub. Limit yourself to two drinks or less of caffeine or alcohol a day because both promote water loss.

HAVE YOUR DIET AND BODY COMPOSITION ASSESSED

Nutrition is not an exact science. No dietitian can say, "I'm going to put you on a 5,000-calorie diet for your ultimate performance." What he or she can do is assess what foods you are eating and your body composition and then look at what you need to do to gain muscle, bulk up, or reduce fat.

It's important to go to a reputable person such as a registered dietitian, preferably one who specializes in sports and cardiovascular nutrition. Anyone with little or no training can call himself a "nutritionist." For a reliable reference, contact the American Dietetic Association for one of the 3,000 or so specialized dietitians across the country, contact your state dietetic association, or look in the Yellow Pages under "Dietitian."

Dietary Assessment

The dietitian will probably ask you to keep a three-day food diary. From that you will receive a printout of the percentage of total calories you get from carbohydrates, protein, and fat; your total calorie intake; and whether you are getting significant amounts of the main nutrients: iron, calcium, vitamin C, vitamin A, thiamine, riboflavin, niacin, sodium, and potassium. Or the dietitian may simply assess the frequency with which you eat certain foods or note the foods you tend to eat more than once a week.

Once your diet has been assessed and found to be balanced, you can take a multivitamin supplement that has 100 percent of the U.S. recommended daily allowance (RDA) of nutrients. Take no more than 100 percent of the fat-soluble vitamins A, D, E, and K, which are stored in the body, because they can build up to toxic levels. The water-soluble vitamins B and C don't build up in the body as much, though they can reach toxic levels, too. The trace elements iron, zinc, copper, iodine, selenium, fluoride, magnesium, molybdenum, and chromium should be kept at recommended levels for safety.

The mechanism of absorption for one nutrient may not be the same as that for another. If your intake of amino acids and trace elements is not balanced, you may inadequately absorb one or the other nutrient.

The recommended daily allowance of vitamins and minerals is not the best guide for athletes since it was devised to avoid vitamin deficiencies, not to enhance performance. Different nutritionists may recommend different levels of vitamins and minerals. But you can use the RDA as an overall guide for adding to a balanced diet. And a good, balanced diet is your highest priority.

Body Weight versus Body Composition

Whether you want to gain weight, lose weight, or maintain weight, you need to look not just at your body weight but at your body composition, that is, how much muscle and how much fat you have. When you participate in any diet or exercise program, you can't rely on the scale. Muscle weighs more than fat, and as you increase muscle mass with exercise, you may weigh more even though your total body fat is dropping.

Changes in body composition can be monitored through body fat determinations. Some health clubs use reputable methods to determine body fat but don't follow the proper protocol when testing. For example, testing body fat after a workout when you're dehydrated will result in a lower-than-normal reading. Also, be wary of wonderful-looking computer printouts that don't mean a thing.

The gold standard for determining body fat is hydrostatic weighing. This is a rather complicated procedure that involves full-body immersion in water. A simple yet reliable method is to have a registered dietitian measure your skin thickness in several areas of the body using calipers. This provides a reading of body fat percentage within a narrow range under controlled conditions.

The dietitian can help you track your body fat by measuring several areas of the body every six to eight weeks. For the Giants, we do body fat measurements at the beginning of off-season training in March and at the end of off-season training in May. We also check during the regular season. Working out four times a week, the Giants' players can make fast gains in the reduction of body fat. A player's weight may stay the same during off-season training, but he may have gained 10 pounds of muscle and lost 10 pounds of fat. He doesn't see a change on the scale, but his body composition has changed dramatically. On the other hand, players may weigh the same but have done nothing to reduce their body fat. This often motivates them to start eating a high-performance diet.

You may train less intensely than the pros but make similar changes in body fat composition. There's no rush; you can do it slowly over time. Knowing your body fat level and watching it change is a good motivation to keep fit.

Overweight versus Overfat

Many people who exercise are overweight but not overfat. Being overweight alone is not a health risk, but being overfat is. You need to have some way of determining whether you need to lose weight or lose fat.

A "thin" person could have lower-than-normal weight for his or her age and sex due to one or more of the following factors: shorter height (shorter bones), a smaller frame (smaller, lighter bones), less muscle, and less body fat. A "heavy" person's weight could be due to one or more of these factors that is higher than normal.

Body fat interferes with athletic performance more than the other factors. The more muscle and less fat you have, the faster and quicker you will be. You'll have a higher tolerance for exercising in the heat. Your heart and muscles won't have to work as hard. And you'll be less prone to injury because you are carrying less dead weight on the lower back, hip, knee, and ankle joints. This is why a body fat determination is so important. Once you know how much of your current body weight is body fat, you will be able to set an ideal body weight goal.

Although you may be trying to lower your body fat, you must maintain a certain level for general health. For men the essential body fat level is at least 3 percent. We don't let the Giants' players go below 6 percent body fat because of possible hydration problems. Big linemen, in particular, tend to get dehydrated in hot weather if their body fat is too low. For women the optimal body fat level is between 9 percent and 12 percent for elite athletes and about 15 percent for amateur athletes. Some women athletes, particularly runners and gymnasts, try to get their body fat levels as low as a man's. This can be dangerous. A woman needs a higher level of body fat to maintain her menstrual function and reproductive capabilities.

If you are 20 percent over your ideal body weight, you are considered obese by doctors. Obesity can lead to heart disease, high cholesterol levels, diabetes, and cancer of the breast, prostate, and colon.

Your body fat goals will differ depending on your sport and whether you are playing for fitness or performance, or just for fun. Sports that require more speed and quickness and less body contact require lower levels of body fat.

For other sports, athletes need body fat for protection. For example, hockey and football players need body fat to protect themselves from the pounding they take from opponents. Although receivers and defensive backs can't have a lot of excess body fat (because it slows them down), defensive linemen need the extra bulk provided by more body fat.

GAIN MUSCLE, LOSE EXCESS FAT

Gaining muscle and losing fat makes you stronger. Therefore, all athletes, not just football players and body builders, should strive to gain muscle and lose fat. To do so, you need to increase your calorie intake through a combination of low-fat, high-protein and low-fat, high-carbohydrate foods and beverages.

Gaining Weight

It's not easy to gain muscle weight. An increase of one to two pounds of muscle per week through a combination of diet and weight training is feasible. Any more weight gain than that is due to excess fat and fluid retention.

Your first priority should be to start an appropriate exercise program. You need to train with weights regularly to stimulate muscle cells to grow. You will waste a lot less time and get much better results if you consult a certified strength and conditioning coach, athletic trainer, exercise physiologist, or physical therapist to set up a safe, productive weight-training program. You need the right type of resistance exercises, such as those listed in the strength-training program of Chapter 1, to build muscle.

Remember, too, that rest is an essential element of training. It helps muscles grow and recover and restores their energy so that you will be ready for the next workout. If you are not getting enough rest, you won't be able to do the necessary workouts to gain weight.

A Weight-Gain Diet

To gain one to two pounds, you need to eat an extra 700 to 1,000 calories a day beyond your normal diet. First, have your diet assessed and any nutritional deficits corrected to ensure that you have a balanced diet. Then you can add extra calories. You need calories for muscle growth and to support the heavy training required to build muscle. Those calories should come mostly from low-fat, high-carbohydrate foods, such as vegetables, fruits and juices, breads, nongranola cereals, rice, pasta, peas, legumes, and other starches.

Incorporate extra foods and beverages into your daily diet by having larger portions, second helpings, more frequent meals, or snacks between meals. Be sure to maintain adequate protein intake to supply the building blocks for more muscle.

An easy, convenient way to work in extra calories is to add a low-fat liquid meal plus extra skim milk and fruit juice to a balanced diet. Examples of low-fat liquid meals are Carnation Instant Breakfast®, Sustical®, and Nutrament®. Or you can eat low-fat foods such as skim or low-fat milk, nonfat yogurt, cooked egg whites or egg substitutes (which should be cholesterol-free and pasteurized), low-fat cottage cheese, and reduced-calorie and reduced-fat cheeses, such as those offered by Weight Watchers® or Lite-Line®.

You may notice that these are the same foods eaten to lose weight. The difference is in the quantity and total number of calories consumed. To gain weight, the source of calories consists mainly of liquids, which allow you to slip down a lot of calories easily. For example, you can drink two glasses of orange juice more quickly than you can eat two oranges. To lose weight, eat bulkier foods with fewer calories, such as vegetables and fruits, rather than juices, because such foods take longer to eat.

Losing Weight

The goals of any weight loss program should be to lose excess body fat while maintaining muscle and keeping up fluid intake. Any program that significantly depletes muscle mass or fluids isn't healthy and will not be effective for long-term weight control.

People get excited when they lose two pounds after a workout. But this sudden weight loss usually is due to loss of fluids, which you will need to replenish. Losing excess fluid is counterproductive because it lowers the body's volume of blood. The blood circulates oxygen to working muscles and takes waste products away, and with a lower blood volume, you can't do that as efficiently. In addition, your heart has to work harder to keep the blood circulating. A low blood volume also lowers your sweat volume so that your body doesn't cool off as quickly.

A weight loss of one to two pounds of fat per week through combined diet and exercise is feasible. If you drop any more weight than that, you are probably losing muscle and fluid, not body fat.

The best way to lose body fat is to decrease your intake of food fats *and* increase aerobic exercise. This dynamic duo is not only the best program for training, performance, and weight control, but for overall health as well.

A Weight-Loss Diet

Where do fats appear in our food? We get fats from meat, fish, poultry, cooking fat and oil, butter and margarine, mayonnaise and salad dressing, nuts and nut butter, whole milk, cream, most cheeses, ice cream, nondairy creamers, pastries, cake, donuts, pies, cookies, chips, and other greasy snacks. A simple way of testing if a food is fatty is to put it on a paper napkin. If it leaves a grease spot, you know it's full of fat.

To lose weight, you need to cut down on the portions of high-fat foods you eat. If you are going to eat fat, at least have it in nutritious foods.

People tend to think of foods high in carbohydrates as fattening. But fats have more than twice the calories (9) per gram than carbohydrates (4) or proteins (4). Foods that supply the most calories tend to have the least nutrition. Alcohol is nearly as bad as fat, with 7 calories per gram. Thus, fat and alcohol have the highest number of calories per gram and provide the least nutrition per calorie.

One way to lose weight is to replace fats with carbohydrates. A registered dietitian can help point out high-fat foods in the diet and offer lower-fat alternatives. For example, you can switch from eating donuts (high fat) to bagels (low fat), or from ice cream (high fat) to frozen yogurt (low fat).

Plugging in a suitable, tasty alternative makes a long-term behavior change feasible. Most people hate sitting down to wimpy food portions. By eating lower-fat foods, you can still have fairly large portions and eat when you're hungry.

Part Two

Common Risks and Basic Safeguards

Conditioning and
Your Health

First Aid: What to Do
Until the Doctor Comes

Conditioning and Your Health

How does the body accomplish what we ask it to do? The body is like an internal combustion engine. It burns fuel and oxygen for energy just as your car engine burns gasoline mixed with oxygen. Just like a car, the body gives off heat as it burns energy. This is why your body temperature rises when you exercise. And, like a car, it gives off waste products as it uses this energy.

Your body utilizes carbohydrates in the diet as its energy source. It converts complex carbohydrates—such as breads, grains, potatoes, and other starches—and sugars in the diet to a fuel substance called glycogen. Glycogen is stored in muscle cells and in large amounts in the liver. The glycogen in muscles combines with oxygen, brought in by the circulating blood from the lungs, and releases energy; this is known as the aerobic energy cycle. The waste products are carbon dioxide and water.

Once the muscle glycogen is exhausted from prolonged exercise, reserve glycogen is released from the liver and carried to muscle cells so that they can continue working. This glycogen release continues until the body's supply of glycogen is totally depleted. At this point, you are basically out of gas.

However, the body has another reserve fuel supply to enable it to keep chugging on. It changes fuels and begins to burn fat instead of glycogen. This is a whole new energy cycle, called the anaerobic energy cycle, in which the waste product released is lactic acid.

The body can easily rid itself of carbon dioxide and water, but it has difficulty getting rid of lactic acid. As you continue to exercise, lactic acid begins to build up in the muscle, and you become more fatigued. This buildup of lactic acid is what causes the burning pain in exhausted muscles and most of the soreness and stiffness you feel the next day.

The longer you can prevent the body from converting to the anaerobic energy cycle, the longer you can put off fatigue and continue to perform at a high level. Thus, you must either improve the supply of oxygen to the muscles or prevent the exhaustion of glycogen reserves. Conditioning the heart can increase the efficiency of oxygen transfer to the muscles. And to keep glycogen stores high, complex carbohydrates should form the bulk of your diet.

The previous chapter gave you specific dietary advice. This chapter looks at the other principles that keep your human engine running smoothly:

- Prevent body heat problems.
- Exercise your heart.

- Understand the mental aspects of exercise.
- Avoid steroids and performance enhancers.

PREVENT BODY HEAT PROBLEMS

Your body has three ways to shed this excess heat: radiation, convection, and evaporation.

In radiation, the increase in body temperature causes the blood vessels in the skin to dilate. This pooling of blood is the reason your skin turns red when you exercise. Large quantities of blood rise to the skin surface, where heat can be radiated to the outside to cool off the body. The problem with radiation is that exercising muscles demand large quantities of blood to supply oxygen and fuel. This reduces the amount of blood available to the skin, so radiation becomes less effective.

Convection relies on the difference between the body's temperature and the air temperature to transfer heat from the body. The closer the air temperature is to 98.6° F (normal body temperature), the less heat is drawn off the body. So as the weather gets hotter and you need to lose more heat, this mechanism becomes less efficient.

We depend mainly on evaporation for temperature control in hot weather. As sweat evaporates, it cools the skin. In hotter weather you sweat more, so this system works well in high temperatures. But if the humidity is high, there is more water in the air, and less sweat is absorbed from the skin through evaporation. With no evaporation, there's no cooling. So exercising on a humid day can be more dangerous than exercising on a hot day. Also, if you keep perspiring without replacing body fluids, you become dehydrated. Since sweat is salty, excessive sweating leads to loss of body salts and potassium, which collectively are called electrolytes.

What you wear while exercising also affects this heat reduction mechanism. If you cover your body with clothes, as football players do from head to toe, or if you wear clothes that don't "breathe," that is, that don't allow sweat to evaporate from the body, you put yourself at risk for a heat problem, either heat exhaustion or heat stroke.

Heat Exhaustion

Heat exhaustion is due to dehydration and the loss of electrolytes. It causes you to feel light-headed and dizzy, and you may even faint. Your cooling mechanisms are working overtime so that you are sweaty, and your skin is cool and clammy. You may also have severe muscle cramps due to the loss of salt and potassium. If you experience these symptoms, stop whatever you are doing, rest in a cool place, and replace your fluids with water or an electrolyte drink such as Gatorade. In severe cases, you may need to have fluids and electrolytes replaced intravenously at a hospital emergency room.

EMERGENCY

Heat Stroke

Heat stroke is a true medical emergency. In this case, all of the heat mechanisms have failed, and the body temperature has risen to the point where the brain's regulating mechanism has been knocked out. Body temperature may go as high as 107° to 109° F. The symptoms of heat stroke are red, hot skin; lack of sweating; and, usually, loss of consciousness. Get someone with heat stroke to the emergency room immediately, where an ice bath, ice packs, or a cooling blanket can be used to help lower the body temperature. Someone with heat stroke could die very quickly without treatment.

Preventing Heat Problems

How can you prevent these heat problems? First, check the temperature and humidity before you exercise. If the temperature and humidity are both high, cut back on your workout for that day or wait till the temperature and humidity have gone down. Wear light, loose clothing that breathes and allows air to circulate.

Second, keep your fluid intake up. Take frequent water breaks, every 15 minutes if possible. You should drink plain water even if you're not thirsty. By the time you become thirsty, it may be too late. You can also drink an electrolyte drink, such as Gatorade, but remember to dilute it, using at least two parts water to one part Gatorade, to help your stomach absorb the high concentration of electrolytes.

Third, do not take salt tablets; they only create more problems. A large amount of salt in the intestines causes the body to extract large amounts of water from body tissues to dilute it, causing further dehydration in the muscles. Adequately salted meals and high-potassium foods, such as bananas, tomatoes, and oranges, should be adequate to maintain your electrolyte levels.

EXERCISE YOUR HEART

Exercise is essential in maintaining the body's overall well-being. Even modest amounts of exercise can substantially reduce your chances of dying of heart problems, cancer, or other diseases.

Certain well-known risk factors lead to heart disease, including obesity, high blood pressure, high cholesterol, low levels of the "good" (HDL) cholesterol, diabetes, cigarette smoking, and family history of heart disease. Exercise has a dramatic effect on almost all of these risk factors:

- It causes weight loss by increasing the number of calories burned.
- Many people can control their blood pressure through exercise and diet without any medication.
- Cholesterol levels change for the better. In particular, aerobic exercise raises levels of HDL (high-density lipoprotein) cholesterol in the blood. This "good" cholesterol carries "bad" LDL (low-density lipoprotein)

cholesterol to the liver, preventing it from clogging arteries.
- Diabetics respond to exercise with lowered blood sugar, less need for medication, and fewer swings in blood sugar levels.
- Most regular exercisers give up smoking because it lowers their stamina, and exercise helps calm their nervous tension.

The only heart disease risk factor that exercise can't conquer is family history. But even if you have a high incidence of heart disease in your family, you can still reduce the other risk factors and be less likely to suffer from heart disease or a heart attack.

The heart is, after all, a muscle, and any muscle can be strengthened by exercise. The stronger the heart gets, the more easily it can do its job—pumping blood to the rest of the body. A well-conditioned heart has a low resting heart rate. The fewer times it has to beat each minute, the less strain is put on it. And a well-conditioned heart is better able to meet the sudden demand of a burst of activity, such as running for a bus or shoveling snow.

Conditioning the Heart

The entire theory behind conditioning the heart is extremely simple. You need to know just two basic terms: predicted maximum heart rate and training range.

The predicted maximum heart rate is the highest number of beats per minute that is safe during any one exercise period. There are two ways to determine this rate. You can undergo a fancy exercise stress test at a cost of $100 to $150, or you can calculate your maximum heart rate with a simple formula: 220 minus your age. For example, a 40-year-old would have a predicted maximum heart rate of 180 beats per minute.

The heart rate must be brought into the training range, which is 70–85 percent of the maximum. This is the heart rate that best conditions the heart. So a 40-year-old, with a predicted maximum heart rate of 180, would have a training range of 126 to 153 beats per minute.

How to Monitor Your Heart Rate

Now the only trick is how to monitor your heart rate. You can buy a heart rate monitor, complete with chest strap and wrist monitor, for $130 to $300. Or you can simply time your pulse. The easiest place to take your pulse during exercise is at the side of the throat, where the carotid artery beats forcefully. Place your index and middle fingers at the base of the neck on either side of the windpipe (see the following figure) and count your heartbeats for 10 seconds. Multiply this number by 6. This tells you the number of heartbeats per minute. Then you can check whether this heart rate falls within your training range.

Risks and Benefits

The type of aerobic activity you choose makes no difference as long as you attain the training range. At the minimum, you need to keep your heart rate in the training range for at least 20 minutes three times a week.

However, recent research shows that even less exercise—12 minutes three times a week—

Neck Pulse

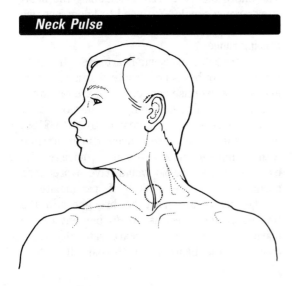

can produce health benefits. This landmark study, carried out by the Institute for Aerobics Research and the Cooper Clinic in Dallas, one of the first large studies to look at women's fitness as well as men's, shows that you can benefit from being just a bit more active. So if you have time for only a short workout, go for it. A little exercise is better than none at all.

If you have any history of heart trouble or orthopedic problems that might make exercise dangerous, see your doctor for a physical exam before starting a program. It was once recommended that any man age 40 or over have an exercise stress test before beginning a rigorous exercise program. However, I now order stress tests only for people who have several heart disease risk factors. Age is not as much a risk as is jump-starting an unconditioned heart. If a sedentary person's heart is only borderline healthy, a conditioning program could put him or her at risk of a heart attack.

Use some common sense when beginning an exercise program. Start slowly and gradually build up to 20 minutes or more during each session. Don't go out for 20 long, hard minutes your very first day. See the section on gradual conditioning on page 7.

Avoiding Burnout

When you constantly train at the high end of your target heart rate, you risk problems with fatigue, muscle injury, and stress. Trying to work out like an elite athlete can run you into the ground.

"No pain, no gain" is not the best way to condition yourself. Fatigue and injuries can result from pushing yourself too hard. You will find that you can achieve better results by cutting back on your exercise intensity. For example, running more than 40 miles a week can triple your likelihood of sustaining an injury. So decreasing your mileage to less than 40 per week will help prevent injuries and ultimately keep you running longer.

Overtraining may also increase your susceptibility to colds. Several studies have shown that intense daily training reduces resistance to infectious diseases such as colds and the flu.

In addition, long training sessions may actually slow you down. One study of U.S. college swimmers found that those who swam up to 10,000 meters twice a day lost arm strength and power. After the swimmers tapered their training to 2,700 meters a day for a few days, they recovered their arm power. Thus, too much training may cause you to burn out and prevent you from reaching your goals.

High-intensity training may also counteract the good feelings you get from exercising. Exercise is a great way to reduce stress and anxiety and to lift your mood. But the same swimming researchers found that increasing training intensity and distance at the end of the season made the swimmers feel more tense, depressed, and angry.

Exercise shouldn't be a chore. It should be fun. If your workout feels like work, change your training schedule or try some new type of exercise that reinvigorates you. One of the advantages of cross-training is the use of more than one sport to keep you physically and mentally active. A bored but well-conditioned athlete won't perform up to par.

UNDERSTAND THE MENTAL ASPECTS OF EXERCISE

Almost all sports are based on competition. Even the recreational jogger or health walker will try to attain his or her personal best and go a little farther or faster, and the individual weight trainer try to get in one or two extra repetitions of a weight workout. Striving to reach peak performance is fine until you push yourself past your capacity. This usually occurs at the end of activity, when your muscles are tired and more prone to injury.

Good Days and Bad Days

There will be days when you feel really good as an athlete and believe that you can do more than you usually do. Despite this euphoria, however, your body may not in fact be capable of suddenly doing the extra exercise. The result often is an injury.

The opposite side of the coin is trying to force yourself to perform on a bad day. Refusing to recognize a bad day also can lead to overfatigue and injury. When you're not feeling up to par, just do what you can comfortably accomplish and leave it at that. Tomorrow will be a better day.

Negative Addiction

Exercise is very helpful in alleviating stress, releasing tensions, and producing a relaxing kind of fatigue. However, some people go far beyond this normal response and become dependent on daily exercise.

One of the by-products of exercise is the production of naturally occurring brain chemicals called endorphins. These morphinelike substances produce a sense of well-being and relaxation and are responsible for the "runner's high." Some people become addicted to daily exercise because of the production of these chemicals. If they don't exercise, they become depressed and irritable, and they may actually have withdrawal symptoms. If they become injured, they will make life miserable for everyone around them until they can get back to exercising daily.

Working through an Injury

Many athletes refuse to take time off because of their drive to keep pushing themselves. I often hear athletes say, "I laid off exercise for three days when I pulled a hamstring, but it didn't get better." It can be difficult to get the message across that a hamstring pull may take three weeks to heal. The athlete just doesn't want to hear it.

And once treatment begins, I inevitably hear: "Do I have to stop, or can I keep playing?" This mental outlook often interferes with even the best treatment because the athlete will try to play before he or she is ready.

AVOID STEROIDS AND PERFORMANCE ENHANCERS

In this era of drug abuse, a new problem has become widespread: the use of anabolic steroids among high school and college athletes. Steroids are the most dangerous group of legal prescription drugs besides the poisonous chemicals used to treat cancer. These drugs are widely available through an underground black market, mostly through weight-lifting gyms. But even in suburban health clubs, the guys in the weight room commonly know where to find steroids.

An increasing number of teenagers are using steroids to enhance their athletic performance and their appearance. An estimated 260,000 teens, mostly boys in grades 7 to 12, use or have used steroids, according to a survey by the National Institute of Drug Abuse. Another study by Penn State and the American Medical Association puts the figure closer to 400,000.

Steroids have become a major problem among high school and college football players. During football season, in the course of examining high school athletes for injuries I spot one or two players a week who are taking steroids. About 10 percent of college football players admit that they use steroids, mostly to improve athletic performance, according to a National Collegiate Athletic Association poll. Even nonathletes concerned about body image are turning to steroids. In fact, this is the group with the largest increase in steroid use.

The Dangers of Steroid Use

Steroids have a wide variety of side effects. The excess of male hormones circulating in the blood can cause a personality change toward increased aggressive behavior. Part of the increase in strength attributed to steroids is due to this aggressiveness; the athlete lifts more because he attacks the weights harder. This aggressiveness may lead teenagers to get into fights and become hard to handle. In high doses, steroids have been reported to cause psychotic episodes.

One of the more serious side effects of steroids is on male reproductive organs. Because of the high level of circulating testosterone, the testicles no longer need to manufacture this hormone, so they begin to shrink. This reduces sperm production and may lead to both impotence and sterility.

In addition, steroids lead to changes in the structure and function of both the kidneys and the liver. These changes can cause chronic health problems in later life and markedly increase the risk of liver cancer.

I believe that the anecdotal reports of heart attacks among athletes will eventually also be linked to steroid use. The incidence of coronary artery disease and heart attacks among 20-year-old steroid users is now being documented. The drug causes a marked rise in total cholesterol levels and a marked drop in levels of HDL cholesterol. Low HDL levels mean that there is nothing to prevent deposits from clogging arteries, including those in the heart. Also, degeneration of the heart muscle itself has been identified in steroid users. This change is irreversible, leaving a heart transplant as the only viable treatment.

Steroid users may also develop a severe form of acne over the upper torso and become prematurely bald. They also are more susceptible to injuries of the bones and tendons because these support structures aren't strong enough to anchor overdeveloped muscles.

I see these problems mostly among football players, shot-putters, discus and hammer throwers, wrestlers, weight lifters, and body builders. If the steroid use is not too prolonged, some of these side effects will reverse themselves once the user stops taking the drugs. However, many problems, such as hair loss and heart problems, are not reversible.

Female Body Builders

A relatively new group of steroid users are female body builders. More muscular female body builders tend to win more competitions. Women can strengthen their upper bodies with weight training, but the only way to bulk up these muscles is by taking male hormones.

Female body builders not only suffer the same side effects as men, but they also lose breast tissue, develop deeper voices, undergo changes in the structure of their reproductive organs, and grow hair on their faces. None of these changes is reversible. Women on steroids also stop having periods, which is reversible when the steroids are discontinued.

The Artificial Human

Is it fair for an athlete to compete against another who is artificially built up? I don't think so. Young athletes tell me, "I have to take steroids because the guy across the line is bigger than me." However, when his larger opponent sees that his rival is getting bigger, he takes steroids to keep up. As a result, the one who was bigger to begin with is still bigger, but both athletes have had their bodies ravaged by steroids.

One reason steroid use has become so widespread is that it fits in with society's attitude of self-gratification. High school and college athletes tell me, "I will do whatever it takes to get ahead." Even after I've explained all of the dangers of steroid use, most of them say they still plan to use the drugs because that's the only way they can see to achieve their goals.

When I talk about the side effects of steroids with teens, they say, "It's not going to happen to me." I had the same feeling of invincibility when I smoked cigarettes. Doctors call this the "Superman syndrome." I stopped smoking almost 30 years ago because I was coughing very badly. Once I quit and discovered how much better I felt, I became a strong antismoking advocate with my patients. The only way to keep teens clean is to make sure that they understand all of the dangers and that there is no way of avoiding them. Whether it's cigarettes or steroids, they have to understand that they are mortal like everyone else.

Parents need to be educated about steroids as well. One mother, who told me her teenage son was into body building, asked me to prescribe "the proper dose of steroids so he wouldn't get into trouble." I told her that I don't prescribe or deal in steroids and attempted to talk her out of finding steroids for her son.

Other Performance Enhancers

The search for a "magic bullet" to improve performance has led athletes to try other drugs. Various vitamins and herbal mixtures sold through catalogs advertised in muscle magazines purportedly improve strength. There is absolutely no evidence that any of them work. An illegal drug called gamma hydroxybutyrate is being sold in body-building and athletic clubs and in some health food stores. The Food and Drug Administration has issued a public health warning stating that this potent drug has powerful side effects, including coma, seizures, and severe breathing problems.

A synthetic version of human growth hormone is said to help turn a soft, mushy body into a lean, lanky physique. Growth hormone has side effects similar to those of steroids plus other side effects that have not yet been carefully studied.

A substance being abused by athletes to enhance stamina and performance is recombinant erythropoietin, known as EPO. This genetically engineered drug was created for people who suffer from kidney failure in order to raise their red blood cell levels. Red blood cells are essential for carrying oxygen, so some athletes and trainers started using the drug to improve the body's ability to carry oxygen.

Injecting the drug does enhance an athlete's performance in aerobic endurance events. Many bicycle racers, marathon runners, and cross-country skiers are suspected of using the drug. Yet doctors and blood specialists have linked EPO to deaths among European professional bicyclists. Thus, even though EPO may raise your aerobic capacity, it may also kill you.

4

First Aid: What to Do Until the Doctor Comes

The first person to treat an injured professional athlete is usually the team physician or trainer. Unfortunately, most amateur athletes are treated by someone with no training and little if any experience in administering first aid to sports injuries. A few areas of the country have trainers available for high school games, but no one is there to manage acute injuries for the recreational athlete.

The primary goals of immediate first aid are to protect the athlete from further injury and to get the person back in action as soon and safely as possible. To be sure this happens, every recreational athlete needs to follow these basic principles:

- Take your time.
- Use the "RICE" formula to reduce swelling.
- Note how the injury happened.
- Use the right pain killers.
- Use first aid for common muscle injuries.

TAKE YOUR TIME

If you become injured, don't allow yourself to be rushed off the floor or field. You may feel that you have to get to the sidelines as quickly as possible to get out of the spotlight. Well-meaning but inexperienced teammates, friends, or officials may rush you in order to get on with the game, particularly if it's a twilight affair with darkness approaching.

Don't be pressured into moving before you are convinced that it's safe. This is particularly important for neck and spinal cord injuries. I have taken as long as 15 minutes, with national television footing the bill, to move an athlete whom I felt had been seriously injured.

In the same vein, take care about "walking off the field." Many recreational athletes and coaches believe that once an athlete is on her feet, she will be okay. But I have seen athletes walk off the field only to collapse when they get to the sidelines. Lie still until you are absolutely sure it's safe to move. If you are not sure, wait for a stretcher.

A broken bone should be splinted before the player is moved. This is a concept basic to all fractures. Any suspicious-looking injury should be treated as a fracture and splinted. The splint can always be removed later; but if you fail to splint and you guess wrong, you may do irreparable damage that leads to permanent disability.

USE THE "RICE" FORMULA TO REDUCE SWELLING

The most basic treatment principle is summed up by the acronym RICE, which stands for *r*est, *i*ce, *c*ompression, and *e*levation. These four, in combination, reduce swelling, which occurs when blood and fluids leak into the injured body part, often a joint.

Swelling is the most important factor in delaying your return to activity long after the pain is gone. A swollen joint has severely limited function. If you can keep the swelling down to a minimum at the time of injury, you will have much less pain and aggravation to deal with as you heal. Anything that can prevent swelling will save you days of recovery later on.

- *Resting* the injury cuts down the circulation to the area. The less circulation, the less leakage occurs from broken blood vessels. Also, when small blood vessels are torn, any motion in the area prevents them from sealing, so they keep bleeding.
- *Ice* constricts blood vessels when first applied. The blood vessels shrink and limit bleeding into the affected area, which reduces swelling.
- *Compressing* the swollen area with an elastic bandage limits the area available for fluid to leak into. Compression causes a higher pressure outside of the torn blood vessels than inside, which makes it difficult for fluid to flow out.
- *Elevating* the damaged area also decreases blood flow. The heart has to pump harder against gravity if the injured area is raised to a level higher than the heart. At the same time, gravity helps any fluid that has accumulated at the injury site to move back toward the torso.

RICE also helps prevent further injury. Rest avoids complications caused by moving the injured part. Ice prevents more bleeding, which can cause calcium deposits to form later. Compression helps support the injury. Elevation prevents you from putting any weight on the injured part, which could damage it more.

NOTE HOW THE INJURY HAPPENED

One of the most helpful yet often overlooked ways to lessen the extent of an injury is to note how the injury happened. Swelling and pain often mask the actual injury, and it may be difficult to examine the injury by the time a player has been brought into the emergency room or doctor's office. The player, his teammates, or coach should be able to say where the athlete was hit, which way he fell, and what he was doing at the time of injury. Often, using this information I can make a precise diagnosis when I am unable to do a total physical examination.

USE THE RIGHT PAIN KILLERS

I suggest three types of pain-killing pills for my patients. I find these drugs to be valuable because they allow me to start aggressive, early rehabilitation of injuries.

Aspirin is the oldest and probably most widely prescribed drug. It not only kills pain but also reduces inflammation. The major side effect of aspirin is stomach upset and even bleeding from the lining of the stomach. If you have problems with regular aspirin, use buffered or enteric coated aspirin intead. Aspirin also interferes with blood clotting and should not be used in large doses during contact sports.

Acetaminophen pills, such as Tylenol®, have the same pain-killing effects as aspirin in most people but do not have as much of an anti-inflammatory effect. They are less irritating to the stomach and have no anticlotting effect.

Ibuprofen is the active ingredient in nonsteroidal anti-inflammatory agents. The various over-the-counter preparations are half-strength versions of the prescription medication Motrin®.

They all have a very strong anti-inflammatory effect and also have pain-relieving properties.

Anti-inflammatories must be taken carefully. They can have severe gastrointestinal (GI) side effects; they may irritate the stomach and cause bleeding as well as ulcers. They can interfere with the production of the coating that protects the stomach and intestine from stomach acid. Anyone with a history of GI problems should not take anti-inflammatory agents, including those sold in drug stores, except under a doctor's direction. The doctor may prescribe accompanying medication to ameliorate the side effects.

When I suggest that athletes take a pain killer, I let them choose whichever one they like best. Most people know from previous experience which drug works well for them.

The only caveat is not to take aspirin along with anti-inflammatory agents. Since these two are chemically similar, adding one to the other could lead to a toxic reaction. So, for example, if you are taking ibuprofen for sore muscles and you get a headache, take acetaminophen instead of aspirin.

USE FIRST AID FOR COMMON MUSCLE INJURIES

How to Treat Muscle Pulls

No matter how diligently you warm up and stretch, or warm down and stretch, you may still pull a muscle from overuse, fatigue, or injury. A muscle pull is probably the most common sports injury next to a bruise, which you can do little if anything to prevent. A muscle pull occurs when a sudden, severe force is applied to the muscle and the fibers are stretched beyond their capacity. If most of the fibers are overstretched and a few are torn, you have a muscle pull. If many of the fibers tear, it becomes a muscle tear.

The universal treatment for a muscle pull or tear is to apply ice. This relaxes the muscle and

helps relieve any spasm. Apply ice to the injured body part and rest it until the pain and swelling subside. You should apply the ice for about 20 minutes at a time for several days to reduce inflammation. Then you can start rehabilitating the body part with a gentle exercise and stretching program.

It is of the utmost importance to stretch the muscle while it heals. A pulled muscle usually goes into spasm, which is a protective mechanism that causes the stretched muscle fibers to contract. If the fibers are not gradually relengthened, the muscle will pull again once you return to activity because it will have healed in a shortened state. If you stretch the healing muscle gradually, not violently, you'll decrease your chances of reinjuring it.

In general, you can return to action when you are able to stretch the injured body part without pain as far as you can stretch the healthy one on the other side of the body.

How to Treat Muscle Spasms

If you show up on Monday at your doctor's office complaining of a "pulled muscle" from running over the weekend, you may have a delayed muscle spasm rather than torn muscle fibers. Most muscle injuries result in some degree of spasm or tightness. In fact, many mild muscle "pulls" actually end up to be low-grade spasms. If you are not sure when the muscle began to hurt, you probably have not torn the muscle.

Some doctors like to give pain killers or anti-inflammatory agents as soon as possible after a muscle spasm starts and then suggest that the athlete rest. Pain killers help prevent truly torn muscles from going into spasm. However, rather than keep my patients out of action with total rest, I prefer to get them involved in a gradual exercise program that uses a combination of icing and stretching.

First, apply a large cold pack to the muscle to numb it. A good way to do this is to make an ice cone by freezing water in a styrofoam cup and peel down the rim, and then rub the muscle with the ice until it is numb.

Next, start moving the sore muscle until you begin to feel tightness or pain. When the pain disappears, hold the injured body part in that position for a 20-second static stretch. A few moments later, contract the muscle slowly but fully, and hold for about 5 seconds. This isometric contraction will help relax the muscle more.

Now move the body part again until you feel tightness or pain. Hold the body part for 10 seconds and then contract the muscle for 5 seconds. Repeat the stretch and contraction again, and then stretch the muscle one last time.

Let the body part rest naturally for 20 seconds and repeat the entire program. You may need to renumb the muscle between sessions.

This method of icing and stretching can also be used initially in muscle pulls and tears.

Within two or three days, the dull ache of the muscle spasm will be partially relieved. Then you can gradually resume full activities.

How to Treat Sore Muscles

Delayed muscle soreness and pain typically occur a day or two after strenuous exercise. The soreness usually subsides by itself within a few days. Mild exercise and liniment may help relieve the soreness.

Most athletes have used liniment to relieve the aches and pains of exercise. The unmistakable smell of liniment pervades locker rooms. I have found a direct correlation between an athlete's age, the ambient temperature, and the amount of smell—the older the player and lower the temperature, the worse the liniment smells.

Almost all professional teams use various balms on injured players, but sports doctors don't fully understand how liniments work. It's difficult to say whether liniment is directly responsible for an athlete's quick recovery and return to action. The actual massaging action of rubbing in

the liniment, working it into muscles, may relax the muscle.

There are two basic types of liniment you can buy in a drug store. The first includes products such as Ben-Gay® and Sports Creme®, which typically contain menthol and an aspirinlike chemical, methyl salicylate. When you rub it in, your skin becomes slightly irritated, which causes an increase in blood flow to the area. This also produces heat, which relaxes stiff muscles. These rubs may also allow some salicylate to enter the bloodsteam. Since salicylate is the active ingredient in aspirin, they may also have some pain-relieving effect.

The second type of rub, including Hot-Stuff® and Atomic Balm®, depends on a substance called capsicum, which is the active ingredient in jalapeño peppers. An extract of this chemical is now being used as a prescription ointment for arthritis pain, which is an indication that these rubs really do work. These hotter rubs have a much stronger irritating effect on the skin to stimulate blood flow. They give off so much heat that you can actually burn yourself, especially if you have fair skin. Go slowly when you use them until you can see how your skin reacts.

In addition to its use as an exercise rub, liniment is touted by some manufacturers as a warmup aid. Liniment can help relax tight muscles and increase circulation. It may shorten your warmup time, particularly in cold weather, and may help increase blood flow after warmdown to reduce the lactic acid residue.

But don't think that because you have applied liniment you are warmed up. A proper warm-up raises overall body temperature, not just the temperature in one muscle group. Think of liniment as a passive warmup for one body part. Combine it with 10 minutes of light exercise, followed by stretching, to warm up the whole body.

Aspirin may be helpful in relieving muscle soreness after a tough workout. This soreness dissuades many people new to strength training from going back to the gym for another session. Most weight lifters have sore muscles for a day or two after working out, and then the soreness disappears. Anti-inflammatory drugs such as aspirin may ameliorate this discomfort somewhat. Several studies have found that taking aspirin after exercise reduces muscle soreness and improves the athletes' range of motion a day or two later.

For additional first-aid tips, look for this symbol throughout the book: ✚

Part Three

What to Know from Head to Toe

The Head and Neck

Related Sports Chapters

Baseball and Softball

Basketball

Boxing and Martial Arts

Cycling

Football and Rugby

Hockey, Lacrosse, and Skating

Running, Jogging, and Track and Field

Skiing

Soccer and Field Hockey

Tennis and Other Racquet Sports

Since the head houses all of the body's vital control centers, any injury to the head other than a mild bump or scrape should be seen by a doctor. I always consider head injuries to be serious until it is proven otherwise since they can be life-threatening. No one has ever laughed at me for being overcautious with a head injury.

EMERGENCY
CONCUSSION

A player who has suffered a head injury may feel better later in the game and may try to sneak back into action. This is especially easy for a football player since there are many players intermittently running on and off the field. To make sure an injured Giants player doesn't return without permission, we take away his helmet. That works for everyone except Lawrence Taylor. When he has had his head "dinged," Taylor, though dazed, will holler at me to let him back in. By the end of the shouting match, I know he's okay, and I've accomplished what I wanted to.

A concussion is any loss of consciousness, even for a moment, or disorientation after a blow to the head. There are many degrees of concussion. A player may be unconscious for several minutes with a severe concussion. Another player may be stunned for a few seconds and have trouble remembering where he is or what he is doing.

There is no way to predict which athletes are likely to suffer concussions. The severity of a concussion depends strictly on how much force is applied to the head and whether it is a head-on or a glancing blow. People who wear helmets, which absorb shock, will probably get milder concussions than those who don't.

Treating a Concussion

The treatment for a concussion is rest to protect against further injury to the head. If you immediately regain consciousness or are out for just a short time, you should be watched carefully for signs of headache, nausea, and further loss of consciousness. These are the danger signs of possible bleeding inside the head. Even if you appear normal after the injury, you should be watched for the next 24 hours for any of these signs.

If you do not recover immediately, you should be transported to a hospital as soon as possible for observation and a neurological examination. A typical neurological exam after a concussion will include checks on your reflexes, muscle strength, balance, and pressure in the back of your eye.

Returning to Action

Even if you recover immediately, you should not be allowed to reenter the game or return to activity under any circumstances. When you suffer a concussion your brain swells, and until the swelling subsides completely, another, lesser blow can cause severe damage to the brain. So if you have had a concussion, you are at high risk for another one until you are completely recovered.

Sometimes, it's hard for me to tell whether a player who has been hit in the head has had a memory lapse. He may insist he is all right and may even answer general questions correctly. That's why we have another Giants player ask the injured player about his assignment in particular situations, and we base the diagnosis on his response.

Although we do allow a professional player back in the game, it is only after we are sure he has recovered. He is constantly monitored, and he is not returned to the game if it is not safe. However, this degree of care is not available at any other level of participation, so it is necessary to keep an injured amateur athlete out as a precaution.

The rule of thumb I use to determine when an athlete can return is

- First concussion: Wait seven days or until any postconcussion symptoms cease, whichever is longer. For example, a touch football player who suffers a concussion on Saturday should miss next Saturday's game, even if it was a mild concussion.
- Second concussion: Wait three weeks or until symptoms cease.
- Third concussion: Remain out of action for the remainder of the season.

Anyone who suffers a severe concussion should not return to sports without a physician's recommendation. The physician usually bases the decision on the results of neurologic tests and a review of the symptoms.

Postconcussion Syndrome

After a concussion, some symptoms may persist, including headache, dizziness, loss of memory of the event, fatigue, and general weakness. For some people, these symptoms clear up and they feel fine, but the symptoms recur when they become active again. This is called postconcussion syndrome.

As soon as these symptoms return, you should stop all activity and rest again. You may need a prolonged period, as much as several months, before the symptoms cease. No athlete should return to heavy physical activity until the symptoms clear completely. Giants quarterback Jeff Hostetler had to sit out four weeks of the 1992 season with postconcussion syndrome.

EMERGENCY

SKULL FRACTURE

A hard blow to the head can fracture the bones of the skull. This is an extremely dangerous injury. A depressed skull bone from a fracture may put pressure on the brain or tear blood vessels in the lining of the skull, causing bleeding on the brain. The pressure and bleeding can cause coma and even death if not relieved.

Blood or clear fluid leaking from the ear or nose may be a sign of a skull fracture. Though I rarely see skull fractures, they do occur, and I consider any severe blow to the head as a possible fracture.

If you suspect a skull fracture, get the player to an emergency room immediately for treatment to relieve the pressure or bleeding on the brain.

✚ BROKEN NOSE

I have been leveled several times on the sidelines while watching Giants games, mostly because I can't see over the heads of the players to see if anyone is coming at me. I remember walking toward the sidelines in 1982 when all of a sudden the players in front of me parted and an opposing defensive back came flying toward me, head first. I turned to get most of my body out of his way, but the edge of his face mask clipped me on the nose and broke it.

A blow to the nose can fracture the nasal bones or the cartilage of the septum, the area dividing the two nostrils. A broken nose often is obvious: The nose appears to be flattened or crooked, there is lots of bleeding from the nose, and breathing is difficult.

Any nose suspected to be broken should be iced down to limit swelling and bruising. Then have the nose x-rayed and examined by a doctor. If the broken bone has been at all displaced, it can cause later breathing problems if it's not fixed in place. Once fixed, the nose should be protected with a splint until it heals completely, which can take four to six weeks.

✚ BROKEN CHEEKBONE

The same athletes who are prone to nose breaks may also break cheekbones. A hard blow to the cheek can fracture the bone.

In case of a break, ice the cheek and apply pressure to reduce swelling and bleeding. Then have the cheek x-rayed. If it's broken, surgery may be required to repair it. The player must rest until it heals, which could take several weeks.

MD BLOWOUT FRACTURE

A blow to the eye or cheek can fracture the bones surrounding the eyeball, called the orbit. A blowout fracture is easy to spot: Since the orbit connects to one of the sinuses, when the victim blows hard through the nose, the eye will suddenly swell shut as air gets into the tissues right under the eye.

As with any fracture, the victim of a blowout must see a doctor for treatment, which may include surgery. If the fractured orbit is displaced, as often happens, it can trap one of the eye muscles. Then the eyes won't move in conjunction, which can cause double vision unless surgically corrected.

MD SCRATCHED CORNEA

A scratched cornea commonly occurs when you get poked in the eye by a finger. This usually is an extremely painful, though minor, injury: but if severe and not cared for, it can lead to loss of vision. You can't differentiate the severity by the amount of pain you feel. If you suffer a scratched cornea, cover the eye with a patch and see a doctor as soon as possible.

Direct blows to the eye from a ball in racquet sports, particularly racquetball, can also cause a variety of severe injuries. To protect their eyes, many athletes now wear protective gear, especially if they have already had an eye injury. Every eye injury must be considered serious. Sight is one of our most precious gifts and should be protected at all times. Again, cover the eye and get to a doctor.

MD CAULIFLOWER EAR

If an unprotected ear is bent over, punched, or caught in a wrestling hold, the cartilage in the ear can break. Bleeding under the skin will result, and if the blood is not drained, scar tissue will form and the ear will take on the look of a cauliflower.

To treat such an injury, apply ice and compression to the ear to limit bleeding, and then get to a doctor to have the excess blood drained from the ear.

MD BROKEN JAW

When Giants tight end Mark Bavaro broke his jaw, he kept it wired for one week and then removed the wires himself so that he could get a good meal. He played with an enlarged face mask for the rest of the 1985 season, but I don't recommend that others follow his example. The average athlete has a much lower pain tolerance than a Mark Bavaro.

A blow to the jaw can break it. You will feel pain on one side of the jaw and may not be able to clench your jaw because of the pain. Or, if you can clench your jaw, your teeth will not meet properly.

A broken jaw must be wired shut by a dental surgeon to allow it to heal, which usually takes six weeks. Many athletes can compete with their jaws wired shut, but their diet is limited to liquids taken through a straw. This can lead to loss of weight and strength. You are not at risk by playing as long as your jaw is wired.

A blow to the jaw can also injure the hinge where the lower jaw fits into the upper jaw, called the temporomandibular joint (TMJ). The ligaments may become torn, causing the joint to slide in and out of place. The jaw may even get stuck in an open position, requiring manipulation by an oral surgeon to close it. This injury usually heals within six to eight weeks, but a mouthpiece may be necessary to hold the jaw in position until the ligaments heal.

TMJ pain is one of the reasons athletes wear mouthpieces. The mouthpiece protects the jaw and teeth and disperses the shock from a blow. This also reduces the possibility of a concussion and is the main reason a boxer uses a mouthpiece: It helps prevent him from being knocked out.

All kinds of mouthpieces are available, from hand-molded, individualized ones for professional athletes to $1 rubber or plastic mouthpieces found in your local drug store. The rubber or plastic mouthpiece, which can be heated to become form-fitting, may not be as good as the customized ones, but any mouthpiece is better than none at all.

I believe that mouthpieces should become part of the uniform for most high school sports and some recreational sports. Yet only high school football and hockey players routinely wear mouthpieces. Certainly in basketball, where elbows are flying everywhere, and in wrestling, everyone should wear some type of mouthpiece. Racquetball players should also wear them as protection against being hit in the face with the ball.

THE NECK

Along with the head, the neck is the area of most of the serious injuries I see. Knee injuries may end careers, but neck injuries may end lives or cause paralysis.

The neck is much less stable and much more prone to injury than the rest of the spine. At the top of the spinal column, the vertebrae in the neck become progressively smaller. The neck is tremendously mobile to allow the head to swivel, so the range of motion between the vertebrae in the neck must be greater than in the lower spine. Also, neck muscles are much weaker than those in the lower back, where the strongest muscles in the body support the spine.

Don't move a person with a neck injury. I consider *every* neck injury to be serious. When you feel neck pain, check for numbness or the inability to move a body part. If either is present, **don't move.** Stay where you are until a trained ambulance or emergency first-aid crew arrives. These medical personnel have the training and equipment to minimize further injury. An injury can easily turn into a permanent disaster if the neck isn't properly stabilized. Moving a fractured neck can cut the spinal cord.

At Giants games, we don't move a player with a suspected neck injury off the field even though we have two doctors and three trainers present. Emergency medical technicians move neck injury victims every day, and we don't, so we wait for them. I strongly urge anyone delivering first aid to a neck injury to wait for professional help.

BROKEN NECK

The most serious neck injury damages the cervical vertebrae in the neck; this is commonly called a broken neck. Each year a few football players, from the high school level on up to the professionals, suffer spinal cord injuries that leave them quadriplegics. However, the most common cause of a broken neck is diving. The diver misjudges the depth of the pool and hits the bottom head first.

A head-on blow causes a compression fracture of the neck, in which the force to the top of the head compresses and shatters some of the cervical vertebrae. This may be as mild as a simple chipping of the vertebrae, or it may cause compression or severing of the spinal cord. Compression or cutting of the cord can cause quadriplegia or even death, depending on where the injury occurs along the spinal column.

An equally severe injury can occur from a blow when the neck is bent down. This is more common in football, where a tackler ducks his head as he makes contact.

SPRAINED NECK

Ligaments hold the vertebrae together, and those ligaments can be sprained or stretched, often by the head snapping backward. If the injury is severe, one vertebra may slide forward out of place and compress the spinal cord—the same injury as a fracture. If the sprain is mild, you will just feel pain and stiffness in the neck area. Anything more than a mild sprain should be seen by a physician.

PINCHED NERVE

An injury that seems like a sprain but is more complex is a pinched nerve. This happens when a cervical disc ruptures or degenerates. Commonly, when a disc ruptures, jellylike material from inside the disc presses on a nearby nerve and causes sharp pain that extends down into your arm. You may feel a sudden onset of severe pain in your neck, or the pain may come on slowly over time.

Any athlete who makes fairly violent neck motions is prone to pinched nerves. A pinched nerve usually responds to some form of cervical traction for two to six weeks, with accompanying physical therapy to reduce muscle spasm. However, if severe symptoms persist, particularly in the arm and the hand, you may need surgery to repair damage to the disc.

NARROWED CANAL

Athletes who have recurrent, short episodes of numbness or weakness in their arms and hands may have a narrowed spinal canal. This condition is called cervical stenosis. A magnetic resonance imaging (MRI) scan will show a narrowing of the cervical canal, which is the area from the base of the skull to the shoulder. The symptom may occur after relatively mild trauma to the neck because the spinal cord does not have adequate room in the canal.

A "BURNER" VERSUS STRETCHED NERVES

There are two nerve injuries to the neck that feel the same at first. Both are caused by a blow to the head or neck, and both cause burning pain down the arm and weakness in the arm and hand. One, a "burner," is a simple injury that won't keep you out of action; but the other, stretched nerves, is a serious injury that requires rehabilitation.

A "burner" or "stinger" is characterized by sudden burning pain down one arm, which feels weak. This is due to a pinched nerve in the neck. Usually, the pain disappears and full strength in the arm returns within five minutes. If your arm strength is normal, then you can return to full activity.

It's very important to know which side of the head was hit and on which side you feel the pain. If you sustain a blow to the *left* side of your head, your head will be knocked toward your right shoulder, and you will suddenly feel the burning pain down your *right* arm. The pain comes from the nerve being pinched as vertebrae in the neck flex sharply to the right.

The similar but more dangerous injury, a brachial plexus stretch, has almost the same symptoms. This time, however, the pain and weakness persist because of stretched nerves. This is a serious injury, and you must not return to action until you have recovered full strength, which may take weeks.

In this case, when you sustain a blow to the *left* side of the head and your head is knocked toward your right shoulder, you feel pain down your *left* arm. This is due to the nerve being stretched on the left side of the neck as the head is pushed to the right.

If you still feel pain at the end of activity, see a doctor. Do not return to action without the doctor's approval. An earlier return may reinjure the nerves and cause permanent damage.

✚ NECK MUSCLE INJURIES

When you wake up in the morning and can turn your head only one way, you are suffering from wryneck, or spastic torticollis, which is due to a pulled muscle or a muscle spasm. The same type of injury can happen in sports, such as when you look up and serve or hit an overhead smash in tennis. You feel the pain on one side of the neck, and your neck may be pulled over slightly to that side. It's particularly painful to turn your head in the direction of the pain. That is, if the pain is on the left side of your neck, you can turn to the right but not to the left.

The proper treatment is to apply ice for 20 minutes at a time and gently stretch the neck (see the stretching program at the end of this chapter). If the pain is severe, you may need medication, such as a muscle relaxant or anti-inflammatory agents, and physical therapy.

✚ TRAPEZIUS TRIGGERS

Severe muscle spasm in a localized area of the neck can cause another injury, called triggers of the trapezius, characterized by a very painful area at the base of the neck or extending out above the collarbone. Any athlete can suffer this injury by pulling fibers in the trapezius muscle or from a direct blow to the muscle fibers in the neck.

The muscle spasm in the neck sets up a reflex arc that feeds on itself. The spasm causes nerves to fire and gives the sensation of pain. This electrical impulse causes other nerve fibers to fire and the muscle to contract more. This, in turn, causes the pain fibers to fire, starting the whole cycle all over again.

For treatment, ice the neck for 20 minutes and then massage it gently with your fingers while stretching the muscle (see Trapezius Stretch).

If the pain is severe, you may need physical therapy, including electrotherapy, which involves electrical stimulation of the neck muscles. Very severe pain may require an injection of cortisone and novocaine.

MD WHIPLASH

The neck muscles, as well as the ligaments that hold the bones of the neck, can become severely strained. A combination of muscle and ligament strain to the neck due to a sudden, violent movement is called whiplash.

This can be a severe injury that takes up to six months to heal. It should be seen by a physician and x-rayed to make sure that the vertebrae in the neck have not slipped out of alignment or become fractured.

The treatment for whiplash is rest for two or three days, followed by physical therapy. Anti-inflammatory drugs can also help ease the discomfort. The injury may also require a cervical collar, which is a high collar that supports the weight of the head and takes the strain off the ligaments.

Preventing Neck Injuries

Probably the best way to prevent a neck injury is to strengthen your neck muscles. The huge necks you see on college and professional football players do not happen by accident. They are the result of long hours of exercise to increase neck muscle strength.

Every athlete should work on improving neck strength. You can do basic exercises by applying resistance against yourself or by working with a partner.

Neck-Strengthening Exercises

Neck Tilt Against Resistance

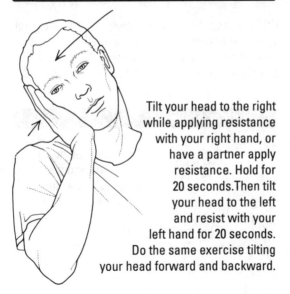

Tilt your head to the right while applying resistance with your right hand, or have a partner apply resistance. Hold for 20 seconds. Then tilt your head to the left and resist with your left hand for 20 seconds. Do the same exercise tilting your head forward and backward.

Shoulder Shrug with Barbell

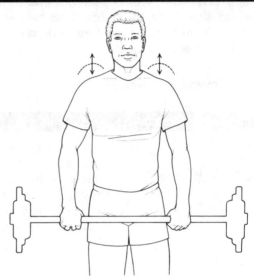

Hold a barbell with 50 to 100 pounds of weight straight down in front of you with your elbows locked. Now shrug your shoulders and hold for five seconds. Do five repetitions for five sets. This helps build up the trapezius muscle in your neck. If you are starting out, you may need to use less weight and build up gradually to the specified weight.

A Stretching Program for Pain Relief

To help alleviate minor neck pain, here are some simple exercises. Probably the best stretch of them all is the Trapezius Stretch. If you have serious neck problems, consult your physician before trying these exercises.

Neck-Stretching Exercises

Trapezius Stretch

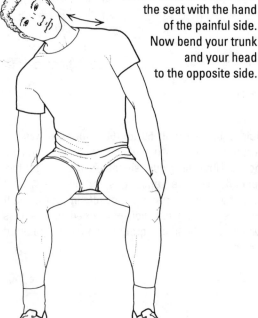

Sit in a chair and hold onto the seat with the hand of the painful side. Now bend your trunk and your head to the opposite side.

Funky Pigeon

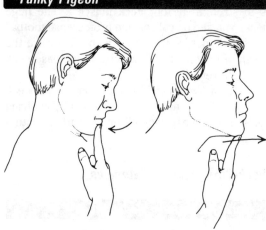

While sitting down, look slowly to the side, first over one shoulder and then over the other, five times back and forth. Then get "funky" like a pigeon: Jut your chin forward and back five times.

Shoulder Shrug

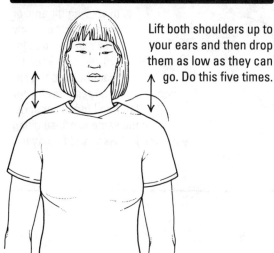

Lift both shoulders up to your ears and then drop them as low as they can go. Do this five times.

Chin Drop

Gently drop your chin to your chest. Now move your chin in a semicircle from shoulder to shoulder five times.

Shoulder Roll

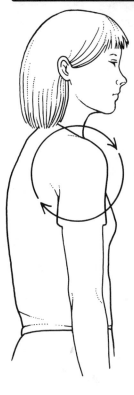

Roll your shoulders by making a circle. Lift both shoulders and roll them forward five times, and then lift and roll them backward five times.

The Shoulder

Related Sports Chapters

Baseball and Softball	Running, Jogging, and Track and Field
Basketball	
Football and Rugby	Skiing
Golf	Swimming and Other Water Sports
Gymnastics and Cheerleading	Tennis and Other Racquet Sports
Hockey, Lacrosse, and Skating	Triathlon
	Volleyball
	Wrestling

The shoulder is a unique joint and is prone to a great many injuries. It's a very shallow ball-and-socket joint. The head, which has little contact with the small socket, can easily slide out of it, which means that the joint is not very stable. The rest of the shoulder socket is formed by ligaments that connect various parts of the bony components of the socket, and cartilage around the small rim of the bony socket.

The shoulder is the only joint in the body not really held together by ligaments. The few ligaments in the shoulder serve only to keep the shoulder from moving too far in any one direction. The ligaments have little to do with holding the joint in place.

The shoulder socket also contains three tendons: the tendons of the long and short heads of the biceps muscle and the supraspinatus tendon. The biceps tendons connect the biceps muscle to the bones of the shoulder and help the biceps flex the forearm. The supraspinatus tendon connects the supraspinatus muscle and the bone of the shoulder, and aids the supraspinatus to move the humerus, the bone between the shoulder and the elbow. Directly below the socket is the brachial plexus, which houses all of the nerves that supply the arm.

The shoulder bones are held together by a group of muscles you read about often in the sports pages: the rotator cuff muscles. These muscles are also responsible for the shoulder's fine movements, such as throwing a ball. Because of the shoulder's shallow socket and lack of ligaments, any weakness of the small rotator cuff muscles makes it easy for the head of the shoulder to slide part way out of the socket, which is a partial dislocation, or subluxation. Or it may slide all the way out, which is a full dislocation.

⊞ ROTATOR CUFF INJURY

Sports in which you bring your arm up over your head, such as baseball, tennis, volleyball, and swimming, are the main contributors to overuse injuries of the shoulder. The rotator cuff muscles are not meant to function under stress with the arm above a line parallel to the ground. If the shoulder joint is continually stressed with the arm in this overhead position, the rotator cuff muscles begin to stretch out. This allows the head of the joint to become loose within the shoulder socket.

If the head of the shoulder is loose, when you extend your arm backward over the shoulder the head will slide forward, catching the tendon of the short head of the biceps between the ball and the socket. The same thing happens if you raise your arm to the side above a line parallel to the ground. The head will drop in the socket, and the tendon of the long head of the biceps will become impinged. The supraspinatus muscle may also become impinged.

This impingement causes the tendons to become inflamed and painful. Baseball pitchers tend to feel the pain in both the long and short heads of the biceps, and tennis players feel the pain particularly in the long head of the biceps. Athletes such as free-style and butterfly swimmers who feel pain deep in the shoulder are impinging the supraspinatus tendon.

Tennis players with this injury tell me they can hit their ground strokes effortlessly, but when they try an overhead stroke or serve, their shoulder hurts. The same thing can happen to golfers in both the backswing and the follow-through, when their arms are above parallel to the ground.

How Not to Treat Rotator Cuff Problems

Many doctors overlook the true problem with a shoulder impingement. They treat the tendinitis (inflamed tendons) with anti-inflammatory agents or cortisone (steroid) injections. But the anti-inflammatories soon wear off, and the next time the individual throws a ball, the tendon is pinched or impinged again. The pain returns, requiring another injection or more anti-inflammatories.

All too often I see a high school or college baseball pitcher with a sore shoulder whose doctor has told him not to throw for a while, just to rest it. So the pitcher stops throwing, the pain subsides, and by the end of the season he's fine. During the off-season, he continues to rest his shoulder. The next spring, after three or four days of throwing, the pitcher's arm hurts again, and he's right back where he started. Consequently, he has to miss the entire season while he restrengthens his rotator cuff muscles.

I have seen untreated impingements ruin the careers of many young, promising athletes. Surprisingly, many of them are swimmers. Swimming is often called the perfect form of exercise because it works both the upper- and lower-body muscles to improve conditioning with little pounding on the joints. However, most young, competitive swimmers who train at great distances

end up with rotator cuff problems. The overhead motion of pulling the arm through the water hour after hour, day after day, eventually causes an impingement of the rotator cuff.

The Right Treatment for Rotator Cuff Injuries

The proper way to treat a shoulder impingement is through an exercise program to strengthen the rotator cuff muscles sufficiently so that the head of the shoulder is held firmly in place and will not slip out of the socket. With no slipping, the tendons will no longer be inflamed or irritated.

Rotator-Cuff-Strengthening Exercises

You can restrengthen your rotator cuff muscles initially at home with a free-weight program. Using 15 pounds as the absolute maximum weight, do the following exercises until fatigue sets in or for 50 repetitions once a day.

Arm Curl (standing)

Hold a dumbbell with your palm facing forward and your hand at your side. Bend your elbow and lift the weight to your shoulder. Slowly lower the weight to the starting position.

Reverse Arm Curl

Hold a dumbbell with your palm facing backward and your hand at your side. Bend your elbow and lift the weight to your shoulder. Slowly lower the weight to the starting position.

Front Lift (palm down)

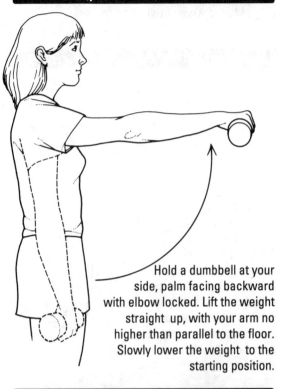

Hold a dumbbell at your side, palm facing backward with elbow locked. Lift the weight straight up, with your arm no higher than parallel to the floor. Slowly lower the weight to the starting position.

Front Lift (palm up)

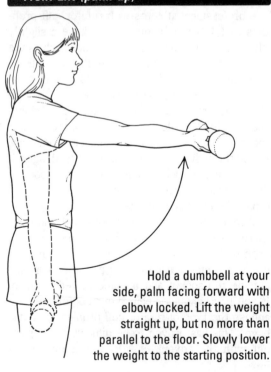

Hold a dumbbell at your side, palm facing forward with elbow locked. Lift the weight straight up, but no more than parallel to the floor. Slowly lower the weight to the starting position.

Lateral Lift

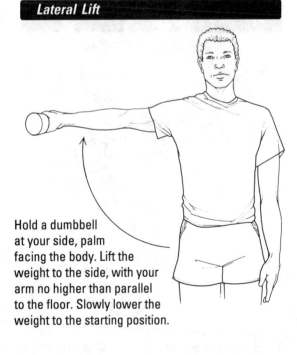

Hold a dumbbell at your side, palm facing the body. Lift the weight to the side, with your arm no higher than parallel to the floor. Slowly lower the weight to the starting position.

Bent-over Lateral Lift

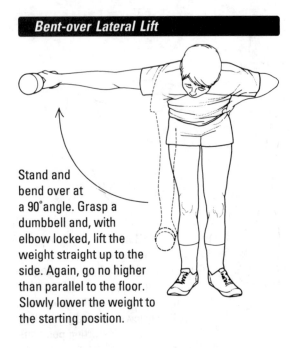

Stand and bend over at a 90°angle. Grasp a dumbbell and, with elbow locked, lift the weight straight up to the side. Again, go no higher than parallel to the floor. Slowly lower the weight to the starting position.

Bent-over Chest Lift

Stand and bend over at a 90° angle. Grasp a dumbbell and, with elbow locked, lift the weight across your chest. Slowly lower the weight to the starting position.

Your doctor may prescribe physical therapy, in which case a physical therapist can design an exercise program for you. Three out of every four rotator cuff problems can be cured with simple exercises.

If the problem has not begun to disappear in six to eight weeks, you may need to use special isokinetic exercise machines, such as Cybex® machines. These machines use a computerized system that senses your effort and, at any given millisecond, adjusts the resistance to meet your force. Also, for some movements of the shoulder, such as the follow-through for a pitcher, muscles are hard to rehabilitate with free weights. Unless you stand on your head, the weight is coming down from the force of gravity and offers no resistance. A Cybex machine provides the proper resistance for any motion.

Some people do not respond to rehabilitation, even with physical therapy, and will require surgery to repair the shoulder joint.

The Pro's Rotator Cuff Injury

The professional athletes with rotator cuff problems that you read about usually have a slightly different injury. For a baseball pitcher such as the Mets' Dwight Gooden, who has thrown millions of pitches over the years, the rotator cuff muscles can become so overdeveloped that they no longer fit into the shoulder socket. As a consequence, they rub along the outside of the socket, and eventually some of the muscle fibers are sawed through as they ride back and forth against the rim of the socket. The only way to correct this is through surgery to enlarge the socket and repair the damaged muscle fibers.

About 1 in 200 people is born with naturally narrow shoulder sockets. For such a person, even when the rotator cuff muscles are not built up, as a professional athlete's are, they can ride outside the socket and become sawed through. If you have shoulder pain, your doctor must diagnose the type of rotator cuff problem you may have. This has proved to be difficult in the past, but with the advent of MRI it is much easier now.

A Rotator Cuff Tear

A torn rotator cuff used to mean the end of a baseball pitcher's career or of weekend tennis matches. Tearing these muscles left the shoulder weak. Today, tearing the rotator cuff muscles is not as much of a problem because of improved rehabilitation programs and much better surgery.

A torn rotator cuff receives the same initial treatment as a stretched one—a good rehabilitation program. Some tears will heal without surgery. The surgery is difficult and should be avoided if at all possible. Consider surgery only if you don't respond well to rehabilitation.

If the tear is not too large, a simpler surgery through a lighted tube, or arthroscope, may be possible. Arthroscopic surgery, which has revolutionized treatment of the knee, is coming into more widespread use for the shoulder. Repairing the rotator cuff muscles through the arthroscope provides a new, less invasive way to treat this injury.

Another potential problem with a rotator cuff tear develops during the recovery period after surgery. When you rest a shoulder, as you must for four to six weeks after rotator cuff surgery, and avoid moving it in certain ways, the shoulder loses its ability to make those movements. The result may be a partially "frozen" shoulder with limited motion. This requires a diligent rehabilitation program, and it can be a long, painful process to get the shoulder to move through its full range of motion.

MD WEIGHT LIFTER'S SHOULDER

Weight lifters also suffer from overuse injuries of the shoulder. In particular, the bench press often leads to shoulder pain in the joint where the collarbone meets the shoulder blade, called the acromioclavicular (AC) joint. The small amount of cartilage between these two bones can tear or degenerate from the stress of weight lifting. When the cartilage is damaged, bone rubs on bone, causing pain.

This injury is not common among well-trained or world-class weight lifters. In fact, I have never seen it in any of the Giants' players, even though bench pressing is an important part of their training. That's because our players are coached in the proper lifting technique.

People who work out on their own are the ones most likely to develop weight lifter's shoulder. They typically do not space their hands correctly on the bar and try to lift too much too soon. Usually, rest for a few weeks and an injection of cortisone provides temporary relief. If the pain becomes chronic, then a small piece of the outer end of the collarbone can be removed surgically. This widens the space between the two bones and relieves the pressure in the joint, enabling you to return to full, pain-free weight lifting.

✚ SHOULDER MUSCLE PULLS

Like any area of the body, the shoulder is subject to muscle pulls. The mechanism is the same: the muscle overcontracts or overstretches, causing muscle fibers to tear. This is typical among wrestlers and in the throwing sports.

The proper treatment is a short rest period, about three to seven days, followed by stretching and then strengthening exercises. As with all muscle pulls, you should warm up and then stretch and lengthen the shoulder muscles to prevent pulling them again.

Because of the complexity and number of muscles around the shoulder that can pull, you need to see a physician to get a diagnosis of which muscles are involved and then a physical therapist for a program specifically designed for those muscles. You cannot rehabilitate torn shoulder muscles yourself. Find out which ones are torn and what to do for them.

MD THE OTHER SHOULDER PAIN: BURSITIS

Some doctors call any kind of shoulder pain "bursitis." However, true bursitis occurs only in the pillowlike sacs of fluid, called bursas, found throughout the body. These sacs vary in size tremendously, from the size of a lemon pit to that of a large lemon. Bursas occur where a tendon has to turn a corner and go around a bone; they allow the tendon to slide freely without wearing itself out as it rubs against the bone. Overstressing these sacs causes them to become inflamed. Once they swell up, they become extremely painful.

Bursitis is different from tendinitis, although both can be very painful. Usually, you don't feel the pain of tendinitis unless you use the tender body part. With bursitis, the body part is painful whether you move it or not. Also, you feel the tenderness of tendinitis all along the length of the tendon, but you feel it in one specific spot with bursitis.

The usual treatment for bursitis is a cortisone injection. You may have heard horror stories about having an injection for bursitis and how painful it is. Unfortunately, most of those stories are true. Putting more fluid into an already-inflamed sac causes a flare-up of severe pain for about a day. Once the cortisone takes effect, however, it cools down the inflammation, and the pain subsides.

I have found that the more humane way to treat bursitis is with cortisone by mouth for the first few days. The pills almost always provide rapid relief, and in many cases the bursitis calms down completely without any need for injections. Some bursitis sufferers, however, may still need injections because of the discomfort. These later injections do not cause as much pain since the inflammation and swelling in the bursa have already been reduced.

✚ SHOULDER "POPS": PARTIAL DISLOCATION

Jill's shoulder was so loose that she could dislocate her joint at will. In my office, I saw the 11-year-old gymnast slide it in and out by her-

self. The damage was so extensive that I knew she would require surgery. However, no doctor wanted to perform surgery because her muscles had not yet fully developed. So I put Jill on a weight-training program. Fortunately, she worked so hard at rehabilitating her shoulder that she never needed that operation.

A sudden force exerted against the shoulder can cause the head to slip momentarily out of the socket, that is, become partially dislocated, or subluxated. The shoulder's structures and shallow socket may allow the head to slip part way up onto the rim of the socket, and then the shoulder snaps back into place spontaneously. It feels as if your shoulder has "popped" out and then "popped" back in. But that's not really what happens. If the shoulder were truly dislocated, with the head all of the way out of the socket, it wouldn't "pop" back in spontaneously. Most people can't put a dislocated shoulder back in place by themselves the way Jill could. Often, it's difficult for even an experienced physician to get it back in place.

Many of the Giants' players have had partially dislocated shoulders. We would like their shoulder muscles to be strong enough that this doesn't happen, but the forces generated on the football field are so great that the players tend to have slippery shoulder sockets. Tight end Mark Bavaro had multiple problems with his shoulders, both of which had to be repaired surgically.

When the shoulder head slides partially out and then snaps back in, it stretches the rotator cuff muscles, and you have the same problem as an overuse injury. The shoulder begins to slide around, causing an impingement and tendinitis. Because the rotator cuff muscles are stretched, the next time the shoulder takes a blow, the head is likely to slide out again. With each blow you take, the rotator cuff gets looser and looser until finally your shoulder is in danger of truly dislocating.

The standard treatment for a subluxated shoulder is rest. But that's not enough. Your resting shoulder may not hurt, but the rotator cuff muscles are not getting any stronger. If the muscles stay loose, the shoulder joint can still slip later on. You must use the exercise program described earlier to strengthen the rotator cuff muscles to prevent future slipping.

These muscles are slow healers. The strengthening program usually takes 6 to 12 weeks, and the shoulder may not be back to full strength for six months or more.

✚ FULL DISLOCATION

A shoulder becomes fully dislocated when the head comes all the way out of the socket. This requires a much greater force than that needed for a partial dislocation.

A dislocation may stretch or tear the rotator cuff muscles. Usually, these muscles are just stretched, particularly among younger athletes. Older athletes, who have more brittle rotator cuffs, are more likely to tear the muscles. The only time I see a tear in a young athlete is in response to a high-impact injury, such as a fall while skiing on snow or water at high speed.

When I started practicing sports medicine, the standard treatment was to immobilize a dislocated shoulder for six weeks. But even after six weeks the shoulder never really worked well again, so we cut the immobilization time to three weeks. Now we know that rest is effective only when the rotator cuff muscles are also restrengthened. I can't emphasize enough that if you have shoulder pain or discomfort, even though it will go away with rest, you must restrengthen your rotator cuff muscles through an exercise program to regain full use of your shoulder.

It used to be that two shoulder dislocations meant surgery. And without rehabilitation after one dislocation, a second one happened quite frequently. Today, even with multiple dislocations, a good rehabilitation program can often tighten the shoulder muscles so that no surgery is necessary.

The problem with rehabilitation is that there is no way to tell beforehand whether it's going to work. A competitive volleyball player who bangs her shoulder diving for a ball may have minimal shoulder slipping or only one dislocation. She may rehabilitate her shoulder with exercise and yet still need surgery. A high school football player can have many dislocations and recover fully through rehabilitation alone.

✚ SHOULDER SEPARATION

"Separation" of the AC joint, where the end of collarbone meets the shoulder blade, is actually a sprain of the ligaments that connect the two bones. "Separation" is an old medical term that has been applied to the widening of the space between the bones. Since this problem involves ligaments, it really should be called a sprain.

As with all sprains, there are three degrees of severity. A mild, or first-degree, sprain causes a minimal stretching of the ligaments without much tearing of fibers, and the joint remains stable. There will be pain and swelling around the joint.

In a moderate, or second-degree, sprain, the ligaments are stretched more and partially torn, and the outer end of the collarbone will partially snap in and out of the joint. I diagnose this type of sprain by first taking an x-ray of both shoulders. Then I have my patient hold a 25-pound weight in each hand, and I take another x-ray. Because the weight pulls the two bones apart, the joint of the affected shoulder will be visibly wider on the second x-ray.

It's much easier to diagnose a severe, or third-degree, sprain. The complete disruption of all of the ligaments around the joint causes the collarbone to stand straight up.

The treatment for first- and second-degree shoulder sprains is rest. You will have to put the shoulder in a sling for one to three weeks, depending on the severity of the injury. Also, in addition to resting the shoulder, you must ice it for 20 to 30 minutes a few times a day in the beginning to ease the pain. These are particularly frustrating injuries because they can take six to eight weeks to heal. You may not be able to raise your arm laterally beyond 90° until the injury has healed.

For a third-degree shoulder sprain, surgical repair of the ligaments is necessary to fix the joint. Up to six weeks of recovery from surgery are necessary before you can begin a restrengthening program. This program consists of range-of-motion and strengthening exercises similar to those used to rehabilitate a shoulder impingement.

✚ BRUISED COLLARBONE

When I was with the Westchester Bulls, we had the only Japanese-American quarterback ever to play professional football. We always had a problem with Sieki Morono, better known as Zeke, because he was a reserve officer in the Marines. Every spring he had to miss two weeks of training camp while he put in his Marine training time.

In our last game of the 1970 Continental League season, Zeke took an extremely late hit and fell hard on his shoulder, severely bruising his collarbone. The injury became complicated when he began to lose calcium in the collarbone. We took an x-ray, which showed a terrible-looking deterioration of the collarbone, and sent it to the Marines, who gave him an immediate medical discharge. What they never knew was that, within six months, Zeke's shoulder had healed completely, and he played for several more seasons without any interruptions for Marine training.

A blow on the head of the collarbone can cause an ugly bruise. The blow causes a painful bone bruise, or contusion, but does not actually sprain the AC joint.

The injury usually heals without difficulty but may lead to a second condition called osteolysis.

This condition causes the bone to dissolve and deteriorate due to a loss of calcium. On an x-ray the collarbone has a frightening, mosslike appearance, and the physician can see the bone loss on the outer end of the bone.

Although this can be quite painful, the bone usually heals and becomes healthy again in 6 to 12 months, as Zeke's did, and the pain subsides. Otherwise, the outer edge of the collarbone can be shaved off surgically to relieve the pain.

✚ BROKEN COLLARBONE

The collarbone has an unusual restorative ability. If it is broken, it does not need to be set perfectly, as other broken bones do. As long as the pieces of the bone are in close proximity, they will bridge any gaps, heal, and form a new collarbone even stronger than the old one. As the bone heals, it grows over the site of the break, which will become somewhat thicker than the rest of the bone.

A broken collarbone is usually a concern only because it prevents you from functioning. However, in severe cases sharp fragments can cause damage to the surrounding tissue. If you feel a sharp pain aggravated by pressure or movement of the shoulder, see a physician. Proper treatment for a broken collarbone is immobilization to allow it to heal. A brace is used to pull the shoulders back and hold the ends of the bone in line. This injury takes six to eight weeks to heal completely, but there is usually enough early healing that the brace can be removed in about three weeks. Since the shoulder joints are not involved in the bracing, you have full use of your arms and shoulders, and no shoulder rehabilitation program is necessary.

The decision of when it's okay to return to activity has changed in recent years. Modern professional football players have the advantage of better protection with better-made shoulder pads, so we try to get them back into action quickly. Wide receiver Mark Ingram broke his collarbone early in the 1988 season, and he came back and played well six weeks later.

Since the healing rate and type of break differs widely, no amateur athlete should return to activity until a physician feels it's safe to do so.

This will vary depending on the sport and how much trauma may be sustained from that sport. A tennis player may get back to her regular game before a flag football player gets back to his.

7

The Back and Ribs

Nearly all injuries to the back are muscular in nature. About 95 percent of low-back pain is the result of muscular problems caused by lack of exercise, weak muscles, or overweight. Back problems can also be due to tense muscles or strain from suddenly overloading these muscles during activity. Muscle fibers may pull or tear, sending the back muscles into spasm and causing pain.

Even though the back muscles are the strongest in the body—you can lift four times more weight with the back than with the arms and shoulders—back injuries have become the leading occupational hazard in the United States: 25 million Americans claim that they lose at least a day's work each year due to back pain. Back pain is the second most common cause of lost time at work among people under age 45 (after the common cold), and 60 percent of people over age 30 have a propensity for back pain.

Fortunately, most simple backaches go away within a few weeks, with or without treatment, and 90 percent of them disappear within two months. A workout that strengthens the lower-back and abdominal muscles can prevent back pain, bring relief to those suffering from pain, and help prevent pain from recurring.

✚ BACK SPASM

When back muscles go into spasm, the force is so great that you may be disabled by excruciating pain. When these muscles go into spasm and shorten, it can cause your back to tilt severely to one side.

The treatment for back spasm is rest for a few days, medication such as aspirin or other anti-inflammatory agents, and possibly muscle relaxants. Use ice for as long as you feel pain. You may also need support from a girdle and physical therapy, which includes ice, then heat, electrical stimulation of muscles, stretching, and deep massage to relax the muscle. This should be followed by an exercise program to strengthen the back, described later in the chapter.

MD SHORT LEG SYNDROME

Another common cause of lower-back pain is a difference in the lengths of the legs. A quarter-inch difference can be significant in an athlete, whereas a nonathlete may get away with a difference of up to a half-inch. The back pain is usually felt on the side of the longer leg. This leg pounds into the ground when you run, throwing that whole side of the body out of alignment. The stress works its way all the way up to your back.

If you stretch your back regularly and still feel back pain, have a sports doctor or trainer measure the lengths of your legs. You can correct the problem by putting a lift in your shoe. At first, correct for only 50 percent of the difference. For example, if you have a quarter-inch difference, put in an eighth-inch lift. If need be, you can use a thicker lift later on. Your back pain should disappear almost immediately. If it doesn't, have a doctor check for other possible back problems.

MD BULGING DISC

Discs are fibrous pillows filled with a gel-like material found between the vertebrae. They act as shock absorbers for the spine, cushioning the vertebrae as they move against each other.

One of the most common back problems is a bulging disc. The wall of the disc bulges out into the spinal column. The disc, however, is not ruptured completely.

The disc bulge looks like a weak spot on the inner tube of a tire. The pressure of this bulge on the spinal cord or on the nerve roots coming out of the spine causes the pain. See your doctor for treatment.

MD RUPTURED DISC

A ruptured, or slipped, disc usually occurs in the lower (lumbar) spine, the area that takes the brunt of twisting and turning. Blown lumbar discs afflict 5 million Americans each year. A lifetime of poor posture, lifting heavy objects, or repetitive twisting motions in sports can weaken the discs and eventually cause a rupture.

A ruptured disc, also called a herniated disc, occurs when the disc capsule breaks open and protrudes into the spinal canal, pressing on nerve roots. Gel oozes out of the disc and causes more pressure on the spinal cord or the nerve roots. Over time, the gel usually disintegrates, and the symptoms may be relieved.

When a disc ruptures, however, the pad between the two vertebrae is gone, and the gradual wearing of bone on bone leads to arthritis. This can cause serious pain if the arthritic spurs of the vertebrae press on the nerve root. The pain will worsen as years go by without treatment.

The pain of a ruptured disc is usually sharp and sudden. Commonly, the pain will be passed along the course of the nerve impinged by the ruptured disc. A disc pressing on the sciatic nerve root causes sciatica, sending pain from the buttock down the leg and into the foot.

A bulging disc cannot be seen on a normal x-ray but can be picked up easily on a computed tomography or MRI scan. Only when the disc has completely disintegrated can the narrowed space between two vertebrae be seen on x-ray. So you may need more than a simple x-ray for your doctor to make the correct diagnosis.

Many ruptured discs will respond to bed rest. When you stand, each disc carries the weight of the body above it. Therefore, you need to take the weight off of the disc. Often, the disc will heal if you lie down until the pain recedes.

A back brace may help relieve the stress on the disc, and physical therapy can help relieve any muscle spasms associated with a ruptured disc. After you have passed the stage of acute pain, you will need to engage in a back-strengthening program.

If your symptoms do not subside, you may need surgery to remove some or all of the disc. What used to be a crude, major operation requiring long disability has become a much more sophisticated, simpler procedure with little difficulty afterward.

The majority of patients get better without surgery, even those with acutely ruptured discs. Surgery is prescribed for the 10 to 15 percent of patients who don't respond to conservative treatment or who feel weakness or numbness in their limbs, which is a sign of neurological problems.

The classic back operation, called a diskectomy, involves an incision in the lower back and removal of a small piece of the vertebra to expose the injured disc. Then the damaged part of the disc is cut out. Surgery now usually involves insertion of an arthroscope into the ruptured disc to suck out the gel and relieve pressure on the nerve.

A nonsurgical procedure popular in Europe is the injection of a papaya derivative called chymopapain into the center of the ruptured disc. This natural enzyme dissolves the gel to relieve the pain. However, this treatment has hazards and is not widely used in the United States.

MD CRACKED BACK

A fracture of the part of the vertebra connecting the front and rear portions of the bone is called spondylolysis. Originally, this was thought to be a congenital failure of the two halves of the vertebra to fuse. Now we believe that this is due to acute fractures caused by back trauma.

I see spondylolysis most commonly among young people who have chronic back pain for no apparent reason. Often, they have taken a fall before feeling any pain. If an x-ray reveals a fractured bone, I have to decide whether the fracture is fresh or old. A bone scan, a simple nuclear medicine procedure, helps identify fresh activity in the bone.

If the fracture is old or congenital, the treatment of choice is a strengthening program with reduced physical activity until the symptoms cease. If the fracture is fresh, the patient must stop all sports or physical activity for six months so that it can be determined whether or not the fracture will heal. Usually, rest alone is not enough to relieve all the symptoms, and a program to strengthen the back muscles is required afterward.

A back brace may be helpful during this time. However, a brace should be used only in the presence of acute pain. Back braces are not useful in the long run because they further weaken the back.

If the fracture doesn't heal, it may lead to another condition called spondylolisthesis, in which the front portion of the vertebra slips forward out of line with the other vertebrae. Most of the stabilizing ligaments of the spinal column are located behind the column. If the connecting bone does not heal, then almost any activity can cause the front part of the vertebra to slip forward.

After an initial period of rest to get the bone to heal, you can resume normal activity. If the vertebra slips, however, you will have to give up certain activities, such as diving and gymnastics, where you have to arch your back violently, and contact sports such as football and basketball, where you might take a heavy blow to the back. If a slipped vertebra progresses despite conservative treatments, you will need to have the vertebra fused surgically.

MD CRACKED WING

A wing is the protuberance at the lower side of each vertebra, and this wing can also crack from a blow to the back. The back muscles and ligaments attach to the spine at the wing, which is also called the transverse process. A wing fracture commonly occurs in football to running backs who are hit with a helmet from behind. Giants' quarterback Jeff Hostetler was put out of action for the last few games of the 1991 season when he broke three wings in his back.

Although very painful, this is not as serious a back fracture. You will need to rest and take anti-inflammatory agents to ease your pain, which typically lasts a few weeks. Once the pain disappears, you can return to activity as long as you put extra padding around the wing to protect it.

MD SCIATICA

Sciatica is not a true back problem but refers to pain along the course of the sciatic nerve. This nerve runs from the buttock down the back of the leg to the foot. Pressure on the sciatic nerve root at the spine causes the pain. It's necessary to find out what is causing the pressure and then treat it. Possible causes include impingement of a disc, an arthritic spur of a vertebra, a muscle spasm, or neurological problems in the spinal cord. Treatment for sciatica itself is not the answer since sciatica is only a symptom of the underlying problem.

Sciatica may be very easy or very difficult to diagnose. If you feel pain only in your thigh, it can be easily confused with a hamstring pull. If the pain goes all the way down the leg to the foot, it is obviously sciatica. Muscles and bones do not extend beyond a joint; only blood vessels and nerves traverse the whole leg, and blood vessels do not cause you pain.

If you feel increased pain upon bending over or while doing a straight leg raise, you may be stretching a nerve. Other indications of sciatica are a weak big toe, trouble in raising the front of the foot, and a diminished ankle reflex.

Preventing Back Problems

The basic prevention for back problems is to develop a strong back. Since most injuries are due to muscle weakness, increased strength is the answer to almost every back problem.

In the past, back doctors and sports medicine experts always recommended exercises that strengthen the flexor muscles of the back. This may be why back treatments have not been very successful. The flexor muscles are the ones that pull the back forward and down. But the body is naturally pulled in that direction by gravity. To lift your trunk into an erect position, you must use the extensor muscles. These are the muscles that you need to strengthen. Once you get through early flexion exercises, you must concentrate on extension exercises.

Recognizing the need to concentrate on extensor muscles has led to a change in the philosophy on how to recondition an injured back. Also, with machines such as the Cybex®, we can work muscles beyond the point of pain. The machine will indicate when you have reached the danger point and should stop exercising.

Also, through the use of electromyograph (EMG) machines, which measure muscular activity, researchers have found that the traditional sit-up used to strengthen the abdominal muscles actually does more harm than good. EMG results show that a sit-up with the fullest range of motion offers more potential for damage than a simple abdominal curl.

A Back-Strengthening Program

Back pain is slightly different in each person, and there are many different types of self-treatments. I prefer ice treatments for 20 to 30 minutes at a time, two or three times a day, for as long as the back is sore. I prescribe heat on the back only to loosen it up before activity once it has healed.

Bed rest for more than a couple of days only weakens your muscles and can be disabling. You need to get out of bed as soon as possible. Surgery should be considered only as a last resort.

If you suffer a back problem, chances are you will wind up on a regimen of daily stretching and strengthening exercises to recondition your back. These exercises are designed to strengthen the muscles that support the back, especially the abdominal muscles; to stretch overly tight muscles and ligaments in the back so that they are less likely to be injured; and to reduce the defects in posture that strain the back. Strong, flexible muscles around the lower back and abdomen stabilize the spine and protect it from injury.

Back-Stretching and Flexion Exercises

You can do back exercises at home to strengthen both your extensor and flexor muscles. To strengthen an acutely injured back, start with stretching and flexion exercises.

Slow Toe-Touch

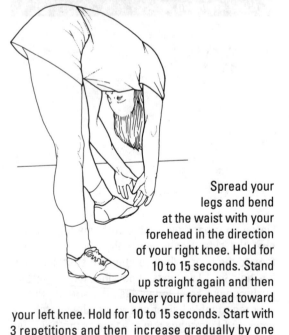

Lower your forehead between your knees while standing. Go as far as you can go, and then grasp behind your knees and try to go a little farther. Hold for 10 to 15 seconds. Start with three repetitions and then increase gradually by one every other day until you reach 12 repetitions.

Hurdler Stretch (standing)

While standing, put one foot on a chair in front of you. Now bend your forehead forward and try to touch it to your knee. Use the same number of repetitions as for the toe-touch exercises. Repeat with the other leg.

Toe-Touch with Rotation

Spread your legs and bend at the waist with your forehead in the direction of your right knee. Hold for 10 to 15 seconds. Stand up straight again and then lower your forehead toward your left knee. Hold for 10 to 15 seconds. Start with 3 repetitions and then increase gradually by one every other day until you reach 12 repetitions.

Knee Pull with Head Curl

This exercise increases flexibility in the hip, lower back, and buttock muscles. Lie on your back with knees bent and feet flat on the floor. Bring one knee up toward your chest and clasp the knee with both hands. As you pull the knee down gently, curl your head up slightly. Hold for 10 to 15 seconds. Return the leg to the starting position and do the same number of repetitions as for the toe touches. Repeat with the other leg.

Pelvic Tilt

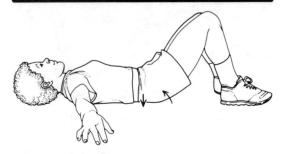

While lying on your back with knees bent and feet flat on the floor, relax the back muscles and tighten your abdominal and buttock muscles to press your back flat against the floor. This will tilt your pelvis forward. Once you have a totally flat back, do the same number of repetitions as for the toe touches.

Back Extension

Stand up straight, arms at your side, and slowly lean your upper body back from the waist. Try to look at the ceiling. Hold for 10 seconds, and then relax and straighten up. Do five repetitions and build up by twos as the stretch becomes easier.

Abdominal Curl

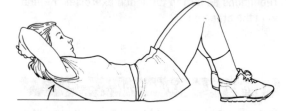

Lie on your back, knees bent and feet flat on the floor, with your hands clasped behind your head. Slowly curl your shoulder blades up off the floor, leaving your back on the floor. Hold for five seconds and slowly lower your head and shoulders. Start with five repetitions, increasing the number by five as the curls get easier.

Extension Exercises

As you become more comfortable and your back muscles begin to lengthen, you can start extension exercises.

Hip Extension

Lie on your back on a table with one leg hanging over the side. Gently lower the leg from the hip toward the floor. When you feel the stretch in your hip, hold for 10 seconds. If possible, have a partner push on your knee to increase the stretch. Return your leg to table height and repeat the stretch five times. Add stretches two at a time as this becomes easier.

Reverse Sit-up

This involves working with a partner, who will have to hold your legs down. Lie on your stomach on a table, with only your legs and pelvis on the table. Have your partner hold your ankles while you bend at the waist off the edge until your forehead is pointing to the floor. Then slowly lift your upper body until it is horizontal again. Do five repetitions and add two at a time as this becomes easier.

Pain-Free Sports

Orthopedists often advise back pain sufferers to avoid sports that put severe stress on the back. However, a back problem should not doom you to a life of inactivity. You can participate in almost any sport if you take some precautions.

Pain-free activities include swimming, walking, cross-country skiing, and stationary cycling. These can all be done without sharp, sudden movements; severe arching of the back; twisting or rotating of the trunk; heavy impact; or unexpected, awkward falls.

Bicycling is almost pain-free because it is a non-weight-bearing exercise; there is no weight on your legs and thighs and no pounding of joints. People who have back problems probably are better off using the upright handlebars on traditional bicycles. Sitting upright places less stress on the back.

Running can lead to back problems from the impact of the foot strike, abnormal foot mechanics, the forcing of imbalanced muscles to work harder, and the attempt to run too fast, not to mention the problems that result if one leg is slightly longer than the other. If you are an avid runner, you may have to curtail your running to every other day, and you should try to run on soft surfaces with good, shock-absorbent shoes.

Tennis can be challenging for anyone with back pain, with all of its twisting, flexing, and extending motions. If you are plagued by a bad back, try to flatten out your serve to eliminate excessive arching and twisting. You may also consider wearing a back brace. Try to pick up balls by holding them between a foot and the racquet rather than bending at the waist.

Aerobic dancing is terrible for all kinds of low-back pain. Try low-impact, not high-impact, aerobics; or, better yet, opt for water aerobics.

Golfers should beware of the torsion placed on the back during the swing. Tone up your abdominal muscles to help prevent back injuries. Remember to bend at the knees, not the waist, when placing a tee in the ground and when lining up a putt.

You are at risk of throwing out your back from basketball, volleyball, downhill skiing, dancing, bowling, football, baseball, or any other sport requiring lots of arching, twisting, and sudden starts and stops. Take it easy at the start of the season, and always ease muscles in and out of activity with warmup, warmdown, and stretching. If you are out of shape, don't push yourself beyond your range of motion.

PREVENTING EVERYDAY BACK STRAIN

Equally important is learning how to perform ordinary movements so that you don't strain your back.

Consistent, good posture is the first step toward maintaining a pain-free back. Keep your shoulders back and your lower back supported by a pillow when sitting.

Carrying heavy loads can be a problem for someone with a bad back. When you lift objects from the floor, squat as close as possible to the object and lift with your legs, not your back. Lift smoothly; the faster the lift, the more stress on your spine.

Know the weight of an object so that you can prepare yourself mentally before lifting it. Don't bend at the waist. The muscles in front of your thighs are among the strongest in the body; let them do the work.

Do not carry heavy briefcases or luggage. Instead, use a luggage roller whenever possible.

When gardening, cleaning the floor, or do-ing other prolonged, back-straining activities near the ground, kneel on one knee rather than bend-ing at the waist. Back problems can be exac-erbated by spending time hunched over a desk that's too low for you. Try to keep your work surface at elbow height. Adjust the height of your chair so that you can sit with your feet flat on the floor and your knees level with your hips. If you have a desk job, take frequent breaks. Get up at least once an hour and walk around for a few minutes.

Avoid wearing high heels, which place greater pressure on the back than flats do.

THE RIBS

The ribs are bones in the chest that attach to the vertebrae. There are 12 ribs on each side of the body. They serve two functions: They act like bars of a cage to protect the lungs and heart from blows, and they help the chest wall expand and collapse so that air can move through the lungs.

The ribs do not attach directly to the breast bone in the front. If they did, the rib cage would be so rigid that you would not be able to breathe. Flexible cartilage connects the end of each rib to the breastbone.

✚ BRUISED RIBS

A blow to an unprotected rib cage can bruise the ribs. The treatment for bruised ribs is to rest them and apply ice until the pain is gone. You can continue activities if you use a pad to protect the ribs. This pad, made of strong plastic with an absorbent material underneath, looks like a flak jacket; it hangs on the shoulders and wraps around the rib cage. Several varieties are avail-able in sporting goods stores.

MD SEPARATED RIB

A severe blow can cause a rib separation, in which the rib tears loose from the cartilage in the front.

You will feel severe pain, usually toward the front of the rib cage, and it will hurt to breathe. When you bend over or rotate your body, you may feel a "pop." It will be particularly painful to go from a lying to a sitting position, so you may have trouble getting out of bed in the morning. If someone puts one hand on your back and the other on your breastbone and squeezes, you will feel tremendous pain.

The treatment is to use a rib belt. This is a strap of elastic, about eight inches wide, that goes around the rib cage. It stretches tight and closes in front with Velcro®. This compresses the rib cage so that it can't expand too far. The belt holds the rib end in place until it heals and lessens the pain of everyday movements.

No matter how much you may want to, you can't participate in sports when you have separated ribs. The resulting pain will be too much to allow you to continue.

EMERGENCY
BROKEN RIB

The ultimate injury from a blow to the rib cage is a broken rib. The pain may occur anywhere in the rib cage depending on where the rib is broken. It may be that more than one rib is broken.

You will feel the same pain as with bruised or separated ribs, only more severe. You should be concerned about sharp ends of broken ribs and should have an x-ray. **Any excessive strain or movement, or another blow, can cause a sharp end to puncture a lung,** **sending you to the hospital for emergency treatment.**

Again, the treatment is to rest (for about six weeks) and to wear a rib belt until the pain is gone. An x-ray must show that the ribs have healed before you can return to activity.

✚ PULLED RIB MUSCLE

The muscle between each pair of ribs, the intercostal muscle, which is the muscle used in respiration, may pull or tear due to overstress. This can happen to a tennis or football player who makes a sudden, violent lateral motion or suddenly rotates the rib cage.

As a result, you will feel tenderness between the ribs, not on them. Again, rest the ribs and ice them until the pain disappears, and use a rib belt until you can move about freely.

The Elbow

The elbow is an important joint to athletes not only because of its use in so many sports, but also because it is a common source of misery, particularly in racquet and throwing sports. The elbow is actually three separate joints, consisting of the junction of the two bones of the forearm and the junction of each of these bones with the humerus, the bone of the upper arm. These three interfaces allow the elbow to bend and straighten and also to rotate, which allows you to move your hand from palm up to palm down.

An elbow injury can also be caused by wrist problems. The muscles that control the wrist originate from the elbow's bones. So many of the problems that arise from excessive wrist strain cause pain in the elbow rather than the wrist.

✚ TENNIS ELBOW

Tennis elbow, the most common elbow injury, is really an inflammation of the muscles of the forearm and the tendon that connects the muscles to the bones in the elbow. These muscles are used to bend the wrist backward and to turn the palm face up. When the muscles and tendon become inflamed from overuse, you feel pain on the outside of your elbow (the lateral epicondyle). The pain is worse when you try to lift things with your palm facing down, so you may have trouble picking up a coffee cup or taking a quart of milk out of the refrigerator.

Tennis elbow also causes pain when you rotate your hand in a clockwise direction, as you would in using a screwdriver or in screwing in a light bulb. You also will feel pain when you clench or squeeze something, such as when you shake hands or hold a racquet or golf club. The pain may become so severe that it makes combing your hair virtually impossible.

Golfers also suffer from tennis elbow, but on the nondominant side; a right-handed golfer will feel the pain in the left elbow. Pulling the club through the swing with the left wrist causes irritation in the left elbow. So a right-handed golfer who feels pain in the right arm or wrist is doing something terribly wrong during the swing.

A tennis player most often aggravates the elbow by hitting the ball late on a backhand swing. The backhand, most players' *bête noire*, is an especially difficult stroke to master. When hitting the ball with your weight on your back foot, you have to compensate by mostly using your arm, and hitting late causes your elbow to be bent. You end up straining the forearm muscles and tendon. You can also get tennis elbow by turning your wrist to put more spin on the serve.

Treatment for Tennis Elbow

Once your elbow becomes inflamed, everyday activities are enough to keep it irritated. Giving up your weekly tennis game to rest your elbow is not enough to solve the problem. Treating tennis elbow requires an exercise program to increase the strength and flexibility of the forearm muscles and tendon. Once they are strong enough to withstand the stress of a bad backhand, the pain will go away and won't return.

Forearm-Strengthening Exercises

You will need a small dumbbell, 5 pounds for men and 2.5 pounds for women. The weight can be gradually increased as your strength improves.

In addition to the strengthening exercises shown here, do Arm Curls and Reverse Arm Curls (see Chapter 6).

Wrist Curl

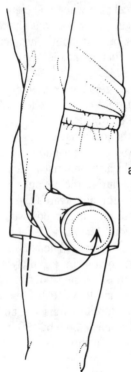

Hold the dumbbell with your arm down by your side and your elbow locked. With your palm facing forward, flex the wrist forward all the way and then let it back down. Repeat 50 times or until the muscle is exhausted.

Reverse Wrist Curl

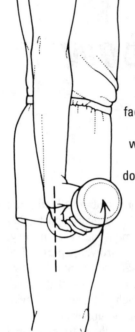

Put your arm down by your side and turn your hand so that the palm faces backward. Holding the dumbbell, flex your wrist forward as far as it will go and then let it down. Repeat 50 times or to the point of muscle exhaustion.

Unbalanced Wrist Rotation

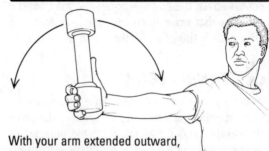

With your arm extended outward, hold the dumbbell by one knob so that the shaft and the other knob come out on the thumb side of your hand. Now rotate your wrist so that the other knob rotates to the left, then all the way to the right, and then back to center again. Do 50 complete left-to-right rotations or repeat until muscle exhaustion.

Roll-up

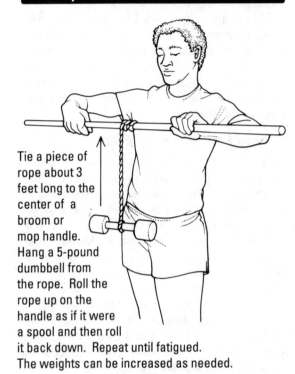

Tie a piece of rope about 3 feet long to the center of a broom or mop handle. Hang a 5-pound dumbbell from the rope. Roll the rope up on the handle as if it were a spool and then roll it back down. Repeat until fatigued. The weights can be increased as needed.

Ball Squeezing

Hold a soft rubber ball and squeeze it continually until your hand is fatigued. Sporting goods stores also carry a substance called hand putty, which can be squeezed in the same way.

Elbow Flexibility Exercises

When you start the exercise program, you may feel some pain because you are overloading the elbow to make it stronger. The following flexibility exercises such as these elbow stretches will help relieve this pain.

In a week to 10 days you should begin to feel better. You may need to use anti-inflammatory agents during those first 10 days of therapy.

Elbow Stretch (palm up)

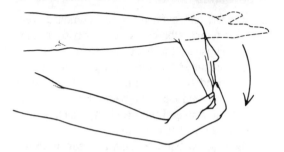

Extend your arm straight out, parallel to the floor with the elbow locked, palm facing up. With your other hand, push the palm and fingers of the extended hand toward the floor. Hold for 15 to 20 seconds.

Elbow Stretch (palm down)

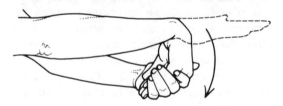

Extend your arm straight out, parallel to the floor with the elbow locked, palm facing down. Push the top of your hand and fingers of the extended hand down toward the floor with your other hand. Hold for 15 to 20 seconds.

"Just Say No" to Cortisone

In the past, and even now, the standard treatment for tennis elbow has been cortisone injections. This is *not* the best long-term treatment. Injecting an anti-inflammatory agent such as cortisone around an inflamed tendon will reduce the inflammation and ease the pain. But this doesn't address the cause of the problem, which is overstressing the forearm tendon.

When the cortisone begins to wear off in four to six weeks, the forces that caused the tendinitis in the first place will remain, causing the pain and stress to recur, and you will need a second injection of cortisone. To remain pain-free, you will have to repeat the whole process again and again. This may be good for your doctor's bank account, but it isn't good for your elbow. Eventually, these cortisone injections can irreparably damage the tendon.

Alternative Treatments

Occasionally, I have patients who are resistant to treatment with the exercise program alone. I then use a cortisone injection to reduce the inflammation so that they can actively work on strengthening the elbow without too much pain. I use cortisone only as a last resort, not as a primary treatment for tennis elbow. I also put some patients into physical therapy, where they can exercise under supervision.

I may also introduce deep friction massage. This is a quite painful technique in which a physical therapist applies deep thumb pressure back and forth across the tendon. The irritation causes increased blood flow to the tendon and promotes healing. Another way of increasing blood flow is electrotherapy, which passes an electric current through the tendon.

Other modalities include iontophoresis, in which a cortisone solution is painted on the skin and then driven through to the tendon with an electric current. This concentrates cortisone around the tendon without subjecting the tendon to the damage of an injection. When all else has failed, I have had success in some patients with a cold quartz laser.

Every one to two years I get a patient who needs surgery to repair tennis elbow. Such a patient has detached some tendon fibers from the bone and has a "dead spot" in the center of the tendon. The only therapy is surgery to clean out the dead area of tendon, followed by reattachment of the tendon.

How to Prevent Tennis Elbow

To prevent tennis elbow, do the same strengthening and flexibility exercises that were outlined for treatment. Also, make sure that you warm up and stretch your arm before playing a vigorous set. You should also seek the advice of a tennis instructor to correct your backhand stroke so that you hit the ball properly. Choosing the proper tennis racquet and string pressure can also prevent tennis elbow; see Chapter 29.

If you have a history of tennis elbow or feel twinges of pain after playing, wait at least half an hour after your match and then ice the elbow down. Icing is more effective once the elbow has returned to normal body temperature.

✚ *TENNIS ELBOW II*

Another type of tennis elbow is characterized by pain on the inner side of elbow (the medial epicondyle). This pain involves inflammation of the muscles and tendon that allow you to pronate the wrist, that is, turn it over so that the palm faces down. I see this elbow pain in tennis players who hit topspin forehands, which require them to turn the racquet head over the top of the ball. Many top-ranked tennis players feel pain on the inner side of the elbow because they hit a lot of topspin shots. For the weekend player, the culprit may be a late forehand that requires snapping the wrist and pronating the forearm.

Other sports that require a snap of the wrist, such as the throwing sports, can also lead to this type of elbow pain. Prevention and treatment measures are the same. The exercises outlined earlier also strengthen and stretch the inner side of the elbow. I also recommend that you work on your biomechanics with a coach, particularly if you feel pain during the throwing motion. Pitchers with good biomechanics can throw for years without elbow problems.

PITCHER'S ELBOW

Baseball pitchers suffer a type of elbow pain that occurs on the inner side of the elbow or on both the inner and outer sides. In the pitching motion, there is a tremendous external rotational force on the elbow that spreads the inner side and compresses the outer side. The ligaments that hold the inner bones together are stretched and become painful. At the same time, compression of the outer side causes the head of the outer forearm bone (radius) to jam against the upper bone (humerus).

The repeated trauma of this compression can cause an area of bone in the humerus to die. This is similar to the injury Bo Jackson suffered in his hip, but it is due to repeated trauma rather than the one blow he took playing football. It is called osteochondritis dissecans. The dead piece of bone can actually fall into the joint, leaving a crater. This causes continued pain and clicking in the elbow. If a fragment gets caught in the joint, it can cause the elbow to lock.

To diagnose this injury, your doctor will have you extend your arm from the side. While you hold the upper part of your arm close to your body, the doctor will push the lower part of the arm away from your body. This reproduces the rotational forces that cause pitcher's elbow.

The treatment for this condition is rest, which will allow the elbow ligament and bone to heal. It may take a full year for the bone to heal. If you have loose pieces of bone inside the elbow, you will need arthroscopic surgery to remove them.

The cause of this injury is throwing too many pitches too often. After the elbow heals, you should watch how many pitches you throw and change your throwing routine so that you are not overusing your arm.

EMERGENCY
LITTLE LEAGUE ELBOW

A young baseball player who throws too often or too hard can irritate the growing part of the elbow bone in the medial epicondyle. This area, called the growth center, widens and enlarges the medial epicondyle. The flexor muscles of the wrist contract to propel the ball. These muscles connect to the medial epicondyle, and the constant yanking pulls the soft growth center apart, causing pain. Also, the irritation of the growth center stimulates it and causes the medial epicondyle to overgrow.

The treatment for this condition, known as Little League elbow, is simply to rest until the condition subsides. This usually takes anywhere from six weeks to six months depending on the severity of the injury.

The best way to deal with Little League elbow is to prevent it. First, young pitchers need to be taught the proper mechanics of throwing. Then they have to be limited in the number of pitches they can throw each week. Little League and high school pitchers are often overused by coaches not familiar with the cause of this strictly biomechanical injury.

Sanctioned Little Leagues now restrict the number of innings a pitcher can pitch per week. But if a young pitcher is wild, he may throw a lot of pitches per inning, many more than a pitcher who has good control. Coaches should limit the number of pitches thrown to 80 twice a week and not simply count the number of innings pitched.

In severe cases, a Little Leaguer may tear the medial epicondyle right off the bone through the soft growth center. You can recognize this injury by swelling, severe pain, and limited arm motion. This is an emergency situation, and the epicondyle will need to be surgically reimplanted.

Rehabilitation, which includes immobilization followed by gradual range-of-motion exercises with an experienced physical therapist, may take six months or longer after surgery. In most cases, the pitcher will be back in action the following year, although he may never be an effective pitcher again.

MD POPEYE ELBOW

Besides his huge forearms and jutting jaw, the cartoon character Popeye the Sailor also has tiny knobs sticking out from behind his elbows. That's the site of a bursal sac called the olecranon bursa. Like any bursal sac, it can become inflamed, causing bursitis. This generally happens as a result of being hit on the end of the elbow. It can also become a chronic condition for people who lean on their elbows when they talk on the phone. This bursal sac becomes inflamed and quite painful, and a noticeable lump develops on the back of the elbow. This condition is known as Popeye elbow.

When the bursitis is due to an acute condition, the excess fluid in the sac will need to be drained with a needle. Then cortisone is injected into the sac, which is the standard treatment for any bursitis.

If the condition is chronic, you may feel little lumps behind the point of the elbow as you move it. These lumps are often misdiagnosed as bone chips, which have to be removed surgically. They really represent a less-threatening thickening in the wall of the bursal sac due to constant inflammation.

To prevent the chronic condition, don't spend so much time leaning on your elbows. If necessary, get a headset for your telephone. This problem has a tendency to recur, so if you have had it in the past, use an elbow pad during sports for protection.

MD THE "FUNNY BONE" SYNDROME

Everyone knows the numbing, tingling pain of hitting the "funny bone" at the end of the elbow. The ulnar nerve traverses the back of the elbow in a groove behind the medial epicondyle. Hitting your elbow in a certain way stimulates the ulnar nerve and causes the numbness, tingling, and pain of the "funny bone" syndrome.

Some athletes may feel as if they have hit their "funny bone" as a result of repeated trauma to the elbow. Scar tissue may form over the nerve and compress it into the canal, allowing it no room to move. This causes fairly severe pain in the elbow. The numbness and tingling radiate down into the fourth and fifth fingers, and you may lose strength in these fingers. This syndrome, called the cubital tunnel syndrome, is similar to carpal tunnel syndrome in the wrist (see Chapter 9). When center Mike Gminski joined the New Jersey Nets, he hit his elbow on the rim of the basket and developed cubital tunnel syndrome: as a result, he missed much of his rookie season.

The treatment is surgery to remove the scar tissue from the nerve. The nerve may have to be transplanted outside of the canal to prevent scar tissue from building up again. The surgery is usually successful, as it was for Gminski, who returned the next year to begin a long, successful career.

✚ HYPEREXTENDED ELBOW

When force applied to the elbow forces it to extend farther than normal, the result is hyperextension. This tears the fibers that hold the front of the elbow joint together and overextends the biceps muscle, which attaches just below the elbow.

A hyperextended elbow will cause pain and swelling. Treat this by resting and icing it intermittently at first. It may require a splint to keep the elbow bent until the pain subsides. Then you must gently stretch until your range of motion returns and you can fully extend the elbow without pain. Then strengthen the elbow with arm curls using weights. Total recovery time is usually three to six weeks, depending on the severity of the injury.

MD *BONE CHIPS*

Bone chips are something you read about frequently in the sports pages, but they are quite rare. They are the result of many years of overuse of the elbow and usually afflict an older, well-known pitcher or tennis player, so they get a lot of publicity. The condition is caused by little pieces of bone breaking off the elbow due to long and repeated stress. Many young pitchers with sore elbows come into my office worried that they have bone chips. Their pain is almost always due to something else, because they rarely have had enough trauma to form chips, unless they have osteochondritis dissecans, described earlier.

Even in old-timers, bone chips are rare. Former major league pitcher Jim Bouton is one of my long-time patients. Nearly age 50, he still pitches regularly in a high-quality semiprofessional league. He always complains about various aches and pains, but even after all these years he has no elbow problems, and he says that his arm feels as good as ever.

✚ *TRICEPS TENDINITIS*

Throwing sports can cause pain in the back of the elbow right above the point of the joint. This is the area where the triceps tendon hooks to the back of the elbow. The triceps muscle and tendon combine to straighten out the elbow. In the throwing motion, the elbow begins at a bent position as the arm is cocked and straightens out as the throw is delivered. This causes stress where the triceps tendon attaches to the elbow. The pain of triceps tendinitis can be severe, primarily for baseball pitchers.

Rest alone is not the answer. As with most forms of tendinitis, triceps tendinitis responds to a structured exercise program. I have athletes do Triceps Curls with fairly light weights for many repetitions. This helps build up the triceps muscles and the tendon so that they can tolerate the overuse from throwing. This exercise program also can help you return to action more quickly if you already have triceps tendinitis.

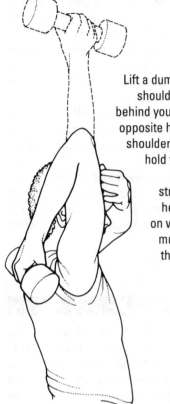

Triceps Curl

Lift a dumbbell up over your shoulder and then drop it behind your head. Place your opposite hand between your shoulder and elbow to help hold your arm up. Then raise the dumbbell straight up over your head, concentrating on working the triceps muscle. Slowly drop the dumbbell behind your head again.

Some pitchers are resistant to this treatment and may need a cortisone injection in the area of the triceps tendon. Once the inflammation disappears, they can use this exercise program to help prevent the injury from recurring.

✚ *BICEPS TENDINITIS*

Pain in the lower portion of the biceps muscle where it attaches to the elbow is a common phenomenon in beginning weight lifters who overstress themselves, and among veteran lifters who make too big a step up in weights. You will usually experience the pain on the day after lifting, and it can be very severe. You will also have a limitation in your range of motion: You will probably not be able to fully straighten or bend your elbow. This is due to swelling and spasm in the muscle fibers that have been over-stressed. If both elbows are affected, you can be virtually disabled. Even eating is nearly impossible because you cannot bend your elbow enough to get a fork to your mouth.

The proper treatment is to ice the elbow for 20 minutes at a time three or four times during the day. By the second day you can start a gentle stretching program.

Do two or three repetitions of the Biceps Stretch every hour, and the muscle fibers will gradually relax and lengthen. It is important that the stretch be even and gradual. Any sudden

movement or force may tear some of the muscle fibers and actually make matters worse.

The next step is to bend and straighten the elbow frequently to restore your range of motion. Do this for three or four days, and the biceps muscle should return to normal. Once it has recovered, you can return to lifting, doing Arm Curls with a slow progression of weight to allow the biceps to adapt to increasing weight (see the strength program in Chapter 1).

✚ TORN BICEPS

A sudden, severe movement of the arm can tear the biceps muscle. One head of the biceps can be literally torn in half. This is usually seen in an older athlete, such as a golfer who hits the ground hard with a club or a tennis player who hits a hard forehand smash, or in a young weight lifter attempting the sudden, violent motion of a clean-and-jerk. The torn muscle causes pain, bleeding, loss of function, and muscle deformity.

You need to take care while recovering from a biceps tear. If the biceps contracts as the swelling subsides, the upper part of the muscle can ball up, causing a defect the size of a small orange on top of the muscle.

Cosmetic surgery can correct the muscle defect, but it cannot bring the muscle back to its original strength. The buildup of scar tissue weakens the muscle. In fact, a torn biceps muscle that has been repaired will likely tear again.

Treatment involves allowing the torn muscle to rest for two or three weeks while it heals. This is followed by a training program to strengthen the other head of the biceps so that it can take over full function of the muscle. Arm Curls are the best exercise to strengthen the biceps muscle (see the strength program in Chapter 1).

I have never seen the second head of a biceps tear in somebody who has torn the first head. If the muscle tears again, it's usually the same head. So muscle strengthening usually works to restore function to the biceps.

Biceps Stretch

Grasp the undersurface of a heavy object, such as a dining room table, and gradually pull yourself back so that your elbow begins to straighten out. Pull on the table until you feel a strain in the muscle above the elbow, and then hold for 20 to 30 seconds.

The Wrist and Hand

Related Sports Chapters

Aerobics	Hockey, Lacrosse, and Skating
Baseball and Softball	
Basketball	Running, Jogging, and Track and Field
Boxing and Martial Arts	
Cycling	Skiing
Football and Rugby	Triathlon
	Volleyball
Golf	Wrestling
Gymnastics and Cheerleading	

The wrist is one of the most complex structures in the body. There are 10 bones involved in moving the wrist joint in various directions. These include the 2 forearm bones and 8 other, small bones. These small bones are extremely sensitive to excessive force or trauma, such as that generated in snapping the wrist in racquet and throwing sports. In addition, there are tremendous head-on forces generated in boxing, football, and wrestling as the wrist grasps and pulls against great strength. Because of all of these forces, the wrist is one of the more frequently injured parts of the body.

✚ SPRAINED WRIST

The most common injury to the wrist is a sprain. With all of the stresses on the wrist in sports, there is a good chance that the ligaments interconnecting the wrist bones will be sprained. Many people have weak wrists because there are few muscles in the wrist to stabilize it.

All but the most minor wrist sprains should be x-rayed because a sprained ligament may pull off a little piece of bone, which changes the injury to a fracture. A sprained wrist may not need anything more than a soft splint. A fractured wrist, however, requires casting.

The treatment of a sprained wrist, as for any sprain, is immediate immobilization, rest, and ice, and then a set of range-of-motion exercises followed by strengthening exercises. Use the same exercises outlined in Chapter 8 for the elbow. These exercises help take the pressure off the wrists to prevent injuries.

The ultimate sprain is a subluxation of the wrist bones. This happens when the ligaments connecting two or more of the small bones become torn completely, and the bones slide out of place. This is a common injury among boxers and usually results from hitting the heavy bag in training. The shock transmitted to wrist bones from hitting this large, mostly immovable object or from body punching during training causes undue stress on the small bones of the wrist. When the boxer hits with the afflicted hand, he feels severe pain.

Several professional boxers have required hand surgery to correct this problem, including then-middleweight Bobby Czyz and heavyweight Scott Frank, as have several top-ranked amateurs.

Athletes in other sports also are subject to this injury. Giants linebacker Carl Banks suffered a wrist sprain in 1990 severe enough to require surgery. That same year, the Detroit Pistons

All-Pro guard Isiah Thomas had a similar injury and surgery. Ageless tennis ace Jimmy Connors had to have his wrist completely rebuilt surgically after years of overuse. The long, arduous rehabilitation from surgery requires the services of a good hand therapist for the athlete to regain full motion in the wrist.

MD BROKEN WRIST

Any severe wrist pain following a fall or blow should be seen by a physician and x-rayed because of the possibility of a fracture. One or both of the two bones in the forearm that lead to the wrist, the radius and ulna, are the most likely to fracture. A wrist usually fractures because of a fall. However, a wrist can also fracture by being hit by a thrown or batted ball, which is what happened to New York Mets pitcher Sid Fernandez. He missed about half of the 1991 season recovering from a broken wrist.

A wrist fracture is often written off as a sprain or a bruise, and the victim may not see a physician for some time. I have seen many patients complain of a sprained wrist that wouldn't heal and that turned out to be fractured.

You may also fracture the small bone in the wrist just behind the base of the thumb, called the navicular bone. This fracture is usually caused by stretching your hand out to break a fall or by hitting your hand against an opposing player's helmet.

Even if you go to a doctor soon after this injury, the navicular fracture may not be apparent on the first x-ray because the fracture line is too fine to see. If you feel chronic pain in your wrist that doesn't respond to simple treatments, have it x-rayed once and then again 10 days to two weeks later to confirm the diagnosis. By this time, the fracture line will have widened as a result of the healing process.

Healing is more difficult for this fracture than for most other fractures in the body because there may not be adequate blood supply to the broken bone. It can take eight weeks to eight months for this bone to heal by itself. There are

new techniques, however, such as implanting an electromagnet in the cast, that speed bone healing. A magnet works by making the underlying filaments of the bone matrix line up with the same polarity. The filaments tend to get jumbled at the fracture line, and if you can get them to line up, they will form a bridge that can cross the fracture line. A magnet is now commonly used when there is no evidence of healing after a reasonable amount of time, about six weeks.

Finally, if the bone does not reknit, it probably will need to be fixed surgically. You may need a bone graft, which entails taking a piece of bone from the pelvis and placing it across the two bone fragments into a groove. This acts to hold the two pieces together and forms a bridge to help the fracture heal.

If left untreated, the navicular fracture will lead to chronic pain in the wrist and the loss of ability to extend the wrist backward.

MD RACQUET WRIST

Tennis or racquetball players may develop pain at the base of the hand below the "pinky" finger. Every time the player hits a ball, the racquet butt bangs into and bruises one of the small bones of the wrist. This usually occurs because the racquet butt is too big for the player's hand.

If the pain is severe, you should see a doctor because the little hook of bone at this spot might be broken. If it is, it will need to be treated as a fracture.

✚ TENDINITIS

The wrist is the passageway for tendons that begin in the forearm and extend into the fingers. The fingers are actually controlled by muscles in the forearm, not in the hand. Overuse of the wrist in sports causes inflammation of the finger tendons attached to these forearm muscles. This results in swelling, pain, and limited function in one or more of the fingers.

Two tendons in the thumb are particularly sensitive to overuse: the extensor and flexor tendons. The extensor tendon moves the thumb away from the second finger, and the flexor tendon moves it toward the second finger. Tendinitis greatly limits your ability to grasp with the thumb. I see many tennis players with pain and swelling on the thumb side of the wrist, which is often caused by gripping the racquet too tightly.

Treatment involves resting and icing the tendon in the wrist, followed by administration of anti-inflammatory agents and immobilization of the thumb and wrist to further reduce the inflammation.

I normally make a small, lightweight thumb splint from pliable plastic that can be removed so that my patient can wash the hand. If the pain is severe, I may also give a cortisone injection.

To prevent the wrist from being overstressed, you need to strengthen the appropriate muscles and tendons. Follow the forearm-strengthening exercises outlined in Chapter 8. Pay particular attention to Ball Squeezing on page 81. Squeeze to the point of fatigue as many times a day as you can to improve your grip strength.

Finger Flexion and Extension Exercises

You can also improve the extension and lateral movement of your fingers by doing exercises with a rubber band. The large rubber bands used by grocery stores on broccoli or celery provide about the right amount of resistance.

Thumb and Fingers Stretch

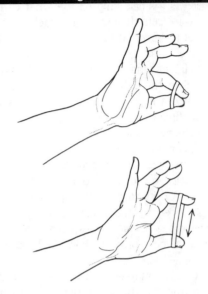

With your palm facing you, hook a rubber band around the thumb and the index finger, and stretch the rubber band between the fingers. Hold for about one second and repeat until fatigued. Then move the rubber band to each of your other fingers and stretch them individually against the thumb.

Adjacent Fingers Stretch

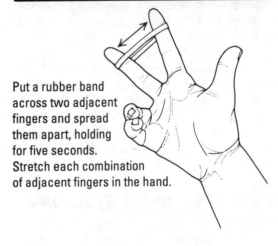

Put a rubber band across two adjacent fingers and spread them apart, holding for five seconds. Stretch each combination of adjacent fingers in the hand.

Thumb and Fingers Flex

To make your fingers stronger in flexion, hook a rubber band around the thumb and one finger, and try to close the finger to the palm. Hold for five seconds. Do the same exercise with each of the fingers of the hand.

MD GANGLION

A ganglion is a small lump on the wrist or hand that can vary from the size of a kernel of corn to the size of a cherry. It can occur on the back or front of the wrist, depending on whether an extensor or flexor tendon is involved. Both of these tendons slide through a sheath lined with cells that produce a slippery, thick fluid. The sheath allows the fingers to make the rapid movements that pianists need and all of us depend on.

If a finger tendon and its sheath become inflamed from overuse or a blow to the wrist, the inflammation can cause part of the tendon sheath to seal off. A cyst forms at this spot because the liquid produced by the sheath is trapped. The cyst, called a ganglion, swells inside the tendon sheath as the cells produce more fluid, and it can become quite painful.

The ganglion may open at one end if there is pressure from overproduction of fluid or from a sudden blow. The increased pressure blows open one end of the cyst, and the fluid runs out. The ganglion then collapses. The problem is that the raw surfaces that have blown out may seal off again, causing the ganglion to reform, and the whole process can repeat itself.

A ganglion is a problem when it becomes painful with activity. As long as it doesn't bother you, you don't need to treat it.

When I first went into medical practice, the treatment for a persistent ganglion was to smash it by hitting it with a book. That's the reason doctors kept *Gray's Anatomy* around after they graduated from medical school. The trick was to hit the ganglion hard enough with the thick book to break up the ganglion without breaking the wrist.

Today doctors inject a ganglion with cortisone, which causes it to disappear. If the ganglion continues to reform after several injections, surgical removal may be necessary.

✚ CARPAL TUNNEL SYNDROME

The finger tendons pass through the wrist in a narrow, tunnel-like enclosure. With chronic overuse or excessive twisting of the wrist, fluid builds up in the sheaths of the tendons, causing the tendons to become inflamed and swollen. Also, the carpal ligament becomes thickened from overuse. Both of these things narrow the tunnel and pinch the main nerve that passes through the tunnel to the fingers.

The result is a painful wrist condition known as carpal tunnel syndrome, named after the carpal ligament that goes across the top of this tunnel. The pain extends up into the forearm and down into the hand, and there may be numbness, tingling, and even loss of strength in the middle and ring fingers.

Carpal tunnel syndrome, also called repetitive motion injury, has been called the occupational disease of the 1980s. Office workers who type at computer terminals, meat cutters, textile workers, musicians, and many others are prone to this injury. The injury is not confined to the workplace, however. Anyone who tightly grips something while exercising may also suffer carpal tunnel syndrome.

The treatment is to rest the affected wrist and apply ice. If the symptoms do not subside, then anti-inflammatory agents may help. Many people will need a splint to minimize or prevent pressure on the nerve and perhaps a steroid injection into the ligament to help reduce the swelling. If the pain persists, surgery to cut the ligament at the bottom of the wrist may be the only way to release the pressure.

To help you avoid repetitive motion injuries, here are a few stretching exercises:

Fingertip Pull. Rest one forearm on a table, and then grasp the fingertips of that hand and pull back gently. Hold for five seconds. Repeat with the fingers of the other hand.

Palm Press. Press your palm flat on a table, as if doing a push-up, and lean forward to stretch the forearm muscles and wrist. Hold for five seconds.

THE HAND

Because the hand is so complex and so vital to everyday activities, all hand injuries should be considered serious and seen by a doctor. You can do irreparable damage by not getting immediate treatment to identify a broken bone. Any rotation of a broken finger bone can compromise that finger's function. Dislocations need to be x-rayed, even if the finger easily pops back into place. A dislocated finger also needs to be immobilized so that the ligaments can heal, or it may dislocate again with much less pressure on the finger.

The locker room saying "It can't be broken because I can move it" is a myth. All kinds of fractures of the hand still allow you to move the hand. If your hand hurts enough that you suspect a broken bone, it's best to have it x-rayed.

EMERGENCY
BROKEN HAND

The long bones of the hand, the metacarpals, are very subject to fracture, almost always due to a head-on blow to the knuckle, as when an angry person lashes out and hits a wall with the fist. I frequently see these fractures as a result of a player smashing his hand into another player's helmet by accident. Having your hand stepped on can also break the bones in the middle of the hand.

The treatment for a broken hand is to cast it for four to six weeks. However, if the break is directly across the shaft of the bone and the ends are jammed together, an athlete may be able to return to activity in a much shorter time with a light, plastic splint to protect it. If, on the other hand, the bones have been twisted apart and there are sharp ends at the fracture, the hand will have to stay in a cast until the fracture heals.

It is up to the physician's discretion as to which treatment method is safer. The type of fracture depends mainly on the direction of the force applied to the hand, not the particular sport you are playing.

BROKEN FINGER

Finger fractures are very common in sports. They commonly occur when a deflected ball hits the end of a finger. Many finger fractures are not serious, particularly those in the tip of the finger. If the finger is properly protected, you can continue to compete. "Buddy taping," or taping an injured finger to the healthy one next to it, usually allows you to return to activity almost immediately. If the fracture is in the second or third finger bone, you will need to splint the finger for four to six weeks to allow the fracture to heal.

MD DISLOCATED FINGER

If a finger is struck with a great deal of force, one of its joints may dislocate. On television, you may have seen a football player come to the sidelines with a finger sticking up at a crazy angle. It's usually simple for the team doctor or trainer to pop the finger back into place. Buddy-taping the dislocated finger to a healthy one stabilizes the joint, and the player can go back into the game.

The finger is always x-rayed later on. A piece of bone at the base of the dislocated finger may break off, and this can cause a bad fracture that extends into the joint. If not taken care of, this can result in great loss of function in the finger and future disability. So if you dislocate a finger, make sure to have it x-rayed to check for a fracture.

JAMMED FINGER

If you "jam" a finger, typically by hitting something head-on at the tip of the finger, it usually becomes very swollen. One of the joints holding the finger bone may not be totally dislocated, but the bone may have snapped partway out of joint and then snapped back in. This injures the cartilage on the end of the bone, as well as the capsule around the joint, and stretches the ligaments that hold the joint together. The result is a swollen, painful finger that may appear normal on an x-ray.

A jammed finger heals very slowly. The finger should be immobilized for 7 to 10 days and then buddy-taped to the finger next to it. I warn my patients that it can take six months for the joint to return toward normal size. And, as with any severely jammed joint, it usually will not return to full function. A jammed finger will always be larger than it was or larger than the joint on the opposite hand. You will lose a few degrees of flexibility in the finger, but not enough to cause any great difficulty in dexterity.

MD TENDON TEARS

A sudden, violent force to the fingers can cause tendons to tear. Any tendon that is torn through must be repaired surgically to prevent loss of finger function. If you have a weakness or an inability to move one of the joints in a finger, you must consider that a tendon may be torn, and you should seek a doctor's advice immediately.

Baseball players often tear the tendon on top of a finger from a blow to the end of the finger. As a result, the tip of the finger droops down, and you can not straighten out the fingertip. Either the tendon itself is torn in half or a piece of bone where the tendon attaches to the tip has been torn off. In either case, the finger must be splinted with the fingertip in the extended position for six weeks. This condition is known as baseball finger and is also seen among basketball and volleyball players who are hit by the ball on the end of the finger.

If the tendon doesn't heal, then you will need surgery to straighten out the fingertip. The only finger that I usually don't recommend for surgery is the "pinky" since loss of function there is not that important for sports.

✚ SKI POLE THUMB

In the early 1970s the New York Nets' reserve center, Eddie Johnson, was a notoriously bad foul shooter. He tried everything to correct his foul-shooting stroke, to no avail. On investigating his problem, we discovered that he had torn the ligaments in his right thumb and was unable to control the ball. He had surgery to repair the damaged thumb, and he markedly improved his foul-shooting percentage. I'd like to say he became one of the best foul shooters in the league. At least he became respectable.

The most common ligament tear in the hand occurs on the inner side of the thumb. This is the so-called ski pole injury suffered by snow skiers when a thumb gets trapped in the loop of the pole during a fall. When the thumb ligaments are torn, you can't press the thumb sideways against the other fingers to grasp an object. This necessary movement of the thumb is what distinguishes the human hand from an animal's paw. Occasionally, basketball players also suffer this injury, as the Nets' Eddie Johnson did.

The immediate treatment is to ice the thumb and splint it. Then get to a doctor. You will have to immobilize the thumb for approximately six weeks and see if the ligament heals. If it doesn't heal, it will have to be surgically repaired.

MD TRIGGER FINGER

Trigger finger is the result of repeated trauma to the palm of the hand. This may be from a tennis racquet jamming into the palm or a baseball repeatedly hitting a catcher's palm. The trauma causes injury to the flexor tendon of one of the fingers. The tendon's sheath thickens, leaving a narrowed area for the tendon, and the tendon itself also thickens. Consequently, it becomes difficult for the thickened part of the tendon to get through the narrowed part of the sheath.

The flexor muscles of the fingers, which are stronger than the extensor muscles, are able to pull on the tendon and bend the finger. But the extensors are not strong enough to pull it back. The finger ends up in a bent position, the same position as a finger that has pulled the trigger on a gun. The only way to straighten out the finger is to pull on it with the other hand.

This injury sometimes responds to cortisone injection, which reduces inflammation in the tendon sheath. If not, the sheath will need to be split surgically to allow free motion of the finger.

✚ BLISTERS AND CALLUSES

Many athletes suffer blisters and calluses on their hands and fingers from gripping balls, clubs, and racquets. Blisters form on skin that is damaged by friction or burns. Sweat makes your skin sticky, and the friction between your hands and the object you are gripping can cause blisters.

There are two theories on treating blisters. One is to leave the blisters alone and let them heal. New skin forms under the blister, and the fluid in the blister gradually becomes absorbed. Eventually, the outer layer of skin sloughs off.

The other theory recommends opening up the blister and letting the fluid drain out. Then you snip away the dead skin, apply an antibiotic cream to the area, and cover it with a dressing.

I prefer the first method because the second one leaves the raw skin under the blister painful and open to infection. If a blister breaks or becomes damaged by further friction, then use an antibiotic ointment and dressing. If it becomes infected, see a physician.

Calluses are areas of skin that have thickened because of constant pressure. The pressure causes the tissues underneath the callus to become tender. If the callus becomes bothersome, you can soften it with a cream or ointment and rub away dead skin with a pumice stone. If this does not help, a physician can trim the callus surgically or chemically.

To prevent these uncomfortable annoyances, you need to find out what is causing them. Tennis players and golfers may not be holding the racquet or club properly, or they may need new grips. Gymnasts should wear gloves and put powder on their hands before exercising on the parallel or high bars. There's not much baseball pitchers can do. Nolan Ryan used to soak his hands in pickle brine, which apparently worked for him, though I can't recommend it for everyone.

Hand Rehab and Injury Prevention

The rehabilitation of hand injuries is so complex that you should seek out a specialist in hand therapy. Under the specialist's direction, you can usually rehabilitate your hand with exercises at home.

There's not much you can do to prevent hand injuries since most of them are caused by accidents. You can use golf or batting gloves to prevent minor problems such as blisters and calluses.

If you feel persistent pain in your hand from racquet sports, get your racquet size evaluated immediately. Don't wait until you develop a fracture.

Strong fingers are important in almost every sport. They are especially important in golf and tennis for holding the club or racquet lightly but securely. Following is one simple finger exercise.

Finger Stretch

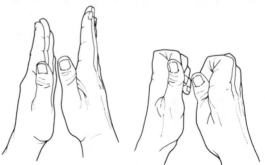

Hold your hands out in front of you, palms facing each other and fingers straight up. Bend fingers down and squeeze them as tightly as you can. Hold for five seconds and then release. Repeat five times a day for stronger fingers and a better grip.

10

The Thigh and Hip

Related Sports Chapters

Basketball

Cycling

Football and Rugby

Hockey, Lacrosse, and Skating

Running, Jogging, and Track and Field

Skiing

Triathlon

Volleyball

Walking, Hiking, and Horseback Riding

The thigh contains the major leg muscles. The hamstring muscle in the back of the thigh is the driving force in all running sports. Your hamstrings help determine how fast and strong a runner you are. The large quadriceps muscle in the front of the thigh straightens the knee, which helps you stand tall. This is the main muscle used in jumping, and it also provides the power when you pedal a bicycle.

✚ HAMSTRING PULL

The hamstring muscles are often ignored in the weight room in deference to their stronger, more aesthetically appealing counterparts, the quadriceps muscles. The hamstrings are implicated in maladies ranging from low-back pain to jumper's knee.

Probably the most common injury in the thigh and hip area, and *the* most common muscle pull, is the hamstring pull. Any rapid running subjects the hamstring muscles to great force; consequently, they are prone to pull. These muscles have an extremely wide range of motion, and they stretch out rapidly during the long running stride as you throw your foot forward.

When you see a great athlete sprinting on television suddenly grab the back of a leg and fall in full flight, the runner has probably pulled a hamstring muscle. Although a hamstring will sometimes tear as a sprinter drives out of the starting blocks, a hamstring usually pulls from overstretching, not overcontracting, the muscle. It's not the first part of the stride, when the muscle contracts, but the second part of the stride, as the leg stretches out, that causes problems.

If you pull a hamstring, it may feel as if the muscle has "popped." You will feel sharp pain and see swelling in the thigh—and maybe even bleeding, depending on the degree of muscle damage. The back of the thigh may turn black and blue, usually right below the area of pain, because blood works its way down by gravity. If you touch the back of the thigh, you may feel a gap in the muscle where the fibers have torn. You will not be able to raise your leg straight off the ground more than 30° to 40° without feeling severe pain.

Rehabilitation begins with the classic combination of rest, ice, and compression. The amount of rest depends on the severity of the pull or tear and is typically two to three days. This should be followed by limited activity until you are free of pain and fully restretched. Icing the muscle for 20 minutes three or four times a day will reduce the chances of aggravating the condition. Then you can start on a gentle stretching program.

You need to start stretching as soon as possible while the muscle is recovering. As long as the stretch is gentle and steady, you can start as early as the second day after your injury, unless you have a major tear. Go into the stretch slowly without jerking the muscle in order to avoid pulling or tearing it again. Stretch to the point of discomfort but not pain.

The best hamstring stretch is the hurdler stretch. This can be done either sitting or standing. See Hurdler Stretch (sitting), in Chapter 1; and Hurdler Stretch (standing), in Chapter 7.

To prevent another pull or tear, you need to warm up adequately and stretch before any activity and, as always, restretch afterward.

Try to keep up your aerobic conditioning and overall muscle tone during your rehabilitation. Cycling and swimming are safe and effective exercises and should be done pain-free to prevent overstressing the injured muscle.

The symptoms of sciatica can mimic a hamstring pull, with pain in the back of the thigh. I see many patients who complain of a pulled hamstring but who really have sciatica.

Sciatica is simply a signal that something is irritating the sciatic nerve. Possible causes include a disc in the lower spine pushing on the nerve root where it comes out of the spinal cord; an arthritic spur on the spine pushing on the nerve root; a muscle spasm in the large lower-back muscles, which pull and stretch the nerve; or a nerve entrapped in the buttock area.

If the thigh pain extends below the knee or if you feel any numbness in your lower leg or foot, the problem is not a hamstring pull but sciatica. If the pain in the back of your leg becomes worse with stretching, then it's probably sciatica and you should see a doctor.

✚ A BRUISED QUAD

A blow to the large quadriceps muscle in the front of the thigh can cause bleeding into the muscle. A blow can crush the muscle fibers against the large, heavy femur bone below. This muscle is prone to heavy bleeding because it is contains many blood vessels. The bleeding causes swelling and sometimes severe pain, and you may be unable to bend your knee fully.

The immediate treatment is to ice the muscle for 20 to 30 minutes with the knee bent as far as it will go. Sports doctors used to think that the leg should not be bent because this would cause complications, including more bleeding and later calcium deposits. Now we know that's not true. With the Giants, we apply ice packs to the thigh and then wrap the leg with the knee fully bent using an elastic bandage to pull the leg back against the hamstring. This compresses the quadriceps muscle and puts enough pressure on the blood vessels to stop the bleeding. We instruct the player to ice the thigh several times a day for as long as he has any discomfort or swelling, and to keep stretching the muscle by flexing the knee as far as it will go.

If you have more than mild swelling or pain, see a doctor for a physical therapy prescription. Blood in the quadriceps will cause calcium deposits to form, which is called myositis ossificans. If this condition is not treated vigorously, the calcium will not allow the fibers in the muscle to extend fully, and you won't be able to bend your knee all the way. This is a difficult condition to treat and can disable you for up to a year.

✚ A QUAD PULL OR TEAR

A quadriceps pull is usually a running or jumping injury. A pull or tear to a quadriceps muscle is less common than a hamstring pull or tear. But the treatment is the same: Rest the muscle for a few days, and then ice and stretch it. Prevention is also the same: Warm up correctly and stretch the muscle in the front of the thigh through an exercise such as the following.

Quadriceps Stretch

Stand next to a wall and pull the foot of the injured leg toward the buttocks with your hand. Balance yourself against the wall with the other hand. Hold for 15 to 20 seconds and then relax. Repeat five times.

EMERGENCY
FEMUR FRACTURE

The thigh bone (femur) is the largest bone in the body. Femur fractures in sports are rare because the bone is so strong. Also, much of the rotary force of the leg is absorbed by the knee and is not transferred to the thigh bone.

This injury causes sharp pain in the leg and usually requires surgery to fix the bone. You will need to rest the leg until it heals, which usually takes several months.

THE HIP

The hip is a very tight, stable ball-and-socket joint. Because the ball of the hip fits so tightly into the hip socket, it doesn't dislocate as easily as the shallow shoulder joint and is much less prone to injury. To dislocate a hip, you almost have to be hit by a truck.

Because a hip dislocation requires immense force, it is very rarely seen in athletics. In all my years of attending football games, I have seen only three hip dislocations. Two occurred on the field during professional games where huge bodies collided with great force. The third one happened to the quarterback for the Newark Bears minor league team. While driving home for the off-season, he was hit by a coal truck in Pennsylvania.

✚ OSTEOARTHRITIS

Osteoarthritis is a degenerative process in the hip caused by wear and tear or by an injury. The surfaces of the joint become rough, causing pain from hip movement. There is no apparent swelling, as with osteoarthritis of the knee, because the tight hip joint has little space for fluid accumulation. Also, the joint is buried beneath very deep muscles, so any swelling is invisible.

All you can do for osteoarthritis of the hip is to take anti-inflammatory agents and decrease your activity. You may need a hip replacement later in life.

MD THE BO JACKSON INJURY

Avascular necrosis was a little-known sports injury until super-athlete Bo Jackson developed it. It is usually caused by a blow to the knee or foot with the leg extended. Bo did not actually take a hit to the hip. He was hit high and knocked off balance while carrying the football. All of his weight came down on one leg, locked at the knee. The full impact of his landing on one foot was transmitted up to his hip. This caused the ball of the hip joint to hit the wall of the socket with great force, compromising the blood supply in the area and causing gradual deterioration of the surrounding cartilage and bone.

You should suspect avascular necrosis if the pain in your hip does not go away after a few weeks or becomes progressively worse. The only means of early diagnosis is an MRI scan. By the time a physician is able to see the changes in a regular x-ray, the disease has become very advanced.

You need to rest without putting any weight on the hip for 6 to 12 months. Bo being Bo, he came back a little sooner than that. There are some surgical procedures that can help your recovery. If the hip doesn't get better, the bone in the ball will eventually be destroyed and you will need a hip replacement, just as Bo eventually did.

EMERGENCY
BROKEN HIP

A broken hip causes severe pain and the inability to move the hip or walk. If you are lying on your back on the field after breaking your hip, your leg may appear to be shortened and your foot rolled to the outside while the other foot points up.

Usually, a broken hip needs to be repaired surgically. This injury is rare among young athletes and usually occurs in the elderly, who have brittler bones. However, a violent force can break even a young athlete's hip.

✚ BUTTOCK PULL

A pull of the muscle in the buttock (gluteal muscle) will cause pain there, particularly in reponse to any physical effort. It will hurt to do a straight leg raise. Doing the Hurdler Stretch (see Chapters 1 and 7) will help relieve this minor problem, which should go away within a week or two.

✚ GROIN PULL

If you make a sudden lateral movement while rotating your leg when running or skating, you can pull a groin muscle. Several different groups of muscles attach to the groin area. The flexor muscles bend the hip, the adductor muscles bring one leg in against the other, and the rotator muscles bring the knee across the opposite leg. To determine which muscle is involved, you must find out which motion brings on the pain.

You must rest a groin pull for several days and then begin a gentle stretching program. This should be followed by a gradual return to activity. As always, the best prevention is a good stretching program before and after activity.

You must first determine which muscles are injured. If it is the flexor muscles, do the Hip Extension exercise described in Chapter 7. If it is the adductor muscles, use the Side Straddle Stretch. The rotator muscles respond to a Yoga Lotus Stretch.

Side Straddle Stretch

Stand with your legs three feet apart, and gradually bend one knee and lean to the side away from the injured hip. Keep your trunk straight. Hold the stretch for 20 to 30 seconds.

Yoga Lotus Stretch

While sitting down, bend your knees so that the soles of your feet are touching each other. Now put your elbows on your knees and gradually push them outward. Hold for 20 to 30 seconds.

✚ ILIOTIBIAL BAND SYNDROME

Dorothy had been running for two years as part of her program for recovery from cancer when she developed a severe pain in her hip. The pain persisted for two weeks, so she went to see her internist, who in turn sent her to a local medical center. There she had an x-ray of her hip, a computerized hip scan, and a bone marrow biopsy of her hip, all of which where negative.

On a friend's recommendation, Dorothy came to see me. I listened to her recount her medical history and litany of testing, and I lightly put my hand on the outside of her hip. She screamed and jumped off the examining table. As I suspected, she had iliotibial band syndrome, a tightening of the band across the hip. With 10 minutes of stretching each day, she was running again in 10 days without pain.

The fibrous band running down the outside of the thigh is called the iliotibial band. It provides lateral stability to the hip so that it can't move too far to the outside. In some people, particularly runners, the band overdevelops, tightens, and saws across the hip bone. Each time the runner flexes and bends the knee, the band rubs against bone, causing pain. Although this condition often causes knee pain, it may also cause pain over the point of the hip. (For more about iliotibial band syndrome, see Chapter 11.)

A snapping pain in your hip is almost always due to the iliotibial band snapping back and forth over the point of the hip. As you stretch the band out, this pain will disappear. (See the stretching program in Chapter 1.)

✚ HIP POINTER

A hip pointer is a blow to the rim of the pelvis that causes bleeding where the muscles attach. The treatment is to rest until the pain subsides, which usually takes one to two weeks. During that time, ice the rim of the pelvis intermittently.

To prevent hip pointers, wear hip pads. Many recreational hockey and football players don't, and they suffer the consequences.

11

The Knee

Related Sports Chapters

Basketball	Soccer and
Cycling	Field Hockey
Football	Triathlon
and Rugby	Volleyball
Hockey, Lacrosse,	Walking,
and Skating	Hiking, and
Running,	Horseback
Jogging, and	Riding
Track and Field	Wrestling

The knee is a complex joint that not only bends and straightens but also twists and rotates. The knee is not a simple ball-and-socket joint, like the hip. It depends heavily on the soft tissues that surround it—the muscles, tendons, and ligaments—because it's a weight-bearing joint that is subjected to many different types of motion. This variety of motion can lead to tearing of the cushioning cartilage inside the knee and of the supporting ligaments on both sides of and inside the knee.

A thick pad of cartilage acts as a cushion and stabilizes the structures between the two bones of the knee. The two lower knuckles of the femur (the thigh bone) are called condyles. These condyles sit on top of the flat surface of the tibia, the large shin bone. Inside the knee, between each condyle and the tibial surface are two half-moon-shaped cartilages, the medial meniscus and the lateral meniscus.

The knee joint is basically held together by four very strong ligaments. The medial and lateral collateral ligaments provide side-to-side stability. They are found on the inside and outside of the knee between the thigh bone and the shin bone. The anterior and posterior cruciate ligaments provide front-to-back stability. They are inside the knee. The anterior cruciate runs from the front of the shin bone to the back of the thigh bone, and the posterior cruciate runs from the back of the shin bone to the front of the thigh bone. They cross in the middle, and that's why they are called "cruciate," which means cross-shaped. The cruciate ligaments allow you to come to a sudden stop and to accelerate suddenly.

Because of its structure, the knee is extremely susceptible to blows from the side. It also can be severely damaged by rotating, twisting forces. The joint is very well designed for its intended functions, but it is the most poorly designed of all the joints in the body to withstand the forces of athletics. When God created the knee, He didn't have football in mind.

The knee is the most commonly injured joint in the body, accounting for about one-quarter of all injuries. Nearly one million knee surgeries are performed each year. Between acute traumatic and overuse injuries, I see about six or seven patients with knee damage every day in my practice. A knee injury is also the injury most likely to end an athlete's career.

✚ *SPRAINED KNEE*

You can sprain your knee by twisting it in a fall, by stepping in a hole while running, or by being hit from the side while playing sports. The knee will swell up, and you will have trouble walking on that leg.

A knee sprain, by definition, is an injury to a knee ligament. The sprain may vary in severity from a slight stretch to a complete tear of the ligament. A mild, or grade 1, sprain simply stretches the ligament and causes pain and swelling. A moderate, or grade 2, sprain partially tears the ligament and is much more disabling. A severe, or grade 3, sprain is a complete rupture and often needs surgical repair.

The most commonly sprained knee ligament is the medial collateral ligament (MCL). This ligament can be sprained by a blow to the outside of the knee, particularly if your foot is planted in the ground when you are hit. The blow causes the knee to move toward the inside of the body and stretches the ligament. You will feel tenderness and pain on the inside of the knee, and the knee will feel like it may buckle or give way to the inside. Anything more than minimal pain should be treated by a doctor.

A sprain of the ligament on the outside of the knee, the lateral collateral ligament, is caused by a blow to the inside of the knee, which forces the knee to the outside. This is much less common than an MCL sprain because it is hard to get hit on the inside of the knee. Usually, your other leg gets in the way and takes the blow.

Here's a good rule of thumb for knee injuries: If you receive a blow to the knee and the pain is on the same side of the knee that was hit, it's probably just a bruise, and the pain will go away rapidly. If the pain is on the opposite side of the knee, consider this a serious injury that needs careful treatment.

The immediate treatment for a sprained knee is the standard RICE formula (see Chapter 4). Rest the knee while it aches and ice it intermit-tently several times a day. Wrap it in an elastic bandage in between icings and keep it elevated as much as possible.

Knee Sprain Rehab

If the MCL sprain is a mild one, an early rehabilitation program using a stationary bicycle and leg extension and curl exercises is all you need.

Begin by riding a stationary bicycle for 20 minutes. Keep the seat high so that your range of motion is minimal. Don't put any drag on the bike; you are simply interested in moving the knee. In the very beginning, you may not be able to pedal all the way around. Just pedal back and forth until you can come over the top. Once you can do this, lower the seat gradually so that you increase the bend in your knee each day until you get back your full range of motion.

Do the Leg Extension while seated at a bench or a table (see the strength-training program in Chapter 1). Once you lift the weight, hold at full extension for three seconds and then very slowly lower your leg. Concentrate on the slow movement down, which is the most important part of the lift. Muscle contraction against weight while the muscle is lengthened builds the most strength.

Ten lifts make a set. Do five sets of this exercise and rest for 30 seconds or more, if needed, after each set. Start with no weight and gradually add weights (5 pounds for men, 2.5 pounds for women) until you reach the amount of weight necessary for you to fail during the last set. Use ankle weights, or a weight boot, or hang an old tote bag or pocketbook filled with weights from the ankle.

Do the Leg Curl while lying on your stomach (see the strength-training program in Chapter 1). Again, do 10 lifts per set for five sets. If you are using a weight machine, you should hold for three seconds with the leg bent. If you are using free weights, this is not necessary.

The purpose of these exercises is to

strengthen the quadriceps muscles in the front of the thigh (leg extensions) and the hamstring muscles in the back of the thigh (leg curls). These muscles, particularly the quadriceps, begin to lose strength within 12 hours of a knee injury. These muscles control the knee and must be restrengthened.

If you have a problem doing the leg extensions, that is, if your range of motion is too limited or you find it too painful, then do isometric quadriceps exercises first.

Isometric Quad Exercise

While sitting in a chair, fully extend your leg and tighten your quadriceps muscle to pull the kneecap up. Hold for one second and then relax. Repeat 50 times. The whole procedure should take about a minute and a half. Do this exercise once an hour while you are awake.

If this exercise is painful with your leg in full extension or if you have trouble controlling the muscle isometrically, you can bend your knee slightly, hook your foot under something too heavy to lift— such as a bed, dresser, or desk—and attempt to lift it. This accomplishes the same thing.

Anything more severe than a minimal knee sprain should be seen by a physician. You will then need to begin a rehabilitation program that consists of more sophisticated strengthening exercises, perhaps using isokinetic machines, bracing, and physical therapy.

MD THE CRUCIAL CRUCIATES

If the force to the side of the knee is more severe, or if you are rotating your knee when you are hit, then the anterior cruciate ligament (ACL) may be stretched or torn. Probably the most severe ruptures I see are caused not by trauma but usually by a heavy athlete, such as a football lineman, running and then planting his foot and turning 90° to go upfield. This twisting can cause a complete ACL rupture. Giants punter

Sean Landetta missed the last half of the 1992 season when he turned to make a tackle and ruptured his ACL without anyone touching him.

If your ACL ruptures, the loud pop may be heard by your teammates. You will feel sudden pain and instability in the knee. The knee will swell up rapidly because the ACL bleeds quickly when injured. Any ACL injury causes symptoms profound enough for you to seek professional help. You cannot treat an ACL injury yourself.

An MRI scan may help determine whether the ligament is stretched or totally torn. If it's torn, it will need to be repaired surgically, although an older athlete may be able to get by without surgical repair. Modern methods of repair through the arthroscope plus new ideas on rehabilitation, such as beginning exercises immediately after surgery, have dropped recovery time from 12 to 15 months to 6 to 7 months. Even so, rehabilitation is a major undertaking.

The arthroscope allows complex surgical repairs to be made through a few small holes in the skin. Arthroscopy works best on the knee because the knee has sufficient space for the scope to slip easily among the bones, cartilage, and other tissues. The benefits of successful arthroscopy include less pain, less chance of infection, a shorter recuperation period, and lower medical bills.

There are also rehabilitation programs for a partially torn ACL. Done under a physical therapist's guidance, they center on the use of isokinetic exercise machines, which are much more efficient than regular free weights or the weight machines in gyms. These machines resemble isotonic devices, such as the Nautilus® leg extension machine, but the isokinetic machines vary the resistance with the amount of pressure applied. The more effort you expend, the more resistance you encounter. Your effort is recorded by a computer and displayed on a screen or printed out on paper.

Once your rehabilitation is complete, very sophisticated knee braces are available that will allow you to return to full activity, even if the ligament has been totally torn and not repaired.

Posterior cruciate ligament (PCL) injuries are very rare and usually are due to a head-on blow to the knee. You will feel pain and some swelling, and you will not be able to accelerate without severe pain. This ligament will usually heal itself.

Two Giants linebackers, Carl Banks and Gary Reasons, had PCL injuries and returned to action in three to four weeks. Only tight end Mark Bavaro's PCL tear did not heal and required surgery. Philadelphia Eagles quarterback Randall Cunningham required surgery because he tore both his PCL and his MCL, which resulted in instability.

MD TORN CARTILAGE

A hit on the outer side of the knee causes the inner side to stretch. This can cause one of two things to happen. The MCL, which is attached to the cartilage, can tear the cartilage as it stretches. Or, when the stretching force is removed, the inner side of the knee can close again with some force, driving the condyle back into the cartilage just as the spring hinge of an old screen door slams the door back into the frame.

The grinding action on the knee as it rotates can also damage cartilage. This grinding action is similar to that of a mortar and pestle, with the cartilage the substance being crushed. The same thing happens when the femoral condyle rotates on the tibia with all of your weight compressing it.

If you tear some cartilage, you will feel pain and see swelling in the knee, but usually not as much as with an ACL tear. The pain may be on the inside or the outside of the knee, depending on which cartilage has torn. You may hear a clicking sound inside the knee when you move it; this is the bone riding over the torn part of the cartilage. When you move laterally or twist your knee, the knee may slip and buckle and even cause you to fall. Many of my patients with torn

knee cartilage complain that they can't make a sharp turn even when walking.

The knee may be locked so that it is impossible to extend it fully or bend it. Remember, the knee is a hinged joint, and if a piece of cartilage tears and flops over, it impedes the hinge from working. Just as sticking a pencil in a door will prevent the door from closing all the way, the knee joint won't open or close fully if a piece of cartilage is stuck between the two bones.

Most cartilage tears do not heal by themselves. Cartilage has a poor blood supply except at the outer rim, so about 90 percent of cartilage tears have no ability to heal. Tearing a cartilage is similar to tearing a fingernail. A torn fingernail won't heal by itself; you have to wait for the nail to grow out, and then you cut off the torn part.

Unfortunately, cartilage does not grow back, but the torn piece still has to be cut out. The most common way is to shave down the ragged edges of the tear with tiny instruments manipulated through an arthroscope. Arthroscopic surgery is minor surgery in an expert's hands. There is no real excuse for opening up a knee for a cartilage repair except in the most unusual cases.

If the tear is at the outer edge of the cartilage, or if it is small, it may heal. Healing requires a rehabilitation program similar to that described for the MCL to restrengthen the muscles around the knee. By following the rehabilitation program, you can usually return to full activity within three or four weeks.

EMERGENCY

THE TERRIBLE TRIAD OF O'DONOHUE

A very severe injury to the knee, and one common among athletes, is called the Terrible Triad of O'Donohue, named after a long-time team physician at the University of Oklahoma and one of the deans of sports medicine. He was the first to describe this injury, which consists of an MCL sprain or tear, an ACL tear, *and* a medial cartilage tear, all due to a single blow to the knee.

This devastating injury requires complete surgical repair. It's impossible to rehabilitate all of these structures and have a functioning knee again without surgery.

EMERGENCY
DISLOCATED KNEE

An extremely severe traumatic injury to the knee, and one of the few true orthopedic emergencies, is total dislocation of the knee. This is caused by a blow that tears the whole knee out of the socket. The lower leg moves away from the upper bone, and the only thing really holding the lower leg together is the skin. This can cut off the blood supply to the lower leg and necessitate amputation if not rapidly relieved.

MD DISLOCATED KNEECAP

The kneecap (patella) is the bone covering the tendon that runs from the quadriceps muscle in the front of the thigh to the bone beneath the knee. This tendon is responsible for holding the leg straight so that you can stand erect, and also for straightening a bent leg for climbing stairs or riding a bicycle.

The back of the kneecap is shaped like a wedge and rides in a V-shaped groove in the front of the lower end of the thigh bone between the two condyles. If the kneecap is hit at an angle, it can be knocked out of this groove. The kneecap almost always dislocates to the outside since the outer lip of the groove is much shallower than the inner lip.

A dislocated kneecap causes pain, and the knee will appear deformed since the kneecap will sit way out to the side. Usually, it can be popped back into place by a doctor without too much difficulty. It may even pop back in by itself on the way to the doctor's office or emergency room. Even if it pops back in, however, you must have it x-rayed to make sure a piece of bone has not been knocked off the undersurface. Occasionally, the kneecap is locked out of place so severely that surgery is needed to put it back in place.

A dislocated kneecap requires immobilization in a splint for about three weeks to allow the tissues on either side of the kneecap to heal. These tissues are responsible for holding it in place, and if they remain torn, the kneecap will be prone to dislocate again. Interestingly, the kneecap groove is much shallower in girls than in boys, so dislocation is a more common, recurrent problem among girls.

After a period of rest, the athlete must strengthen the quadriceps with a program similar to the one outlined for the knee ligaments. Start with isometrics and then progress to Leg Extensions (see Chapter 1). These exercises will tighten the kneecap back down by increasing the tone of the muscles pulling on the tendon underneath it. This will hold the kneecap in the groove so that it won't be likely to pop out again.

MD BROKEN KNEECAP

The kneecap may fracture from a head-on blow. Usually, this causes pain and swelling, and the kneecap will need to be x-rayed. The x-ray must be interpreted by someone very familiar with kneecaps. In many people, the kneecap naturally forms in two pieces and never unites, and this can be misinterpreted as a break.

A broken kneecap needs to be immobilized and may even need surgical repair, depending on the direction of the fracture line. If the fracture line is vertical, immobilization should be enough. If the fracture line is horizontal, then the two pieces will be pulled apart by the quadriceps and will need to be wired together until they unite.

MD *LOOSE BODY IN THE KNEE*

If an athlete has sudden episodes of knee pain and knee locking, there may be a loose body floating inside the joint. The onset of these symptoms may not appear for months to a year after a traumatic injury, such as a blow to the knee. Just as suddenly as the pain comes on, it disappears and you have your full range of motion again.

These on-again, off-again symptoms are due to a loose body in the knee getting caught between the upper and lower bones, causing pain. When the body floats back up into the hollow space in the knee, out of the way, the pain is relieved.

The loose body may be a piece of cartilage that has torn off or a piece of bone that has chipped off. The bone may have been injured before. It gradually dies, and a piece can fall off the bone and float inside the knee.

You may be able to feel the loose piece along the edge of the knee joint. It may feel like a pea that suddenly floats into the knee under the pressure of your weight and then suddenly disappears.

Arthroscopic surgery is necessary to remove the loose piece and stop the symptoms.

RUNNER'S KNEE

The most common overuse injury to the knee, and the most common cause of knee pain, is runner's knee or walker's knee, known medically as chondromalacia patella or patello-femoral syndrome. This is caused by misalignment of the kneecap in its groove. The kneecap normally goes up and down in the groove as the knee flexes and straightens. If the kneecap is misaligned, it will pull off to one side and rub on the side of the groove. This causes both the cartilage on the side of the groove and the cartilage on the back of the kneecap to wear out. On occasion, fluid builds up and causes swelling in the knee.

As a result, you will experience pain around the back of the kneecap or in the back of the knee after running. You also will have difficulty going up and down stairs and running hills. It will become painful to sit still for long periods with the knee bent. This is called the "theater sign" of runner's knee because people can't sit through an entire movie or play without getting up to move around. Half of the people you see outside their cars along the roadside are not going to the bathroom; they are stretching their legs to relieve the discomfort of runner's knee.

The basis of the problem is not the knee but the foot. An inward roll of the foot and ankle causes the shin bone to rotate to the inside, which turns the knee to the inside as well. The kneecap ends up sliding at an angle instead of straight up and down.

Treatment involves correcting the foot strike by propping up the foot with an arch or orthotic device inside the running shoe. This prevents excessive pronation and keeps the knee in alignment. I suggest you start with a commercial arch support and progress to a hand-made orthotic if you don't get suitable relief.

You also need to do exercises to strengthen the inner side of the quadriceps muscle. The muscle in the front of the thigh hooks in the kneecap and helps align it into the center of the groove. Normally, you strengthen the quadriceps with the full Leg Extension described in Chapter 1. However, in runner's knee, as the quadriceps contracts, it pulls the kneecap back into the groove and grinds it against the side as you lift your calf. Therefore, you cannot do the full range of leg extensions with the knee bent without worsening your symptoms.

There is a way to get around this. The inner side of the quadriceps muscle comes into play only in the last 30°, or six to eight inches, of a full leg extension. At this point the kneecap is up out of the groove. The idea is to work the quadriceps only within these last six to eight inches of the lift, as described in the 30° Leg Extension.

30° Leg Extension

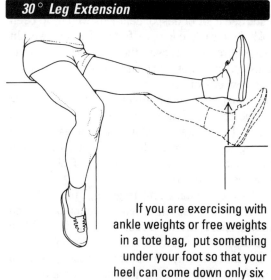

If you are exercising with ankle weights or free weights in a tote bag, put something under your foot so that your heel can come down only six to eight inches after your leg is fully extended. I recommend that you sit on something high, such as a kitchen table or a desk, so that you have enough room for a bag to hang from the ankle without hitting the floor. Then take a chair or stool and pile books on it to a height of six to eight inches below your heel when your leg is fully extended. As you come down, your heel will hit the books and stop your knee from bending.

If you are exercising on a bench with a leg machine, put a cinder block or box under the bar so that your leg stops six to eight inches below full extension.

If you are exercising on a weight machine, first lift the stack of weights to full extension. Then have someone else put a second pin into the stack so that when the weights come down six to eight inches, the pin blocks them from going any further.

Do the previously described muscle-strengthening program of five sets of 10 repetitions with enough weight so that your muscle is exhausted during the fifth set. When the exercise gets easy, increase the weight. Do this once a day every day until you are free of pain. Then do it two or three times a week to keep the quadriceps muscle strong.

If you are doing other leg-strengthening routines, stay away from leg presses or squats, which put stress on the bent knee. Bending the knee more than 30° will cause symptoms to flare up, so any kind of bent-leg exercise is bad.

The same principle goes for riding a stationary bicycle. The seat should be high enough so that you bend your knee as little as possible. Avoid using a StairMaster® because climbing steps is particularly worrisome. A stepper that allows you to adjust the height of the step is acceptable if you use a very short step.

A large dose of aspirin is helpful in stimulating the regeneration of cartilage in the kneecap. Take two plain or buffered aspirin pills with food or milk four times a day until your knee is better. If you have stomach problems, buffered aspirin is better than plain aspirin.

✚ JUMPER'S KNEE

Inflammation of the tendons that hook into the upper and lower ends of the kneecap is called jumper's knee. Both of these tendons, the quadriceps and patellar tendons, help to straighten the leg. When these tendons are overstressed, they become inflamed. The sudden, violent vertical leap straightens out the knee, and may cause minute tears that irritate the tendons. It usually hurts more going up than coming down since you must exert a greater force to get up into the air.

The treatment is to rest long enough to get over the acute pain. Anti-inflammatory agents may help reduce the pain. Then you can ice the knee intermittently for as long as it is tender. This will enable you to begin a weight-lifting program to strengthen the tendons and muscles.

Use a leg extension exercise similar to the one described for runner's knee, but extend through the knee's full range of motion. The quadriceps controls the entire action of the knee, and that's the muscle you need to work on to tolerate the stress of jumping again. Leg curls are not as important, but it's a good idea to keep the balance between the hamstrings and the quadriceps muscles.

The same strengthening program can also help prevent a recurrence by ensuring that the tendons are not overstressed.

MD OSGOOD-SCHLATTER DISEASE

Seen only in adolescents, Osgood-Schlatter disease is not really a disease but a syndrome. It was named before doctors fully understood what it was all about. It is an overuse syndrome related to the growth process.

The lower end of the patellar tendon attaches to a knob on the surface of the tibia. As a child grows, this knob becomes larger to give the tendon more to attach to. The constant yanking on this tendon from running and jumping, which adolescents do a lot of, can cause some irritation in the knee.

Every time the child with this syndrome straightens the leg, say, to go up stairs or ride a bicycle, the pain becomes worse. The dull ache may come and go, depending on how active the child is. However, the worse the syndrome gets, the more it hurts.

Also, the knob becomes stimulated to grow and protrudes below the knee. The lump on the shin bone will be tender to the touch.

Luckily, this is a self-limiting syndrome. It always disappears by age 17 in males and age 16 in females, when the knob stops growing. By then, the tendon is yanking on a solid piece of bone, and the pain goes away, although the protuberant knob will always be there.

In the old days before sports medicine, children with Osgood-Schlatter's disease were banned from activity. They were put in a long leg cast for six weeks, which was cruel and unnecessary punishment. No one knew how long it took to heal, and the doctor couldn't detect healing through the cast. Worst of all, the leg muscles atrophied.

Some old-time doctors still immobilize the leg. I still see a lot of despondent kids who have been told they can't compete for a year or two. In fact, there is no reason they can't return to full activity. Only those who have severe pain require a few weeks of rest.

I don't stop young athletes from participating in sports until I hear them say, "It hurts too much. I don't want to play." As long as they are willing to put up with the discomfort, I let them play since there is no possibility of permanent damage to the knee.

To keep a young athlete going, I prescribe ice after activity, aspirin or anti-inflammatories, and maybe short periods of rest for a few days. When the child finally says, "No more," I immobilize the knee with a splint, which prevents the knee from bending and the tendon from pulling on the knob. I leave the splint on until the knob no longer is tender to the touch, although the splint is taken off every day to allow the child to shower. When the knob doesn't hurt, the child is ready to return to action. This may take a few weeks or more.

The pain may come back in a few weeks, months, or years, or it may never come back. Of all the kids I see, 99 percent get through Osgood-Schlatter disease without needing a knee splint. Most kids get by and continue to play. In addition to icing and anti-inflammatories, I recommend buying a good pair of basketball or wrestling knee pads. They should be worn low over the knob because hitting it is extremely painful and aggravates the syndrome.

✚ ILIOTIBIAL BAND SYNDROME

Pain along the outer side of the knee is often due to iliotibial band syndrome, particularly among runners. The pain usually begins 10 to 20 minutes into the run and gets progressively worse until you are forced to stop. As soon as you stop running, the pain almost always goes away, and it won't bother you again until your next run. Ten to 15 minutes into the run, the pain comes back and intensifies the more you run. If the condition persists, the pain will come on earlier and earlier into your run.

The cause of the pain is an overly tight iliotibial band. This is the hard band of fiber at the outside of the thigh extending down to the knee. The band starts at the rim of the pelvis, crosses the point of the hip, comes down the thigh across the outer side of the knee, and attaches below the knee. It helps keep the hip from moving too far to the outside, sort of like the check rein you see on the outside of a racehorse's leg.

Sometimes the band overdevelops and tightens with exercise. When you run, the band saws against the bony ridge on the outside of the knee as you bend and straighten your leg. It rubs hard enough to irritate the knee and may cause similar pain over the point of the hip.

Treatment is quite easy: All you need to do is stretch the band (see the Knee-over-Leg Stretch [Iliotibial Band Stretch] in the stretching program in Chapter 1). You will feel discomfort or pain in the buttock area right behind the bony prominence of the hip due to the band stretching.

Since the band is all one piece, stretching it in the upper part will loosen it all the way down, and you will no longer feel pressure against the side of the knee. Do three repetitions of the Knee-over-Leg Stretch, holding for 20 to 30 seconds. Do this five or six times a day until you can feel that the band is loose and it no longer causes pain during a run. This stretch should become part of your daily routine. If the pain is not better in 10 to 14 days, see a doctor.

MD *OSTEOARTHRITIS*

Osteoarthritis is the wear-and-tear degeneration of the knee. Spurs of bone form along the edges of the knee joint and wear down the cartilage. This can be aggravated by an injury to the knee. Also, bowlegged people may develop severe osteoarthritis of the knee because the bowing causes increased pressure of the inner part of the tibia against the medial femoral condyle. This wears out the inner cartilage and causes bone to grate on bone, leading to arthritis.

Bone spurs or pieces of worn-down cartilage can break off and float around in the knee. This causes pain during activity and swelling of the joint. Anti-inflammatory agents will help ease the pain. If an x-ray reveals that you have a large amount of debris in the knee, arthroscopic surgery can clean out the joint and provide relief for up to a few years. Then your knee may need to be cleaned out again.

If the pain becomes so severe that it interferes with activity, the knee may have to be replaced with an artificial joint.

MD *"HOUSEMAID'S KNEE"*

A large sac of fluid may form in the front of the kneecap due to a sudden blow or trauma to the knee. The medical term for this condition is pre-patellar bursitis. Common among roofers, floorers, and carpet layers, who work on their knees, this used to be called "housemaid's knee," a reference to maids scrubbing floors on their knees.

Trauma to a bursal sac in front of the kneecap irritates the kneecap and causes fluid to form in the sac. Treatment is drainage of the bursal sac with a needle, and then injection of cortisone into the sac if it continues to fill with fluid. If the condition persists and can't be controlled with cortisone, the sac must then be removed surgically.

12

The Lower Leg

Related Sports Chapters

Basketball

Football
and Rugby

Hockey, Lacrosse,
and Skating

Running,
Jogging, and
Track and Field

Skiing

Soccer and
Field Hockey

Tennis
and Other
Racquet Sports

Triathlon

Volleyball

Walking,
Hiking, and
Horseback
Riding

If you are a runner or jogger and your shins hurt, check your feet. They are almost always the culprit behind shin pain and the key to recovery.

Practically all of the pains that occur on the inner side of the shin bone (tibia) are due to improper foot strike, the way the foot hits the ground when you walk or run. These are overuse injuries, and the symptoms depend on the amount of stress you place on your legs and the problems you have with your foot strike. A sedentary person with a severe foot abnormality may have no leg pain, whereas a marathon runner with a mild foot abnormality may suffer severe shin pain.

Pronation is the inward roll of the foot as it hits the ground. Two different foot problems cause excessive pronation. A person with a *pronating foot* has an overly mobile foot and ankle and loose ligaments. The foot rolls to the inside when weight is applied to it, as during walking or running. People with pronating feet may say they are flat-footed, and they may be, but often the arch of the foot appears to be rolled down because the ankle collapses inward. The feet and ankles naturally tip inward like those of a beginning ice skater.

The other problem is *Morton's foot*, which is characterized by the second toe being longer than the big toe. If you have Morton's foot, your foot will roll to the inside when you come up on your toes to push off for the next step. (See Chapter 14 for more about specific foot problems.)

Excessive pronation can lead to three lower leg injuries: shin splints, tibial stress syndrome, and tibial stress fracture.

✚ SHIN SPLINTS

"Shin splints" is a catch-all term used by coaches and runners for any pain on the inner side of the shin. A true shin splint injury is quite rare.

What people call shin splints are actually pains in the muscles near the shin bone. They can be caused by running or jumping on hard surfaces or simple overuse. They usually occur in people unaccustomed to training, although they can also plague experienced athletes who switch to lighter shoes, harder surfaces, or more concentrated speed work.

The pain is felt on the inner side of the middle third of the shin bone, which is where the muscle responsible for raising the arch of the foot attaches. When the arch collapses with each foot strike, it pulls on the tendon that comes from this muscle.

The arch collapses to absorb the shock of the foot hitting the ground. As you come up on your

111

toes for the next stride, the muscle attached to the arch fires and pulls the arch back up to ready it for the next impact. This muscle responds totally to the stretch of the tendon as the arch flattens.

In the pronating foot, the arch stays down because the foot is rolled to the inside. Consequently, the muscle starts to fire while there is still weight on the foot, and it is unable to bring the arch up. Because of its multiple firings during each foot strike and its pull against great weight, the arch muscle tears some of its fibers loose from the shin bone. This causes small areas of bleeding around the lining of the bone and pain.

The key element of treatment is an arch support to prevent excessive pronation and pull on the tendon. This usually solves the problem almost immediately. Many athletes do well with a simple commercial arch support. Those who have a more serious problem may need an orthotic device custom-made by a sports podiatrist.

✚ BONE STRESS SYNDROME

Most runners with shin pain have tibial stress syndrome. Excessive pronation causes the shin bone to rotate inward with each step while the upper part of the leg remains almost fixed. This abnormal twist of the bone, coupled with the fact that you come down with two to four times your body weight on your leg when you run, puts stress on the shin bone and causes irritation and pain.

Again, treatment is an arch support or orthotic device, depending on the degree of foot disability. This will support the foot and stop the rotation of the shin bone. As soon as the rotation stops, the soreness will begin to disappear, and you should be pain-free in two to three weeks.

MD STRESS FRACTURE

If you overstress any substance repeatedly, it will become fatigued and crack. In the case of the leg, if the twisting of the tibia is severe and is repeated enough times, the bone will crack.

Your body can compensate for this stress to some extent. X-ray studies of the shin bone show that the bone thickens in an attempt to strengthen itself. But if you continue to run and the bone fails to strengthen itself sufficiently, it can develop a minute, often microscopic, crack, or stress fracture.

The problem with identifying a stress fracture is that the crack is so small that it typically cannot be seen on an x-ray until it begins to heal itself a few weeks later. If your leg x-ray is negative and you still feel shin pain, then you should have a bone scan. This is a simple, safe x-ray procedure that will reveal a stress fracture within 24 to 48 hours of injury.

You should suspect a stress fracture if the pain level of bone stress syndrome suddenly increases. Also, if you previously felt pain only while running and you now feel it while walking, you should suspect a stress fracture.

A tibial stress fracture requires rest. You cannot run through it; it will only get worse, and the crack in the bone will get larger. If the pain becomes severe, you may need crutches to walk. Otherwise, a break from running for six to eight weeks should be enough. You can cycle or swim for exercise, if this causes you no pain.

As the fracture heals, treat the foot strike problem with one of the support devices mentioned earlier. If you don't correct your foot strike, you will likely fracture the bone again.

For many years, shin splints and bone stress syndrome were treated with aspirin, ice, and wrapping of the calf muscle. I have found that propping up the foot is much more successful in correcting the excessive pronation. Many patients respond as well to commercial arch supports costing $15 to $40 as they do to orthotic devices that cost $200 to $300. Only if your foot deformity is severe or if pronation occurs mostly as you rise up on your toes will you need an orthotic.

✚ *PAIN ON THE OUTSIDE OF THE LEG*

Another type of pain occurs on the outer part of the lower leg and is due to stress on the small bone on the outside of the leg (fibula). This, however, is due to pounding and shock transmission up the outside of the leg rather than twisting.

This type of pain occurs mostly among people with a supinating foot, which is a foot that rolls to the outside because the arch is too tight. This is a high-arched, rigid foot that will not collapse on impact. Look at your shoes and see if they are badly turned over to the outside. If they are, you are landing on the outside of your foot when you run. Since the arch of a supinated foot does not collapse to sustain the shock of the foot strike, the shock is transmitted up the outside of the lower leg and can result in bone pain and a possible stress fracture of the fibula.

Treating this condition is much more difficult. You can prop up a loose arch, but you cannot make a tight arch collapse. The best treatment is to provide maximum padding for shock absorption at the outer side of the foot. An air-sole shoe or a very soft-soled shoe is not the answer because the outside of the sole soon collapses, increasing supination. If the padding is not effective, you may need an orthotic device to protect the foot.

Fibula pain is less debilitating because the fibula is not a true weight-bearing bone. The pain should disappear in two to three weeks with proper padding under the foot.

▄▄ EMERGENCY ▄▄

✚ *COMPARTMENT SYNDROME*

The lower leg is unique in that the various muscles are contained in thick, fibrous tubes called compartments. The design of these compartments doesn't allow them to expand very much, so overdeveloped muscles will be somewhat compressed within the compartments.

When you exercise the lower leg, the muscles become engorged with blood, and the pressure on the veins doesn't allow the blood to leave the muscle. Blood continues to enter the muscle from the arteries, where the pressure is higher than that inside the compartment. Blood continues to fill the compartment because it has no way to escape. This builds up until blood from the arteries can no longer get into the muscle. Without the oxygen carried through the arteries, the muscles can become damaged. Eventually, the muscle fibers die if the condition is not corrected.

The pressure inside the compartment causes pain in the muscles in the outer front part of the shin. This area swells up and becomes very sensitive to any pressure.

Treatment for compartment syndrome is to elevate the leg and ice it for several hours. The swelling should go down, and your leg will be less tender to the touch. If it does not respond within the first few hours, you *must* see a doctor. This is a surgical emergency. If the compartment is not opened up to relieve the pressure within, the muscles will die and you will have total, permanent loss of function of these leg muscles.

Compartment surgery is also done in athletes who have recurrent, milder episodes. A good example is long-distance runner Mary Decker-Slaney, who had both legs treated surgically at age 15 because of recurrent problems with compartment syndrome.

This is probably the most dangerous of all overuse injuries that I see. Luckily, it is quite rare.

✚ *LEG MUSCLE PULLS AND TEARS*

Muscle pulls and tears commonly occur in the major muscles of the calf, the gastronemius and the soleus. These muscles make up the large bulge in the back of the lower leg and are responsible for lifting the heel and driving you forward as you run.

Pulls and tears represent different degrees of the same injury as muscles are suddenly overstretched beyond their limits. The degree of overstretching determines whether the muscle is pulled or actually torn.

Treatment depends on the severity of the injury. You should rest for a few days to begin with and then begin a gentle, gradual stretching program. Calf stretches are best done with the Wall Push-up. Once the muscle is adequately restretched, it should be restrengthened. Toe Raises are the easiest way to do this.

Do the Wall Push-up one leg at a time. If you stretch both legs at the same time and one calf is tighter than the other, which is likely if you have a pulled muscle, you are limiting the stretch in the good leg to what you can do with the bad leg.

As always, adequately stretching the muscle is also the best way to prevent a pull or tear.

Wall Push-up

Toe Raise

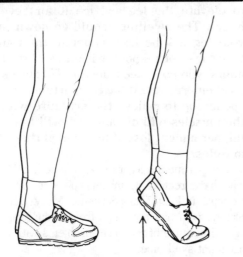

Stand on your toes for 10 seconds and then come down flat on the floor. Repeat until you feel real fatigue in your calf muscles.

As the calf muscles begin to strengthen, you can put all of your weight on the affected leg and keep the other leg off the floor. Then you can hold dumbbells or a barbell to increase your body weight. Use the unaffected leg for balance, but do all of the lifting with the affected calf.

Place one foot as far away from a wall as you can and still keep your rear heel flat on the ground and the other leg a few inches from the wall. Bending your elbows, lean into the wall and support yourself with your hands, but don't let your rear heel come off the ground. Hold the stretch for 10 to 15 seconds and push back up. Reverse legs and repeat.

✚ *CALF CRAMPS*

Calf cramps are dangerous because the sudden muscle pain can be so severe that a runner falls and risks other injury. No one has pinpointed the exact cause of muscle cramps. A number of factors may be at work, including dehydration, electrolyte imbalance in the blood, physical conditioning, and improper diet.

Calf cramps usually occur after periods of repeated heavy exercise. I see plenty of muscle cramps during the first two weeks of football practice. Some of the players sweat profusely or are on low-salt diets, and the cramping may be related to these factors. Or it could just be a matter of getting the calf muscle accustomed to working hard again. I tell the players to drink more water before, during, and after practice, and this generally limits the cramping.

Many people assume that a nutritional deficiency is the main cause of muscle cramps, but that's not the case. Over-exercise, fatigue, poor conditioning, and water loss should first be eliminated as causes before you check for any nutritional deficiencies.

The calf muscle often twitches uncontrollably, which is a signal that it may go into spasm. When the muscle does cramp, stretch it out gently by doing Wall Push-ups. Then massage the muscle with your thumbs and forefingers from the top down toward your feet until the pain passes.

✚ *ACHILLES TENDINITIS*

The Achilles tendon, the largest tendon in the body, connects the gastrocnemius and soleus muscles to the heel and transfers the force of their contractions to lift the heel.

Achilles tendinitis is an inflammation of the tendon and is a prime symptom of an overuse injury. The most common cause is excessive pronation of the ankle and foot, which cause the Achilles tendon to pull off-center. This condition may also be due to over-stress from frequent jumping.

The treatment for Achilles tendinitis is to rest until it feels better and to ice the tendon several times a day during this time. You can use anti-inflammatory agents to relieve swelling and pain. Stretch the tendon as well with Wall Push-ups or Heel Drops. Heel Drops can be done from a stair, a telephone book, or a 2 × 4 board. Or you can lean forward on an inclined plane.

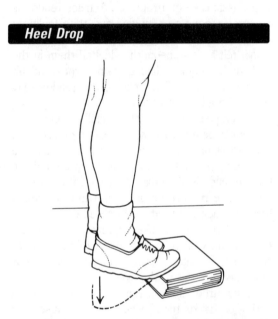

Heel Drop

Stand with your forefeet on a raised surface, as if you were going to do a back dive off a diving board. Let your weight take your heels down below the level of the surface so that the back of your calf is stretched. Hold for 10 to 15 seconds and come back up. Repeat until your calf is fully fatigued.

An arch support or orthotic device may help correct the pronation that caused the tendinitis. Whether you need an arch support or an orthotic depends on the severity and complexity of your foot disability, not on the severity of your tendinitis. A severely pronating foot with lax ligaments will probably respond well to an arch support. A foot that pronates less but has a variety of other problems may not benefit as much from a simple arch. I suggest that everyone try an arch first and, if that doesn't work, then go on to an orthotic.

MD *ACHILLES RUPTURE*

The classic case of a ruptured Achilles tendon is a person stepping or lunging and then feeling a snap at the back of the calf. Athletes often report that it felt as if someone had kicked them in the back of the heel or had thrown a rock and hit them in the heel. The snap of the tendon may sound like a bone breaking.

A complete tear of the Achilles tendon is thought to be due to an accumulation of frequent, small tears or inflammations that have weakened the tendon. Scar tissue may build up around the tendon, and swelling may be apparent above the heel. Once rupture occurs, you can often feel a hole between the tendon's severed ends.

One sign of an Achilles rupture is the inability to stand on your toes. However, this test is not completely reliable. Also, when you walk, your foot may turn out to the side.

A ruptured Achilles tendon can be confused with a partial rupture because it may cause little pain at first. In fact, an Achilles rupture is quite often misdiagnosed. In one survey of European primary care doctors, less than half of them made the correct diagnosis. Most of these doctors diagnosed the injury as a sprained ankle. Thus, the initial minimal pain can lead both doctors and patients to regard this very serious injury as trivial.

The only foolproof way to know if you have ruptured this tendon is to lie on your stomach with your foot off the end of a bed, toes pointing down, and have someone squeeze your calf. The front of the foot normally will move down. If there is no flex in the foot, then the tendon is torn. You can also compare the two legs. Squeeze the uninjured leg first to observe the

flexing movement, and then squeeze the injured leg to see whether it moves.

The best treatment for an athlete is surgical repair. (There is a method used for the elderly in which the tendon is placed in a cast, but this is not adequate for an athlete.) Ideally, you should have the operation within two weeks of the injury. You will be in a cast for six to eight weeks. For the first few weeks the cast will extend above the knee, and then it will be reduced to below the knee.

After eight weeks you can start range-of-motion and stretching exercises. These will be difficult and should always be done with a physical therapist. It may be six months or more until you can return to athletic activity. Coming back from a ruptured Achilles tendon is one of the most difficult recoveries for an athlete.

MD *TENNIS LEG*

A small tendon, the popliteus tendon, runs parallel to the Achilles tendon on the inside of the leg. It probably no longer has any function, and there is some argument over whether everyone has this tendon. But if you have it and you overstress it suddenly, it can snap.

A popliteus rupture usually is seen in a tennis player and occurs as he or she makes the first, hard step toward the net—hence the name "tennis leg." It is also referred to as a disease of the aging athlete because it becomes more common with advancing age. Young athletes almost never rupture the popliteus tendon.

The symptoms of a popliteus rupture are similar to those of an Achilles rupture. The victim may complain of being hit in the back of the calf with a tennis ball, and the blow can feel as severe as when the Achilles tendon snaps. You also may not be able to stand on your toes and may have a similar gait as someone with an Achilles tendon rupture. The base of the bulging muscle on the inner side of the calf will be quite tender, and you may see a small black and blue spot there.

The treatment is to ice the calf intermittently for the first few days and to rest it. You may need to walk with a cane or crutches during this time. A shoe with an elevated heel also helps to prevent stress. As soon as you can tolerate it, start a gentle stretching program. As the pain diminishes, you can increase your intensity until you attain full flexibility.

Normally, the tendon will heal with this routine in 10 to 21 days. However, I tell my patients not to go back to athletics until they can stretch the affected side without pain as far as they can stretch the good side. If you go back too soon, you are likely to rupture the tendon again.

As usual, the best prevention is to warm up and stretch properly. This injury is most prevalent among tennis players probably because they are notoriously bad at stretching. This injury should be examined by a physician to differentiate it from an Achilles rupture.

EMERGENCY

MD *LEG FRACTURES*

Giants offensive lineman John (Jumbo) Elliott missed a major part of the 1990 season because of a fibula fracture. He was out of action longer than most people who suffer this injury because, as he weighs in at 300-plus pounds, every bone in his body is weight-bearing. In his first game back, against Buffalo, Jumbo gave up a sack for a safety to All-Pro defensive lineman Bruce Smith. But he played well against him for the rest of the game. In the locker room after the game, as he was icing his leg, he told me that his leg had been sore and he couldn't move the way he usually did. I asked him how he had handled Smith so well. This behemoth of a man looked at me and coyly said, "Cunning, sheer cunning."

Breaking either the tibia or fibula is a traumatic injury that requires medical treatment. A fracture of the tibia is serious because this bone heals slowly and sometimes poorly because of the sparse blood supply in some areas of the bone. Commonly seen among skiers, this fracture is called a boot-top fracture since the leg breaks right at the top of the rigid ski boot. Before the advent of rigid boots, skiers used to fracture their ankles. Now their ankles are protected, so they fracture the tibia.

A fracture of the fibula is less serious because the fibula is not a true weight-bearing bone. Normally, an athlete can return to activity within four or five weeks of a fibula fracture with padding to protect the leg from further damage.

13

The Ankle

Related Sports Chapters

Baseball and Softball	Tennis and Other Racquet Sports
Basketball	
Football and Rugby	Triathlon
Hockey, Lacrosse, and Skating	Volleyball
Running, Jogging, and Track and Field	Walking, Hiking, and Horseback Riding
Soccer and Field Hockey	

The ankle's unique structure allows you to move your foot in many directions. The foot's up-and-down movement enables you to walk by first striking the ground with the heel and then pushing off from your toes. Without this movement, you would be able to walk only with your foot flat on the floor.

The other important ankle movements are rolling the foot to the inside and to the outside. This allows you to adjust your foot to uneven surfaces so that you can walk on the side of a hill or step on a pebble and not fall.

And there's the rub. When the foot rolls to the outside on an uneven surface, it may continue to roll over until it has stretched and sprained the not-so-strong ligaments on the outside of the ankle. The presence of small holes in playing fields leads to many sprains. Even on a flat surface such as a basketball court, a player can always step on someone else's foot and turn the ankle over. Ankle sprains account for as much as one-fifth of the injuries seen at sports medicine clinics.

In the ankle, three bones form what is called a "mortise" joint. The dome of the ankle bone (talus) sits in a squared-off socket formed by the two bones of the lower leg (tibia and fibula). The joint is held together by three moderately strong ligaments on the outside of the ankle and one very large, very strong ligament on the inside.

ANKLE SPRAINS

All the years I was with the New York and New Jersey Nets, we kept a small garbage can filled with ice and water in the locker room during games. Every sprained ankle was immediately doused in it. This is not a particularly humane treatment, but it really cuts down on disability and swelling, and no one has come up with a better solution.

All-Pro forward Rick Barry particularly hated sticking his ankle into the ice water, and he always belly-ached about doing it. But our long-time trainer, Fritz Massmann, would hear none of it. Superstar or not, Rick's ankle was treated the same as anyone else's.

The ankle suffers only two types of injury: a sprain and a fracture. But it's very difficult to differentiate the two. A large, swollen ankle may only be sprained, whereas a healthier-looking ankle may be broken. For this reason, I recommend that every ankle injury, except the most minimal sprains, be x-rayed. As a kind of mental exercise, I try to predict whether an ankle is broken or sprained before I have it x-rayed. I'm wrong more often than with any other joint, even though I've seen tens of thousands of ankle injuries. There really is no way to predict

119

accurately, so every ankle injury must be x-rayed before a fracture can be ruled out.

If an athlete goes down with a severe ankle injury, the ankle should be splinted and the athlete sent to an emergency room. It may look silly, but nobody will laugh at a sprained ankle with a splint on it, and splinting will help protect the ankle if it's broken.

There are three grades of ankle sprain. When a jogger steps gently off a curb and "twists" her ankle, she simply stretches the ligaments, with no real tearing. That's a mild, or grade 1, sprain. When a tennis player lunges out over a poorly planted foot, partially tearing the fibers of the ligament, that's a moderate, or grade 2, sprain. When a volleyball player jumps and lands on another player's foot, twisting and forcing her ankle violently to the court, most or all of the fibers tear. That's a severe, or grade 3, sprain. A moderate sprain requires vigorous treatment and a severe sprain may put you in a cast or require surgery.

Treat a sprained ankle right, and you can be on your feet in a few days and back in action in a few weeks. A severe or mistreated sprain, however, may not heal for six months or more. Therefore, all but the mildest sprains should be medically checked.

Outward Sprain

The most common ankle sprain happens when you roll off the outer part of your foot and sprain the ligaments on the outside of the ankle. You will have swelling and pain in the outer area of the ankle, and you may have black and blue marks around the injury. Within a few days, your foot and toes may also be discolored. Don't sound the alarm; this is just blood from the broken vessels flowing downward due to gravity. It is my experience that many people don't bother to treat a sprain at first, and then, when blood shows up in the foot, they panic and rush in to see me.

If you feel pain on the inside of the ankle as well, you absolutely should have it x-rayed. When the foot rolls over, the central bone of the an-

kle can knock against the tibia on the inside of the ankle. This may bruise the bone or even break a piece off of it, which turns the injury into a fracture.

Inward Sprain

An injury from rolling off the inside of your foot is much less common than an outward sprain and usually results in a fracture rather than a sprain. The inside ligament is actually stronger than the inside bone, and rather than spraining, it may pull off a piece of bone where it attaches. This type of ankle sprain always requires an x-ray.

Forward Sprain

A third type of sprain results when you catch the front of your foot on the ground and roll over your toes. This pulls the tendons in front of the ankle and tears the ankle capsule, the membrane that surrounds the ankle bones. The capsule forms a closed compartment around the ankle's structures and helps to stabilize the ankle. It also secretes the fluid that lubricates the joint. A forward sprain can take two to three times as long to heal as the other two types of sprains.

The Steps to Recovery

The best immediate treatment for an ankle sprain is RICE (see Chapter 4). Your goal is to limit internal bleeding and swelling. If the sprain is severe, you may need to splint the ankle.

Rest your ankle immediately. A sprain's intense pain eases after a few minutes, and you may be tempted to keep walking or playing. Hours later, you may find yourself with a swollen, discolored ankle too sore to stand on. If you stay off the ankle until the swelling stabilizes, usually you can walk easily within 24 hours. You may need crutches for a day or two.

Ice your ankle until the swelling disappears. The ice curtails bleeding by narrowing blood vessels and helps reduce swelling. Fill a plastic bag with crushed ice and strap it onto the ankle with a towel or elastic bandage. Or you can use a bag of frozen peas or carrots from the supermarket.

Some doctors recommend icing the ankle for 24 hours and then using heat. I prefer ice therapy throughout treatment. Continue icing your ankle for 20 minutes or until it starts to feel numb, and then take off the ice pack and give the ankle enough time to regain some warmth, usually about 20 minutes. Keep icing for 20 minutes on and 20 minutes off for 48 hours or until the ankle returns to normal size.

Compress the ankle in between icings and at night by wrapping it with an elastic bandage, which limits the swelling and bruising.

Elevate the ankle so that it's above your hips and, if possible, above your heart. At night, rest it on pillows or put a suitcase under the mattress at the foot of your bed.

As soon as you can, begin range-of-motion exercises. These can help reduce stiffness and restore mobility.

You should try to put weight on the ankle as soon as possible, depending on the severity of the sprain. If you need crutches, put a little weight on your ankle as you use them to walk as soon as it feels comfortable. Do not put your full weight on the ankle until you can walk with a normal heel-to-toe gait. Do not "duck walk" by turning your foot to the side in order to be rid of the crutches.

Ankle-Strengthening Exercises

Once your range of motion is near normal, you can begin strengthening exercises.

Ankle Lift

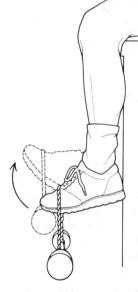

Take a piece of rope about 1.5 feet long, and either tie a 5-pound weight to each end or loop the rope around a 10-pound weight. Sit on a counter and drop the rope over the top of the toes (while wearing an athletic shoe). Lift the weight with your ankle as many times as you can.

Alphabet Range-of-Motion Exercise

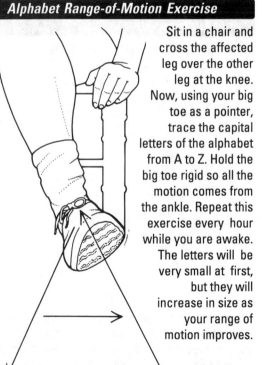

Sit in a chair and cross the affected leg over the other leg at the knee. Now, using your big toe as a pointer, trace the capital letters of the alphabet from A to Z. Hold the big toe rigid so all the motion comes from the ankle. Repeat this exercise every hour while you are awake. The letters will be very small at first, but they will increase in size as your range of motion improves.

Ankle Turn

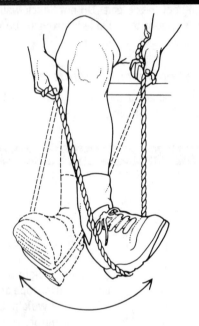

While sitting on a counter, take a long rope, put it under the arch of the shoe of the affected foot, and hold the ends of the rope at about knee height. Turn your ankle as far as it will go to the inside. Now pull on the inside part of the rope and force your ankle to the outside, working against the resistance of the rope. When your foot is all the way out, pull on the outside part of the rope as you bring your foot back to the inside, again working against resistance. Keep the inward and outward movements going until your ankle is fatigued.

Foot Lift (outward)

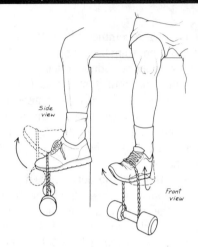

While sitting on a counter, hang a weight on your toes, point your foot up, and turn your ankle as far as it will go to the outside. Repeat as many times as you can. Start with a 5-pound weight and work your way up to heavier weights.

Foot Lift (inward)

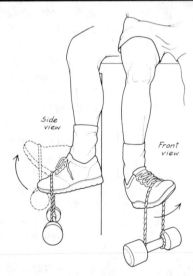

While sitting on a counter, hang a weight on your toes, point your foot up, and turn your ankle as far as it will go toward the inside. Repeat as many times as you can. Start with a 5-pound weight and work your way up to heavier weights.

Also do the Toe Raise and Heel Drop (see Chapter 12), alternating them until your ankle is fatigued. As your ankle gets stronger, lift up your good foot and put all your weight on the injured ankle.

Each of these exercises should be done to the point of total muscle fatigue, so that you can't do even one more.

Balancing is important in retraining an injured ankle to sense where the foot is in relation to the ground. Practice by balancing on one foot with your arms stretched out to the sides until you lose balance or become fatigued. When your ankle gets better, do this exercise with your eyes closed.

If the sprain is severe or if you need to return to activity quickly for a big event, you should consider a good physical therapy program. All of the preceding exercises can be done on machines, which are much more effective than weights and pieces of rope. For balance training you can stand on a balancing board, which is a board that rests on a cylinder and allows you to roll back and forth. These exercises can be combined with electrotherapy, range-of-motion exercises, and massage under the direction of a physical therapist, who knows when and how hard to push you.

Preventing Another Ankle Sprain

The tried-and-true method of protecting a sprained ankle is to wrap the ankle tightly in athletic tape. But that requires learning the intricacies of proper ankle taping. What's more, tape tends to loosen with activity. As an alternative, use a lace-up cloth brace, which can be tightened during a time-out. Elastic braces or bandages are of little value in preventing reinjury because they stretch if the ankle starts to turn over again.

If your ankle is still weak, you can use an Air-Cast®, which consists of two sets of inflatable bladders that are laced together and run up both sides of the ankle. This $20 brace holds the ankle firm and allows you to run. You can wear it until your ankle is fully restrengthened.

If you have problems with recurring sprains, an orthotic device with a lateral flange or built-up area over the side of the heel can prevent the ankle from turning over. Persistent sprains may require surgical repair of the ankle ligaments.

People with tight ligaments, such as those with a supinating or Morton's foot, may have continuing problems. The supinating foot tends to land on the outside and predisposes the ankle to turn out over the foot. Similarly, the person with a Morton's foot is susceptible to ankle sprains because the foot lands on the outside, which makes the ankle prone to turn outward.

Ankle sprains should be taken seriously. Follow an aggressive rehabilitation program to speed recovery and reduce the chances of reinjury. Push yourself just to the point of pain; otherwise, rehabilitation may be too conservative and keep you out of action longer than necessary. Maintain your cardiovascular fitness through cycling and water workouts while you rehabilitate your ankle.

MD BROKEN ANKLE

In sports an ankle can break if it is turned severely with great force. This happens in basketball when a player comes down from a rebound and lands on the side of another player's foot, turning the ankle with the force of his full weight. A football or soccer player can break an ankle if his cleats are dug into the ground and someone falls on or rolls into his ankle. In baseball, catching the cleats while sliding into a base is a common cause of broken ankles.

Common signs of a difficult-to-spot broken ankle include a recurrent, diffuse ache in the ankle that increases with exercise; swelling after exercise, followed by pain-free periods; limited movement; bruising in the ankle; and an unremitting ache.

There are many types and combinations of fractures, from simple, small chips to complex situations that require surgery. All ankle fractures require medical care and prolonged casting or surgery. It is outside the scope of this book to discuss all of the various ankle fractures. Suffice it to say that if you break your ankle, you need to see a doctor.

Most important, be sure to undertake an adequate rehabilitation program after the cast is removed from your ankle. Your ankle will be weak because the muscles will have atrophied, and you will have lost full range of motion. You must bring the ankle back up to 100 percent strength in order to compete at your previous level without the threat of reinjury.

Many orthopedists, however, do not follow through on rehabilitation. I see patient after patient whose doctor felt that his responsibility ended once the cast was off and the bone had healed. An athlete can't return to activity and compete in that weakened condition. So make sure that you see a doctor who specializes in sports injuries.

14

The Foot

Related Sports Chapters

Aerobics

Baseball and Softball

Basketball

Cycling

Football and Rugby

Running, Jogging, and Track and Field

Soccer and Field Hockey

Tennis and Other Racquet Sports

Triathlon

Volleyball

Walking, Hiking, and Horseback Riding

The foot is the most complex structure in the lower body. It is made up of many bones that interact, unlike the rest of the structures of the lower body, in which only two or three bones interact.

The main function of the foot is to absorb the shock of the body's weight landing on it. The foot supports up to four times your body weight when you are running fast, and it must bear at least 1,800 foot strikes for every mile you walk or run. It also must lock itself into a rigid position when you come up on your toes to push off so that it can act as a lever for propulsion. And the foot must roll from outside to inside as your body weight comes forward from the heel to the front of the foot. It's really a physiological wonder.

✚ FOOT ABNORMALITIES

A structural abnormality of the foot can cause stress all the way up the leg into the back. The lower extremity can be viewed as a set of building blocks placed one on top of the other: the foot, ankle, calf, leg, knee, thigh, hip, and lower back. When one building block does not function as it should, the blocks above it also do not function properly because they have an insecure base. Imagine if the Eiffel Tower had been built with one of the lower segments unevenly balanced. Any segment above it would be unstable.

Nearly all overuse injuries of the lower extremities are due to an abnormality in the way the foot hits the ground. To correct a foot problem, you may need to put something in your shoe to change the way the foot functions.

Common Types of Foot Abnormalities

Pronating Foot

The pronating foot has loose ligaments and, because it doesn't have the proper support, rolls to the inside. The foot appears to be flat because the arch becomes compressed when the foot rolls over. But when the weight is taken off the foot, the arch reappears. A person with true flat feet has no arch at all.

When a person with a pronating foot stands, it looks as if he or she is learning how to ice skate. The inward roll of the foot causes the entire leg to rotate to the inside. The kneecaps point toward each other. Everything in the person's leg and hip is pulled out of line.

A pronating foot can be propped up with an arch support under the inside of the foot. This keeps the foot in line when it strikes the ground and prevents the leg from rolling inward.

Supinating Foot

The supinating, or cavus, foot, which rolls to the outside, is the mirror image of the pronating foot. The ligaments are tight, and the foot is rigid with a high arch, which causes the person to walk on the far outer portion of the foot. Because the arch is too tight, it cannot collapse when the foot hits the ground. With no arch to absorb the shock of each step, the shock is sent straight up the outside of the leg.

The supinating foot requires soft padding under the outside of the foot. If you have this problem, I suggest you take a $4 Dr. Scholl's Flexo Arch® and glue a quarter-inch of soft foam padding along the outside edge of the arch. This will cause your foot to roll back slightly toward the middle and will provide some padding to reduce the pounding on your leg, or you may need an orthotic device to take some of the weight off of the outer side of your foot.

Morton's Foot

Morton's foot is characterized by the second toe being longer than the big toe. The problem is that the bone behind the big toe (first metatarsal) is too short. This inherited trait occurs in about 25 percent of the population and causes problems in more people than the other two foot abnormalities combined.

When you walk or run, you create forward momentum by pushing off with the big toe, which is called toeing off. Just before toeing off, you place all of your weight on the head of the first metatarsal. In people with Morton's foot, the first metatarsal is too short to provide the leverage needed to shift the weight to the bottom of the big toe. Instead, the foot buckles to the inside, and the weight rolls along the inner side of the big toe. This is similar to what happens with the pronating foot, but a Morton's foot doesn't pronate until weight is placed on the toes.

People with Morton's foot first strike the ground with the far outer part of the foot. This is probably an unconscious attempt to correct the inward roll of the foot, but it doesn't help prevent the pronation on toeing off. Instead, the person ends up walking across the foot, landing on the outside of the heel and then toeing off on the inside of the big toe, instead of walking with a straight-footed, heel-to-toe gait.

Walking on the inner side of the big toe of a Morton's foot usually forms a large callus there. The big toe will also be pushed toward the second toe, and the pressure on the inside of the big toe may cause bunions on the inside of the foot.

If you have Morton's foot, you may get by with a commercial arch support along with a foam pad under the big toe. More likely, you will need an orthotic that has an arch support and is built up under the big toe joint. When your foot starts to buckle, the built-up area will force you to push straight off your foot.

Flat Feet

Bones, muscles, and tendons under the foot create an arch in most people. Some people, however, are born with "fallen arches," or flat feet. Contrary to popular belief, flat feet are not a problem for athletes. In fact, flat feet usually are more flexible, have greater range of motion, and are better able to absorb the shock of running and jumping.

It is the athletes with high arches who are more injury-prone. An unusually high-arched foot is more rigid and has less range of motion during quick, agile movements. Also, a foot that's precariously balanced on the heel and ball has poor shock-absorbing ability.

Many children start off with flat feet, but the vast majority develop normal arches as they grow. Until recently, flat-footed children were frequently treated with orthotics and perhaps surgery to create a higher arch. But few studies have shown that wearing a particular shoe or arch support can make a significant difference in the development of an arch. Most doctors now feel that flat-footed people should not limit their activities and do not need special treatment. Seek medical care only if your feet hurt.

Telltale Signs of Foot Abnormalities

One of the best ways to diagnose foot problems is to look at the wear pattern in a pair of athletic shoes. A pronating foot wears out the inside of the heel and toe, and the shoe breaks over to the inside. If the shoe is placed flat on a table top, it will lean to the inside, particularly the heel counter. A supinating foot wears out the outside of the shoe, from the heel all the way down to the toes. This shoe will lean to the outside. A Morton's foot wears out the shoe on the outside of the heel and midsole, and then straight across the sole to the inside of the big toe (see the figure below).

I ask people who are having foot problems to bring their running or tennis shoes with them to my office. Often, they bring in a new pair of shoes because they are ashamed to show me how badly ruined their old shoes are. Of course, a brand new pair of shoes tells me absolutely nothing about their foot problems.

Orthotics

Orthopedists have begun to question the safety, expense, and usefulness of the rigid, custom-made inserts that have become trendy among athletes. Orthotic devices contain carefully placed divots and bumps designed to shift your weight in a way that forces you to walk or run more naturally. They are made from a variety of materials, from layered foam to leather-covered cork to hard plastic.

Orthotics are not the answer to all foot problems. In fact, about 80 percent of the people who spend hundreds of dollars for custom-made devices would do just as well with a soft arch support. Many commercial arch supports are available for $15 to $40 at drug or sporting goods stores.

I usually don't send anyone to be fitted for an orthotic until he or she has failed to improve with a stock arch support. If the foot problem is so complex that a simple stock arch will be ineffective, then I order an orthotic right away.

If you have persistent foot pain that you can't trace to an episode of trauma, put some type of arch in your athletic shoe. If nothing changes, then your pain is not due to an overuse injury, and you need to see a doctor to find out what's wrong. If the pain diminishes or even gets worse, then you probably have an overuse injury. Any change in pain is a sign that the arch support has had some effect. If the pain goes away, continue using the arch support. If the pain gets worse, see a sports podiatrist for a properly fitting orthotic.

In looking for a podiatrist to make an orthotic, it's important to find someone who deals with athletes. A running orthotic is very different from a walking orthotic. If you choose someone who

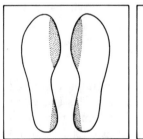

Pronating Foot

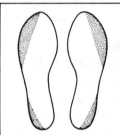

Supinating Foot

Morton's Foot

Normal Foot

doesn't understand the mechanics and stresses of running, you may end up spending a lot of money for little or no pain relief. Also, wearing an orthotic insert should never be painful. If it is, take it back and have it adjusted.

✚ FOOT PAIN

Pain in the front of the foot just behind the toes (metatarsalgia) can be due to the stress of placing weight on the toes when you run. Usually, you will feel the pain in your second or third toe. The heads of the metatarsal bones in these toes may drop slightly, and the excessive weight placed on them as you come up on your toes causes pain. A pad behind the heads of these toes will lift them and take the weight off, and this usually relieves the pain.

✚ BRUISED FOOT

A batter who fouls a ball off the foot, a soccer player who continually kicks the ball, or a person whose foot is stepped on can develop a nasty-looking bruise. If you bruise your foot, ice it for four or five days and rest it until you can walk normally.

EMERGENCY
BROKEN FOOT

Any bone in the foot, from the toes to the heel, can be broken. Broken bones in the foot other than the toes require immediate medical attention and casting. The length of time you will have to spend in a cast depends on the bone involved. Four to six weeks is customary. Each break is different your time to recovery may be a great deal longer.

✚ BROKEN TOE

A broken toe usually only needs to be buddy-taped to the next toe. Put gauze between the two toes before taping them together; otherwise, sweat will cause the skin to soften and flake away.

✚ BLACK TOENAILS

I frequently see long-distance runners whose toenails turn black and fall off. This is due to the toenail banging into the toe box of the runner's shoe. The constant banging causes bleeding under the toenail, which makes it turn black.

The problem is an undersized shoe. As you run, your foot spreads out and swells up slightly, so your running shoes should be one size larger than your dress shoes. Sizes vary from brand to brand, so always carefully try on a new shoe. Regardless of a shoe's stated size, if your toenail turns black after running, the shoe is too small.

People with Morton's foot have an additional problem. The toe boxes of running shoes are all designed with the assumption that the big toe is the largest toe. In the person with Morton's foot, the second toe is largest, so most athletic shoes do not fit properly. If you have Morton's foot, try on a lot of styles and see which one is the most comfortable.

✚ TURF TOE

"Turf toe" is the vernacular term for a sprained joint at the base of the big toe. This injury has always been around, but it became more common with the replacement of natural grass playing fields with artificial turf.

The injury is due to the unforgiving interface between the athletic shoe and a hard surface. When you run on natural grass with cleats on, the grass gives. If you look at the ground, you will see dirt packed down by cleat holes. This means that some of the stress of toeing off has been absorbed by the ground. The hard surface of artificial turf doesn't give, and the entire stress of toeing off is transferred to the toe joint.

The aggressive push-off with the big toe places an overwhelming force on the toe ligament, and the joint can sprain. This injury is very painful and slow to heal. You need to rest your toe until the pain is gone. When it begins to heal, you can tape the toe down so that it can't extend upward. A sports podiatrist can provide a strapping technique and a special appliance to hold the toe down and speed your return to action.

✚ *PLANTAR FASCIITIS*

The plantar fascia is the elastic covering on the sole of the foot that holds up the arch. It runs the length of the foot, from just behind the toe bones to the heel bone. This shock-absorbing pad can become inflamed, a condition called plantar fasciitis, causing a dull ache along the length of the arch.

The ache is due to overstretching or partial tearing of the plantar fascia. This injury usually happens to people with rigid, high arches. They feel the pain when putting weight on the foot or when pushing off for the next stride. When the arch starts to come down, it stretches the plantar fascia and pulls on its fibers. The torn fibers may go into spasm and shrink. With every step, the plantar fascia tears a little more and causes intense pain.

If you suffer from this injury, you will feel the pain particularly upon arising or after sitting for a long while. With the weight off your feet, the plantar fascia will start to heal. But each time you again put weight on your foot, the torn fibers will be pulled apart as the arch collapses.

The treatment is to put an arch support under the foot immediately to prevent the arch from collapsing and the plantar fascia from stretching. Also, put an arch support in your slippers and wear them as soon as you get out of bed. Even a few steps without support can stretch the plantar fascia. By using arch supports, you will likely feel relief within two to three days.

Plantar fasciitis is particularly common among middle-aged people who have been sedentary and who suddenly increase their level of physical activity. Running and jogging lead to most of the injuries. Inappropriately fitting shoes or a weight gain of 10 to 20 pounds can also contribute to the condition.

🆔 *"HEEL SPUR"*

One of the most common complaints I hear is about heel pain. The patient will say, "My doctor told me I have a heel spur, and he wants to operate. What should I do?"

The first thing you should do is *not* have surgery. The pain under the surface of the heel may or may not stem from a heel spur. A heel spur is a hook of bone that irritates the heel. More likely, however, the pain is from an irritated, overstretched plantar fascia.

The pain originates under the surface of the heel where the plantar fascia hooks into the heel bone. Constant pulling on the plantar fascia where it attaches to the heel can cause the heel bone to overgrow and form a spur. This can be seen on an x-ray. For most people, however, the pain is simply due to overstretching the plantar fascia when the arch comes down, not to the growth of a spur. An arch support can hold up the plantar fascia and keep it from overstretching. Even if an x-ray shows an actual heel spur, you may not need surgery.

Some doctors recommend a heel cup, which holds and cushions the heel within the shoe. But a heel cup may make things worse. Many heel cups are rounded on the bottom, which causes increased pronation in the heel and stretches the plantar fascia even farther.

If your heel is very painful, you may need a cortisone injection to reduce the inflammation in the plantar fascia. This, however, is a last resort. You will still need to use an arch support to prevent the pain from recurring.

✚ *HEEL BURSITIS*

Pain in the back of the heel where the Achilles tendon attaches to the heel bone can be due to bursitis. Under the Achilles tendon is a small bursal sac, about the size of a bean, that protects the tendon from rubbing on the heel bone. When the Achilles tendon goes out of alignment, a situation usually due to pronation, it puts undue stress on the bursa, and the sac becomes inflamed and painful.

This bursitis sometimes responds to an arch support, which brings the Achilles tendon back into alignment. More often, however, it requires a small injection of cortisone, like any other bursitis.

MD *HEEL STRESS SYNDROME*

Stress syndrome is another cause of pain in the heel. It occurs on both the inside and outside of the heel bone, but more severely on the inside. You will feel pain when your heel hits the ground, and the pain will worsen from running. This pain is due to excessive pronation of the foot. The heel rolls to the inside, and the force of your weight is delivered at an angle rather than straight down.

I often see this problem in young children in the spring and fall because the pronation problem is aggravated by cleats. If a child has a pronating foot, the broad base of a shoe or sneaker tends to stabilize the foot. When the child wears cleats, however, there is minimal contact between the surface of the shoe and the ground, and the foot is allowed to slide much further toward the inside. Children with pronating feet who go out for football, soccer, or baseball pound on their heels and feel the pain.

This heel stress in children is often misdiagnosed as an inflammation of the growth center in the heel, called Sever's disease. This is a rare disorder. The heel pain is much more likely to be due to the stress of running.

Again, the answer is to put an arch under the foot to correct the pronation. Some children who can barely walk will be free of pain after two to three days of using the arch. I also recommend that children with heel pain practice in sneakers and wear cleats only during games.

MD *STRESS FRACTURE OF THE FOOT*

If you have felt mild pain in your foot for days or even weeks while running, and you then feel a sudden, severe pain in the front part of your foot during a run, you probably have a stress fracture of the foot.

When excessive force is transmitted to the second, third, or fourth metatarsal bone, the bone can crack from overfatigue. When you come up to toe off, most of your weight is on the first metatarsal, behind the big toe. This bone is very thick and heavy to provide support. If the bone is too short, as in the Morton's foot, your weight will be transmitted to the other toe bones, which are not as heavy, and they can crack.

If you suffer a stress fracture, both the upper and the lower surfaces of your foot will be tender, and you may have some swelling. You will need to get an x-ray of the foot, and sometimes even a bone scan, to confirm the diagnosis.

A stress fracture needs rest for four to six weeks to allow the fracture to heal. Crutches are necessary only if you feel severe pain when you walk. Casting is usually not necessary. However, you will need an orthotic to redistribute your weight so that the bone doesn't crack again when you return to activity. Early use of an orthotic will give you relief while the fracture heals.

A stress fracture of the fifth metatarsal, behind the little toe, is a more serious injury. This results from an excessive load on the outside of the foot, such as with the supinating foot. These fractures heal poorly and require early medical attention. Simple rest is not the answer. You may be in a cast and on crutches for anywhere from six weeks to several months. Many of these fractures are treated surgically, with a screw used to hold the fragments together.

✚ *TOE TENDINITIS*

Tenderness and swelling along the top of the foot *only* is usually due to tendinitis, an inflammation of the tendons that raise the toes. It will hurt if you hold your toes down with your fingers and try to pull them back up against resistance.

The cause may simply be that you are lacing your shoes too tightly. Or you may have poor padding under the tongues of your shoes.

The treatment is to ice the tendons intermittently until the pain and swelling subside and to take anti-inflammatory agents. I also suggest that you go to an upholstery store and get a wad of foam to put under the tongues of your shoes.

Choosing an Athletic Shoe

I remember when sneakers or "tennies" were the shoe of choice for athletes. Made of thin rubber soles and thin canvas tops with white laces, they were worn for every sport. They were the original cross-trainers.

When I first took up jogging, the Nike Waffle Trainer® had just come out and I, along with everyone else, thought it was the greatest advance in comfort yet. Today, however, no one would consider using this shoe, or a canvas tennis shoe, because of its flimsy construction and lack of padding.

Athletic shoe design has become a high-tech specialty. There are now new air soles, gel soles, fluid soles, and gimmicks such as the Pump®. There are so many different makes and models and shoes for so many different sports that we now have a hybrid called the cross-trainer, which is good for a lot of sports but not great for any one. I still can't see the need for separate shoes for walking and jogging.

And the cost of shoes has gone out of sight. When I was young, the only children who wore sneakers to school were those who were too poor to afford real shoes. Today, everyone wears sneakers to school. It's not uncommon for a high-top basketball shoe worn only to school to cost more than $100, and adult athletic shoes can cost more than $150—quite a difference from the $9.99 Converse® tennies I used to wear.

By wearing proper athletic shoes, you can reduce the risk of all the injuries that stem from a poor foot strike and lead to pain all the way up the leg to the back. Here are some necessary features for sports-specific shoes:

- In running shoes, look primarily for good cushioning and good stability. The soles should curve up in the front and back, with a slightly elevated heel; heel counters should be firm; and the edges should be sharp for stability. The shoes should be lightweight with soft, breathable, and flexible uppers. They should have good midsole cushioning and soles that are grooved or studded.

  If your foot tends to pronate, choose a shoe with a straighter last and extra firmness along the inner edge for more stability. If your foot tends to supinate, choose a shoe with a curved last that forces your foot inward and with a soft midsole and heel counter.

- Walking shoes should be made to suit the heel-to-toe gait of walking. They should have adequate flexibility in the forefoot and adequate room between your toes and the top of the shoe. The shoes should be lightweight and have strong heel counters, good midsole cushioning, slightly elevated heels, and flexible soles that curve up at the heel and toe. The upper should be made of breathable materials with a hard, reinforced area to protect the toe.

- Tennis shoes should provide good lateral support and good shock absorption. They should be heavy and strong with flat soles and a hard, squared-off edge. Also look for a reinforced front, a cushioned midsole, a firm heel counter, and a sole with circles to facilitate turning.

- Racquetball shoes should have lightweight uppers, good midsole cushioning, and tacky, round-edged soles that are thinner and more flexible than those of tennis shoes.

- Volleyball shoes should be lightweight and flexible with reinforced toes, well-cushioned midsoles, and soles made of ridged gum or rubber with rounded edges for good lateral support.

- Aerobics shoes are a lightweight combination of tennis and running shoes. They should have good shock absorption, and stabilizing straps may be good for the side-to-side action of low-impact aerobics. Good aerobics shoes will have slightly elevated heels; firm heel counters for stability; lots of midsole cushioning; and wrapped, soft rubber soles for lateral support.

- Basketball shoes should be heavier than tennis shoes, with good shock absorption, ankle support, traction, and stability. This means good lateral support, hard rubber cup-ridged soles, and sturdy midsoles.

- Football shoes should have thick, rigid, leather uppers with sturdy heel counters and spiked rubber soles.

- Baseball shoes should have uppers made of leather or nylon and leather, soles with sharp edges for good traction, a long tongue flap that folds back over the laces to keep dirt out, and soles with cleats of molded plastic or hard rubber.

- Cycling shoes should have stiff soles for efficient pedaling. Racing shoes should have a very stiff sole and touring shoes a little more flexibility. The snug-fitting, stiff uppers should be made of leather or leather and nylon with no cushioning. Shoes for mountain biking may use more durable materials. Many cycling shoes have Velcro snaps for a snug fit. The shoe should also fit snugly into the toehold on the pedal, and the soles should have grooves to help grip the pedals.

- Weight-training shoes need a wide base for stability and a firm midsole for support. Stabilizing straps can lock in the heel to provide a firm footing.

- Cross-trainers pack flexibility, stability, and cushioning into one pair of shoes. Choose shoes with restraining straps for good lateral support and with reinforced toes. You need a shoe that provides adequate cushioning, especially in the heel and ball of the foot.

Part Four

Sport-by-Sport Injuries

Aerobics

Baseball and Softball

Basketball

Bowling

Boxing and Martial Arts

Cycling

Football and Rugby

Golf

Gymnastics and Cheerleading

Hockey, Lacrosse, and Skating

Running, Jogging, and Track and Field

Skiing

Soccer and Field Hockey

Swimming and Other Water Sports

Tennis and Other Racquet Sports

Triathlon

Volleyball

Walking, Hiking, and Horseback Riding

Weight Lifting and Body Building

Wrestling

15

Aerobics

Setting calisthenics to music has created a new, more appealing form of exercise: aerobics. Aerobics caught on because it has the appeal of dance, offers the companionship of a group, and costs very little, as long as you don't buy the ultra-fashionable exercise outfits and shoes.

Calisthenics alone does not allow you to achieve your target heart rate for a long enough time to provide conditioning. By combining calisthenics with repetitive dance routines, you can achieve your target heart rate and maintain it.

Aerobics is now one of the most popular forms of exercise. Approximately 27 million women and men are enrolled in aerobics classes, and that doesn't include the countless individuals who exercise at home to aerobics videotapes.

But the growing popularity of aerobics has led to problems. Although the aerobics originators were trained in exercise physiology and kinesiology (the study of body motion), the movie and television personalities who sell millions of videotapes and books for home use have had no such training—and neither have many of the aerobics instructors in health clubs. As a result, many aerobicizers do too much, too fast, too soon, and they injure themselves.

The jumping and bouncing routines of high-impact aerobics on a hard gym floor have also led to multiple injuries, mostly to the lower body.

Original aerobic shoe designs are partly to blame. Shoe manufacturers saw a huge market in aerobic shoes and, unfortunately, designed the shoes more with fashion sense than with function in mind.

These problems have led to so many injuries that, at one time, aerobics instructors replaced gymnasts as the athletes with the highest incidence of sports injuries. More than 75 percent of aerobics instructors have sustained at least one injury while teaching aerobics.

MD *INNER EAR DAMAGE*

There is a strong association between high-impact aerobics and damage to the structures of the inner ear. Jarring the skeleton transmits vibrations all the way up to the skull and the tiny bones of the inner ear. This may disturb the inner ear's delicate, finely tuned balance mechanism, resulting in dizziness and hearing loss in some people who are heavy aerobicizers.

It's still unclear whether the ear damage sustained from hours of vigorous jumping is permanent or will clear up if activity is curtailed. The exercise makes most aerobicizers feel so much better emotionally that they seem unwilling to give it up, even if it does affect their hearing and balance.

135

PULLED MUSCLES

The most common aerobics injury is a pulled or strained muscle. Almost any muscle in the body can become injured during aerobics, but most injuries occur in the legs, back, and stomach. These usually result from using muscles that have never been used before or going further with a muscle than ever before. The jumping, twisting, and turning of aerobics causes a sudden, violent stretch of the muscle. I see these muscle injuries most commonly in beginners who get "into" the music and get carried away—and then have to be carried away, literally.

A pulled muscle can take a few days to a few weeks to heal, depending on how badly you pulled it and how quickly you treat it. You must stretch the muscle as it heals so that you won't reinjure it when you resume aerobics.

The most severe injuries from aerobics occur in the lower back. If your back continues to hurt after being treated for a muscle pull, see a qualified health professional. You may have a disc problem or ligament damage from the violent, twisting motion of aerobics.

See pages 43, 69, 70

THIGH AND HIP PAIN

The excessive rotation of an abnormal foot strike against the floor can be transferred up into the thigh and hip. Pronation causes the thigh and hip as well as the foot to roll to the inside. This constant stress and twisting can cause the thigh and hip bones to crack, which is known as a stress fracture.

See page 97

AEROBICS KNEE

A form of runner's knee (chondromalacia patella) is a very common cause of knee pain during aerobics. Aerobics aggravates this condition by introducing movements that put weight on the leg with the knee bent more than 30°. These move-

ments are still commonly included even in low-impact aerobics routines.

See page 106

ILIOTIBIAL BAND SYNDROME

Pain in the outer side of the knee or over the point of the hip is due to iliotibial band syndrome. Aerobics activities can cause this band, which extends from the rim of the pelvis to below the knee, to overdevelop, tighten down, and rub on the point of the hip or the outer projection of the knee. Either of these areas can then become sore.

See pages 99, 108

AEROBICS SHINS

When high-impact aerobics were in vogue, the injury commonly referred to as shin splints, and the tibial stress syndrome and tibial stress fracture that can accompany it, was a frequent problem due to the impact of the foot on the floor. The impact of pounding the floor improperly is transferred up the leg into the shin, causing pain. The advent of low-impact aerobics (where one foot stays on the floor at all times), step aerobics, more shock-absorbent floors, and better shoe design has reduced the number of shin injuries.

To correct for shin pain, you need to change the mechanics of your foot as it hits the floor. This will ease the pain shooting up your leg. If you have a pronating foot, which rolls to the inside, you are likely to feel the stress in your tibia. If you have a supinating foot, which rolls to the outside, you will likely feel the pain in your fibula.

See pages 111–113

STRESS FRACTURES OF THE FOOT

Stress fractures of the foot can result from the hard impact of the foot on the floor. This injury is characterized by sudden, severe pain during class that recurs afterward whenever you put weight on the foot. If the pain does not go away in a few days, have your foot x-rayed. You may also need a bone scan to help your doctor make the proper diagnosis.

See page 130

STEP AEROBICS

One of the hottest types of aerobics is step aerobics. More than 4 million people have become step aerobicizers. Step, or bench, aerobics requires you to step on and off a bench using a variety of foot and leg movements. It offers a high cardiovascular workout with low body impact. Stepping represents the aerobic equivalent of a seven-mile run and the impact equivalent of a three-mile walk. Many step programs include hand weights, which help develop the arms and upper body.

In a typical step aerobics class, you hop on and off a bench 8 to 12 inches high to the beat of music. To do your step training at home, you can use a simple adjustable bench, offering heights of 2 to 8 inches, or even stairs. Small, portable units you can carry around easily or store in the closet are available for about $50. Some come with a step aerobics workout on videotape for home use.

Stair-steppers, such as StairMaster, rank as the most-used type of exercise equipment in health clubs. These machines are great for developing the calves, thighs, and buttocks and give you a good cardiovascular workout. The machine gives you a readout of how many calories you have expended; the equivalent number of floors you have climbed; and the equivalent number of miles you have walked, jogged, or run. You can buy a stair-stepper for home use for $200 to $2,000.

You can use this machine to work various muscle groups. To tone buttock muscles, take higher steps. To work abdominal muscles, take shorter steps. If you put your feet forward, you take pressure off the calf muscles and shift it to the hips, quadriceps, and hamstrings. Stand facing away from the machine to work the lower-back muscles.

When stair-stepping, make sure your knees stay over your toes. If you place your foot ahead of your knee and then lift up, you could strain your knee or hip. If you have a history of knee or hip problems, you should probably stay off stair-steppers and walk instead. If you begin to feel knee or hip pain from any kind of step aerobics, this form of exercise is not for you.

Another caveat: Many people set resistance or time limits beyond their capabilities. To keep up with the machine, either they shorten their steps and cut the exercise's range of motion, or they support themselves by leaning on the machine. When you support one-quarter of your weight with your arms, you lose 30 percent of the machine's efficiency. So stand straight, use the handrails for balance only, and choose a workout level that does not force you to lean on the machine.

WATER AEROBICS

More and more aerobics instructors around the country are offering water workouts as a safe, energetic alternative to regular aerobics classes. Water (or aqua) aerobics are hard on the muscles but soft on the joints, and you can achieve a greater range of motion than on land.

The natural buoyancy of water helps people with sports injuries—as well as pregnant women, older people, those who are overweight, and those who suffer from arthritis—get a complete, safe workout. Children can also participate if they are tall enough to stand chest-deep in the water.

Most water aerobics programs mix conditioning exercises with muscle-toning movements that involve jumping, twisting, punching, kicking, and running in the water. All of these exercises are performed in the shallow end of the pool.

It's important to find a program that includes 20 minutes of continuous exercise to put you within your cardiovascular training range. The program should have a warmup of 5 to 10 minutes, a variety of water activities, and then a warm-down of 5 to 10 minutes. You won't be able to work out in the water for as long as you can on land, so start off slowly and stop when you get tired or develop sore muscles.

In water your body weight is reduced to only 10 percent of what it is on land. So exercising in water is often more comfortable than exercising on land. A water temperature in the low 80s enables you to stay cool while working out, no matter how hot it is outside. You sweat, but you don't notice it. On the other hand, you have to be willing to exert yourself, and not just float, to get the full aerobic benefit.

A typical water aerobics class will have you wear a special vest to increase your buoyancy and allow you to jog in the water. These flotation devices allow even those who can't swim to feel comfortable doing shallow-water routines. You should also wear shoes, either special aquatic footwear available in sporting goods stores or standard aerobic dance shoes.

With the addition of special equipment, you can increase your resistance even more to build strength and increase flexibility. The faster you move your arms and legs, the greater the resistance and the better the workout. Water fins, hand and leg paddles, special lightweight armbands, and ankle boots can provide buoyancy and enhance the water's natural resistance. Some programs use balls, dumbbell-shaped floating weights, plastic bottles, boots, and gloves to increase water resistance. These devices help provide both an upper- and a lower-body workout.

If you are interested in water aerobics, contact your local "Y" or health club with a swimming pool. Many private swim clubs and community pools now offer water aerobics classes. Water aerobics instructors should be experienced at teaching exercise classes and should have some training in basic first aid or cardiopulmonary resuscitation (CPR).

How to Improve Your Workout

Invest in a good pair of aerobics or cross-training shoes to prevent impact injuries to your lower body. You need a shoe with good shock absorption in the heel, a wide toe, strong arch support, and a firm sole. The problem with most shoes is that they are too soft. A shoe may be comfortable, but if the shoe is too soft, the foot does what it wants to do instead of what it's supposed to do. Once you find a good quality shoe, then look for comfort. And once you find a well-fitting, comfortable shoe, don't change it because this year's shoe style has changed.

Whenever possible, look for low-impact aerobics classes. Better yet, try water aerobics, which is the least jarring on your joints.

Preventing Aerobics Injuries

The large number of injuries to aerobics instructors prompted a revolutionary changeover to low-impact activities. Low-impact aerobics involves a lot of stepping, side-to-side and step-touch motions, and leg bending to shift body weight. Padded floors have replaced hard gym floors, and aerobics shoes have been designed to absorb more shock.

To avoid being injured from aerobics, find a facility that offers various levels of aerobics classes and experienced instructors who can start you at the right level. Resist being moved up to a higher class if you are having difficulty. The mark of a seasoned instructor is knowing how hard to push. If you feel persistent pain in your muscles or joints, stop exercising and have the pain evaluated.

Look for an instructor with training in teaching aerobics and certification by a reputable national organization such as the American Aerobic Association. Many aerobics instructors also have a college degree in physical education or exercise physiology.

Avoid being overly competitive in class. Aerobics is a way of improving your health, not a competitive sport. You want to be in the best shape possible, but that doesn't mean you have to be in as good a shape as the person next to you.

An Individualized Aerobics Program

The basic problem of an aerobics class is that it is designed for a group. You have to adapt your workout to fit the type of class. And routines on videotape are even less forgiving; at least an instructor can give you a variation on a particular movement.

If you decide to take up aerobics, or to change classes, make sure that the instructor takes the following factors into account:

- *Your age*. This means your physical age as well as your chronological age. Most health clubs now offer classes for the elderly as well as for the young.

- *Your basic conditioning*. There's no reason an older athlete in reasonably good shape shouldn't take a tough aerobics class. But don't try to push yourself beyond your limits. You can always rest and catch up with the rest of the class.

- *Your flexibility*. Many young aerobics instructors have dance training and can do things with their bodies that most people can't. Again, stay within your limits.

- *Your strength*. Some new aerobics classes strengthen and tone muscles as well as condition the heart. If your muscles are sore for several days after a class, consider dropping down a level.

- *Your body's own peculiarities*. Let the instructor know if you have any orthopedic problems, such as recurrent lower back pain, or any biomechanical abnormalities, such as runner's knee.

Know your target heart rate, and monitor your heart rate while you exercise to make sure you stay within that zone. In a mass aerobics class, no one will monitor your heart rate; you have to do it yourself. A good aerobics instructor will stop the class and let you monitor your heart rate. If you are aerobicizing at home, stop every five minutes to check your pulse and calculate your heart rate.

Aerobics Variety

If you're bored with your current aerobics class, look for one with a different twist or a different style of music. Some aerobics classes stress sports movements, combining push-ups, abdominal exercises, jumping drills, squat thrusts, dips on benches, and sprinting. Others use circuit workouts, providing muscle toning and strengthening along with cardiovascular work. You use a body ball, rubber bands, or a jump rope for 45 seconds each, alternating these exercises with aerobics movements.

Several new devices for home aerobics are available, such as slick plastic floor pads for gliding side-to-side, a plastic sleeve filled partly with water, and a long metal bar covered with soft foam. These and other devices are available for $50 to $90, and some of them come with videotapes.

Plyometrics is a form of low-impact aerobics in which you propel yourself upward with the force of high-impact aerobics but land softly. This involves a high-intensity, deep jump off a box. As soon as you hit the floor, you immediately spring upward again. This is similar to a basketball jump, but slower and more controlled.

Jazzercise® blends jazz dance choreography with aerobics, muscle toning, and stretching exercises. The music in Jazzercise classes runs the gamut from Broadway show tunes, to country and western, to jazz and soul music. The fluid movements do not shock the body.

16

Baseball and Softball

As a throwing sport, baseball puts tremendous stress on the arm, particularly a pitcher's arm. Although the softball pitching motion is underhand, a windmill pitcher, who brings the arm all the way up and around the head, also puts tremendous stress on the arm and shoulder. Besides the pitcher, other players throw regularly and may also injure their arms. With 38 million Americans playing these sports, that's a lot of sore arms.

ARM ABUSE

Most injuries in baseball come from overusing the throwing arm. The throwing motion can be divided into phases to show what happens to the arm and shoulder.

In the windup, you bring your throwing arm back behind your body. In the cocking phase, you turn your arm to put your hand behind your head. This puts your elbow out in front of your wrist and into extreme external rotation. In the acceleration phase, you move the ball forward while it is still in your hand. A professional pitcher can accelerate a ball from a dead stop to more than 90 miles an hour. In the release phase, your wrist snaps forward as you release the ball. Finally, in the follow-through or deceleration phase, your arm comes down and across your body.

The bulk of throwing injuries are due to stretching the rotator cuff muscles. The rotator cuff muscles were previously thought to be stretched during the acceleration phase of the throwing motion, but recent studies show that they are actually injured during the deceleration phase. Stopping the arm after you release the ball is what tears up the shoulder.

Treating Shoulder Pain

To strengthen the rotator cuff muscles, baseball players should do the home exercise program described in Chapter 6 with light weights. Anything above these weight limits will bring the larger muscles of the shoulder into play and eliminate the rotator cuff muscles.

If your shoulder hurts, it is not necessary to determine whether your rotator cuff muscles are simply stretched or are torn. Both injuries are rehabilitated through the same exercise program. Once you have rehabilitated the rotator cuff muscles and are playing baseball or softball again, changing your follow-through by keeping the arm in the middle of your body and following all the way through may help relieve the pain. Or seek coaching help to improve your mechanics.

See page 59

The Pro's Pain

A different type of shoulder pain occurs mainly among professional pitchers or amateurs who have pitched for many, many years. The rotator cuff muscles sit in a bony arch in the shoulder. After many years of throwing, the muscles can become overdeveloped so that they don't fit in the arch any more. This requires surgery to enlarge the arch and provide more room for the rotator cuff muscles.

See page 62

Windmill Pitchers

In softball, the normal underhand pitcher's delivery does not cause shoulder problems. But a windmill pitcher may suffer rotator cuff injuries because she comes over the top with her pitch and has to decelerate her arm after letting the ball go. Windmill pitchers should use the standard rehabilitation program for rotator cuff pain.

See page 59

ELBOW PROBLEMS

Baseball players may suffer a tennis-elbow–like syndrome. The flexor muscles of the wrist pull the wrist forward and help turn the hand over as it releases the ball. These muscles are attached to the inner side of the elbow, the medial epicondyle, which can become inflamed and painful from overstress. Baseball coaches and sports doctors used to believe that this elbow pain was caused by throwing too many curve balls. Now we know that it's the repeated flexing of the wrist that causes the stress.

The ligaments that reinforce the inner side of the elbow can also be stretched or torn from throwing. If the pain persists, it may be a symptom of another condition, called osteochondritis dissecans. This is rare, but it does occur among young pitchers.

Pitchers also may experience pain in the back part of the elbow. The severe external rotation of the elbow pushes it to the outside and swings a hook of bone, the olecranon process, to the

inside, causing it to rub on the inner side of the elbow groove. This irritation can eventually lead to arthritis or bone spurs in the elbow.

The triceps muscle, in the back of the upper arm, attaches to the olecranon process in the elbow. This is the muscle that extends the elbow to put extra power in your throw. The attachment of the muscle at the elbow can become irritated, as any tendon can from overuse.

Baseball players are also susceptible to Popeye elbow, which is the inflammation of a small bursal sac over the olecranon process.

See pages 83–85

LITTLE LEAGUE ELBOW

Little League elbow is a type of pitcher's pain that results from the repeated yanking on a growth center in the elbow, and has become a particular problem among high school pitchers. Little Leagues now limit the number of innings a youngster can pitch, but there is no limitation on high school pitchers. After about 75 pitches, a high school pitcher should be taken out of the game, whether or not he is tired, to protect his arm. Several weeks of rest is the proper way to ease any severe pain.

Unfortunately, subtle pressure is often applied to young athletes, particularly at playoff time. The star pitcher is not told that he has to pitch again right away, but it's put to him in such a way that he can't refuse. As a result, he ends up hurting his arm by throwing too much in one week.

See pages 83, 84

CARPAL TUNNEL SYNDROME

Repeated bending of the wrist from throwing a ball may lead to carpal tunnel syndrome. The carpal tunnel in the wrist carries the main nerve that flexes the fingers and tendons. If you feel wrist pain and numbness in the third and fourth fingers, you must rest your wrist and apply ice.

See page 90

BASEBALL FINGER

A head-on blow to the tip of the finger, which often happens to catchers going after foul tips, can tear the extensor tendon in the finger or detach it from the bone. This tendon's job is to straighten the tip of the finger. If it is injured, you will not be able to fully extend your finger. You must see a doctor to make sure that you have not broken a bone and also to get proper treatment.

See page 92

✚ SLIDING INJURIES

The most severe baseball injuries to the lower body come from sliding into a base. Catching a foot under the bag may cause a severe ankle sprain by stretching the ligaments on the outside or the inside of the ankle. Usually, it is the front ligaments of the ankle that are sprained, since the front part of the foot gets caught under the bag. You must have the ankle x-rayed to rule out a fracture. If the ankle doesn't give out from sliding into a base, you may break the bones of the lower leg above the ankle.

Almost anyone who has ever slid into a base knows about strawberries. These are huge abrasions on the hip that result from sliding on ground that's too hard. The treatment is to clean and disinfect the reddened area, and then apply an ointment and cover the strawberry with a sterile bandage so that it won't become infected. Sliding pads can help protect against strawberries, but most players refuse to wear them.

KNEE INJURIES

Knee injuries are rare in baseball. They most frequently result from a batter's violent rotation when he swings and misses. His knee gives out, and he goes down with torn cartilage.

See page 104

HEEL PAIN

For me, springtime means young baseball and softball players with heel pain. This is the time of year when they trade in their sneakers for cleats. In young players, heel pain is often assumed to be an inflammation of a growth center in the heel bone, which is called Sever's disease. However, in almost all cases, the actual reason for the pain is foot pronation. When people with foot pronation begin running in cleats, which are much less stable than flat sneakers, their heels roll to the inside, and they feel the heel pain almost immediately.

Put an arch support under the foot to correct the problem. If a child's pain disappears within a few days, then the child does not have Sever's disease. If the pain persists, have a sports doctor investigate the cause.

See page 130

TURF TOE

Baseball players who play primarily on artificial turf are prone to turf toe, which is a sprain of the big toe that results from the hard running surface.

See pages 128, 129

How to Improve Your Game

Conditioning

Baseball is primarily a sprint, rather than an endurance, sport. The longest you will have to run is 360 feet, slightly more than 100 yards, when legging out an inside-the-park home run. In between pitches and waiting to bat, you do a lot of standing around. But when the time comes, you have to run in short spurts. Thus, you don't need to do much distance work, but you do need to practice running sprints. Do 50-yard dashes, resting in between, until you are exhausted.

Even though they know that baseball requires fast bursts, most players don't condition themselves well. Softball players are even worse off since many do not even consider themselves athletes.

Because baseball and softball are running sports, you need to work on your leg strength. Concentrate on the Leg Extension, Leg Curl, and Leg Press (see the strength-training program in Chapter 1), Ankle Lift with weights (see Chapter 13), and 90–90 Wall Sitting (see Chapter 20).

You also need a program of exercises to strengthen your arm. These exercises should include those prescribed for rotator cuff injuries. Doing these exercises in the off-season is a good way to strengthen the shoulder. You can supplement them with shoulder exercises from the strength-training program in Chapter 1.

Baseball players have carefully avoided arm strength training in the past. They felt that it would make their arms muscle-bound and interfere with the fluid throwing motion. With today's stretching programs and techniques of full range-of-motion exercise, this is no longer a valid argument. All baseball players will profit by having stronger arms. Not only will they throw farther and faster, but they will have fewer shoulder and elbow injuries.

Warm Up Your Arm

Warming up the arm is essential. A good baseball player throws at one-quarter speed, then half-speed, and then three-quarters speed before he throws full out. Baseball is often played in cold weather and players who just go out and throw without warming up may end up with sore or injured arms. When I covered high school games in New Jersey, I don't think I saw more than three or four true first basemen. Almost all of them were sore-armed pitchers who couldn't throw very far.

To improve your arm flexibility, you should stretch your shoulder. Following are three basic shoulder stretches you should do after warming up.

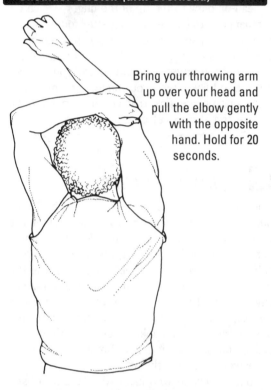

Shoulder Stretch (arm overhead)

Bring your throwing arm up over your head and pull the elbow gently with the opposite hand. Hold for 20 seconds.

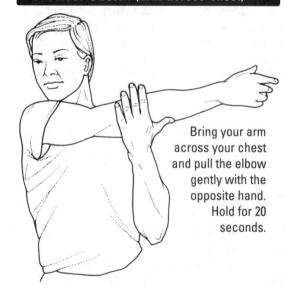

Shoulder Stretch (arm across chest)

Bring your arm across your chest and pull the elbow gently with the opposite hand. Hold for 20 seconds.

Shoulder Rotation Stretch

Face a doorway or post, grasp the doorway or post, and rotate your body away from the door or post to stretch the front of the shoulder. Hold for 20 seconds.

Warm down the same way, with throws at three-quarters speed, then half-speed throws, and finally one-quarter-speed lobs. Then stretch your shoulder again.

After pitching, you should ice your shoulder. Wait 20 to 30 minutes before icing. If you allow the muscles to return to body temperature, the icing is much more effective.

If you notice persistent shoulder pain from pitching, have a pitching coach look at your follow-through. A good pitching coach knows the proper mechanics and can make on-the-spot corrections.

Safer Softball

Nearly three out of four injuries to the 40 million Americans who participate in organized softball games result from sliding into a base. Most softball players don't know how to slide properly, and many players decide to slide too late. Being in poor condition and drinking beer on the sidelines may also contribute to the problem.

These injuries could be practically eliminated through the use of breakaway bases instead of anchored bags. A study from Michigan showed that playing softball on fields with stationary bases led to 23 times more injuries than playing on fields with breakaway bases. So if you play in a league or set up your own game, make sure to use bases that move so that you avoid sliding injuries.

17

Basketball

When James Naismith invented basketball more than 100 years ago, he didn't foresee 7-foot, 270-pound players who run like deer. Because today's athletes are bigger, stronger, and faster, they injure themselves more often than their nineteenth-century counterparts did. Naismith also probably never thought his game would become the most-played sport worldwide. Basketball is played by nearly 40 million people in the United States alone.

Basketball has evolved from an outside set-shooting game to an under-the-basket dunking contest. As big players jockey for rebounds, they make a great deal of contact. A player driving to the hoop may collide violently with an opponent or, if he is knocked off balance, come down on a hardwood floor. In addition, the game is played in a confined space, so there are many things to run into. The pole holding the basket, the scorer's table, and the bench are all close to the court and represent dangerous obstacles for fast-moving players.

Overuse injuries are magnified in basketball because of the hard surface the players must run on. Most gyms have hardwood floors laid directly on concrete. If there is a wooden base underneath, the court is slightly less rigid. In either case, the floor does not give sufficiently to cradle the impact on the foot as a player pounds up and down the floor.

Professional teams play on a floor built up on risers. This is a much softer, more forgiving surface that allows professionals to play more than 80 games a year without suffering perpetually sore joints.

HEAD INJURIES

Basketball players can bang their heads going after loose balls, or a player can take an elbow to the head, usually while rebounding. These clashes cause cuts and bruises, which should be cleaned and iced down; concussions; and broken noses, cheeks, and jaws.

If you suffer a concussion, be careful about returning to play ball. You are at increased risk of another concussion from a lesser blow to the head.

Any nose, cheek, or jaw suspected to be broken should be iced down with pressure applied to reduce swelling and bleeding. Then it should be x-rayed.

Occasionally, a basketball player will be poked in the eye, resulting in a scratched cornea. The immediate treatment is to patch the eye shut. Then have an eye specialist check on the extent of the damage. Goggles can be worn to protect the eye from further injury.

See pages 49–51

SHOOTER'S SHOULDER

When you go up for a shot with your arm straight up and an opponent knocks your arm backward, you may end up with a partial or full shoulder dislocation. The same thing can happen when you go up for a rebound with your arms stretched over your head.

Once the shoulder is back in joint, the treatment is to strengthen the rotator cuff muscles with an exercise program. Rest may ease your pain, but your shoulder muscles will still be weak. Without restrengthening, the shoulder will likely go out on you again. The shoulder is a slow-healing joint, and rehabilitation may take several months.

See pages 64, 65

BASKETBALL BACK

People with long legs are more likely to have one leg that is slightly longer than the other. This discrepancy can lead to lower-back pain. Measuring your leg lengths and putting a heel lift in the shoe of the shorter leg can correct this problem.

Tall people also have long backs and need more muscle to stabilize the spine. A basketball player who comes down off balance from a rebound commonly strains a muscle and may even rupture a disc. All the jumping and twisting exerts tremendous torque on the back, and a player's muscles may not be adequately developed to absorb all the shock.

A back exercise program is therefore important for basketball players. A lower-back stretching program should be incorporated into the exercise routine, and both arching and flexing exercises should be used to strengthen the back.

See pages 69–71

WRIST INJURIES

Sprained and even broken wrists commonly result from players falling to the floor. They instinctively put out their hands to stop their momentum, and the wrist absorbs the shock.

It's difficult to distinguish a sprained wrist from a broken wrist without an x-ray. Because there are so many tendons and bones in the wrist, it's one of the hardest areas of the body in which to diagnose an injury. If you damage your wrist, see a sports doctor who knows the difference between the two injuries.

A basketball player may break the small navicular bone just behind the base of the thumb. This fracture may take from eight weeks to eight months to heal by itself. If it doesn't heal, surgery will be needed to help the bones knit back together.

See pages 87, 88

FINGER FRACTURES

Almost all veteran basketball players have broken a finger. This injury typically occurs when a deflected pass hits the end of a finger, or a tendon can rupture and a piece of bone can break off with it. If your finger gets hit by a ball, ice it down until the swelling subsides. If the pain persists, see a doctor and have the finger x-rayed to see whether it is broken.

See pages 91, 92

DISLOCATED FINGER

If the ball hits your finger and moves it sideways, a dislocation may result, commonly in the joint closest to the hand. Immediately pulling on the finger usually puts it back in joint and relieves the sharp pain. However, you should have the finger x-rayed because it may also be broken, and you can lose the motion in an untreated broken finger.

The swelling may take four to eight months to go down. Don't be alarmed. The finger may always be a little bit bigger than it was, and you may lose some mobility, but not enough to throw you off your game.

See page 91

HAMSTRING PULL

Hamstring pulls are common among basketball players because of their sudden acceleration, for example, as they drive to the basket.

The treatment is rest and ice, followed by a stretching program. When you can stretch the injured side without pain as far as you can stretch the healthy one, you are ready to return to action.

To prevent another hamstring pull, you can apply a sports cream, such as Ben-Gay®, before playing to keep the muscle warm and fluid. Many players now wear rubber thigh sleeves under their shorts to keep the thigh warm and give it some support.

See page 95

KNEE INJURIES

Knee injuries are less common in basketball than in football, but they do occur and can be severe. Usually they result from the player taking a blow to the knee from the side. Since a sneaker doesn't fix your foot to the floor, the foot can rotate, which reduces the impact somewhat.

You can also injure a knee by suddenly changing direction while running. This may cause an anterior cruciate ligament (ACL) tear or a cartilage tear. An ACL tear requires reconstructive surgery, and it may take six months or more of strenuous physical therapy before you recover fully. Initially, a knee brace will become a part of your standard basketball equipment. Eventually, a well-repaired knee can do without a brace.

A moderately severe knee injury may not be immediately evident. You may have a sizable cartilage tear and have no problem with your knee for quite a while. Then the next time you stress the knee, it gives out on you.

As a jumping sport, basketball often leads to jumper's knee, a condition where the tendons that hook into the top and bottom of the knee become inflamed. To ease this tendinitis, rest until the acute pain subsides, and ice your knee intermittently while it is tender. Pain-killing anti-inflammatory agents may also help. Then you need to strengthen the tendons and muscles of the knee using the Leg Extension and Leg Curl exercises described in the strength-training program in Chapter 1.

All knee injuries should be treated by a doctor. The knee is not a joint that lends itself to self-treatment. You may be able to do a prescribed rehabilitation program at home, but there is no standard program for all knee injuries. If your knee hurts for more than a few days, or if you feel pain after two playing sessions, see a doctor.

See pages 103, 104, 107, 108

CALF PULL

The stress of leaping can cause a muscle pull in your calf. Rest for a few days and ice the calf muscle often during this time. Then begin a stretching program using Wall Push-ups. Stretch the muscle for 20 seconds at a time, doing five repetitions at least six to eight times a day, to lengthen the calf muscle.

See pages 113, 114

ANKLE SPRAIN

The ankle sprain is the basketball player's bête noire. It usually results from a player stepping on another player's foot while coming down from a jump or while running up the court.

Anything but the most minimal ankle sprain should be seen by a doctor and x-rayed to check for a possible fracture. Treatment includes the traditional RICE formula described in Chapter 4, followed by early range-of-motion exercises. You can bear weight on the ankle once you can walk with a normal heel-to-toe gait. Muscle-strengthening exercises are important in preventing another sprain. Taping or bracing the ankle may also help support the ankle while you are recovering.

See pages 119–123

ACHILLES TENDINITIS

Basketball players can suffer Achilles tendinitis from two causes: turning the foot over while running and straining the Achilles tendon while jumping.

Two useful stretching exercises are the Wall Push-up and the Heel Drop in Chapter 12.

Repeated tendinitis can weaken the Achilles tendon and cause scar tissue to form. A player may go up for a jump shot one day and all of a sudden the tendon ruptures. Each year I see about a half-dozen basketball players with Achilles ruptures, which is one of the most severe injuries in sports. It is likely that surgery will be needed to repair the ruptured tendon, and full recovery may take six months or more.

See pages 115, 116

STRESS FRACTURES

Basketball players must pay heed to foot pain. They have a high incidence of stress fractures, the injury that shortened Bill Walton's career. If you experience a sudden pain in the front part of the foot while running, it may be a stress fracture. If both the top and bottom of the foot hurt and the foot swells up, have it x-rayed to see whether any bones have cracked.

The most common stress fracture among basketball players occurs in the bone behind the little toe. An informal survey of team doctors in the National Basketball Association found that, of all lower-body fractures, more than half were to the fifth metatarsal, behind the little toe. A Penn State study revealed that NBA players come down on their feet with as much as 14 times their own body weight after a lay-up. The NBA is now studying the connection between such high-impact landings on hard floors and stress fractures.

See page 130

How to Improve Your Game

Like other running sports, basketball requires superb conditioning. You must be able to exert a burst of speed to get by the person guarding you and also have the endurance to run the court for an entire game. You can perform running drills that combine these facets.

Endurance running drills are just long, slow runs, from three to five miles a day, that get your heart into the training range. This gives you the strong base of aerobic conditioning that is necessary for stamina. Once you have built up your base level, start interval training. Repeated sprints of varying distances with short rests in between will give you the speed and quick recovery you need for basketball.

You also need to develop a good first step and side-to-side agility. Here are drills to make you more agile and to improve your lateral movement:

Figure Eight

Run a figure-eight pattern the length of the court until you are tired.

"Suicide"

Run at full speed from the foul line to the midcourt line, turn quickly, and run back to the foul line. Do this until you are tired.

Carioca

Cross one foot over the other while moving quickly from side to side. Do cariocas the width of the court until you are tired.

Reaction Drill

Do this with a partner. While you run lightly in place, have your partner make hand signals—right, left, back, forward—and then you shuffle a few steps in the indicated direction. Do this drill for 30 to 60 seconds, and then switch with your partner.

Basketball is, of course, a jumping sport, so you need to strengthen your legs. In particular, work on your calf muscles to increase your vertical leap. Plyometrics are good rhythmic drills that increase calf muscle strength to improve jumping ability. Following are three plyometrics exercises:

Plyometrics Exercises

Drum Major Strut

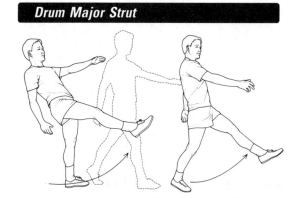

With your legs stiff, lean back and strut forward like a drum major for three or four lengths of the court.

Box Jumping

Stand on a box or bench, bend your knees, and jump down to the floor, again bending your knees as you land. Turn around quickly and jump back up onto the box or bench, bending your knees deeply again. Repeat until you are tired.

Moon Walking

Bound three or four lengths of the court as if you were walking on the moon.

I can't emphasize enough the value of an overall strength training program for basketball players. Your legs must be strong to jump high, and your upper body needs to be strong for boxing out and rebounding. Professional teams now work on strength training in the off-season as well as during the season. Most teams also take a strength coach with them on the road. The strength coach hooks up with a local health club that allows the players to work out there.

18

Bowling

Bowling is an extremely repetitive sport in which you use the exact same motion on each delivery, if you're good at it. Therefore, bowling mostly involves repetitive overuse injuries. Rarely will you experience an acute traumatic injury, unless you drop a ball on your foot. And, believe it or not, I have seen several bowlers break their feet this way.

Bowling is enjoying a rebirth among baby boomers, who grew up playing the sport and are now introducing it to their own children. Some 40 million Americans bowl more than once a year.

MD CRAPSHOOTER'S ELBOW

Bowlers who develop a weak arm and shoulder after a night at the lanes should see a doctor about possible nerve damage. The repetitive, explosive release of the heavy ball can cause nerve damage in the arm and shoulder.

Releasing the bowling ball with a bent-over posture can stretch the nerves between the neck and the armpit and can cause forearm weakness and numbness. Crapshooters develop a similar weakness and numbness in the elbow from constantly throwing dice, so doctors call this illness "crapshooter's elbow."

As a result of this nerve damage, you may be unable to raise your bowling arm, and you may feel numbness in your bowling thumb and forefinger, as well as a burning sensation over your bowling shoulder.

The best prescription is rest until the pain subsides, followed by physical therapy. You should completely recover from the nerve damage within several months.

BOWLER'S ELBOW

Many bowlers develop a pain on the inner side of the elbow (medial epicondylitis) similar to that seen in baseball pitchers. The muscles that flex the wrist attach by a tendon to the inner point of the elbow. Both the weight of the ball and the active flexing of the wrist on delivery overstress the flexor muscle and its tendon in the elbow. These structures become inflamed and painful.

Injecting the elbow with cortisone to control the inflammation is not the answer. The proper treatment is a forearm strengthening and flexibility program so that the arm can tolerate the stress of throwing a heavy bowling ball again and again. A strong forearm won't be overstressed and won't feel any pain. Do the exercises for tennis elbow in Chapter 8.

See page 82

CARPAL TUNNEL SYNDROME

Carpal tunnel syndrome is a very common injury in bowling, which is one of the few sports in which the repeated effort by the wrist is sufficient to cause cumulative damage.

The repetition of the bowling motion—supporting the heavy ball on the fingers and then propelling it—causes wrist tendons to become swollen. In addition, nerve inflammation sends pain down into the third and fourth fingers of the bowling hand and up into the forearm along the nerve. You may also feel numbness, tingling, and weakness in these two fingers.

The treatment is to immobilize the wrist with a splint for several weeks and to take anti-inflammatory agents. All bowlers should also use a splint when they bowl to prevent excessive movement in the wrist.

See page 90

BOWLER'S THUMB

When you release the bowling ball, your thumb violently pops out of the thumb hole. This motion can sprain the ligaments on the inner side of the thumb. This is similar to the ligament sprain skiers suffer from getting the thumb caught in the strap of the ski pole. However, the skiing injury is an acute traumatic injury, whereas bowler's thumb is a cumulative injury. A bowler's thumb

ligaments are not torn violently but are stretched and frayed from continued, repetitive use.

Bowler's thumb may respond to rest for four to six weeks, splinting for three weeks, and anti-inflammatory agents. Better placement of the thumb hole so that the thumb doesn't jerk out may also help. A severe injury may require surgery to repair the ligament.

See page 92

BOWLER'S KNEE

The recurrent stress to the knee as a bowler bends to deliver the ball can irritate the kneecap in people who are prone to develop runner's knee. This injury is primarily due to misalignment of the kneecap. The tightening of the quadriceps muscle in the front of the thigh as the knee bends into the sliding position causes the bowler's kneecap to be pulled back into its groove. If the kneecap is at all misaligned, it will rub the groove.

Supporting the arch in the foot can prevent the kneecap from getting out of alignment. An arch support or orthotic device in the bowling shoe can adjust the bowler's foot position as she slides to release the ball. The 30° Leg Extension in Chapter 11 can help build up the muscles around the knee to keep the kneecap in place.

See pages 106, 107

How to Improve Your Score

The most important step you can take as a bowler is to keep your elbow strong. The weight program outlined for treatment of tennis elbow in Chapter 8 is of great value as a year-round exercise to prevent injury. Also, by strengthening these muscles, you will develop more power and better control of the ball.

Bowlers flex the shoulder muscles and contract the biceps in order to propel the ball down the lane. You can strengthen your shoulder and

arm by doing the exercises (Arm Curl, Reverse Arm Curl, and Front Lift) outlined in Chapter 6.

Focus your stretching program on your shoulder and arm. When you take your warmup tosses, you are preparing your shoulder and arm to stretch more. After a few tosses, do the shoulder stretches described in Chapter 16.

To loosen up your forearm, do the elbow stretches illustrated in Chapter 8.

19

Boxing and Martial Arts

In boxing, the aim is to inflict punishment by landing blows to the head and upper body. It is no wonder that boxers have a high injury rate.

Amateur and recreational boxers fight with different objectives than do professionals. In professional boxing, meting out punishment is part of the game. The point of amateur boxing is to outbox your opponent with a minimum of injuries. Recreational boxers are looking to improve their conditioning and coordination with a full-body workout.

In addition, amateur and recreational boxers use more protective equipment. They are required to wear headgear; larger, more heavily padded gloves; and a mouthpiece. These devices are all intended to soften the force of a blow to the head.

Also, an amateur or recreational bout is shorter than a professional bout. Amateurs and recreational boxers fight 3 two-minute rounds. Limiting the bout to six minutes virtually eliminates the fatigue factor for well-trained fighters. Professionals fight 12 three-minute rounds. Many serious injuries and most boxing-related deaths come about late in fights, so amateur fights are much safer.

Despite these precautions, many types of injuries occur even among amateur boxers.

A KNOCKOUT

A knockout is, by definition, a concussion. Any boxer who is "out on his feet" has suffered a concussion. If you have been knocked out, you should be examined carefully by a neurologist. A professional boxer who has been knocked out is required to wait three to six months, depending on where the fight took place, before he can fight again.

Cumulative head trauma is another problem. Repeated blows to the head can cause the brain to rock against the side of the skull. This kills brain cells due to bleeding in the brain and leads to small areas of scarring. The result is the "punch-drunk" syndrome, where the boxer's loss of brain tissue is sufficient to interfere with his mental function. Most professional boxers who have fought more than 50 times, even though they may show no outward signs of brain damage, have inhibited thinking ability and may suffer from headaches, blurred vision, or memory loss.

Some studies suggest that the neurological problems of amateur boxers are less dramatic because of stricter precautionary measures, such as mandatory headgear, limited bouts, and premature stopping of fights.

The most severe head injury is a brain hemorrhage from a violent blow to the head, which can result in paralysis or death. These are rare among amateur boxers, except for those who don't wear headgear.

See pages 49, 50

BROKEN NOSE

The nose is a prominent, unprotected target. Consequently, almost every boxer, if he fights long enough, will suffer a broken nose.

Ice down a broken nose to limit the swelling and bruising, and get to a physician, who will set it. You should not box again until the fractured bone heals, which takes about eight weeks.

See pages 50, 51

EYE PROBLEMS

A contusion or black eye from a blow to the head can cause bleeding into the eyelids. Treat a black eye with intermittent icing until the bruise disappears. Unless you have a vision problem, you don't need to see a doctor.

However, scrapes and cuts of the cornea, which are usually caused by loose laces on the boxing glove or the opponent's thumb, are serious. All injuries to the eye itself should be seen by a doctor. Thumbless gloves are an attempt to cut down on this injury, but they are not very popular among boxers.

The most common serious eye injury among boxers is a detached retina. This is the injury suffered by world champion "Sugar" Ray Leonard. This injury requires surgical repair, and the victim should refrain from fighting. "Sugar" Ray, however, returned to professional boxing, knowing that he risked blindness every time he fought.

A boxer may also fracture the bony structure (orbit) around the eye, which is called a blow-out fracture. This calls for medical treatment, which may include surgery.

See page 51

BROKEN CHEEKBONE

The cheekbone can break from a hard blow. This fracture should be iced down until it can be treated by a doctor. Surgery to elevate a depressed cheekbone may be necessary.

See page 51

BROKEN JAW

A mouthpiece helps to protect against, but can't prevent, a broken jaw. You can determine whether you have a broken jaw by trying to clench your teeth. If you can't clench them, or if your teeth feel out of alignment, your jaw is probably broken.

A broken jaw must be wired shut to heal. In many sports you can compete with your jaw wired shut for protection. This is not the case in boxing, since wiring cannot protect your jaw from another blow. In addition a boxer is likely to lose weight from the liquid diet required for someone whose jaw is wired shut.

See pages 51, 52

✚ CUTS AND BRUISES

A glancing blow of the glove can cause a deep facial cut and quickly end a fight. That's why a good cut man is so highly regarded among professionals. You can put petroleum jelly on your face in between rounds to keep your opponent's gloves from tearing your skin.

When you suffer a cut, apply pressure to stop the bleeding. Then treat it with an antiseptic ointment and a bandage. Wait until it heals completely before you return to the ring.

If you get a bruise, ice it down intermittently. Wait until the color disappears before you fight again.

MD CAULIFLOWER EAR AND PUNCTURED EARDRUM

If you don't wear headgear, as you should, then a blow to the ear can cause bleeding in the ear.

If you don't go to a doctor to have it drained, the blood can form a hard mass, resulting in what is called a cauliflower ear.

The pressure of a fist against an exposed ear may also rupture an eardrum. If you have problems with your hearing, see an ear, nose, and throat specialist. Once your eardrum has been punctured, hearing loss will occur. However, over time and with no further injury, the eardrum itself may heal.

See page 51

SHOULDER INJURIES

Shoulder injuries are not uncommon among boxers. A muscle can tear from the rapid deceleration of the shoulder as a blow lands against an opponent's body. The arm stops more suddenly than the shoulder, and this can tear the shoulder muscles or the rotator cuff muscles inside the shoulder joint.

Treat a torn shoulder muscle by resting it until the pain disappears, and ice it intermittently during this time. Then stretch and strengthen the muscle as it heals.

See pages 59–63

SEPARATED OR BROKEN RIBS

Rib separations are fairly common among boxers. The front end of the rib is connected to the breastbone by a piece of cartilage, and this cartilage can be torn from a sharp blow or series of blows to the rib.

A rib can actually break from a hard blow. This injury is more dangerous than a separated rib because the broken rib can become displaced and puncture a lung.

It can sometimes be difficult to tell whether a painful rib is separated or broken, so you need to get an x-ray. Either injury is treated with rest (about six weeks) and a rib belt. Once the pain is gone, you should not put on your boxing gloves again until an x-ray shows that the rib has healed completely.

See pages 76, 77

EMERGENCY
RUPTURED SPLEEN

The spleen sits under the left rib cage. This soft organ is prone to injury from a sharp strike, such as an uppercut to the left ribs.

A ruptured spleen bleeds profusely and may cause death if it is not removed rapidly and the bleeding stopped. If it is at all damaged, the spleen must be removed. Since the spleen has no vital function, it's possible to live without one.

Even if it doesn't rupture immediately, a spleen that is bruised by a light blow during sparring may rupture later on. Therefore any spleen injury must be examined by a doctor. If the x-ray scan reveals that the spleen has been seriously bruised, it will need to be rescanned to verify that it has healed adequately for you to return to the ring.

MD ## DAMAGED LIVER

The liver sits under the right rib cage. Although the liver is stronger than the spleen, a blow to the right ribs can tear its surface. Surgery may be needed to repair the tear and stop the bleeding or to remove part of the liver, if the damage is severe. Any suspected liver damage should be seen by a doctor immediately.

MD ## INJURIES TO OTHER ABDOMINAL ORGANS

The stomach and intestines may be injured by heavy blows to the abdomen. Bruising these organs can cause bleeding in the lining around the stomach or intestine. See a doctor immediately if you suspect internal bleeding.

A blow to the solar plexus, which is a nerve center in the abdomen, is responsible for many a knockout. The blow puts the solar plexus temporarily out of service, short-circuiting the nervous system. Usually, nerve function is restored within a few minutes. If this happens to you while sparring, rest until you feel normal and then pick up where you left off.

WRIST INJURIES

A boxer may sprain his wrist ligaments from hitting an opponent or the heavy bag. If you sprain your wrist, rest it for two to three weeks, or longer if it remains painful. Ice it intermittently during this time. You may also need to have it splinted by a doctor to allow the ligaments to heal, which takes about three weeks. To rehabilitate and strengthen your wrist, do the Wrist Curl, Reverse Wrist Curl, Roll-Up, and Ball Squeeze exercises found in Chapter 8.

The small bones of the wrist may slide out of place if the ligaments holding them together are partially torn. This partial dislocation, which often is the result of constantly hitting the heavy bag, causes pain at the base of the hand when you hit. New training techniques have moved away from punching the heavy bag, which doesn't give at all when your fist hits it. This is a serious injury that requires surgical repair.

See pages 87, 88

INJURIES TO THE HITTER

Injuries occur to the hitter as well as to the "hittee." Boxers almost always have sore hands, and broken bones in the hand are quite common. The metacarpal bones, which are the long bones in the palm of the hand that form the knuckles with the fingers, can break from the force of a blow on the knuckle.

Most commonly, boxers break the fourth and fifth metacarpals; consequently, these are known as "boxer's fractures." These fractures must be set, casted, and rested for at least eight weeks.

See page 91

CONDITIONING PROBLEMS

Whenever I would see a boxer doing roadwork in army boots, I cringed. The heavy boots with no arches gave no support to the boxer as he ran mile after mile. It took me years of haranguing to convince fight promoter Lou Duva to put his fighters, including a young Evander Holyfield, into running shoes for their long workouts. Evander obviously learned his lesson about good training. For his first heavyweight championship bout, he used such unconventional conditioning methods as aerobics, yoga, flexibility exercises, and heavy weight training.

Boxers have traditionally trained incorrectly. They do long miles of daily roadwork, and although running long distances is good for building up cardiovascular conditioning, boxing is basically a burst activity. You go full out in two- to three-minute spurts, and then rest for one minute. You don't fight in one long, continuous segment, and you shouldn't train that way.

A boxer needs interval training consisting of two- to three-minute bursts of activity, with one minute of rest in between, to simulate a fight and improve his anaerobic conditioning. He should get his aerobic conditioning up first by running long distances and then begin interval training, running sprints, just as for any burst activity sport.

Many boxers work long, frequent sessions with the heavy bag to increase their punching power. As a result they may punch harder, but they also are likely to injure their hands and wrists. Instead of punching the heavy bag, a boxer should spend more time in the weight room.

RECREATIONAL BOXING

Any recreational boxer who spars is subject to the injuries that have been described so far. Even recreational boxers who don't spar may suffer the same hand, wrist, and shoulder problems from hitting practice.

More women are turning to boxing workouts as part of an overall fitness program and for cross-training purposes. A boxing workout provides both physical and health benefits, particularly cardiovascular improvement. Boxing works the muscles of both the upper and the lower body and improves balance, agility, and hand-eye coordination.

Boxing develops quickness and stamina, and it strengthens the upper body without building big, bulky muscles. Look at a typical boxer. He isn't muscle-bound; he has a lean, well-proportioned torso. In addition to increasing strength and endurance, boxing is also a good way to relieve stress.

Boxing-based training programs are popping up at health clubs and spas across the country. They incorporate the techniques used by amateur and professional boxers into safe, well-rounded exercise programs. These typically include skipping rope, punching a speed bag and a heavy bag, shadowboxing, and doing sit-ups, all under the guidance of a trainer. Participants may also go a few rounds in the ring, throwing combinations of punches into the trainer's oversized, padded gloves.

Boxing gyms used to be men's clubs, but now women are being encouraged to join. Don't expect the same fancy facilities that a health club has; these gyms still have a no-nonsense atmosphere. Contact your state athletic commission for a list of licensed gyms. Then contact a local gym and ask about the availability of trainers. You will probably have to pay a small fee to join the gym and an hourly rate to the trainer for individual sessions. The gym should provide all the equipment. All you need bring is a T-shirt, shorts, and a pair of athletic shoes with good side-to-side stability.

Your local college may offer a boxing class that allows you to spar against classmates. Classes usually consist of a warmup such as calisthenics, work on the light and heavy bags, rope jumping, shadowboxing, and sit-ups, as well as short bouts followed by a warmdown and stretching period.

MARTIAL ARTS

There are literally hundreds of types of martial arts. All of them depend on speed, balance, and leverage rather than brute strength.

Like boxing, the martial arts offer the advantage of working your upper body as well as your lower body. You usually work your way through meditation, stretching exercises, and then punching, kicking, and blocking at various speeds, as if you were shadowboxing.

The martial arts are good conditioning activities that help you build strength, increase muscle tone and flexibility, and improve your balance. In addition, you are likely to lose weight and relax your body while acquiring good self-defense skills.

To find a martial arts school, look in the Yellow Pages. Then go watch some classes and find out what skills each teacher emphasizes so that you choose a style that suits you.

All of the boxing injuries listed in this chapter are also seen in the martial arts, and they can be severe, since participants typically wear no headgear. In addition, injuries occur to the lower body because the feet also are used as weapons.

HAND INJURIES

Hand injuries in the martial arts differ slightly from those in boxing because blows are delivered with the side of the hand as well as with a closed fist. Fractures commonly occur in the fifth metacarpal, the bone behind the little finger. These fractures, just as in boxing, need to be casted for four to six weeks. You will probably need to wait at least eight weeks before you can start hitting with the hand again.

See page 91

KNEE INJURIES

All of the ligament and cartilage injuries described in Chapter 11 occur in the martial arts. Anything but the most superficial knee injury should be seen by a doctor.

Runner's knee is very common in the martial arts because of the characteristic bent-knee stance and rapid, forceful kicks. This movement causes the same stress as the frog kick in the breast stroke detailed in Chapter 28.

The proper treatment is to correct the foot position to ease the stress on the knee. The problem is that most martial arts are done barefoot. Wearing an arch or orthotic in your shoe in daily life will allow your knee pain to subside so that you can function on the mat without a shoe.

See pages 102–104, 106–107

BROKEN TOE

Toes are broken more than occasionally in the martial arts. The usual treatment for a broken toe is to ice it until the pain is gone and then to buddy-tape it to the toe next to it, with gauze between the two toes so that the skin doesn't rub.

The big toe doesn't buddy-tape well and may require medical treatment. This may include re-aligning the broken bone and keeping weight off the toe for three to four weeks.

See page 128

How to Improve Your Skills

The first thing both boxers and martial artists need to work on is coordination. Both hand-eye and hand-foot coordination are essential. If you don't have good coordination, these are probably not good sports for you.

Hand-eye coordination can be improved by one of the training programs developed by sports optometrists and now used by the U.S. Olympic team. These techniques increase your peripheral vision so that you can see over a wider range and decrease your hand's response time to a visual stimulus. This allows a boxer or martial artist to see a punch coming in time to stop it before it lands. It also means that if you spot an opening, you can respond to it more quickly than your opponent can defend against your attack. Ask your optometrist about these special eye-training programs.

Shadowboxing, particularly in front of a mirror so that you can inspect your stance, will certainly help a boxer's hand-foot coordination. The same goes for martial artists, who should practice punches and kicks in front of a mirror.

Often a fighter gets hurt because he's off balance after he throws a punch or kick and he can't recover to defend himself. Training on a biomechanical ankle platform stabilizer (BAPS) board and a side-ski machine can improve your balance. A BAPS board is a large, flat board balanced on a hemisphere. When you stand on the platform, it can tip to any side. The object is to stay balanced as you move about on the board. A side-ski machine allows you to move your weight from side to side as you balance yourself, approximating the motion of downhill skiing.

Boxers have long avoided working with weights out of fear of becoming muscle-bound. Today's weight-training techniques, and Evander Holyfield's success, have dispelled this outdated notion. Full range-of-motion weight lifting, followed by full-body stretching after a workout, can increase your strength without shortening your muscles. And you won't lose any punching speed. Almost every sport now uses weight training. Boxers and martial artists certainly could benefit from it as well.

20

Cycling

Almost everyone learns to ride a bicycle as a child and owns a bicycle at some point in his or her life. It may be just pieced together, but it has two wheels and pedals and gets you from one place to another. For most children, bicycling is the primary means of independent transportation.

With the emergence of the U.S. cyclists in the top ranks of the Olympics, the prominence of Greg LeMond in European road racing, the increased interest in triathlons, and the popularity of mountain bikes, cycling has become a much more widespread sport. More than 85 million Americans now consider themselves cyclists.

The construction of bicycles has improved tremendously. Not only have engineering changes made cycles more efficient, but new materials have led to the creation of stronger and lighter-weight frames. Advances in technology have produced bicycles with up to 18 gears and mountain bikes that can be used in the countryside on rough terrain.

Studies have shown that up to 20 percent of cycling injuries result from collisions with cars. The rest are due to collisions with stationary objects or to the rider being thrown from the cycle. Falls result from skidding on slippery pavement or from hitting a pothole, a rut, or an object in the road that you don't see in time.

✚ SCRAPES AND BRUISES

Scrapes and bruises are the most common cycling injuries. Although sport cyclists usually wear bicycling pants and long-sleeved shirts to protect their skin, most children don't. They usually just wear shorts and T-shirts, and they can lose large patches of skin in falls. No matter what you wear, however, there is nothing you can do to prevent a bruise if you hit the hard surface of the roadway at a fairly high speed.

Scrapes should be washed clean and disinfected and then treated with an antibiotic cream. Treat bruises with ice for 20 minutes at a time until the swelling goes down.

MD BROKEN BONES

If the force of your fall is great, you can break almost any bone in the body. The bones most likely to break in a cycling accident are in the hands, wrists, arms, ankles, or legs as you attempt to break your fall.

Any injury that causes severe pain or an apparent deformity could be a fracture and should be examined, x-rayed, and treated by a doctor.

DEHYDRATION

Cyclists are susceptible to dehydration problems. Make sure to drink plenty of fluids before you go out for a long ride and carry a filled water bottle. Take a drink every 15 minutes or so. For rides longer than two hours, you may want to mix an electrolyte drink with the water.

See pages 34, 35

HEAD INJURIES

Head injuries are all too common among cyclists and account for two-thirds of hospital admissions from cycling accidents. More than 1,000 people die each year while cycling, and three out of four die as a result of head injuries.

I see somewhat fewer head injuries among serious cyclists, who are more careful to wear helmets. However, only 10 percent of all cyclists wear helmets, and only 2 percent of children under age 15 wear them. A cycling helmet is of the utmost importance. Because of the high incidence of head injuries, many states are considering cycling helmet laws similar to those governing motorcyclists.

Falling and hitting your head on a paved road can cause a concussion or even a skull fracture. A concussion can be mild or severe, depending on how hard you fall. If you lose consciousness or are disoriented after a fall, get to a doctor's office.

See pages 49, 50

NECK AND SHOULDER PAIN

Neck and shoulder pain is quite common among cyclists and is usually due to the horizontal position the body must assume on a bicycle with dropped handlebars. When riding in this position you have to extend your head up to see in front of you. You also have to support a great deal of your weight with your arms and shoulders, which leads to muscle fatigue.

This combination of strains causes pain in the back of the neck that spreads down through the trapezius muscles, the broad muscles in the upper part of the shoulder above the shoulder blade. A stretching and strengthening program for the neck and trapezius muscles will help relieve the pain. You can also raise the handlebars to allow you to sit in a more upright position.

See pages 53, 54, 56

BACKACHE

In addition to causing neck and shoulder pain, cycling with your body in the horizontal position can lead to pain in the upper and lower back muscles. Again, stretching and strengthening exercises and a higher handlebar position should alleviate the pain.

See pages 72–75

✚ HAND PROBLEMS

Pain, numbness, or weakness in the hand from cycling usually occurs along the side of the hand and may extend into the fourth and fifth fingers. This is due to the position of the hand on the handlebars, which compresses a nerve at the base of the palm.

Padded cycling gloves can help relieve the pressure on this nerve. If the pain persists, put your handlebars in a more upright position.

Usually, the hand pain goes away with rest. Because this is a nerve injury, there's nothing you can do about it except to stop doing what caused it.

✚ SEAT PAIN

Cycling with your body in a horizontal position also puts all of your weight at the cycle's saddle on the ischial tuberosities. These are the bones that form the bottom of your pelvis. You can feel these bony knobs on either side of the rectum, where the hamstring muscles and other structures attach to them. As these bones press against the saddle, the structures attached to them are crushed between the bone and the seat, as are the buttock muscles (gluteals) and fat pads that cover these bones. This causes pain and soreness in the area.

Padded cycling pants are helpful, but they may not be enough to relieve the symptoms. You can change the shape of the cycle's saddle or add a padded seat cover. Raising the handlebars to move your weight further back may help. If all else fails, you must rest until the symptoms clear and then reduce your cycling time to prevent a recurrence.

Beginning cyclists may develop "saddle sores," which can be mild or severe. If you experience chafing on your buttock, use talcum powder or a lubricating ointment to reduce the friction between your body and the cycle's saddle.

✚ PENILE NUMBNESS

An injury that befalls some serious male cyclists is penile numbness. The nerve behind the scrotum can become compressed against the cycle's saddle, causing numbness of the scrotum and penis.

This is usually due to the front of the saddle being too high. You simply need to lower that part of the saddle. Because this is a nerve injury, the only treatment is to rest until the symptoms disappear and then change to a more comfortable seat position.

HIP PAIN

Hip pain due to iliotibial band (ITB) syndrome is fairly common. The rotation of the hip and knee as you pedal causes this thick band to rub on the bony prominence of the hip and the outer side of the knee. About 20 minutes into a ride you will feel pain in your hip or the outer side of the knee, and the pain will get progressively worse until you are forced to stop. Once you stop, the pain quickly disappears. The ITB responds fully to stretching.

See page 99

RUNNER'S KNEE

The malady known as runner's knee (chondromalacia patella) is very common among cyclists. This is usually due to excessive pronation of the foot and the use of the quadriceps muscles in a bent-knee position.

The U.S. Olympic training center in Colorado Springs corrects for pronation in elite cyclists by wedging the pedals. There are several good cycling shops that can do the same for recreational cyclists.

Raising the seat to decrease the amount of bend in the knee is also helpful. The higher the seat, the less stress is exerted on the kneecap and the less pain you feel.

To compensate for the pronation, you can support your foot with an arch or orthotic. You can strengthen your quadriceps muscles with the program of 30° Leg Extensions described in Chapter 11, which puts the leg through only the last 30° of the lift.

See pages 106, 107

✚ FOOT PAIN

Pain and numbness in the foot are usually caused by strapping your cycling shoe to the pedal too tightly. Adjust the strap so that it does not put pressure on the top of the foot. Or you can switch to the type of pedal that has an attachment for the sole of the shoe, which eliminates straps.

STATIONARY CYCLING

Stationary cycling is a convenient aerobic exercise outlet. It is widely used by avid cyclists when the weather prevents outdoor exercise and by those who want to work out at home. Rows of stationary cycles, or exercycles, have become part of the standard equipment found in good health clubs.

A basic stationary cycle sells for $150 to $300 and easily fits into the corner of a room. On the simplest cycles, you sit upright and pedal. Pressure against the wheels provides resistance as you pedal. On some models, a fan substitutes for the front wheel and creates resistance by blowing air. The faster you pedal, the more air that blows. Typically, a device attached to the cycle measures your time, distance, speed, and revolutions per minute.

Another type of stationary cycle combines both leg pedals and arm levers to propel the cycle's wheels. This cycle allows you to exercise both the upper and lower body at the same time. There are also upper body cycles where only the arm levers move the pedals. These are especially useful for people who have a lower-body injury or disability.

Among the newer stationary cycles are the recliner or recumbent cycles. For these cycles, you sit in a chair with your legs stretched out in front of you to pedal. This cycling position eases tension on the back and is recommended for people with lower back problems. These cycles also work the buttock and thigh muscles harder than upright cycles.

In the higher price range ($1,000 and up), you can find cycles that measure the rider's pulse rate. A wireless device picks up the heart rate when you place your hands on metal plates embedded in the cycle's handlebars. The machine automatically speeds up or slows down based on your heart rate.

Other types of computerized cycles vary resistance over the course of the ride. This reproduces the sensation of outdoor cycling with hills and speed changes. Some cycles add a video monitor that shows you the scenery as you pedal.

One problem with stationary cycling is that it can get boring. I like to do two things at once when I use a stationary cycle—listen to music, read a magazine, or watch television. Try weight lifting, pumping light dumbbells overhead to strengthen the shoulders (in a manner similar to the Military), the Arm Curl (sitting) and Triceps Curl for the arms, and a sitting version of the Flat Fly for the chest muscles.

See pages 11, 17, 85

INDOOR CYCLING INJURIES

Stationary cycling leads to many fewer injuries than outdoor cycling. Dogs, cars, and potholes are not a problem, and there are no traumatic injuries from falling off. Stress to the back, neck, shoulders, and hands does not usually occur.

What I have seen are two injuries common to regular cyclists—kneecap pain in those prone to runner's knee, and hip pain due to iliotibial band syndrome.

How to Improve Your Cycling

Strength Training

To increase your cycling efficiency, you should work on your leg strength first and foremost, since this is your means of locomotion.

Strengthen the quadriceps muscles by doing the Leg Extension, Leg Press, and Squat, which are illustrated in the strength-training program in Chapter 1. You can also do 90–90 Wall Sitting (see page 165).

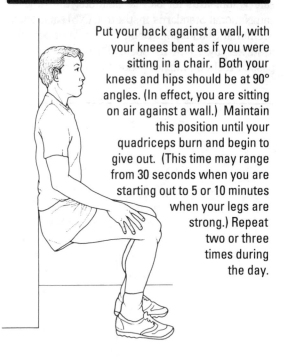

90–90 Wall Sitting

Put your back against a wall, with your knees bent as if you were sitting in a chair. Both your knees and hips should be at 90° angles. (In effect, you are sitting on air against a wall.) Maintain this position until your quadriceps burn and begin to give out. (This time may range from 30 seconds when you are starting out to 5 or 10 minutes when your legs are strong.) Repeat two or three times during the day.

Cycling also calls for strong buttock muscles as well as solid calves for pedaling. To strengthen the buttocks, nothing is better than squats. For calves, do the Toe Raise described in Chapter 12, while holding weights on your shoulders as you would while doing Squats.

The Bicycle

There are literally hundreds of cycles on the market, and you need to choose the proper style and gearing for the terrain you intend to ride on. To cycle in hilly or mountainous country, you need a mountain bike, with its fat, knobby tires and low gears. If you plan to ride on broad, flat streets, choose a touring bike or one of the new hybrids, which combine the features of mountain and touring bikes. If you want to race, obviously you should buy a road racer.

A properly fitting cycle is extremely important. There is no other sport in which the athlete and the machine are so close to being a single entity. Ask your cycle shop owner to adjust the seat, handlebars, and pedals for you. Not only will this make you a better cyclist, but it will reduce your down time due to injuries.

The frame is the right size if you can straddle it with your feet flat on the floor and with an inch of clearance at the crotch. For a mountain bike, there should be two or three inches of clearance. As for proper seat height, you should be able to extend your leg fully while standing on the bottom pedal. If the frame is too short or the seat too low, you may develop chronic knee pain.

If your shoulders cramp up, the bicycle's stem, which is the bar between the seat and the handlebars, may be too short. Riding a bike with too long a stem can cause lower back pain. To correct either of these problems, adjust the seat height or install a stem of the proper length.

Safety Gear

Bicycling gear can help protect you from injury. Wear bright-colored clothes so you can be seen. If you ride on the street, goggles can protect your face from stones or small objects thrown into the air by cars. Wear biking pants and long-sleeved shirts to cover your skin and prevent cuts and scrapes. Proper padding in biking pants can also ease buttock pain. If you are among the more than 3 million people who cycle to work, wear clips on the cuffs of your pants to prevent them from flapping and getting caught in the pedals.

A good-fitting helmet is a must. The helmet should have spongy pads attached to the inside with Velcro so that they can be adjusted. The helmet's strap should adjust easily, and both the chin strap and buckle should remain securely fastened when you ride.

There are two basic types of bicycle helmets. Helmets with hard shells tend to be heavy and don't offer as much protection from serious injury as those with thin, elastic shells. The lighter thin shells, which are covered by a thin layer of semirigid plastic, resist penetration by sharp objects and absorb impact better than hard shells.

Two organizations conduct tests and set safety standards for bicycle helmets: the American National Standards Institute (ANSI) and Snell Memorial Foundation. Look for a helmet bearing a sticker by ANSI or Snell. That means it has passed tests on impact protection and strapping.

21

Football and Rugby

Legendary Green Bay Packers coach Vince Lombardi used to tell his players: "Football is not a contact sport. Kissing is a contact sport. Football is a collision sport." When two huge people run head-on into each other, the impact can be tremendous.

Although it is a violent sport, football does not lead the sports injury list. Yes, a lot of football players get injured, but other athletes have higher injury rates, such as gymnasts and aerobics instructors. And many football injuries can be prevented, particularly for the nation's more than 1 million amateur football players.

I don't mean to give the impression that football isn't a dangerous sport. Each year, a few dozen football players under age 30 die suddenly. (About the same number die playing basketball.) Many of these players, however, had undiagnosed heart conditions, and any physical exertion would have led them to the brink of death.

Although injuries do occur in football, the boys who play in organized Pop Warner football leagues do not have a high injury rate. I see more cycling and skateboarding injuries in this age group. Because they are smaller and don't run very fast, the boys don't hit each other very hard. Also, these leagues match players by age and size.

I generally see the most severe football injuries in high school freshmen, who may have to go up against bigger, more physically developed opponents. If a skinny, 120-pound 15-year-old has to go up against a muscular, 180-pound 15-year-old, it's obvious who is more likely to be injured.

Because football is a collision sport, all but the most superficial bumps and bruises should be seen by a health professional, either a trainer, a nurse, a doctor, or an emergency medical technician.

HEAD INJURIES

Despite the introduction of water, air, and suspension helmets, which have improved head protection, head injuries do occur in football and can be very dangerous. The most common head injury is a concussion. A player who suffers a concussion must not return to the game under any circumstance and should be watched after the game for signs of neurological changes. If the player is sleepy, is nauseous, vomits, has a severe headache, or is confused, he should go to the hospital immediately. Before he plays again, he will have to be cleared for action by a doctor.

See pages 49, 50

167

NECK INJURIES

For most of his career, Giants All-Pro linebacker Harry Carson had a useless deltoid muscle in one shoulder. The muscle, which comes out of the point of the shoulder, had totally atrophied. A violent blow to Harry's neck early in his career tore the nerve that supplies this muscle.

In practice, Harry trained other muscles to help lift the arm. When Harry wore his football uniform, no one knew the difference since one shoulder pad was built up more than the other. Now that he's in the real world and he wears a suit, you notice that one shoulder is much smaller than the other.

A "Burner" versus a Stretch

In a televised game it is common to see a player run off the field with his arm down at his side, only to return a few minutes later. Such a player has suffered a "burner," which is a burning pain down the arm caused by a pinched nerve in the neck. This usually results from the player taking a hit that rolls his head and neck to the side that experiences the pain. The severe pain disappears in a few minutes, and the player's arm and grip strength return completely. As soon as the pain is gone, he is ready to go back in.

We do two tests on the sideline to check a player's grip and arm strength. To test grip strength, I have the player squeeze two of my fingers with each of his hands and I see if there's a difference. To test arm strength, I have the player hold both arms straight out and I push down on each arm. If one arm stays up and the other goes down, the second arm is still weak.

A more serious injury with the same symptoms is a brachial plexus stretch. In this case, the pain and weakness don't quickly disappear, and the pain is felt on the same side of the neck as the blow. The impact, usually from making a tackle, stretches the network of nerves (brachial plexus) that supply the arm.

This injury may take weeks or months to heal. Nerves are the slowest-healing tissues, and there's nothing you can do but rest. You must wait until your arm strength returns completely. A weak arm is more susceptible to a second injury, which could cause permanent nerve damage.

A player returning from a burner or a brachial plexus stretch should wear a roll collar to protect the neck. The collar should ride up to the back rim of the helmet; a small collar tied down to the shoulder pads, which is the way most high school players wear it, has no value. A collar with high sides, like an orthopedic collar, prevents you from flexing your neck too much in any one direction.

Causes of Neck Injuries

Neck injuries end lives or lead to paraplegia more commonly among young players, who don't know the proper techniques to protect themselves. The pros are more likely to sprain their necks rather than break them because they tackle with the head up.

Poor tackling technique is the main cause of compression fractures among football players. You hear coaches say, "Put your head in the ball carrier's numbers," which means to catch him right in the chest with the top of your helmet. This is called spearing and is illegal, but it is still taught by some coaches. The spearer can break his neck, and the ball carrier can break his breast bone if he is hit below the shoulder pads.

Ducking the head during a tackle can also cause a fracture. This injury usually happens to a small defensive back, particularly a high school player, who faces a much larger tight end or running back coming right at him. The defensive player runs up to make the tackle and, at the last minute, decides this is not such a good idea. So he closes his eyes and ducks his head as he makes the hit, and he ends up breaking his neck. A new chin strap that prevents a player from dropping his head too low may help prevent this injury.

Another way players break their necks is by taking a knee to the crown of the head. Helmets are specifically shaped to deflect this kind of blow, but they don't always work as intended.

Heads are now so well protected by helmets that players are not afraid to use them as weapons. Neck injuries are on the rise while head injuries are on the decline. No helmet design can protect the neck. I'd prefer that players take the face mask off the helmet and learn other tackling techniques, as rugby players have done. I'd rather see a broken nose than a broken neck.

If you are a football player and you experience neck pain, do not take off your helmet. A properly fitted helmet is tight and will exert a great deal of pressure on the neck if it is not removed correctly. Leave this to the doctor in the emergency room. The face mask is held on by rubber loops, and these can be cut to remove the mask. Then you can be attended to without risking further injury to the neck.

See pages 53, 54

SHOULDER INJURIES

Separation

A sprain or tear of the ligament that connects the collarbone to the shoulder joint can lead to separation of the shoulder. This usually occurs from falling on the point of the shoulder or falling on the point of the elbow, which drives the shoulder upward.

You can do nothing to treat this sprain but rest. If the sprain is mild, rest for 7 to 10 days. If it is moderate, rest until you are free of pain and full motion is possible. Ice the shoulder intermittently to help ease the initial pain.

Only if the ligament is completely ruptured in a severe sprain should you have surgery. Six weeks after the surgery, you can begin shoulder-strengthening exercises.

Dislocation

A less common injury is a dislocated shoulder. When the rotator cuff muscles are stretched, the shoulder may come partway out of joint and then pop back in by itself, which is a partial dislocation. If the shoulder fully dislocates, a doctor will need to put it back in the socket.

Once the shoulder is back in place, rest it for two weeks. Then rehabilitate the shoulder by strengthening the rotator cuff muscles.

See pages 64–66

BACK PROBLEMS

Lower-Back Pain

Football is a lifting sport: At times you have to literally lift up your opponent and move him out of the way. This overworks the muscles in the back and leads to muscle strains and spasms.

Football players need to work on a back-strengthening and flexibility program. Weight lifting helps build strong, heavy muscles, but the muscles must also be lengthened with back stretches.

A discrepancy in the lengths of your legs, even as little as a quarter-inch, can also cause lower-back pain. If you still feel pain after stretching your back regularly, have the lengths of your legs measured by a trainer or sports doctor.

A Cracked Back

If you are hit in the back with a helmet, you can crack the body of a vertebra. This fracture, called spondylolysis, can be seen on an x-ray. However, since some people are born with this type of spinal deformity, you may need a bone scan to determine whether the injury is new or old. If the injury is old or congenital, you can keep on playing. If it is new, you must rest for six months while the fracture heals.

If the fracture doesn't heal, then the vertebra may slip forward and compress the spinal cord. If this happens, hang up your football shoes. Any subsequent back injury could lead to paralysis. Engaging in other sports is fine, except for diving and gymnastics, in which you have to arch your back violently. If there is no vertebral slip, you may continue all activities, including football.

I see a few young football players with this injury every year. Usually, the victim is an offensive lineman who gets hit while trying to lift a defensive lineman out of the way.

Another type of back fracture involves the wing at the lower part of a vertebra, which is where the back muscle attaches to the spine. If you are hit in the back, this wing can crack. This usually happens to running backs who get hit with a helmet from behind.

This is a more painful but less serious injury. Rest your back and take anti-inflammatory agents to help ease the pain, which usually disappears within a few weeks. Once the pain is gone, you can play, with extra back padding to protect the wing.

See pages 69, 71

HIP POINTER

A fall on the hip or some other blow to the pelvis can cause a painful hip pointer, which is a bruise to the rim of the pelvis. That's why all football players, including recreational players, should wear hip pads.

See page 99

EMERGENCY
BRUISED KIDNEY

A helmet blow to the kidney can bruise it. This painful injury can be serious because the kidney could rupture, requiring emergency surgery.

If you feel sharp pain inside your body after taking a hit on the side, seek medical help immediately. You should have your urine checked for signs of blood, including microscopic amounts. Then you need to rest and avoid any contact until the pain and bleeding are gone. This may take a week or two, or even longer, depending on the severity of the kidney bruise.

In 1985 Giants quarterback Jeff Hostetler sustained a bruised kidney in an exhibition game, and he missed the entire season because of persistent pain and blood in his urine.

BRUISED RIBS

A quarterback can suffer bruised ribs when he is hit while making a throw. The same thing can happen to a wide receiver when he stretches to catch the ball. Raising the arm in the air lifts the shoulder pad and exposes the ribs.

All professional quarterbacks now wear flak-jacket-type rib pads. Most wide receivers take their chances and, when they run a pass pattern over the middle and the quarterback throws the ball too high, simply brace themselves for a blow to the ribs.

See page 76

WRIST SPRAIN

A sprained wrist is a common injury among linemen. A lineman's job in pass blocking is to put his hands forward to hold off an onrushing opponent. With a 290-pound opposing player charging like a bull, you can see why an offensive lineman is susceptible to sprained wrists.

Touch football or high school football players often use elastic bandages to support their wrists, but this has little effect, as the bandage simply stretches.

Most of the Giants' offensive linemen now wear plastic braces to protect their wrists. The brace prevents the wrist from being extended back too far, to the point of spraining, yet preserves the wrist's normal range of motion. These braces are custom-made. A plaster cast is molded to the wrist, and then cut off and shipped to a brace manufacturer. The cost of these individually designed braces makes them prohibitive for most amateur athletes.

See pages 87, 88

BRUISED QUAD

A football player who takes a blow to the thigh from a helmet can get a bruised quadriceps. This is particularly common among high school players; the equipment may not fit properly, and the thigh pad slips to one side, allowing the helmet to strike the quadriceps muscle. Many pro football players wear oversized thigh pads to protect against this injury. Giants running back O. J. Anderson has very large thighs, but some of that size is due to heavy padding.

See page 96

LEG MUSCLE PULLS

Pulled leg muscles cost players more playing time than any other injury. That's why we have the Giants spend so much time on flexibility exercises.

If one of the bunchy muscles in the leg (calf, thigh, hamstring, groin) is put in an awkward position, it will pull. In football, this often occurs when the leg is stretched out as a ball carrier is tackled. Also, football is one of the few sports often played on a wet, icy surface, so your feet can easily come out from under you.

In running sports such as football, a player has a tendency to lengthen the stride and stress the hamstrings. Also, any sudden twisting or sideways movement can stress the groin muscles.

The treatment for a pulled muscle is to rest it and ice it frequently over several days. On about the third day after the injury, begin a slow, gentle stretching program. When the muscle feels better, you can begin to restrengthen it with resistance exercises. When you can stretch the pulled muscle without pain as far as you can stretch the one on your good side, you're ready to be reactivated.

See pages 96–99

KNEE INJURIES

Knee injuries are occupational hazards in football. From high school players to the pros, knee injuries have ended more careers than any other type of injury.

All knee injuries should be iced and examined by a doctor as soon as possible. Even minimal trauma to the knee can cause serious damage. For a less serious injury, an adequate rehabilitation program can bring the knee back to full strength and prevent a second injury.

Runner's Knee

A person with runner's knee experiences pain around the back of the knee or behind the kneecap after running. The pain is due to the kneecap rubbing on the side of its groove due to an improper foot strike. The amount of pain depends on the degree of pronation and the length of time spent running each week.

The pain may not bother football players much in the off-season, but they feel it as soon as they put on cleats. When you run in cleats, only a small area of your foot comes in contact with the ground, decreasing stability.

Playing on grass is worse than playing on artificial turf. If a cleat on the inside part of your shoe digs into the ground, your foot will tend to roll toward the inside. On the hard surface of artificial turf, no cleat digs in more than any other.

Jumper's Knee

The quadriceps and patellar tendons that connect, respectively, above and below the kneecap can become inflamed from overuse. This is known as jumper's knee, as it is these tendons and the muscles attached to them that lift the body in the jumping motion. The patellar tendon can also become irritated if you fall on it, which happens often in football.

Knee Tears

Most knee injuries involve the cartilage or ligaments and result from a blow to the outside of the knee with the foot planted in the ground. If you feel pain on the same side as the blow, you probably have just bruised your knee. Rest it and ice it intermittently for a few days. However, if the pain is on the side opposite the blow, the knee joint has probably broken open. Consider this a serious injury.

The second most common means of injury is stressing the knee by rotating it quickly. Typically, a lineman plants his foot and turns to go upfield. He can tear his knee apart even without anyone hitting him.

The most common injury from this type of lateral rotation of the knee is a cartilage tear, which can cause your knee to buckle or lock up on you. Get to a doctor as soon as possible. The wonders of arthroscopic surgery can remove the torn part of cartilage and get you back in action in three to four weeks.

Ligament injuries are rarer but are much more serious. Even the mildest sprain or smallest tear to a ligament requires rest and a strenuous rehabilitation program under a physical therapist's guidance. Large ligament tears call for surgical repair to stabilize the knee. Some of these tears cannot be fixed through the arthroscope and require 6 to 12 months of rehabilitation to strengthen the knee. For others, new arthroscopic procedures and rehabilitation techniques can reduce the rehabilitation time to less than 6 months.

Terrible Triad of O'Donohue

When someone says they "blew out a knee," they usually mean that they tore a ligament or two. But the worst possible knee injury involves tearing two ligaments, the medial collateral *and* the anterior cruciate, *and* the medial cartilage all at once. This devastating injury is called the Terrible Triad of O'Donohue, named after the doctor who described it, and requires complete surgical repair and a long period of rehabilitation.

Dislocated Kneecap

A dislocated kneecap is a fairly common football injury. A blow to the inside of the knee can cause the kneecap to dislocate to the outside. Usually the kneecap pops back in place by itself, or a physician can pop it back in. If the muscles around the knee go into spasm, a muscle relaxant can make it easier to put the kneecap back in place.

Sometimes surgery is needed to repair the tissues that hold the kneecap in place. Even if your kneecap pops back in, have it x-rayed to make sure that a piece of bone has not been knocked off under the surface.

Bracing the Knee

In 1983 the Giants' medical staff strongly recommended that all linemen wear protective knee braces. Only about half of them did. Then defensive lineman Dee Hardison was hit on the knee in training camp. The hit completely destroyed his steel brace, yet he didn't even need to ice the knee. The next day, everyone else came to see the staff for knee braces.

The jury is still out on the question of whether a brace can protect a healthy knee against injury. The knee is the most common site of injury, particularly the medial collateral ligament. A brace can protect this ligament from a blow from the side.

Some studies suggest that braces may not prevent knee injuries among football players. However, the most definitive study, done at West Point, did show a positive effect from using the lateral knee brace as a preventive. I know of at least four Giants whose careers were saved by wearing a brace to protect the knee from severe hits.

I feel that bracing is particularly effective for linemen and linebackers, and I believe that these players, at all levels, should wear them. High school teams that have the money should purchase braces and require *all* players to wear them. Weekend flag football players probably don't take shots to the knee that often and can do without braces, unless they already have knee injuries.

See pages 103–105, 106–108

SHIN SPLINTS

"Shin splints" is a generic term for various kinds of lower leg pain related to a poor foot strike.

If you are a pronator, or if you have a Morton's foot and roll to the inside of your big toe, try a commercial arch support in your football shoe. If this does not ease your pain in a few weeks, have a sports doctor take an x-ray to check on the possibility of a fracture. If there is no fracture, a podiatrist can prepare a custom-made orthotic.

If you feel pain on the outside part of your lower leg, you may be stressing the small fibula bone. You probably have a supinating foot with a high, rigid arch, causing you to run predominantly on the outside of your foot. Put padding along the outside edge of your football shoe. If the pain does not disappear within a few weeks, see a podiatrist for an orthotic.

See pages 111–113

ANKLE INJURIES

During the 1989 season, Lawrence Taylor had a piece of broken bone in his ankle but insisted on playing. Our orthopedic surgeon, Dr. Russell Warren, felt that LT could do no further damage. LT decided he could deal with the excruciating pain and played on a heavily braced ankle. I certainly do not recommend this for any ordinary mortal. LT, however, does not fit into that category.

A player who steps into a divot or turns hard upfield can sprain an ankle. Usually the foot and ankle will roll to the outside, spraining the ligaments on the outside of the ankle. Anything but the most minimal sprain should be x-rayed to make sure the ankle isn't broken.

Some football players, such as offensive linemen, may be able to continue playing on a badly sprained ankle. But most players need to cut back and forth diagonally, which requires a healthy ankle.

If a Giants player says he can't run on a sprained ankle, we don't force him to return to the game. If he says it hurts, it's hard for me to refute him. On the other hand, if he says he can play, then it's up to the medical staff, along with the coach, to decide whether to send him in again. If the sprain is severe, we take a precautionary x-ray before making our decision. We don't want a player running on a broken ankle.

See pages 119–124

ACHILLES TENDINITIS

Pain, swelling, and tenderness in the tendon above the heel indicates Achilles tendinitis. The tendon becomes inflamed either from tightness or from excessive pronation of the ankle.

If you experience these symptoms, rest your Achilles tendon and ice it several times a day until it feels better. Anti-inflammatory agents can help relieve the pain and swelling.

If you are a pronator, put an arch support in your football shoe to correct the inward roll of your foot. You also need to work on stretching your Achilles tendon and calf muscle: Use the Wall Push-up and the Heel Drop.

See pages 115, 116

HEEL PAIN

Players commonly complain of heel pain early in the football season. Usually, the pain is due to excessive pronation of the ankle, which puts undue strain on the inside of the heel. Wearing cleats can aggravate this condition.

Football shoes now come in three different widths and are equipped with a heel counter to stabilize the heel. Particularly if you have a pronating foot, you need to try different shoes and choose the one that gives you the best support. Then put an arch support inside the shoe. Your pain should disappear almost immediately.

If you have a problem with persistent heel pain, practice in sneakers and wear cleats only for games.

See page 130

ARCH PAIN

A dull ache in the arch of the foot is due to stretching or tearing of the tissue that holds up the arch, the plantar fascia. This elastic tissue runs along the length of the bottom of the foot.

You need to prop up the arch to relieve the pain. An arch support prevents the arch from collapsing and, therefore, the plantar fascia from stretching. You can also use athletic tape along the length and across the bottom of the foot to support the arch.

See page 129

TURF TOE

"Turf toe," which is a sprain of the joint at the base of the big toe, usually occurs on artificial turf. Artificial turf, which is usually laid on macadam, is much less forgiving than grass. Running backs, receivers, and defensive backs who drive off the big toe to get a quick first step are the most susceptible to turf toe. I rarely see turf toe in nonprofessional players because only a small percentage of high school games are played on artificial turf.

See pages 128, 129

EMERGENCY
HEAT EXHAUSTION AND HEAT STROKE

Football players have a special problem with heat. Summer practices and warm-weather games played with a full load of equipment covering the body can lead to heat exhaustion or heat stroke (see Chapter 3).

If the weather is hot, keep as much skin surface exposed as possible. Wear short-sleeved mesh shirts and short socks, and take your helmet off as soon as you leave the playing field. If possible, cut off the bottom of your shirt to expose your stomach. Every square inch of exposed body surface is important.

Salt tablets have no place anywhere near a football field. They actually contribute to dehydration. The large dose of salt can be absorbed from the stomach only in a dilute solution, and your body must bring in fluid from the tissues to dilute the salt. This makes you more susceptible to heat exhaustion.

Heat exhaustion results from the loss of fluids and natural body salts (electrolytes) through sweating. Your skin becomes cold and clammy, and your muscles cramp up. You may lose coordination and become disoriented. If you are suffering from heat exhaustion, stop playing immediately, drink liquids, and get to a cool, dry environment.

Heat stroke is a medical emergency that represents failure of the body's internal thermostat. The player's skin becomes hot and dry, he stops sweating, and he loses consciousness. Body temperature may rise to 108° F. Unless the body temperature is brought down quickly, the player may die.

If a player has these symptoms, immerse him in ice and get him to an emergency room. Notify the hospital that you are on the way so that the technicians can prepare cooling equipment. Minutes count. This is one of the leading causes of death on the football field.

PREVENTING FOOTBALL INJURIES

Football injuries can be prevented through sound coaching techniques, enforcement of the rules, use of proper equipment, and the presence of health professionals at games and practices. In Pop Warner games, coaches should stay on the field to instruct young players on proper blocking and tackling techniques. The coaches should join the huddle and then stand 10 to 15 yards behind the play. The goal of these games is to instruct players, not to motivate them to win.

If you are involved in any form of organized football, from a Pop Warner team to a weekend flag football league, make sure that the officials enforce the rules. Clipping, or hitting a player in the legs from behind, can break a leg or tear knee ligaments, depending on what gives way. Grabbing the face mask can break a neck. Piling on can break a leg. Head slapping with the forearm can perforate an eardrum. If the officials overlook such infractions, players may think they can get away with anything.

If your equipment is not first-class, your team should not be on the field. Playing with inexpensive, shoddy equipment can be worse than playing with none. Helmets should be reconditioned and recertified every two years. Protective pads can wear down, and pants can lose their stretch so that the thigh pads slip, leaving a player vulnerable to a disabling thigh bruise.

The equipment should also fit properly. In high school, the freshmen usually get the short end of the stick; they get what's left over after the upperclassmen are outfitted. With their oversized helmets and shoulder pads, they look like those bobbing-headed dolls you see attached to dashboards.

The area that needs the most improvement is availability of medical help on the scene. Some 60 percent of all high school football injuries occur during practice, when no trainer, nurse, doctor, or emergency medical technician is present. Without proper screening of injuries, high school players often aggravate injuries or suffer additional injuries.

At the recreational level, medical supervision of games is practically unheard of. The players and coaches must be responsible for applying first aid and getting help for an injured player.

ULTIMATE FRISBEE

Tossing a Frisbee® in the park hardly seems dangerous, but I have seen some very serious injuries from the competitive form of Frisbee, called ultimate Frisbee. This game, which basically is football played without pads and using a Frisbee rather than a ball, can lead to shoulder separations and dislocations as well as arm and wrist fractures from hitting the ground with the arms extended.

A mild shoulder separation may need only rest, but a severe one may require surgical repair. Shoulder dislocations need a period of immobilization followed by an intensive rehabilitation program to strengthen the rotator cuff muscles, as illustrated in Chapter 6. Any broken bone should be splinted immediately. If you feel severe pain, even if there is no sign of a deformity, have the bone splinted and x-rayed to check for a fracture.

RUGBY

Rugby is similar in many ways to football, but the tackling technique is very different and leads to different injuries. Neck injuries are almost unheard of because a rugby player does not use his head to tackle an opponent. He learns to tackle with his head up and out of the way, using his shoulder instead. Without a helmet, the head is not a weapon as it is in football.

SHOULDER INJURIES

Because the shoulder takes the brunt of a rugby tackle, it is a major problem area. Hitting an opponent without the protection of a football player's shoulder pads leads to collarbone bruises, shoulder separations, and even partial or full shoulder dislocations.

See pages 64–66

KNEE INJURIES

Knee injuries are less common in rugby than in football because of the open-field tackling technique. Most rugby tackles are made around the upper body rather than around the legs. A low tackle might lead to a blow to the head from a knee, so rugby players use their shoulders and arms to drag the ball carrier down.

Also, a rugby play doesn't begin with tightly packed formation at the line of scrimmage, where so many injuries occur in football from a blow to the side of the knee. The only tight formation in rugby is the scrum, and it is here that most knee injuries occur, as a player falls on or is pushed into the side of another player's knee, leading to sprains and tears.

See pages 103–108

ANKLE SPRAINS

Ankle sprains are common because rugby is a running sport that is often played on uneven, uncared-for fields.

See pages 119–123

✚ *CUTS AND BRUISES*

The lack of protective equipment and the constant banging of bodies in rugby leads to cuts and bruises all over a player's body. Stop any bleeding by compressing the cut, and ice down a bruise for 20 minutes at a time, off and on, for a day or two to limit swelling.

How to Improve Your Game

The most important thing a football player can do is improve his conditioning. Statistics show that injuries tend to occur at the end of a half because players are fatigued.

Proper warmup, warmdown, and flexibility exercises can help you avoid muscle pulls. Warmdown and stretch after exercising to avoid soreness and stiffness the next day.

Weekend football players need total body stretching, but should concentrate on the lower body, which is where most muscle pulls in football occur.

Strength training is equally important, and it may be the reason the Giants won their two Super Bowls. The Giants were a very strong second-half team because they would wear down opponents with their strength and endurance. Because of the excellent training program organized by strength coach Johnny Parker, the Giants' players believed that they were better than the other team. If you think you are better, you will play better.

The pros never used to train with weights during the season. Then someone discovered that players grow weaker as the season progresses. Now we have players work out with weights at least two days a week all season long to maintain their strength.

An overall strength-training program, working both the upper and the lower body, is important for football players at all levels. Use lighter weights and do many repetitions. This approxi-mates what you will be doing on the field better than trying to lift a heavy weight once. Youngsters can start training with light weights at age 11, but not before.

Running backs and defensive backs need to work on both upper- and lower-body strength. The upper body needs strength to make tackles or to take hits, depending on which side of the line you are on. The lower body must be strong so that you can run fast.

Linemen, linebackers, and tight ends need a full-body workout plus extra back strengthening, since much of their activity involves lifting.

Wide receivers need good lower-body strength to run fast and total body flexibility so that they can take hits while up in the air. Quarterbacks should work on improving arm strength to help them throw the ball farther.

Ultimate Frisbee depends on quickness and agility. Run intervals of sprints to work on your quickness and conditioning, and practice the agility drills in Chapter 17.

Rugby players need to improve their conditioning and endurance. Long-distance running, followed by interval speed work, is the best way to accomplish this.

A rugby player should work on improving both upper- and lower-body strength. Lower-body strength provides the power to carry a would-be tackler, and upper-body strength helps improve the arms and shoulders to make it easier to tackle a ball carrier.

22

Golf

Over the past few decades, some sports have become popular and then faded (such as racquetball), and others have peaked and leveled off (such as tennis and running). Golf is one of the few recreational games that has continued to grow. Now that the baby boomers have reached their forties, golf is having its own boom, particularly among women. Nearly 30 million golfers now play the game regularly, despite the high costs, crowded links, long wait times, and even longer playing times. Along with the game's growth has come an increase in the number of golf-related injuries.

A golfer's score ultimately is determined by his or her athletic talent, by the amount of time he or she devotes to practicing and playing, and by the level of his or her physical fitness. Unfortunately, most golfers overlook the fitness component and try to get by on natural talent and regular play. However, the more rounds you play without working on your conditioning, the greater are your chances of injury.

Golf is associated with a high incidence of biomechanical injuries because of the unnatural movements of the golf swing. It is the only sport in which the nondominant side is the power side, that is, a right-handed golfer derives most of her power from the left side of the body. So muscles that usually aren't used as much are subjected to great force. The golf swing also leads to muscle pulls and lower back problems.

MUSCLE PULLS

Muscle pulls are not that common in golf and are quite preventable. Muscles in the trunk, back, and occasionally the calf can pull due to sudden, violent contractions from overstretching on the backswing.

If you pull a muscle while playing golf, you will need to rest for a few days and ice the sore muscle—20 minutes on, 20 minutes off—as often as possible during that time. Then you can begin a stretching program to relengthen the muscle. Once you can stretch the injured muscle painlessly as far as you can the muscle on the opposite side of the body, you are ready to play again.

Duffers with poor body mechanics during the swing place considerably more stress on their backs than do professional golfers. To avoid serious back trouble, I suggest you take a series of lessons to improve your golf swing.

See page 43

ROUGH ROTATOR CUFF

Any time the arm is swung above a line parallel parallel to the ground, the rotator cuff muscles in the shoulder may become stretched. It's usually a right-handed golfer's left shoulder that hurts because the left arm is moving with more force than the right arm during the follow-through.

The treatment is to strengthen the rotator cuff muscles to tighten the shoulder joint (see Chapter 6). Most likely, a physical therapist will need to prescribe a set of specific exercises to rehabilitate these muscles.

A golfer who digs the club into hard ground can tear the rotator cuff muscles. The injury is marked by severe pain and loss of motion in the shoulder. The approach to treatment is to rehabilitate and restrengthen the rotator cuff muscles. Occasionally these muscles will need to be operated on.

See pages 59–63

"GOLFER'S ELBOW"

A golfer's nondominant arm can develop a form of tennis elbow. The pain appears on the outside of the left elbow of a right-handed golfer and is due to the excessive demand placed on the extended left wrist as it pulls the club through the swing. The tendon becomes inflamed where it attaches to the outside of the elbow, causing tendinitis.

The correct treatment is a physical therapy program, which may include ultrasound treatments and electrotherapy, and a weight program to strengthen the extensor muscles of the wrist, as outlined in Chapter 8. Once these muscles are strong enough to handle the force of swinging the club, the pain will disappear and will not recur.

You must combine this weight program with a stretching and flexibility program for the wrist and forearm, because a great deal of the pain and disability are due to spasm in the muscles and tendon.

See pages 79–82

WRIST DAMAGE

The nondominant wrist can also develop ligament damage. A right-handed golfer will feel pain in the back of the left wrist. The treatment is to rest the wrist for one week and to do strengthening exercises, such as the Wrist Curl, which is found in Chapter 8.

This injury must be distinguished from a ganglion, which is a benign cyst that commonly grows on the back of the wrist. The tendon sheath in the wrist can become irritated by the violent motion of a golf swing, causing a ganglion.

See pages 87, 88, 90

WALKING WOES

A golfer with a sore leg may have shin splints or runner's knee from walking long distances up and down hills. A commercial arch support or a customized shoe insert can help correct a poor foot strike. Using a golf cart instead of walking also eases the pain. However, the only general exercise you get from golf is walking the course, and a cart eliminates even that little amount of aerobic conditioning. Walking also offers the benefit of keeping your back muscles warm and supple.

See pages 106, 107, 111, 112

How to Improve Your Game

Strength Training

Strength is just as important in golf as accuracy. Not only will it enable you to hit the ball farther (Lawrence Taylor claims to have hit a drive 400 yards), but it will cut down the number of injuries.

Strengthening the legs is most important. The power of the golf swing comes from the legs. Taller players therefore have a mechanical advantage over smaller players. You can improve your leg strength by doing the Toe Raise with or without weights to strengthen the calf muscles, as described in Chapter 12, and the Leg Extension and Leg Curl, which are part of the strength-training program in Chapter 1, to improve your quadriceps and hamstring muscles.

Many golfers have bad backs. Swinging a club can put stress on your back equal to eight times your body weight. Also, the jolting contact of the club against the ground can send tremors up your spine. And bouncing around bent over the wheel of a golf cart puts a lot of unnecessary stress on your back muscles. To strengthen your lower back, do back extension exercises, including the Reverse Sit-up, as well as abdominal muscle exercises, as illustrated in Chapter 7, to help take the pressure off the back muscles.

If you use your large trunk muscles when hitting the ball, you can generate much more power than you can with the smaller muscles of the arms and shoulders. Following are three exercises you can do to strengthen your trunk muscles.

Bent-Waist Rotation

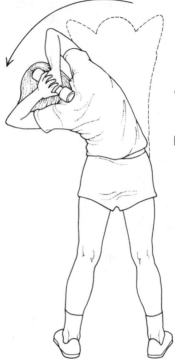

Bend at the waist and hold a small weight (10 pounds for men, 5 pounds for women) at the back of your neck. Rotate from side to side until your muscles are exhausted.

Thigh Thinner

This is a straight leg lift. Lie on your side and lift one leg up. Do five sets, with 10 to 20 repetitions per set. Repeat with the other leg.

Runner

This exercise strengthens the rotator muscles on the sides of the stomach. Lie on your back, hands behind your head. Raise your right knee toward your chest and keep your left leg straight. Now touch your left elbow to your right knee, and then repeat with the opposite leg and elbow until your muscles are exhausted.

To generate power as you pull the club through the swing, you need strong shoulders. The most important exercise is the Lateral Lift, described in Chapter 6. Start with a small weight (10 pounds for men, 5 pounds for women) and gradually build up to more.

The forearms and wrists are particularly important in golf because they are used to give the ball added impetus. They also control the path of the swing and the accuracy of the shot. The best exercises to strengthen these muscles are the Wrist Curl, Reverse Wrist Curl, and Unbalanced Wrist Rotation, described in Chapter 8.

In general, a golfer should be interested not in bulking up but in doing a high number of repetitions with lighter weights. Do the preceding exercises three times a week, particularly in the off-season.

Weight machines in the gym may be easier to work with, but they limit the direction in which force can be applied to your muscles. Free weights allow you to vary the path of motion of the weight and thus more easily adjust to strength differences between the two sides of your body.

If you do nothing else, at least do the trunk rotation and the forearm and wrist exercises. These exercises done year-round are the best way to stay limber during the off-season.

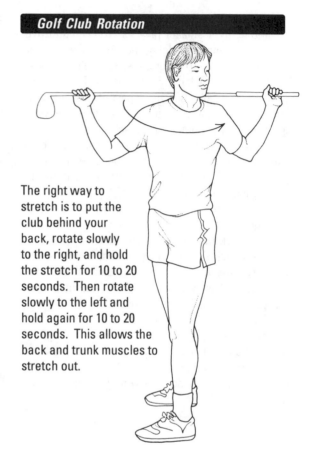

Golf Club Rotation

The right way to stretch is to put the club behind your back, rotate slowly to the right, and hold the stretch for 10 to 20 seconds. Then rotate slowly to the left and hold again for 10 to 20 seconds. This allows the back and trunk muscles to stretch out.

Pre-Round Stretching

A pre-round stretching program is the best way to avoid a traumatic muscle pull. Most golfers, if they do stretch, tend to overstretch their muscles before a round. There is a right way and a wrong way to stretch before hitting a golf ball. The way most golfers stretch their backs is more destructive than helpful. Typically, a golfer puts a club behind the back and rotates back and forth. You would be better off not stretching at all. Every time you rotate during this ballistic stretch, receptors fire and shorten the muscle, which is the opposite of what you want.

The following group of exercises is designed specifically to help golfers stretch correctly and thereby improve their performance on the course.

To further loosen your trunk muscles, do the Side Stretch detailed in Chapter 1.

To stretch your calf muscles, do the Heel Drop described in Chapter 12.

To stretch your buttock muscles, do the standing Hurdler Stretch in Chapter 7.

To stretch your hamstring muscles, do a standing Hamstring Stretch (see following illustration).

Hamstring Stretch

While standing, grab your knees and try to touch your forehead to your knees. Hold for 10 to 20 seconds.

To stretch your shoulder muscles, follow the shoulder stretching program outlined in Chapter 16.

If you arrive at the course just before your tee time, you should warm up your muscles rather than stretch them. A warm, loose muscle will stretch itself out during practice swings. You are better off running in place or doing jumping jacks than trying to stretch cold muscles. Of course, the best thing is to get to the course in time to both warm up and stretch your muscles.

Unfortunately, most golfers don't warm up at all. People who don't stretch or work out with weights are notorious for not loosening up before going out for a round of golf. Most professional golfers, on the other hand, take at least 45 minutes to warm up and stretch before they hit the course.

23

Gymnastics and Cheerleading

Denise, age 17, came to me complaining of constant back pain. When I looked at an x-ray and saw how chewed up her back was, at first I thought she had cancer. Then I looked more closely and saw that she had multiple, small fractures all along her spine. I asked Denise about her athletic history, and she told me she was a gymnast. The constant arching of her back during gymnastics maneuvers had cracked the bones in her back. Her injuries were so severe that she was forced to stop all gymnastics permanently.

Gymnasts suffer a multitude of injuries and have the highest injury rate of all athletes, including football players. Cheerleaders perform many of the same activities and therefore suffer similar injuries. Both sports require strength, balance, timing, and extreme flexibility.

THE PROBLEMS OF GYMNASTICS

Above all else, a gymnast must be flexible. It is your innate flexibility, not your size, that determines whether you can make it as a gymnast. You can stretch your muscles and tendons to make them longer, but the looseness of your joints is genetically determined. If you flex your joints too

far, you incur an injury. All but the most flexible or "loose-jointed" athletes drop out of gymnastics because they can't compete.

Many adult women gymnasts are tiny because their growth has been stunted. Rigorous training at an early age prevents them from menstruating because they don't have enough body fat to reach normal estrogen levels. This prevents the normal growth spurt.

As for women who go into gymnastics with a normal menstrual cycle, the heavy exercise may cause them to have spotty periods, or their periods may stop altogether. If they ease up their exercise intensity, their periods usually become normal again and they continue to develop sexually. But they may never make up lost growth because the growth centers in their long bones close sooner than they should. That's partly the reason well-known gymnasts such as Cathy Rigby and Olga Korbut are tiny even as adults.

I believe that the pressure of competition contributes to a high injury rate among gymnasts. Gymnastics is set up for early competitions rather than exhibitions. I suspect that the urge to compete pushes young children to try moves they are not yet ready for. They usually try them out in practice, which is where 95 percent of gymnastics injuries occur. Some gymnasts may be slightly injured but are afraid to say so for fear of missing a competition, and they injure themselves even more. This early, hard push to compete also leads to a high dropout rate.

MUSCLE PULLS AND TEARS

Gymnasts are likely to pull or tear muscles anywhere in the body due to the stresses of sudden, violent manuevers. The standard treatment applies: Rest the muscle and ice it down intermittently for a few days, and then start an early stretching program to relengthen the muscle.

You need to stretch six to eight times a day during rehabilitation. Stretch the muscle until you feel uncomfortable, and then stop. When you can painlessly stretch the injured muscle as far as you can the one on the opposite side of the body, you are ready for action again.

Gymnasts have a problem with stretching. Their joints are so loose that it's almost impossible for them to stretch an injured muscle fully. The muscle may stretch only as far as the joint allows it to, not as far it needs to stretch to recover from an injury.

A gymnast may tear a muscle severely enough to require surgery, although this is rare. This may happen to a quadriceps muscle in the thigh. Scar tissue that builds up in a weak area in the muscle may need to be removed.

See pages 43, 96

WHIPLASH

A fall from a height that snaps the head back can cause a whiplash injury. A gymnast sustaining such a fall may dislocate or fracture a cervical vertebra in the neck.

This is a grave injury and should be treated only by emergency medical personnel. If you hit your head hard on the floor and your neck snaps back, do not move until an ambulance arrives and an expert can stabilize your neck. Continued medical care under the direction of a physician will be necessary.

See page 54

SHOULDER INJURIES

Gymnastics, with its emphasis on speed combined with intricate movements, is characterized by a high incidence of shoulder injuries. In no other sport is an athlete so suddenly forced to support his or her entire body weight on the shoulders. For this reason, gymnasts suffer severe rotator cuff muscle injuries.

Stretched or torn rotator cuff muscles lead to tendinitis in the shoulder. You can control the pain and inflammation with rest and anti-inflammatory agents. But treatment requires a special exercise program to restrengthen these muscles, which hold the joint together.

Doing a handstand on the uneven bars after decelerating from a high speed places tremendous stress on the shoulders. The shoulder can rotate 360°, but it is not designed to do so while supporting the entire body weight. Continually overstressing the shoulder can partially dislocate it by weakening the rotator cuff muscles, which loosens the joint.

The tremendous rotational stress of activity on the rings and bars may completely dislocate a shoulder. In this case, the shoulder is completely out of joint, and a doctor must put it back in place. Rehabilitation is necessary to restore strength to the shoulder muscles and prevent another dislocation. If a dislocation recurs, surgery to tighten the joint may be necessary.

See pages 59–63, 65

BACK INJURIES

Although stories abound of gymnasts who are crippled by low-back pain by the time they reach their late 20s, this may not be due to their training. Anyone with hypermobile joints is prone to develop back problems. Because of the tremendous torque gymnasts exert on their backs, they commonly suffer injuries all the way up the spine to the skull.

A gymnast who falls to the floor on her back can fracture one or more of the wings of the vertebrae. Or a gymnast may fracture the part that connects the front and rear portions of the vertebra, an injury called spondylolysis.

Sometimes the front part of the vertebra slips forward with activity in those who already have spondylolysis. This condition, called spondylolisthesis, leaves the spine unstable. If rest and back-strengthening exercises fail to correct the problem, the vertebra may need to be fused surgically and the gymnast, unfortunately, will have to give up gymnastics.

Landing on your behind from the height of the rings or uneven bars can compress the vertebrae so much that they fracture. You may even chip off a piece of vertebra. This is known as wedging.

Arching the back violently, particularly on dismounting, can cause this injury to the rear rather than the front part of the vertebra. Arching flexes and extends the spine so much that the vertebrae bang into each other. Most gymnastics schools now discourage arching on landing to avoid this severely painful injury.

Stress fractures of the spine and pelvis are rare, but they can disable a gymnast for up to two years. These are weight-bearing joints, so they heal slowly. If you have persistent pain in your back or pelvic area, have a doctor perform a bone scan to check for a stress fracture.

See pages 71, 72

✚ PELVIC PAIN

It hurts me just to look at a gymnast whack into the bottom bar of the uneven bars. Swinging into this bar can cause bruises or blood clots in the front of the pelvis. If you get such bruises, ice them intermittently until they disappear and stay off the uneven bars until you are completely pain-free. Rest is particularly important because repeated episodes of bleeding can cause many serious complications, including calcification of muscles and impaired function of internal organs.

ELBOW INJURIES

If the elbow gives way while you are doing a handstand, either on the floor, rings, or bars, you can sprain the ligaments on the inside of the elbow. A mild sprain simply requires rest. A more severe sprain may require you to wear a splint for several weeks. After the healing begins, you should strengthen the elbow with an exercise program. The best exercises are the Arm Curl and Reverse Arm Curl described in Chapter 6.

This injury often is confused with tennis elbow, which is an inflammation of the muscles of the wrist where they attach to the elbow. A gymnast develops tennis elbow when a sudden stress on the wrist stretches it up and back, causing pain on the inside of the elbow. Stressing the wrist forward can cause pain on the outside of the elbow. The correct treatment for tennis elbow is the program of range-of-motion and strengthening exercises in Chapter 8.

Hitting the mat on your arms with the elbows locked can hyperextend the elbow, that is, force it to extend farther than it is designed to go. If this happens, rest and ice the elbow, and then do strengthening exercises until the elbow has healed.

Gymnasts also develop a form of pitcher's elbow. Two of the bones in the elbow joint (radius and ulna) bang into each other, causing a dead area in the elbow. The dead bone may chip off, and the chips may float inside the elbow, causing pain and clicking in the joint.

A fracture of the olecranon process in the back of the elbow can also cause bone chips. If these floating chips get caught in the joint, the elbow can lock. You will need to have the chips removed surgically, but you can return to action as soon as you recover from the surgery.

See pages 79–85

WRIST SPRAINS AND PAINS

Gymnasts commonly sprain wrists from applying force to the wrist in tumbling routines such as cartwheels. As with any sprain, the proper treatment is RICE, followed by the strengthening exercises in Chapter 9. If you get a severe sprain, you must have it x-rayed, just as you would a severe ankle sprain. The wrist has many small bones with many ligaments that can sprain or tear.

Tumbling is an activity that suddenly places the entire body weight on the wrists. This can lead to tendinitis in the wrist and elbow. Weight lifters may lift their own body weight and golfers may apply tremendous torque to the wrists, but only gymnasts combine the two movements.

Painful wrist motion may be due to a ganglion, which is a cyst in the tendon sheath on the back or front of the wrist. The ganglion forms as a result of trauma to the wrist tendon. A ganglion usually responds to a cortisone injection, but it may need to be removed surgically.

Landing on an outstretched hand can also break a tiny wrist bone at the base of the thumb. A fracture of this navicular bone causes pain and tenderness in the wrist behind the thumb and makes it difficult to extend the wrist backward.

This is a difficult injury to diagnose because the break in the bone may not show up on an x-ray until several weeks after the injury. If your doctor suspects you may have fractured this bone, make sure he or she orders a second x-ray a few weeks after the first one.

Healing is especially difficult for this injury due to poor blood supply to that area of the wrist. The bone usually knits in two months but may take as long as six to eight months. If it does not heal, surgery to fuse the parts together will be necessary if you wish to continue your gymnastics career.

See pages 87–91

KNEE TEARS

Knee injuries are not common but can occur if the gymnast comes down with the knee hyperextended when tumbling or dismounting. Although the most common injury is an anterior cruciate ligament (ACL) tear, a gymnast may tear other ligaments, as well as cartilage.

See pages 103, 104

RUNNING INJURIES

Because gymnastics is basically a running sport, it can lead to running-related injuries such as shin splints and runner's knee. These injuries are due to problems with the foot striking the floor. Gymnasts usually feel the pain in their shins or knees when running to vault over the horse or during floor exercises.

Since gymnasts compete barefoot (vaulters may wear a flat shoe), it is difficult to correct any foot strike problems. I suggest that the gymnast wear an arch or shoe insert in a vaulting shoe or very light sneaker during practice to relieve the pressure of daily pounding on the legs.

See pages 106, 107, 111–113

ANKLE SPRAINS AND FRACTURES

Ankle sprains and even fractures are common among gymnasts, who often land off-balance or on the edge of the mat. All but the mildest ankle injuries should be examined by a physician and x-rayed. A sprained ankle can be treated by RICE, range-of-motion exercises, and then strengthening exercises. A broken ankle will need to be casted for 6 to 12 weeks, and then restrengthened with the same exercise program used for a sprained ankle.

See pages 119–124

FOOT FRACTURES

The repeated trauma of landing hard from dismounts off the balance beam, vault, rings, and uneven and parallel bars can cause stress fractures of the long bones of the foot. An off-balance landing may also cause toes or other bones to break.

See page 130

CHEERLEADING

The selection process for cheerleaders is not as rigorous as that for gymnasts. Cheerleaders tend to have tighter joints, and they may not work on their flexibility or warm up adequately. Consequently, cheerleaders suffer more pulled muscles, inflamed tendons, and sprained ligaments than gymnasts.

In addition, cheerleading is a burst-type sport. There are long downtimes while the game goes on. If you don't keep warm during inactive periods, you risk pulling a muscle. Cheerleaders at football games in cold weather have to keep their bodies warm and their muscles loose.

CHEERLEADING INJURIES

In general, cheerleaders suffer injuries similar to those of gymnasts. They have a higher incidence of hip and groin injuries due to performing splits, often from a height. If you have a foot imbalance, such as a pronating foot, the trademark stamping of the foot on a hardwood basketball floor can cause severe shin splints or stress fractures of the leg. You can correct this by taking anti-inflammatory agents to relieve the initial pain and then by wearing an arch support or orthotic in your sneaker.

Modern cheerleading, with its gymnastics-like routines, is a high-risk sport. A fall from the top of a pyramid or a missed catch after being thrown by another cheerleader can lead to a traumatic head injury or a broken neck. Cheerleaders have died from falling from the upper part of a pyramid, and there is a movement to ban pyramiding below the college level.

See pages 49, 50, 97–99, 111–113

How to Improve Your Routines

Both gymnasts and cheerleaders should concentrate on strength training to improve their performance and prevent injuries. For gymnasts, strength and balance are the major factors in competition. Cheerleaders especially need to increase their strength, particularly in their upper bodies. If the bottom person in a pyramid doesn't have a strong back, the whole pyramid can collapse, causing injuries to many.

Most gymnasts and cheerleaders start training at a young age. Girls age 11 and up can lift weights to increase their strength without bulking up their muscles. As long as a girl has normal levels of estrogen circulating in her blood, her muscles will become stronger but still look the same.

At the college level, most cheerleaders are also gymnasts who are good athletes. At the high school level, however, the strength and flexibility training required of gymnasts does not carry over to cheerleaders. Cheerleaders need to consider themselves athletes and condition themselves as gymnasts do. They have to train like any other competitive athlete: lift weights, stretch their muscles, and condition their bodies.

To prevent muscle pulls, both gymnasts and cheerleaders need to work on flexibility and warmup, particularly between bursts of activity. Warmup means what it says: keep your body temperature up.

Then they need to do a total body-stretching program. Usually gymnasts are so flexible that they only need minimal stretching after warming up. Cheerleaders probably need a prolonged stretching period so that they can maintain their flexibility during inactive periods.

24

Hockey, Lacrosse, and Skating

Hockey is a high-speed, high-impact sport. The bigger you are and the faster you go, the greater is the impact from something or somebody hitting you. Although hockey players are not as big as football players, they travel at higher speeds while gliding on ice and therefore experience much greater impacts. And ice is one of the hardest playing surfaces in sports.

The arena and the equipment also can lead to high-impact injuries. The boards around professional hockey rinks have some give in them, but this is not necessarily true for rinks at lower levels. When I played hockey as a youth in the Adirondack Mountains area, the boards were frozen into the ice. When you hit them, you knew it. Also, a hockey player can't skate out of bounds to avoid a check, as a football player can to avoid a tackle.

The metal goal cage is on magnets at the professional level but may be fixed to the ice at lower levels. When you are checked into it or skate into it, it does not move.

The puck is made of hard rubber with sharp edges and is frozen so that it slides better, which makes it even harder. It can come at you at a very high speed: a good slap shot moves at more than 100 miles per hour.

The sticks are used as weapons. Although there are penalties for high sticking and slashing, the fact that there are penalties indicates that violations do happen regularly.

The skate blades are razor-sharp. Professional players sharpen their blades between periods to ensure a sharp skating edge. Those edges can become a terrible hazard when a player falls and his skates turn up.

Dropping the gloves and fighting has, unfortunately, become a part of the game. This leads to the same traumatic injuries seen among boxers.

HEAD INJURIES

The usual head injuries from hockey are concussions and skull fractures. The head can hit the ice or the boards, both of which are hard, or it may be hit by a stick or the puck.

The introduction of helmets has helped to cut down the number of head injuries. Although helmets are no longer mandatory in the National Hockey League, most players still wear them. Helmets are mandatory at the peewee, high school, college, and professional minor league levels, but not at the recreational level, and many recreational players still do not wear helmets. I implore any hockey player to wear a helmet.

See pages 49, 50

FACIAL INJURIES

A hockey player can suffer cuts on his face from the puck, a stick, or a skate. Or he may end up with bruises and broken bones from hitting the ice or the boards or being hit by a stick or another player's fists.

A player can avoid facial injuries by wearing a mask, which is mandatory for young, inexperienced players but not for older ones. Not many recreational players use masks, and only goalies customarily wear them in professional hockey.

Small cuts need to be cleaned and then iced until the swelling subsides. Large, deep cuts may need stitches. Bruises should also be treated with ice. If they are severe, a doctor should take x-rays to check for any broken bones.

See pages 51, 52

DENTAL INJURIES

In the past, hockey players were notorious for their missing teeth. Being hit in the mouth by the puck, a stick, or a fist usually led to a gap-toothed smile.

Most professionals now wear mouth guards, but many recreational players do not. There is no question that mouth guards save teeth, and every hockey player should wear one. It doesn't have to be fitted, like the ones the pros wear. Even the less expensive, generic mouth guards can save you a trip to the dentist.

COLLARBONE COLLISIONS

A hockey player who falls on the point of his elbow may stretch or tear the ligaments connecting the collarbone to the shoulder, which can separate the shoulder.

A hockey player can also break his collarbone from hitting the boards or another player with a shoulder check. Hockey shoulder pads are not as heavy as football pads, so they do not protect the shoulder as well. A collarbone may also fracture from being hit squarely with the puck.

See pages 65–67

BACK PROBLEMS

Lower-back and disc problems are common among hockey players because of the bent-over position they maintain while skating and stickhandling, not to mention their frequent collisions with the boards.

If your back is sore, it could be bruised or sprained, a muscle could be pulled, or you could have a more serious injury, such as a disc problem. Since it's difficult to tell the difference, all seemingly minor back injuries that last longer than a few days should be seen by a doctor.

See pages 69–71

HIP POINTER

A hip check or a hip-first crash into the boards can damage the rim of the pelvis, leading to a hip pointer. To avoid this painful injury, every hockey player should make hip pads a part of his uniform.

See page 99

KNEE INJURIES

You might expect hockey players to have a low incidence of knee injuries; when the knee is struck from the side, the foot slides on the ice, lessening the blow. However, hockey players often get their skates caught against the boards, where the foot can't slide. Or a stick can get caught in the skate blade and twist the knee violently, which is similar to the high torque applied to the knee when a ski doesn't release from its binding. All but the most minor knee injuries should be seen by a doctor.

"Housemaid's knee" is also common among hockey players. Though they wear knee pads, they frequently bang their knees on the ice or the boards lining the rink, and this can result in a large, fluid-filled swelling in front of the kneecap.

See pages 102, 103, 109

BROKEN LEG

Fractures of the lower leg are particularly common in hockey. These result from the leg striking the boards or the goal cage or being hit hard by a stick. Usually, it's the small bone in the leg (fibula) that breaks.

Since the fibula is not weight-bearing, a player can usually return to activity within four or five weeks. A sports doctor or a trainer can devise a guard to protect the leg during play.

See page 117

BROKEN FOOT

A foot may fracture from being hit by the puck. Often, a slap shot or wrist shot coming at high speed skims off the ice and slams into the side of the skate boot. Even the rigid boot cannot protect against a hard-driven puck, although the newer fiberglass boots do offer better protection than the old leather boots.

A broken bone in the foot requires immediate medical attention and casting, probably for four to six weeks.

See page 128

PREVENTING HOCKEY INJURIES

To avoid injury from playing hockey, first and foremost avail yourself of all of the protective equipment, particularly a helmet, a face mask, and a mouthpiece. A macho attitude will not save your teeth from being knocked out, but a mask will.

Play at a level where you can compete and defend yourself. If necessary drop down a level and work your way back up. Play only in leagues where the rules are stringently enforced. Also, make sure the playing surface, the boards, and the goals are in good condition.

In addition, make sure *you* are in good condition so that you don't get overtired. A fatigued player loses coordination and makes mistakes in judgment that can lead to injuries.

LACROSSE

Lacrosse is very similar to hockey. In fact, indoor or box lacrosse is played in a hockey rink without the ice; has teams of six men, the same as hockey; and is played according to basic hockey rules using a lacrosse ball and the heavier lacrosse stick.

Playing in a cleated shoe instead of a skate leads to more ankle and knee injuries in lacrosse than it does in hockey. Ankle sprains, knee sprains, ligament ruptures, and cartilage tears are also much more common in lacrosse. Some injuries have similar incidence rates in the two sports: shoulder separations and dislocations from falling and cuts and bruises from being hit with a stick.

Lacrosse is a continuous running sport and can lead to foot and heel pain, tibial stress syndrome, and runner's knee (see Chapter 25 for specific treatments).

RECREATIONAL ICE SKATING

Most traumatic injuries to recreational skaters are due to lack of skill. By increasing skill, skaters can easily avoid these injuries.

Most recreational skaters use figure skates, which can contribute to injuries. The double-edged, rocker-type figure-skating blade has points in the front, and you must keep your weight back. This can be a problem for people who learned how to skate on hockey or racing skates, which allow you to glide on the front of the blade.

If you glide too far forward on a figure skate, you may catch a point in the ice and abruptly fall forward. You may fall on your face and suffer facial or head injuries. Minor cuts and bruises on the face and head should be cleaned and iced until the swelling subsides. If you have a headache for a few days or any vision problems, have a doctor check you for a possible concussion.

If you put your hands out to stop your fall, you may sprain or break a wrist. Make sure to get the wrist x-rayed to rule out the possibility of a fracture.

HEADACHES

If you come home from an indoor skating session with a headache and you are tired, nauseous, and short of breath, you may be suffering from carbon monoxide poisoning. The engine of the Zamboni machine that smooths the ice emits carbon monoxide gas, just as a car does. This odorless, colorless, poisonous gas can collect indoors. If you develop symptoms that suggest carbon monoxide poisoning, consider switching to a rink that uses a battery-powered resurfacer, which does not emit carbon monoxide. Or, if you can, skate outdoors.

WEAK ANKLES

People who tend to overpronate their ankles have a difficult time controlling ice skates. Properly fitting skates, which hold the ankle firmly, along with ankle-strengthening exercises, such as those used to treat a sprained ankle, can be helpful. You may need to place an arch support or orthotic device in your skate to avoid rolling your ankle to the inside.

See pages 121, 122

FIGURE SKATING

Figure skaters make gymnastic moves at high speeds and come down on a hard surface, not a soft mat; therefore, they suffer many traumatic injuries. Also, they don't land on a flat foot but, rather, on a thin blade with two edges. You never figure-skate on the whole width of the blade. You skate either on the inner edge or on the outer edge, changing edges as you change direction. If you come down from a jump so far over the edge that it cannot bite the ice, the blade slides out, and you can fall and injure yourself.

BROKEN WRIST

Figure skaters instinctively extend their hands to break a fall, as all skaters do. A crash to the ice from the height of a jump can break a wrist. The treatment is to cast the wrist for six to eight weeks or longer, depending on the bone that was broken.

See page 88

SPRAINED KNEE

A figure skater can sprain a knee by twisting in the air and stopping suddenly when the blade edge catches the ice. This is much like a football player catching a cleat in the ground while twisting the body. If the knee overrotates, ligaments can sprain or cartilage may tear.

If your knee swells up, you hear a clicking noise inside the knee, and it buckles when you move it, you may have torn cartilage.

See pages 102–104

RUNNER'S KNEE AND JUMPER'S KNEE

A form of runner's knee is extremely common among figure skaters and is usually due to excessive pronation of the skate while the knee is bent. An orthotic can improve the foot position within the skate, and quadriceps exercises can be used to strengthen the knee.

Figure skating is also a jumping sport and therefore causes stress on the tendons under and above the kneecap. This can result in the pain and disability of jumper's knee. The treatment is to rest the knee until the pain subsides, ice it as long as it's tender, and take anti-inflammatory agents. This should be followed by a leg extension program to strengthen the knee.

See pages 106–108

FOOT PAIN

Figure skaters commonly feel a pain on the top of the foot. This usually is due to an inflammation of the tendons that extend the toes, which cross over the bones on top of the foot.

If you experience this symptom, you probably are lacing your boots too tightly or have inadequate padding under the tongue. Pressure against the tendons causes them to become inflamed, resulting in pain. Use ice and anti-inflammatory agents until the pain subsides, and put a foam pad under the tongue of your skate.

See pages 130,131

IN-LINE SKATING

Many ice skaters have also taken up one of the latest fitness fads, in-line skating, for their off-season conditioning. In-line skating, or roller blading, is a high-speed, low-impact workout that's great for cardiovascular conditioning and muscle strengthening. And it feels good—whooshing along a road or in the park with the bicyclists, far ahead of the runners.

A 12-mile skate is the aerobic equivalent of about a 6-mile run and avoids the strain on your knees. The boots are lightweight, and the polyurethane wheels absorb shock well. Practice sprinting, and you add to your anaerobic conditioning. Skate long distances, and you enhance your aerobic capacity.

In-line skating is good for overall leg toning and for building strength and power. It tightens the hamstrings, develops the quadriceps muscles, improves the muscles around the hip joint, and tightens the buttocks. You can even strengthen your upper body by using rubber-tipped ski poles. The swaying motion of poling works the triceps and the erector muscles in the spine, which are important for good posture.

In-line skating is a low-impact sport, but it can also be a sudden-impact sport. Common injuries include scrapes, bruises, and broken bones caused by falls. For your own safety, wear cycling or leather gloves, a lightweight bicycle helmet, knee and elbow pads, and stiff plastic wrist pads, which both protect against wrist injuries and help absorb the impact of falls. Although few in-line skaters wear helmets, all should, and they will soon be mandatory in races.

Since in-line skates are faster, smoother, and more maneuverable than conventional roller skates, stick to flat, paved, lightly traveled roads at first. In-line skating is easier for a beginner than ice skating or traditional roller skating, so an accomplished skater should be able to pick it up rather quickly.

The biggest problem facing in-line skaters is stopping. You cannot skid to a stop as you do on ice skates. The most effective brake you have is the heel stop, which is usually located at the rear of the right skate. Ask your local skate shop to show you how to use the brake. The dealer can probably recommend a qualified in-line skating instructor as well.

If you take all the precautions, in-line skating is not a dangerous sport. Always wear protective safety gear and never attempt any fancy movements unless you have practiced them. And always look ahead to plan a possible escape route.

How to Improve Your Game

Hockey has one of the best warmup periods of any sport, beginning with a skate-around and ending with shooting drills. These raise the body temperature adequately and increase blood flow to the muscles. Before play begins, however, you should stop and stretch.

The most important muscles to stretch are in the groin. These are the most frequently pulled muscles in hockey. Hamstring pulls are not as common as they are in running sports because hockey players take a shorter stride. You should stretch your entire leg but concentrate on groin stretches, the Yoga Lotus Stretch, and the Side Straddle Stretch, as described in Chapter 10.

Hockey is a sport that depends on leg strength. Increase quadriceps strength with the Leg Extension and Squat, and hamstring strength with the Leg Curl (all three in Chapter 1); increase calf strength with the Toe Raise, described in Chapter 12. Do the Toe Raise while holding as much weight as you can to increase the workload on the calf muscle. Or stand on one leg at a time so that your entire body weight is being lifted by one leg.

The wrists generate the power for most shots in hockey. The stronger your wrists, the more powerful your shot will be. Do the Wrist Curl, Reverse Wrist Curl, Unbalanced Wrist Rotation, and Roll-up with a broomstick, as outlined in Chapter 8. The heavier the weight, the stronger your wrist will become.

Lacrosse depends on strength and endurance. A bigger, stronger player is better equipped to withstand the body contact the sport demands. Both upper- and lower-body weight training is essential, as it is in hockey. Also, a lacrosse player should run long distances slowly to build aerobic conditioning and stamina, and then intersperse these distances with intervals of sprints to improve speed.

Recreational skaters also need to warm up properly before going into a heavy workout and should strengthen their legs in the same way as a hockey player.

25

Running, Jogging, and Track and Field

More than 25 million Americans run regularly, and 70 percent of them sustain an injury sometime during their running careers. Anatomical flaws, particularly in the feet, lead to the great majority of problems. The surface you run on, the shoes you wear, and the way you train also influence your risk of incurring a running injury.

One out of three runners can expect to visit a sports doctor this year because of a running-related injury. Despite all the coaching and training tips, world-class runners are just as likely as recreational runners to suffer injuries. In general, sprinters suffer hamstring strains and tendinitis, middle-distance runners commonly have backaches and hip problems, and marathoners complain of foot and leg problems.

Contrary to popular belief, runners are no more susceptible to arthritis than nonrunners. The old doctrine that "the more you use a joint, the faster it will wear out" is probably not true. Running seems to keep bones strong. Studies of marathon runners show no degeneration of their knees. It may be that long-time runners have the genetic traits to be runners and that people whose joints are more susceptible to running problems tend to drop out of the sport.

BACK PAINS

When the jogging craze first hit, I saw many people with lower-back pain. I measured the lengths of the two legs, and they were the same. I couldn't figure out what was causing the pain.

Then I asked where they were running. Many of them were running along the slanted edge of roads. They would run near the curb, cross the street, and then run back along the curb on the other side. One leg, in effect, was always shorter than the other when they ran. I prescribed running against the traffic and coming back with the traffic, and their backs improved.

Lower-back pain is usually caused by a difference in the lengths of the legs. A difference as small as a quarter-inch can be significant for a runner. The back pain is usually felt on the side of the longer leg, which takes more pounding.

When a runner with back pain has a pronating foot on one side and a supinating foot on the other side, I suspect a leg length discrepancy. The body is trying to compensate by shortening the long leg with pronation and lengthening the short one with supination. People with a shorter leg also tend to bend the knee of the longer leg while standing to even out the difference.

You must have the lengths of your legs measured while standing. Your family doctor or a sports doctor can measure them for you. The measurement should go from the spine in front of the pelvis to the floor just inside the prominence of the ankle. The treatment is to put a lift in the heel of the short leg.

I also watch young runners carefully. As they grow, their leg lengths may even out, in which case they need no treatment. If the discrepancy gets worse, I prescribe a heel lift.

If you have a back problem, it may be more than a leg length discrepancy. If a lift doesn't ease your pain, see a doctor. You may have a disc problem, spondylolysis, or a muscle weakness.

See pages 69, 70

ILIOTIBIAL BAND SYNDROME

One of the most commonly misdiagnosed problems among runners is iliotibial band syndrome. This is characterized by pain in the bony prominence of the hip or the outer side of the knee. A sharp pain comes on gradually with each run. You may get in a mile or two before you feel the pain, and then it becomes progressively worse than before. As soon as you stop running, the pain goes away. But each time you run, the pain becomes worse than before. As you will quickly find out, you cannot run through the pain of iliotibial band syndrome.

The iliotibial band runs down the outside of the thigh from the rim of the pelvis to below the knee and provides lateral stability to the hip. In active runners, this fibrous band overdevelops and tightens down. Each time you flex and extend your leg, the band is sawed across the bone of the hip or the center of the knee, resulting in pain.

The easy treatment is to stretch the band. As with a rubber band, if you stretch one part,

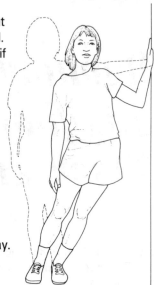

Iliotibial Band Stretch (standing)

Stand sideways about three feet from a wall. Lean into the wall as if you were doing a one-handed push-up, and let your hip drop in toward the wall as far as it will go. This stretches the band on the leg closer to the wall. Hold the stretch for 15 to 20 seconds. Do three repetitions, four to five times a day.

the entire band stretches. The Knee-over-Leg iliotibial band stretch is presented in Chapter 1. Above is a standing stretch for runners. It is not as effective as the floor stretch, but if you are not in a position to lie on the floor or the ground, the standing stretch is better than not stretching at all.

Once the pain is gone, put iliotibial band stretches into your regular routine before and after a run.

See pages 99, 108–109

FEMUR FRACTURE

Most of the rotational force from an abnormal foot strike is absorbed by the knee, but some can be transferred to the thigh bone, or femur, causing a stress fracture. This injury requires resting the leg until the sharp pain disappears, which usually takes a few months. Again, correcting the foot strike will prevent a recurrence.

See page 112

HAMSTRING AND QUAD PULLS

The most common muscle pull for runners is a hamstring pull. The hamstring is the main driving force in running, so it's important for you to warm up and stretch this muscle before going out for a run.

A sudden, sharp pain in the back of the thigh that causes you to hobble is a sure sign of a hamstring pull. You must rest until the severe pain stops and you can get around, which usually takes a few days. Ice the sore muscle initially as much as you can. Then gently stretch it to the point of discomfort, not pain, and restrengthen it with the Leg Curl, as described in Chapter 1.

If you find a black-and-blue area on the back of your thigh, you probably have torn the hamstring muscle. This may take weeks to heal. If the pain persists, have a doctor check for sciatica, as the sciatic nerve runs down through the thigh. The symptoms of sciatica can mimic a severe hamstring pull or tear.

Runners are less likely to pull a quadriceps muscle, but it does happen. The treatment is the same as for a hamstring pull.

See pages 95–97

KNEE PROBLEMS

If you step in a hole or on a stone while running, you may fall and twist your knee. The knee will swell up, and you will have trouble bearing weight on it. These are signs of a sprained knee, which you need to treat with the RICE formula described in Chapter 4.

If you have pain under the kneecap, you probably have the most common sports injury, runner's knee (chondromalacia patella). The cartilage in the kneecap wears down because the kneecap is tracking improperly. With raw bone rubbing on raw bone, your knee aches with each stride you take.

Even though the pain is in your knee, the cause of the problem is the way your foot strikes the ground. A pronating or Morton's foot rolls the knee inward and destroys the alignment of the kneecap, pulling it off to one side. You feel the pain either on the inside or on the outside of the kneecap, depending on where it's rubbing the hardest. You may also feel pain in the back of the knee due to fluid build-up, or it may be referred pain: Your body senses the pain in the back of the knee in the same way a person feels the pain of a heart attack down the left arm.

You need to correct an improper foot strike with an arch support or orthotic, and then build up the inner side of the quadriceps muscle in the front of the thigh. Do the 30° Leg Extension, described in Chapter 11. You also can take two aspirins, four times a day, to ease the pain.

Although jumper's knee is more common in jumping sports (hence the name), it can interfere with a runner's routine. The sudden, severe stress of straightening the leg with each stride tears the tendons above or below the kneecap away from the bone, causing inflammation.

If you develop jumper's knee, you must rest until you get over the pain. Ice the knee off and on during this time, and take anti-inflammatory agents to reduce swelling. Then you can begin to restrengthen these tendons with a full leg extension program.

See pages 102, 103, 106–108

CALF PULLS

If you don't warm up and stretch before a run, you are liable to pull a calf muscle. If the pull is severe, rest your leg and ice it intermittently for a few days. Then gently stretch the injured muscle. It's important to stretch it while it's healing; otherwise, the next time you go for a run, it will pull again because it's too short. When you can painlessly stretch the muscle as far as you can stretch the one on the other side of the body, you are ready to resume running.

Do the Wall Push-up and the Heel Drop in Chapter 12 to stretch the calf muscles.

See pages 113–115

COMPARTMENT SYNDROME

When you run regularly, you build up the muscles in the lower leg, and these muscles fill the space within the compartments on the side and front of the leg. Running increases blood flow to the working muscles, and they become engorged. This increases the pressure in the leg compartments and can cause severe pain.

Not many competitive runners develop compartment syndrome. But because it can be a true medical emergency, you should be cautious about any lower-leg pain.

Some runners are born with tight compartments. Others develop a chronic problem with compartment syndrome and must have surgery to continue running. Once the compartments are opened, the thick casings won't regrow, so the problem is solved.

See page 113

SHIN SPLINTS

In the running world, "shin splints" is a catch-all term used to describe pain on the inner side of the shin. True shin splints are caused by overuse of the muscle that pulls the arch back up. This muscle contracts with every stride in response to the stretching of the tendon attached to it.

The common treatment for shin splints is to put an arch support in your running shoe. This props up the foot so that the muscle doesn't keep contracting. The first time you run with the arch support, you may feel some residual pain, but it should stop within a few days. Stretching the calf muscles helps relieve the pain.

Only 5 to 10 percent of runners have true shin splints. The vast majority have tibial stress syndrome or a tibial stress fracture. The excessive inward roll of the pronating or Morton's foot causes the whole lower leg to rotate inward, twisting the tibia. This causes the tibia to become painful and, if continued long enough, can cause a stress fracture.

One way to tell which injury you have is to note when you feel the pain. If it hurts only when you run, you probably have stress syndrome. If it also hurts when you walk, it may be a stress fracture. Less than 1 percent of runners develop stress fractures, but you should be aware of the possibility.

If you have stress syndrome, you can prop up your foot with an arch support and keep running, using pain as your guide. If the pain doesn't get any worse, keep going. The stress syndrome should heal within a few weeks. If the pain worsens, have your shin examined by a doctor. The doctor may need to take a bone scan to make sure you don't have a stress fracture.

See pages 111–113

STRESS FRACTURE OF THE FIBULA

A runner with a supinating foot pounds the outside of the foot into the ground. This transmits shock up the outer bone of the shin, leading to a stress fracture of the fibula. This injury is much easier to diagnose. Just press along the bone on the outside of your calf. But don't press too hard, because you will feel intense, shooting pain if you have this condition. Rest for four to six weeks, put padding in the outer edge of your running shoe, and you will be back on track.

See page 117

ANKLE SPRAINS

An ankle sprain means that you have overstretched or torn ligaments in the ankle. Typically, you mildly sprain an ankle from stepping in a hole and moderately sprain it from slipping off the edge of a curb. Rarely will a runner suffer a severe sprain, because running does not impose enough force to tear ligaments.

If you have recurrent ankle sprains, you can wear an orthotic with a lateral flange at the side of the heel, which prevents the ankle from rolling over. Elastic bandages may feel good, but they provide little support; they stretch right along with the ankle as it is spraining. An inflatable stirrup (Air-Cast) or a lace-up brace holds the ankle more firmly in place and gives you real support when you run.

See pages 119–123

ACHILLES TENDINITIS

The Achilles tendon in the back of the heel can become inflamed either by excessive foot pronation or by a shortening of the tendon.

If you are a pronator, an arch support will relieve the pain. Have someone look at your Achilles tendon as your foot hits the ground when you run. If the tendon flares to the outside at the heel, that means your foot is turning in, and you are a pronator.

If you are not a pronator and you feel this pain, you probably are not stretching enough. The Achilles tendon will shorten if you don't stretch the calf muscles. Women who wear high heels or high boots also tend to feel this pain. The high heel props the foot up so that the Achilles tendon doesn't stretch when the foot hits the floor.

The Wall Push-up and Heel Drop in Chapter 12 are the best stretches for Achilles tendinitis. Runners should do five repetitions of these exercises, holding the stretch for 15 to 20 seconds, six to eight times a day.

Inserting heel lifts into your running shoes will help alleviate the pain. Buy four packages of Dr. Scholl's® heel pads and put a pair of pads, stuck together, in each shoe. You must even out the height in your shoes, even if you feel the pain on only one side.

See pages 115, 116

HEEL PAIN

Pain under the surface of your heel is commonly said to be due to a heel spur. This occurs when the plantar fascia pulls too hard at its attachment to the heel bone. This overstimulates the bone and causes a hook or spur to grow. This piece of bone hurts when you put pressure on it while running.

However, it's more likely that any heel pain you feel while running is from the inflamed plantar fascia, rather than a bone spur. The treatment for this type of pain is an arch support. Heel spurs almost never require surgery.

Pain from placing weight on the inner side of the heel is due to excessive pronation of the foot. This spot becomes tender to the touch. Supporting the arch prevents the pronation and provides relief within a few days.

See page 129

FOOT ABNORMALITIES

When I see a young runner with Morton's foot, I tell her she is in good company. About 25 percent of the population inherits Morton's foot. One of the most famous individuals with this condition was the Italian sculptor Michelangelo. Look at his David and other statues, and you will know what a Morton's foot looks like. I spent one vacation roaming the museums and inns of Florence looking at statues. I could always tell a Michelangelo by looking at the feet.

Virtually all of the problems I see in runners occur in the lower body. It's not surprising that 95 percent of these problems are due to the foot striking the ground improperly.

Three types of foot problems plague runners. A *pronating* foot rolls toward the inside. A *supinating* foot rolls to the outside. A *Morton's* foot is a combination of these two abnormalities. The foot strikes the ground on the outside and then rolls all the way across to the big toe, which is shorter than normal.

You can correct a pronating foot by propping it up with an arch support. However, for 10 percent of runners, an arch support provides too little lift, and for another 10 percent an arch provides too much lift. These 20 percent of runners will need a custom-made shoe insert, or orthotic device. If you need an orthotic, make sure to see a sports podiatrist who understands how to fit an orthotic to meet a runner's needs.

To correct a supinating foot, put padding under the outer part of your foot to absorb the shock. Use this modified arch in your running shoe.

Someone with a Morton's foot may get by with an arch support but will probably find that they need an orthotic with a built-up area under the big toe.

See pages 125, 126

FOOT FRACTURE

A sudden, severe pain in the front part of your foot during running, preceded by a period of mild pain, is a clear signal of a stress fracture. The upper and lower surfaces of your foot will be tender, and the upper surface may be swollen.

This injury is particularly common among runners with Morton's foot. The thick long bone just behind the big toe is designed to support large amounts of weight. But in a Morton's foot, the thinner long bones behind the other toes must bear more weight than they are meant to. This stress can cause the thinner bones to crack.

By using an orthotic to redistribute the weight, you can continue to run with a lower risk of recurrence.

See page 130

ARCH PAIN

Runners typically feel two types of arch pain. One is the dull ache that results from overstretching the plantar fascia, which holds up the arch. The other is a sudden, sharp pain in the bottom of the foot and is usually due to a torn plantar fascia. You will feel either of these pains

when your weight is on your foot or when you push off for the next stride.

The treatment is to use an arch support or to strap your foot with tape. Run strips of athletic tape from behind the toes to the back of the heel in a fanlike pattern. Then run more strips across the bottom of the foot. Using a simple arch support, however, is much less trouble than taping. With your arch supported you should be running without pain within a few days.

See page 129

BIG TOE PAINS AND SPRAINS

Pain in the big toe joint is common among people with Morton's foot. Side stress on the toe as the foot rolls over strains the ligaments that hold the inner side of the joint together. The big toe is designed to move up and down, not from side to side.

A big push off the big toe places enormous force on the ligament, and the joint can sprain. This injury is better known as "turf toe."

To treat either of these problems, rest the toe until the pain disappears. Meanwhile, ice it occasionally for 20 minutes at a time to reduce the pain and swelling, and take anti-inflammatory agents. When you first return to running, tape the toe down so that it can't come up when you push off it. You also should wear an orthotic in your running shoe to correct the abnormal movement of your foot.

See pages 128, 129

TENDER TOES

Tenderness, possibly accompanied by swelling, on the upper surface of the foot *only* is usually a sign of tendinitis of the toes. You may be lacing your shoes too tightly or wearing too little padding under the tongue. Rest and ice the tendons occasionally until the pain and swelling subside, and take anti-inflammatory agents if necessary. Put a foam pad under the tongue of your running shoe to prevent the pain.

See pages 130, 131

CROSS-COUNTRY

Cross-country runners have an extremely high injury rate. Covering long distances daily during training, as well as running two meets a week for high school athletes, causes the body to break down as the season progresses. Injuries can take place on the first day of practice when the coach sends runners out for a 7-mile run, and the sore muscles that result may last throughout the season.

Any lower-extremity pain should be attended to early on. Trying to run through the pain can lead to disabilities and severe injuries. During the season runners may develop runner's knee, shin pain, and stress fractures of the foot, shin, leg, and even the pelvis.

Hilly courses can intensify the pain of runner's knee, since running downhill aggravates this condition. Shin pain may indicate the need for an arch support or orthotic to prevent a tibial stress fracture.

A stress fracture in any body part can be difficult to diagnose with an x-ray and may require a bone scan. A runner who feels constant pain while walking as well as while running should stop training and, if a stress fracture is confirmed, hang up his or her running shoes for the rest of the season.

Running on natural, uneven terrain can cause ankle sprains and even broken bones from falls, as well as cuts and bruises.

TRACK AND FIELD

Track and field athletes suffer all of the same injuries as runners, as well as some others, depending on the demands of the individual event.

Sprints

Muscle pulls are the most common injury for sprinters. The speed and length of the stride require rapid, violent contraction and then stretching of the leg muscles, which may pull or tear as a result.

Young sprinters (under age 16) may injure their growth plates. The drive out of the starting blocks can pull the iliac spine off its growth plate, and running longer sprints can pull the rim of the pelvis off its growth plate. These painful injuries, which can be diagnosed through close inspection of an x-ray, require four to eight weeks of rest to heal.

See pages 95–97, 255–257

Hurdles

Hamstring and hip muscle pulls are fairly common in hurdling because the lead foot must make a long stretch over the hurdle. Hitting a hurdle can lead to a fall, resulting in deep cuts and bruises.

See pages 95, 96, 98

Long Distances

The constant repetition of step after step over long distances can lead to runner's knee, tibial stress syndrome, and tibial stress fractures. Orthotics can help correct any problems with the foot strike.

See pages 106–107, 112

High Jump

In the high jump, leg muscle pulls may occur in conjunction with the old-fashioned straddle jumping technique. The newer flop technique, where the jumper lands on the back of the neck and shoulders, may cause soreness in these body parts.

See pages 95–97

Long Jump

A high-speed explosive maneuver requiring a long stride, the long jump involves a high incidence of lower-body muscle pulls.

See pages 95–97

Pole Vault

The most dangerous of all events, the pole vault requires speed as well as tremendous upper-body strength. In addition to the hazard of lower-body muscle pulls, the great stress on the shoulder can cause tendinitis and a partial dislocation.

A fall from the top of a pole can lead to all sorts of traumatic injuries. I have seen several high school vaulters who broke their necks by landing in the wrong position or by missing the pit.

See pages 53, 63–65, 95–97

Field Events

All of the field events require a combination of explosive speed and tremendous strength. The javelin throw is hard on the shoulder and leads to the same overuse injuries seen in tennis and baseball players, as outlined in Chapter 6. The shot put and hammer throw also place demands on the shoulder, as well as on the muscles of the back and the lower body, and can lead to muscle tears and tendon injuries.

See pages 59–62, 63, 69

How to Improve Your Performance

Conditioning

Preventing running injuries is easy if you warm up, warm down, and stretch properly. Slowly jog until you break a sweat, and then stop and stretch. Do a total body stretch, but concentrate on the lower body up through the lower back.

At the end of your run, slow down to a jog or walk for five minutes. Then it's imperative to stretch again. While you run, your muscles tend to shorten. Stretching after you run will prevent stiffness and soreness the next day.

Listen to your body. There will be days when your body is just not ready to run. If you force it, you may injure yourself. Most runners feel terrible for about the first mile. If you feel better during the second mile, keep going. If you feel worse, it may be time to head back home.

Leg strength is essential to runners. The extensor muscles in the leg drive your forward stride. The calves, hamstrings, quadriceps, buttocks, and lower-back muscles need to be strengthened to improve your performance.

Distance running improves your stamina and conditioning, but if you are interested in competitive running, even "fun runs," you need to do interval training to increase your speed. Interval training is running for short bursts followed by a slow run.

Take one or two days a week and do mostly interval training. Start with one 100-yard sprint in the middle of your normal run and gradually do more and longer sprints with each run. Build up to four fast quarter-miles interspersed with slow quarter- or half-miles. With practice, you will find your comfort level.

You may find that the backs of your thighs hurt more after interval training. It's not because you are using different muscles, but because the fast bursts work the hamstrings more. Make sure to stretch the hamstrings after interval training.

Cross-country runners should aim to build up their aerobic conditioning to allow them to run farther without shifting to the anaerobic energy cycle. Build up a good aerobic base and then add interval speed work, alternating sprints with longer distances.

For sprinters and hurdlers, as well as jumpers and vaulters, stretching and flexibility exercises of the lower body are of utmost importance. Remember to warm up and stretch before practice as well as before meets, and keep your muscles warm in between races or attempts. Long-distance runners should pay particular attention to increasing their leg strength. For field events, overall strength training is a must, in addition to flexibility exercises.

Choosing Shoes

A proper shoe is crucial to an injury-free running program. Both the design and fit should be individualized. New shoes should feel comfortable both when you stand and run. Most runners choose a shoe that's one size too small. You need to allow a quarter-inch between the longest toe and the end of the shoe, because your feet swell when you run. Many shoe stores will let you road-test a shoe for a few blocks.

Running shoes should be constructed to absorb the shock of running and to stabilize the foot. The shoes should have a flexible, thick sole; a sturdy heel counter; a cushion for the Achilles tendon; a sole that is wider than the top; a comfortable arch support; a raised heel; and plenty of room in the toe. Training shoes generally have more cushioning and provide more shock absorption than racing shoes.

The shoes should also be matched to the surface you run on. A ripple sole is designed for cement and asphalt, and a waffle bottom is meant for grass and dirt.

The hardness of the running surface does not matter that much. The cushioning of running shoes has advanced to the point where an asphalt surface feels almost the same as grass. Many running injuries result from stepping in a hole or on a rock and falling. Running on a smooth surface, such as an asphalt road, makes it easier to pay attention to your running technique. Also, running barefoot on the beach is just asking for trouble. Because the sand is loose, running puts an unnatural strain on your calves and Achilles tendon. And if your foot pronates or supinates, sand provides absolutely no support for it, so any problems with your foot strike are automatically magnified.

Recreational runners with normal feet and no lower-body problems need not spend $300 on a running shoe. However, if you have leg problems, need ankle support, or have a foot abnormality, you need to look for a special running shoe.

There are different shoes for different types of feet, and you have to find the right one for you. If you pronate excessively, choose a shoe with a more rigid heel counter and a straighter last. A supinating foot needs a shoe with much cushioning, such as an air-sole, to disperse the landing shock. A person with Morton's foot really has a pronation problem and requires the same type of shoe as a pronator.

26

Skiing

The sport of downhill skiing, the ultimate escape for many athletes, has grown to include nearly 10 million participants. Despite its popularity, snow skiing has a reputation for injuries, and 2 or 3 out of 1,000 downhill skiers become injured. Many accidents occur on very gentle runs, where a skier may simply lose control and fall or strike a tree. These injuries often occur late in the day, when a skier's muscles are fatigued. Each year a number of deaths result from multiple head and neck injuries caused by skiers losing control.

Recently, the number of head, neck, and shoulder injuries from skiing has increased dramatically, while the number of leg injuries has declined. Thanks to improved hill grooming and slicker ski surfaces, skiers can cover more of the mountain more quickly. Better ski bindings, which release the foot more readily during a fall, have led to fewer lower-extremity injuries. Despite improvements in technology, however, bindings are not all they could be. New boots have spared the ankle only to pose a danger to the knee and leg.

There are many reasons skiing leads to injuries. It is a high-impact sport; that is, you are likely to have a high-speed impact with the ground or with a natural obstacle, such as a tree,

a rock, a fence, or another skier. The leverage of the ski attached to the foot applies a high level of torque to the joints. There is also a high rate of repetitive overuse injuries due to the pounding exerted on the knees in the crouch position.

What's more, many skiers tend to ski beyond their abilities. They want to be out on the expert slopes but can't handle them. They hurt not only themselves but others when they get out of control. Fast skis, overcrowded slopes, and reckless hotdoggers also contribute to the incidence of ski injuries.

HEAD INJURIES

Although competitive skiers wear helmets, a recreational skier wears nothing more on his head than a fancy wool cap. A blow to the head from hitting the ground can cause a concussion, and a skull fracture can result if the ground is hard enough or if the skier hits a tree or a rock. Facial fractures are common from blows to the nose, cheek, or jaw.

These are all serious injuries and require medical attention. Even a mild concussion needs treatment. If you recover rapidly and ski down by yourself, you should stop skiing for the day and rest for one week or until you have no symptoms of dizziness or disorientation when you exercise.

See pages 49–52

NECK SPRAINS

A whiplash injury can sprain your neck, causing stiffness and pain when you move it. You might even break your neck due to a high-impact injury. Unless the symptoms are very mild, your neck should be x-rayed.

If the injury is extremely mild, ice your neck, 20 minutes on and 20 minutes off, and rest it for a few days. You can also wear a soft neck collar. By day 3, you can begin to stretch your neck muscles gently to restore your range of motion.

See pages 53, 54

BROKEN OR SEPARATED COLLARBONE

A skier who falls on a shoulder can break the collarbone. If your shoulder looks as if it has dropped down and you feel pain between the breastbone and the shoulder, you probably have broken your collarbone.

If you fall directly on your shoulder, or if you fall on the point of the elbow and drive the upper arm into the shoulder, you may separate the collarbone where it hooks into the shoulder joint.

You will feel pain at the tip of the shoulder where the collarbone attaches. You will have trouble moving your arm, particularly out to the side, although any motion can be very painful if the separation is severe.

See pages 65–67

SHOULDER DISLOCATION

A partial shoulder dislocation occurs when the head of the arm bone (the humerus) that fits into the shoulder socket is forced partway out of the socket by a blow to the shoulder. You may feel the shoulder snap back in spontaneously or as you move it. This injury stretches the rotator cuff muscles, which hold the shoulder joint together. To tighten the joint, you will need to carry out an exercise program to restrengthen the rotator cuff muscles.

When the head of the bone comes all the way out of the socket, the shoulder is dislocated. This injury stretches the rotator cuff muscles severely. The shoulder will not pop back in by itself, and it may be difficult for a doctor to put it back in. Rotator cuff tears are usually seen among older athletes, but a high-impact ski injury can tear a rotator cuff even in a young athlete.

A rotator cuff tear or severe stretch requires a closely supervised rehabilitation program to restrengthen these muscles, and it may require surgery.

See pages 59–62, 64, 65,

KNEE INJURIES

Some of the most severe knee injuries I have seen are from skiing. I never go through a ski season without seeing a number of knee injuries that require surgery. All but the most minor knee injuries must be seen and diagnosed by a doctor.

Two-thirds of all ski injuries occur in the lower limbs, and knee ligament injuries are the most common. The increase in knee injuries has been attributed to the modern high ski boot with its forward-leaning position.

Knee injuries from skiing are usually due to severe torque to the knee when bindings fail to release the foot in a fall. When your foot is fixed to the ski, turning your body or the ski to a position the rest of the body can't follow applies a severe rotary force to the knee. The damage can vary from a simple knee sprain to a tear of the medial collateral ligament (MCL), of cartilage, or even of the anterior cruciate ligament (ACL). The ACL is most likely to tear when you land on one leg and quickly pivot in the opposite direction.

Skiing is an extremely difficult sport for people with runner's knee because it puts tremendous force on the kneecap. Crouching with the thigh muscles contracted pulls the kneecap back into the groove, causing irritation. My patients with runner's knee tell me that after two days of skiing their knees ache so much that they have to take a couple of days off before they can get back on the slopes.

The treatment is to strengthen the quadriceps muscles that support the knee and, when necessary, to use an orthotic device to control the foot. Many ski shops sell boot orthotics, but these are not designed by foot experts. These may be effective if your foot problem is mild, but if it is severe, you will need a true orthotic made by a sports podiatrist.

See pages 102–104, 106–107

SKIER'S THUMB

A skier can easily injure the thumb in a fall if it gets caught in the strap of the ski pole. This common injury tears ligaments at the base of the thumb. You will not be able to touch the thumb to the second finger, and you will have no strength at all in the thumb.

Ice the thumb and get to a doctor. Your thumb will need to be splinted for about six weeks before the doctor can tell whether it will tighten and heal by itself. If not, you will need to have the thumb ligament surgically repaired.

See page 92

BOOT TOP FRACTURE

You can break almost any bone of the body in a high-impact injury, but the bones most likely to break are the tibia and fibula in the leg—the so-called boot top fracture. If the boot is rigidly fixed to the ski and the binding does not release, both bones will snap just above the boot top if enough force is applied.

This serious injury leaves the leg unstable because both bones are broken. Also, the tibia heals very slowly in this area of the leg. Often, a surgical plate must be put in to stabilize the leg.

See page 117

CROSS-COUNTRY SKIING

All of the injuries discussed so far also occur among cross country skiers, but they are usually less severe because of the slower speed and lower impact of cross-country skiing. Cross-country skiers do suffer more muscle strains because they use their arms and legs more actively than downhill skiers.

The only injury that is common to cross-country skiers and not seen among downhillers is an ankle sprain. The rigid boot used in downhill skiing doesn't allow the ankle to turn over; the forces are transmitted higher up and often result in a leg fracture. The low, soft shoe used in cross country skiing, however, allows the ankle to sprain.

SNOWBOARDING

More than 200,000 Americans have joined the ranks of snowboarders, who proficiently ride what amounts to a small surfboard adapted to snow. They use the same slopes as downhill skiers, and snowboarding is increasingly accepted at ski areas as the equipment improves and instructors become certified.

The injury patterns from snowboarding are similar to those from downhill skiing, with slightly fewer lower-extremity injuries and slightly more head and upper-extremity injuries. The snowboarding injury rate is estimated at 1 or 2 out of 1,000, although there actually are more injuries than this because only one-quarter to one-half of all significant injuries are reported.

How to Improve Your Skiing

Conditioning

Strengthening exercises should be done in the off-season. The muscles subjected to the greatest stress in skiing are the quadriceps. These leg muscles handle all of the strain in the bent-knee position and absorb the shock of bumps and moguls because they control how much the knee bends.

First do the Leg Extension in Chapter 1, 10 lifts per set for five sets, with whatever weight is necessary for you to fail in the last set.

An isometric exercise to strengthen the thighs, described in Chapter 20, is 90–90 Wall Sitting; another good exercise is the One-Legged Knee Bend.

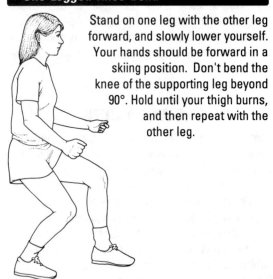

One-Legged Knee Bend

Stand on one leg with the other leg forward, and slowly lower yourself. Your hands should be forward in a skiing position. Don't bend the knee of the supporting leg beyond 90°. Hold until your thigh burns, and then repeat with the other leg.

A lot of unnecessary trauma and injury could be avoided if skiers would prepare for the season by getting in shape. Many skiers do nothing to condition themselves prior to the ski season.

Building strong muscles and increasing cardiovascular and muscle endurance can reduce injuries and add to the enjoyment of skiing.

If you prepare properly before the season, you will be less vulnerable to a serious injury. Work to improve your flexibility, coordination, strength, and general fitness. This will substantially reduce the chance of limb and ligament damage when you fall, as you inevitably will.

A general flexibility and stretching program will help prepare your body for the twists and turns of skiing. Before you hit the slopes, remember to warm up to increase blood flow to the muscles.

You can also work to improve your skills and correct bad habits in the off-season. With this in mind, many skiers have taken up in-line skating, or roller blading. When you are going downhill on in-line skates, you need to make tight, complete, careful turns. The turning maneuvers in downhill skiing are almost identical to those of skating, where you bow the body into the curve with your weight on one leg. The weight shifting, the sense of edging, the forward-leaning stance, and the forward and backward balance of skating are characteristics that carry over to skiing. Cross-country skiers can practice with in-line skates along with ski poles adapted for the pavement.

Your local health club may have exercise machines that mimic the motions of cross-country skiing. Similar machines for home use are also available.

Check Your Equipment

Your performance in skiing depends on the quality of your equipment. Have your equipment checked every year to ensure that the ski bindings are properly set. In practically every case I see of a bad knee injury from skiing, the patient tells me, "I fell, and my binding didn't release."

All skiers should wear goggles or sunglasses

that prevent reflected sunlight from reaching the eye. Normal sunglasses reduce glare from the front but do not protect the eye from glare from the side. A maximum-protection UV sunblock cream is essential in preventing severe sunburn. Apply a sunscreen lotion with a sun protection factor of at least 15 before you ski and throughout the day.

Don't Hotdog

It makes good sense to stay within your limits when skiing. Don't overski slopes you can't handle. The reckless young men between the ages of 16 and 30 who fly down the hills are the ones who get hurt the most often. Also, I see a lot of middle-aged men trying to recall their 20s by taking runs on difficult slopes.

Fatigue is a tremendous factor in ski injuries. More tired skiers on the slopes means more accidents. Getting one last run in because you paid so much for the lift ticket can be a ticket to serious injury if you are overtired. Psychologically, you may feel that you are able to perform, but muscle fatigue affects your control. If you try to make the last run of the day the best one, you are probably overdoing it.

27

Soccer and Field Hockey

Not every soccer player can be a Pelé, but soccer is one of the fastest-growing participation sports nationwide, particularly among youngsters. Soccer leagues, from preschool to industrial to senior leagues, have sprung up across the country, mostly in the suburbs. The fervor of the 1994 World Cup competition in the United States will likely add to the interest in soccer. Along with this growth have come more soccer-related injuries, particularly to girls. And although soccer is perceived to be safer than football, particularly for children, soccer injuries can be severe.

There are several reasons for soccer's popularity. It doesn't require particular physical characteristics. Smaller players can compete on an equal basis with larger ones, which is not true for such sports as football and basketball.

Soccer requires minimal equipment and therefore is inexpensive. A local recreational department is more likely to have a soccer program than a football program, because the latter is much more expensive to run.

Soccer is a sport that both boys and girls can play. In many soccer leagues, young girls play alongside boys. The introduction of women's soccer teams in college, along with the availability of scholarships, has given more high school players an incentive to stick with the sport. In fact,

women's soccer was the fastest-growing team sport in high schools and colleges in the 1980s. More than 6 million females, from school-age to teen-age, now play soccer. With the U.S. team winning the first women's world soccer championship in 1991, even more women in this country are likely to take up soccer.

However, parents should not be led to think that girls and boys can play soccer and never get hurt. Soccer is a collision sport and can lead to many types of injuries.

HEAD BANGING

Banging heads with an opponent while trying to head the ball can result in a variety of injuries, including a concussion. A soccer player who has a momentary loss of consciousness should not return to play until he or she has been cleared by a doctor.

Soccer players can also break noses, cheekbones, or jaws from clashing in the air over the ball. These fractures are all serious injuries that call for x-rays and treatment by a doctor.

Knocking heads can also cause cuts and bruises. If the cut is not deep, stop the bleeding with a towel, and then cleanse and cover the cut with gauze. If it is deep, it may require stitches.

211

Ice bruises off and on until the swelling goes down, and rest until they are no longer very tender.

The repeated trauma from heading the ball may lead to subtle brain damage similar to that seen in boxers. In a study of former Norwegian soccer players, 30 percent showed signs of minor brain damage, including headaches, dizziness, and neck pains. A player can head the ball several thousand times in a season. The Norwegian players averaged more than 5,000 headers per season over their 15-year careers.

See pages 49–52

SOCCER SHOULDER

When you go up to head a ball and come down on your shoulder or elbow, you can sprain the ligaments connecting the collarbone to the shoulder joint, separating the shoulder.

A partial dislocation of the shoulder is often confused with a separation. A partial dislocation occurs when the shoulder slides partially out of joint and then pops back in by itself. This stretches the rotator cuff muscles, which hold the joint together.

If you don't strengthen the rotator cuff muscles, each time you fall on your shoulder you will stretch them more and more. Finally, your shoulder will dislocate fully, with the head of the arm bone coming all the way out of the shoulder socket. A dislocated shoulder will not go back in by itself.

See pages 64–66

QUAD AND HAMSTRING PULLS

Pulled leg muscles are common in any running sport. Soccer demands sudden acceleration and direction changes, which make you prone to muscle pulls.

Ice a sore muscle, 20 minutes on and 20 minutes off, until the pain subsides, and rest it during that time. As soon as the muscle can tolerate it, begin a stretching program to relengthen the muscle.

See pages 95–97

KNEE INJURIES

Soccer players suffer the same kinds of knee injuries as football players do. If you take a blow to the knee from the side with your cleats dug into the ground, you can damage ligaments or cartilage in the knee. If you feel pain on the side of the knee that took the blow (usually the outside), the injury probably is just a bruise. Ice it down for a few days, and rest it until you can cut back and forth again.

However, if you feel the pain on the opposite side of the knee, you have probably sprained ligaments and possibly torn cartilage. The immediate treatment for a sprained knee is the RICE formula described in Chapter 4 and the use of a splint to immobilize the knee. If the knee does not improve within a day or two, see a doctor. Or if the swelling or pain is severe, see a doctor immediately. One sign of torn cartilage is buckling of the knee when you try to turn on it, even when walking.

Any injury to a knee ligament must be considered serious. The medial and lateral collateral ligaments may heal with a rehabilitation program without surgery, but you cannot fully recover from these injuries without supervision.

A sudden rotation of the knee with your foot fixed to the ground, such as when you plant your foot to go upfield, can cause the worst of all knee injuries. The torque on the knee can tear the medial collateral ligament, the anterior cruciate ligament, *and* the medial cartilage. This injury, known as the Terrible Triad of O'Donohue, leaves you with a totally unstable knee. You will need surgery to repair each of the damaged structures and a rehabilitation program to strengthen the knee muscles.

See pages 102–105

BROKEN LEG

One of the most serious soccer injuries is a fracture of both bones in the lower leg. This injury is similar to the boot top fracture from skiing, and it is what ended Joe Theisman's career as a quarterback. In soccer, it occurs when two players going for the ball at the same time clash. If your opponent misses the ball and kicks you with enough force, it can break both the tibia and fibula bones.

You will need to have the leg splinted before you can be transported to a hospital. Then you will need a cast or possibly surgical insertion of a pin or plate to hold the bone fragments together. These bones may take months to heal.

If you are kicked on the outside of the leg, you will usually fracture only the fibula. This is not as serious since the fibula does not bear weight. The treatment is a cast or, if the fracture is not serious, just non-weight-bearing with crutches. In four to six weeks you may be able to return to play with a hard shin guard.

See page 117

⊞ BRUISED LEG

Since soccer is a kicking sport, you're bound to get kicked in the lower leg, usually in the shin. Cuts and bruises in the shin can be painful, and they heal slowly because of poor blood supply to that area. If your opponent's cleat was dirty, which is likely, you must clean any cuts carefully and watch for signs of infection, which include redness, swelling, and heat around the cut.

Getting kicked in the calf can also cause bleeding and bruising in the muscle. First stop the bleeding by compressing the muscle with an elastic bandage. Then ice and elevate the calf. Continue icing intermittently for several days and then begin to stretch the muscle. When you bruise a muscle, it goes into spasm and shortens, so you need to relengthen it as it heals.

ACHILLES TENDON RUPTURE

I commonly see Achilles tendon ruptures among older soccer players. In my area there are several senior soccer leagues, with players who are in their seventies. A lifetime of running in unstable soccer shoes and the accumulation of pulls and partial tears of the tendon weakens it. You should take care of any small injury to the Achilles or else, somewhere down the road, you may have to pay the price.

If your Achilles tendon does rupture, you will need surgery to repair it if you plan to play again. Recovery from this injury is very difficult and requires a prolonged rehabilitation program. Some older players willing to hang up their soccer shoes may get by with casting the tendon for six to eight weeks and then going through rehabilitation.

See page 116

ANKLE SPRAINS

Probably the most common soccer injury is a sprained ankle. Almost all soccer games below the college level are played on grass. Stepping in a hole or divot can force the ankle to turn over, spraining the ligaments. A player who steps on the side of an opponent's foot when going for the ball can also sprain an ankle.

All but the mildest ankle sprains, which allow you to continue to play, should be x-rayed to check for a broken bone. If there is no fracture, the standard RICE formula detailed in Chapter 4 is the initial treatment and should be followed by range-of-motion and ankle-strengthening exercises.

See pages 119–123

RUNNING INJURIES

Soccer players suffer the same overuse injuries as players in all running sports, including arch pain, stress fractures of the foot, heel pain, shin splints, runner's knee, iliotibial band syndrome, and lower back pain. Virtually all of these problems can be solved by propping up the arch of the foot so that it strikes the ground properly.

The peculiar design of soccer shoes tends to aggravate running injuries. One function of a sport shoe is to correct any abnormal action of the foot, such as pronation. Soccer shoes, however, are too soft to protect against excessive foot roll. In many young soccer players, heel pain is misdiagnosed as damage to the growing area in the heel bone or as a fracture. The pain actually is due to stress on the heel bone from excessive pronation of the foot.

The placement of the numerous low cleats in a soccer shoe also causes instability. The cleats are much closer together than those in a football shoe, which means you are running on a narrow base. Also, the narrow, pliable shank of a soccer shoe does not resist the torque of your foot rolling over. Football shoes come in three midsole widths, but most soccer shoes use a European design that comes in only one width.

Finally, soccer shoes have no built-in arches, as do running shoes. An arch can prevent the excessive pronation of the foot that leads to running injuries.

> *See pages 69–70, 99, 106-107, 108, 111–112, 129, 130*

TURF TOE

Soccer played on an artificial surface can lead to a sprained big toe, or turf toe, due to the stress of running on a hard surface.

> *See pages 128, 129*

GOALIE INJURIES

Guarding the goal puts the goalie in a unique position. In addition to being vunerable to all of the preceding injuries, goalies have problems peculiar to their position.

When diving to stop shots, goalies often land on their hips and suffer cuts, scrapes, and bruises over the hip bones. In some cases, blood collects in a goalie's hip and must be drained. The immediate care for cuts and scrapes is to stop the bleeding and cleanse and cover the injured area. Ice bruises intermittently until the swelling goes down and rest until the area is no longer tender. Goalies should wear adequate padding to protect their hips.

Because they dive so often, goalies have a much higher incidence of partial and full shoulder dislocations. They also dislocate and break fingers from the impact of the ball coming at them at high speed. You may be able to pull on a dislocated finger and put the joint back in place. Buddy-tape it to the finger next to it, and you can get back in the game. But make sure to have the finger x-rayed, because it may be broken.

Landing on the point of the elbow can leave a goalie with Popeye elbow, a form of bursitis that causes little knobs to swell up behind the elbow. This may also cause little bits of bone to chip off of the elbow. The elbow should be rested until the swelling goes down and iced during that time. Most likely, the blood and fluid will also need to be drained from the area. A goalie should wear elbow pads to protect against this injury.

Goalies may also suffer the same shoulder and elbow injuries seen in the throwing sports, but they are relatively uncommon in soccer.

> *See pages 64, 65, 84, 91*

FIELD HOCKEY

Field hockey is an open-field game that's similar to soccer in many respects. As in soccer, the object of the game is to score a goal, but a stick, rather than the foot, propels the ball. Field hockey, like soccer, is a running game in which the contact is supposed to be incidental, yet injuries occur quite often.

Runner's knee and shin splints, and the related tibial stress syndrome and tibial stress fracture, are common field hockey ailments because of the constant running. An orthotic can correct the foot strike to relieve these pains, and leg-strengthening exercises can help prevent a recurrence.

A slash of a field hockey stick can easily bruise another player's leg. A bruise should be iced immediately and the leg rested. I have even seen sprained knees and cartilage tears from blows by the stick to the outside of the knee.

An ankle sprain can result from stepping on another player's foot or in a rough spot on the field. Treat the ankle sprain with the RICE fomula in Chapter 4, followed by an aggressive range-of-motion and strengthening program, as illustrated in Chapter 13. A severe sprain should be x-rayed to check for a fracture.

How to Improve Your Game

Since soccer is a running game played on a huge field with practically no time allowed for rest, cardiovascular conditioning is of the utmost importance. Soccer players are never out of the action for long. You may be able to rest momentarily when the play is across the field, but you're quickly on the go again.

You need to work on your agility and speed as well as your endurance. You not only need to be able to run fast, but you must also be able to dribble and kick the ball at the same time, all while evading opponents.

As part of your training, practice running both long distances and sprints. Or you can incorporate both into one workout. Jog for a quarter-mile and then sprint for 50 yards. Repeat to the point of muscle exhaustion.

Work on your distance before you begin sprint work. This will give you a good aerobic base for sprinting.

Running uphill is great for endurance and good for the legs. However, it can be hard on the knees, so be alert for any kneecap pain. Also, if you run uphill, you must run down again, which causes pounding on the knees.

Warmup activity for soccer can be anything

from a slow jog around the field to calisthenics. Make sure to stretch out the lower body.

Since you need strong legs, concentrate strength-training workouts on the lower body. In particular, do the Leg Extension, Leg Curl, and Leg Press, which are part of the strengthening program of Chapter 1; Toe Raise with weights, as described in Chapter 12; and 90–90 Wall Sitting, as illustrated in Chapter 20.

Exercises that strengthen the neck muscles can help soccer players with their headers. Work with a partner and do the neck exercises outlined in Chapter 5.

Look for soccer shoes with wide cleats, built-in arches, and a wide shank for better foot stability, although such shoes may be hard to find. If you develop a running-type injury, wear sneakers or cross-trainers during practice, and wear soccer shoes only during games.

A field hockey player needs to improve her running skills. She should run long distances to build a good aerobic base for endurance, and then intersperse these distances with sprints to increase speed. Pay particular attention to strengthening the legs and arms during strength training.

28

Swimming and Other Water Sports

Swimming has been the favorite participation sport of Americans for three decades. Some 30 million people in the United States swim for fitness, and 70 million swim at least once a year. Among women, swimming is the single most popular athletic activity; about 40 percent of women listed it as their number-one sport in a recent Gallup poll.

Swimming has also become an "upscale" activity, with significantly greater participation among higher-income, better-educated groups, perhaps because people in these groups are more likely to own pools or can afford to go to swim clubs and health clubs with pools.

Swimming is probably the most nearly perfect form of exercise, especially at the recreational level:

- It is a non-weight-bearing exercise and imposes no stress on the bones and joints. Even people with bad backs can exercise in the water without fear of injury.

- It exercises and strengthens the upper and lower body.

- It is an exercise in which it is easy to reach the training range and maintain it.

- It is an effective weight-control exercise. An hour of vigorous swimming burns about as many calories as running six miles in an hour.

- It is a form of meditation. It calms your nerves in addition to providing a good workout.

- It is a good exercise for people with exercise-induced bronchospasm.

Exercise-induced bronchospasm is a condition where exercising causes wheezing and coughing. People with this condition are unable to warm and moisten the air to the lungs when they breathe hard. It's especially bothersome in cold, dry weather. People who can't exercise outdoors in cooler weather can swim indoors, where the warm, moist air around a pool prevents these symptoms.

Swimming has additional advantages. With an indoor facility, it can be done year-round independent of the elements. Nor is age a barrier. In-water calisthenics are excellent for older athletes who cannot do distance swimming for some reason. There also is much less stress on the body when it is supported by water, and this can help speed rehabilitation of injuries suffered in other sports.

The risks for recreational swimmers are minimal. I occasionally treat an ear infection caused by excessive water in a swimmer's ear. Lack of facilities is more of a problem for swimmers. Some areas of the country just don't have any indoor pools available. As for those that do, the facilities are often crowded and expensive.

DIVING DISASTERS

Swimmers may suffer disastrous injuries from diving into the pool. If your head hits the bottom, you can incur a severe head or neck injury ranging from a mild or severe concussion to a skull fracture or a broken neck, or cervical fracture. These injuries require immediate medical treatment and usually land the diver in an intensive care unit.

To avoid these injuries, do not dive into a pool if you don't know how deep the water is. Diving in at a steep angle from the side can cause your head to hit bottom.

See pages 49, 50

✚ SWIMMER'S EAR

Dampness can cause bacteria to infect the outer ear canal. Once your ear has become infected, most doctors prescribe antibiotic drops. A less expensive and more effective treatment is Burow's solution, which can be found in any pharmacy. This solution changes the acidity of the ear canal and kills the bacteria.

To prevent a recurrence of the infection, plug your ears with lamb's wool and lanolin when you swim, and wear a bathing cap. You can also use alcohol to dry the ear canal. Put some drops into the ear after swimming and then dry the ear with the corner of a tissue. Do *not* use a Q-Tip®. Putting anything deep into your ear can be dangerous.

IRRITATED EYES

Many people are sensitive to the high concentration of chlorine in swimming pools. If your eyes become red and irritated, an over-the-counter medication can clear them up. To prevent the problem, buy a good pair of swimming goggles.

Goggles are necessary for swimmers, especially competitive swimmers, who spend hours at a time in the water. The chemicals in pools, salts in the ocean, and other eye irritants found in most outdoor waters can cause allergic reactions, resulting in an inflamed eye, and may permanently damage the cornea. Wearing swim goggles limits the amount of water that reaches the eye and reduces the possibility of infection.

SWIMMER'S SHOULDER

Although swimming is not considered a sport that leads to injuries, competitive swimmers do incur problems, particularly with their shoulders. About half of the competitive swimmers over age 12 suffer from shoulder pain. One reason is that the concept of training for competitive swimming has changed. Swimmers now swim tremendous distances in training programs, some more than 10 miles a day.

The most common injury in swimmers is a rotator cuff problem. The rotator cuff muscles, which hold the head of the shoulder in the joint, are not meant to be overstressed with the arm at an angle above parallel to the ground. All swimming strokes, except the breaststroke, place the arm in this over-the-head position and stress these muscles as the arm is pulled through the water. The stress on the rotator cuff muscles is similar to that imposed by the throwing motion in baseball or the serve in tennis.

When the swimmer's arm is in a full overhead position, the small rotator cuff muscles become stretched, allowing the head to slip around in the shallow socket. As it slips, it catches the biceps tendons, pinching them and causing pain.

The treatment is to rest the shoulder for several weeks and then modify the training program by using a kickboard or doing the breaststroke to maintain conditioning. This should be combined with the shoulder-strengthening program for the rotator cuff muscles in Chapter 6. In the home strengthening program, men should limit the amount of weight to 15 pounds, and women and young swimmers should use only 10-pound weights. If heavier weights are used, the rotator cuff muscles will be assisted by the bigger shoulder muscles, and the exercise won't be as effective.

If the home strengthening program with free weights is not effective, you may need physical therapy with exercises done on isokinetic machines. When you return to swimming, decrease your distance at first and then increase it very gradually.

Another rotator cuff problem is an impingement syndrome. Repeated, heavy exercise over the years can cause the rotator cuff muscles to overdevelop to the point where they no longer fit in the bony cage in the shoulder. If this happens, you will need surgery to enlarge the space in the shoulder if you wish to continue to swim.

See pages 59–62

COLLARBONE PAIN

Continuously placing the arm in the full overhead position compresses the two ends of the shoulder bones together where the collarbone hooks into the shoulder. This causes the bone ends to become irritated and painful, and the small cartilage between the two bones can degenerate or tear. In severe cases, the outer end of the collarbone dissolves, which is called osteolysis.

The management for this condition is to change your training program. Stay out of the water for a week. Use a kickboard for conditioning, but continue to rest the arm until the pain is gone. Use ice and anti-inflammatories during this time. If these treatments are unsuccessful, the joint may respond to a direct injection of cortisone. This will cut down on the inflammation in the bone and the joint. In severe cases surgical widening of the joint will be necessary.

See page 66

SWIMMER'S KNEE

The syndrome known as swimmer's knee primarily occurs among people who use the breaststroke. Similar to the process that leads to runner's knee, it is caused by the breaststroker's frog kick, which requires a sudden snap of the knee as the leg straightens out. The frog kick causes the kneecap to shift and to rub on the side of the groove, causing pain under the kneecap.

This injury requires rest until the pain eases, icing, and anti-inflammatories. Aspirin seems to have a healing effect. Try eight aspirins a day until the pain subsides. Also try a swimming stroke that uses a straight leg kick until the knee has healed.

To reduce pain on land, treat the problem as you would runner's knee: Use an arch support or orthotic device in your shoe and do quadriceps-strengthening exercises.

See pages 106, 107

IN-WATER REHABILITATION

Horse trainers were among the first to recognize the benefits of hydrotherapy: They had thoroughbreds with sore ankles run through the surf. Now both racehorses and human athletes exercise in pools. Some professional baseball players swing a bat underwater to increase their strength, since water offers 12 to 14 times the resistance of air.

Water aerobics classes are now popping up in health clubs. An hour of exercise in the water equals two or three hours on land. As you move your limbs through water, you tone your entire body, and your chances of injury are virtually nil.

One advantage of rehabilitating an injury underwater is that you can begin range-of-motion exercises without placing weight on injured body parts. Not only is there no weight bearing in the water, but the buoyant effect of the water reduces the suspended weight of the affected part, so that you can move it with less stress. This allows you to begin your rehabilitation much earlier than on land. For example, if you are rehabilitating a pulled muscle in the hip, you may not be able to lift the weight of your leg and bring it through its complete range of motion in the air. Since your leg weighs much less underwater, you *can* do the exercise in a pool.

Many professional athletes, such as basketball All-Pros Michael Jordan and Bernard King and All-World Athlete Bo Jackson, have rehabilitated knee, hip, back, and leg injuries in water. With the body supported by water, you avoid the pounding of the foot as it strikes the ground. Sports rehabilitation centers may offer a water tank with a treadmill on the bottom. You can simulate the same workout by putting on a life vest, holding on to the side of a pool, and exercising without the effects of gravity.

CANOEING AND ROWING

Canoeing and rowing are popular water sports that place a great strain on the body parts that generate the power of the stroke.

In using either the single-bladed canoeing paddle or the double-bladed kayaking paddle, the shoulders and upper back bear the brunt of the work. This places stress on the rotator cuff muscles in the shoulder and can lead to a partial dislocation. Pulling the paddle through the water can also stress the elbow and cause biceps tendinitis. The constant rotation of the wrist may result in tendinitis or carpal tunnel syndrome. The strengthening programs for the rotator cuff muscles in Chapter 6 and the elbow in Chapter 8 can relieve the stress on these muscles and tendons. Carpal tunnel syndrome requires rest and possibly an injection of cortisone to reduce swelling.

The constant kneeling in a canoe can cause housemaid's knees, a form of bursitis. This also responds to a cortisone injection. Use of a kneel-ing pad in the bottom of the canoe can help prevent a recurrence.

Rowing injuries occur mostly in the back and the knees. Rowers, who tend to be tall and have long backs, are susceptible to pulled back muscles. These should be treated with ice, stretching, and then restrengthening, as described in Chapter 7. A rower will occasionally rupture a disc, which usually requires surgery.

Driving the legs from a flexed to a straight position can irritate the kneecap if it's misaligned and can lead to a form of runner's knee. You can correct this problem by wearing an orthotic while rowing, as well as in everyday shoes, and by doing the limited leg extension exercises in Chapter 11.

BOARD SAILING AND SURFING

Board sailing, or wind surfing, combines surfing and sailing into a new way to have fun on the water. Attaching a sail to a surfboard allows the board sailor to zoom through the waves with more speed and control than a surfer has.

Board sailing injuries occur mostly in the shoulder. Shoulder stress from controlling the sail against a sudden gust of wind can lead to rotator cuff muscle strains and shoulder tendititis. The constant pulling on the sail can also cause a form of tennis elbow on the inside of the elbow. The standard rotator-cuff–strengthening program described in Chapter 6 can be used to treat the shoulder injuries, and the elbow exercises described in Chapter 8 can treat the tennis elbow.

Surfers must get used to being thrown against the sea floor or being hit by a surfboard. The seriousness and site of the injury determines the treatment. Bruises should be iced immediately and rested; a deep cut or fracture needs immediate medical attention. There's not much a surfer can do to prevent injuries except to avoid surf that is beyond his or her capabilities.

How to Improve Your Swimming

Swimming works all of the body parts, so you need a total-body conditioning program. It is extremely important to keep the rotator cuff muscles and shoulder joints tight, so you should make shoulder-strengthening exercises part of your regular workout routine. You should use free weights rather than an exercise machine, since the free weights allow you to isolate the rotator cuff muscles. Exercise machines require you to lift too much weight, thus forcing you to use other shoulder muscles in addition to your rotator cuffs.

Swimmers know that they can swim farther and faster if they train with weights. The U.S. women swimmers have become the leaders in the women's weight-training movement because of their recent success. Many world records have been broken since women began to train with weights regularly.

As in any sport, warming up and stretching are important. A few minutes of stretching before and after swimming will make your stroke smoother and more efficient and will help relieve muscle soreness.

If you are just starting to swim, try to swim continuously for at least 10 minutes. Once you can do that comfortably, increase your swim time by 2 minutes every third session. Then try to add a set of 10 sprints of about 50 yards each. Rest for about 30 seconds in between.

Canoers need a program to strengthen the upper body to increase both the strength of their pull through the water and their endurance. Rowers need general strength training, since leg drive, back strength, and upper-body strength are all important. Back flexibility exercises will also help prevent muscle pulls.

Board sailors also need upper-body strengthening and should concentrate on the upper trunk, shoulders, and arms.

Lower-body strength is the key to controlling the surfboard. Surfers should do leg extensions, leg curls, leg presses, and calf raises. Since surfing requires good balance, I recommend the balance training described in Chapter 19 as well.

Get a Stroke Coach

More recreational swimmers are turning to swimming coaches to boost their performance. A coach can provide a structured, systematic fitness routine. A coach can also help you set realistic goals and then help you achieve them. For triathletes, a coach may be necessary to guide the transition to a new sport.

If you don't have good stroke mechanics, your time spent swimming will be more of a chore than a pleasure. All parts of your stroke are integrally linked. Head position and kick determine how high you ride in the water. The timing of your breathing affects your alignment and, to some extent, the path of your arms as you swim.

A coach can teach you how to cover the same distance with fewer strokes, making you a more efficient swimmer. Even older swimmers can become faster by learning to be more efficient through improved technique.

To find a coach, check with your local "Y," high school, or college. The most reliable coaches are certified by the American Swimming Coaches Association.

29

Tennis and Other Racquet Sports

Tennis and other racquet sports have a large following among recreational athletes. More than 30 million Americans participate in racquet sports. Racquet sports bring into play almost all of the muscle groups of the body. A half hour of tennis singles against a similarly skilled opponent three times a week can improve your health and endurance. Racquetball and squash are even better for conditioning; few sports burn calories at such a high rate.

Accidents do happen on the court, and the recreational nature of these sports can make players particularly susceptible to injury.

EYE INJURIES

Eye injuries happen in all racquet sports, though less frequently in tennis than in racquetball. Anyone playing a racquet sport should wear some type of eye protection. Even tennis players should wear goggles or eye guards. Injuries can occur from the ball or the racquet striking the eye. They can cause severe, permanent damage.

If you are hit in the eye, apply ice intermittently for several days to reduce swelling. If your vision is very blurry, or if it remains blurry after one day, see an eye specialist immediately.

Wearing eye guards can prevent virtually all eye injuries. Most eye guards or goggles com-pletely cover the eyes with a pane of clear, shatter-resistant glass or plastic. They cost from $10 to $40 in sporting goods stores.

See page 51

NECK PAIN

Looking up to hit an overhead or a serve can pull a neck muscle. This injury, called wry neck, is the same pain that you may feel upon waking and that allows you to turn your head in only one direction.

To treat wry neck, ice the stiff side and then gently stretch the neck away from the stiff side. That is, if your right side is stiff, try to place your left ear on your left shoulder.

See page 54

ROTATOR CUFF PROBLEMS

One of the most common sites of pain among tennis players is the shoulder. The shoulder's rotator cuff muscles may be strained from the serving or other overhead motion, but not from ground strokes.

You will feel the pain in the front of your shoulder or the outside of your upper arm. The pain is usually due to a slight dislocation of the shoulder and an impingement of the biceps tendon. Less frequently, you will feel pain in the back of the shoulder from an impingement of the supraspinatus tendon.

You can strengthen the rotator cuff muscles with the weight program in Chapter 6, or you may need to undergo physical therapy with isokinetic machines. If exercise fails, you may need surgery to repair the muscles.

See pages 59–62

TENNIS ELBOW

Many racquet sport injuries happen because the muscles and tendons in the forearm are not strong enough to withstand the impact of the ball against the racquet.

Tennis elbow is usually the main topic of conversation in tennis clubs. About half of all tennis players suffer from tennis elbow at some time. Those in the 35-to-50-year-old age group are the most likely to complain of elbow pain.

The tendons that extend the wrist and turn the palm up become inflamed, usually from hitting a backhand improperly or trying to slice the serve. The tendon that attaches these muscles to the outside of the elbow also becomes inflamed.

These structures become irritated because the forearm is not strong enough to meet the demands placed upon it. Tennis elbow often results when a player tries to step up in class and then finds that the ball is coming at him harder. The elbow ends up absorbing most of the shock. Also, the player may be a little late hitting the ball because of its speed.

Once you develop tennis elbow, the activities of everyday life are enough to keep the elbow irritated. So just putting your racquet away and resting is usually not enough to solve the problem.

The proper treatment of tennis elbow is an exercise program with light weights to strengthen elbow muscles and tendons. These exercises should include the Arm Curl and Reverse Arm Curl from Chapter 6 and, from Chapter 8, the Wrist Curl, Reverse Wrist Curl, Unbalanced Wrist Rotation, and Ball Squeezing, which also helps develop the forearm flexor muscles.

Extending the fingers against a strong rubber band is also a helpful exercise, as illustrated in Chapter 9. Other excellent exercises for tennis elbow are the Elbow Stretches in Chapter 8.

Only in resistant cases do I ever inject cortisone into a tennis elbow. Physical therapy may also be necessary for very resistant cases. To help prevent this injury, you may want to take a backhand lesson to review proper swing technique.

Wearing an elastic elbow band, either a single band or a double band with a bar, is definitely beneficial for tennis elbow. These bands compress the muscles and reduce the shock transmitted to the tendon.

I suggest that a tennis player ice the elbow 15 to 20 minutes after play. I usually tell my patients to apply ice as soon as they get home. Fill a plastic bag with a mixture of ice and water, and keep the elbow cool for up to 30 or 40 minutes.

A second type of tennis elbow causes pain on the inner side of the elbow, similar to the pain experienced by baseball pitchers. This is an inflammation of the muscles and tendons that flex the wrist forward and turn the palm down. The pain is usually the result of turning the hand over the top of the racquet while hitting topspin shots on the forehand side.

This condition can be treated with the same exercise and flexibility program just described. You may also want to take a lesson to correct any technical flaws in your topspin stroke.

See pages 79–83

WRIST AND HAND PAIN

A sore wrist is a common tennis injury. The wrist may be sprained or sore from overuse. A sprain causes sudden pain and is due to one specific move. An overuse pain comes on gradually and gets progressively worse as you continue to play.

A sprain should be iced until the pain subsides and rested for several days. Then begin the strengthening program of wrist curls and rotations in Chapter 8. An overuse injury requires more prolonged rest (for several weeks), administration of anti-inflammatory agents to ease the pain, and the same strengthening program.

Pain in the fleshy part of the palm behind the thumb is usually due to an oversized grip on the racquet. The obvious remedy is to reduce the size of the grip.

Pain at the base of the hand behind the pinky finger may indicate a severe injury. The butt of the racquet continually hitting the hook of the small hamate bone can break the bone. A sports doctor will need to take an x-ray to see whether the bone is broken. If it is, it will need to be treated as a fracture. If it is just bruised, rest the hand until the pain subsides and then use a racquet with a smaller butt.

See pages 87, 88

RUNNING INJURIES

Tennis is more of a running game than a hitting game. You are constantly running to hit shot after shot. Therefore, many injuries incurred in tennis are running injuries, such as arch pain, stress fractures of the foot, ankle sprains, runner's knee, thigh and hamstring pulls, and back strain. And you can tear up a knee playing tennis as badly as you can in football from the sudden directional changes.

Many foot problems can be avoided with a good pair of tennis shoes. Look for shoes with lateral stabilizing straps, a strong toe box, a midsole for cushioning, a heel stabilizer, and rubber soles with a pivot ball in front. Cheap, poorly built shoes can compound foot problems.

Ankle sprains are common among tennis players due to sudden side-to-side direction changes. Anything but the mildest sprain should be x-rayed.

The ankle may actually be broken, particularly if the inner side is swollen.

Many tennis players complain of pain around the kneecap during and after playing. Some say they feel the pain deep in the knee or behind the knee. The pain usually comes on gradually, and the player may feel fluid in the knee from time to time. These are the signs of runner's knee. The constant bending of the knees in tennis causes the kneecap to pull out of alignment.

The sudden directional changes, twisting and turning, and stops and starts of tennis can lead to cartilage and ligament damage in the knee. These traumatic injuries should be treated immediately with ice and mild compression to avoid swelling. Then see a sports doctor. The knee is a very complex joint, and proper diagnosis and treatment of knee injuries is essential in enabling you to return to full activity. I see more and more tennis players wearing fancy knee braces to support rehabilitated knees.

A quick stop with the knee bent can cause the quadriceps muscle in the front of the thigh to pull or even tear. If your legs are not properly warmed up and stretched, and you lunge for a ball, you may pull a hamstring muscle in the back of the thigh. Anyone who has pulled a hamstring understands the benefits of warming up and stretching before going all out on the court.

If your leg starts to hurt about 20 minutes into the game and keeps getting worse, you probably have iliotibial band syndrome. Once you stop playing, the pain usually disappears—until your next match, and then the pain starts up again in the middle of the match. The easy treatment is to stretch the band.

Suddenly twisting the back, hitting a ball off-balance, or skidding to a stop can cause back strain. You may experience severe, shooting pain. You probably have pulled a back muscle, and you need to rest and ice your back for a few days and take anti-inflammatory agents. Begin a back-stretching program like the one in Chapter 7 as soon as possible.

Tennis players often complain of chronic back pain, which may be due to a difference in the lengths of the legs. A small discrepancy in the leg length can cause pain, usually on the side of the longer leg. A heel lift in the shoe of the shorter leg can correct for this discrepancy. Do not permanently attach the lift inside your tennis shoe. Rather, use the lift in all of your shoes to relieve the pressure on your back.

See pages 69, 70, 95–97, 99, 106–107, 108–109, 119–123, 129

TENNIS LEG

The two major causes of racquet sports injuries are failure to warm up properly and overstressing joints and muscles due to the nature of the sports. Many tennis players hit eight balls over the net and think they are ready to go. A cold, unstretched muscle is just waiting to be torn.

"Tennis leg" is a term used to describe a calf muscle or a tendon that is torn when the player rushes the net, and it is seen almost exclusively among tennis players. It feels as if you were hit in the back of the leg by the ball. This injury can be prevented with an adequate warmup and stretching program.

See pages 116, 117

RACQUETBALL AND SQUASH INJURIES

Racquetball and squash players suffer basically the same injuries as tennis players. They are particularly prone to wrist, hand, and eye injuries.

However, one type of injury seen among racquetball and squash players, and not tennis players, is the result of running into the wall. This usually involves a blow to the shoulder, but the head, hip, or knee may also be injured.

A hard blow can loosen the shoulder joint by partially dislocating it. If your shoulder hurts for more than a few days, see a doctor and begin a shoulder rehabilitation program.

Possible head injuries include a mild or severe concussion. Anything but the mildest head injury should be seen by a doctor.

Hips and knees are usually just bruised and probably will respond to ice and rest.

Racquetball and squash players also suffer more serious eye injuries than tennis players. The ball in these sports is smaller and harder than a tennis ball, so the blow to the eye is much more concentrated. No one should step onto a racquetball or squash court without eye protection. Open-frame goggles are totally useless since the ball, when hit at high speed, can compress and come right through the opening. Clear plastic goggles provide far better eye protection.

Getting hit by the racquet or by your opponent is also a common source of injury in these sports. Whenever I hear my opponent yell, "Around!" I cringe, half-expecting the ball to hit me in the back of the head. The small, confined area of the court and the side-by-side struggle for the center of the court encourage banging, which causes cuts and bruises. Immediate first aid should take care of cuts, but you may need stitches if they are deep. Treat bruises with ice and rest.

HANDBALL AND PADDLE TENNIS

Handball players suffer the same kinds of injuries as racquetball and squash players. In four-wall handball, players often run into a wall and are vulnerable to a concussion, a partial shoulder dislocation, and hip and knee bruises. Eye protection is a must, as the hard ball comes off the wall at high speed.

In both four- and one-wall handball, players crouch low to hit the ball, which puts stress on the knee. This can aggravate an existing runner's knee condition. An ankle sprain is another common handball injury due to the player's rapid changes in direction.

Paddle tennis players suffer injuries similar to those experienced by tennis players, and they are much more likely to suffer from tennis elbow. Unlike the strings of a tennis racquet, the heavy paddle doesn't give, and this, along with the harder ball, increases the stress transmitted to the elbow. Some of my patients develop elbow problems year after year while playing paddle tennis but have no problems from regular tennis.

BADMINTON

Backyard badminton may cause ankle sprains from the player's sudden stops or directional changes. Competitive badminton players may suffer rotator cuff muscle injuries and biceps tendinitis as in any other sport where the arm is constantly brought up over the head.

How to Improve Your Game

Equipment

Using better equipment and improving your stroke technique can reduce the risk of racquet sport injuries.

Tennis elbow sufferers should use a composite or graphite racquet since these transmit the least amount of shock to the elbow. (Wooden racquets are the best at absorbing the shock, but they are no longer available.) The racquet should be strung loosely and should be no larger than midsize. An oversized racquet not only has a bigger "sweet spot" in the center but also has a much larger, elbow-shocking hitting area around the rim. Also, a ball hit out on the rim of an oversized racquet is a shot you probably would have missed with a smaller racquet, which would have spared your elbow.

Manufacturers are now producing lighter, stronger tennis racquets with increased padding to enhance shock absorption. You may want to try one of the racquets with a different style of stringing, such as one strung in a diagonal direction, which are designed to reduce the shock transmitted to the arm.

Racquetball, squash, and handball players should make sure to wear shatterproof eye guards. Also, racquetball and squash players should avoid open-throat racquets, which allow the ball to zoom through when it is hit at a high speed.

Speed Training

Running is an integral part of racquet sports. Wind sprints are particularly good for training. After warming up, run four or five 200- to 300-yard sprints at an easy pace. Work up to a series of 8 to 10 fast sprints once or twice a week. Do not stop abruptly; walk or jog for a minute or two in between sprints. When you finish, warm down and stretch.

Game-Day Warmup

Before playing a racquet sport, go through your typical warmup and stretching program. Then run a series of half- and full-court sprints and shuttle drills, side-stepping from one sideline to the other.

As part of your game-day warmup, do the Lunge Stretch described in Chapter 1 to loosen your leg muscles and to help reduce the risk of a strained groin muscle. Start with one set of 10 lunges in each direction and build up to three sets of 10 to 15.

Before you actually play, go through a series of shadow strokes without the ball. Then hit the ball at half-speed, and do some serves to warm up your shoulder and back muscles. Then stretch the shoulder as described in Chapter 6. Also do a complete lower-body stretch program, as illustrated in Chapter 12, emphasizing calf stretches to reduce the likelihood of a "tennis leg" injury.

After playing, take time to warm down and stretch to keep your muscles limber.

Tennis Strength

The best way to improve your tennis game is not simply to play more tennis. You need a total-body strength-training program to help you hit the ball harder, move faster, and beat the players who are now beating you. In tennis, muscle strength has to be accompanied by muscle stamina. That is built by using light weights and doing many repetitions. Top players such as Ivan Lendl and Andre Agassi now travel with strength-training coaches to enhance their games.

To avoid upper-body muscle strains, incorporate calisthenics from Chapter 1 such as push-ups, pull-ups, abdominal crunches, and torso twists into your regular workout routine. For strength training, do trunk rotations and shoulder-strengthening exercises. These should include the Arm Curl and Reverse Arm Curl from Chapter 6 and the Flat Fly, Lateral Raise, and Military from Chapter 1, although you should *not* do militaries or use a lat pulldown machine if you have any shoulder pain. If possible, do the Bench Press in Chapter 1 as well.

One warning: Don't lift weights and then go out and play tennis. You temporarily lose some fine motor control when you lift weights, and you also tire out muscles. Lift on the days you don't play, or lift after you have played.

Enhancing upper-body strength and agility will improve any racquet-sport player's game. Use the strength-training program in Chapter 1 regularly both during the season and in the off-season to increase and maintain strength. Also do the agility drills in Chapter 17 to improve your ability to change direction quickly.

30

Triathlon

The triathlon is a new sport that grew out of the thirst for new ways to compete. It was devised for runners who became bored with 5- or 10-kilometer races and sought new means of competition. The sport is growing by leaps and bounds; about 400,000 Americans now train for triathlons, and it may well become *the* sport of the 1990s.

The whole concept of cross-training can be traced to triathletes. Until recently, most athletes trained for just one sport and suffered a high rate of overuse injuries because of the constant repetition. Alternating activities, going from swimming to biking to running, helps triathletes reduce their overuse injuries. Cross-training also helps relieve the monotony of repeating the same training program over and over again.

A SPORT FOR EVERYONE

A popular misconception is that triathlons are only for elite athletes. Anyone who enjoys fitness and takes the time to train can complete a triathlon. The average triathlete is 35 years old, enters triathlons primarily for fitness reasons, and trains for an average of 14 hours a week.

One-third of triathletes are women. Female triathletes range from high school students to full-time mothers to businesswomen and professionals. Women, however, should be wary of developing amenorrhea (lack of menstrual periods) from overtraining. Stress fractures and runner's knee are also more common among female triathletes.

Not every triathlon is like the Hawaiian Ironman, the grueling combination of a 2.4-mile swim, a 112-mile bike ride, and a 26-mile run. Other, much shorter, triathlons cater to the growing number of competitors of all ages. These include sprint triathlons (half-mile swim, 12-mile ride, and 3-mile run) and Olympic-distance races (0.9-mile swim, 25-mile ride, and 6-mile run).

THE COMPLETE EVENT

The triathlon brings into play virtually every part of the body, which makes it probably the most complete sporting event. Swimming builds the upper body, specifically the chest and shoulders. Running primarily works the extensor muscle groups of the lower body, namely, the lower-back muscles, the buttock muscles, the hamstrings, and the calves. Biking brings in the flexor muscles, particularly the quadriceps, which are not strengthened that much from running.

As a general conditioning sport, the triathlon is much better than any of its three separate components. Each of the three sports requires good aerobic training, but there is little crossover from the lower to the upper body in aerobic training. Triathlons train both the lower body and the upper body aerobically.

The diversity of activities allows you to train even if you have an injury. For example, if you suffer tibial stress syndrome from running, and all you did for exercise was run, you would have to wait until the injury healed and then change the amount you ran. But a triathlete can train by swimming or biking until the tibial pain subsides.

Another example is shoulder pain from swimming. Instead of being forced to stay out of the water or to use a kickboard, a triathlete can bike or run until the shoulder improves. A triathlete can always do some type of training activity while rehabilitating.

Doctors know that athletes decondition by 50 percent in a matter of a few weeks while resting an injury. One of the precepts of sports medicine is to substitute other activities to keep injured athletes from deconditioning. Even when hurt, triathletes can usually continue to condition themselves.

TRIATHLON INJURIES

Triathletes suffer all of the injuries associated with the three individual sports. By combining three sports, you increase the variety of potential injuries. However, the incidence of each type of injury is lower, and the injuries are usually less extensive.

Surveys of top triathletes show that they often experience lower-back pain, sciatica, knee injuries, iliotibial band syndrome, plantar fasciitis, ankle tendinitis, and stress fractures.

Refer to the swimming, cycling, and running chapters for more details about specific injuries. Keep in mind, however, that triathletes have an advantage. Where the treatment for an overuse injury indicates "rest," substitute "change activity" as the treatment for triathletes.

Since each sport accentuates different muscles, start slowly on a new sport. You can be aerobically fit and in good shape for the sport in which you are experienced, but you may develop soreness in muscles you never knew you had. Novice cyclists can experience hand problems, such as carpal tunnel syndrome caused by gripping the handlebars too tightly, as well as lower-back strain and buttock muscle strain from riding too many miles. Beginning runners are vulnerable to problems ranging from foot injuries to runner's knee to tibial stress fractures aggravated by pounding the feet against the ground. New swimmers may develop shoulder pains from bringing the arm up over the head.

Cramping due to muscle fatigue is a common problem for triathletes. About two-thirds of all competitive triathletes report cramping, usually during the run phase of a race. Drink lots of liquids and eat potassium-rich foods, such as bananas, oranges, and tomatoes, a few days before an event to help prevent your muscles from cramping.

If muscles do cramp during a race, slow your pace. It may be necessary to stop. A stitch in the side is usually a sign of spasms in your diaphragm muscles, which help expand and contract the lungs. Breathe slowly and regularly, and you'll work your way through the cramp.

*See pages 69–72, 99, 106–109
119–120, 129–130*

TOO MUCH TRAINING

Some triathletes, like marathoners, feel compelled to put in prodigious weekly distances. But the more they do, the more overuse problems they can experience. Runners who attempt to maintain their normal mileage while adding swimming and cycling to their routines put themselves at increased risk of overuse injuries.

Distance runners and swimmers are the most prone to be obsessed with their mileage. However, there is a point at which you gain nothing from doing more. You know you are overtraining when you always feel tired while exercising, you have difficulty falling and staying asleep, and your resting heart rate is elevated.

Chronic fatigue is a common syndrome among endurance athletes due to changes in their immune function. They become more susceptible to viral infections and suffer many coughs and colds. Take a week off after a triathlon race or a day off after a heavy training day. This can prevent minor injuries from escalating into major ones.

How to Improve Your Times

Balanced Training

The trick to becoming a good triathlete is to train to your highest level in each sport but to stay below your injury threshold. That is, train to your capacity, but don't overtrain and thereby risk repetitive, overuse injuries.

Many triathletes hold back on their running programs because running has the highest injury rate of the three sports. As a result, however, they may be undertrained for the running portion of events and lose precious time.

Each triathlete must determine the level at which he or she can train for each sport to get maximum performance while minimizing injuries. Balancing your training along this fine line can make you a better performer. This comes with experience and knowing how much your body can do.

You should monitor your pulse while training. Often, you'll find that when you take up a new sport, you hit your target heart rate faster and at a lower resistance than you expected. This is particularly important in swimming, which trains both the upper and lower body.

You must spend enough time with each activity to achieve muscle growth and strengthening. You need to do an activity at least twice a week. Once you have strengthened your muscles sufficiently to handle a new activity, you can slowly incorporate another new activity into your training.

Triathletes can safely train at 75 to 90 percent capacity for five days a week. This schedule might cause injuries and burnout if you limited yourself to one activity, but with cross-training, you can maintain your aerobic conditioning while giving the muscles you worked on yesterday some time to recover today. Rest is as important as the workout. Without it, your muscles are continually torn down. Recovery is built in to cross-training because different sports use different muscles.

Once you have competed in a few races and wish to improve your time, you many want to try a triathlon camp. Most of these who attend camp do so to learn more about training techniques and to maximize their potential. You will spend a weekend or a week with elite athletes and experts who will examine your swimming, biking, and running techniques and discuss good nutrition and other training tips.

Targeted Conditioning

There are certain areas of the body you should concentrate on to increase your strength for each sport. For swimming, you need to work on the shoulders, to strengthen your pull through the water; the triceps, for that last push of the stroke; and the wrists, to help you flick your hand as it comes out of the water.

For propulsion in cycling, you need strong quadriceps muscles, which you develop with leg extensions. You also need a strong upper body for climbing hills and controlling the handlebars. You should also work on shoulder and arm strengthening.

For running, extension exercises strengthen the lower back; leg curls strengthen the hamstrings to power your stride; and toe raises build strong calf muscles, which give you that extra push at the end of your stride. Strong biceps can help control your arm swing to improve your running rhythm.

Equipment

Many triathletes use large swim goggles that seal on the bony structure of the eye. These rugged goggles are more comfortable for longer swims and also provide good peripheral vision. However, they are slightly more difficult to seal than the smaller swimming goggles that cover only the eye sockets.

You can get swim goggles with tinted lenses to cut down on sun glare. I recommend goggles with fog-resistant, optical-grade lenses. Some people try to wear contact lenses underneath non-prescription swim goggles. Others prefer prescription lenses built into their swim goggles.

Look for triathlon wetsuits with the zipper in the front rather than the back. This makes the suit easier to peel off before you switch to biking. These "tri" suits also have very flexible arms to facilitate swimming motions. You can also buy a specially padded swimsuit that you can also bike and run in. This can save time in transition from one event to the next.

Another way to save time is to use lace locks. These plastic guides allow you to pull on your running shoes and lace them all in one motion so that you don't have to stop to tie your shoes.

Nutrition

Some triathletes suffer from anemia due to iron deficiency or have digestive tract problems because they tamper with their diets to produce the maximum amount of energy. Others become vegetarians without understanding the dangers of dietary restrictions: Avoiding fish and chicken can rob the body of valuable protein, calcium, and iron. Triathletes need a balanced diet that is very high in calories, is rich in iron, and has large amounts of protein and calcium.

31

Volleyball

Volleyball is an increasingly popular and competitive sport. The success of both the men's and women's U.S. Olympic teams in the 1980s sparked a volleyball boom on courts and beaches across the country. Competitive beach volleyball is now a professional sport for both men and women. The level of play of competitive volleyball is far removed from the backyard games of yesteryear. With bodies flying in the air and collapsing onto the court, competitive volleyball is a sport with a fairly high injury rate. The stress on the arm from spiking the ball while up in the air and the constant bending of the back and knees also cause overuse injuries.

BACK STRAIN

Like any jumping sport, volleyball leads to back strains from the pounding the back takes as a player comes down. Volleyball players also arch and twist their backs to go up for spikes and then uncoil to violently whip through the ball. This also can lead to lower-back muscle strain.

Volleyball players need to develop their back muscles to help stabilize the spine. A back exercise program is important, incorporating both extension and flexion exercises from Chapter 7.

Persistent back pain that does not respond to a lower-back stretching program should be checked by a doctor.

See page 69

SORE SHOULDER

Like any sport that brings the arm up over the head, volleyball has its share of rotator cuff injuries. The little rotator cuff muscles that hold the shoulder joint together can become stretched. This allows the head to slip within the shoulder socket and pinch the biceps tendons where they come through the joint.

This is a very common injury in volleyball because of the overhead position of the arms in blocking, serving, and spiking. The force of an oncoming volleyball against the hand in a block transmits tremendous shock to the shoulder joint. And no other athletic skill is quite like the spike. You must hit the ball as hard as you can over the net while in midair. You don't have the advantage of using the floor, as you do when throwing, so you must bend and twist your body in the air to help generate the power that can deliver 100 mile-per-hour spikes. Whipping the arm through the ball while in the air for a spike or a jump serve can strain the rotator cuff muscles. I highly recommend following the shoulder-strengthening program in Chapter 6 during the off-season to prevent this all-too-common injury.

See pages 59–62

BROKEN AND DISLOCATED FINGERS

Finger fractures and dislocations occur often in volleyball due to the impact of the ball at a fairly high speed. All of these injuries need to be seen by a doctor and x-rayed. Buddy-taping a broken or dislocated finger to the finger next to it may be all that is required to protect it.

A direct blow to the end of a finger from a volleyball may cause a "jammed" finger, in which the cartilage on the end of the bone is damaged and the ligaments that hold the joint together are stretched. Or it may lead to a form of "baseball finger," in which the tendon on the top of the finger is ruptured, causing the tip of the finger to droop.

See pages 91, 92

JUMPER'S KNEE

Jumper's knee is a familiar injury to volleyball players. Jumping from a crouched position to block or spike the ball causes the quadriceps muscles to contract with great force as they straighten out the knee. Either the kneecap, the quadriceps tendons, or the patellar tendon can become inflamed from the repetitive, excessive force against them, causing pain. This will respond to the strengthening program in Chapter 11.

See pages 107, 108

ANKLE SPRAIN

Volleyball players usually sprain their ankles from coming down on the side of another player's foot under the net. If the sprain is mild, use the usual RICE formula of Chapter 4, and then be-

gin early range-of-motion and ankle strengthening exercises in Chapter 13. Treat your ankle right, and you will probably be back bumping and setting in a few weeks.

If the sprain is more severe, you should see a doctor and have it x-rayed.

See pages 119–123

✚ BRUISES AND BROKEN BONES

All kinds of bumps, bruises, and fractures can result from diving or falling on the hardwood floor of a volleyball court. This is a hazard with all hard playing surfaces, but it is a particular problem in volleyball because of all the diving, rolling, and sprawling on the court. Players just learning how to dive are also liable to bang and cut up their chins, requiring stitches.

If the bruise is mild, just ice it until the swelling goes down. If the pain remains severe after icing, have a doctor take an x-ray to check for a possible broken bone.

Beach volleyball players, of course, have it easier since the sand is much more forgiving.

BEACH VOLLEYBALL

Popularized by Sinjin Smith and Randy Stoklos, beach volleyball is one of the fastest-growing sports today. Dozens of men and women now earn a living playing professional beach volleyball, not to mention the bonuses they receive from all those endorsement and modeling contracts.

Beach players suffer the same injuries as indoor players, except they don't have as many cuts and bruises due to the softness of the sand. However, they are prone to ankle sprains from turning an ankle on the sand's uneven surface.

They also have to worry about the heat and the sun. Make sure to drink plenty of liquids before and after playing beach volleyball. During play, stop every 15 minutes to have something to drink, either water or an electrolyte drink such as Gatorade.

You must also protect yourself against the sun. Wear a sunscreen with an SPF of at least 15. If you go into the water to cool off, put the sunscreen on again. Several companies now make special sports sunscreens, which supposedly hold up against sweat. I still recommend that you put sunscreen on lavishly and often during a day at the beach.

With only two players covering the court, and with the traction problems caused by sand, you have to be in great condition to play beach volleyball. Try to work out two or three times a week within your training range to improve your cardiovascular conditioning.

How to Improve Your Game

Power, which is a combination of strength and speed, is critical in volleyball. With all the fast, explosive movements that characterize the game, it may not seem as if volleyball players need to be strong, but overall body strength is quite important. You must not only develop your legs to help you jump higher, but you need to work your upper body as well to strengthen the back and shoulders. Training with weights during the season, as well as in the off-season, can help maintain your strength and power. And a stronger athlete is a more explosive athlete.

Strength training also helps prevent injuries. Strengthening the quadriceps, which extend the knee, and the hamstrings, which flex the knee, will result in a more stable, less injury-prone knee. A volleyball player must also have strong, flexible hips and back to withstand the stresses of the game. Do arching and back extension exercises regularly. The abdominal strengthening exercises in Chapter 7 are also important for supporting the back.

When you stretch after warming up, emphasize the lower back, hip flexors, hamstrings, groin, Achilles tendon, calf, and shoulders.

Exercises that mimic volleyball movements also are helpful. The deep jumps of plyometrics described in Chapter 17 develop your legs and your jumping skills.

To jump higher, you have to practice jumping as you would during a game. That means practicing your footwork for blocking and spiking and then jumping as high as you can. It's best to pick a high target, such as a basketball backboard. Jumping to a target is a lot harder than just jumping into the air. Notice how high you are able to jump, and try to jump this high 10 times in a row. Work your way up to at least four sets of 10 jumps, and you can increase your jump by two to three inches within a few weeks.

32

Walking, Hiking, and Horseback Riding

Walking is probably the best form of exercise next to swimming, and it certainly is a more accessible activity. More than 50 million Americans walk for fitness and incorporate walking into their ordinary routines, such as going to work or to the store.

Once you start walking and learn to appreciate its convenience and benefits, it becomes second nature. It's a sport you can pursue for the rest of your life.

Walking offers all the fitness benefits of jogging and avoids the pounding on your body and the risk of knee or other joint injuries. When you walk, you transfer your body weight from one foot to the other, as distinct from jogging or running, where each stride transfers three to four times your body weight to the lower body. Walking is also highly effective protection against the bone loss of osteoporosis.

Brisk walking can bring you into the cardiovascular training range just as effectively as jogging, if you walk at a fast pace, and without excessive strain or fatigue. If you're out of shape, it's a painless way to start shedding pounds and toning up muscles. You burn about 100 calories a mile while walking briskly, which is on a par with jogging. The only difference is that walking takes a little longer to burn off those calories.

Walking is a year-round sport. Indoor walking enables people who might not otherwise exercise because of very hot, cold, or inclement weather to continue their routines. Many malls offer free walking time before shopping hours. Malls provide a flat, even walking surface and a climate-controlled, comfortable environment without the obstacles of car or bicycle traffic or dogs.

And the only equipment you need is a good pair of walking shoes.

WARM UP BY WALKING

Walking is one of the few sports that doesn't require any prolonged warmup or stretching program. Walking *is* your warmup. And since you don't put much strain on your muscles when walking, you don't need to stretch them out first.

However, a good warmdown at the end of a walk is important. You should walk slowly for about five minutes to warm down and allow your heart rate to return to normal.

After warming down, stretch your Achilles tendons, shins, calves, quadriceps, hamstrings, trunk, and upper body, as illustrated in Chapter 1. Hold each stretch for 20 seconds and then switch to the opposite body part.

BACK PAIN

Some walkers develop lower-back pain. If you do, you should check the lengths of your legs. A difference in leg length is the most common cause of back pain in walking, as it is in jogging and running. This can be corrected by putting a lift in the heel of the shorter leg.

See pages 69, 70

TRAUMATIC INJURIES

An ankle sprain is the most common traumatic walking injury and is due to walking on uneven surfaces. If you step on a stone or in a hole, you can turn over your ankle and sprain it.

The only other traumatic injuries associated with walking are getting hit by a car or cyclist or being bitten by a dog. If you fall, you may suffer cuts and bruises, but they are usually minor.

See pages 119–123

OVERUSE INJURIES

Because of the repetitive nature of walking and the high number of strides per mile, walkers may suffer lower-body overuse injuries. These include arch pain, stress fractures of the foot, heel pain, shin splints, and runner's knee.

All of these conditions can be alleviated by supporting the foot. Try a commercial arch support first. If that does not correct the problem, have a sports podiatrist make you an orthotic device.

See pages 106, 107, 111, 112, 129, 130

STARTING A WALKING PROGRAM

Being overambitious when you start a walking program can cause an injury or lead to enough discomfort that you lose interest in walking. If you feel stiff and sore a few days into your program, you may give up. Walking too fast, too far, too soon has killed many people's motivation to get into a regular routine.

Don't worry about distance in the beginning. The total time walked is more important than the distance. Start by walking at a comfortable pace for about 10 minutes. Yes, you probably can do more than that, but do yourself a favor and don't try. When you are comfortable, increase your walking time by one to two minutes every other day until you are walking about 20 minutes.

Next, get in the habit of checking your pulse, and gradually increase your pace until you are within your training range (see Chapter 4). Once you are within your training range for 20 minutes and you have established the pace necessary to maintain your heartbeat there, gradually increase your distance as much as you wish. Go an extra mile or two at a comfortable pace, and don't push yourself. You should be able to converse comfortably while walking.

RACE WALKING

Women's race walking has gained popularity in recent years and debuted as an Olympic event in 1992. The percentage of body fat among women race walkers is approximately the same as that of elite women distance runners.

You don't have to be an Olympic-caliber walker to enter a race. More and more races are divided into age groups to allow participants to compete more closely. Most race walkers do it just for fun and fitness.

The rules of race walking require you to keep one foot on the ground at all times and to keep the knee of the supporting leg straight. You must learn a technique that entails rotating the hips and striding out while pumping your arms with your elbows held at 90° angles.

You can teach yourself how to race-walk with the help of a book or video, or your local health club or "Y" may offer a race walking clinic.

HIKING

Hiking moves a walking program to a higher level. Hikers usually cover greater distances and expend more energy than walkers because the terrain is usually much more difficult.

Hiking has all the advantages of walking, plus it helps you attain a higher level of fitness because of the increased effort and longer exercise time. But most people can't afford the time to hike every day, and some can't hike year-round because of the climate.

Hikers have a much higher propensity for traumatic injuries than walkers because of the nature of hiking trails. Ankle and knee sprains are much more common because of the unevenness of the terrain. Upper-body and even head injuries can result from falls on rough terrain. In addition, carrying a pack can disturb your balance and cause a fall. Also, the abundance of branches and rocks on hiking trails leads to higher prevalence of scrapes and bruises among hikers than among walkers.

You can't do much to prevent these injuries except to be careful where you hike and to watch where you step. Don't get too carried away by the magnificent scenery. On the other hand, just looking at the ground while hiking isn't much fun, so you have to scan back and forth from the ground to the horizon.

OVERUSE INJURIES

Hikers have a high incidence of overuse injuries because of the long distances they travel. These are the same injuries seen among walkers. Runner's knee can be a severe problem because hiking downhill aggravates this injury.

The way to prevent these injuries is to wear a good hiking boot to protect the foot and an arch support or orthotic to control any abnormality in the foot. The new sneaker-weight, high-top hiking shoes offer just as much protection from sprains as the traditional heavy combat or hunting-style boots.

HORSEBACK RIDING

Almost all of the injuries from horseback riding are due to being thrown from, stepped on, or kicked or bitten by a horse. These injuries can range from simple bruises to serious fractures. Fatal head and neck injuries are also possible, and a movement is afoot in a number of states to make riding helmets mandatory.

One idiosyncratic injury seen infrequently among riders is the formation of huge calcium deposits in the lower buttock right where the hamstring muscle attaches to the pelvis. This injury occurs when the rider is thrown from the horse and lands flat on his or her buttock. This harsh landing crushes the soft tissues, causing heavy bleeding in the buttock. The buttock tissue can calcify, leading to permanent discomfort when the rider sits on a horse or uses the hamstrings.

Some riders try ultrasound treatments in an effort to break up the calcium deposits. Anti-inflammatory agents can be used to ease the pain. The injury is usually not severe enough to require surgical removal of the deposits.

How to Improve Your Walking and Riding

Learning proper fitness-walking technique will help you get the most out of your walking program. Keep your shoulders relaxed (back and down), your head level, and your chin up. Align your shoulders directly over your hips with your spine straight. Bend your arms at the elbow at a 90° angle, keeping your fingers curled gently. Swing your arms like a pendulum with each step. Become more aware of your arms and the energy of the upper body as it powers you forward.

Strength is one of the keys to becoming a better rider. Upper-body strength will help you control a huge, very strong animal. Use the strength training program in Chapter 1. Hip strength allows you to squeeze with the knees to maintain your seat. You can strengthen the adductor muscles in the hip with an abductor-adductor hip machine, which can be found in health clubs. Or you can isometrically strengthen the adductors:

Hip Strengthener

Sit down and place a soccer ball or basketball between your knees and squeeze. Hold for 15 to 20 seconds. Repeat five times a day.

Get a Good Pair of Shoes

An inexpensive pair of walking shoes may seem like a bargain, but it may cripple your walking program. A good shoe is absolutely essential and may even correct some defects in the way your foot strikes the ground. A $40 or $50 pair of walking shoes from a reputable manufacturer is a worthwhile investment. Various manufacturers use different shoe lasts, so try on a number of brands until you find the one your foot feels comfortable with.

A good walking shoe should provide side-to-side stability and have cushioning in the midsole; a flexible, nonskid sole; and a strong heel counter with a low back tab.

33

Weight Lifting and Body Building

The injuries suffered by weight lifters and body builders are usually the result of using too much weight. Although you can increase your strength by using lighter weights with many repetitions, you can achieve bulk and muscle definition only by using heavy weights for a few repetitions. However, you have to take care when using massive amounts of weight.

MUSCLE AND TENDON TEARS

The strain of that last repetition may cause a muscle fiber tear in the tendon attached to the muscle. These partial tears are treated by a short period of rest followed by a stretching program, since an injured muscle tends to shorten. Then the muscle must be restrengthened to return to normal function.

The ultimate injury is a complete tear of a muscle or tendon. This requires surgical repair.

See pages 43–45

JOINT SPRAINS

The ligaments around joints are commonly sprained in weight lifting due to overstress.

These sprains are treated in the same way as any other sprain, beginning with the RICE formula described in Chapter 4.

See page 42

SHOULDER INJURIES

As in any other sport where the arm goes over the shoulder, lifting weights over the head can cause shoulder pain, tendinitis, or a partial dislocation. Military presses, lat pull-downs, and even the basic clean-and-jerk movement all stress the shoulder.

See pages 63–65

ELBOW PAINS

Tennis elbow is a common condition among weight lifters due to the stress placed on the muscles that flex and extend the wrist in exercises for strengthening the biceps. See the strengthening and flexibility exercises for tennis elbow in Chapter 8.

See pages 79–82

RUNNER'S KNEE PAIN

Runner's knee can become quite aggravated by repetitions of squats, leg extensions, and leg presses. If the front part of the knee begins to hurt, you should stop doing squats until the pain subsides. Also, you should limit leg extensions and presses so that your leg moves through only the last 30° of the extension or press, as described in the 30° Leg Extension exercise in Chapter 11.

See pages 106–107

BACK INJURIES

Weight lifters need to be wary of back muscle pulls and ruptured discs. The most serious problems stem from squats. If the weight shifts while you are down in the squat position, a violent force can be applied to the back. Squat racks help prevent this problem, but even they are not a total safeguard. Squat machines, where the lifter lies on his back and lifts the weight with his legs, seem to be the best solution.

See pages 69–71

How to Improve Your Workout

Moderation in Weight Lifting

Weight lifters and body builders need to guard against pushing too hard. If you progress too quickly in your weight-training program, you may overstress joints and muscles. If you are injured and have to rest during recovery, you will lose much of the muscle development you gained.

Your body needs a day to recover after a weight workout. You can safely do split workouts, working the upper part of the body one day and the lower part of the body the next.

34

Wrestling

Wrestlers have the reputation of being tough and able to withstand pain—and for good reason, since wrestling is a sport with a high incidence of injuries. According to the list of injuries compiled by the National Athletic Trainers Association, wrestlers suffer more injuries than football players at the high school level.

The typical wrestling injury is due to levered force rather than sudden impact. Wrestlers tend to become injured from the slow, continued strain on joints and muscles rather than from the explosive injuries characteristic of football.

HEAD INJURIES

Concussions are not common among wrestlers, but they do occur. Wrestling headgear covers primarily the ears and does not protect the head as a football helmet or boxing headgear does.

Skull fractures are rare because of the padding of the wrestling mat. The only time I see a skull fracture is when a wrestler comes off the mat and hits his head on the hard gym floor.

Broken noses, on the other hand, are fairly common because of the head clashing that takes place during matches. Stop any bleeding by applying pressure to the nose, and apply ice to bruised areas. Then have the nose x-rayed.

See pages 49–51

CAULIFLOWER EAR

One of my biggest bugaboos with wrestling is cauliflower ear. The only way a wrestler can suffer this injury is by not wearing headgear. I see around 15 young wrestlers every season who need to have blood drained from their ears regularly to avoid cauliflower ear. Young wrestlers tend to think they won't be challenged as hard in practice, and they don't wear headgear because it irritates them. Wrestlers are required to wear headgear during matches, and matches are often stopped to allow wrestlers to reset their headgear. There's a good reason for this: Headgear is designed to protect the ears.

See page 51

NECK INJURIES

Stress on the neck from hitting the mat or from a half-nelson or cradle-type hold can sprain neck ligaments. This is basically a whiplash injury. The muscles in the back of the neck, along with the ligaments that hold the cervical spine in place, become overstressed and strained.

The stress of bending the neck forward or landing on the back of the neck can break off a piece of bone in the neck. Usually, it is the protruding bone at the back of the cervical vertebra that breaks rather than the body of the vertebra itself.

Do not move someone with a severe neck injury. Check to see whether the wrestler can move all of his extremities. Even if he can, call emergency medical technicians and wait for them to move the injured athlete.

A "burner" or a more dangerous brachial plexus stretch can occur in wrestling. A "burner" is caused by a pinched nerve in the neck, which sends pain down the arm. The pain is felt on the side of the body opposite the side that took the blow and disappears rapidly. As soon as the individual's strength returns and the pain is gone, he may wrestle again.

If, however, the wrestler feels this pain on the side of the body that took the blow, this is a sign of nerve damage and is a serious injury. He must not wrestle again until his symptoms completely disappear and his strength is back to 100 percent. Recovery time depends on the severity of the injury and may range from a few days to six months. In severe cases, the damage may be permanent.

See pages 53, 54

SHOULDER INJURIES

The most common site of injury in a wrestler's upper body is the shoulder. Muscle strains, a partial dislocation, or a full dislocation can result from the rotational force applied to the shoulder in certain holds, such as the half nelson. These three injuries represent increasing degrees of the same process. Rehabilitation consists of exercises, such as those in Chapter 6, to strengthen the rotator cuff muscles in order to tighten the shoulder joint.

Landing on the point of the shoulder or the elbow can force the shoulder up and separate it. If the fall is hard, the wrestler may even break a collarbone.

See pages 59–67

ELBOW INJURIES

A wrestler can injure an elbow by forcing it to go too far in a certain direction. Hyperextending the elbow tears up the front part of the capsule surrounding the elbow joint and the ligaments holding the bones together. Forcing the elbow out and away from the body sprains the ulnar collateral ligament on the inner side of the elbow.

The treatment for a hyperextended elbow is to keep it splinted for at least two weeks to allow it to heal. Then begin range-of-motion and gradual strengthening exercises. For an elbow ligament sprain, the treatment is basically the same except that the splint is kept on as long as three weeks, depending on how quickly the ligament stabilizes.

In severe cases, the elbow can become dislocated. This is a medical emergency. As the bones slip out of the socket, they can impinge on arteries and cut off the blood supply to the forearm and hand. The blood supply must be restored, or the victim will lose the use of his forearm and hand.

If the stress on the elbow is great, the bones can give way, resulting in a fracture.

The elbow is a complex joint. Do not attempt to rehabilitate it without consulting a doctor. There are rehabilitation exercises in Chapter 8 that you can do at home under the guidance of a doctor and a physical therapist.

See page 84

WRIST INJURIES

Two common wrestling injuries are a sprained wrist and a broken wrist. Wrist sprains typically occur when your opponent pulls back on your hand, and fractures are usually caused by falling on the wrist.

As with any sprain, all but the most minor injury should be x-rayed in case a piece of bone has been pulled off, which makes the injury a fracture. For example, the bony tip of the wrist can be pulled off from overstress of the ligaments that attach to it.

A wrestler can break both bones of the wrist (Colles' fracture), producing what doctors call a silver fork deformity. The lower end of the wrist and hand become bent so that they are higher than the forearm. This gives the arm the look of an upside-down fork. The treatment entails re-aligning the bone to correct the deformity, casting the wrist for up to six weeks, and then doing range-of-motion and strengthening exercises to restore function.

Navicular fractures commonly occur when a wrestler tries to break a fall and lands on his outstretched hand. The navicular bone behind the base of the thumb heals slowly; it can take eight weeks to eight months to fully recover from this injury. A surgeon may need to graft a bone to the fractured wrist or insert a pin to help it heal.

A wrestler can fix a dislocated finger immediately by pulling it back into joint. If the dislocation is serious, it will require medical attention. The wrestler should ice the finger off and on until he can see a doctor.

See pages 87, 88, 91

KNEE INJURIES

Wrestlers are more likely to sprain their knees than tear ligaments or cartilage. All but the most minor knee injuries should be seen by a doctor.

It's important that a sprained knee be examined before it swells up too much. Examining a sprained knee is hardest on the day after the injury. By then it's sore, and the swelling makes it difficult for the doctor to see what's happened inside.

The wrestler or coach should tell the doctor how the injury happened. This is helpful in ensuring a correct diagnosis. In particular, he should note the side of the pain in relation to the side on which force was applied to the knee. If the

pain is on the same side, the injury is probably a bruise, and it should be iced intermittently until the swelling and discoloration disappear.

Pain on the opposite side denotes a much more serious injury. The wrestler probably has stretched or torn knee ligaments from the force of the blow. If the knee clicks, buckles, locks, or gives way to the inside or outside, he probably has torn cartilage.

"Housemaid's knee," or pre-patellar bursitis, is also a hazard for wrestlers since one contestant always starts on his knees.

See pages 102–104, 109

ANKLE SPRAINS

The wrestling shoe is high but provides little support for the ankle because it is soft so that it can grip the mat. An ankle sprain may occur as a result of tripping or stepping on the side of an opponent's foot or from stepping on the edge of the mat. The ankle turns over and sprains on the outside.

Treat a mild sprain with the RICE formula in Chapter 4, followed by the range-of-motion and strengthening exercises illustrated in Chapter 13. A more severe sprain may require prolonged rehabilitation or even a cast and surgery.

Don't bear full weight on the ankle until you can walk with a normal heel-to-toe gait. You should tape the ankle or wear a lace-up brace when you return to action to prevent another sprain.

See pages 119–123

WEIGHT CONTROL

Besides acute injuries, the biggest problem among wrestlers is weight control. Many wrestlers try to get down to the lowest possible weight so that they can be stronger than their opponents. In effect, they try to get the power of a 160-pounder into a 140-pound body instead of trying to increase their natural power at 160 pounds.

The coach of one of the most successful wrestling teams in my area understood that the amount of lean body mass compared to body fat is more important than a wrestler's weight. He built a wrestling dynasty by forbidding his athletes to struggle to make weight. Instead, he helped them pick their ideal weight class and showed them how to improve their strength at that level.

Methods to control a wrestler's never-ending quest to make weight have been tried in various states. For a long time New Jersey had what was called the 5 percent rule: No wrestler was allowed to lose more than 5 percent of his body weight. This didn't work very well because it allowed a tiny 100-pound flyweight to lose 5 pounds when he might not have 2 pounds of available fat to lose. At the same time, an overweight 200-pound heavyweight could lose only 10 pounds when he may really need to lose 35 pounds to get down to his normal body weight.

Another method used is doctor certification of a wrestler's ideal body weight. A doctor estimates the wrestler's body fat and determines his appropriate weight class. The parents of young wrestlers must also agree that the wrestler can go down to this level.

This method depends on the doctor's ability to estimate how much weight the wrestler can lose safely. The doctor must not be swayed by the coach's and wrestler's desires to aim for an unrealistic weight level. That's why parents are involved, as a safeguard. This is the most widely used method and, in the absence of programs to measure body fat, is probably the most successful.

The only sensible way to determine a wrestler's proper weight is to measure his body fat. Then he will know the lowest possible weight he can achieve without losing strength.

Wrestlers will do almost anything to help them make weight on the day of a match. They will starve themselves, not realizing that they are depleting their carbohydrate stores and thereby making themselves weaker. They dehydrate themselves by wearing a rubber suit to make them sweat, or they may even take diuretics and laxatives just before the weigh-in.

The problem with all of these methods is that rather than getting to a specific weight and maintaining it, the wrestler binges after the weigh-in in hopes of becoming stronger. He also drinks a lot of water to rehydrate himself. If the weigh-in is a few hours before the match, he fills his stomach with food and water, which decreases the amount of blood available for the muscles in his limbs and weakens him further. After the match, he binges again because he hasn't eaten for days. He may regain five or six pounds that night. He must then lose that weight in three days to make weight again.

This is very destructive. A young, growing athlete should pick a weight, maintain it, and stop yo-yoing.

How to Improve Your Performance

Wrestling is a sport in which strength, speed, and endurance are all important. It requires intense, short bursts of activity. Energy output is extremely high during a six-minute match at the high school level.

Strength training is crucial. If the wrestler can increase his strength, he won't have to decrease his weight as much and then constantly worry about making weight. Gaining strength and controlling weight is the key to optimal performance.

Wrestlers need strong legs, but they particularly need to work on upper-body strength.

All upper-body exercises are important, but wrestlers should focus on those involving the shoulder and the arm in the strength-training program in Chapter 1.

A full flexibility program is important to accommodate the stresses on the joints from various holds. Again, concentrate on improving shoulder flexibility.

Conditioning should consist mostly of interval training as wrestling involves short periods of maximum effort. Run long distances to build endurance, interspersing these runs with short sprints.

Sports Medicine for Everyone

Female, Child, and Elderly Athletes

How to Select a Sports Specialist

35

Female, Child, and Elderly Athletes

A woman's, child's, or senior's sports injuries are basically the same as a young man's. But there are some peculiarities due to differences in anatomy, including problems related to the menstrual cycle, growth spurts, and aging bones. The female, child, or elderly athlete also has certain nutritional needs that a young man doesn't.

THE FEMALE ATHLETE

RUNNER'S KNEE

Runner's knee is much more common among women than men because a woman's pelvis is wider, making the angle between the thigh and the calf sharper. This increases the tendency for the kneecap to pull out of line and rub on the side of its groove, causing knee pain.

See pages 106, 107

DISLOCATED KNEECAP

Dislocated kneecaps are also more common. The groove that the kneecap rides in is much shallower in women than in men. The kneecap therefore has less lateral stability.

See page 105

TENNIS ELBOW

Tennis elbow is usually associated with lack of forearm strength. I see it particularly among women who play mixed doubles. When the ball comes at a woman with more force than she is used to, the shock of the ball hitting the racquet is transmitted up through her forearm. Since the ball is coming so fast, her weight is typically back and she is late getting her racquet head around. On the backhand, if the ball hits the racquet while the elbow is still bent, the shock is transmitted to the outer area of the elbow, causing elbow pain.

See pages 79–82

✚ INCONTINENCE

Women athletes also have more problems with incontinence. About one-third of women experience leaking of urine from the bladder during running or high-impact aerobics. The jarring shakes urine out of the bladder.

The leaking can usually be brought under control with exercises that tone the pelvic muscles, which tend to stretch and loosen from childbirth. Contract the muscles in your pelvis for 10 seconds. It should feel as if you are trying to stop the flow of urine. Rest for 10 seconds. Repeat the exercise several times every day for several weeks.

A vaginal tampon or diaphragm may eliminate the problem. If the leaking usually occurs late during a long run, stop to urinate at some point. If need be, you can switch to swimming or cycling, which are not as strongly associated with incontinence. There also are medications available to help control incontinence.

✚ MENSTRUAL IRREGULARITIES

A major problem among women who are ultra-slim and who exercise heavily is amenorrhea, or disruption of the normal menstrual cycle. I see this particularly among long-distance runners and triathletes.

Intensive physical activity before puberty can delay a girl's first period by a year or more and lead to an irregular menstrual cycle. Numerous theories have been advanced to explain the relationship between exercise and amenorrhea. There seems to be a change in the control of the pituitary and the ovaries, resulting in a dramatic fall in estrogen levels.

A very thin woman with little body fat may experience a hormone imbalance. To maintain the natural rise and fall of hormones during the menstrual cycle, a woman must maintain a body fat content of about 22 percent. Too much exercise along with a rigorous diet may reduce a woman's body fat and cause ovulation problems. Women runners with a body fat content of 17 percent or less will not menstruate.

The good news is that this exercise-induced fertility problem appears to be reversible. As soon as you cut down on exercise and gain a few pounds, your body fat will build up again and your period will return to normal. If it doesn't, you should see a gynecologist. You may have other medical problems that need attention.

MD BONE LOSS AND STRESS FRACTURES

A menstrual disturbance in a young female athlete can increase her risk of bone loss and stress fractures. Amenorrhea in a young athlete usually leads to insufficient bone mineral density. With aging, she will lose bone tissue and be vulnerable to osteoporosis, a bone wasting disease. In the short term, she will be vulnerable to stress fractures. Fifty percent of competitive runners with irregular periods sustain stress fractures, compared to 30 percent of runners with normal periods. These runners have a bone mineral content comparable to that of postmenopausal women more than twice their age.

It is thought that postmenopausal women are the most commonly affected by osteoporosis because their ovaries no longer produce estrogen. Estrogen is vital to proper bone growth because it allows calcium to be absorbed from the intestines, and calcium is a necessary ingredient in building the skeleton. I recommend that every amenorrheic athlete raise her daily calcium consumption to 1.5 grams to maintain a normal calcium balance.

Along with estrogen and calcium supplements, exercise helps to optimize bone mass. Weight-bearing exercises, such as walking, dancing, and jogging, are particularly valuable in reducing bone loss in middle-aged and postmenopausal women, and may help to prevent osteoporosis.

SPECIAL PROTECTION AND PRECAUTIONS

Upper-Body Strength

Women can build their legs to be extremely strong, but they cannot, in general, develop their upper-body strength as much as men because of basic physiologic differences. The human male has an innate potential to develop bigger shoulders, chest, and arms than the human female.

Through weight training, women can increase their upper body strength markedly without bulking up as men do. This is because women have little circulating male hormone, which is a required for bulking up. The huge upper bodies you see on female weight trainers are due to steroid use. As long as a female athlete has a normal level of circulating female hormones and doesn't take any artificial male hormones, she will increase her strength and not her bulk through weight training.

Good Nutrition

Women may need to supplement their diets for peak athletic performance. Most women need a high calcium intake. Dairy foods such as lowfat milk, calcium pills, or even a few Tums® (which have a high calcium content) a day should provide the calcium a woman needs.

A female needs a higher concentration of iron in her diet than a male, and this is especially true for athletes. A heavily exercising female athlete breaks down blood cells at a higher rate than a sedentary woman. This, combined with loss of blood during the menstrual cycle, requires increased intake of iron. I recommend that female athletes take in 15 milligrams of iron per day, either through the diet or supplements.

Some women are still resistant to a high-carbohydrate diet. The idea that a high-starch diet can be nonfattening is hard for some women to comprehend. Traditionally, when women attempted to diet, they gave up bread, potatoes, and rice. These old dietary prejudices may be hard to overcome.

Protecting the Breasts

Any woman must be concerned with protecting her breasts during sports. Sports bras now provide much-needed breast support. The first sports bra was made in the mid-1970s by sewing two jock straps together. Since then, the market has been flooded with sports bras of different shapes and sizes.

Sports bras are designed to minimize breast motion. They press the breasts against the chest, and they cradle and restrain each breast separately within a cup. A good sports bra is sturdy but not constricting and allows a full range of motion. Most are made of nonabrasive, breathable materials.

Since there are so many sports bras available, evaluate each one before you make a purchase. When trying on a bra, run in place or do jumping jacks. You want to make sure you get all the support you need.

Pregnancy Care

Most women can continue to exercise while pregnant. Several world-class athletes, such as runners Mary Decker-Slaney and Joan Benoit-Samuelson, have given birth to healthy babies and gone right back to competing. A pregnant athlete simply needs to consult her doctor, follow some simple guidelines, and pay attention to her body for signs of fatigue.

In 1985 the American College of Obstetrics and Gynecology (ACOG) developed a set of guidelines for women who plan to exercise during pregnancy. These guidelines recommend a target heart rate during pregnancy that is 25 to 30 percent lower than the nonpregnant target. You need to find your own comfortable exercise level. For a fit woman, 30 minutes is probably safe because the blood flow to the uterus is not significantly reduced within this time.

Keeping fit and maintaining good muscle tone is an important part of health care during pregnancy. Exercise prepares the body for labor, promotes good bowel function, aids in sleep, and makes a woman feel better in general. Women who exercise regularly during pregnancy have fewer cesarean births, less pain during delivery, shorter hospital stays, and slightly heavier babies compared with nonexercising women. Studies show that women who continue to run or participate in aerobic dance programs at intensities between 50 percent and 85 percent of maximum aerobic capacity do not increase their risk of early birth.

Strengthening muscles will help a woman deal with the low-back pain and other problems encountered during pregnancy due to weight gain and an altered center of gravity. There's no reason for a pregnant woman to avoid lifting heavy objects. That old myth should be put to rest.

Women who are in a regular exercise program certainly shouldn't take nine months off. If a woman is planning a pregnancy, she should exercise to get in shape before she becomes pregnant and then maintain her fitness during pregnancy.

Most prenatal classes, in addition to offering a selection of aerobically based exercises, have mothers-to-be work on specific muscle groups. These include three major areas: the shoulders and back, the abdominals, and the muscles at the base of the pelvis.

The safest sports during pregnancy are those that offer smooth, continuous activity as well as conditioning. Walking, swimming, cross-country skiing, and cycling are all excellent.

Exercising after Birth

Fit women tend to rebound quickly from childbirth. Most postpartum classes offer strength-training routines and exercises similar to those of prenatal classes. These classes help women build strength in the abdominal, back, and shoulder muscles, which is necessary for hoisting a baby around. An aerobic activity can help a woman shed the extra pounds gained during pregnancy. Within a month of giving birth, a woman should be able to see improvements in her aerobic capacity.

Many women who breast-feed are fearful that exercise may hinder their milk supply. But active women actually produce more milk than inactive women.

Before a woman starts any postpartum workout, the ACOG recommends that she check with her doctor.

Relieving Menstrual Woes

A regular, moderate exercise program can help relieve the painful, disabling symptoms of premenstrual syndrome as well as those of menopause. Exercise causes the pituitary gland to release endorphins, a group of substances chemically similar to morphine and thought to be the source of the elusive runner's high. Studies show that exercise can help ameliorate the aches and abdominal cramps associated with menstrual changes.

THE CHILD ATHLETE

The biggest problem I see with children is lack of exercise and conditioning. In an age when adults have become more involved in fitness, today's children are more obese and less physically fit than their older brothers and sisters, as well as their parents.

One reason for this is that watching television or playing computer games has replaced after-school play. Children will sit for hours amusing themselves in front of a television. Studies have shown that the more television children watch, the more likely they are to be overweight.

Another reason many children are in sorry shape is that physical education classes are no longer mandatory in most states. New Jersey is one of the few states that still requires mandatory gym classes. Yet even in New Jersey, one quarter of the gym class time is taken up by driver's education and one quarter by health education, so students really only get two quarters of physical education each year.

The whole concept of physical education in schools is due for an overhaul. Even in those areas where physical education is mandatory, children don't get enough uninterrupted class time to do much good. After they change clothes and have attendance taken, there probably is only about 20 minutes for actual exercise before they have to take a shower and change back to their street clothes. They exercise within the training range for only about 6 or 7 minutes of the available class time.

Even methods of punishment need to be rethought. If a child misbehaves in physical education class, the teacher usually makes him run laps. The child's punishment should be that he *can't* run or play at all.

The goal of physical education classes should be to teach children about the value of exercise and fitness so that they will continue to exercise on their own after they graduate. It would be much more beneficial to get students into cardiovascular conditioning and weight-training programs in high school and to give them instruction in lifestyle and life sports, such as tennis and golf.

Whether it's individualized weight training or team sports, it's important that children do something physical. Numerous studies show a correlation between academic performance and participation in high school sports and achievement in extracurricular activities. Children learn tremendous lessons concerning teamwork, sportsmanship, and social interactions, as well as the discipline of being coached and following instructions, lessons that will help them in later life.

GROWTH PLATE INJURIES

Despite rumors to the contrary, too much exercise does not stunt growth. In fact, exercise enhances growth. Problems arise only when young athletes push themselves to the point of overuse injuries.

The trauma of long-term training can damage joints that aren't completely developed. Before age 13, any activity that requires repetitive jumping, falling, or high-intensity training can affect a child's physical development by putting stress on the growth plates, the growing areas at the ends of bones at the joints. This is less of a problem among older teens, who have gone through most of their growth spurts.

The most common growth plate injury is Osgood-Schlatter disease, which causes swelling and marked tenderness in a lump of bone just below the knee. This piece of bone is the tibial tubercle, the area where the tendon from the kneecap attaches to the shin bone. It contains a growth center that controls the growth of the tubercle itself, not the whole leg. As the child gets bigger and heavier, the knob has to become bigger for the attachment of the tendon. In some children, the repetitive yanking of the kneecap tendon as they flex and extend the knee while running causes the growth center in the tubercle to become irritated. When a growth center is irritated, it becomes painful and is stimulated to overgrow.

Osgood-Schlatter disease, like most growth plate injuries, is self-limiting; that is, it always goes away by itself. By the time the child reaches age 17, the growth center closes, and the tendon is then pulling on a solid knob of bone. The pain disappears, but the lump under the knee does not. It is a permanent fixture in the child's bone.

This disease is self-limiting also because the more it hurts, the harder it is for the child to play. In the past, doctors limited what kids could do, and some kids sat out as much as two years waiting for the growth center to close. There is absolutely no reason for this, and we now allow a child to do whatever he or she can.

Only when the child says, "I can't play any more. It hurts too much," do I prescribe a knee immobilizer. The immobilizer keeps the knee straight and prevents the tendon from yanking on the growth center, which relieves the pain. This also prevents the child from running around, so the pain doesn't recur. The immobilizer is taken off every night to allow the child to shower and to test the tibial tubercle. When the bump under the knee is no longer tender to the touch, the child can return to activity.

Ice and aspirin or anti-inflammatory agents are also used to relieve any pain. Virtually all children can continue to play through this disability

I also recommend that the youngster wear a good pair of basketball or wrestling knee pads over the bump. Hitting the bump on the floor not only hurts tremendously but further irritates the condition.

See page 108

LITTLE LEAGUE ELBOW

A young pitcher who throws the ball too often or too hard may feel pain on the inner side of the elbow. The elbow may swell and be tender to the touch. The muscles that flex the wrist attach to a growth center on the inner side of the elbow. Throwing too much irritates this growth center, causing the area to overgrow and become painful.

The treatment is to rest the elbow by not throwing. If the pain is not severe, icing the elbow and taking anti-inflammatory agents will allow the pitcher to continue to play, but at a position where he doesn't have to throw very often, such as first base.

If the pain becomes severe, the child must cease activity entirely. Some young pitchers throw so hard that they tear the knob of bone off the elbow. The bone must then be reattached surgically and the elbow allowed to heal, and the child must refrain from throwing altogether.

See pages 83, 84

MD SLIPPED CAPITAL EPIPHYSIS

The growth plate in the neck of the thigh bone where it attaches to the hip can slip from overactivity. This disease, called slipped capital epiphysis, causes pain in the hip and sometimes in the knee as well. It also requires surgical repair. The pain prevents the child from doing any running at all. I tend to see this more often in very heavy children. The growth center is at an angle and is subjected to a shearing force when excessive weight is placed upon it.

SEVER'S DISEASE

Many children come to me with heel pain from running. I see it particularly in the spring and fall, when they begin running in cleats for football, soccer, or track. Many doctors diagnose this as an inflammation of the epiphyseal plate in the heel, which is known as Sever's disease. Pounding against the growth plate in the heel bone causes inflammation.

However, Sever's disease is extremely rare, and 99 percent of children with heel pain from running simply pronate their ankles too far. The ankle rolls to the inside, which leads to pounding on the heel. The stress of the heel hitting the ground is transmitted up through the thinner, inner portion of the heel bone, rather than the stronger middle portion, which causes pain.

Children who wear cleats are more susceptible to pronation because the points of the cleats have less contact with the ground than the wide, flat base of a sneaker. Put a pronator in cleats, and the shoe rolls even more to the inside.

If the child puts an arch support inside the shoe to prevent pronation, the heel pain usually goes away within two or three days, and the child is able to continue running. There is no way the pain could disappear so quickly if the growth center were inflamed from Sever's disease. Sometimes, I suggest that a youngster practice in sneakers and use cleats only during games.

See page 130

MD PELVIC PAIN

Young runners may experience severe pain in the upper rim of the pelvis. This area becomes tender to the touch because the upper rim of the pelvis is partially pulled away from the lower rim right at the site of the growth center in the hip.

This hip problem requires rest for six to eight weeks, and the child must stop running. Once the growth center is back to normal, the child can run again. Normally, this growth center closes at about age 15, and the child is no longer at risk of this problem.

CHILDHOOD ASTHMA

Asthma should not in any way restrict a child's ability to exercise and compete. An asthmatic child should be allowed to exercise at any level he or she is capable of, as long as he or she follows a physician's advice. If respiratory problems are severe, bronchodilating medications in pill form or administered through inhalers can increase a child's capacity to breathe normally and to compete.

There is one caveat: Asthma medications may affect performance, so I tell my patients with childhood asthma to use medications during practice or playtime before they use them during competition. Only then will the child know how he or she responds to the medications while exercising. Also, the use of some asthma medications is banned from higher levels of competition, so the athlete must know what he or she can use effectively. Then, along with a physician, the asthmatic athlete can make appropriate adjustments in the amount and type of medication.

Exercise-Induced Asthma

Asthma attacks usually result from exposure to environmental factors, but they may be induced by exercise. This condition, which I see fairly often among children, is called exercise-induced asthma. Mild symptoms can be managed by reducing the intensity of the exercise or with the help of an inhaler. To prevent an attack, I recommend a slow, prolonged warmup and a longer, but slightly less vigorous, aerobic activity period. An inhaler can be used before exercise, if necessary.

If you are participating in an organized sport or activity, let the coach or instructor know of this condition. Also make sure someone knows the location of the inhaler and whom to call in case of an emergency.

Children and others who are susceptible to exercise-induced asthma are unable to warm and moisten large amounts of air inhaled during exercise. The condition is worse in cold weather, and often bothersome only at low temperatures. Many people who experience exercise-induced asthma during the winter can exercise indoors without any symptoms. Indoor swimming is particularly helpful because of the warm, moist air surrounding the pool.

Athletes with exercise-induced asthma can exercise safely by using the same bronchodilating drugs prescribed for asthmas of other origins.

SPECIAL CONCERNS AND PRECAUTIONS

Pressure to Perform

From Little League age on up, children are pressured to participate in organized, competitive athletics. Everything today seems to be organized, with weekly games and rigidly scheduled leagues. Yet sports competition should be no more or less stressful than performing in the school play or playing in the school band.

The pressures of organized leagues can be difficult for children. It's not that they don't want to have fun, but that the parents and coaches take the fun out of the game for them. With so much pressure on them to win, they tend to burn out at an early age. I see children over and over again who don't want to play a particular sport any more. They come into my office with symptoms of injuries or overuse syndromes. They are afraid to tell the coach or their parents that they don't want to play, so they hide behind recurrent injuries. Parents need to be sensitive to the hidden language behind the excuses children use to avoid practice or competition.

Sports are supposed to be fun. According to a study of 10,000 students of ages 10 to 18 concerning their feelings about sports, "fun" is the critical factor in the decision to play or to drop out of a sport. For those who play, "fun" means improving skills, staying in shape, taking satisfaction in individual performance, and competing against others. Even among the most dedicated athletes, winning takes a back seat to "having fun," self-improvement, and the excitement of competition.

For those who drop out, the aspect of sports that is "not fun" is pressure—pressure to perform, to win, and to practice too much. There is no sense of play left.

An experiment from the 1970s shows the beneficial effects of fun. Philadelphia had two rival baseball leagues, one run by the Little League and the other run by the Police Athletic League (PAL). The Little League drafted players for teams and had playoffs for a championship. The PAL also drafted players, but every two weeks they broke up the teams and redrafted players so that everyone had different teammates and different coaches. There was no real pressure to win since teams changed character every two weeks.

When these children entered high school, their baseball skills were judged to be equal. Without pressure to perform, the PAL players had learned just as much. And they had half as many injuries as the Little Leaguers had.

Another prevalent problem involving pressure on young athletes concerns distance running. Young runners may begin by jogging with their parents. Then they start running races. It's not uncommon to see five-year-olds running 10-kilometer races.

No one knows the effect of long-distance running on children, but I suspect it is not good for them. Most children run until they are tired, flop down, rest, and then get up and run again. They listen to their bodies. We don't yet know all the ramifications of putting children into a training regimen so that they can compete in long races. What does the continuous pounding do to their growth plates? Running around on soft grass is not the same as running a 10-kilometer race on a hard road. Long-distance running can subject a growing body to unrelenting stresses and strains.

Run a child long and hard enough, and eventually he or she will develop stress fractures, back strain, knee injuries, and chronic tendinitis. If you do run with your child, which can be fun for both of you, let the child set the pace and intensity.

Fatigue

Fatigue is a common problem among young athletes. Teens need sleep to help their bodies grow. They also need extra energy to help their bodies grow, and this comes from a good, healthy diet.

Some teens lack sufficient iron in their bodies. Even though their iron deficiency may not be severe enough to produce anemia, it can slow their growth, deplete their energy supply, and lead to poor sports performance. Although iron deficiency is usually associated with girls, boys also lose iron during strenuous exercise.

In general, I don't think vitamin supplements are appropriate for young athletes. Most of them eat a lot, and as long as they eat a balanced diet, they don't need vitamin supplements. For a picky eater, supplements may be beneficial.

Children cannot be regarded as little adults. The American Academy of Orthopedic Surgeons has outlined some physiologic distinctions. Children must sustain higher heart and breathing rates than adults, so they burn more calories and tire faster. Children are less efficient at using the muscle fuel glycogen, so, even taking into account the size difference, they cannot produce as much muscle power as adults.

Sensitivity to Temperature

Children take longer to adjust to abrupt increases in heat and humidity and therefore have an increased risk of dehydration in hot weather. Children also don't generate as much heat in the winter, so they should dress warmly in extremely cold weather.

Fears about Football

I am often asked about the safety of Pop Warner football. It is supposedly dangerous because of the risk of blows to the extremities, which can cause growth plate injuries. But I really see few injuries among these youngest football players. These children don't weigh very much or run very fast; consequently, they don't run into each other hard enough to hurt themselves much. I applaud the use of equipment and the supervision these players get. Their games are much safer than the sandlot games that are played without proper equipment and supervision, where anything goes.

High school players suffer more injuries, often because bigger players go up against smaller players of the same age. About one-third of the nation's one million high school football players are sidelined by an injury at least once, but the majority of injuries are not serious. About half are sprains and strains, and about one-third are cuts and bruises. Less than 10 percent are major injuries that require the athlete to miss a few weeks of action. Two out of three injuries are suffered during practice, when there usually are no trainers available, and the remainder occur during games, which are supervised by trainers and emergency medical personnel.

In contrast, high school track and field athletes are more likely to suffer a serious injury, such as a broken bone, and will be sidelined longer. On average, an injured football player is out for about a week, whereas a track athlete stays out for three or four weeks.

Sudden Death

Despite the attention it receives in the media, sudden death is a rare occurrence among young athletes. Only 1 or 2 out of 200,000 athletes under age 30 dies suddenly each year. About 5 in every 100,000 young athletes have a heart condition that places them at risk for sudden death, and only 1 in 10 of them dies suddenly.

Safeguards for Playing

Each year more than 20 million boys and girls in the United States participate in nonschool recreational and competitive sports. Yet most volunteer coaches are unaware of a young athlete's vulnerability to injury, especially overuse injury. The coaches that supervise community sports programs are usually less experienced and knowledgeable than school phys ed instructors. Parents should assess the qualifications and techniques of their children's coaches and sports teachers.

Every youth sports program should require a child to have a physical exam before he or she can play. This provides a pediatrician the opportunity to check for problems associated with specific sports and to assess a child's overall health. Facilities and equipment should be well maintained. Policies should be established for first aid, referral, and treatment of injured players. Ideally, a certified athletic trainer should be on hand for games, although this is not generally feasible. Every athlete should go through warmup and warmdown exercises before and after practices and games.

The Dangers of Steroids

An increasing concern among parents is the popularity of anabolic steroids and other performance enhancers. The medical issues surrounding the use of these insidious drugs don't seem to concern young athletes. Very few side effects of steroid use are immediately apparent, so young athletes are more likely to continue using steroids, ignoring the serious long-term medical implications. For more about steroids and their effects, see Chapter 3.

Influencing adolescent athletes' attitudes toward steroids requires more than merely presenting information about the medical consequences of their use. Providing alternatives to performance-enhancing drugs, such as advice about good nutrition and strength-training techniques, may be more effective in discouraging steroid use. Approaches that enhance self-esteem, similar to those used in substance abuse programs, may help to keep adolescent athletes off steroids.

Fortunately, steroid use is not difficult to detect. If your teenage son has undergone an aggressive personality change, has put on 30 pounds of solid muscle in the past year, and has developed severe acne on his upper body, chances are he hasn't just been eating his Wheaties. These are clear signs of steroid abuse. Other physical signs of steroid use in a teenage boy are hair loss, breast growth, and smaller testicles, which may lead to impotence.

Infant Exercise

Infant exercise programs are all the rage today, but I see no reason for them. Infants move as much as they are capable of, and toddlers never seem to stop. I'd like to see a fit adult try to keep up with a toddler. He'd poop out in half a day.

There is no evidence that gym and swim classes will speed a baby's development of strength and balance, according to the American Academy of Pediatrics. Children develop skills in crawling, walking, jumping, and running through normal play. Each child is different and will progress at his or her own rate.

What's more, very young children could sustain injuries from overly strenuous exercise. Broken bones, muscle strains, and dislocated limbs have resulted from infant exercise programs.

Like any other child who grew up in the cold part of the country, I learned to ice-skate at age 3. My parents gave me an old kitchen chair to push around the ice until I was able to let go and not fall down. In the summer, we all splashed around in the water until someone began to move, and then we all did what he did. That's how I learned to swim. I firmly believe that the best sports training for infants or young children is simply to allow them to do what comes naturally.

THE OLDER ATHLETE

Molly, an 83-year-old tennis player, came to me because her elbow was bothering her. She played tennis every afternoon with her girlfriends, and she had begun to feel pain right after playing. I put Molly on a light weight-training program using dumbbells and stretching, and I told her to come back in a few weeks. When she returned, she said her elbow hurt even more. So I sat her down and had her describe her rehabilitation program to find out exactly what she was doing. Rather than doing 50 repetitions of the exercises I had given her, she was doing 500. No wonder her elbow pain was worse! I found it hard to yell at a well-meaning Jewish grandmother, so I asked her granddaughter to make sure Molly did only as much as she was supposed to do, not 10 times more. Within a few months, Molly was again frolicking pain-free on the tennis court.

There is a common misconception that older people should remain sedentary because exercise could cause injuries and place undue strain on the heart. However, research now shows that much of what doctors have ascribed to aging is actually due to inactivity. Time and time again, I am visited by an elderly patient who complains that her doctor said she shouldn't exercise because she is too old, that exercise is not good for her. This is a trap many doctors fall into. Exercise is good for people regardless of their age.

If your doctor takes the easy way out and says, "Don't exercise," you may be better off finding a new doctor. Most doctors can carefully determine what you can do physically and design a safe exercise program for you.

Some doctors flatly state that anyone over 35 or 40 should check with a doctor before beginning a new exercise program. I don't agree. If you have been exercising regularly for many years, you probably can continue to exercise quite safely without a doctor's prescription. Only those people with known chronic diseases, such as high blood pressure, heart disease, lung disease, and diabetes, need to consult a doctor first.

Someone who decides late in life to take up exercise needs to avoid undue stress on the heart. A sedentary older person who decides to start exercising regularly should have a complete, thorough checkup, particularly to ascertain the status of the heart.

This does not mean that if you have heart disease you can't exercise. Exercise will benefit someone with mild to moderate heart disease by strengthening the entire cardiovascular system. Your doctor can set limits and outline appropriate levels of exercise. You should start your exercise program at a low level and advance very slowly so that you don't overstress your body.

MIDDLE-AGED ATHLETES

Athletes in their forties and fifties should continue to exercise at whatever level they are capable of. They should not feel that because they are over 40 they have to cut back.

If an athlete is exercising at competitive level at age 39 or 49, the change in the level of exercise at age 40 or 50 should be totally insignificant. Keep doing what you have been doing until, for some reason, you can't do it any more. However, with increasing age, it becomes more and more important to listen to your body. It will tell when you are abusing it and when you should begin to back off. Injury or sickness can also cause an athlete to reduce his or her exercise level.

Pitcher Nolan Ryan and boxer George Foreman have shown that athletes in their forties can compete with men half their age. But Nolan and George are anomalies. Emulating them may lead to injury and frustration, which the aging athlete certainly doesn't need.

ELDERLY ATHLETES

Elderly athletes are capable of participating in virtually all of the sports young people do. But they do need to take care to warm up properly. The warmup and warmdown periods should be almost as long as the exercise session itself. Take 10 to 20 minutes to warm up, then exercise for 20 to 30 minutes, and take another 10 to 20 minutes to warm down.

An older athlete's injuries may take longer to heal, so be careful to rehabilitate yourself fully, and slowly, before returning to activity.

Also, the elderly are much more likely to suffer from heat stress and dehydration than younger people. So make sure to drink plenty of liquids before and during exercise.

THE BENEFITS OF EXERCISE

We have to get away from the idea that if you can't run a marathon, you aren't fit. An elderly person needs only take a few brisk walks each week to increase his or her odds of living a long, healthy life. Almost any daily activity can increase the workload on the muscles and raise the heart rate. The elderly can keep fit by doing ordinary, useful activities such as mowing the lawn, cleaning the bathroom, and working in the yard.

Exercise strengthens the heart and lungs, lowers blood pressure and cholesterol, thickens bones, tones muscles, and may improve memory. Moderate exercise also seems to boost the immune system and improve the reflexes of elderly athletes. Because of these benefits, elderly people who exercise tend to outlive their inactive contemporaries by two or three years. Even if they don't live longer, they will probably live better and remain independent longer. Thus, exercise improves the quality as well as the quantity of life.

Weight Loss

Weight loss is very important for the elderly. Everyone tends to put on weight with age, and it becomes more difficult to lose weight with the advancing years. New data out of the Framingham Heart Study reveal that being overweight at age 65 is accompanied by a significant increase in mortality.

Exercise is still the best way to lose weight. A regular exercise program combined with a good, healthy diet will help you to keep your weight down.

It doesn't matter what you do as long as you burn calories. Walking is just as good as running. The only difference is that it takes a little longer to burn calories through walking.

A good diet is an essential part of any exercise program. Elderly people who successfully strengthen their muscles usually also eat well. Food provides the basic building blocks for muscle.

Muscle Strength

Stronger muscles enable the elderly to perform daily tasks more easily. Also, increased strength can help prevent falls, the leading cause of injury in older people. Just by lifting one-pound dumbbells and increasing the weight gradually, an elderly person can markedly increase his or her strength. I have found that bedridden people respond well to light weight training, and I recommend that all older athletes incorporate light weight training into their regular activities.

Exercise all the major muscle groups two or three times a week for 20 to 30 minutes a session. Work on muscles of the chest, back, and trunk as well as the limbs. Light toning exercises are all that's necessary to increase strength.

Certain people with chronic diseases should be carefully evaluated before they are allowed to begin a strength-training program. These include people with high blood pressure, those with uncontrolled angina, and those who have recently had a heart attack.

Even very feeble people in their late eighties and nineties can benefit from light weight training. In one study, a group of frail nursing home residents, ages 86 to 96, achieved dramatic gains in strength, muscle mass, and walking speed after an eight-week program of supervised, high-resistance leg training. By the end of two months, most participants had achieved a three- to fourfold increase in leg strength.

Just as younger athletes must "use it or lose it," an ongoing conditioning program proved necessary to maintain these improvements in muscle strength. After a month of inactivity, the nursing home residents' leg strength dropped by one-third.

These findings show that improvements in muscle strength, size, and mobility from exercise are not restricted to younger athletes. They also challenge the theory that muscle strength must decline with age. As we age, there is an unavoidable, biologically determined decline in muscle size; this is true even for elite athletes over age 40. Muscle strength declines 30 to 40 percent over the average adult's life span. However, an increasingly sedentary lifestyle causes muscles to atrophy more quickly, and older people tend to lose more strength than necessary simply because they decrease their activity level.

Well-Being

Even if you don't reach that peak range known as the exercise "high," a good exercise program can increase your physical and emotional well-being. Healthy older people say that they look better and that they have more energy, endurance, and flexibility. They sleep better, are more satisfied with life, and experience less anxiety.

In addition to its health benefits, exercise increases your self-esteem. It's a good feeling to know that your body is not deteriorating. You can still do things and be active. You show yourself and others that you are not ready for a wheelchair just yet.

Even if you are over age 65, you can control your physical and physiological destiny through exercise. Working out regularly can keep you physiologically younger. Exercising slows the various aging processes, such as the deterioration of muscle and connective tissue and the increase of fat. And it's never too late to begin.

Simple stretching, range-of-motion, and deep-breathing exercises were shown to significantly improve the health and mobility of people in their seventies and beyond who were overweight, who had never exercised regularly, and who had serious chronic ailments, including arthritis, high blood pressure, heart disease, and diabetes.

Sharper Reflexes

Fitness helps to shorten reaction time by improving circulation in the brain. An active person of age 65 can have quicker reflexes than an unfit person 40 years his junior.

Aerobic exercise can improve short-term memory, reaction time, and mental flexibility. People who exercise regularly process information faster than those who don't. Active people can react quickly enough to break a fall with their hands, whereas inactive people are more likely to fall with full force on their hips, which often results in permanent disability. So keeping the body active helps keep the brain active.

Special Benefits for Exercising Women

Exercise may benefit women even more than men. Walking and running help reduce bone loss and prevent osteoporosis. Bone densities are much higher in exercising women than in those who are sedentary.

Also, women who exercise regularly starting at a young age are less likely to develop breast cancer. Obesity increases the risks of breast cancer, and exercise helps women remain lean. Researchers have reported lower rates of breast and reproductive system cancer in women who were athletes in college compared to their non-active classmates.

In addition, elderly women who regularly perform endurance exercises have been found to undergo greater changes in cholesterol level compared with middle-aged women who exercise.

Additional Health Benefits

Many elderly people have stomach and intestinal tract problems. The increase in circulation brought on by exercise increases the tone of the gastrointestinal tract and prevents many of these problems.

A person who has had a stroke or some muscular dysfunction certainly can benefit from exercise. Individualized exercise programs can help post-stroke patients return to a lifestyle as close to normal as possible.

There is no evidence that aerobic exercise such as running, swimming, cycling, or walking causes arthritis or joint damage. Exercise, within reasonable limits, is good because it preserves the health of joints and muscles. I have found that people who suffer aches and pains from mild osteoarthritis do well if they keep their joints active.

36

How to Select a Sports Specialist

When an injury does not respond to home treatment, then it's time to seek medical advice. Your family doctor or hospital emergency room personnel may be able to diagnose and treat simple problems. For more subtle or debilitating problems, a qualified sports medicine specialist may be necessary. For serious injuries that may require surgery, you should go to an orthopedic surgeon whose practice is devoted full-time to sports medicine.

Finding a reputable sports medicine specialist can be difficult. Although the ranks of sports doctors have grown from a few hundred in the early 1970s to more than 10,000 today, there is no formal certification in sports medicine. Any doctor who wants to tap this increasingly lucrative market can simply hang out a shingle that says "Sports Medicine." But a sign on the door is no guarantee that the treatment you get inside will cure your tennis elbow or runner's knee.

As a result of this situation, many patients are confused and angry about their care. Typically, a patient comes to me and says, "I went to two other sports doctors, and they didn't do any of the things you did. How can they be sports doctors?" That's a difficult question to answer. Most people don't want to hear that anyone can be a sports doctor. They want to know how to find a good doctor who can help them.

THE TEMPTATION OF TECHNOLOGY

A pseudo sports doctor who doesn't know why, for example, a patient has a sore ankle may be tempted to resort to modalities such as ultrasound or electrical stimulation to cure the patient. Such an approach can only evoke bad feelings.

One of the basic tenets of sports medicine is to make an early, accurate diagnosis and to prescribe a specific treatment. The doctor who is scattered in his approach to treatment is not practicing true sports medicine.

Many pseudo sports doctors order a battery of tests on the principle that it is better to be safe than sorry. Many of the estimated 500,000 arthroscopy procedures done each year, at $2,500 and up, may be unnecessary. As with all surgery, you should consider obtaining a second opinion even if your doctor is convinced that arthroscopy is necessary.

There is an effort underway to cut back on these tests because sports doctors now realize that they have been ordering too many. The true sports doctor uses arthroscopy as a diagnostic tool only when noninvasive diagnostic procedures have failed. Arthroscopy is basically used to correct a specific problem after an accurate diagnosis has been made.

TYPES OF SPORTS SPECIALISTS

There are various types of sports medicine specialists, and each has its own qualifications and training requirements. Before you select a specialist, examine his or her qualifications carefully.

Primary care sports doctors usually are trained in family practice, internal medicine, or physiatry, which is a branch of medicine that treats diseases and body defects with a physical therapy approach. These doctors have an interest in injury prevention, conditioning, flexibility, biomechanics, and nutrition. Their aim is to bring athletes to their peak performance level and to keep them injury-free. They usually do not treat sports injuries that require surgery.

Orthopedic surgeons are doctors who specialize in the bones and the joints. Sports orthopedists have special medical training in sports injuries. They perform operations and repair fractures, and they can treat any type of sports injury. However, sports orthopedists are usually not as concerned with strains, sprains, and overuse injuries as are primary care doctors.

Osteopaths are doctors who utilize both medical approaches and manipulative approaches in caring for athletes, although in recent years, manipulation has been left primarily to chiropractors. There is almost no difference between the medical training of a doctor of osteopathy (D.O.) and that of a medical doctor (M.D.).

Chiropractors are trained in spinal manipulation. In the sports field, they have branched out to manipulation of the limbs and joints as alternative treatments. A chiropractor (D.C.) has gone to a school of chiropractic medicine and is not licensed to prescribe medication or to perform surgery.

Podiatrists are doctors who limit their practice to parts of the body below the knee. They spend four years studying this area, whereas an M.D. spends the same time studying the entire body. Sports podiatrists are particularly knowledgeable about injuries related to running sports and the treatment of conditions that stem from foot problems.

Physical therapists are trained in rehabilitation techniques. They have a broad knowledge of anatomy and are experts in modalities for bringing an injured athlete back to health. They must take special courses to be licensed in physical therapy.

Athletic trainers are skilled in conditioning techniques; injury prevention, including taping and bracing; on-the-field diagnosis; and first aid for acute sports injuries. Trainers also understand how to rehabilitate athletes so that they can return to action from injuries. They are certified through a special training program to aid sports doctors.

A good sports medicine clinic should offer a team approach to patient care, using the expertise of all of the types of sports specialists. The primary care doctor can mix and match these techniques and steer you in the right direction to receive the highest level of care. This has been the basis of the success of my practice over the years.

HOW TO LOCATE A SPORTS SPECIALIST

The first sanctioned board-certifying examination in sports medicine will be offered in 1993. Board-certified family physicians, internists, pediatricians, and emergency medicine specialists will be eligible for a certificate of added qualification in sports medicine. Osteopaths will be able to earn a similar secondary certification in sports medicine. These exams will help control the specialty and let an injured athlete know who is a qualified sports doctor. To pass these board exams, a doctor will need special training and a good working knowledge of sports medicine. Until now, sports medicine practitioners have arranged their own training, and this has contributed to the wide variation in skills seen among the sports medicine fraternity.

The best recommendation for a sports doctor may come from a friend who has just been treated for a sports injury. Or your family doctor or local medical center may be able to make a referral.

The American Orthopaedic Society for Sports Medicine and the American Medical Society for Sports Medicine can provide you with names of members in your area. The American College of Sports Medicine (ACSM) provides a similar service, though not all of the members are doctors. A medical journal, *The Physician & Sportsmedicine,* publishes an annual list of sports medicine clinics across the country.

Doctors who belong to these two medical societies, as well as the American Academy of Sports Physicians, are the most likely to have up-to-date information, skills, and training. Young doctors in the field should have at least a year-long fellowship at a sports medicine clinic as part of their postgraduate training.

There are many fellowships available at orthopedic sports medicine clinics and a growing number at primary care sports medicine clinics across the country. In the late 1980s there were only a handful of primary care specialty fellowships, including the one that our sports medicine department ran. Now there are several dozen, and more are being added each year.

These fellows have a depth of knowledge in sports medicine. This usually encompasses the physiology of exercise and how to apply it to the training and conditioning of athletes; the functional anatomy and pathology of biomechanical sports injuries; and the diagnosis, first aid, and full rehabilitation of traumatic injuries. Fellows may provide medical coverage of local sports events or be the team doctor for a local team. They often conduct research into sports injuries and the problems of sports and exercise.

If you can't find a doctor who has a fellowship in sports medicine, find one in your area who is a team doctor. Many of today's team doctors learned how to treat athletes on a trial-and-error basis, as I did, and never received a fellowship in sports medicine. The doctors who dash out onto the field to tend to a fallen player, from high school sports to the professionals, may be ortho-

pedic surgeons, family physicians, cardiologists, or eye doctors. Even a high school team doctor who is not trained in sports medicine is used to handling injuries and shows an interest in helping athletes, which is the first step to becoming a good sports doctor.

Certainly, a doctor who takes care of a professional or college team should be well qualified. You can call some local sports teams and ask where their athletes are treated. The ACSM is looking into the prospects of certifying team doctors, which will further help to clarify who is a well-qualified sports specialist.

Another good source is your local running or cycling club. These clubs usually have identified the best local sports doctors and refer their members to them. They know who gets good results and who doesn't.

If you choose a doctor who tells you to go home and stay off your injury for three weeks, choose again. An important part of being a sports doctor is understanding the psychology of athletes, who are determined to play at all costs. Doctors who are not accustomed to treating athletes tend to take the safest course and simply say, "Don't play." They often fail to consider how much of an athlete's life is dedicated to keeping fit and having fun.

WHAT TO LOOK FOR IN A SPORTS SPECIALIST

You can arm yourself with questions to ask about a sports medicine specialist's qualifications:

- *Who will treat me, a physician or a nonphysician?* Many insurance companies won't cover care that isn't ordered by a physician. Check with your insurance carrier before receiving treatment from a nonphysician.

- *What are the doctor's professional affiliations?* It's a good sign if your sports doctor is a member of one of the medical specialty groups mentioned earlier, although there are good sports doctors who have no professional affiliation.

- *Does the doctor have special training?* Look for a doctor with a fellowship in sports medicine, either through orthopedic surgery or family practice. Also, a sports medicine specialist should deal with all areas of sports medicine, not just cardiovascular fitness.

- *Does the doctor or clinic offer a full range of diagnostic and rehabilitation services?* The most comprehensive sports medicine clinics include an orthopedic surgeon, an internist, a podiatrist, a physical therapist, and a trainer. A sports medicine clinic is no more reliable than its individual practitioners and should be closely scrutinized. Also, check whether the clinic has state-of-the-art isokinetic machines, such as Cybex, for rehabilitation.

- *How much will the treatment cost?* A sports doctor shouldn't charge any more for a procedure than any other doctor. If you have doubts, ask your insurance carrier what the customary fee is for a particular procedure.

- *How much time does the doctor spend on sports medicine?* Only a few practitioners are full-time sports specialists. Many spend about 30 to 40 percent of their time practicing sports medicine.

- *Does the doctor have any special areas of practice?* You should choose a specialist to meet your needs. If you have a knee injury, seek out an orthopedist who specializes in knee problems. If you are having irregular menstrual periods, find an obstetrician-gynecologist who specializes in women's sports problems.

Index

BARRON'S

MAT

MILLER
ANALOGIES TEST

10TH EDITION

Robert J. Sternberg, Ph.D.
Dean of the School of Arts and Sciences,
Professor of Psychology at Tufts University

Karin Sternberg, Ph.D.
Sternberg Consulting, LLC

BARRON'S

All inquiries should be addressed to:
Barron's Educational Series, Inc.
250 Wireless Boulevard
Hauppauge, New York 11788
www.barronseduc.com

ISBN-13: 978-0-7641-4235-2
ISBN-10: 0-7641-4235-6

International Standard Serial No. 1533-7715

Printed in the United States of America

9 8 7 6 5 4 3

FSC
Mixed Sources
Product group from well-managed
forests and other controlled sources

Cert no. SW-COC-002507
www.fsc.org
© 1996 Forest Stewardship Council

Contents

Introduction

WHAT THIS BOOK CAN DO FOR YOU

This book is designed to help bring you to the point where your performance on the *Miller Analogies Test (MAT)* is the best of which you are capable. If the book succeeds in doing so, it has succeeded admirably, and so have you.

Many individuals do not reveal their true abilities on the *MAT* and other standardized tests. There are several reasons why this is so:

1. *The mystique of standardized tests.* One reason for underperformance stems from the aura of mystery that surrounds standardized tests. The mystique of standardized tests evolves from three common misconceptions. The first misconception is that the tests evaluate the whole person. In fact, the tests evaluate just a small segment of the person's behavior, and their evaluation of this small segment of behavior is, as we shall soon see, highly fallible. A second misconception is that there is nothing one can do to improve one's test performance, since the tests measure something that is innate rather than something that is learned. In fact, there is a great deal you can do to improve your test score, and in reading this book and in working on the practice tests, you are already doing it. The third misconception is an emotional one—it is the feeling of awe that people often have when faced with something they don't understand. By the time you are done with this book, however, you will understand the *Miller Analogies Test* very well, and what once seemed mysterious to you will be quite familiar.

   There are certain basic facts about the *MAT* that anyone who is to take the test ought to know. Some of these facts are readily available to the public through various pamphlets provided by the test publisher, but others are not. Many of the most important facts are among the least well known. Parts Two and Four of this book contain the basic facts that you ought to know about the *MAT*.

2. *Unfamiliarity with test-taking strategies and skills.* Many individuals never acquire the test-taking strategies and skills that would enable them to optimize their performance on the *MAT*. As a result, they make blunders that reflect their deficiencies in test-taking rather than in intellectual ability. Part Three of this book shows you just what an analogy is, the types of analogies that appear on the *MAT*, and the strategies you can employ to systematically

V

approach *MAT* problems. Included are helpful hints that will prove useful to you in preparing for and then taking the actual test.

Part Five will help you in learning the words commonly used on the *MAT* and in reviewing some of the basic facts from the content areas used in the test. As you will see, the number of questions from each content area is small, and an extensive review of all possible areas is simply unfeasible.

TIP

Although there are 120 items, only 100 are scored. The other 20 are experimental items. It is not possible to tell which items are scored and which are experimental.

3. *Lack of practice in taking MAT-type tests.* It is one thing to have developed a repertoire of test-taking strategies and skills, but it is another to readily apply them. Part Six of this book contains ten practice tests that are similar in difficulty, content, and form to the actual *MAT*. Like the actual test, each practice test has 120 items, is timed for 60 minutes, and requires a multiple-choice answer selection process from among four possible alternatives. As in the real test, answers are recorded on a separate answer sheet. By taking these tests, you will have an opportunity to utilize the test-taking strategies that you will acquire. You will build up a facility with *MAT*-type questions so that when you take the actual test, you will not have to waste time and points warming up to the types of questions that appear.

Before reading about the *MAT* and how to improve your performance on it, take the pretest in Part One to give yourself a sense of what the *MAT* is like. You will then stand to profit more from the suggestions that follow.

Answer Sheet
PRETEST

1 Ⓐ Ⓑ Ⓒ Ⓓ	31 Ⓐ Ⓑ Ⓒ Ⓓ	61 Ⓐ Ⓑ Ⓒ Ⓓ	91 Ⓐ Ⓑ Ⓒ Ⓓ
2 Ⓐ Ⓑ Ⓒ Ⓓ	32 Ⓐ Ⓑ Ⓒ Ⓓ	62 Ⓐ Ⓑ Ⓒ Ⓓ	92 Ⓐ Ⓑ Ⓒ Ⓓ
3 Ⓐ Ⓑ Ⓒ Ⓓ	33 Ⓐ Ⓑ Ⓒ Ⓓ	63 Ⓐ Ⓑ Ⓒ Ⓓ	93 Ⓐ Ⓑ Ⓒ Ⓓ
4 Ⓐ Ⓑ Ⓒ Ⓓ	34 Ⓐ Ⓑ Ⓒ Ⓓ	64 Ⓐ Ⓑ Ⓒ Ⓓ	94 Ⓐ Ⓑ Ⓒ Ⓓ
5 Ⓐ Ⓑ Ⓒ Ⓓ	35 Ⓐ Ⓑ Ⓒ Ⓓ	65 Ⓐ Ⓑ Ⓒ Ⓓ	95 Ⓐ Ⓑ Ⓒ Ⓓ
6 Ⓐ Ⓑ Ⓒ Ⓓ	36 Ⓐ Ⓑ Ⓒ Ⓓ	66 Ⓐ Ⓑ Ⓒ Ⓓ	96 Ⓐ Ⓑ Ⓒ Ⓓ
7 Ⓐ Ⓑ Ⓒ Ⓓ	37 Ⓐ Ⓑ Ⓒ Ⓓ	67 Ⓐ Ⓑ Ⓒ Ⓓ	97 Ⓐ Ⓑ Ⓒ Ⓓ
8 Ⓐ Ⓑ Ⓒ Ⓓ	38 Ⓐ Ⓑ Ⓒ Ⓓ	68 Ⓐ Ⓑ Ⓒ Ⓓ	98 Ⓐ Ⓑ Ⓒ Ⓓ
9 Ⓐ Ⓑ Ⓒ Ⓓ	39 Ⓐ Ⓑ Ⓒ Ⓓ	69 Ⓐ Ⓑ Ⓒ Ⓓ	99 Ⓐ Ⓑ Ⓒ Ⓓ
10 Ⓐ Ⓑ Ⓒ Ⓓ	40 Ⓐ Ⓑ Ⓒ Ⓓ	70 Ⓐ Ⓑ Ⓒ Ⓓ	100 Ⓐ Ⓑ Ⓒ Ⓓ
11 Ⓐ Ⓑ Ⓒ Ⓓ	41 Ⓐ Ⓑ Ⓒ Ⓓ	71 Ⓐ Ⓑ Ⓒ Ⓓ	101 Ⓐ Ⓑ Ⓒ Ⓓ
12 Ⓐ Ⓑ Ⓒ Ⓓ	42 Ⓐ Ⓑ Ⓒ Ⓓ	72 Ⓐ Ⓑ Ⓒ Ⓓ	102 Ⓐ Ⓑ Ⓒ Ⓓ
13 Ⓐ Ⓑ Ⓒ Ⓓ	43 Ⓐ Ⓑ Ⓒ Ⓓ	73 Ⓐ Ⓑ Ⓒ Ⓓ	103 Ⓐ Ⓑ Ⓒ Ⓓ
14 Ⓐ Ⓑ Ⓒ Ⓓ	44 Ⓐ Ⓑ Ⓒ Ⓓ	74 Ⓐ Ⓑ Ⓒ Ⓓ	104 Ⓐ Ⓑ Ⓒ Ⓓ
15 Ⓐ Ⓑ Ⓒ Ⓓ	45 Ⓐ Ⓑ Ⓒ Ⓓ	75 Ⓐ Ⓑ Ⓒ Ⓓ	105 Ⓐ Ⓑ Ⓒ Ⓓ
16 Ⓐ Ⓑ Ⓒ Ⓓ	46 Ⓐ Ⓑ Ⓒ Ⓓ	76 Ⓐ Ⓑ Ⓒ Ⓓ	106 Ⓐ Ⓑ Ⓒ Ⓓ
17 Ⓐ Ⓑ Ⓒ Ⓓ	47 Ⓐ Ⓑ Ⓒ Ⓓ	77 Ⓐ Ⓑ Ⓒ Ⓓ	107 Ⓐ Ⓑ Ⓒ Ⓓ
18 Ⓐ Ⓑ Ⓒ Ⓓ	48 Ⓐ Ⓑ Ⓒ Ⓓ	78 Ⓐ Ⓑ Ⓒ Ⓓ	108 Ⓐ Ⓑ Ⓒ Ⓓ
19 Ⓐ Ⓑ Ⓒ Ⓓ	49 Ⓐ Ⓑ Ⓒ Ⓓ	79 Ⓐ Ⓑ Ⓒ Ⓓ	109 Ⓐ Ⓑ Ⓒ Ⓓ
20 Ⓐ Ⓑ Ⓒ Ⓓ	50 Ⓐ Ⓑ Ⓒ Ⓓ	80 Ⓐ Ⓑ Ⓒ Ⓓ	110 Ⓐ Ⓑ Ⓒ Ⓓ
21 Ⓐ Ⓑ Ⓒ Ⓓ	51 Ⓐ Ⓑ Ⓒ Ⓓ	81 Ⓐ Ⓑ Ⓒ Ⓓ	111 Ⓐ Ⓑ Ⓒ Ⓓ
22 Ⓐ Ⓑ Ⓒ Ⓓ	52 Ⓐ Ⓑ Ⓒ Ⓓ	82 Ⓐ Ⓑ Ⓒ Ⓓ	112 Ⓐ Ⓑ Ⓒ Ⓓ
23 Ⓐ Ⓑ Ⓒ Ⓓ	53 Ⓐ Ⓑ Ⓒ Ⓓ	83 Ⓐ Ⓑ Ⓒ Ⓓ	113 Ⓐ Ⓑ Ⓒ Ⓓ
24 Ⓐ Ⓑ Ⓒ Ⓓ	54 Ⓐ Ⓑ Ⓒ Ⓓ	84 Ⓐ Ⓑ Ⓒ Ⓓ	114 Ⓐ Ⓑ Ⓒ Ⓓ
25 Ⓐ Ⓑ Ⓒ Ⓓ	55 Ⓐ Ⓑ Ⓒ Ⓓ	85 Ⓐ Ⓑ Ⓒ Ⓓ	115 Ⓐ Ⓑ Ⓒ Ⓓ
26 Ⓐ Ⓑ Ⓒ Ⓓ	56 Ⓐ Ⓑ Ⓒ Ⓓ	86 Ⓐ Ⓑ Ⓒ Ⓓ	116 Ⓐ Ⓑ Ⓒ Ⓓ
27 Ⓐ Ⓑ Ⓒ Ⓓ	57 Ⓐ Ⓑ Ⓒ Ⓓ	87 Ⓐ Ⓑ Ⓒ Ⓓ	117 Ⓐ Ⓑ Ⓒ Ⓓ
28 Ⓐ Ⓑ Ⓒ Ⓓ	58 Ⓐ Ⓑ Ⓒ Ⓓ	88 Ⓐ Ⓑ Ⓒ Ⓓ	118 Ⓐ Ⓑ Ⓒ Ⓓ
29 Ⓐ Ⓑ Ⓒ Ⓓ	59 Ⓐ Ⓑ Ⓒ Ⓓ	89 Ⓐ Ⓑ Ⓒ Ⓓ	119 Ⓐ Ⓑ Ⓒ Ⓓ
30 Ⓐ Ⓑ Ⓒ Ⓓ	60 Ⓐ Ⓑ Ⓒ Ⓓ	90 Ⓐ Ⓑ Ⓒ Ⓓ	120 Ⓐ Ⓑ Ⓒ Ⓓ

Answer Sheet

PRETEST

1	Ⓐ Ⓑ Ⓒ Ⓓ	31	Ⓐ Ⓑ Ⓒ Ⓓ	61	Ⓐ Ⓑ Ⓒ Ⓓ	91	Ⓐ Ⓑ Ⓒ Ⓓ
2	Ⓐ Ⓑ Ⓒ Ⓓ	32	Ⓐ Ⓑ Ⓒ Ⓓ	62	Ⓐ Ⓑ Ⓒ Ⓓ	92	Ⓐ Ⓑ Ⓒ Ⓓ
3	Ⓐ Ⓑ Ⓒ Ⓓ	33	Ⓐ Ⓑ Ⓒ Ⓓ	63	Ⓐ Ⓑ Ⓒ Ⓓ	93	Ⓐ Ⓑ Ⓒ Ⓓ
4	Ⓐ Ⓑ Ⓒ Ⓓ	34	Ⓐ Ⓑ Ⓒ Ⓓ	64	Ⓐ Ⓑ Ⓒ Ⓓ	94	Ⓐ Ⓑ Ⓒ Ⓓ
5	Ⓐ Ⓑ Ⓒ Ⓓ	35	Ⓐ Ⓑ Ⓒ Ⓓ	65	Ⓐ Ⓑ Ⓒ Ⓓ	95	Ⓐ Ⓑ Ⓒ Ⓓ
6	Ⓐ Ⓑ Ⓒ Ⓓ	36	Ⓐ Ⓑ Ⓒ Ⓓ	66	Ⓐ Ⓑ Ⓒ Ⓓ	96	Ⓐ Ⓑ Ⓒ Ⓓ
7	Ⓐ Ⓑ Ⓒ Ⓓ	37	Ⓐ Ⓑ Ⓒ Ⓓ	67	Ⓐ Ⓑ Ⓒ Ⓓ	97	Ⓐ Ⓑ Ⓒ Ⓓ
8	Ⓐ Ⓑ Ⓒ Ⓓ	38	Ⓐ Ⓑ Ⓒ Ⓓ	68	Ⓐ Ⓑ Ⓒ Ⓓ	98	Ⓐ Ⓑ Ⓒ Ⓓ
9	Ⓐ Ⓑ Ⓒ Ⓓ	39	Ⓐ Ⓑ Ⓒ Ⓓ	69	Ⓐ Ⓑ Ⓒ Ⓓ	99	Ⓐ Ⓑ Ⓒ Ⓓ
10	Ⓐ Ⓑ Ⓒ Ⓓ	40	Ⓐ Ⓑ Ⓒ Ⓓ	70	Ⓐ Ⓑ Ⓒ Ⓓ	100	Ⓐ Ⓑ Ⓒ Ⓓ
11	Ⓐ Ⓑ Ⓒ Ⓓ	41	Ⓐ Ⓑ Ⓒ Ⓓ	71	Ⓐ Ⓑ Ⓒ Ⓓ	101	Ⓐ Ⓑ Ⓒ Ⓓ
12	Ⓐ Ⓑ Ⓒ Ⓓ	42	Ⓐ Ⓑ Ⓒ Ⓓ	72	Ⓐ Ⓑ Ⓒ Ⓓ	102	Ⓐ Ⓑ Ⓒ Ⓓ
13	Ⓐ Ⓑ Ⓒ Ⓓ	43	Ⓐ Ⓑ Ⓒ Ⓓ	73	Ⓐ Ⓑ Ⓒ Ⓓ	103	Ⓐ Ⓑ Ⓒ Ⓓ
14	Ⓐ Ⓑ Ⓒ Ⓓ	44	Ⓐ Ⓑ Ⓒ Ⓓ	74	Ⓐ Ⓑ Ⓒ Ⓓ	104	Ⓐ Ⓑ Ⓒ Ⓓ
15	Ⓐ Ⓑ Ⓒ Ⓓ	45	Ⓐ Ⓑ Ⓒ Ⓓ	75	Ⓐ Ⓑ Ⓒ Ⓓ	105	Ⓐ Ⓑ Ⓒ Ⓓ
16	Ⓐ Ⓑ Ⓒ Ⓓ	46	Ⓐ Ⓑ Ⓒ Ⓓ	76	Ⓐ Ⓑ Ⓒ Ⓓ	106	Ⓐ Ⓑ Ⓒ Ⓓ
17	Ⓐ Ⓑ Ⓒ Ⓓ	47	Ⓐ Ⓑ Ⓒ Ⓓ	77	Ⓐ Ⓑ Ⓒ Ⓓ	107	Ⓐ Ⓑ Ⓒ Ⓓ
18	Ⓐ Ⓑ Ⓒ Ⓓ	48	Ⓐ Ⓑ Ⓒ Ⓓ	78	Ⓐ Ⓑ Ⓒ Ⓓ	108	Ⓐ Ⓑ Ⓒ Ⓓ
19	Ⓐ Ⓑ Ⓒ Ⓓ	49	Ⓐ Ⓑ Ⓒ Ⓓ	79	Ⓐ Ⓑ Ⓒ Ⓓ	109	Ⓐ Ⓑ Ⓒ Ⓓ
20	Ⓐ Ⓑ Ⓒ Ⓓ	50	Ⓐ Ⓑ Ⓒ Ⓓ	80	Ⓐ Ⓑ Ⓒ Ⓓ	110	Ⓐ Ⓑ Ⓒ Ⓓ
21	Ⓐ Ⓑ Ⓒ Ⓓ	51	Ⓐ Ⓑ Ⓒ Ⓓ	81	Ⓐ Ⓑ Ⓒ Ⓓ	111	Ⓐ Ⓑ Ⓒ Ⓓ
22	Ⓐ Ⓑ Ⓒ Ⓓ	52	Ⓐ Ⓑ Ⓒ Ⓓ	82	Ⓐ Ⓑ Ⓒ Ⓓ	112	Ⓐ Ⓑ Ⓒ Ⓓ
23	Ⓐ Ⓑ Ⓒ Ⓓ	53	Ⓐ Ⓑ Ⓒ Ⓓ	83	Ⓐ Ⓑ Ⓒ Ⓓ	113	Ⓐ Ⓑ Ⓒ Ⓓ
24	Ⓐ Ⓑ Ⓒ Ⓓ	54	Ⓐ Ⓑ Ⓒ Ⓓ	84	Ⓐ Ⓑ Ⓒ Ⓓ	114	Ⓐ Ⓑ Ⓒ Ⓓ
25	Ⓐ Ⓑ Ⓒ Ⓓ	55	Ⓐ Ⓑ Ⓒ Ⓓ	85	Ⓐ Ⓑ Ⓒ Ⓓ	115	Ⓐ Ⓑ Ⓒ Ⓓ
26	Ⓐ Ⓑ Ⓒ Ⓓ	56	Ⓐ Ⓑ Ⓒ Ⓓ	86	Ⓐ Ⓑ Ⓒ Ⓓ	116	Ⓐ Ⓑ Ⓒ Ⓓ
27	Ⓐ Ⓑ Ⓒ Ⓓ	57	Ⓐ Ⓑ Ⓒ Ⓓ	87	Ⓐ Ⓑ Ⓒ Ⓓ	117	Ⓐ Ⓑ Ⓒ Ⓓ
28	Ⓐ Ⓑ Ⓒ Ⓓ	58	Ⓐ Ⓑ Ⓒ Ⓓ	88	Ⓐ Ⓑ Ⓒ Ⓓ	118	Ⓐ Ⓑ Ⓒ Ⓓ
29	Ⓐ Ⓑ Ⓒ Ⓓ	59	Ⓐ Ⓑ Ⓒ Ⓓ	89	Ⓐ Ⓑ Ⓒ Ⓓ	119	Ⓐ Ⓑ Ⓒ Ⓓ
30	Ⓐ Ⓑ Ⓒ Ⓓ	60	Ⓐ Ⓑ Ⓒ Ⓓ	90	Ⓐ Ⓑ Ⓒ Ⓓ	120	Ⓐ Ⓑ Ⓒ Ⓓ

Pretest

Directions: In each of the following questions, you will find three initial terms and, in parentheses, four answer options designated *a*, *b*, *c*, and *d*. You are to select from the four answer options the one that best completes the analogy with the three initial terms. To record your answers, use the answer sheet provided.

Time: 60 minutes

1. GRAY : ELEPHANT :: (*a*. white, *b*. brown, *c*. green, *d*. gray) : GRIZZLY BEAR

2. (*a*. ratatouille, *b*. vermouth, *c*. lemonade, *d*. gin) : EAT :: MANHATTAN : DRINK

3. MOON : PLANET :: (*a*. asteroid, *b*. sun, *c*. planet, *d*. Orion) : STAR

4. JOHN : (*a*. Jackson, *b*. Adams, *c*. Pierce, *d*. Garfield) :: ANDREW : JOHNSON

5. 1 + 2 : MARCH :: 12 − 3 : (*a*. September, *b*. October, *c*. November, *d*. December)

6. CANNON : CANNON :: STIMULI : (*a*. stimulation, *b*. stimuluses, *c*. stimulate, *d*. stimulus)

7. GRAPES : WINE :: (*a*. alcohol, *b*. hops, *c*. alfalfa, *d*. kemp) : BEER

8. SCROOGE : GREEDY :: (*a*. Antony, *b*. Portia, *c*. Cassius, *d*. Macduff) : TREACHEROUS

9. (*a*. hurricane, *b*. hail, *c*. sleet, *d*. thunder) : RAIN :: BLIZZARD : SNOW

10. BLANC : ALPS :: EVEREST : (*a*. Andes, *b*. Himalayas, *c*. Jungfrau, *d*. Caucasus)

11. i : e :: (*a*. $-\infty$, *b*. π, *c*. 1, *d*. $\sqrt{-1}$) : 2.71828

12. (*a.* Na, *b.* Al, *c.* O_2, *d.* N) : SALT :: H : HYDROCHLORIC ACID

13. UROLOGIST : (*a.* bladder, *b.* urine, *c.* heart, *d.* ears) :: OPHTHALMOLOGIST : EYES

14. A : C :: ALPHA : (*a.* lambda, *b.* kappa, *c.* omicron, *d.* gamma)

15. (*a.* coin, *b.* bullion, *c.* currency, *d.* check) : CASH :: PROBABLE : CERTAIN

16. SKINNER : ENVIRONMENT :: (*a.* Galton, *b.* Locke, *c.* Watson, *d.* Spence) : HEREDITY

17. DOG : NOUN :: (*a.* newspaper, *b.* at, *c.* the, *d.* is) : ARTICLE

18. IRISH : (*a.* setter, *b.* Guernsey, *c.* mutt, *d.* St. Bernard) :: LABRADOR : RETRIEVER

19. PERSHING : (*a.* French, *b.* U.S., *c.* English, *d.* Canadian) :: WELLINGTON : ENGLISH

20. MORNING STAR : EVENING STAR :: VENUS : (*a.* Mercury, *b.* Mars, *c.* Jupiter, *d.* Venus)

21. HYPERBOLE : HYPERBOLA :: STATEMENT : (*a.* statements, *b.* curve, *c.* exaggeration, *d.* ellipse)

22. $\bar{X}$: SAMPLE :: (*a.* μ, *b.* σ, *c.* λ, *d.* ρ) : POPULATION

23. METHYL : ETHYL :: GRAIN : (*a.* turpentine, *b.* alcohol, *c.* rain, *d.* wood)

24. SHORTEST : (*a.* February, *b.* August, *c.* April, *d.* December) :: LONGEST : JUNE

25. (*a.* nadir, *b.* zenith, *c.* summit, *d.* hilt) : BOTTOM :: APEX : TOP

26. PERCENT : 100 :: PROPORTION : (*a.* 0, *b.* 1, *c.* 0.1, *d.* 0.01)

27. RATIONAL : $\sqrt{100}$ :: IRRATIONAL : (*a.* $\sqrt{1}$, *b.* $\sqrt{-4}$, *c.* $\sqrt{50}$, *d.* $\sqrt{0}$)

28. ENORMITY : (*a.* great wickedness, *b.* great largess, *c.* great size, *d.* great passion) :: VILIFICATION : SLANDER

29. VANILLA : TEA :: (*a.* stem, *b.* root, *c.* flower, *d.* bean) : LEAF

30. NOON : EVE :: 12:21 : (*a.* 8:34, *b.* 10:01, *c.* 7:54, *d.* 11:29)

31. (*a.* soap, *b.* aspirin, *c.* base, *d.* litmus) : ACID :: LYE : ALKALINE

32. SAM : AIR :: ABM : (*a.* sea, *b.* land, *c.* ballistic, *d.* missile)

33. STEP : STAIRCASE :: (*a.* notch, *b.* support, *c.* poles, *d.* rung) : LADDER

34. OCHER : (*a.* yellow, *b.* green, *c.* blue, *d.* gray) :: LAVENDER : PURPLE

35. MARE : EWE :: HORSE : (*a.* goat, *b.* sheep, *c.* pig, *d.* deer)

36. RAVIOLI : (*a.* spaghetti, *b.* linguine, *c.* cannelloni, *d.* enchilada) :: MANICOTTI : TORTELLINI

37. (*a.* bacteria, *b.* viruses, *c.* fungi, *d.* rickettsiae) : TYPHUS :: BACTERIA : TUBERCULOSIS

38. TWO : IMPEACH :: (*a.* zero, *b.* one, *c.* three, *d.* four) : CONVICT

39. 0 PROOF : 0% :: 50 PROOF : (*a.* 10%, *b.* 25%, *c.* 75%, *d.* 100%)

40. BENEDICT : ALFREDO :: EGGS : (*a.* oeufs, *b.* clams, *c.* ziti, *d.* fettuccini)

41. INDUCE : INDUCT :: (*a.* adduce, *b.* reason, *c.* persuade, *d.* deduct) : INSTALL

42. (*a.* maroon, *b.* crimson, *c.* pink, *d.* scarlet) : RED :: GRAY : BLACK

43. STOP : POT :: STOOL : (*a.* feces, *b.* toilet, *c.* chair, *d.* loot)

44. PICASSO : (*a.* Bosch, *b.* Daumier, *c.* Tintoretto, *d.* Dali) :: GUERNICA : GARDEN OF EARTHLY DELIGHTS

45. $3x^2$: $6x$ :: $5y$: (*a.* 5, *b.* 10, *c.* $5y^{1/2}$, *d.* $10y^{1/2}$)

46. UNICORN : (*a.* mythical beast, *b.* duet, *c.* zebra, *d.* union) :: SINGLETON : BICYCLE

47. (*a.* Holland, *b.* Yugoslavia, *c.* Denmark, *d,* Switzerland) : ALPINE :: GREECE : MEDITERRANEAN

48. M.D. : EARNED : (*a.* D.D., *b.* Ph.D., *c.* D.D.S., *d.* O.D.) : HONORARY

49. (*a.* Don Juan, *b.* Pablo, *c.* Sancho, *d.* Dulcinea) : DON QUIXOTE :: WATSON : HOLMES

50. SONATA : (*a.* movement, *b.* sonatina, *c.* coda, *d.* solo) :: NOVEL : NOVELLA

51. NOVICE : EXPERT :: (*a.* teacher, *b.* apprentice, *c.* journeyman, *d.* layman) : MASTER

52. CLUB : (*a.* diamond, *b.* heart, *c.* spade, *d.* ace) :: LOWEST : HIGHEST

53. GOSLING : GOOSE :: SHOAT : (*a.* goat, *b.* sheep, *c.* horse, *d.* hog)

54. C : LEMON :: A : (*a.* liver, *b.* lettuce, *c.* orange, *d.* cake)

55. PACIFIC : OCEAN :: (*a.* Mercury, *b.* Jupiter, *c.* Uranus, *d.* Neptune) : PLANET

56. ICHTHYOLOGIST : (*a.* sentences, *b.* algae, *c.* insects, *d.* fish) :: ZOOLOGIST : ANIMALS

57. ELECT : SELECT :: TIE : (*a.* lose, *b.* win, *c.* sty, *d.* rope)

58. MALLET : (*a.* hunting, *b.* rugby, *c.* cricket, *d.* croquet) :: BAT : BASEBALL

59. BAROMETER : AIR PRESSURE :: TACHOMETER : (*a.* speed of descent, *b.* speed of rotation, *c.* acceleration, *d.* inertia)

60. EMERALD : GRUE :: (*a.* ruby, *b.* sapphire, *c.* amethyst, *d.* diamond) : BLEEN

61. MARTIN : DAVID :: (*a.* Dombey, *b.* Micawber, *c.* Magoun, *d.* Chuzzlewit) : COPPERFIELD

62. (*a.* 2:00, *b.* 3:00, *c.* 5:00, *d.* 6:00) : SEATTLE :: 4:00 : CHICAGO

63. VENUS : (*a.* Uranus, *b.* Mars, *c.* Saturn, *d.* Pluto) :: LOVE : THE DEAD

64. SUBORN : (*a.* give birth to, *b.* prove, *c.* bribe, *d.* demand) :: SUBORDINATE : INFERIOR

65. A : O :: (*a.* E, *b.* OA, *c.* B, *d.* RH) : AB

66. (*a.* coal, *b.* petroleum, *c.* black opal, *d.* uranium) : BLACK GOLD :: PYRITE : FOOL'S GOLD

67. MALACHITE : GREEN :: LAPIS LAZULI : (*a.* blue, *b.* red, *c.* yellow, *d.* amber)

68. LONGITUDE : LATITUDE :: (*a.* 110°, *b.* 90°, *c.* 70°, *d.* 50°) : 20°

69. VALENTINE : SECOND :: NICHOLAS : (*a.* first, *b.* sixth, *c.* tenth, *d.* twelfth)

70. MARK : (*a.* Munich, *b.* Berlin, *c.* Zurich, *d.* Basel) :: FRANC : PARIS

71. (*a.* biology, *b.* chemistry, *c.* physics, *d.* astronomy) : HERSCHEL :: SURGERY : LISTER

72. METER : KILOMETER :: LOG 10 : (*a.* e, *b.* 10, *c.* 10^3, *d.* $\sqrt{10,000}$)

73. (*a.* Ash Wednesday, *b.* St. Bartholomew's Day, *c.* Maundy Thursday, *d.* All Saints' Day) : EASTER :: FIRST : LAST

74. GHOST : SPIRIT :: GHOUL : (*a.* body, *b.* vampire, *c.* nightmare, *d.* grave robber)

75. GERUND : (*a.* adverb, *b.* pronoun, *c.* conjunction, *d.* noun) :: PARTICIPLE : ADJECTIVE

76. N.Y. : N.J. :: N.H. : (*a.* N.D., *b.* N.C., *c.* N.M., *d.* N.W.)

77. (*a.* Abelard, *b.* Aquinas, *c.* Erasmus, *d.* Eusebius) : HELOÏSE :: TRISTAN : ISOLDE

78. GOBI : (*a.* Africa, *b.* Asia, *c.* South America, *d.* Central America) :: SAHARA : AFRICA

79. X : X^2 :: STANDARD DEVIATION : (*a.* mode, *b.* median, *c.* variance, *d.* chi square)

80. LEONINE : (*a.* vulpine, *b.* porcine, *c.* supine, *d.* bovine) :: LION : FOX

81. AUGUST 8 : LEO :: (*a.* January 8, *b.* April 8, *c.* October 8, *d.* December 8) : SAGITTARIUS

82. CHESS : CHESSMEN :: GO : (*a.* cards, *b.* stones, *c.* pegs, *d.* balls)

83. CIPHER : NAUGHT :: (*a.* zero, *b.* all, *c.* most, *d.* one) : NONE

84. SEVENTH-DAY ADVENTIST : (*a.* Friday, *b.* Saturday, *c.* Sunday, *d.* Monday) :: MUSLIM : FRIDAY

85. (*a.* 10, *b.* 11, *c.* 12, *d.* 13) : DUODECIMAL :: 13 : DECIMAL

86. (*a.* shawl, *b.* belt, *c.* cloak, *d.* sash) : BURNOOSE :: CAP : BUSBY

87. LEGHORN : (*a.* cattle, *b.* goat, *c.* sheep, *d.* fowl) :: ANGORA : GOAT

88. LISZT : HUNGARY :: MENOTTI : (*a.* U.S.A., *b.* Greece, *c.* Spain, *d.* England)

89. MELODY : (*a.* immediate, *b.* successive, *c.* retrogressive, *d.* momentary) :: HARMONY : SIMULTANEOUS

90. SINUSITIS : SINUS :: MENINGITIS : (*a.* liver, *b.* heart, *c.* artery, *d.* membrane)

91. APPROXIMATE : EXACT :: (*a.* analog, *b.* analogous, *c.* analogical, *d.* analogy) : DIGITAL

92. (*a.* is as, *b.* is almost, *c.* is virtually, *d.* is) : IS LIKE :: METAPHOR : SIMILE

93. CONGRESS : U.S.A. :: DIET : (*a.* Germany, *b.* Turkey, *c.* Japan, *d.* China)

94. MAYOR : (*a.* Montevideo, *b.* Sussex, *c.* Casterbridge, *d.* Marseilles) :: HUNCHBACK : NOTRE DAME

95. INDUCTION : DEDUCTION :: HUME : (*a.* Locke, *b.* Leibniz, *c.* Berkeley, *d.* Mill)

96. STOP : (*a.* h, *b.* j, *c.* t, *d.* v) :: FRICATIVE : F

97. (*a.* $\frac{1}{2}gt^2$, *b.* ra, *c.* $\frac{1}{4}g^2k$, *d.* pc) : D :: MA : F

98. FIDELIO : BORIS GODUNOV :: BEETHOVEN : (*a.* Rimski-Korsakov, *b.* Shostakoviev, *c.* Prokofiev, *d.* Mussorgsky)

99. MISER : AVARICIOUS :: SYCOPHANT : (*a.* plutonic, *b.* veracious, *c.* unctuous, *d.* sybaritic)

100. (*a.* genitive, *b.* dative, *c.* ablative, *d.* vocative) : ACCUSATIVE :: INDIRECT : DIRECT

101. (*a.* wheat, *b.* barley, *c.* oats, *d.* rice) : SAKE :: JUNIPER BERRIES : GIN

102. A RAISIN IN THE SUN : THE GRAPES OF WRATH :: (*a.* Morrison, *b.* Hansberry, *c.* Miller, *d.* Hare) : STEINBECK

103. SHARP : TACK :: COOL : (*a.* cucumber, *b.* stone, *c.* stream, *d.* milk)

104. SASQUATCH : NORTH AMERICA :: YETI : (*a.* South America, *b.* Europe, *c.* Australia, *d.* Asia)

105. CRETE : (*a.* Turkey, *b.* Syria, *c.* Greece, *d.* Albania) :: SICILY : ITALY

106. $a^2 + b^2$: (*a.* hypotenuse squared, *b.* rectangular area, *c.* circumference cubed, *d.* spherical volume) :: $(y - y_1) / (x - x_1)$: SLOPE

107. (*a.* tomato, *b.* peanut, *c.* chestnut, *d.* ginger) : PARSNIP :: TURNIP : POTATO

108. KEEL : FRAMES :: BREASTBONE : (*a.* human, *b.* ribs, *c.* pectorals, *d.* backbone)

109. PUSILLANIMOUS : (*a.* brave, *b.* hungry, *c.* joyful, *d.* jealous) : PERFIDIOUS : LOYAL

110. MARS : VENUS :: EARTH : (*a.* Jupiter, *b.* Saturn, *c.* Mercury, *d.* Neptune)

111. CACOPHONOUS : NOISOME :: SOUND : (*a.* sight, *b.* feel, *c.* smell, *d.* taste)

112. CAT : MOUSE :: (*a.* squirrel, *b.* bandicoot, *c.* lemur, *d.* mongoose) : SNAKE

113. ELEPHANT : (*a.* piano, *b.* tusk, *c.* table, *d.* hoof) :: WHALE : LAMP

114. (*a.* Padua, *b.* Siberia, *c.* Verona, *d.* Narnia) : OZ :: SHANGRI-LA : ATLANTIS

115. AURORA BOREALIS : (*a.* Northern Lights, *b.* Gulf Stream, *c.* Black Forest, *d.* El Niño) :: CRANIUM : SKULL

116. PUMMELO : CITRUS FRUIT :: (*a.* rutabaga, *b.* grain, *c.* lentil, *d.* artichoke) : LEGUME

117. KENNEDY : (*a.* House Representative, *b.* Senator, *c.* Mayor, *d.* Governor) :: CLINTON : GOVERNOR

118. ARGES : CYCLOPS :: MEDUSA : (*a.* gorgon, *b.* minotaur, *c.* siren, *d.* hydra)

119. I.E. : (*a.* English, *b.* Italian, *c.* Latin, *d.* Greek) :: RSVP : French

120. (*a.* weary, *b.* tenacious, *c.* harmonious, *d.* sprightly) : JOCUND :: VERITABLE : AUTHENTIC

Answer Key
PRETEST

1.	B	31.	B	61.	D	91.	A
2.	A	32.	C	62.	A	92.	D
3.	C	33.	D	63.	D	93.	C
4.	B	34.	A	64.	C	94.	C
5.	A	35.	B	65.	C	95.	B
6.	D	36.	C	66.	B	96.	C
7.	B	37.	D	67.	A	97.	A
8.	C	38.	A	68.	A	98.	D
9.	A	39.	B	69.	D	99.	C
10.	B	40.	D	70.	B	100.	B
11.	D	41.	C	71.	D	101.	D
12.	A	42.	C	72.	C	102.	B
13.	A	43.	D	73.	A	103.	A
14.	D	44.	A	74.	D	104	D
15.	D	45.	A	75.	D	105	C
16.	A	46.	B	76.	C	106.	A
17.	C	47.	D	77.	A	107.	D
18.	A	48.	A	78.	B	108.	B
19.	B	49.	C	79.	C	109.	A
20.	D	50.	B	80.	A	110.	C
21.	B	51.	B	81.	D	111.	C
22.	A	52.	C	82.	B	112.	D
23.	C	53.	D	83.	A	113.	A
24.	D	54.	A	84.	B	114.	D
25.	A	55.	B	85.	B	115.	A
26.	B	56.	D	86.	C	116.	C
27.	C	57.	C	87.	D	117.	B
28.	A	58.	D	88.	A	118.	A
29.	D	59.	B	89.	B	119.	C
30.	B	60.	B	90.	D	120.	D

EXPLANATION OF ANSWERS FOR PRETEST

In the following explanations of answers, explanations concerning the correct response are in a large font. Explanations regarding distracters (incorrect responses) that are not self-explaining or could be misinterpreted are in a smaller font in order to highlight the explanations of the answers that are correct.

1. GRAY : ELEPHANT :: (*a.* white, ***b.* brown**, *c.* green, *d.* gray) : GRIZZLY BEAR

   (**b**) An elephant is gray; a grizzly bear is brown.
   General Information—Description

2. (***a.* ratatouille**, *b.* vermouth, *c.* lemonade, *d.* gin) : EAT :: MANHATTAN : DRINK

   (**a**) Ratatouille is something one eats; a Manhattan is something one drinks.
   General Information—Description

3. MOON : PLANET :: (*a.* asteroid, *b.* sun, ***c.* planet**, *d.* Orion) : STAR

   (**c**) A moon revolves around a planet; a star is a celestial body of hot gases.
   An asteroid is a small object in the solar system revolving around the sun, which is mostly composed of rock. Orion is a constellation of stars in the sky.
   Natural Science—Description

4. JOHN : (*a.* Jackson, ***b.* Adams**, *c.* Pierce, *d.* Garfield) :: ANDREW : JOHNSON

   (**b**) John Adams and Andrew Johnson were both U.S. presidents.
   The names of the other presidents were Andrew Jackson, Franklin Pierce, and James Garfield.
   Humanities—Completion

5. 1 + 2 : MARCH :: 12 − 3 : (***a.* September**, *b.* October, *c.* November, *d.* December)

   (**a**) March is the third (1 + 2) month of the year; September is the ninth (12 − 3) month.
   General Information—Description

6. CANNON : CANNON :: STIMULI : (*a.* stimulation, *b.* stimuluses, *c.* stimulate, ***d.* stimulus**)

   (**d**) *Cannon* is the plural form of *cannon. Stimuli* is the plural form of *stimulus.*
   General Information—Class

7. GRAPES : WINE :: (*a.* alcohol, *b.* **hops**, *c.* alfalfa, *d.* kemp) : BEER

(**b**) Wine is made from grapes; beer is made from hops.
General Information—Description

8. SCROOGE : GREEDY :: (*a.* Antony, *b.* Portia, *c.* **Cassius**, *d.* Macduff) : TREACHEROUS

(**c**) Scrooge (in *A Christmas Carol*) was greedy; Cassius (in *Julius Caesar*) was treacherous. Macduff is a character in Shakespeare's *Macbeth* who kills Macbeth in the final act. Portia is the wife of Brutus (Julius Caesar's famous assassin) in Shakespeare's *Julius Caesar*. Antony is a soldier and ruler of the Roman Empire in Shakespeare's *Antony and Cleopatra*.
Humanities—Description

9. (*a.* **hurricane**, *b.* hail, *c.* sleet, *d.* thunder) : RAIN :: BLIZZARD : SNOW

(**a**) A hurricane is characterized by strong wind and heavy rain; a blizzard is characterized by strong wind and heavy snow.
General Information—Description

10. BLANC : ALPS :: EVEREST : (*a.* Andes, *b.* **Himalayas**, *c.* Jungfrau, *d.* Caucasus)

(**b**) Mont Blanc is the highest mountain peak in the Alps; Mount Everest is the highest mountain peak in the Himalayas. The Alps are a mountain range in Europe. The Andes are a mountain range in South America. The Himalayas are a mountain range in Asia. The Jungfrau is a mountain in the Swiss Alps and the Caucasus is the mountain range that separates the continents of Asia and Europe.
General Information—Description

11. i : e :: (*a.* $-\infty$, *b.* π, *c.* 1, *d.* $\sqrt{-1}$) : 2.71828

(**d**) The quantity *i* is equal to $\sqrt{-1}$; the quantity *e* is (approximately) equal to 2.71828. The quantity of π is approximately equal to 3.14159. The symbol ∞ represents infinity.
Mathematics—Equality/Negation

12. (*a.* **Na**, *b.* Al, *c.* O_2, *d.* N) : SALT :: H : HYDROCHLORIC ACID

(**a**) Salt is a compound containing sodium (Na); hydrochloric acid is a compound containing hydrogen (H). O_2 stands for oxygen, N stands for nitrogen, and Al stands for aluminum.
Natural Science—Part/Whole

13. UROLOGIST : (***a.* bladder**, *b.* urine, *c.* heart, *d.* ears) ::
OPHTHALMOLOGIST : EYES

 (**a**) A urologist treats the bladder; an ophthalmologist treats the eyes.
General Information—Description

14. A : C :: ALPHA : (*a.* lambda, *b.* kappa, *c.* omicron, ***d.* gamma**)

 (**d**) *A* is the first letter and *c* is the third letter of the Roman alphabet;
alpha is the first letter and gamma is the third letter of the Greek alphabet.
Lambda is the 11th letter of the Greek alphabet, kappa the 10th letter, and omicron is the
15th letter.
Humanities—Class

15. (*a.* coin, *b.* bullion, *c.* currency, ***d.* check**) : CASH :: PROBABLE :
CERTAIN

 (**d**) A check has probable value in a financial transaction (it is not certain to
clear). Cash has certain value. A bullion is a pure form of a precious metal and
therefore has a certain value. A coin is a metal disc usually issued by a government that is
used as money. A currency is the form of money used in a country.
General Information—Description

16. SKINNER : ENVIRONMENT :: (***a.* Galton**, *b.* Locke, *c.* Watson,
d. Spence) : HEREDITY

 (**a**) Skinner is known for his belief that environment largely shapes behavior;
Galton believed that heredity largely shapes behavior. John Locke was an English
philosopher and empiricist. John Watson was an American psychologist who established the
school of behaviorism. Kenneth Spence was an American psychologist who developed the
theory of Stimulus Control.
Social Science—Description

17. DOG : NOUN :: (*a.* newspaper, *b.* at, ***c.* the**, *d.* is) : ARTICLE

 (**c**) *Dog* is a noun; *the* is an article. *Humanities—Description*

18. IRISH : (***a.* setter**, *b.* Guernsey, *c.* mutt, *d.* St. Bernard) :: LABRADOR :
RETRIEVER

 (**a**) An Irish setter and a Labrador retriever are both kinds of dogs.
General Information—Completion

19. PERSHING : (*a.* French, *b.* **U.S.**, *c.* English, *d.* Canadian) ::
WELLINGTON : ENGLISH

(**b**) Pershing was a U.S. general who led the American Expeditionary Force in World War I; Wellington was an English general who served in the Napoleonic wars.
Humanities—Description

20. MORNING STAR : EVENING STAR :: VENUS : (*a.* Mercury, *b.* Mars, *c.* Jupiter, *d.* **Venus**)

(**d**) Venus is known both as the morning star and as the evening star.
General Information—Similarity/Contrast

21. HYPERBOLE : HYPERBOLA :: STATEMENT : (*a.* statements, *b.* **curve**, *c.* exaggeration, *d.* ellipse)

(**b**) A hyperbole is a type of statement; a hyperbola is a type of curve.
Mathematics—Description

22. X̄: SAMPLE :: (*a.* μ, *b.* σ, *c.* λ, *d.* ρ) : POPULATION

(**a**) X̄ is a symbol for a sample mean; μ is a symbol for a population mean. σ stands for the standard deviation of a population. λ stands for eigenvalues and Lagrange multipliers. ρ stands for a correlation coefficient in statistics. Note that these Greek letters have additional meanings in other sciences.
Mathematics—Description

23. METHYL : ETHYL :: GRAIN : (*a.* turpentine, *b.* alcohol, *c.* **rain**, *d.* wood)

(**c**) *Ethyl* is *methyl* without the initial *m*; *rain* is *grain* without the initial *g*.
Nonsemantic

24. SHORTEST : (*a.* February, *b.* August, *c.* April, *d.* **December**) ::
LONGEST : JUNE

(**d**) The shortest day of the year occurs in December. The longest day of the year occurs in June.
General Information—Description

25. (*a.* **nadir**, *b.* zenith, *c.* summit, *d.* hilt) : BOTTOM :: APEX : TOP

(**a**) The nadir is the lowest point, or bottom of something; the apex is the highest point, or top. A zenith is the direction pointing directly above a particular location. A summit is the highest point of a mountain. A hilt is the handle of a sword.
Vocabulary—Similarity/Contrast

26. PERCENT : 100 :: PROPORTION : (*a.* 0, ***b.* 1**, *c.* 0.1, *d.* 0.01)

    (**b**) The highest possible percent is 100; the highest possible proportion is 1.
    Mathematics—Description

27. RATIONAL : $\sqrt{100}$ :: IRRATIONAL : (*a.* $\sqrt{1}$, *b.* $\sqrt{-4}$, ***c.* $\sqrt{50}$**, *d.* $\sqrt{0}$)

    (**c**) $\sqrt{100}$ is a rational number; $\sqrt{50}$ is an irrational number. A rational number can be expressed as a ratio of two integers (which are natural numbers like 1, 2, 3, and their negatives). An irrational number is a real number that cannot be expressed as a fraction and therefore is not a rational number.
    Mathematics—Description

28. ENORMITY : (***a.* great wickedness**, *b.* great largess, *c.* great size, *d.* great passion) :: VILIFICATION : SLANDER

    (**a**) Enormity is great wickedness; vilification is slander.
    Vocabulary—Similarity/Contrast

29. VANILLA : TEA :: (*a.* stem, *b.* root, *c.* flower, ***d.* bean**) : LEAF

    (**d**) Vanilla is from a bean, tea from a leaf. *General Information—Description*

30. NOON : EVE :: 12:21 : (*a.* 8:34, ***b.* 10:01**, *c.* 7:54, *d.* 11:29)

    (**b**) *Noon* and *eve* are both palindromes (they read the same spelled backward and forward), as are 12:21 and 10:01.
    Nonsemantic

31. (*a.* soap, ***b.* aspirin**, *c.* base, *d.* litmus) : ACID :: LYE : ALKALINE

    (**b**) Aspirin is acid; lye is alkaline.
    General Information—Description

32. SAM : AIR :: ABM : (*a.* sea, *b.* land, ***c.* ballistic**, *d.* missile)

    (**c**) The second letter in the acronym *SAM* (surface-to-air missile) stands for air; the second letter in the *ABM* (anti-ballistic missile) stands for ballistic.
    General Information—Part/Whole

33. STEP : STAIRCASE :: (*a.* notch, *b.* support, *c.* poles, ***d.* rung**) : LADDER

    (**d**) A staircase has steps; a ladder has rungs.
    General Information—Part/Whole

34. OCHER : (***a.* yellow**, *b.* green, *c.* blue, *d.* gray) :: LAVENDER : PURPLE

    (**a**) Ocher is a shade of yellow; lavender is a shade of purple.
    Vocabulary—Description

35. MARE : EWE :: HORSE : (*a.* goat, ***b.* sheep**, *c.* pig, *d.* deer)

    (**b**) A mare is a female horse; a ewe is a female sheep.
    Vocabulary—Description

36. RAVIOLI : (*a.* spaghetti, *b.* linguine, ***c.* cannelloni**, *d.* enchilada) ::
    MANICOTTI : TORTELLINI

    (**c**) Ravioli, cannelloni, manicotti, and tortellini are all stuffed pasta dishes.
    General Information—Class

37. (*a.* bacteria, *b.* viruses, *c.* fungi, ***d.* rickettsiae**) TYPHUS ::
    MYCOBACTERIA : TUBERCULOSIS

    (**d**) Typhus is caused by rickettsiae (parasitic bacteria), tuberculosis
    by mycobacteria.
    Natural Science—Description

38. TWO : IMPEACH :: (***a.* zero**, *b.* one, *c.* three, *d.* four) : CONVICT

    (**a**) Two presidents of the United States have been impeached
    (Andrew Johnson and Bill Clinton); no president has been convicted.
    Humanities—Description

39. 0 PROOF : 0% :: 50 PROOF : (*a.* 10%, ***b.* 25%**, *c.* 75%, *d.* 100%)

    (**b**) Something that is 0 proof has a 0% concentration of alcohol;
    something that is 50 proof has a 25% concentration of alcohol.
    General Information—Description

40. BENEDICT : ALFREDO :: EGGS : (*a.* oeufs, *b.* clams, *c.* ziti, ***d.* fettuccini**)

    (**d**) Eggs Benedict and fettuccini Alfredo are both food dishes.
    General Information—Completion

41. INDUCE : INDUCT :: (*a.* adduce, *b.* reason, ***c.* persuade**, *d.* deduct) :
    INSTALL

    (**c**) To induce is to persuade; to induct is to install. To adduce means to cite
    or to allege in order to support an argument; to deduct is to take away, as from an
    amount; to reason means to think logically.
    Vocabulary—Similarity/Contrast

42. (*a.* maroon, *b.* crimson, ***c.* pink**, *d.* scarlet) : RED :: GRAY : BLACK

    (**c**) Pink is red mixed with white; gray is black mixed with white.
    General Information—Description

43. STOP : POT :: STOOL : (*a.* feces, *b.* toilet, *c.* chair, ***d.* loot**)

   (**d**) *Pot* is all but the first letter of *stop* reversed; *loot* is all but the first letter of *stool* reversed.
   Nonsemantic

44. PICASSO : (***a.* Bosch**, *b.* Daumier, *c.* Tintoretto, *d.* Dali) :: GUERNICA : GARDEN OF EARTHLY DELIGHTS

   (**a**) Picasso painted *Guernica*. Bosch painted *The Garden of Earthly Delights*. Daumier is famous for his works depicting the life of Don Quixote; Tintoretto is known for his painting of the last supper (and da Vinci created a painting with the same title!); Dali is famous for his bizarre, surreal images, often of soft watches like in *The Persistence of Memory*.
   Humanities—Description

45. $3x^2 : 6x :: 5y : (\boldsymbol{a.\ 5},\ b.\ 10,\ c.\ 5y^{1/2},\ d.\ 10y^{1/2})$

   (**a**) The expression $6x$ is the first derivative of $3x^2$; 5 is the first derivative of $5y$.
   Mathematics—Description

46. UNICORN : (*a.* mythical beast, ***b.* duet**, *c.* zebra, *d.* union) :: SINGLETON : BICYCLE

   (**b**) A unicorn and a singleton both refer to one of something; a duet and a bicycle both refer to two of something.
   General Information—Equality/Negation

47. (*a.* Holland, *b.* Croatia, *c.* Denmark, ***d.* Switzerland**) : ALPINE :: GREECE : MEDITERRANEAN

   (**d**) Switzerland is an Alpine country; Greece is a Mediterranean country. Croatia is an eastern European country. Denmark is located in northern Europe and Holland is located in western Europe.
   General Information—Description

48. M.D. : EARNED :: (***a.* D.D.**, *b.* Ph.D., *c.* D.D.S., *d.* O.D.) : HONORARY

   (**a**) An M.D. (Doctor of Medicine) degree is earned; a D.D. (Doctor of Divinity) degree is honorary. A Ph.D. is a Doctor of Philosophy, a D.D.S. is a Doctor of Dental Surgery, and an O.D. is a Doctor of Optometry.
   General Information—Description

49. (*a.* Don Juan, *b.* Pablo, *c.* **Sancho**, *d.* Dulcinea) : DON QUIXOTE :: WATSON : HOLMES

    (**c**) Sancho was the sidekick of Don Quixote; Watson was the sidekick of Holmes. Don Juan, the protagonist of a legend, is a rogue and likes to seduce women. Pablo is a character from John Steinbeck's novel *Tortilla Flat*. Dulcinea is a character who is referred to in *Don Quixote* but does not actually appear.
    Humanities—Description

50. SONATA : (*a.* movement, *b.* **sonatina**, *c.* coda, *d.* solo) :: NOVEL : NOVELLA

    (**b**) A sonatina is a short sonata; a novella is a short novel. A movement is a self-contained part of a larger composition. A coda is a musical passage that brings a piece to a conclusion. A solo is a (part of a) piece played or sung by one artist alone.
    Humanities—Description

51. NOVICE : EXPERT :: (*a.* teacher, *b.* **apprentice**, *c.* journeyman, *d.* layman) : MASTER

    (**b**) An apprentice is a novice; a master is an expert.
    Vocabulary—Similarity/Contrast

52. CLUB : (*a.* diamond, *b.* heart, *c.* **spade**, *d.* ace) :: LOWEST : HIGHEST

    (**c**) In bridge, the club represents the lowest suit and the spade represents the highest suit.
    General Information—Description

53. GOSLING : GOOSE :: SHOAT : (*a.* goat, *b.* sheep, *c.* horse, *d.* **hog**)

    (**d**) A gosling is a young goose; a shoat is a young hog.
    Vocabulary—Description

54. C : LEMON :: A : (*a.* **liver**, *b.* lettuce, *c.* orange, *d.* cake)

    (**a**) A lemon is a very good source of vitamin C; liver is a very good source of vitamin A.
    General Information—Description

55. PACIFIC : OCEAN :: (*a.* Mercury, *b.* **Jupiter**, *c.* Uranus, *d.* Neptune) : PLANET

    (**b**) The Pacific Ocean is the largest of the oceans; Jupiter is the largest of the planets.
    General Information—Description

56. ICHTHYOLOGIST : (*a.* sentences, *b.* algae, *c.* insects, **d. fish**) ::
ZOOLOGIST : ANIMALS

    (**d**) An ichthyologist studies fish; a zoologist studies animals of all types.
    Natural Science—Description

57. ELECT : SELECT :: TIE : (*a.* lose, *b.* win, **c. sty**, *d.* rope)

    (**c**) *Elect* is pronounced like *select*, minus the initial *s* consonant sound;
    tie is pronounced like *sty*, minus the initial *s* consonant sound.
    Nonsemantic

58. MALLET : (*a.* hunting, *b.* rugby, *c.* cricket, **d. croquet**) :: BAT : BASEBALL

    (**d**) Croquet is played with a mallet, baseball with a bat.
    General Information—Description

59. BAROMETER : AIR PRESSURE :: TACHOMETER : (*a.* speed of descent,
b. speed of rotation, *c.* acceleration, *d.* inertia)

    (**b**) A barometer measures air pressure; a tachometer measures speed
    of rotation.
    General Information—Description

60. EMERALD : GRUE :: (*a.* ruby, **b. sapphire**, *c.* amethyst, *d.* diamond) :
BLEEN

    (**b**) In Nelson Goodman's famous paradox, an emerald can now be
    construed as grue (green until the year 2000 and blue thereafter),
    whereas a sapphire can be construed as bleen (blue until the year 2000
    and green thereafter).
    Humanities—Description

61. MARTIN : DAVID :: (*a.* Dombey, *b.* Micawber, *c.* Magoun,
d. Chuzzlewit) : COPPERFIELD

    (**d**) *Martin Chuzzlewit* and *David Copperfield* are both titles of novels by
    Charles Dickens. *Dombey and Son* is a novel by Charles Dickens; Wilkins Micawber is a
    character in *David Copperfield*, and Francis Magoun was a writer and professor at Harvard.
    Humanities—Completion

62. (**a. 2:00**, *b.* 3:00, *c.* 5:00, *d.* 6:00) : SEATTLE :: 4:00 : CHICAGO

    (**a**) When it is 2:00 in Seattle, it is 4:00 in Chicago.
    General Information—Description

63. VENUS : (*a.* Uranus, *b.* Mars, *c.* Saturn, ***d.* Pluto**) :: LOVE : THE DEAD

    (**d**) In Roman mythology, Venus was the goddess of love; Pluto was alleged to be the god of the dead. Saturn was the god of agriculture and harvest, Uranus was the god of the sky, and Mars was the god of war.
    Humanities—Description

64. SUBORN : (*a.* give birth to, *b.* prove, ***c.* bribe**, *d.* demand) :: SUBORDINATE : INFERIOR

    (**c**) *Suborn* and *bribe* are synonyms, as are *subordinate* and *inferior*.
    Vocabulary—Similarity/Contrast

65. A : O :: (*a.* E, *b.* OA, ***c.* B**, *d.* RH) : AB

    (**c**) A, O, B, and AB are all blood types.
    Natural Science—Class

66. (*a.* coal, ***b.* petroleum**, *c.* black opal, *d.* uranium) : BLACK GOLD :: PYRITE : FOOL'S GOLD

    (**b**) Petroleum is black gold; pyrite fool's gold.
    General Information—Similarity/Contrast

67. MALACHITE : GREEN :: LAPIS LAZULI : (***a.* blue**, *b.* red, *c.* yellow, *d.* amber)

    (**a**) Malachite is green in color; lapis lazuli is blue.
    General Information—Description

68. LONGITUDE : LATITUDE :: (***a.* 110°**, *b.* 90°, *c.* 70°, *d.* 50°) : 20°

    (**a**) Lines of longitude and latitude are at right (90°) angles to each other, as are lines at 110° and 20°.
    Mathematics—Description

69. VALENTINE : SECOND :: NICHOLAS : (*a.* first, *b.* sixth, *c.* tenth, ***d.* twelfth**)

    (**d**) St. Valentine's Day occurs during the second month of the year; St. Nicholas Day occurs during the twelfth month.
    General Information–Description

70. MARK : (*a.* Munich, ***b.* Berlin**, *c.* Zurich, *d.* Basel) :: FRANC : PARIS

    (**b**) The mark was the unit of currency in Germany, of which Berlin is the capital; the franc was the unit of currency in France, of which Paris is the capital.
    General Information—Description

71. (*a.* biology, *b.* chemistry, *c.* physics, ***d.* astronomy**) : HERSCHEL :: SURGERY : LISTER

    (**d**) Herschel is famous in the field of astronomy; Lister is famous in the field of surgery.
    Natural Science—Description

72. METER : KILOMETER :: LOG 10 : (*a.* e, *b.* 10, ***c.* 10^3**, *d.* $\sqrt{10,000}$)

    (**c**) A kilometer is 1000 meters; 10^3 is 1000 times log 10.
    Mathematics—Equality/Negation

73. (***a.* Ash Wednesday**, *b.* St. Bartholomew's Day, *c.* Maundy Thursday, *d.* All Saints' Day) : EASTER :: FIRST : LAST

    (**a**) Ash Wednesday is the first day of Lent; Easter is the last day.
    General Information—Description

74. GHOST : SPIRIT :: GHOUL : (*a.* body, *b.* vampire, *c.* nightmare, ***d.* grave robber**)

    (**d**) A ghost is a spirit; a ghoul is a grave robber.
    Vocabulary—Similarity/Contrast

75. GERUND : (*a.* adverb, *b.* pronoun, *c.* conjunction, ***d.* noun**) :: PARTICIPLE : ADJECTIVE

    (**d**) A gerund is a verb form that can act like a noun; a participle is a verb form that can act like an adjective.
    General Information—Description

76. N.Y. : N.J. :: N.H. : (*a.* N.D., *b.* N.C., ***c.* N.M.**, *d.* N.W.)

    (**c**) N.Y., N.J., N.H., and N.M. are all abbreviations for two-word states of which the first word is *New*.
    General Information—Class

77. (***a.* Abelard**, *b.* Aquinas, *c.* Erasmus, *d.* Eusebius) : HELOÏSE :: TRISTAN : ISOLDE

    (**a**) Abelard and Heloïse were lovers, as were Tristan and Isolde. Abelard was a medieval philosopher and theologian. Tristan and Isolde are characters in a legend. Desiderius Erasmus was a Dutch Renaissance humanist and Catholic theologian. Eusebius Caesarea was the bishop of Caesarea Palestine and through his work provided a basis for Church History. Saint Thomas Aquinas was an Italian Catholic priest and proponent of natural theology.
    Humanities—Class

78. GOBI : (*a.* Africa, ***b.* Asia**, *c.* South America, *d.* Central America) :: SAHARA : AFRICA

(**b**) The Gobi Desert is in Asia; the Sahara Desert in Africa.
General Information—Description

79. X : X² :: STANDARD DEVIATION : (*a.* mode, *b.* median, ***c.* variance**, *d.* chi square)

(**c**) A variance is a standard deviation squared.
Mathematics—Description

80. LEONINE : (***a.* vulpine**, *b.* porcine, *c.* supine, *d.* bovine) :: LION : FOX

(**a**) *Leonine* means "like a lion"; *vulpine* means "like a fox." *Porcine* means "like a pig," *supine* means "lying on the back," and *bovine* means "like a cow."
Vocabulary—Description

81. AUGUST 8 : LEO :: (*a.* January 8, *b.* April 8, *c.* October 8, ***d.* December 8**) : SAGITTARIUS

(**d**) Someone born on August 8 is born under the sign of Leo; someone born on December 8 is born under the sign of Sagittarius. Aries (March 21–April 20); Taurus (April 21–May 21); Gemini (May 22–June 21); Cancer (June 22–July 22); Leo (July 23–August 21); Virgo (August 22–September 23); Libra (September 24–October 23); Scorpio (October 24–November 22); Sagittarius (November 23–December 22); Capricorn (December 23–January 20); Aquarius (January 21–February 19); Pisces (February 20–March 20).
General Information—Description

82. CHESS : CHESSMEN :: GO : (*a.* cards, ***b.* stones**, *c.* pegs, *d.* balls)

(**b**) The game of chess is played with chessmen; the game of go is played with stones. *General Information—Description*

83. CIPHER : NAUGHT :: (***a.* zero**, *b.* all, *c.* most, *d.* one) : NONE

(**a**) *Cipher, naught, zero,* and *none* all refer to nullity.
Vocabulary—Class

84. SEVENTH-DAY ADVENTIST : (*a.* Friday, ***b.* Saturday**, *c.* Sunday, *d.* Monday) : MUSLIM :: FRIDAY

(**b**) Sabbath occurs on Saturday for a Seventh-Day Adventist, and on Friday for a Muslim.
General Information—Description

85. (*a.* 10, ***b.* 11**, *c.* 12, *d.* 13) : DUODECIMAL :: 13 : DECIMAL

    (**b**) The number 11 in duodecimal (base 12) notation equals the number 13 in decimal (base 10) notation.
    Mathematics—Equality/Negation

86. (*a.* shawl, *b.* belt, ***c.* cloak**, *d.* sash) : BURNOOSE :: CAP : BUSBY

    (**c**) A burnoose is a type of cloak; a busby is a type of cap.
    General Information—Description

87. LEGHORN : (*a.* cattle, *b.* goat, *c.* sheep, ***d.* fowl**) :: ANGORA : GOAT

    (**d**) A leghorn is a type of fowl; an angora is a type of goat.
    General Information—Description

88. LISZT : HUNGARY :: MENOTTI : (***a.* U.S.A.**, *b.* Greece, *c.* Spain, *d.* England)

    (**a**) Liszt was a noted composer from Hungary; Menotti is a noted composer from the United States.
    Humanities—Description

89. MELODY : (*a.* immediate, ***b.* successive**, *c.* retrogressive, *d.* momentary) :: HARMONY : SIMULTANEOUS

    (**b**) Melody is successive; harmony is simultaneous.
    Humanities—Description

90. SINUSITIS : SINUS :: MENINGITIS : (*a.* liver, *b.* heart, *c.* artery, ***d.* membrane**)

    (**d**) Sinusitis is an inflammation of the sinus; meningitis is an inflammation of a membrane.
    Natural Science—Description

91. APPROXIMATE : EXACT :: (***a.* analog**, *b.* analogous, *c.* analogical, *d.* analogy) : DIGITAL

    (**a**) An analog computer yields approximate results; a digital computer yields exact results.
    Natural Science—Description

92. (*a.* is as, *b.* is almost, *c.* is virtually, ***d.* is**) : IS LIKE :: METAPHOR : SIMILE

    (**d**) A metaphor often uses the linking verb *is*; a simile links two concepts by *is like*. A metaphor compares seemingly unrelated subjects. A simile compares two unlike things as well, but similes do not equate the subjects as metaphors do.
    Humanities—Description

93. CONGRESS : U.S.A. :: DIET : (*a.* Germany, *b.* Turkey, **c. Japan**, *d.* China)

   (**c**) The main legislative body of the United States is the Congress; the main legislative body of Japan is the Diet.
   General Information—Description

94. MAYOR : (*a.* Montevideo, *b.* Sussex, **c. Casterbridge**, *d.* Marseille) :: HUNCHBACK : NOTRE DAME

   (**c**) *The Mayor of Casterbridge* and *The Hunchback of Notre Dame* are both titles of books.
   Humanities—Completion

95. INDUCTION : DEDUCTION :: HUME : (*a.* Locke, **b. Leibniz**, *c.* Berkeley, *d.* Mill)

   (**b**) Hume, an empiricist, used induction as his major mode of reasoning. Leibniz, a rationalist, used deduction as his major mode of reasoning.
   Humanities—Description

96. STOP : (*a.* h, *b.* j, **c. t**, *d.* v) :: FRICATIVE : F

   (**c**) The sound of *t* is a stop; the source of *f* is a fricative. A fricative is a sound that is produced by forcing air through a narrow passage. A stop is a consonant produced by stopping the flow of air at some point.
   Social Science—Description

97. (**a. $\frac{1}{2}$ gt^2**, *b.* ra, *c.* $\frac{1}{4}$ g^{2}k, *d.* pc) : D :: MA : F

   (**a**) Distance fallen by an object equals one-half the force of gravity times the amount of time squared; force equals mass times acceleration.
   Natural Science—Equality/Negation

98. FIDELIO : BORIS GODUNOV :: BEETHOVEN : (*a.* Rimski-Korsakov, *b.* Shostakovich, *c.* Prokofiev, **d. Mussorgsky**)

   (**d**) *Fidelio* is an opera by Beethoven; *Boris Godunov* is an opera by Mussorgsky.
   Humanities—Description

99. MISER : AVARICIOUS :: SYCOPHANT : (*a.* plutonic, *b.* veracious, **c. unctuous**, *d.* sybaritic)

   (**c**) A miser is avaricious; a sycophant is unctuous.
   Vocabulary—Description

100. (*a.* genitive, **b. dative**, *c.* ablative, *d.* vocative) : ACCUSATIVE ::
INDIRECT : DIRECT

(**b**) In Latin, the dative case is used for indirect objects; the accusative case
is used for direct objects.
Humanities—Description

101. (*a.* wheat, *b.* barley, *c.* oats, **d. rice**) : SAKE :: JUNIPER BERRIES : GIN

(**d**) Just as the beverage gin is made from juniper berries, so is the beverage
sake made from rice.
General Information—Part/Whole

102. A RAISIN IN THE SUN : THE GRAPES OF WRATH :: (*a.* Morrison,
b. Hansberry, *c.* Miller, *d.* Hare) : STEINBECK

(**b**) Lorraine Hansberry wrote *A Raisin in the Sun* and John Steinbeck wrote
The Grapes of Wrath.
Humanities—Description

103. SHARP : TACK :: COOL : (**a. cucumber**, *b.* stone, *c.* stream, *d.* milk)

(**a**) The phrases "sharp as a tack" and "cool as a cucumber" can both be used
to describe people.
General Information—Completion

104. SASQUATCH : NORTH AMERICA :: YETI : (*a.* South America,
b. Europe, *c.* Australia, **d. Asia**)

(**d**) The myth of the existence of a hairy hominid called sasquatch
originated in North America just as the myth of the existence of a
hairy hominid called yeti originated in Asia.
General Information—Description

105. CRETE : (*a.* Turkey, *b.* Syria, **c. Greece**, *d.* Albania) :: SICILY : ITALY

(**c**) Crete is a large island that is part of Greece and Sicily is a large island
that is part of Italy.
General Information—Description

106. $a^2 + b^2$: (**a. hypotenuse squared**, *b.* rectangular area, *c.* circumference
cubed, *d.* spherical volume) :: $(y - y_1) / (x - x_1)$: SLOPE

(**a**) The expression $a^2 + b^2$ is equal to hypotenuse squared just as
$(y - y_1)/(x - x_1)$ is equal to slope.
Mathematics—Equality/Negation

107. (*a.* tomato, *b.* peanut, *c.* chestnut, ***d.* ginger**) : PARSNIP :: TURNIP : POTATO

(**d**) Ginger, parsnips, turnips, and potatoes are all edible root vegetables.
General Information—Class

108. KEEL : FRAMES :: BREASTBONE : (*a.* human, ***b.* ribs**, *c.* pectorals, *d.* backbone)

(**b**) The keel is the structural centerline of a ship, to which the frames are attached. The breastbone is a structural midline of the body, to which the ribs are attached.
General Information—Part/Whole

109. PUSILLANIMOUS : (***a.* brave**, *b.* hungry, *c.* joyful, *d.* jealous) : PERFIDIOUS : LOYAL

(**a**) Pusillanimous means the opposite of brave, just as perfidious is the opposite of loyal.
Vocabulary—Similarity/Contrast

110. MARS : VENUS :: EARTH : (*a.* Jupiter, *b.* Saturn, ***c.* Mercury**, *d.* Neptune)

(**c**) Mars, Venus, Earth, and Mercury are all terrestrial or "rocky" planets. Jupiter, Saturn, and Neptune are gas planets.
Natural Science—Class

111. CACOPHONOUS : NOISOME :: SOUND : (*a.* sight, *b.* feel, ***c.* smell**, *d.* taste)

(**c**) Something cacophonous is an unpleasant sound. Something noisome is an unpleasant smell.
Vocabulary—Description

112. CAT : MOUSE :: (*a.* squirrel, *b.* bandicoot, *c.* lemur, ***d.* mongoose**) : SNAKE

(**d**) Cats are frequently kept to ward off mice just as mongooses are kept to ward off snakes.
General Information—Description

113. ELEPHANT : (***a.* piano**, *b.* tusk, *c.* table, *d.* hoof) :: WHALE : LAMP

(**b**) The elephant was once poached so that its ivory could be used for keys on pianos. The whale was once poached so that its oil could be used to burn in lamps.
General Information—Description

114. (*a.* Padua, *b.* Siberia, *c.* Verona, *d.* **Narnia**) : OZ :: SHANGRI-LA : ATLANTIS

(**d**) Narnia, Oz, Shangri-La, and Atlantis are all fictitious places of literature. Padua and Verona are cities in Italy. Siberia is a part of Northern Asia located in Russia. *Humanities—Class*

115. AURORA BOREALIS : (*a.* **Northern Lights**, *b.* Gulf Stream, *c.* Black Forest, *d.* El Niño) :: CRANIUM : SKULL

(**a**) Aurora Borealis is the term of Latin origin used for the Northern Lights. Cranium is the term of Latin origin used for the skull. *Natural Science—Similarity/Contrast*

116. PUMMELO : CITRUS FRUIT :: (*a.* rutabaga, *b.* grain, *c.* **lentil**, *d.* artichoke) : LEGUME

(**c**) A pummelo is a citrus fruit just as a lentil is a legume. *General Information—Class*

117. KENNEDY : (*a.* House Representative, *b.* **Senator**, *c.* Mayor, *d.* Governor) :: CLINTON : GOVERNOR

(**b**) Before becoming president, Kennedy and Clinton were a senator and a governor, respectively. *General Information—Description*

118. ARGES : CYCLOPS :: MEDUSA : (*a.* **gorgon**, *b.* minotaur, *c.* siren, *d.* hydra)

(**a**) Arges was a cyclops just as Medusa was a gorgon. The Minotaur is a mythical creature with the head of a bull and the body of a man. A siren is a mythical sea nymph that lures sailors to their demise. Hydra is a mythical monster with nine heads; when one head is struck off it is replaced by two new ones. *Humanities—Class*

119. I.E. : (*a.* English, *b.* Italian, *c.* **Latin**, *d.* Greek) :: RSVP : French

(**c**) The commonly used acronym "i.e." is derived from Latin just as the commonly used acronym "rsvp" is derived from French. *Nonsemantic—Nonsemantic*

120. (*a.* weary, *b.* tenacious, *c.* harmonious, *d.* **sprightly**) : JOCUND :: VERITABLE : AUTHENTIC

(**d**) Jocund means sprightly just as veritable means authentic. *Vocabulary—Similarity/Contrast*

Item Classifications

PRETEST

Item Classification Chart

		RELATIONSHIP					
		Similarity/ Contrast	Description	Class	Completion	Part/ Whole	Equality/ Negation	Nonsemantic
C O N T E N T	Vocabulary	25, 28, 41, 51, 64, 74, 109, 120	34, 35, 53, 99, 80, 111	83				
	General Information	20, 66	1, 2, 5, 7, 9, 10, 13, 15, 24, 29, 31, 39, 42, 47, 48, 52, 54, 55, 58, 59, 62, 67, 69, 70, 73, 75, 78, 81, 82, 84, 86, 87, 93, 104, 105,112, 113, 117	6, 36, 76, 107, 116	18, 40, 103	32, 33, 101, 108	46	
	Humanities		8, 17, 19, 38, 44, 49, 50, 60, 63, 88, 89, 92, 95, 98, 100, 102	14, 77, 114, 118	4, 61, 94			
	Social Science		16, 96					
	Natural Science	115	3, 37, 56, 71, 89, 90, 91	65, 110		12	97	
	Mathematics		21, 22, 26, 27, 45, 68, 79				11, 72, 85, 106	
	Nonsemantic							23, 30, 43, 57, 119

Achieving Success on the *Miller Analogies Test*

• Facts about the *MAT*	• The 12 biggest mistakes test-takers make
• How to solve analogies	
• Practice in analogical thinking	• Advice on preparing for the *MAT*
• Thirty helpful hints	• Improving your intellectual skills

FACTS ABOUT THE *MAT*

History of the *MAT*

The *MAT* was developed for use at the University of Minnesota, where it was first administered in 1926. At the time, its use was restricted to this university. However, the test received a great deal of attention from psychologists and educators, and it was subsequently made more widely available on a restricted basis. Today, it may be administered only at licensed centers, and distribution of the test booklets is carefully regulated. New forms of the test have been issued periodically over the years, each of which has test items of equal average difficulty and of similar content.

Description of the Test

The *MAT* is a 120-item, 60-minute verbal analogies test. All questions are in the form A : B :: C : D (A is to B as C is to D), with one of the four terms missing. Four possible options are given for the missing term. Of the 120 items, 100 count toward your score and 20 are experimental and do not count.

Your task is to select the option that best completes the analogy. Answers are recorded on a separate answer sheet. You are not allowed to make any marks in the test booklet. The answer sheet is later scored either by hand or by machine.

What the *MAT* Measures

According to the *Miller Analogies Test Manual* (1970), the "*Miller Analogies Test (MAT)* was developed to measure the scholastic aptitude at the graduate school level . . . The test items require the recognition of relationships rather than the display of enormous erudition [p.3]."

As is often the case with standardized tests, theory is rosier than practice. While there is no question but that the "recognition of relationships" is required, its importance relative to that of plain (and some not so plain) knowledge (or "enormous erudition," if you prefer) is probably overstated in the Manual.

Meer, Stein, and Geertsma (1955) investigated the relationship of *MAT* scores to scores on each subtest of the *Wechsler-Bellevue Intelligence Scale* (Wechsler, 1944), a former version of what has been among the most popular and highly respected intelligence tests (yes, some people actually do respect such things). These authors found by far the strongest relationship between scores on the *MAT* and scores on the Vocabulary subtest of the Wechsler-Bellevue. The second strongest relationship was with the scores on the Information subtest. The correlation between scores on the *MAT* and those on the verbal reasoning (Similarities) subtest of the Wechsler-Bellevue was not statistically significant!

Although this study was conducted on a restricted population, and therefore must be interpreted with caution, it points out something you will soon discover on your own: Vocabulary and, to a lesser extent, general information play an important role in determining *MAT* scores. No matter how good you are at reasoning, you first have to recognize and comprehend the concepts with which you are supposed to reason. You will probably find some (if not many) items on which your difficulty does not involve reasoning with the concepts, but of understanding them in the first place.

In one respect, all of this is not as bad as it sounds. Numerous studies have found that vocabulary is the best single predictor both of general intelligence and of performance in a fairly wide variety of tasks. This fact will probably be of more comfort to those who view themselves as walking dictionaries (or even better, walking encyclopedias) than to those whose vocabularies haven't kept up with their razor-sharp reasoning abilities.

Reasons for Taking the *MAT*

Most people who take the *MAT* do so for one of four reasons:

1. **Graduate Study.** The most common reason for taking the *MAT* is to support an application for admission to a graduate level academic program at either the masters' or doctoral level.

2. **Scholarship Aid.** A second common reason for taking the *MAT* is to support an application for financial aid in pursuing a graduate program.

3. **Business.** A third use of the *MAT* is as a selection or placement device in a business firm or agency. For example, an industrial organization may require the test of applicants to their management traineeship program.

4. **Guidance.** A fourth use of the *MAT* is for personal guidance by a college adviser or placement office.

If a school to which you are applying requires the *MAT*, you have no choice but to take it. But some schools offer you a choice of either the *GRE* or the *MAT*. In that case, you can take one or both. If you have the choice, here are the considerations that might incline you toward the *MAT*.

1. If you are weak in mathematics, the *MAT* is the preferred choice. One of three tests of the *GRE* is *Quantitative Reasoning,* whereas the *MAT* has just a few mathematically oriented items.

2. If you are particularly strong in vocabulary and general knowledge of the world, the *MAT* is the way to go. Although it is billed as a test of reasoning, vocabulary and general knowledge weigh heavily in the score, probably even more than does reasoning.

3. If you have difficulty taking tests that are long and grueling, the *MAT* is probably the better option. It is only 1 hour, versus 2 ½ hours of testing time for the *GRE.*

4. If you have found analogies to be a particular strength of yours, the *MAT* is also the way to go, as it is all analogies.

5. If you are weak in writing skills, you may wish to choose the *MAT* because, unlike the *GRE,* it does not require writing an essay.

More schools require the *GRE* than the *MAT,* so if you have the time or money only for one test, you may want to choose the *GRE.*

No matter what the reason for taking the test, it is usually not taken before the senior year in college unless it is administered through a special program that has received explicit authorization from The Psychological Corporation.

About the *MAT*

The following information is a summary of information contained in the Candidate Information Booklet, 2008–2009, for the *Miller Analogies Test* (2008).

THE TEST

The test is available in both pencil-and-paper and computer versions. It is usually administered through Controlled Testing Centers (CTC). Each CTC formulates its own schedule for testing, its own application process, and its own fee structure. Applications to take the test are made to the CTCs rather than to The Psychological Corporation, except in rare cases described below. Today, there are more than 600 CTCs in the United States, Canada, and overseas. Locations of CTCs can be found in the Candidate Information Booklet, which can be downloaded from the Web.

It is up to the CTC to offer either the paper-and-pencil format of the *MAT,* the computer-based format, or both. What the CTC offers depends on their preference—the paper-and-pencil test is not being phased out. No matter in which format the *MAT* is presented to you, the test items will be the same. There are different versions of the *MAT* to make sure that you won't be presented with the same items again if you take the test more than once, but the versions that exist are identical for the computer-based and the paper-and-pencil version. The advantages of the paper-and-pencil version, we believe, are that it is easier to go back and forth between items and that you can better get an overview of the whole test. However, if you are so used to doing everything on a computer that paper-and-pencil format makes you uncomfortable, you might then wish to choose the computer, if you have the option.

THE PUBLISHER

The publisher of the test is The Psychological Corporation, which belongs to NCS Pearson, Inc. The company was founded in 1921 and is the oldest publisher of commercial tests in the United States. The Psychological Corporation develops many of the tests used in the testing industry today, such as the *Wechsler Adult Intelligence Scales* and the *Metropolitan Achievement Tests*. It has a reputation for creating sound tests that are carefully researched and validated. However, like most testing companies, it tends to be rather conservative in the kinds of tests it publishes. The *Miller Analogies Test*, for example, is a very old test. It was already an old test when the first author worked at The Psychological Corporation during the summers of 1968 and 1969!

Testing Centers

At present, there are more than 600 testing centers in 50 states and in several foreign countries. Special arrangements can be made in foreign countries where there are no regular centers, but you should allow at least a month for arrangements of this kind to be made. If you reside more than 100 miles from a test center, or if you are not able to reach such a center within a month, special arrangements may also be made, but again you should allow ample time for these to be completed.

A complete list of testing centers may be obtained at *www.milleranalogies.com*, by calling 1-800-622-3231, or by writing to *MATscoring.services@pearson.com*. You should also contact them if you have made arrangements to take the *MAT* but have not received the bulletin of information regarding the test. The website for the test, which contains comprehensive information, is *www.milleranalogies.com*

Alternative Testing Site

If you reside more than 100 miles from a CTC, you have the option of requesting of The Psychological Corporation an alternative testing site. In this case, you may actually find an individual to administer the test to you. The individual must be cleared by the company. It might be, for example, a faculty member at your college or university, an administrator at the school, or a U.S. Embassy administrator or consulate. The fee for such a testing is a stiff $149. The procedure for setting up such an alternative testing site is rather elaborate and is described in the Candidate Information Booklet.

SERVICE AND FEES

Normal Fees

Fees are set by each CTC. Generally, today they are around $75 to $90, on average. However, there are additional fees that can quickly add to the cost of taking the test.

Accommodations

Special accommodations can be made at most CTCs if you need them. Such accommodations include a Braille, large-print edition, or audio edition for the visually impaired. It is even possible to arrange for a reader. Other accommodations can be made as well for those with specific disabilities or disorders.

RETESTING

After you have taken the *MAT*, you will receive a Retest Admission Ticket by mail. If you apply to retake the *MAT*, you must present the Retest Admission Ticket and tell the testing center that you are taking a retest. This ticket will ensure that you are not given the same form of the test twice within a period of one year. If you retake the same form within a year, your score will be invalidated. There is a fee of $25 for a replacement retest admission ticket, so do not lose the ticket when you receive it!

Individuals who have taken the *MAT* previously are expected to indicate this at the time of testing and to specify their reason for desiring to be retested. Once you have taken the *MAT*, you will be sent a Retest Admission Ticket by mail. By means of this ticket, the Test Administrator can give you a different version of the *MAT* than the one you completed previously. If you begin the test but then clearly recognize the form as one you took previously, you should tell the examiner. In no case should you take the same form of the test twice. To do so will result in the invalidation of your more recent score.

Information for the Handicapped

Nonstandard administrations can be arranged for the handicapped, but the testing center must be notified well in advance so that appropriate preparations can be made. Both Braille and enlarged-print editions of the *MAT* are available. If you are unable to mark your answer sheet yourself, you may make oral responses to an examiner, who will then mark the answer sheet for you. Oral administration of the *MAT* by a reader provided by the Testing Center is permitted.

Information for Those Who Speak English as a Second Language

You will not be permitted to use a dictionary or any other aids while taking the *MAT*. Although scores obtained by an individual for whom English is not a first language are always difficult to interpret, these scores would be completely uninterpretable if the test-takers were allowed to use English-language aids. If your command of the English language does not reflect your true verbal abilities, you will obviously be at a competitive disadvantage in taking the test, although you will very likely find yourself at a similar disadvantage when entering the academic or employment situation for which the *MAT* is required.

Since there are no foreign-language editions of the *MAT*, you must take the test in English. However, any competent test user aware of your linguistic background will take into account when interpreting your score the fact that English is not your native language. It would be to your advantage to make this fact known to the appropriate official at any institution to which your score is sent.

Test Dates

The *MAT* is administered throughout the year by appointment. Since testing dates and times vary from one center to another, you will have to consult a local center for this information.

Score Reports

When you report for the test, you will be given an *Examinee's Report* to address to yourself. It will be returned to you with your score recorded on it in a few days after you take the test.

Scoring

NORMAL SCORING

Scoring is done electronically, whether you take the test in paper-and-pencil format or via computer. If you take the test electronically, you will receive a Preliminary Score Report when you have completed the test. Those scores still need to be verified by The Psychological Corporation, however. Whether you take the test in paper-and-pencil form or electronically, it normally takes 10–15 days from the time you take the test until you receive your final score report.

The following information is contained in the score report.

Scale Scores

On the *MAT*, scaled scores range from 200 to 600. The average score is 400. Percentile ranks from 1 to 99.

Percentile for Intended Major

This tells you the percentage of people who scored below you in the major field in which you plan to concentrate.

Percentile for Total Group

This percentile is relative to all examinees who have taken the test, regardless of major.

The average score is 400 (cf. with the average on the GRE, which is 500). The theoretical range is 200 to 600, but extreme scores are very rare because the standard deviation is only 25 points, meaning that roughly two-thirds of all scores fall between 375 and 425, and roughly 95% of all scores fall between 350 and 450. Scores over 475 or under 325 will be extremely rare, each achieved by only a fraction of 1% of test-takers. According to Meagher and Perez (2008), in the 2001–2003 normative sample (i.e., the sample on the basis of which raw scores were converted to standard scores), the range of scores was 231 to 563. However, the bottom and top scores were the extremes—no one scored lower than 231 or higher than 563 of more than 126,000 candidates.

NORMATIVE DATA

As noted above, scores on the *MAT* show a theoretical range of 200 to 600, but very few people score under 325 or over 475. Meagher and Perez (2008) have provided means (average scores) for different fields. They found averages of 397 for business applicants, 400 for education applicants, 414 for humanities applicants, 403 for applicants in the natural sciences, and 399 for applicants in the social sciences.

HAND SCORING

If when you receive your score you believe there is a mistake, you can write to The Psychological Corporation and request that your test be rescored by hand. There is a $35 fee for this service. For the most part, such requests are not worth the bother. Machine scoring is typically accurate. But if your score appears totally off to you, it is probably worth the money, if only for the peace of mind.

REPLACEMENT SCORE REPORTS

If after four weeks from the date of testing you have still not received your score report, or if you receive a score report in a timely fashion but it is damaged, you can request a replacement at no charge if you send your request within six weeks of taking the test. Otherwise, there is a charge of $25. You can find the request from for your Score Report at *www.milleranalogies.com*

SCORE RECIPIENTS AND TRANSCRIPTS

The fee for the test includes a score report to you as well as to as many as three institutions. However, for the institutions to be included in your official score report, they must be specified at the time you take the test. If you request them later, you will have to pay a fee of $25 per score report. Only accredited institutions of higher education and approved scholarship and fellowship organizations are entitled to receive score reports.

At the time of testing, you may list up to three addresses to which you want official score reports sent. It is essential that you know at this time the correct and complete address of any institutions to which you want the score sent. You cannot expect the testing center to supply this information. The charge for reporting scores at the time of testing to as many as three institutions is included in the test fee.

Should you later decide that you wish additional score reports sent out, you will have to mail a request to The Psychological Corporation. You can find the request form at *www.milleranalogies.com*

The fee is $25 for each report. Requests and payments should be addressed to Pearson, Miller Analogies Test, P.O. Box 7247-6707, Philadelphia, PA 19170-6707. Money orders are required.

Scores of tests taken more than 5 years ago will not be reported, since these scores may not be accurate reflections of current ability. You must therefore take the test again if you need a score reported but have not taken the test during the preceding 5 years. If you took the test more than 2 years but less than 5 years ago, the old score will be reported, but you are strongly urged to retake the test nevertheless. If you take the test twice within 2 years, both scores will be reported.

NO SCORE OPTION

You may, at the time of testing, request that your test not be scored. If you do, the test will not be scored and there will be no reportable record of your having taken the test. However, there will be no refund and you cannot change your mind later. You will then be sent a blank score report and a retest admission ticket, should you decide to retake the test.

This means you must go into the testing session with the plan for no scoring. If you think you really messed up, you should cancel. But if you think you did reasonably well, definitely do not cancel. There is no guarantee you will do better next time, and you may do worse.

CANCELLATION OF SCORES

The Psychological Corporation reserves the right to cancel scores. Scores may be cancelled for a variety of reasons. They include (a) taking a retest without submitting a retest admission ticket, (b) repeating the same form of the *MAT* within a 1-year period, (c) the occurrence of an irregularity in the administration of the test, or (d) a score gain that seems questionable. A questionable score gain is one that is 50 points or greater than the previous score. If your score is invalidated for reasons of questionable gain, you may take a third test at no charge. If your third score is within 25 points of the second one, the second score is validated. If it is not, no scores will be released. Exceptions can be made in special cases.

Practice Tests

You can take either or both of two practice tests offered by the publisher, Harcourt Assessment. At the time we are writing this book, the cost for each test is $23.99. The website to access for more information is *http://tpc-etesting.com/matopt/*. The tests will be scored for you by the test publisher. New practice tests are scheduled to be made available in 2009.

What to Bring to the Test Center

1. **Bring all necessary forms and identifications.** You will receive the necessary forms in the mail. Don't forget to bring them to the test, as well as other information you may want to supply, such as addresses of the universities to which you want the scores sent. Do not bring notes, dictionaries, or the like; they are not permitted.

   Bring *two* forms of identification with you, at least one of which has a photo and your signature. The best forms of identification are government-issued ones, such as a driver's license or passport. Credit-card photos are not accepted as a form of photo identification. You will not be admitted to the testing until you show the two forms of identification.

2. **Bring a watch.** There may not be a clock in the room, or it may not be easily visible. Having your own watch ensures that you will be able to check the time easily. A watch will also help you to pace yourself as you work on the test and will enable you to fill in any unanswered questions before the end of the testing period.

3. **Bring two or three pencils with good erasers.** If you are taking the paper-and-pencil version, bring several sharpened #2 pencils with good erasers. Do not bring mechanical pencils or pens of any kind. The last thing you need during the test is to worry about not having a pencil or eraser easily available, so you should not even consider skimping on pencils or erasers.

4. **Bring your Retest Admission Ticket.** If you are retaking the test, be sure to bring your Retest Admission Ticket. This is extremely important so that you do not risk the test score's being invalidated.

What Not to Bring

Do not bring calculators, books, papers, notes of any kind, cell phones or other digital personal assistants, cameras, pagers, or any other similar kinds of materials into the testing room. Also, do not bring food or beverages into the room where you will be tested. Visitors are not permitted in the testing room either, so leave your friends, loved ones, and chauffeurs outside!

When You Are at the Test Center

GUIDELINES FOR BEING AT THE CTC

When you go to the CTC, you should observe certain guidelines. First you should arrive on time. If you arrive late, the policy is to not admit you. Thus, if you are traveling from a distance, be sure to leave more than enough time for your arrival.

Listen carefully to all the instructions you are given. You will be asked to provide various kinds of information, and it is important that you are prepared to provide it in order to ensure that your score is properly reported and validated. You will need to know your social security number, if you have one.

With either the paper-and-pencil or computer versions, you must sign your name. In the case of the paper-and-pencil version, you sign by hand, and in the case of the computerized version, you sign by clicking a signature box. If you do not sign, your scores will be held up.

Make sure that you ask any questions you have before the test begins, because you will not be allowed to ask questions after it has begun. Also you cannot leave the testing room until after the test is over. So please—if you need to go to the bathroom, go before the testing starts. Do not plan to wait until afterward. You do not want to be spending the testing session thinking about these kinds of needs.

At the risk of stating the obvious, you are forbidden to give or receive aid during the test. If you do either, you will be required to terminate the testing session, your test will not be scored, and you will not receive a refund.

HOW TO SOLVE ANALOGIES

What Is an Analogy?

An analogy is a problem of the form A is to B as C is to D. For notational convenience, the problem is often written as

$$A : B :: C : D.$$

This is the way problems are presented on the *MAT*.

Processes Involved in Solving Analogies

Some years ago, the senior author did a detailed analysis of the mental processes people use to solve analogies (Sternberg, 1977). He found that, overwhelmingly, people use a common and fairly straightforward strategy.

Consider the analogy **Washington : 1 :: Lincoln : (a) 5, (b) 10, (c) 15, (d) 23** as an example.

Step 1. *Encode the first analogy term.* You see the term "Washington," so you access meanings available to you in long-term memory, such as that Washington is the name of the first president, the name of a city, and the name of a state.

Step 2. *Encode the second analogy term.* You see the term "1," and you access meanings available to you in long-term memory, such as that 1 is the first whole number, that it can be a unitary quantity of things, and that it is also often used to refer to something that is the best of a bunch.

Step 3. *Infer the relation between the first and second analogy terms.* You try to figure out how Washington might be related to 1. You might now think of two possible relations, given your encoding: that Washington was the first (#1) president and that a bust of Washington appears on a $1 bill.

Step 4. *Encode the third term of the analogy.* You see that the third term is "Lincoln."

Step 5. *Map the relation between the first and second halves of the analogy.* You now can begin to relate the concept of *Lincoln* to the various relations between *Washington* and *1*. Of the inferred relations, both are still viable. Lincoln was also a president and also appears on a bill.

Step 6. *Encode the answer options.* You see the terms "5," "10," "15," and "23," and know what each of the numbers is.

Step 7. *Apply the relation you inferred between *Washington* and *1* in the second half of the analogy. You now can try out the mapped version of the inferred relations on each of the options.

Note at this point the importance of knowledge to success on the *MAT.* To get this item correct, you had to know something about *Washington.* Now you have to know something about *Lincoln.* If you know that Lincoln is on the $5 bill, you have a possible answer, namely, (a). But unless you know that Lincoln was the 16th president, you may wonder whether one of the other options represents the ordinal position of his presidency. And if you do not know that Lincoln is on the $5 bill and you do not know that he was the 16th president, you may find any of the options potentially attractive. So in this item as in all *MAT* items, knowledge as well as reasoning is needed for a correct response.

Step 8. *Discriminate among the answer options.* At this point, you decide which option best satisfies the constraints of the inferred relation. If you know both that Lincoln is on the $5 bill and that he was the 16th president, you can select (a) with confidence.

Sometimes there is an (optional) additional step after 7 and before 8. If you solve an analogy and believe that none of the answer options is correct, then you do that additional step.

Step 8a. *Justify one option as best although not optimal.* In this case, you choose the best answer, even if you believe it is not a perfect answer.

Step 9. *Respond.* Mark "(a)" or whatever your preferred answer is on the answer sheet.

Four Ways of Presenting Analogies

On *MAT* analogies, one of the four terms, A, B, C, or D, will be missing. In its place will be four options. Your task will be to select the option that best fits the analogy. The following analogy might be presented in any of four ways.

EXAMPLE

BLACK : WHITE :: DARK : LIGHT
1. BLACK : WHITE :: DARK : (*a.* gray, *b.* shaded, *c.* light, *d.* heavy)
2. BLACK : WHITE :: (*a.* somber, *b.* blue, *c.* gray, *d.* dark) : LIGHT
3. BLACK : (*a.* color, *b.* white, *c.* gray, *d.* coal) :: DARK : LIGHT
4. (*a.* gray, *b.* black, *c.* heavy, *d.* somber) : WHITE :: DARK : LIGHT

The correct options, of course, are *c, d, b,* and *b,* respectively.

Ways of Perceiving Relationships

You may conceive of the relationship between the terms of the above analogy in two ways. First, you may say to yourself something like "White is the opposite of black, and light is the opposite of dark." Instead, you may say "Black is dark and white is light." Either way you will arrive at the same answer.

The first way looks at the two terms on the left (A : B) as one unit and the two terms on the right as a unit (C : D). The second way looks at the first and third terms as a unit (A : C) and the second and fourth terms as another unit (B : D). The important thing is to discover a relationship that is the same between the two terms in each unit.

Sometimes it is more convenient to solve an analogy in one way, and sometimes in the other.

EXAMPLE

1. DOCTOR : PATIENT :: LAWYER (*a.* judge, *b.* jury, *c.* district attorney, *d.* client)

If the analogy is presented in this form, it is easier to consider the first and third terms as one unit, and the second and fourth terms as another.

A Common Mistake

A common mistake made by those who are relatively unfamiliar with analogies is to try to find a relationship between the first and fourth or the second and third terms. Don't do this. Often an incorrect answer option is waiting to be picked by those who use this kind of faulty reasoning.

In solving analogies, keep the following diagram in mind:

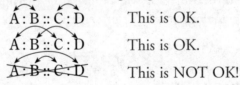

The analogy DOCTOR : PATIENT :: LAWYER : CLIENT is acceptable. The analogy DOCTOR : LAWYER :: PATIENT : CLIENT is acceptable. The analogy DOCTOR : PATIENT :: CLIENT : LAWYER is *not* acceptable. The third and fourth terms of an analogy may not be reversed, nor may the first and second terms. You can look for relations between A and B, C and D, A and C, and B and D in an analogy. You should **not** look for relationships between A and D or between B and C.

Errors Stemming from Reversals

Errors stemming from reversals are frequent.

EXAMPLE

BIRD : SPARROW :: (*a.* boy, *b.* species, *c.* mammal, *d.* phylum) : HUMAN BEING

The relationship is that a sparrow is a type of bird, and a human being is a type of mammal.

Someone might carelessly interpret the analogy as requiring him or her to infer that a sparrow is a type of bird and a boy is a type of human being. This relationship is correct, but it is not the one posed by the analogy.

Examples

It is important to realize that an analogy cannot be inverted. That is, in the analogy A : B :: C : D, the relationship of A to B must be the same as that of C to D. Or the relationship of A to C can be the same as that of B to D.

But the relationship CANNOT BE that A is to B as D is to C, or A is to D as B is to C. Inversions are not allowed. Consider some examples:

EXAMPLE

CAT : SIAMESE :: (*a.* animal, *b.* boxer, *c.* angorra, *d.* pedigree) : DOG

The correct answer is *a*. The reason is that a Siamese is a kind of cat and a dog is a kind of animal. The tempting distracter is *b*. But note that if you were to choose *b*, you would be committing an inversion. View the analogy as taking the form A : B :: C : D. The relationship cannot be A (CAT) is related to B (SIAMESE) in the same way that D (DOG) is related to C (BOXER). Rather, it must be that A (CAT) is related to B (SIAMESE) in the same way that C (ANIMAL) is related to D (DOG). It cannot be that A is related to B as D is related to C.

EXAMPLE

PROTON : ATOM :: DIAL : (*a.* numeral, *b.* watch, *c.* band, *d.* time)

The correct answer is *b*. A proton is part of an atom and a dial is part of a watch. Note that the inverted form—PROTON is to ATOM as DIAL is to NUMERAL—does not work, because the analogy does not permit A to be related to B in the same way as D is related to C.

EXAMPLE

(*a.* tree, *b.* hemlock, *c.* maple, *d.* trunk) : DECIDUOUS :: SPRUCE : EVERGREEN

The correct answer is *c* because a maple is a kind of deciduous tree and a spruce is a kind of evergreen. Note that *a* does not work because it inverts the analogy. It would make a tree a superset of deciduous trees, but a spruce is not a superset but rather a subset of evergreen trees.

EXAMPLE

STREPTOCOCCUS : BACTERIUM :: HERPES : (*a.* type I, *b.* virus, *c.* bacteria, *d.* simplex)

The correct answer is *b* because streptococcus is a type of bacterium and herpes a type of virus. Note that one cannot invert the analogy. Thus, Type I is a type of herpes virus, but one is not allowed to have an analogy where A relates to B and D relates to C. Hence, the correct answer must be *b*.

What Makes an Analogy Difficult?

Miller analogies differ widely in difficulty. In general, one analogy may be more or less difficult than another analogy for any one or more of five reasons.*

1. **Difficulty of Words**—You may simply be unfamiliar with the meanings of some or all of the words in the analogy. In this case, you may be stumped by vocabulary limitations before you even begin to figure out relationships. For example, the analogy IDOLATRY : IDOLS :: OPHIOLATRY : (*a.* icons, *b.* fire, *c.* serpents, *d.* darkness) would be easy for most people to solve if they knew that *ophiolatry* is serpent worship. The difficulty of the analogy resides in the unfamiliarity of a single word.

2. **Difficulty of Relation between *A* and *B***—You may know the meanings of the *A* and *B* (first two) terms of the analogy, but be unable to figure out the relationship between them. Consider, for example, the analogy TRAP : PART :: TEN : (*a.* net, *b.* twenty, *c.* whole, *d.* lost). The terms are all easily recognizable. The difficulty of the analogy is in recognizing that the relationship between the first two terms is that the second is the first spelled backward.

3. **Difficulty of Relation between *A* and *C***—An analogy may be difficult because it is not immediately obvious how the *A* and *C* (first and third) terms match up. Consider, for example, the analogy GARMENT : WEAR :: POTION : (*a.* clothing, *b.* liquid, *c.* drink, *d.* magic). The terms *garment* and *potion* have little in common. Recognizing that one wears a garment does not immediately help you to decide what to do with *potion*. You must recognize that the rule that relates the first half of the analogy to the second half is that "*B* is what one does with *A*." One wears a garment, and drinks a potion.

4. **Difficulty of Relation between *C* and *D***—Sometimes you may be able to infer the relation between *A* and *B*, but have difficulty applying the analogous relation from *C* to *D*. Consider, for example, the analogy GOVERNOR : PRESIDENT :: LEGISLATURE : (*a.* Capitol, *b.* Congress, *c.* House, *d.* Speaker). The terms of the analogy are all familiar ones, and the relations between *A* and *B* and between *A* and *C* are straightforward. The difficulty of

---

*Sternberg, R.J. Component processes in analogies reasoning. *Psychological Review*, 1977, 84, 353–378.
Sternberg, R.J. *Intelligence, Information Processing, and Analogical Reasoning: The Componential Analysis of Human Abilities.* Hillsdale, N.J.: Lawrence Erlbaum Associates, 1977.

this analogy is in applying the analogy rule from *legislature* to the best answer. Options *a*, *b*, and *c* are all fairly plausible, but reflection will reveal that *b* is the best answer. Option *a*, *Capitol*, refers to a specific building; option *c*, *House*, refers to only one of two congressional bodies. *Congress* (option *b*) is the national legislative body, however, and a legislature is a state legislative body.

5. Difficulty of Relation between D and Ideal Answer—Occasionally, you may come upon an analogy that for one reason or another seems to have no "perfect" answer. Consider, for example, the analogy MINUTE : HOUR :: FOOT : (*a.* yard, *b.* day, *c.* inch, *d.* length). The best answer is option *a*, although one could argue that this answer is far from perfect, since there are 60 minutes in an hour, but 3 feet in a yard. When none of the answer options seems quite right, you must either reconsider the way you have interpreted the analogy or else simply pick the answer that seems closest to the ideal one.

How to Select the Correct Answer

1. **Read all the options.** You must choose the best of the four alternative options presented. Keep in mind that item-writers make a deliberate (and usually successful) effort to make the incorrect options as plausible as possible. This fact has an important implication: *Read all the possible answer choices before selecting one.* Ace and Dawis (1973) found that analogies in which the last option is the correct one tend to be most difficult. A likely reason is that people sometimes don't bother to read through all the answers; they pick a plausible but incorrect option before they ever get to the last and correct option.

2. **Check the parts of speech.** In selecting an option, be systematic. When you don't know what all the terms mean, or when the relationship between them is not obvious to you, try to use context cues to figure things out. Remember that while not all terms of the analogy have to be of the same part of speech, they can be of no more than two parts of speech (except for nonsemantic analogies). Therefore, if an option you are considering introduces a third part of speech, it is probably incorrect.

3. **Infer the type of analogy.**

EXAMPLE

THRIFTY : (*a.* wasteful, *b.* economical, *c.* cheerful, *d.* wealthy) ::
SLATTERNLY : UNTIDY

Suppose that you don't know what the word *slatternly* means. You need not give up on the analogy either by skipping it or by answering randomly. The first inference you can make is that it is probably a Vocabulary item (see Content Category I, page 67). As you will soon learn by taking the practice tests, Vocabulary items frequently turn out to be Similarity or Contrast items (see Relationship Categories I-1 and I-2, page 75), and they are more likely to be items of the former kind (synonyms) than of the latter kind (antonyms). So a reasonable inference to make would be that *slatternly* means untidy, and that therefore option *b* is the correct answer, since *thrifty* means economical. Of course, you might not want to rule out the possibility of an antonym.

4. **Consider the sounds of words.** One thing you can do (and this really works on many occasions) is simply to look at the word *slatternly* and decide whether it *sounds* more like a word meaning tidy or one meaning untidy. Most people will choose *untidy*, and they will be correct. The answer to this problem is option *b*.

5. **Guess intelligently.** Suppose the item had been presented in this form:

EXAMPLE

THRIFTY : ECONOMICAL :: SLATTERNLY : (*a.* cheerful, *b.* quickly, *c.* circular, *d.* untidy).

The problem is now more difficult, with fewer context cues available. However, you can still approach the item systematically. First, you can reasonably eliminate option *b*. You know that *thrifty* and *economical* are adjectives, and three of the four answer options are also adjectives. *Quickly*, however, is an adverb, probably included as an incorrect option because it ends in *-ly*, as does *slatternly*. Next, you can reasonably eliminate option *c*. Although it is an *adjective*, it describes a property of an object, whereas *thrifty* almost always describes a characteristic of a person. You are now left with two options and have to make a choice, based on your past experience with words. When you finally choose an answer, you will still be guessing, but you will be guessing intelligently rather than blindly. Guessing can improve your score if you do it intelligently. Because there is no penalty for guessing, make an educated guess on any item when you are unsure of the correct answer. Try not to leave any items unanswered. Guessing intelligently can only improve your score.

6. **Use word association.** You will probably encounter some analogies on the *MAT* in which you find yourself simply unable to infer the relationship between the given terms. When all else fails, a strategy that is slightly better than wild guessing is to try word association. In using this strategy, you attempt to select the option that seems most closely related (in whatever way) to the given terms of the analogy.

The psychologist A. Willner had individuals take a form of the *MAT* as a word association test. Rather than try to solve the analogies, subjects were instructed to pick the answer option that seemed most highly associated to the given element. Willner found that on one of every four items, the correct answer (as keyed for the analogies test) was picked with greater than chance frequency. The indication is that, at least on some items, the word association technique will help you to do better than would random guessing. It is by no means a powerful strategy, however, and should be used only when your attempts to discover any kind of relationship have failed.

For example, consider the very first item of the Pretest. Suppose you were not sure of the exact relation being sought. If you selected option *b* because the color brown has the highest association with bears, in general, or grizzly bears, in particular, you would get the item correct, as brown is the color of the grizzly bear as well as being more highly associated with bears than are the other colors.

Allocating Your Time

A common problem in taking a test such as the *MAT* is one of time allocation. In particular, how much time do you allocate per item? You have 60 minutes for 120 items, meaning that you have to complete two analogies per minute in order to finish. And you really want to finish because items not answered are items lost. Moreover, looking at an item and getting an idea of what is on it provides a much better basis for taking a chance on an item than just answering at random!

If you have a choice between the paper-and-pencil version and the computer version, we would recommend you take the paper-and-pencil version. It is easier to get an overview of all the items, and it is easier to return to items. It makes time allocation easier.

First, always go in order because items are in order of difficulty. Your chances of getting items right are better on earlier than on later items. If you see an analogy and cannot answer it rather quickly—in 20 seconds or so—then make a notation somewhere of the item number. We recommend you use two different types of notations. One is for items for which you have an idea of what the correct answer is. The other is for items where you believe you pretty much have no idea of the correct answer. Then, when you go back, start with the items for which you have some idea of the correct answer. Do the items for which you have little idea last. But always answer the item once you have looked at it because you may not have time to go back. If you do have time, you can change your answer later. It is best to answer all items because it is the rare item for which you have absolutely no idea whatsoever of what the correct answer is.

A big mistake is to get hung up on a hard item. Sometimes, when taking a test, we lose track of the time. Losing track of time can be disastrous on a test such as the *MAT.* Each item counts the same, so it is absolutely not worth your time to spend a great deal of time on an item at the expense of other items. This is doubly true because, for all you know, the item may be one of the 20 experimental ones that do not count in any case. If you have answered all the other items, it is fine to spend that extra time. But if you haven't, be sure you answer all items to the best of your ability before you linger over any one item.

Sometimes, when people go back, they come up with a different answer than their initial one. A question they sometimes ask is whether to change the answer. We recommend you change the answer only if you are confident that the second answer is better than the first. There is some research to suggest that initial answers are better than redo answers.

Practice in Analogical Thinking

Directions: In each of the following the first two terms are related, sometimes in multiple ways. The third term is like the first two terms in some way but different from them in another. See how the third term is (a) like the first two terms and (b) different from them.

1. LEMON : TANGERINE :: PEACH

2. JUICE : MILK :: PANCAKES

3. DANCE : LEAP :: TURNED

4. PLANETS : ASTEROIDS :: SUN

5. ¾ : 0.75 :: 0.25

6. CENTIMETER : MILLIMETER :: INCH

7. DEGAS : MONET :: COURBET

8. SATURN : MERCURY :: PLANETS

9. BRASS : TUBA :: PERCUSSION

10. MISSISSIPPI : HUDSON :: HURON

11. MORGAN : MUSTANG :: MALTESE

12. WHELK : LIMPET :: KELP

13. STAMP : PHILATELIST :: NUMISMATIST

14. PURPLE : GREEN :: RED

15. DISCOVERY : ATLANTIS :: VIKING

16. CALDECOTT : NEWBERY :: PULITZER

17. LIMESTONE : SANDSTONE :: MARBLE

18. PHALANGES : METATARSALS :: FEMUR

19. MILK : CHEESE :: WHEAT

20. VITAMIN A : VITAMIN D :: VITAMIN C

21. ARTERIOSCLEROSIS : MYOCARDIAL INFARCTION :: CARDIOVASCULAR DISEASE

22. CARBON MONOXIDE : NITROGEN OXIDE :: ASBESTOS

23. MONOPHONIC : HOMOPHONIC :: DUPLE METER

24. INCUS : STAPES :: PINA

25. PRESIDENT'S DAY : VALENTINE'S DAY :: MARTIN LUTHER KING, JR., DAY

26. WOOD-CARVED RELIEF : CORK INLAY :: TEXTURE DRAWING

27. WATERCOLOR : TEMPERA :: CHARCOAL

28. EQUILATERAL TRIANGLE : SQUARE :: RHOMBUS

29. SPAN : CUBIT :: STONE

30. PHAEDO : REPUBLIC :: POETICS

31. SOPHOCLES : ARISTOPHANES :: HIPPOCRATES

32. TUNDRA : TAIGA :: TROPICAL RAIN FOREST

33. DONATELLO : MASACCIO :: RAPHAEL

34. DADA : SURREALISM :: SOCIAL REALISM

35. LYMPHOCYTES : MONOCYTES :: ERYTHROCYTES

36. SPRUCE : PONDEROSA :: HICKORY

37. PECK : BUSHEL :: FLUIDRAM

38. TROPIC OF CANCER : ARCTIC CIRCLE :: INTERNATIONAL DATE LINE

39. STARS AND STRIPES : OLD GLORY :: STARS AND BARS

40. FLINT : MATCHES :: LIGHTNING

41. DOMINICAN REPUBLIC : CUBA :: CHAD

42. OFFSIDE : CLIPPING :: GOALTENDING

43. KENYA : BRAZIL :: AUSTRALIA

44. FILMORE : VAN BUREN :: MARSHALL

45. TALLAHASSEE : COLUMBUS :: HOUSTON

46. IONESCO : BECKETT :: IBSEN

47. STIGMA : STYLE :: ANTHERS

48. CIRRUS : CIRROCUMULUS :: NIMBOSTRATUS

49. ORTHOCLASE : QUARTZ :: CALCITE

50. ST. PETER'S : SISTINE CHAPEL :: SANTA MARIA DELLA SALUTE

ANSWER KEY WITH EXPLANATIONS

1. A lemon, tangerine, and peach are fruits. Lemons and tangerines are citrus fruits, but peaches are not.

2. Juice, milk, and pancakes are foods. Juice and milk are liquid; pancakes are solid.

3. *Dance, leap*, and *turned* are verbs. *Dance* and *leap* are present tense; *turned* is past tense.

4. Planets, asteroids, and the sun are heavenly bodies. Planets and asteroids revolve around a star (the sun), whereas the sun is a star.

5. $\frac{3}{4}$, 0.75, and 0.25 are numbers less than 1. $\frac{3}{4}$ equals 0.75, whereas 0.25 does not.

6. Centimeter, millimeter, and inch are units of measure. Centimeter and millimeter are units in the metric system; inch is a unit in the English system.

7. Degas, Monet, and Courbet were painters. Degas and Monet are considered impressionists; Courbet, a realist.

8. Saturn and Mercury are planets; planet is the superordinate category.

9. A tuba is an instrument in the superordinate category "brass." Percussion is a different category of musical instruments.

10. The Mississippi, Hudson, and Huron are all bodies of water. The Mississippi and Hudson are rivers; Huron is a lake.

11. Morgan, Mustang, and Maltese are all breeds. Morgan and Mustang are breeds of horses. Maltese is a breed of dog or cat.

12. Whelk, limpet, and kelp are found in the ocean. Whelk and limpet are marine gastropods that live in shells. Kelp is seaweed.

13. A philatelist and a numismatist are collectors. A philatelist collects or studies stamps; a numismatist, coins.

14. Purple, green, and red are colors. Purple and green are secondary colors; red is primary.

15. Discovery, Atlantis, and Viking are space vehicles. Discovery and Atlantis are space shuttles; Viking is a planetary probe.

16. The Caldecott, Newbery, and Pulitzer are awards given to literature. The Caldecott and Newbery are given specifically to children's books, whereas the Pulitzer is not.

17. Limestone, sandstone, and marble are rocks. Limestone and sandstone are sedimentary rocks; marble is a metamorphic rock.

18. The phalanges, metatarsals, and femur are bones. The phalanges and metatarsals are bones in the foot; the femur is a bone in the leg.

19. Milk, cheese, and wheat are foods. Milk and cheese are members of the dairy nutritional group; wheat is not.

20. A, D, and C are vitamins. Vitamins A and D are fat-soluble; C is a water-soluble vitamin.

21. Arteriosclerosis and myocardial infarction are examples of the superordinate category "cardiovascular disease"—a disease of the heart and blood vessels.

22. Carbon monoxide, nitrogen oxide, and asbestos are air pollutants. Carbon monoxide and nitrogen oxide are gases that contribute to outdoor air pollution. Asbestos is usually an indoor air pollutant; also, asbestos is not a gas.

23. Monophonic, homophonic, and duple meter are examples of basic musical elements. Monophonic and homophonic are examples of musical texture; duple meter is an example of musical rhythm.

24. The incus, stapes, and pina are parts of the ear. The incus and stapes are parts of the inner ear; the pina is part of the outer ear.

25. President's Day, Valentine's Day, and Martin Luther King, Jr., Day are observed as special days in the United States. President's Day and Valentine's Day are in February; Martin Luther King, Jr., Day is in January.

26. Wood-carved relief, cork inlay, and texture drawing are art techniques. Wood-carved relief and cork inlay are three-dimensional; a texture drawing is two-dimensional.

27. Watercolor, tempera, and charcoal are media of artwork. Watercolor and tempera are types of paints, but charcoal is not.

28. An equilateral triangle, a square, and a rhombus are polygons. An equilateral triangle and a square are regular polygons; a rhombus is not a regular polygon because its angles do not have the same number of degrees.

29. Span, cubit, and stone have been used as units of measure. Span and cubit are measures of length; stone is a measure of weight.

30. The *Phaedo*, the *Republic*, and the *Poetics* are literary works associated with Greek philosophy. The *Phaedo* and the *Republic* are Platonic dialogues, whereas the *Poetics* was written by Aristotle.

31. Sophocles, Aristophanes, and Hippocrates were Greek. Sophocles and Aristophanes were masters of dramatic art; Hippocrates is identified with science and medicine.

32. Tundra, taiga, and tropical rain forest are examples of biomes. Tundra and taiga are cold-climate biomes; tropical rain forests are warm-climate biomes.

33. Donatello, Masaccio, and Raphael were Italian painters. Donatello and Masaccio are associated with 15th century Italian art and are considered painters of the "Proto-Renaissance." Raphael's work is classified as 16th century, High Renaissance.

34. Dada, surrealism, and social realism are 20th-century art movements. Dadaists and surrealists fought against conventional, accepted meanings in their art. Social realists believed that art has a social purpose and meaning.

35. Lymphocytes, monocytes, and erythrocytes are blood cells. Lymphocytes and monocytes are white blood cells; erythrocytes are red blood cells.

36. Spruce, ponderosa, and hickory are trees. Spruce and ponderosa are pines; hickory is a broad-leaf tree.

37. Peck, bushel, and fluidram are all units of measure. Peck and bushel are units of capacity (dry measure); fluidram is a unit of liquid measure.

38. The Tropic of Cancer, the Arctic Circle, and the International Date Line are divisions of the earth. The Tropic of Cancer and the Arctic Circle divide the earth horizontally; the International Date Line divides the earth vertically.

39. Stars and Stripes, Old Glory, and Stars and Bars are names given to American flags. Stars and Stripes and Old Glory denote the flag; Stars and Bars was a name for the Confederate flag.

40. Flint, matches, and lightning can start fires. Flint and matches are human means of starting a fire; lightning is a natural means.

41. The Dominican Republic, Cuba, and Chad are countries. The Dominican Republic and Cuba are in the Western Hemisphere; Chad is in Africa.

42. Offside, clipping, and goaltending are penalties imposed in sports. Offside and clipping are used in football; goaltending, in basketball.

43. Kenya, Brazil, and Australia are countries. Kenya and Brazil are located on the equator. Australia is in the Southern Hemisphere.

44. Filmore, Van Buren, and Marshall have served as high officials of the U.S. government. Filmore and Van Buren were presidents. Marshall was a Supreme Court judge.

45. Tallahassee, Columbus, and Houston are cities in the United States. Tallahassee and Columbus are capital cities; Houston is not.

46. Ionesco, Beckett, and Ibsen are playwrights. Ionesco and Beckett are considered modern playwrights (1944–1975). Ibsen preceded Ionesco and Beckett but is considered the "father of modern drama" because he introduced social problems into his plays.

47. Stigma, style, and anthers are all parts of a flower. Stigma and style are considered parts of the "female" flower (carpel); the "male" plant structure (stamen) is tipped with anthers that produce pollen.

48. Cirrus, cirrocumulus, and nimbostratus are clouds. Cirrus and cirrocumulus are high-altitude clouds; nimbostratus clouds often occur at low altitude.

49. Orthoclase, quartz, and calcite are minerals. Orthoclase and quartz are silicate minerals; calcite is a carbonate mineral.

50. St. Peter's, the Sistine Chapel, and Santa Maria Della Salute are cathedrals. St. Peter's and the Sistine Chapel are in Rome; Santa Maria Della Salute is in Venice.

THIRTY HELPFUL HINTS

Certain strategies are effective for raising scores on the *Miller Analogies Test*. Here are thirty of the most important ones.

HINT 1. *Don't wait until the last minute to prepare for the test.*
Research shows that you will do better if you spread your studying a little at a time over a longer period, rather than cramming all your studying into a shorter time right before the test. Therefore, start preparing at the earliest possible date!

HINT 2. *When you take practice tests, duplicate actual testing conditions as closely as possible.*
You best prepare yourself for the actual test if you take the practice tests under realistic conditions. Taking a standardized test means more than just answering a set of questions. It means you will be in an unusually stark testing room and will have to answer questions under time pressure. Actual testing conditions typically produce some degree of anxiety. Too much anxiety can hurt test scores, but so can too little anxiety. If you are too relaxed, you may find yourself not putting in maximal effort. Therefore, it is to your advantage to replicate actual testing conditions as closely as possible. When you take the practice tests, it is important that you strictly observe the time limit. Simulate all aspects of the testing situation as closely as possible and don't allow distractions (such as phone calls or errands).

HINT 3. *Realize that you can improve your score.*
One of the greatest sources of defeat is the belief that intellectual skills are fixed and hence unmodifiable. Once you believe that, it becomes true for you, because you make no effort to improve your intellectual performance.

Carol Dweck (1999) has studied thousands of students and found that they can be placed into two groups with respect to their beliefs about their abilities. One group believes that abilities are fixed; the other group believes that abilities are modifiable. When tasks are easy, the two groups of students do about equally well. But when tasks are difficult, the group that believes in the modifiability of abilities outperforms the group that believes that abilities are fixed. The reason is that the group that believes in the modifiability of abilities is willing to take on difficult challenges, whereas the group that believes in the fixedness of abilities is afraid to undertake tough challenges. People in this group are afraid they will look stupid if they try something hard. Believing that you can improve your intellectual skills is the first step toward improving them.

In fact, there is good evidence that intellectual abilities are modifiable (Grotzer & Perkins, 2000; Perkins & Grotzer, 1997; Sternberg, 1997; Ramey, 1994). It is to your advantage to act on this evidence.

HINT 4. *Be mindful when you take the test.*

How many times have you gone over the results of a test and felt like kicking yourself because you missed easy questions—questions to which you knew the answer? People often find that a major proportion of the test items they answer incorrectly are answered incorrectly not because they did not know the answer, but because their attention slipped or they got careless. Ellen Langer (1989, 1997) has referred to such behavior as *mindless*.

When we behave mindlessly, we act as though we are on automatic pilot—doing things without thinking. Have you ever been driving for a while and then discovered that you missed making a turn, or that you have lost track of what you are doing? Or have you ever been reading and gotten to the end of a page or even a book chapter, only to realize that you have only the foggiest idea of what you have just read? These are examples of mindless behavior.

You might think that people would not show such behavior during tests, but they do. Sometimes people let their minds stray even when the potential stakes in the situation are very high. Think about the catastrophes that can result from being mindless when driving! Make the decision that for the 60 minutes you take the test, you will be completely *mindful* and will concentrate fully on the test.

HINT 5. *Take responsibility for your test score.*

Julian Rotter (1990) has found that some people tend to be what he refers to as *internals*, whereas others tend to be *externals*. Internals take responsibility for their own successes and failures, whereas externals tend to blame other people or circumstances for their successes and failures. Research has consistently shown that *internals* tend to outperform externals in a variety of kinds of life tasks.

First, you need to take responsibility for your test preparation. There are always factors that will get in the way. You will have other things to do; perhaps you will have started preparing later than you should have; perhaps some catastrophic event has recently happened in your life or the life of a loved one. Whatever problems may emerge, it is essential that you take responsibility for preparing. This is the only way you can become truly prepared.

Second, you need to take responsibility for what happens the day of the test. I remember when I took the *Miller Analogies Test* some years ago I was seated at a desk that was too small for me. It was uncomfortable and I cursed my luck for getting stuck with such a small desk, not to mention the occasional noises of construction that came from outside. But then I realized that I had to take responsibility for my own performance. In many testing situations, *something* goes wrong. It may be different things on different days. Maybe you didn't sleep enough, or maybe the desk is too small, or the room too noisy, or the illumination less than adequate. For the 60 minutes you take the test, put all of this stuff out of your mind. Just focus on the test. The mark of the expert test-taker is deciding that, for the time that the test is in progress, he will focus on the test and put other things out of his mind.

HINT 6. *Be motivated, regardless of the stakes.*

Several years ago, the undergraduates in my department (the Psychology Department at Yale) invited me to give a talk to a group of them. I was honored to have been asked to speak and showed up at the appointed time. Unfortunately, no one else showed up except the woman who had organized the talk. She was extremely apologetic and started to give me a number of possible explanations for why no one else showed up.

At first, I felt hurt, but then I started to laugh. I said that I was actually very grateful that only she had shown up. The reason was that I could expect (or, at least, hope) that any talk I ever gave in the future would have at least as good and probably a better turnout. I now would be able to motivate myself to give my best possible talk, if at least two people (the organizer plus one other person) showed up! If at least two people turned out, it would be better than the turnout that ill-fated day. And sure enough, whether I get two people or two thousand, I give it my best shot. Regardless of the stakes, I give every talk my best shot, remembering the time that only the organizer showed up.

Some of you will be taking the *Miller Analogies Test* for extremely high stakes. The test may play a pivotal role in your being admitted or not admitted to the graduate school of your choice, or it may determine whether or not you get financial aid. Others of you will be taking the test for lower stakes. Perhaps only schools you do not care so much about require this particular test, or perhaps you are not even sure you want to go to graduate school in the first place, so a low score will not bother you so much.

Remember my lesson from the speaking engagement, though. If it is worth your time to take the test, it is worth your time to give the test your best shot. You should prepare for the experience with whatever resources you can bring to bear. Too often, people sabotage themselves, telling themselves that something is not important. This way, if they do not do well on it, they do not feel so bad. Don't fall into self-sabotage. Give the *MAT* your best shot, regardless of the stakes.

HINT 7. *Combat test anxiety with visualization and relaxation.*

If you tend to be test anxious, there are steps you can take to help yourself combat your test anxiety. Spend some time each day imagining yourself in the actual testing situation, and try to relax while you visualize yourself actually taking the test.

If that image is too stressful, start with less threatening images and build up to the image of yourself taking the test. For example, you might first imagine yourself three weeks before the test, preparing for the test. That image should be less threatening. So try to relax. Then imagine yourself two weeks before, then one week before, then right at the test. In each case, try to relax as you construct your image.

This description is a simplification of a psychotherapeutic technique called *systematic desensitization*. If you find that this self-help technique does not enable you to relax, you might seriously consider going for a few sessions of therapy to a behavior therapist or a cognitive-behavioral therapist. These therapists can help you alleviate your anxiety.

HINT 8. *Eat something light before the test, avoiding large amounts of sugar.*

Taking a standardized test consumes a great deal of your energy. The day of the test is not the day to fast or to skip breakfast. You need the energy you get from the meal. But don't eat a heavy meal right before a test. You want your energy going to the test, not to digestion. Also, avoid large quantities of sugar. Sugar can give you an immediate high after you consume it, but often leads to a slump somewhat later. You cannot risk feeling the slump while you are taking the test.

HINT 9. *Go to the restroom before you start the MAT.*
You also do not want to waste time getting up and going to the restroom—or needing to go! Make every effort to take care of your restroom needs before the test begins.

HINT 10. *Keep in mind that early items will tend to be easy and later items, difficult.*
You should answer test items in the order that they are presented because they are in average order of difficulty. Thus, for the hypothetical "average" person, the items will be in exact order of difficulty. But because there really is no completely average person, each person will find the order of difficulty a bit different.

An important implication of the principle that items are in order of difficulty is that, if you find an early item to be very hard or a late item to be very easy, you may be misperceiving the point of the question. If you perceive an early item as very difficult, you may be reading things into the item that simply are not there. Ask yourself whether there might be some easier way to see the problem. If you see a later item as very easy, you may be failing to appreciate whatever it is that makes the item difficult, and you may choose a sucker response as your answer choice. Ask yourself whether you might be missing something important in the question. So keep in mind that early items ought to be, on average, relatively easy, and later items, on average, relatively difficult.

Consider two examples. Suppose the following analogy occurs relatively early in the test.

HIT : HIT :: TALK : (*a.* speak, *b.* lecture, *c.* talked, *d.* silent)

This analogy is a straightforward one but not a totally obvious one. At first glance, it might look like it is unbelievably simple, representing simply a repetition of a word. But it becomes obvious quickly that it does not involve merely a repetition, because none of the answer options is *talk*. It is not a synonym analogy either, because HIT is not a synonym for HIT, but, at first glance, the same word.

Option *c* should give the answer away. TALKED is the past tense of TALK, just as HIT is the past tense of HIT. That's all there is to the analogy. There is nothing more, nothing deep. Select option *c* and move on.

Now suppose the following analogy comes rather late in the test:

(*a.* France, *b.* Russia, *c.* Italy, *d.* St. Helena) : NAPOLEON BONAPARTE :: ENGLAND : SIGMUND FREUD

The analogy at first appears to be straightforward. Napoleon was from France. But wait a minute. Sigmund Freud was not originally from England. He was from Austria. So the analogy is not about where a person was from, at least, not originally. The analogy requires you to know that Sigmund Freud, although he was born in Austria, died in England. Napoleon Bonaparte died on the island of St. Helena. The analogy, then, is quite difficult.

HINT 11. *Read every question completely*.

Look at *all* the answer options presented for each question. Remember, distracters (wrong answers) are there, literally, to distract you. Sometimes, the first option (or the second or the third) may look good and you may be inclined to save yourself time by selecting it. *Don't do it*. The distracter may be a near miss. Consider an example:

PEN : INK :: PENCIL : (*a*. lead, *b*. eraser, *c*. paper, *d*. graphite)

A test-taker in a hurry might quickly select option *a* because at first glance, it looks right. But in analogies, you are looking for the *best* answer, and you cannot know what the best answer is until you have read all the answer options. If you take the little additional time it requires to read all the options, you will discover that option *d* is graphite, which is a good competitor for being correct.

So which is the better option, "lead" or "graphite"? Well, in this case, ink is the substance contained inside the pen. The substance inside a pencil is graphite, not lead. The "lead" of a pencil is made of graphite. Thus, a pen uses (writes with) ink in the same way that a pencil uses (writes with) graphite, not lead. But if you do not read the whole test item, you may never get to choose the better answer.

HINT 12. *Read every question carefully*.

You need to read every question not only completely, but carefully. Consider an example.

TERRIBLE : HORRIBLE :: INGENUOUS : (*a*. clever, *b*. sophisticated, *c*. naïve, *d*. foolish)

If you read this item carelessly, you may quickly choose *clever* as the correct answer, and end up getting it wrong. *Clever* would have been the best response had the third word in the stem of the analogy been INGENIOUS, but the word is INGENUOUS, not INGENIOUS. The best answer is thus the synonym for INGENUOUS, namely, NAÏVE. You need to read the words carefully.

Suppose you do not know what INGENUOUS means. In this case, you will have to guess. Use the process of elimination. If, at least, you read the question carefully, you will know that the word for which you need a synonym is *not* INGENIOUS, so that *clever* probably is *not* the best answer, but rather, a distracter. At least you have eliminated one distracter and can choose from among the remaining three. It is also a good guess that *foolish* is wrong, because *foolish* is the opposite of *ingenious*; but we have now determined that the item most likely has nothing to do with being ingenious. Hence, your best bet is either option *b* or option *c*. As it turns out, option *c* is the best answer.

Here is another example:

FROWARD : (*a*. obedient, *b*. backward, *c*. disobedient, *d*. frontward) :: AHEAD : BEHIND

If read carelessly, the whole analogy appears to be about antonyms with respect to directions of movement. But that is not what the analogy is about. The first word is FROWARD, not FORWARD. And FROWARD means not easily controlled or contrary. The best answer is therefore *a*, because *obedient* is an antonym to FROWARD. Again, you must read each word carefully.

You may not know what FROWARD means. In this case, though, you can guess by using the process of elimination. Because you know that FROWARD is *not* FORWARD, it is a safe guess that you can eliminate the options pertaining to direction, namely, *b* and *d*. So *a* or *c* is probably the best answer. In fact, *a* is correct.

HINT 13. *Don't avoid questions just because they initially look difficult.*
Sometimes, a question that looks difficult when you first glance at it proves not to be very hard at all. Therefore, before deciding to skip a question and come back to it, make sure that the question actually is difficult. Consider an example:

VENUS : BEAUTY :: PLUTO : (*a*. prosperity, *b*. underworld, *c*. war, *d*. hearth)

Maybe your first reaction is that you just don't remember all those Greek and Roman gods. But wait a minute. Look at the item. You may find that you remember a few of them, and the one you remember is that Pluto was supposed to be the god of the underworld.

HINT 14. *Watch out for reversals.*
Remember that the direction of the relationship must be the same on both sides of the analogy. Do not trip yourself up by reversing directions. Consider an example:

METER : (*a*. millimeter, *b*. centimeter, *c*. decimeter, *d*. kilometer) ::
YEAR : MILLENNIUM

It is very easy to trip yourself up on this analogy, because option *a*, *millimeter*, has the same initial letters, *mill*, as has the stem term MILLENNIUM. The option therefore sounds right if one is not sensitive to reversals. But a millennium is one thousand years. Because order counts, the second term must represent a thousand of the first term (METER), just as the fourth term (MILLENNIUM) represents a thousand of the third term (YEAR). The correct option thus must represent one thousand meters, not one-thousandth of a meter. The correct option therefore is *d*.

HINT 15. *Look for all valid relationships but only for valid relationships.*
Remember that you can look for relationships either between the first and second and then the third and fourth terms, or between the first and third and then the second and fourth terms. All these relationships are *valid* for solving an analogy. But you *cannot* look for relationships between the first and fourth or between the second and third terms. These relationships are *invalid* for solving an analogy.
Consider the following analogy:

FOUR : 120/15 :: 32 : (*a*. 2^6, *b*. One hundred twenty-eight, *c*. Twenty-four, *d*. LXIV)

The basic analogy here is one of doubling. The second term is double the first and the correct option for the fourth term is double the third. Thus, removing differences of notation, 4 : 8 :: 16 : 32. But there is an option designed to trick test-takers who might look for a relationship between the first and fourth or between the second and third terms. This option is *b*. The third term (32) is four times the second term (120/15), and option *b*, one hundred twenty-eight, is four times the third term (32). Note also that the second and third terms are in Arabic numerals, and that if one selects option *b* (One hundred twenty-eight) or even option *c* (Twenty-four), one will have the first and fourth as well as the second and third terms in the same system of notation. But these relations are irrelevant. The only relations that matter are between the first and second terms and the third and fourth terms, on the one hand, and the first and third terms and the second and fourth terms, on the other. The correct answer is *d*.

HINT 16. *Analyze item contents and relations carefully.*
Remember that not all terms of the analogy have to be from the same content area. Do not be fooled by clang associations just because they seem to be from the right content area. Also, analyze the relations carefully. Consider an example:

ANNA KARENINA : LEO TOLSTOY :: (*a*. Scarlett O'Hara, *b*. Melanie Wilkes, *c. Gone with the Wind, d. War and Peace*) : MARGARET MITCHELL

The analogy starts off with a name that is both the name of a character and the name of a book by Leo Tolstoy. At this point, one cannot tell whether the correct relation is about being a character in a book or about being the name of the book. The second half of the analogy clarifies the issue. The options contain two names of characters that are from *Gone with the Wind*, as well as the title of the book by Margaret Mitchell. Because options *a* and *b* cannot both be correct, the analogy must be about titles of books, so the correct option is *c, Gone with the Wind.*

This analogy can be confusing. First, Scarlett O'Hara is so highly associated with *Gone with the Wind* that she can quickly appear to provide an attractive answer option. Moreover, it is quite possible that the correct relationship is one of characters in a novel. But the appearance of the name Melanie Wilkes, who is less closely associated with the novel, renders Scarlett O'Hara a less plausible option. The analogy thus appears to be about book titles, not about characters. Unless one carefully considers both the contents and the relations in the analogy, however, it is easy to get the analogy wrong.

HINT 17. *Examine parts of speech.*
Remember that many words can serve as multiple parts of speech, and that you need to check the various meanings of a word to ensure that you are using the word in its proper meaning and part of speech. Check that parts of speech match properly. An option is wrong if it does not correctly match the needed part of speech, even though the option may be otherwise plausible. Consider an example:

WAG : (*a*. tail, *b*. rattle, *c*. roll, *d*. joker) :: HARM : INJURE

This is quite a difficult analogy that easily confuses the test-taker. The most frequent use of the term WAG is as a verb, and the second half of the analogy contains two verbs, reinforcing the notion that, apparently, the entire analogy involves verbs.

Because HARM and INJURE are synonyms, the relation must be one of synonymy. But the problem is that neither *rattle* nor *roll* is a good synonym for WAG. Both are somewhat related, but neither really comes anywhere close to being a synonym. So there is no option that fits WAG as a verb. The test-taker must realize that WAG is being used as a noun and therefore that the synonym must also be a noun. A WAG is a joker.

HINT 18. *Be systematic.*
Try to be systematic in selecting the correct option. Use word association only if all else fails.

Consider an example:

LIBERATE : FREEDOM :: LIAISE : (*a.* connection, *b.* captivity, *c.* limit, *d.* destine)

This analogy is difficult in part because many test-takers will never have used or perhaps even seen the word LIAISE. It is an uncommon word, used primarily in Great Britain, and hence one can be forgiven for not knowing it. But you can be systematic and use your prior knowledge to try to solve the analogy.

First of all, LIAISE sounds like a verb, like LIBERATE. Because FREEDOM, the pair of LIBERATE, is a noun, you will want an option that is a noun. That removes option *d*, which is a verb. Because you know that liberating an individual or groups establishes a kind of freedom for that individual or group, you want to figure out what you would establish when you liaise. You probably know that a liaison is a person who establishes a connection. Therefore your best bet is to infer that to liaise is to establish a liaison, or a connection. You choose option *a*, which is the correct option.

HINT 19. *Pace yourself.*
Because you will have 60 minutes to answer 120 items, you should average no more than 30 seconds per analogy. Some items will take more time, some less. Do not get bogged down on a few difficult items. This can be a tremendous waste of time. If an answer just does not come to you, come back to the particular question when (or if) you have time.

For example, suppose you come across the analogy:

K : POTASSIUM :: (*a.* So, *b.* Sd, *c.* Na, *d.* Hg) : SODIUM

You took chemistry and you are pretty sure that, if you really set your mind to it, you can retrieve the chemical symbol for sodium. The problem is that it just isn't coming to you. So you stare at the item and stare some more, and try to think of everything you learned in chemistry, hoping that the association will come to you.

You're wasting your time. You might wish to pick whatever answer looks the best to you, flag the item, and move on. You are much better off going on to other items, and coming back to this one if you have time. You could stare at the item for five minutes, and still not remember that the chemical symbol for sodium is Na.

HINT 20. *Use all the time you are allotted.*
Never hand in your test booklet early. If you have time at the end of the test, review your answers, particularly to questions that you found to be difficult.

HINT 21. *Forget about other problems in your life.*

If, while you are taking the test, you start thinking about anything but the test (e.g., a misunderstanding with a friend or a money problem), STOP! You can think about these other things later. Give the test 100 percent concentration.

HINT 22. *Answer every question.*

If you have only a couple of minutes left, and have not reached questions near the end, then fill in answers to these items anyway. If you left any items unanswered that you already looked at, fill in answers to those items too. There is no penalty for incorrect answers, and by leaving items unanswered you are wasting possible points.

HINT 23. *Wear a watch.*

It is amazing how people can fail to take even the simplest steps to help them improve their score. They may spend hours studying for the test and even taking sample tests, and then neglect to wear a watch when they are tested. You must wear a watch or bring a pocket watch or other clock. There may not be a clock in the testing room, or it may not be easily visible. If the clock is not easily visible, do you really want to waste time trying to decipher the time from it? It is the watch that enables you both to pace yourself and then to fill in at the end answers to questions you may not have reached. Remember that to fill in these answers a minute or two before time is up is called *test-wiseness*, but to do so at any time after time is up is called *cheating*. Therefore, make sure you're test-wise.

HINT 24. *Bring three sharpened #2 pencils.*

Bring at least two and preferably three #2 pencils with good erasers. If your pencil lead breaks, do not expect the examiner to have a replacement. You simply cannot afford to have to find a pencil sharpener while you are taking the test. And there is no guarantee you will find one. Moreover, you don't need the anxiety of worrying about broken pencils. Never use a pen in filling out the test—use a #2 pencil only.

HINT 25. *Don't panic.*

If you find you don't know the answer to the first question, or to the second, or to the third, don't worry. Although items are arranged in order of difficulty, this ordering is of *average* difficulty. What is difficult for one person may be easy for another, and vice versa. The test is tough to begin with, so you can expect to find questions you can't answer scattered throughout the test.

HINT 26. *Be self-confident.*

Even if you're a notoriously poor test-taker, after working through this book, you will have done pretty much all you can to ensure that you perform up to your full potential. That's the most you can ask of yourself.

HINT 27. *If you don't do as well as you had hoped, retake the test.*

If things do not go as well as you had hoped, you can always retake the test. People typically do substantially better the second time they take a test. These "practice effects" are particularly notable on the *Miller Analogies Test*. Thus if things do not go as you had hoped, try again. Chances are you will do better the second time around.

HINT 28. *Remember that the test score is only one factor that is considered in admissions and financial aid decisions.*
Decisions about admissions and financial aid are almost always based on many factors. Thus, you should not believe that your whole future will hinge on how you do on the *MAT*. After making your best effort, keep in mind that in most cases the test score is not a decisive factor in admissions and financial aid decisions.

HINT 29. *Don't confuse test scores with measures of intelligence.*
Tests such as the *Miller Analogies Test* measure only a part—and arguably a relatively small part—of intelligence. These tests do not measure creative abilities or common-sense abilities, for example. These test scores account for only a relatively small proportion of the sources of individual differences that determine who succeeds to a greater or lesser extent in life (Gardner, 1983, 1999; Sternberg, 1997, 2000). Indeed, these tests account for only about 10 percent of the variation among individuals in their success. If you do well on the *MAT*, congratulations. If you don't, remember that there is much more to intelligence than what this or other similar tests measure.

HINT 30. *If you bought the book, then you have the right attitude toward life.*
If you bought this book, then your attitude toward life is that you can do better if you work at it. Ultimately, that will probably count for a lot more than a test score. Albert Bandura (1997) has shown that one of the best predictors of success in life is a sense of *self-efficacy*, the belief that one can do what one needs to get done. Your buying this book shows that you believe that, with hard work, you can do better. And that is the attitude that will help you succeed in life.

References

Bandura, A. *Self-efficacy: The Exercise of Control.* New York: W. H. Freeman and Company, 1997.

Dweck, C. S. *Self-theories: Their Role in Motivation, Personality, and Development.* Philadelphia: Psychology Press, 1999.

Gardner, H. *Frames of Mind: The Theory of Multiple Intelligences.* New York: Basic, 1983.

Gardner, H. *Intelligence Reframed: Multiple Intelligences for the 21st Century.* New York: Basicbooks, 1999.

Grotzer, T. A., & Perkins, D. A. Teaching of intelligence: A performance conception. In R. J. Sternberg (Ed.), *Handbook of Intelligence* (pp. 492–515). New York: Cambridge University Press, 2000.

Langer, E. J. *Mindfulness.* New York: Addison-Wesley, 1989.

Langer, E. J. *The Power of Mindful Learning.* Needham Heights, MA: Addison-Wesley, 1997.

Perkins, D. N., & Grotzer, T. A. Teaching intelligence. *American Psychologist*, Vol. 52, 1125–1133, 1997.

Ramey, C. T. Abecedarian Project. In R. J. Sternberg (Ed.), *Encyclopedia of Human Intelligence* (Vol. 1, pp. 1–2). New York: Macmillan, 1994.

Rotter, J. B. Internal versus external control of reinforcement: A case history of a variable. *American Psychologist,* Vol. 45, 489–493, 1990.

Sternberg, R. J. *Successful Intelligence.* New York: Plume, 1997.

Sternberg, R. J. Successful intelligence: A unified view of giftedness. In C. F. M. van Lieshout & P. G. Heymans (Ed.), *Developing Talent, Across the Life Span* (pp. 43–65). Hove, UK: Psychology Press, 2000.

THE 12 BIGGEST MISTAKES TEST-TAKERS MAKE

1. **Believing that test scores are the measure of a man or woman.** All societies share certain "conventional wisdom." Some of it is true; some of it is not. For example, in 1787, a "three-fifths compromise" was enacted that, for determining political representation in the House of Representatives, would count each slave as three-fifths of a person. This was silly, and yet it was actually written into law. Societies do things at times that later seem odd. Our society believes, properly, we think, that tests have a useful role in high-stakes educational decisions, but some people start to view tests as measuring the worth of a person. Is the score of someone, which is three-fifths of someone else's worth only three-fifths as much? The answer, of course, is no. But you need not only to know that, but to feel it. Your worth as a person is *not* determined by your test scores. Many people with lower test scores go on to do great things. Some with higher test scores go on to do little.

2. **Believing the hype that the tests measure all they are supposed to measure.** Don't believe the hype. People are either analytical thinkers or not analytical thinkers. And can't someone be a good analytical thinker without having the vocabulary and general information to do well on this particular test? Certainly. It will not identify analytical thinkers who do not speak English. And how about those for whom English is a second language? Our society hypes various products, including tests. Don't get sucked in. No test is perfect. No test identifies analytical or any other kinds of thinkers in a foolproof way. The test is a means to help you get into graduate school or to help you get a scholarship or fellowship. It's not a whole lot more than that.

3. **Believing that test scores are immutable.** Many students believe the statements that test publishers sometimes make that using books or taking courses to improve scores really cannot make much of a difference in test scores. Not so. Test-taking is a learnable skill, just as is riding a bicycle or using a word-processing program on a computer. Almost every skill is learnable and modifiable. Test-taking is no exception. At the same time, it is better to expect reasonable gains than unreasonable ones. If your goal is to increase your score 10 or 15 points out of 100, that is quite reasonable, and you may attain this goal. If your goal is to increase your score 30 or 40 points, for most people, that will not be a realistic goal.

4. **Being overconfident or underconfident.** People who are overconfident set themselves up for a fall. They do not take the challenge of the test seriously enough, thinking that without hard work and preparation they will ace the test. Often, they end up being disappointed. People who are underconfident often choke when they take this test or any other. They become so nervous that they cannot perform at their optimum level. So they create for themselves a self-fulfilling prophecy.

5. **Taking the test close to the deadline for which the score must be submitted.** All tests have a standard error of measurement. That means that sometimes you will do better than you could have expected to do, and other times you will do worse. If you do worse, you can always retake the test. But you cut off your chance of doing that if you take the test too close to when the score is due. In that case, if you get a score that is lower than you had hoped for, you do not allow yourself the option to take it again. Don't wait until the last minute. Take the test early so that if you need to take it again, you will have time.

6. **Drinking a lot of coffee or tea before taking the test.** Research shows that caffeine can help mental performance. So a little coffee or tea before the test may actually help your score. But do not consume too much caffeine. First, it may make you jumpy and actually hurt your performance. Second, it may leave you wanting to go the bathroom and you will not be permitted to go during the testing session. Third, if you are not used to it, you may have side effects such as feeling restless, irritable, or trembling of the hands—the last thing you need when you take a test.

7. **Cramming at the last moment.** Just don't. Research shows that last-minute cramming is not helpful and can actually hurt you. Don't study in the last 24 hours before the test. Just get plenty of rest and go to the test refreshed. You need to have a study plan that starts you early and not at the last moment.

8. **Spending too much time on hard items.** If you get stuck on an item, move on. You then can later return to it. There are 120 items to be completed in 60 minutes. That is 2 per minute. You cannot afford to waste lots of time on hard items.

9. **Not reading items carefully.** Don't waste points on sloppy reading of items. Many people, on later finding out the answers to a test, feel like kicking themselves for getting items wrong for which they knew the answer, because they did not read the item carefully. You cannot afford to waste points on sloppy reading of items.

10. **Leaving items blank.** There is *no* penalty for wrong answers. Do *not* leave any blanks. When time is soon going to be up, make sure you answer every question, even if you answer at random.

11. **Not budgeting time.** You have 30 seconds per item. That's it. So you have to keep budgeting your time so as not to waste time. Don't let yourself get

behind. If an item is too hard, move on. Near the end, fill in an answer at random if you cannot get back to it.

12. **Eliminating answer options that are correct.** Distracters—wrong answers—are chosen on the Miller Analogies Test to be attractive. That means it may be tempting to eliminate as incorrect an answer option that is actually correct. Unless you are confident that an option is wrong, do not eliminate it. It you cannot eliminate even one answer option *for sure,* guess at random. You will have a 1 out of 5 chance of getting the item right.

Reference

www.MillerAnalogies.com.
http://harcourtassessment.com/haiweb/Cultures/en-US/dotCom/milleranalogies.com.htm

ADVICE ON PREPARING FOR THE *MAT*

That the *MAT* is not just a test of your reasoning abilities is probably evident to you from doing the pretest in this book. The *MAT* also assesses your vocabulary and your store of general information, as well as specific information in diverse areas. A person whose native language is not English and whose culture is not mainstream will find the *MAT* extremely difficult, even if the aid of a dictionary were allowed. The level of vocabulary on the test is high; in addition, the definition used for a particular word is not always the most salient or obvious.

In using this book, you are strongly advised to keep a notebook of words you don't know along with their definitions. Use a dictionary to look up words you're not sure of. Study these words regularly, and use them as much as possible, in order to add them to your vocabulary. Also study the vocabulary given in this book as well as the words in the practice tests. The vocabulary on pages 87–104 contains words often used in graduate-level tests and, in addition, provides you with useful synonyms and antonyms.

Five other techniques are also useful in learning new words:

1. Use mnemonics as much as possible, visualizing the words and their meanings as vividly as you can.
2. Group together similar words to study. Also, put together words with similar roots and related meanings.
3. Make flashcards with words on one side, definitions on the other. Study the cards during any free time you have.
4. Whenever possible, study the words with their antonyms and synonyms.
5. Read a good newspaper regularly, such as *The New York Times* or *The Wall Street Journal,* to reinforce the vocabulary you have learned.

Not all these techniques work for everyone; some are better than others for different people. But the benefits of increasing your vocabulary are enormous—you will raise not only your *MAT* scores but other test scores as well.

Fighting Test Anxiety

Almost everyone is familiar with test anxiety. You walk into the examination room and your heart starts beating rapidly, you start sweating, and you start thinking about how poorly you are about to do on the exam. This is detrimental to your test-taking. You may know all there is to know, but if you go into the exam overly anxious, you will not do as well as you should. It is normal for a test-taker to have a mild amount of anxiety; it's what gets a person through an exam. However, too much anxiety can have a crippling effect when a person focuses on negative thoughts and ignores positive ones.

Causes of an individual's test anxiety may be one's exaggeration of the consequences of the exam, the demands one has placed on oneself, or the evaluation of oneself in terms of one's performance on the exam. The most effective way to handle test anxiety is with professional help (e.g., a clinical psychologist). Psychologists have found several techniques, most of which are based on relaxation, to be effective in battling test anxiety. One such technique is systematic desensitization.

Systematic desensitization teaches an individual to be able to relax in the presence of whatever causes the anxiety—in this case, an exam. The individual seeking this therapy is initially taught to relax while imagining anxiety-producing scenarios. The scenarios are graded. Some produce mild amounts of anxiety, whereas others produce extreme amounts of anxiety. Individuals work their way up from the least to the most anxiety-producing scenarios. The client begins by imagining the scenario that produces the least amount of anxiety while relaxing, and if that does not cause anxiety, the person imagines the next scenario on the scale. If it does cause anxiety, the client repeats imagining scenarios until he or she can do so without experiencing anxiety. The client gradually works through all of the scenarios until all of them can be imagined without a great deal of anxiety. It typically takes weeks or even a few months to get through all of them.

For example, a woman seeking treatment for test anxiety may first be told to imagine herself driving to the test center. If she does not feel anxiety while imagining this, she may then imagine getting out of the car, then imagine walking to the building, then imagine walking to the examination room, etc. She will go through this progression of scenarios until she can imagine herself picking up her pencil and taking the test without too much anxiety. At this point, her anxiety about taking tests should diminish.

Although this process works best when it is done with professional help over many sessions, you can learn from it. Its greatest lessons are that you should acquaint yourself with the testing process, and you should relax before an exam, not just a few minutes before sitting down to take it, but weeks in advance. Imagine all the details about the examination day that you can think of. For example, picture how you will get ready to go to the testing center, how you will get there, and how you will get through the paperwork. You should also take the practice tests in this book very seriously; they are very comparable to the real *MAT*. Take the practice tests under real test-taking conditions. For instance, find a quiet place, do not allow any distractions, set a time limit, and pretend you are in the examination room taking the real test. If you take all the practice tests in this book in that manner, when it comes time to take the real one, you will feel more comfortable with the test and the procedures.

Other recommendations that you may want to consider are:

1. Do not wait until the last minute to study. If you wait, you will get flustered by all the studying there is to do, and you will not be able to study as effectively. Study with a positive attitude. Of course there will be information you don't know—no one knows everything—but learn as much as you can, and remember that there is a lot that you do know.

2. As you go to the test center, keep a positive attitude. Do not panic. You have done all the preparing you could do. Remember, the *MAT* is only one part of your entire portfolio. You have accomplished a great deal to get to where you are today, including higher education or employment. Those taking your *MAT* score into consideration will also take into consideration everything else you have accomplished. Think ahead to after the exam. When the exam is over, and it is no longer looming over your head, you will still be the same person. This exam will not drastically change your life.

3. When you take the *MAT*, try to put aside other problems in your life. Give this exam your full concentration. Continue to relax. Have self-confidence. Answering a question you know should fuel your confidence. When you come to a question you don't know, as everyone does, do not let it discourage you. Make an educated guess and then move on.

IMPROVING YOUR INTELLECTUAL SKILLS

Recommended Reading

Most people read this book in order to attain as high a score as possible on the *Miller Analogies Test*. Many readers are also interested in improving the general level of their intellectual skills. Whereas the material in this book is aimed primarily at raising your score on the *MAT*, and only secondarily at improving your general intellectual skills, other books with the primary aim of improving your general intellectual skills are available. Although such books are not intended to improve your score on any one particular test, sharpening your intellectual skills can help you on a large variety of tests, including the *MAT*.

SUCCESSFUL INTELLIGENCE

By Robert J. Sternberg, published as a paperback by Plume, 1997. This book contains further ideas about mind improvement based on the author's triarchic theory of human intelligence.

Other Test Preparation Books

Numerous other books containing problems of various kinds, including other test preparation books, can be quite helpful in improving general thinking skills. Thus, for the person whose goal is general improvement in thinking, Barron's other test preparation books, such as *How to Prepare for the Graduate Record Examination*, are recommended as supplements.

Kinds of Analogies Found on the Miller Analogies Test

- Content of *MAT* analogies
- Practice in recognizing content areas
- Relationships used in *MAT* analogies
- Practice in using and recognizing relationships
- Distribution of categories

CONTENT OF *MAT* ANALOGIES

Success on the *MAT* requires familiarity with a broad range of subjects. There are different ways of classifying the subject areas. The following list of the general content areas covered by the *MAT* shows just one way to group these areas conveniently.

I Vocabulary

II General Information

III Humanities

    A. History
    B. Literature
    C. Mythology
    D. Philosophy
    E. Religion
    F. Art
    G. Music
    H. Grammar

IV Social Sciences

A. Psychology
B. Sociology
C. Economics
D. Linguistics
E. Anthropology
F. Political Science

V Natural Sciences

A. Biology
B. Physics
C. Chemistry

VI Mathematics

VII Nonsemantic

The following examples will give you an idea of what each area covers:

1. *Vocabulary:*

   STRIDENT : (*a.* wide, *b.* shrill, *c.* confident, *d.* rigid) :: TURBULENT :
   AGITATED
   Answer: (**b**). This analogy deals with similarities in meaning. *Strident* and
   shrill are synonyms, as are *turbulent* and *agitated.*

2. *General Information:*

   JAPAN : ORIENT :: FRANCE : (*a.* Europe, *b.* Continent, *c.* Paris,
   d. Occident)
   Answer: (**d**). This analogy concerns locations of countries. Japan is a
   country in the Orient. France is a country in the Occident.

3. *History:*

   (*a.* T. Roosevelt, *b.* F. Roosevelt, *c.* Wilson, *d.* Eisenhower) : SQUARE
   DEAL :: TRUMAN : FAIR DEAL
   Answer: (**a**). This analogy involves presidential programs. T. Roosevelt
   introduced what he called the Square Deal. Truman introduced what he
   called the Fair Deal.

4. *Literature:*

NAPOLEON : FRENCH ARMY :: MAJOR BARBARA : (*a.* Salvation Army, *b.* English Army, *c.* American Army, *d.* Children's Army)
Answer: (**a**). This analogy is about army affiliations of officers. Napoleon was an officer in the French Army. Major Barbara, in Shaw's play by the same name, was an officer in the Salvation Army.

5. *Mythology:*

ZEUS : HERA :: JUPITER : (*a.* Venus, *b.* Minerva, *c.* Juno, *d.* Diana)
Answer: (**c**). This analogy requires recognition of two different names for the same god. Zeus was the Greek name and Jupiter the Roman name for the king of the gods. Hera was the Greek name and Juno the Roman name for his wife.

6. *Philosophy:*

LOCKE : INDUCTION :: (*a.* Berkeley, *b.* Bentham, *c.* Hume, *d.* Spinoza) : DEDUCTION
Answer: (**d**). This analogy deals with methodologies used by major philosophers. Locke was an empiricist philosopher and hence his mode of reasoning was primarily inductive. Spinoza, a rationalist philosopher, relied primarily on deductive reasoning in order to draw conclusions.

7. *Religion:*

ADAM : (*a.* Eve, *b.* Eden, *c.* Heaven, *d.* Israel) :: OEDIPUS : THEBES
Answer: (**b**). This analogy concerns places from which people were expelled. Adam was expelled from Eden. Oedipus was expelled from Thebes.

8. *Art:*

RENOIR : IMPRESSIONIST :: (*a.* Monet, *b.* Bosch, *c.* Van Gogh, *d.* Munch) : EXPRESSIONIST
Answer: (**d**). This analogy involves schools of famous painters. Renoir was an impressionist painter. Munch was an expressionist painter.

9. *Music:*

(*a.* coda, *b.* aria, *c.* overture, *d.* coloratura) : OPERA :: PREFACE : BOOK
Answer: (**c**). This analogy is about introductions to works of art. An overture introduces an opera. A preface introduces a book.

10. *Social Sciences:*

FREUD : OEDIPUS COMPLEX :: (*a.* Jung, *b.* Horney, *c.* Adler, *d.* Allport) : INFERIORITY COMPLEX
Answer: (**c**). This analogy requires recognition of originators of terms describing psychological complexes. Freud coined the expression *Oedipus complex*; Adler coined the expression *inferiority complex*.

11. *Biology:*

(*a.* stomach, *b.* throat, *c.* lung, *d.* gullet) : PHARYNX :: WINDPIPE : TRACHEA
Answer: (**b**). This analogy deals with organs in the body. The pharynx is the throat. The trachea is the windpipe.

12. *Physics:*

MECHANICAL ADVANTAGE : RESISTANCE :: (*a.* distance, *b.* rate, *c.* effort, *d.* seconds) : TIME
Answer: (**a**). This analogy concerns variation between physical concepts. Mechanical advantage varies directly with resistance (when effort is held constant). Distance varies directly with time (when rate is held constant).

13. *Chemistry:*

HCl : HYDROCHLORIC :: H_2SO_4 : (*a.* hydrofluoric, *b.* hydrocyanic, *c.* sulfuric, *d.* nitric)
Answer: (**c**). This analogy involves chemical symbols for acids. HCl is the chemical formula for hydrochloric acid. H_2SO_4 is the chemical formula for sulfuric acid.

14. *Mathematics:*

$2^1 : 2^3 :: 1^2 :$ (*a.* 0, *b.* 1, *c.* 2, *d.* 4)
Answer: (**d**). This analogy is about equivalent ratios. 2 is to 8 as 1 is to 4.

15. *Nonsemantic:*

DEER : DEER :: OX : (*a.* oxen, *b.* oxes, *c.* oxae, *d.* oxena)
Answer: (**a**). This analogy requires recognition of plurals of words. The plural of deer is deer. The plural of ox is oxen.

NOTE

One thing to keep in mind while solving analogies is that the two relationships that comprise the analogy need not come from the same content domain. In the analogy presented as an example of literary content, NAPOLEON : FRENCH ARMY :: MAJOR BARBARA : SALVATION ARMY, the left side of the analogy is taken from the content domain of history, while the right side, the one requiring selection of a correct answer, comes from the content category of literature.

PRACTICE IN RECOGNIZING CONTENT AREAS

Directions: The following quiz consists of 30 pairs of words. Your task is to write next to each pair of words the relationship between the words and then to classify the pair of words in terms of the 15 content categories just described. The purpose of the quiz is to get you thinking actively about the different content areas from which *MAT* items are drawn. There are two examples of each content area. An answer key is given at the end of the quiz.

Word Pair	*Relationship*	*Content Area*
1. PIAGET : STAGE THEORY	_____	_____
2. NEON : INERT	_____	_____
3. MARS : WAR	_____	_____
4. DESCARTES : RATIONALIST	_____	_____
5. ANDES : SOUTH AMERICA	_____	_____
6. RESISTANCE : OHMS	_____	_____
7. SKIN : ORGAN	_____	_____
8. MITIGATE : ASSUAGE	_____	_____
9. EROICA : BEETHOVEN	_____	_____
10. SAWYER : FINN	_____	_____
11. PETER : THE GREAT	_____	_____
12. KORAN : ISLAM	_____	_____
13. IMAGINARY : COMPLEX	_____	_____

	Word Pair	*Relationship*	*Content Area*
14.	PERSONA : PERSONAE	_____	_____
15.	MUNCH : EXPRESSIONIST	_____	_____
16.	LINCOLN : REPUBLICAN	_____	_____
17.	STEP : PETS	_____	_____
18.	PATON : SOUTH AFRICA	_____	_____
19.	DURKHEIM : SUICIDE	_____	_____
20.	TRENCHANT : INCISIVE	_____	_____
21.	AORTA : ARTERY	_____	_____
22.	MICHELANGELO : DAVID	_____	_____
23.	TREBLE : BASS	_____	_____
24.	BASE : EXPONENT	_____	_____
25.	HOLLANDAISE : CREAM	_____	_____
26.	MONK : MONASTERY	_____	_____
27.	CAMUS : EXISTENTIALIST	_____	_____
28.	FORCE : MASS × ACCELERATION	_____	_____
29.	PLUTO : HADES	_____	_____
30.	WATER : HYDROGEN	_____	_____

ANSWER KEY WITH EXPLANATIONS

Relationship	*Content Area*
1. Piaget's theory of intellectual development is a stage theory.	SOCIAL SCIENCES (10)
2. Neon is an inert gas.	CHEMISTRY (13)
3. Mars was the god of war in Roman mythology.	MYTHOLOGY (5)
4. Descartes was a rationalist philosopher.	PHILOSOPHY (6)
5. The Andes Mountains are in South America.	GENERAL INFORMATION (2)
6. Resistance is measured in ohms.	PHYSICS (12)
7. The skin is an organ.	BIOLOGY (11)
8. *Mitigate* and *assuage* are synonyms (meaning "to make less severe or to improve").	VOCABULARY (1)
9. Beethoven wrote the Eroica Symphony.	MUSIC (9)
10. Tom Sawyer and Huck Finn are characters in novels by Mark Twain (named after these characters).	LITERATURE (4)
11. Peter the Great was a Russian czar.	HISTORY (3)
12. The Koran is the holy book of Islam.	RELIGION (7)
13. *Imaginary* and *complex* are two kinds of numbers.	MATHEMATICS (14)
14. *Personae* is the plural form of *persona*.	NONSEMANTIC (15)
15. Munch was an expressionist painter.	ART (8)
16. President Lincoln was a member of the Republican Party.	HISTORY (3)
17. *Pets* is *Step* spelled backwards.	NONSEMANTIC (15)

Relationship	*Content Area*
18. Paton is a famous South African author.	LITERATURE (4)
19. Durkheim is the author of *Suicide*.	SOCIAL SCIENCES (10)
20. *Trenchant* and *incisive*, both of which mean "penetrating," are synonyms.	VOCABULARY (1)
21. The aorta is an artery in the body.	BIOLOGY (11)
22. Michelangelo was the sculptor of *David*. (Alternatively, David was an artist, as was Michelangelo.)	ART (8)
23. Treble and bass are musical clefs.	MUSIC (9)
24. In the numerical expression x^y, x is the base and y the exponent.	MATHEMATICS (14)
25. Hollandaise is a cream sauce.	GENERAL INFORMATION (2)
26. A monk lives in a monastery.	RELIGION (7)
27. Camus was an existentialist philosopher.	PHILOSOPHY (6)
28. In physics, force = mass × acceleration.	PHYSICS (12)
29. Pluto (the Roman name) and Hades (the Greek name) were the god of the underworld.	MYTHOLOGY (5)
30. Water is composed in part of hydrogen gas.	CHEMISTRY (13)

NOTE

In some cases, more than one content area could be justified. For example, Camus was also an existentialist writer, and hence item 27 could have been classified under LITERATURE. Also, multiple relationships are sometimes possible, meaning that you may have discovered a relationship other than or in addition to the one mentioned in each item.

RELATIONSHIPS USED IN *MAT* ANALOGIES

Analogical reasoning requires you to recognize many possible relationships between pairs of concepts. Unfortunately, classification of relationships is not nearly so straightforward as classification of content areas. There have been numerous attempts to classify the possible ways in which words can be related, but none of the systems is completely successful. To quote George Miller, "Words are related to one another in an amazing number of ways."

The classification system outlined on the following pages, similar to one proposed by George Miller, comprises 14 specific categories, which are organized into 7 general groups. Such a scheme, which makes use of a relatively small number of categories, strikes a balance between being too general and being too particular in describing a relationship.

I Similarity/Contrast

1. Similarity
2. Contrast

II Description

3. Predication

III Class

4. Subordination
5. Coordination
6. Superordination

IV Completion

7. Completion

V Part/Whole

8. Part—Whole
9. Whole—Part

VI Equality/Negation

10. Equality (equivalence)
11. Negation

VII Nonsemantic

12. Sound Relationships
13. Letter Relationships
14. Word Relationships

The following examples will give you an idea of what each relationship means.

1. *Similarity*
Relationships are between synonyms or words that are nearly the same in meaning.

HAPPY : GLAD :: DULL : (*a.* razor, *b.* blunt, *c.* sharp, *d.* bright)
Answer: (**b**). This analogy deals with similarities in meaning. *Happy* and *glad* are synonyms, as are *dull* and *blunt.*

2. *Contrast*
Relationships are between antonyms or words that are nearly the opposite in meaning.

WET : (*a.* dry, *b.* moist, *c.* towel, *d.* water) :: STOP : GO
Answer: (**a**). This analogy concerns contrasts in meaning. *Wet* and *dry* are opposites, as are *stop* and *go.*

3. *Predication*
Terms of the analogy are related by a verb or verb relationship. One term *describes* something about the other term. Most analogies fall in this category. Some of the variations are as follows: A is caused by B; A makes B; A rides on B; A eats B; A is a source of B; A induces B; A studies B; A is made of B; A uses B.

AUTOMOBILE : ROAD :: TRAIN : (*a.* conductor, *b.* track, *c.* engine, *d.* ticket)
Answer (**b**). This analogy involves surfaces on which vehicles travel. An automobile travels on a road, and a train travels on a track. The implicit verb is *travels.*

DOG : BARK :: (*a.* cat, *b.* giraffe, *c.* frog, *d.* rabbit) : MEOW
Answer: (**a**). This analogy involves sounds made by animals. A dog barks. A cat meows.

4. *Subordination*
Relationships are those in which an object A is a type of B.

(*a.* lizard, *b.* toad, *c.* sponge, *d.* trout) : FISH :: FROG : AMPHIBIAN
Answer: (**d**). This analogy is about types of animals. A trout is a type of fish and a frog is a type of amphibian.

5. *Coordination*
The first two terms are one type of thing and the last two are another.

LETTUCE : CABBAGE :: PEAR : (*a.* fruit, *b.* peach, *c.* radish, *d.* carrot)
Answer: (**b**). This analogy requires recognition of members of classes. Lettuce and cabbage are both types of vegetables, while a pear and a peach are both types of fruit.

6. *Superordination*
Relationships are those in which A is a category into which B falls.

BIRD : ROBIN :: MOLLUSK : (*a.* fish, *b.* water, *c.* sponge, *d.* snail)
Answer: (**d**). This analogy deals with category membership. Bird is a category that includes the robin; mollusk is a category that includes the snail.

7. *Completion*
Each term of this kind of analogy is part of a complete expression.

SAN : FRANCISCO :: (*a.* San, *b.* Santa, *c.* La, *d.* Los) : ANGELES
Answer: (**d**). This analogy concerns full names of cites. *San* and *Los* complete the names of two cities, San Francisco and Los Angeles, respectively.

8. *Part-Whole*
Relationships are those in which A is a part of B.

DAY : WEEK :: MONTH : (*a.* hour, *b.* minute, *c.* year, *d.* time)
Answer: (**c**). This analogy involves parts of larger amounts of time. A day is part of a week, and a month is part of a year.

9. *Whole-Part*
Relationships are those in which B is a part of A.

(*a.* hour, *b.* minute, *c.* year, *d.* time) : MONTH :: WEEK : DAY
Answer: (**c**). This analogy is about parts of the calendar. A month is part of a year. A day is part of a week.

10. *Equality*
Relationships involve mathematical or logical equivalence.

$\frac{1}{2}$: $\frac{1}{4}$ :: 0.26 : (*a.* 0.52, *b.* 0.18, *c.* 0.13, *d.* 0.11)
Answer: (**c**). This analogy requires recognition of mathematical equalities. Whereas $\frac{1}{4}$ is equal to one-half of $\frac{1}{2}$, 0.13 is equal to one-half of 0.26.

11. *Negation*
Relationships involve logical or mathematical negation.

EQUAL : UNEQUAL :: GREATER THAN : (*a.* less than, *b.* equal to, *c.* greater than or equal to, *d.* less than or equal to)
Answer: (**d**). This analogy deals with possible relationships between pairs of numbers. Any number is either *equal* to or *unequal* to another number. Any number is either *greater than* or *less than or equal to* another number.

12. *Sound Relationships*
Two words are related because they sound similar in some way. The relationship is nonsemantic in that it has nothing to do with the meanings of the words.

TOE : ROW :: LO : (*a.* now, *b.* crow, *c.* boy, *d.* you)
Answer: (**b**). This analogy concerns vowel sounds in words. All the terms have a long ō vowel sound.

13. *Letter Relationships*

The letters of one term are permuted or in some other way transformed to form the letters of another term.

PAT : TAP :: RAT : (*a.* trap, *b.* skunk, *c.* tar, *d.* eat)
Answer: (**c**). This analogy involves backward spelling of words. *Tap* is obtained by spelling *pat* backwards, *tar*, by spelling *rat* backwards.

14. *Word Relationships*

These usually express grammatical relationships between words.

EAT : ATE :: MEET : (*a.* meat, *b.* meet, *c.* met, *d.* meets)
Answer: (**c**). This analogy involves past tenses of verbs. *Ate* is the past tense of *eat* and *met* is the past tense of *meet*.

NOTE

You will need to recognize much more specific relationships than those described above. However, if you understand the preceding relationships, you will have a general framework into which you can fit specific relationships.

PRACTICE IN USING AND RECOGNIZING RELATIONSHIPS

Directions: The following quiz consists of 28 pairs of words. Your task is to write next to each pair of words the relationship between the words and then to classify the pair of words in terms of the 14 relationship categories just described. The purpose of the quiz is to get you thinking actively about the different ways in which pairs of words on the *MAT* can be related. There are two examples of each relationship. An answer key is given at the end of the quiz.

Word Pair	Relationship	Classification
1. COVER : BOOK	_____	_____
2. RUE : CHEW	_____	_____
3. AIRPLANE : FLIES	_____	_____
4. DAFFODIL : LILAC	_____	_____
5. EMPTY SET : NULL SET	_____	_____
6. CLUE : HINT	_____	_____

Word Pair	*Relationship*	*Classification*
7. LAID : DIAL	_____	_____
8. EARLY : LATE	_____	_____
9. LADDER : RUNG	_____	_____
10. NEGATIVE : NONNEGATIVE	_____	_____
11. BETTER : BEST	_____	_____
12. HUMAN : MAMMAL	_____	_____
13. NEW : ORLEANS	_____	_____
14. STAR : DWARF	_____	_____
15. CARPENTER : HAMMER	_____	_____
16. X or Y : Not X and Not Y	_____	_____
17. CIRCLE : SEMICIRCLE	_____	_____
18. CRATE : FREIGHT	_____	_____
19. FURNITURE : CHAIR	_____	_____
20. MELIORATE : IMPROVE	_____	_____
21. STICK : STUCK	_____	_____
22. HEAVENLY : HELLISH	_____	_____
23. FINGER : HAND	_____	_____
24. TAP : PAT	_____	_____
25. ABRAHAM : LINCOLN	_____	_____
26. $\sqrt{64} : 2^3$	_____	_____

	Word Pair	Relationship	Classification
27.	CLUB : WEAPON	_____	_____
28.	POLLACK : COD	_____	_____

ANSWER KEY WITH EXPLANATIONS

Relationship	*Classification*
1. A cover is a part of a book.	PART—WHOLE (8)
2. *Rue* and *chew* rhyme.	SOUND (12)
3. An airplane flies for its locomotion.	PREDICATION (3)
4. A daffodil and a lilac are both kinds of flowers.	COORDINATION (5)
5. The empty set and the null set are mathematically equivalent.	EQUALITY (10)
6. *Clue* and *hint* are synonymous.	SIMILARITY (1)
7. *Dial* is *laid* spelled backwards.	LETTER (13)
8. *Early* and *late* are antonyms.	CONTRAST (2)
9. A ladder is composed in part of rungs.	WHOLE—PART (9)
10. All real numbers that are not negative are nonnegative.	NEGATION (11)
11. *Better* is the comparative form and *best* the superlative form of *good*.	WORD (14)
12. A human is a kind of mammal.	SUBORDINATION (4)
13. New Orleans is a city.	COMPLETION (7)
14. A dwarf is a kind of star.	SUPERORDINATION (6)

NOTE

In some cases, more than one classification can be justified. For example, an empty set and a null set (item 5) can be viewed as synonymous, and hence as related via category 1 (Similarity). Also, multiple relationships are possible in some cases, meaning that you may have discovered a relationship other than the one mentioned in the explanation.

Relationship	*Classification*
15. A carpenter uses a hammer.	PREDICATION (3)
16. The logical negation of "X or Y" is "Not X and Not Y."	NEGATION (11)
17. A circle can be divided into two semicircles.	WHOLE-PART (9)
18. *Crate* and *freight* rhyme.	SOUND (12)
19. One kind of furniture is a chair.	SUPERORDINATION (6)
20. *Meliorate* and *improve* are synonyms.	SIMILARITY (1)
21. *Stuck* is the past tense of *stick*.	WORD (14)
22. *Heavenly* and *hellish* are antonyms.	CONTRAST (2)
23. A finger is part of a hand.	PART-WHOLE (8)
24. *Pat* is *tap* spelled backward.	LETTER (13)
25. Abraham Lincoln was a president of the United States.	COMPLETION (7)
26. $\sqrt{64}$ and 2^3 both equal 8.	EQUALITY (10)
27. A club is a kind of weapon.	SUBORDINATION (4)
28. Pollack and cod are both kinds of fish.	COORDINATION (5)

DISTRIBUTION OF CATEGORIES

All *MAT* items are classified both by content and relationship. The items on the *MAT* practice tests in this book are also classified in this way. A content/relationship item categorization is included in the explanatory answer for each question. Following each practice test is an Item Classification Chart that shows the breakdown of item categories.

Each content/relationship item categorization grid consists of a matrix of the 7 major content areas and 7 major relationship categories described in the preceding sections. Because there are 7 content areas and 7 relationship areas, there are 49 cells in the overall matrix. However, you will notice that some cells in the charts are empty, while others contain many entries. This occurs because content and relationship areas are not "independent." Certain types of item content and relationship never go together, and hence no items fall in the corresponding cells. Other types of item content and relationship are frequently associated, and hence the corresponding cells are filled with entries. For example, Mathematics items frequently fall into the Equality/Negation relationship category, but never into the Sound/Letter/Word category.

As a rule, more items fall into the General Information content category than into any other content category. With respect to content, General Information and Humanities (including history, literature, mythology, philosophy, religion, art, and music) are usually the largest categories, and Nonsemantic is the smallest. On the most recent forms of the *MAT*, there are no Nonsemantic items at all. However, older forms of the *MAT* are still in use, and hence such items are included in the practice tests. With respect to relationship, Description is usually the largest category and Sound/Letter/Word the smallest. Again, the latter category does not appear on the most recent forms of the *MAT*.

For several reasons, there is always a certain amount of ambiguity in the assignment of items to categories. One reason is that different individuals may arrive at the correct answer to a given item via alternative routes, and thus use different relationships to reach the same conclusion. A second reason for the ambiguity is that there is not always a clear line of demarcation between different categories. What is General Information to one person may appear to be Humanities, for example, to another. Hence, item classification is a useful tool in understanding the "anatomy" of an item, but only up to a certain point.

It is not recommended that you make extensive use of the Item Classification Charts during your preparation for the *MAT*. The primary purpose of these charts is to give you an idea of the breakdown of items on typical forms of the *MAT*, not to assist you in pinpointing your strengths and weaknesses. There are two reasons why you should not use the charts for diagnostic purposes. First, on the *MAT* (and on the practice tests) items within the various categories are not of equal difficulty, so that part scores on various categories are not directly comparable. For example, Mathematics items tend to be the most difficult ones, and hence more errors are to be expected on them. Second, it would not be worth your time to study a textbook or other aid in an area in which, if you used the charts diagnostically, you perceived yourself as weak. On a typical form of the *MAT*, there will be only a few items from any one specific content area, and so the probability of your learning from a textbook skimmed a few days before the test exactly what is covered on the particular form of the *MAT* you will take is exceedingly small.

The best way to prepare for the various types of content and relationship that will appear on the *MAT* is to take as many of the practice tests as you have time for, preferably all of them, and to make sure that you understand each error you have made. The Explanation of Answers following each Answer Key will help you to understand your errors. Once you have taken the tests and studied the kinds of items that give you difficulty, you can be confident that you will do your best on the *MAT*.

References

Kuncel, N.R., Hezlett, S. A., & Ones, D. S. (2004). Academic performance, career potential, creativity, and job performance: Can one construct predict them all? *Journal of Personality and Social Psychology*, 86(1), 148–161.

Meagher, D., & Perez, C. (2008). *An introduction to the MAT.* Presentation at the Annual Meeting of the National Association of Graduate Admissions Professionals, May 2.

The *Miller Analogies Test*

PART 4

- Validity
- Stability of *MAT* scores
- What *MAT* scores mean
- A word of caution
- A note to be reread when you get your score

SUCCESS OF THE *MAT* AS A MEASURING INSTRUMENT

Many studies have looked at how well the *MAT* predicts graduate school performance. A much smaller number have looked at the test as a predictor of success in occupational settings. Since the number of such studies is limited, we shall be concerned only with research of the former kind.

A review of the literature on the validity of the *MAT* (how well it measures what it is supposed to measure) safely permits one uninformative generalization about the usefulness of the *MAT* in various types of situations: About the only way to find out how valid the *MAT* will be in a given situation is to try it and find out. There are no stunning and clear-cut patterns in the results, perhaps in part because what one school calls basket weaving another calls textile engineering. While situational generalizations are not possible, however, more global statements can be made.

Validity

On the average, the *MAT* accounts for slightly more than 5% of the variance in various types of graduate school performance. In the large majority of studies, it accounts for more than 1%, but less than 15%, of this variance. This means that the *MAT* generally affords a low level of predictive accuracy to those who use it.

The best predictive scholastic aptitude tests account for up to 20% or even 25% of the variance in school performance, so that on this basis the *MAT* does not rank with the best tests as a predictor. However, these "best tests" tend to be predictors of high school and sometimes undergraduate grades. At this level, straightforward verbal ability tends to be as good a predictor as anything else. In graduate school, however, professors look for such exotic traits as creativity in designing experiments (in science) and level of rapport achieved with patients (in medicine). Even straightforward course work requires more complex combinations of abilities than are usually needed in high school and undergraduate programs. As a result, graduate school performance is harder to predict in part because all students who go on to graduate school tend to be high in ability, so there is not so much range in performance to predict!

It may surprise you to learn that, on the whole, the *MAT* is about as good a predictor of graduate school performance as any other test around, and that even undergraduate grades usually provide only a little better prediction. The simple fact is that *nothing* provides consistently good prediction of performance in graduate-level programs, and educators resort to the *MAT* and similar tests on the assumption that some prediction is better than none at all. This is true as long as the test results are not misused. If the test scores are considered in conjunction with various other sources of information, if they are interpreted as indicating a range rather than a specific level of ability, and if the limitations on their validity are fully appreciated, then they can be somewhat helpful in spite of their usually low predictive power. If the scores are misused, usually by their being overinterpreted, then they certainly illustrate an application of the maxim that "A little knowledge is a dangerous thing." Fortunately, gross misinterpretation is becoming increasingly rare as educators become more sophisticated in the use of standardized tests.

Now that you have become aware of some limitations surrounding *MAT* and other test scores, you won't feel it necessary to hide in a dark corner if your test score isn't what you'd hoped for, and you won't sell autographs (not quite yet, anyway) if your score is much better than you'd imagined possible. Your score can give you and others who interpret it properly some guidance as to how you might perform in graduate work or employment. Many other factors—motivation, study habits, intellectual curiosity, personal sense of well-being, and the like, as well as abilities not tapped by the *MAT*—will also enter into your future success in whatever program you enter.

Meagher and Perez (2008) have reported relatively recent validity data for the *MAT*. The validity data are reported on a scale of 0 to 1, where 0 indicates no relationship between two variables and 1 indicates a perfect relationship. In 2005–2006, across studies, the average correlation between *MAT* scores and graduate-school GPA was 0.27, compared with 0.21 for the Graduate Record Examination (*GRE*) verbal, 0.27 for the *GRE* quantitative, and 0.11 for the *GRE* analytical-writing scores. The correlation for previous graduate GPA was 0.30. These correlations indicate somewhat modest but statistically significant relationships between the test scores and graduate GPA. Available data suggest that the *MAT* and the *GRE* verbal section measure very similar but not identical psychological constructs. The *MAT* puts more emphasis on general knowledge, the *GRE* verbal on in-depth reading skills.

A detailed study on the validity of the *MAT* was conducted by Kuncel, Hezlett, and Ones (2004). They found a correlation of 0.70 between the *MAT* and the *GRE* verbal test, which is a relatively strong relationship. When they corrected for various statistical factors, the correlation went up to 0.88, suggesting that the two tests measure almost the same construct. The *MAT* also correlates moderately to highly with other tests of verbal ability. The correlation with the *GRE* quantitative test was 0.42, which is moderate and indicates some but far from complete overlap. Correlations with measures of graduate-school performance were generally in the high 0.20s. The *MAT* also showed modest but significant correlations with work performance, ranging from 0.15 to 0.33. A curious finding of this study was that higher *MAT* scores were associated with *longer* times to degree completion (with a correlation of 0.35). It is unclear what this means, other than that people who scored higher took longer to finish their degrees!

Stability of *MAT* Scores

As the preceding section states, scores on a given form of the *MAT* usually account for only 1% to 15% of the variance in diverse criteria of performance in graduate school. However, there is something for which such scores usually account for 85% to 90% of the variance, and that is scores on another form of the *MAT*. There you have it. Scores on one form of the *MAT* are excellent predictors of scores on another form of the *MAT*. But you should realize just what this tidbit means. It means that, when a group of people take the test twice (a different form each time), their ranks within the group will probably not change much. However, even if their *ranks* in relation to each other remain stable, their scores may not. Most people gain around 5 points on a second administration. Does this mean you should take the test twice? Probably not. First, you will have capitalized on much of this *practice effect* by reading this book and working at the practice tests it contains. Second, educators and administrators using the test realize that people tend to gain in score from one testing to the next, and they are therefore likely to discount small gains. Large gains, however, are another story, and often indicate that for one reason or another, one of the scores is not representative of the candidate's true ability. In such cases, the higher score almost always counts as much as or more than the lower score. For this reason, if you feel reasonably confident that you were at some sort of disadvantage during the first administration, you may want to consider taking the test again. However, such retesting will be a waste of time and money unless the disadvantage was genuine. You should remember that, even if your score was not quite what you'd hoped for, it is only one of many factors considered in making most admissions, financial aid, and employment decisions.

What *MAT* Scores Mean

Your score on the *MAT* will be reported to you as a *raw score*—you are informed of the number of questions you answered correctly, which may range anywhere from zero to one hundred. Before learning what the score means, you should learn what it does *not* mean.

The first thing for you to do is to rid yourself of any preconceptions you may have about percentage scores. A frequent one is that 90—100% = A, 80—89% = B, 70—79% = C, 60—69% = D, and anything below that is failing. Unfortunately, some *MAT* preparation books foster rather than dispel such erroneous notions. For example, one such book provides five practice tests, and suggests that a score of 475 (95%) is excellent, 425 (85%) is good, 350 (70%) is passing, and anything less is failing. Forget it! These standards may or may not be appropriate for the practice tests in that particular book, but they have no conceivable relation to the *MAT*.

In the first place, there is no such thing as a failing score on the *MAT*. Although a very few institutions may establish cut-off scores (a practice of dubious merit), almost none rely on the *MAT* to the exclusion of other sources of information. Such total reliance would be irresponsible and counterproductive. Second, what is an excellent score in one program may be just average in another, and quite low in a third. *MAT* scores simply cannot be interpreted in absolute terms. They can be interpreted only in relation to those of other individuals applying to programs similar or identical to your own.

Because raw scores are virtually uninterpretable taken by themselves, the test publisher provides percentile equivalents for various groups of individuals who have taken the *MAT*. What is a percentile equivalent? It is the number of people out of 100 whose scores your own score exceeds. Thus, if your score places you in the 56th percentile, this means that your score was higher than those of 56% of the people who were in the particular reference group for which the percentiles were computed. In general terms, the middle score in a group is the 50th percentile, and the highest score is the 100th percentile.

A Word of Caution

A final word of caution is in order with regard to the prediction of your *MAT* score. Obviously, one way to make this prediction is to average your scores on the practice tests in this book, but such a procedure is risky. Items on actual editions of the *MAT* are pretested by giving them as experimental items to large numbers of individuals who take the *MAT*. Only experimental items that precisely match older items are used on new forms of the test. The various forms of the *MAT* are thus referred to as *equated*.

Since the *MAT* is a restricted test, it was of course not possible to equate the practice tests in this book to actual *MAT* forms, and hence estimates of *MAT* scores obtained by averaging scores on these practice tests will be imprecise. Experience indicates that scores on the practice tests tend to run slightly lower than actual *MAT* scores. You might therefore look at your scores on these tests as conservative estimates of what you can expect your *MAT* score to be. Of course, in some cases, individuals may do worse on the actual test; the prediction game, as you know by now, is a very uncertain one. The important thing, however, is not that you go into the test knowing what your score will be (you'll find out just a few days after you take the test), but that you go in knowing that you will get a score that reflects your intellectual ability and not an inability to take tests. After working through this book, you can be confident that you will do your very best on the actual test.

A Note to Be Reread When You Get Your Score

If you did well, congratulations. You have good reason to be proud of yourself. The *MAT* is one of the most difficult ability tests around, and a high score is a genuine accomplishment.

If you didn't do as well as you'd hoped, don't despair. Follow the simple steps below:

STEP 1: Look back and observe how well the *MAT* predicts (or, rather, doesn't predict) graduate school performance. It's not that the *MAT* is worse than other similar tests. It's just that all of these tests don't predict that well. You should be feeling a little better already.

STEP 2: Ask your friendly local librarian for a copy of the January 1973, issue of *The American Psychologist*, and check out the article by David McClelland, "Testing for Competence Rather Than for 'Intelligence.'" McClelland's main point is simple. While aptitude tests provide some (but not much) prediction of performance in school, their ability to predict success in life (as measured by virtually any criterion except test scores and grades) is practically zero. So keep your test score in perspective. In the long run, it isn't that important.

Review for the
Miller Analogies Test

PART 5

- What this review contains
- Vocabulary
- Special collective nouns
- *-ology* words
- Word demons
- Selected foreign words and phrases used in English
- Alphabets and their characteristics
- Geography
- History
- Social sciences
- Art and architecture
- Literary forms and figures
- Music
- Science
- Mythology

WHAT THIS REVIEW CONTAINS

As stated earlier in this book, the *MAT* is a test of vocabulary and general information as well as specific information in diverse areas. It is not possible to review the content of all the subjects that may be included in a *MAT* exam. The reviews provided in this chapter are intended as brief refreshers. They may help you recall important names, events, and terms in different areas of study.

VOCABULARY

The vocabulary list below consists of words often used in graduate tests. For some entries, synonyms, antonyms, or other related words are provided as an added help in handling analogy questions.

abdicate   to denounce; to discard; to abandon

aberration   something not typical; a deviation

abhorrence   repugnance; detestation

abjure   to renounce upon oath

abnegation   self-denial

abrogate   to break, as a treaty or law

abscond   to depart secretly; to hide (oneself)

absolve   to set free from an obligation or the consequences of guilt

abstain   to refrain deliberately from an action or practice, usu. as a form of self-denial

abstemious   sparing or moderate, especially in eating or drinking (antonym: **gluttonous**)

abstruse   hard to understand or grasp; esoteric

abut   to border on; to terminate at the boundary or point of contact

abysmal   immeasurable; bottomless

accolade   an award or honor; high praise

acquiesce   to agree silently; to accept tacitly

acrid   unpleasantly pungent in odor or taste

acrimonious   caustic, biting in feeling or manner

acrophobia   the fear of heights

acumen   keenness

adamant   unyielding; stubborn

addle   to throw into confusion; to confound

adduce   to offer as example or proof

adjure   to command solemnly; to advise earnestly; to beg

admonition   warning against oversight

adroit   showing skill, cleverness, or resourcefulness

adulation   excessive praise

adumbrate   to intimate or foreshadow; to obscure

aestivate (estivate)   to spend the summer in an inactive state

affable   being pleasant and friendly with others

agglomeration   a collection in a mass, heap, or cluster; aggrandizement

agoraphobia   the fear of open spaces

alacrity   liveliness or eagerness; readiness (antonym: **lassitude**)

allegory   a symbolic expression or description

allusion   an indirect reference to something else; a hint

alms   charity; something given to the poor (usu. refers to small change)

alpinism   mountain climbing

altruistic   unselfish; concerned with the welfare of others

ambergris   a product of sperm whales used in the manufacture of perfume

amphora   an ancient two-handled Greek jar

anathema   a ban or curse; a denunciation accompanied by excommunication

andiron   a metal support used for holding logs in a hearth

androphobia   the fear of men

anneal   to toughen or to strengthen

anodyne   a pain reliever

anomaly   an aberration; a deviation; an irregularity

antipathy   firm dislike; hatred (antonym: **sympathy**)

antiseptic   free from germs, exceptionally clean

antithesis   the direct opposite

aphelion   the point in a planet's orbit that is farthest from the sun

apocalyptic   of, or relating to, a revelation or discovery

apocryphal   of doubtful authenticity; spurious

apogee   the point in a satellite's orbit that is farthest from the center of the earth

apothegm   a short, instructive pithy saying

aquiline   hooked; like an eagle

arachnophobia   the fear of spiders

archon   the chief magistrate in ancient Athens; any ruler

arid   dull; unimaginative; extremely dry

arrogate   to claim or seize without justification; to usurp

artifice   cleverness; ingenuity

assiduous   diligent

assuage   to ease the intensity of; to appease; to pacify (antonym: **exacerbate**)

astraphobia   the fear of lightning

atrophy   a wasting away; degeneration

attenuate   to lessen in amount, force, or value; to weaken

audacity   daring spirit

austral   southern (antonym: **boreal**)

axiom   a self-evident rule or truth; a widely accepted saying

azure   sky blue

baleful   menacing; harmful

balmy   soothing; mild

banal   trite; commonplace

bellicose   inclined to start wars or fights (antonym: **pacific**)

beneficent   beneficial (antonym: **deleterious**)

benign   gracious; favorable; not threatening to health (antonym: **malignant**)

benison   spoken blessing

bibliophile   one who loves books

biennial   occurring every two years

bifurcate   divided in two branches; forked

biped   having two feet

blighted   withered or rotten; destroyed; frustrated

blithe   happy; merry; cheerful

bombastic   pompous; overblown; turgid

boreal   northern (antonym: **austral**)

boycott   to engage in a concerted refusal to have dealings with (a person, store, organization) as a sign of disapproval [derived from Charles C. Boycott, an English land agent who was ostracized in Ireland because of his refusal to lower rents]

broach   to make known for the first time; to open up (a subject) for discussion

bromidic   lacking originality; trite

brontophobia   the fear of thunder

brook   to bear or tolerate; to put up with

brusque   abrupt or short in manner or speech

buccal   pertaining to the cheeks or side of the mouth

bucolic   pastoral; relating to rural life

buffoon   a clown or ludicrous figure; someone who amuses with jokes or tricks

bulbous   rotund; round like a bulb

bumptious   aggressive and assertive in an offensive way (antonym: **shy; self-effacing**)

buoyant   (1) having the ability to float; (2) cheerful; gay

burgeon   to grow and flourish

burnish   to make shiny or lustrous; to polish

burnoose   a hooded Arabic cloak

cassock   a loose robe worn by priests

cabal   group united to plot, esp. the overthrow of authority

cache   (1) a hiding place; (2) something hidden in a secure place

cacophony   a harsh-sounding mixture of words, voices, or sounds

caduceus   the emblem of the medical profession (a staff with intertwined snakes and wings at the top)

cajole   to persuade a reluctant person to do something; to coax

caliber   the diameter of the bore of a gun

gauge   the size of a shotgun; measure of the interior diameter of the barrel

calumny   a lie told to damage another's reputation; slander

candid   frank

canonical   orthodox; authoritative

capitulate   to cease resisting; to surrender (often after negotiations)

capricious   unpredictable; governed by a whim

captious   critical; fault-finding

carp   to complain

cashmere   a fine wool from a cashmere goat [derived from Kashmir, India]

catharsis   purification of emotions, esp. through art

bathos   sentimentalism; overdone pathos; triteness; anticlimax

pathos   something that evokes pity, compassion, or sorrow

catholic   universal (antonym: **provincial; parochial**)

caustic   acrid; biting

cavil   to raise trivial objections; to nitpick

cerulean   resembling the blue of the sky

chaff   waste material from the threshing of wheat

dross   waste material from molten metal

slag   scoria; refuse from the melting of metals or reduction of ore

tailings   waste material from the preparation of ores or grains

chalice   a bowl-shaped drinking cup

chartreuse   yellow-green

chastise   to criticize harshly; to castigate

chauvinism   excessive or blind patriotism [derived from Nicholas Chauvin, a character in a French play]

chicanery   trickery; artful deception

chimerical   fantastically visionary; wildly fanciful

choleric   easily angered or irritated

Cimmerian   (1) *adj.* shrouded in gloom and darkness; (2) *n.* a mythical people described by Homer as dwelling in gloom

stygian   (1) dark and gloomy; (2) relating to the Styx (in Greek mythology, the river of the underworld)

circumlocution   an indirect expression; wordy or evasive language

circumspect   considering all options; cautious

clandestine   surreptitious; secret

claustrophobia   the fear of closed places

clemency   an act of leniency; mercy

cloy   to satiate

glut   to oversupply; to satiate

coalesce   to grow together; to unite into a whole

coda   a passage that concludes a musical or literary work

cogent   pertinent; compelling; convincing

cognizant   perceptive; observant

colloquial   of or relating to conversation; characteristic of informal speech

collusion a secret agreement, esp. for an illegal purpose

compulsion an impulse to perform an irrational act

  phobia an inexplicable fear of something

conjoin to join or act together

contentious argumentative; quarrelsome

contumacious rebellious; stubbornly disobedient; renegade

conundrum a puzzle; a riddle

cooper a maker of casks or barrels

corroborate to confirm; to back up with evidence

cowl (1) a hood; (2) a cover for an engine

croupier a collector and payer of bets at a casino

culinary having to do with the kitchen or cooking

cynophobia the fear of dogs

cynosure the center of interest

dauntless fearless

dearth severe shortage

debacle a violent breakdown; a sudden overthrow

debauchery wild living; corruption by sensuality

debilitate to weaken (antonym: **invigorate**)

debonair suave; courteous; sophisticated

deciduous falling off or shedding at a certain season; ephemeral; not
  permanent

declaim to make a bombastic speech

decorous proper; in good taste; correct

defalcate to embezzle; to abscond with money

deleterious harmful (antonym: **beneficial; salubrious; salutary**)

delineate to describe; to portray; to sketch

deliquesce to melt away or dissolve; to become soft, esp. with age

delusion a deception; a false psychotic belief regarding oneself or others

demur to object; to take exception

denim a durable, twilled, usually cotton fabric woven with white filling thread
  [derived from *serge de Nime* (Nîmes, France)]

denouement the unfolding or outcome of a series of events

denounce to express strong disapproval, esp. publicly

depraved morally corrupt or evil

deprecate to play down; to belittle

depredate to lay waste; to plunder

desiccate to dry out

despot a ruler with absolute power

desultory lacking plan, regularity, or purpose; random

dexterous mentally skillful; artful; clever

dialectic logical argumentation

diametric completely opposed; at opposite extremes

diaphanous sheer; extremely delicate

diatribe a bitter denunciation (antonym: **panegyric**)

dichotomy division, esp. into two contradictory groups

didactic intended to teach, moralize, or preach

diffident shy; lacking in self-confidence

dilatory   tending to cause delay (antonym: **expeditious**)

dilettante   one who is involved in a variety of things, none of them seriously; dabbler

diminution   a decrease; a lessening

dint   a force; a power

disavow   to deny

discomfit   to confuse, to deject; to frustrate; to deceive

discourse   to converse; to discuss formally

disingenuous   lacking in candor

disinterested   unbiased

dissemble   to feign or pretend

dissenter   one who goes against an opinion; nonconformist

dissuade   to persuade someone not to do something

djellabah   a loose-fitting gown worn in North Africa (see also **burnoose**)

doctrinaire   dogmatic

doggerel   comic, loose verse

dolt   a stupid person

doughty   fearless; valiant

dour   stubbornly unyielding; uninviting

draconian   severe (as a code of laws); cruel

dray   a vehicle used to haul goods

   teamster   a person who drives a truck as an occupation

ductile   malleable

dunce   a dull-witted or stupid person [derived from John Duns Scotus, whose writings were ridiculed in the 16th century]

duplicity   concealment of one's true intentions by misleading words or actions; deception

ebullient   lively; enthusiastic; boiling up

eclectic   selecting from many sources what seems to be the best; catholic

ecumenical   (1) having to do with a body of churches; (2) worldwide or general in extent or application

edification   instruction; improvement; enlightenment

efface   to make indistinct by wearing away; to erase or remove

effervescent   lively; bubbly (antonym: **effete**)

effete   exhausted; worn-out (antonym: **effervescent**)

effluvium   a disagreeable or noxious vapor; escaping gas

effusive   overflowing; very demonstrative

egregious   conspicuously bad; flagrant

egress   (1) *n.* exit; (2) *v.* to go out from

elan   dash; vigorous spirit

elegy   a lament for the dead

elucidate   to shed light upon; to make clear

emanate   to send out; to emit

eminent   prominent; famous; standing above others in some quality or position

encomium   formal expression of praise

endue   to provide; to endow

enervate   to exhaust, weaken, or unnerve (antonym: **invigorate**)

engender   to bring into being; to produce

enigma   a baffling situation; something that is hard to explain or solve

entreat   to request earnestly

ephemeral   lasting a short time; transient

epiphany   a sudden, and often divine, enlightenment or realization

epitome   a typical or ideal example

equivocal   ambiguous; deliberately confusing; able to be interpreted in more than one way

erratic   unpredictable; wandering; arbitrary (antonym: **static; stable**)

eschew   to avoid; to shun

eulogy   formal expression of praise

euphemism   (1) the substitution of a positive expression for something that may be interpreted as negative or distasteful; (2) the expression that is substituted

evanescent   fleeting; hardly visible; ephemeral

exacerbate   to make more violent or more severe (antonym: **assuage; appease**)

excoriate   to wear off the skin

exculpate   to exonerate; to clear of guilt or blame

exegesis   an interpretation of a text

exigent   urgent; requiring prompt action; taxing

expedite   to speed up; to hasten

expiate   to make amends for

expletive   a syllable or word that fills a vacancy but does not add to the sense of what was said

explicate   to explain

expunge   to strike out; to obliterate or erase

extemporaneous   with little preparation

extirpate   to destroy completely

facetious   humorous; not serious

factitious   artificial; sham (antonym: **authentic**)

fagoting   a type of embroidery

fallacious   erroneous; deceiving; misleading

fallible   capable of making a mistake or error

fastidious   hard to please; fickle

fatuous   silly; inane

fealty   allegiance

feasible   practical; workable

feckless   worthless; feeble

fecund   fruitful; fertile

fervid   very hot; intense in feeling or emotion; impassioned

fetid   having an offensive odor

   vapid   flat; uninteresting; insipid

fetish   (1) a charm; a talisman; an amulet; an object thought to deflect evil or bring luck; (2) a fixation; an object of obsessive desire; a preoccupation

fiduciary   a trustee

fitful   irregular; spasmodic

flaccid   limp; flabby (antonym: **resilient**)

flag   to weaken; to slow down

flagon   a flask with a handle and lid

   tureen   a casserole or bowl usually used to serve soup

flibbertigibbet   female fool

foible   a minor flaw or shortcoming in character; a weakness

foment   to instigate, incite, or arouse

foray   (1) *v.* to ravage for spoils; to pillage; (2) *n.* sudden, sometimes brief, invasion

forbear   an ancestor or forefather

fortuitous   happening by chance; unplanned

fractious   unruly; quarrelsome

franchise   the right to vote; a special privilege granted to a few; the right to market certain goods in a particular region

fraught   laden; charged

frenetic   frantic; frenzied

fricative   produced by forcing air through a constricted passage

froward   habitually disobedient; not willing to compromise

frugal   economical; thrifty; sparing

fuchsia   vivid reddish purple

fugacious   disappearing after a short time; short-lived; evanescent

fulminate   to denounce; to send forth invectives; to explode

fulsome   (1) abundant; copious; (2) morally offensive; disgusting

furtive   sly; shifty

gainsay   to deny; to contradict

galvanize   (1) to stimulate or excite; (2) to coat with zinc

gamut   the entire range

garner   to collect; to accumulate

garrote   to strangle and rob

garrulous   wordy; extremely talkative; gabby (antonym: **taciturn**)

gauche   lacking social grace; crude; awkward

gaunt   excessively thin; lean

gelding   a castrated male horse

genre   an artistic category or type

genuflect   to go down on one's knee; to kneel, usu. in obedience or respect

germane   closely related; relevant; fitting

glabrous   smooth; referring to a surface without hair or projections

   hirsute   roughly hairy

goad   to urge, egg on, or incite to do something (antonym: **curb**)

gorgon   one of three snake-haired sisters whose glance turned the beholder into stone

gourmand   one who eats and drinks excessively; glutton

gratuitous   not required by the circumstances; unwarranted; unnecessary

gregarious   liking companionship; sociable

griffin   a mythical animal having the head and wings of an eagle and the body and legs of a lion

   chimera   (1) a fire-breathing monster with the head of a lion, the body of a goat, and the tail of a serpent; (2) illusion or mental fabrication.

   minotaur   a monster, half man and half bull, confined in a labyrinth

guffaw   a loud, boisterous burst of laughter

guile   deceitful cunning; cleverness

gulch   a deep pit; a ravine

hackneyed   overused; trite; commonplace

haiku   a type of unrhymed Japanese poem consisting of three lines

halcyon   peaceful; tranquil

harangue   a ranting speech without much real meaning

harbinger   someone or something that foreshadows what is to come

Hellene   a native or inhabitant of Greece

heretic   one who goes against an established religion or belief; nonconformist

hermeneutics   the study of principles of interpretation (e.g., of the Bible)

hermetic   sealed off from external influence; airtight; abstruse or occult

herpetophobia   the fear of snakes

hiatus   a gap or interruption in time or in a continuum

hibernate   to spend the winter in a dormant, inactive state

hierarchy   a graded or ranked classification determined on the basis of age,
economic status, or class

hirsute   hairy (antonym: **glabrous**)

hoary   gray or white with age

homily   an inspirational discourse; a sermon

homogeneous   of uniform structure or composition

homophobia   the fear of homosexuals

homophones   words that sound alike but have different meanings

  homonyms   homophones; also, words that are spelled the same but have
  different meanings (e.g., *cleave, quail, bear*)

hone   to sharpen

hyaline   transparent or almost so; glassy

hybrid   anything that is the product of at least two different sources

hydroponics   cultivation of plants in liquid nutrients

hyperbole   an exaggeration

hypertrophy   an exaggerated increase or complexity

hypocritical   pretending to have qualities or virtues that are not possessed;
dissembling

hypothetical   based on conjecture; conditional

  empirical   based on expertise, observation, or experimental evidence

iconoclast   one who destroys religious images or attacks established beliefs

  vandal   one who destroys property

idyllic   carefree and lighthearted; peaceful

igneous   referring to rock formed from molten magma; volcanic

  metamorphic   referring to rock formed from sedimentary rock and changed
  through pressure or heat

ignominious   infamous; despicable

imbue   to permeate or influence

imminent   about to happen (usu. referring to something threatening)

immiscible   incapable of being mixed

immutable   not susceptible to change

impassive   apathetic; expressionless

impecunious   having little or no money

impermeable   impervious; not permitting passage through

impolitic   unwise; injudicious

imprecate   to curse

improvident   not providing for the future; careless

  prescient   having foresight or foreknowledge of the future

impugn   to attack, esp. as false or lacking integrity

inanition   a loss of vitality from lack of food and water

incarnadine   blood red

inchoate   beginning; insipient; only imperfectly formed

incipient   just beginning; in the early stages; commencing

incisive   keen; direct; decisive

incommodious   troublesome; inconvenient

incongruous   not like the others in a group; out of place; incompatible

incontrovertible   unquestionable; indisputable

incorrigible   unruly; delinquent

inculcate   to teach and impress by repetition

indemnify   (1) to secure against loss; (2) to compensate for hurt or loss

indigenous   having originated naturally in a particular environment

indigent   impoverished

induction   (1) an initiation into military service; (2) reasoning from parts to whole

  ordination   an initiation into religious service

ineluctable   inescapable; inevitable

inimical   hostile; unfriendly (antonym: **amicable**)

iniquitous   vicious; wicked

innuendo   a veiled allusion; insinuation

insurgent   a person who revolts against established authority

intractable   hard to manage; unruly; obstinate

intransigent   stubborn; uncompromising

intrepid   fearless (antonym: **timorous**)

inure   to accustom to accept something undesirable; to habituate

invective   insulting or abusive language

invidious   offensive; envious; obnoxious

irascible   easily angered; choleric; malevolent

jalousie   a type of blind or shutter having adjustable slats or louvers and usu. made of glass

jargon   specialized terminology of a certain group; a lingo

jejune   immature; juvenile

jenny   a female donkey

jettison   to sacrifice cargo to lighten a ship or vehicle

jetty   a projection or structure extending into a body of water

jezebel   a shameless, brazen woman

jocose   humorous; witty

jocular   habitually happy or cheerful

jocund   gay; cheerful

judicious   wise; sagacious; prudent

junk   (1) trash; something that is not worth saving; (2) a type of Chinese ship

junta   a political group or committee, esp. after a revolution

juxtapose   to place right next to something

kaleidoscope   (1) a succession of changing patterns or scenes; (2) a changing pattern or scene

kindle   to activate or inspire; to arouse

kindred   (1) *n.* relatives; kinship; (2) *adj.* similar in nature; like

kinetic   related to motion

knave   a sly, deceitful man or boy

kudos   praise; compliments

labyrinth   a place full of intricate passageways; something extremely complex or intricate

laconic   concise (antonym: **verbose; redundant**)

lambent   flickering; softly bright or radiant, as a candle

lampoon   harsh, satirical writing, usu. attacking an individual

lascivious   lewd; lustful; wanton

lassitude   fatigue; weariness (antonym: **alacrity**)

laudable   worthy of praise

lethargic   slow moving; sluggish

levity   lightness; lack of seriousness; frivolity

libertine   a person who is not restrained by convention or morality

licentious   lacking moral restraints, esp. sexual ones; lustful

ligneous   woodlike

limpid   clear and simple in style; transparent; serene and untroubled

   lucid   clear; sane; translucent; luminous

   pellucid   reflecting light evenly; easy to understand

litigate   to try in court; to contest in law

littoral   relating to the shore or coastal region

loggia   a roofed, open gallery, like a porch

loquacious   talkative

lucre   monetary gain; profit

ludicrous   laughable; ridiculous

lugubrious   gloomy; sorrowful

lurid   (1) gruesome; shocking; (2) ghastly pale

magenta   deep purplish red

malefactor   an evil-doer; a criminal

malfeasance   wrongdoing; official misconduct

malignant   evil; injurious; tending to produce death (antonym: **benign**)

mandatory   necessary; obligatory

marred   injured; blemished; damaged

martinet   a strict disciplinarian

masticate   to chew

maudlin   foolishly sentimental or morose

maverick   a rebel; a nonconformist

megalomaniac   one who exhibits delusions of omnipotence or grandeur

mercurial   quickly changing; inconstant

meretricious   attractive only on the surface; superficial; pretentious

meticulous   extremely concerned with details; well organized

miasma   a depleting or corrupting influence or atmosphere

millennium   a thousand years
miscreant   a heretic; a villain; one who commits illegal acts
misogynistic   characterized by hatred of women
mitigate   to soften; to lessen the severity of
moot   questionable; debatable
mordant   biting in manner or style; incisive
motility   movement
munificent   lavish; generous; liberal
nadir   (1) the lowest point; (2) a point in the sky opposite the zenith
naiad   a water nymph
napery   table linens
necromancy   magic; witchcraft
  chiromancy   palmistry
necrophobia   the fear of death
necropolis   a cemetery
nefarious   wicked; vile
neophyte   a novice
nexus   a connection or link
niggardly   stingy
noisome   offensive; harmful
nomenclature   a standardized system of symbols for a particular subject, usu.
  art or science
nonfeasance   failure to perform an act that should have been completed
notorious   widely and unfavorably known
nuance   a subtle distinction, variation, or quality
nugatory   inconsequential; trifling
nullify   to void legally; to make of no consequence
numismatist   one who studies and collects coins and tokens
nuncupative   not written; oral
nyctophobia   the fear of darkness
obdurate   persistent; unyielding
obfuscate   to confuse (antonym: **clarify**)
objurgate   to denounce harshly; to declaim; to castigate
obliterate   to destroy completely; to cause to disappear
obloquy   (1) abusive language; (2) bad repute
obscurant   tending to make obscure
obsequious   obedient; subservient
  sycophant   a servile, self-seeking flatterer
obtrude   to force, usu. oneself or one's ideas on another without request
obviate   to make unnecessary
ocher   earthy yellow or red
ochlophobia   the fear of crowds
officious   meddling; interfering
olfactory   relating to the sense of smell
oligarchy   form of government in which control is placed in the hands of a few,
  esp. associated with corruption
omnipotent   all-powerful

omnipresent   being all places at once

omniscient   knowing everything

omnivore   one who eats both animals and vegetables

onerous   burdensome; oppressive

onomatopoeia   the use of words whose sounds convey their meanings (e.g., *buzz, hiss*)

ontogeny   the development of an organism

onus   a burden; an obligation

ophidiophobia   the fear of snakes

opprobrium   disgrace due to a shameful act

opus   a major work, esp. a set of musical compositions

ornithophobia   the fear of birds

oscillate   to swing back and forth; to vary

osmosis   diffusion through a membrane

ossify   to become hard as a bone

ostentatious   showy; pretentious

oviparous   producing eggs that hatch outside the maternal body

palindrome   a word, sentence, or number that reads the same backward and forward (e.g., *mom*)

palliate   to cover up with excuses; to extenuate

panegyric   high praise; a tribute; an encomium (antonym: **diatribe**)

paradigm   an example; a pattern; an archetype

paradox   (1) something true that appears to be false; (2) something false that appears to be logical

pariah   an outcast

parry   (1) to ward off; (2) to escape by dodging

parsimony   the quality of being careful with money; thrift (antonym: **extravagance**)

partisan   one who is committed to a particular person, cause, or idea

parvenu   one recently risen to an unaccustomed position and not yet possessing the requisite dignity or characteristics; upstart

paucity   a small amount; a scarcity

pecuniary   having to do with money

pedantic   characterized by an ostentatious display of learning

pedometer   an instrument used to measure the distance walked

penultimate   next to last

peremptory   precluding a right of action, delay, or debate; admitting of no contradiction

perfidious   faithless; disloyal; treacherous

peripatetic   wandering; itinerant

peruse   to read carefully; to study

pervade   to spread throughout

petulant   ill-tempered; irritable; fractious

philatelist   one who studies and collects stamps

   -phile   a love of or affinity for (e.g., *philogyny*: love of women)

   -phobe   a fear of or aversion to

philistine   (1) characterized by material rather than spiritual or artistic values; (2) narrow-minded or uninformed with respect to a specific topic area

piscatorial   of or relating to fish

platen   (1) a roller on a typewriter; (2) a flat plate

platitude   the state of being dull, banal, or trite

plethora   a superfluity; an excess

plumb   (1) *n.* a lead weight used to find the true vertical; (2) *v.* to measure the depth of; to fathom

polemic   strong argument in refutation of another; disputation; practice of engaging in controversy

poltroon   a coward

potlatch   (1) a ceremonial feast, with gifts, of northwest coast Indians; (2) a festival or celebration

precipitous   steep

precocious   exhibiting maturity at an early age

prescience   the anticipation of upcoming events; foresight

prevaricate   to deviate from the truth; to lie

probity   honesty; uprightness; rectitude

prodigal   recklessly wasteful; very generous

profusion   a great amount; an abundance

prognosticate   to forecast; to prophesy

propinquity   closeness; proximity

proxy   a person authorized to act for another (e.g., to vote corporate stock)

pseudonym   a fictitious or pen name

surname   (1) a family name; (2) an added name or nickname

puce   dark red

puerile   childish; juvenile

pundit   an expert; an authority; a critic; a savant

purloin   to steal

purview   a range of authority, competence, or responsibility; scope

pusillanimous   cowardly; fearful

Pyrrhic   usu. referring to a victory won at excessively high cost

quaff   to drink heartily

quagmire   a bog; a difficult or entrapping situation; a predicament

qualm   (1) a sudden onset of illness, esp. of nausea; (2) a feeling of unease about a point of conscience

quandary   a state of confusion or doubt

quell   to suppress

querulous   complaining; whining

quintessence   the essence of something in its most concentrated form; the purest representative from a certain category

quisling   a traitor [derived from Vidkum Quisling, a Norwegian who collaborated with the Nazis during World War II]

quittance   a release from debt or obligation

quixotic   foolishly impractical and idealistic; capricious

quizzical   (1) eccentric; odd; (2) inquisitive; questioning

quondam   former; sometime

quorum   the minimum number of a group that must be present to conduct business legally

quotidian   daily

rancorous   with ill-will; with enmity (antonym: **benevolent**)

raze   to demolish completely; to destroy

recalcitrant   obstinately defiant of authority; resistant

recidivism   repeated relapse, as in tendency to repeat criminal activity

reciprocal   (1) mutual; shared; common; (2) inversely related

recondite   obscure; concealed; incomprehensible; esoteric

recumbent   lying down; leaning; resting

recusant   marked by refusal to obey authority

redolent   having a pleasing scent; fragrant

refurbish   to freshen or make new; to renovate

relegate   to assign to a place of insignificance; to banish

relume   to light or light again; to rekindle; to reestablish

remonstrate   to object; to protest

reprehend   to voice disapproval of

reprobate   a villain; an immoral person

repugnant   distasteful; abhorrent; obnoxious (antonym: **congenial**)

rescind   to take away; to remove

resilient   able to recover easily from hardship or misfortune; flexible

restive   tense

revile   to use abusive speech; to rail; to scold

ribald   rude or offensive; indecent

risible   capable of laughing or provoking laughter

rookery   a breeding place among rocks for mammals (e.g., seals) or birds

roseate   overoptimistic; cheerful

rotund   round; plump; chubby

ruminate   to reflect on something; to ponder

saboteur   one who willfully hinders, through destruction or obstruction, industrial production or a nation's war effort

  fifth column   supporters of an enemy that engage in sabotage within defense lines or national boundaries

sagacious   wise; astute; perspicacious

salubrious   healthy; promoting well-being; salutary (antonym: **deleterious**)

sanctimonious   (1) devout; holy; (2) hypocritically devout or holy

sanction   to authorize or approve

sanguine   hopeful

sardonic   disdainful; sarcastic

satiric   using ridicule or sarcasm to convey criticism; lampooning

saturnine   gloomy; sullen; morose

savant   one with detailed knowledge in a specialized field

  prodigy   highly talented child

  virtuoso   one who is highly skilled in the practice of an art, esp. music

scintilla   a minute trace or jot; an iota

  tittle   a particle

sectarian   of or relating to a sect or a smaller group within a larger group that adopts only certain beliefs; narrow-minded

sequester   (1) to set apart from others; to segregate; (2) to confiscate

sidereal   related to the stars; astral

sophomoric   (literally "wise fool") believing one's level of knowledge and maturity to be higher than it actually is

soporific   marked by, or causing, sleepiness or lethargy; drowsy

sordid   wretched; vile; foul

spelunker   one who studies and explores caves as a hobby

splenetic   hot-tempered; easily angered

spurious   false; forged; counterfeit

staid   sedate; serious; grave

sterile   unimaginative; unfruitful; bare (antonym: **fecund; fertile**)

stolid   dull; unemotional; immovable

stoma, stomata   a minute opening in outside surface of a plant (e.g., a leaf) for the passage of gases

striated   referring to muscle with alternate light and dark bands, as opposed to smooth muscle

strident   loud; harsh; grating

stygian   hellish

superfluous   more than necessary; extra

surfeit   overabundant supply; immoderate indulgence

surmise   to imagine; to make inferences based on insufficient evidence

surreptitious   secret; covert (antonym: **brazen; overt**)

sybaritic   voluptuous; sensual

sycophant   servile flatterer; parasite

synthesis   the combination of parts to form a whole, or of thesis and antithesis to form a higher truth

tacit   unspoken; implied (antonym: **explicit**)

taciturn   silent; having little inclination to talk (antonym: **garrulous**)

tactile   perceptible by touch; tangible

tangential   touching only the edge; marginally relevant

tangerine   a deep orange to almost scarlet mandarin orange [derived from Tangiers, Morocco]

tawdry   appearing gaudy or cheap

temerity   audacity; effrontery; boldness (antonym: **caution**)

tempest   storm

temporal   referring to time, as opposed to eternity; secular

tenet   a doctrine upheld by members of an organization

tepid   moderately warm; lukewarm

termagant   a shrew; a nagging woman, as Xanthippe (Socrates' wife); a virago; an ogress; a harpy

terrestrial   having to do with the earth

terse   (1) polished; refined; (2) short and to the point; concise

therapeutic   used in the treatment of diseases or disorders; curative

timbre   the quality of a sound or tone, distinctive of a particular voice or instrument

timorous   fearful; timid (antonym: **intrepid**)

tirade   a long, intemperate speech; diatribe

torpid   dormant; lacking energy; lethargic; apathetic; dull

   vapid   lacking vitality; flat; uninteresting

torque   (1) *n.* a twisting or turning force; (2) *v.* to cause to rotate or twist

torrid   oppressively hot

tort   a civil wrong for which the injured party is entitled to compensation

tractable   docile; malleable; obedient (antonym: **unruly**)

transient   lasting only a short time; changing; ephemeral; transitory

trenchant   (1) caustic; penetrating; (2) separate; distinct

triskaidekaphobia   the fear of the number 13

troglodyte   someone who lives in solitude

truculent   cruel; brutal; belligerent

turbid   muddy

turpitude   baseness; corruption; depravity

umbrage   (1) a feeling of offense or annoyance; (2) a shadow; a hint; a suspicion

unctuous   oily; smug; suave

undulate   to move in wavelike motions; to fluctuate

unduly   excessively

unequivocal   clear; obvious; certain

ungainly   hard to handle; unwieldy; clumsy

ungulate   hooflike; referring to hoofed animals

urbane   polished; polite or finished in manner

utopian   referring to paradise or an impossible ideal

uxoricide   the murder of one's wife

vacillate   to waver; to fluctuate; to oscillate

vacuous   stupid; lacking intelligence

vagrancy   the state of being homeless (legally, a misdemeanor)

vapid   insipid; spiritless

venal   corruptible

venerate   to honor

venial   forgivable

verbose   wordy (antonym: **laconic**)

vernal   suggestive of youth

viable   (1) capable of living; (2) able to stand or develop independently

vicarious   experienced through another medium; experienced through imaginary participation in the events of another's life

vilify   to slander; to verbally abuse; to defame

virago   a loud, overbearing woman; a termagant

viscous   thick; having a gummy consistency

vitriolic   caustic; biting

viviparous   producing living young, as most mammals, some reptiles, and a few fishes

volatile   easily aroused; explosive

volition   choice or decision; will

voracious   ravenous; gluttonous; insatiable
vulpine   foxlike; crafty
wan   pale; sickly
wanton   flirtatious; lascivious
whet   to stimulate; to incite; to make more intense, esp. an appetite
wizened   shrunken and wrinkled with age
wright   a worker, esp. in wood; used in combination with another word
     (e.g., *wheelwright, playwright*)
wroth   intensely angry; incensed
xanthic   yellowish
xenophobia   the fear of strangers
yean   to give birth, used of sheep or goats
yore   time long past
yowl   to cry out loudly; to wail
zealot   one who is enthusiastic, sometimes fanatical, about a cause
zenith   (1) the highest point; (2) the highest point reached by a celestial body
     (antonym: **nadir**)

SPECIAL COLLECTIVE NOUNS

bed of roses
bevy of beauties
cache of jewels
clew of worms
clutch of eggs
coven of witches
covey of quails
drift of swans
gaggle of geese
kindle of kittens
leap of leopards
litter of puppies
lock of hair
muster of peacocks
parcel of penguins
pod or **gam** of whales
pride of lions
rafter of turkeys
shoal or **school** of fish
string of pearls
swarm of bees
walk of snails

-OLOGY WORDS

The suffix *-ology* means the study of or the science of. The root of the word gives you the key to the field of study. The suffix *-ist* added to the name of the field of study refers to someone who works in that area. For example, the root *herpe* means reptile. Herpetology is the study of reptiles, and a herpetologist is one who studies snakes.

In the following definitions, "the study of" or "the science of" is understood.

alalogy   algae
anthropology   human beings—their distributions, origins, classifications,
     physical characteristics, environmental and social relations, and cultures
archaeology   remains of past human life and activities
axiology   values and value judgments (e.g., in ethics)
bacteriology   bacteria
biology   living organisms and vital processes

cosmology   nature, origin, structure, and space-time relationships of the universe

cryptology   codes and ciphers

cytology   cell and its functions

deontology   ethics

enology   wines and wine making

entomology   insects

epistemology   the nature, grounds, and limits of knowledge

eschatology   end of the world

ethology   animal behavior under natural conditions

etiology   causes of phenomena

geology   earth and its history

gerontology   aging and the problems of the aged

hagiology   saints and other revered persons

herpetology   reptiles and amphibians

histology   living tissue

homology   similarity in structure (thought to be due to common origin)

horology   measurement of time

ichthyology   fishes

kinesiology   principles of mechanics and anatomy in relation to human movement

limnology   fresh waters

mammalogy   mammals

morphology   structures and forms of plants and animals; word formation in a language

mycology   fungi

numismatology   coins

oncology   tumors

ontology   nature and relations of being

ophthalmology   structure, function, and diseases of the eye

ornithology   birds

paleontology   fossils

parasitology   parasites and parasitism

pathology   diseases

philology   language, speech, linguistics, and literature

physiology   functions and activities of living organisms

primatology   primates, especially other than recent humans

radiology   use of radiant energy (X rays, radium, etc.) in the diagnosis and treatment of disease

teleology   final causes or purpose in nature

thanatology   death and dying

toxicology   poisons, their effects, and the problems involved

urology   urinary system

virology   structure and function of viruses

zoology   animals

WORD DEMONS

Some words are frequently misused because they sound alike, are spelled almost the same, or are very close in meaning. The following is a list of such words. You should be familiar with the correct spelling, meaning, and use of each word.

adapt   to change or adjust
   When she moved to the foreign country, she had to adapt to new customs.
adept   skilled
   He was adept in all aspects of carpentry.
adopt   to accept or embrace, to accept formally
   The couple hopes to adopt several children.
   The council voted to adopt the new amendment.

adverse   unfavorable, unfriendly, opposing
   She overcame several adverse conditions to win the race.
averse   opposed
   The councilwoman was averse to the new proposal.

advice   suggestion
   The best advice I can give you is to read as much as you can.
advise   to counsel, to give suggestions
   We advise you to start studying for the test as soon as possible.

affect   influence, be of importance to, produce an effect on
   The rain will affect the picnic plans.
affect   to make a pretense of, to fake, to feign
   She affects a British accent.
effect   result, consequence; to bring about, to produce
   The farmers felt the effect of the drought.
   The drought effected a major change in the farmers' life.

affront   insult, offense
   His comment was an affront to the speaker.
confront   to face
   He will confront the student with the evidence.

allusion   reference to
   The author uses several allusions to Greek mythology in his story.
illusion   unreal image
   She has the illusion that I like jazz; I don't.

apprise   to let know, to inform
   The judge will apprise the jury of the pertinent statutes.
appraise   to estimate the value of
   The painting was appraised at two million dollars.

chronic   constant, long-lasting
Parking is a chronic problem in the inner city.
acute   short-lived, perhaps severe
He had acute appendicitis.

coherent   intelligible, meaningful, logical
The newscaster gave a coherent report of the accident.
inherent   innate, essential, intrinsic
Freedom of speech is an inherent part of the Bill of Rights.

complacent   contented
The students were complacent about their grades.
complaisant   willing, obliging
All day long the complaisant horse pulled the vegetable cart.

complement   to complete, to go well with
Two angles complement each other when they add up to 180 degrees.
Cranberries complement a turkey dinner.
compliment   a remark of courtesy or respect, praise
I'd like to compliment you on the excellent job that you did.

continual   repeated, happening often
His continual absence from classes resulted in his suspension.
continuous   uninterrupted, ceaseless
The continuous hum of the machine gave her a headache.

credible   believable, plausible
The child's story simply was not credible.
creditable   worthy of credit or praise, commendable
The teacher did a creditable job in preparing the students for the test.
credulous   ready to believe, gullible, easily convinced
The credulous woman accepted the neighbor's story without question.

denote   to refer to explicitly
The word *black* denotes the characteristic of an object that reflects no color.
connote   to suggest
The word *black* has been taken to connote wickedness or evil.

depredation   sack, plunder, robbing
The effects of the Huns' depredation of the villages were obvious.
deprecation   disapproval, disparagement
The deprecation of the new exhibit hall by all of the townspeople was disheartening to the architect.

detract   to take away from, to diminish
The cracked sidewalks detract from the appearance of the house.
distract   to divert, to turn away from
The student was unable to concentrate because the loud noises from the street distracted him.

discreet prudent, careful, tactful
The attorney was discreet in his questioning of the young girl.
discrete separate, distinct, separate
The party was composed of two discrete groups—the progressives and the conservatives.

disinterested impartial, having nothing to gain
The chairperson was completely disinterested in the outcome of the committee vote.
uninterested not interested in, unconcerned, incurious
The boy was completedly uninterested in the subjects he had to study.

elicit to draw out
She questioned him for an hour but was unable to elicit any information.
illicit unlawful, illegal
The police will crack down on all illicit parking.

eminent prominent, illustrious, preeminent
Gandhi was an eminent statesman.
imminent close at hand, impending
The jury's verdict is imminent.
immanent inherent, innate, intrinsic
Psychologists are studying behavior patterns to determine which are immanent and which are acquired.

farther to a greater distance
The runway was only one-half mile farther than the site of the plane crash.
further more, additionally (in time or degree)
The council will discuss the budget further in the next meeting.

fewer smaller in number
There are fewer students in school now than 10 years ago.
less more limited in amount
Inflation is less now than in the late 1970s.

flammable combustible, able to burn
inflammable combustible, able to burn
You must be careful when storing flammable material.
(The antonym of *flammable* and *inflammable* is *unflammable*.)

flout to scorn, to treat with disdain
Her unconventional dress flouted the guests' sensibilities.
flaunt to show off, to exhibit
The boy flaunted his new scout badge.

homogeneous   of the same kind, uniform, unmixed, similar in structure
It was a homogeneous class, all the students having basically the same socioeconomic and educational background.
The classes were homogeneously grouped according to abilities.

heterogeneous   mixed or varied in composition
The class was heterogeneous, with students from different economic and educational backgrounds.
The crowd outside the theater was a heterogeneous group of students and townspeople.

imply   to hint, to suggest, to indicate
The teacher's frown implied that the girl's answer was wrong.

infer   to conclude from known facts or premises
From the evidence presented, the judge inferred that the defendant was guilty.

ingenious   clever
The ingenious monkey figured out how to reach the bananas by constructing a platform.

ingenuous   frank, artless, naive
The ingenuous child told his grandmother that he didn't like her dress.

ludicrous   ridiculous
Italian western movies may seem ludicrous to an American.

lugubrious   gloomy
The music was lugubrious, suitable for a funeral.

perquisite   privilege that comes with a job
Members of Congress receive mailing privileges as a perquisite.

prerequisite   necessity, something required beforehand
Mathematics is a prerequisite for most physics courses.

precipitate   to bring on, to hasten, to quicken
The Great Depression precipitated the rise of fascism in Germany.

precipitous   steep
Prices during the inflation period rose precipitously.

persecute   to harass, to badger, to victimize
The Puritans came to America after they were persecuted for their religious beliefs.

prosecute   to put on trial, to indict, to bring legal action against
The state will prosecute him for drug trafficking.

perspective   viewpoint
From the perspective of the Native American, land is sacred.

prospective   future, expected
The prospective merger of the two companies caused a flurry of activity on the stock market.

precede   to go in front of
  An incubation period usually precedes the onset of the disease.
proceed   to go ahead
  After you reach the center of town, proceed three more blocks to the hotel.

prescribe   to order or advise (as in medicine)
  The physician will prescribe a drug to combat the infection.
proscribe   to condemn, to disapprove, to outlaw
  During the Middle Ages, the Catholic Church proscribed certain books by scientists.

supplement   to add to something
  He will supplement his regular school work with night and summer courses.
supplant   to replace, to usurp the place of
  Robots will supplant workers in some factories.

venal   capable of being bribed, corrupt
  The judge was accused of being venal and accepting large sums of money.
venial   forgivable
  His continual tardiness was often annoying but venial.

SELECTED FOREIGN WORDS AND PHRASES USED IN ENGLISH

addenda   a list of additions (Latin)
ad hoc   for a particular purpose (Latin)
aficionado   an ardent devotee (Spanish)
agent provocateur   one who incites another person or an organization (French)
alfresco   outdoors (Italian)
alter ego   a second self; a trusted friend (Latin)
amour-propre   self-esteem (French)
angst   dread, anxiety (German)
a priori   based on theory rather than observation (Latin)
au courant   informed of the latest (French)
baksheesh   tip, gratuity (Persian)
bête noire   a strongly detested person or thing (French)
bildungsroman   personal development novel (German)
bona fide   in good faith (Latin)
bon vivant   an epicure; a lover of good living (French)
bravura   a display of spirit and dash (Italian)
casus belli   a pretext or reason that justifies or allegedly justifies an attack of war (Latin)
caveat emptor   let the buyer beware (Latin)
chef d'oeuvre   chief work; masterpiece (French)
chutzpah   gall, arrogance, audacity (Yiddish)
comme il faut   as it ought to be; proper (French)
contretemps   an inopportune or embarrassing situation (French)

corpus delicti   the evidence necessary to prove that a crime has been committed (Latin)

coup de grâce   a final, decisive blow or event (French)

cul-de-sac   a dead end (French)

de facto   actual (Latin)

déjà vu   illusion of having experienced something already (French)

de jure   technically (Latin)

de rigueur   necessary, obligatory (French)

dernier cri   the last word; the newest fashion (French)

déshabillé   undressed or partially undressed (French)

doppelgänger   a counterpart of a living person (German)

enfant terrible   a bad child; one whose behavior is embarrassing (French)

errata   a list of errors (Latin)

ex cathedra   by virtue of one's position or office (Latin)

faux pas   a social blunder (French)

fiasco   disaster (Italian)

idée fixe   an idea that dominates one's mind, especially for a long time (French)

in extenso   at full length (Latin)

in extremis   near death (Latin)

ingenue   the stage role of an ingenuous girl; a naive girl (French)

in loco parentis   in the place of a parent; acting as a guardian (Latin)

in medias res   in the middle of things (Latin)

in re   in reference to (Latin)

insouciance   indifference; lack of concern (French)

in vacuo   in a vacuum (Latin)

junta   group (usually military) that assumes leadership after a coup or overthrow of a government (Spanish)

laissez-faire   a policy of free trade or noninterference (French)

leitmotif   recurring theme (German)

mélange   a mixture or medley, often of incongruous elements (French)

ménage   a household (French)

mirabilis dictu   wonderful to relate (Latin)

modus operandi   a method of procedure, working, or operating (Latin)

ne plus ultra   the highest point that can be attained; the acme (Latin)

noblesse oblige   nobility obligates; the behavior and graciousness of the nobility (French)

nolo contendere   no contest; legally, not contesting a charge against one, but without pleading guilty (Latin)

nom de plume   a pen name (French)

non sequitur   something that does not logically follow (Latin)

nuance   a subtle distinction (French)

pax vobiscum   peace be with you; peace (Latin)

persona non grata   an unacceptable or unwelcome person (Latin)

pièce de resistance   the main course or dish; the most valuable object (French)

presto   rapidly, quickly (Italian)

prima facie   on the face of; at first view (Latin)

pro bono publico   for the public good (Latin)

pro forma   done as a matter of form (Latin)

pro rata   proportionally according to a factor (Latin)

pro tempore (pro tem)   for the time being; temporarily (Latin)

punctilio   a fine point; a minute detail of conduct (Italian)

quid pro quo   something given or received for something else; substitute (Latin)

raison d'être   reason for being (French)

rapprochement   establishing a cordial relationship; developing mutual understanding (French)

rara avis   an unusual specimen (Latin)

rendezvous   an appointment for two or more people to meet at a particular place (French)

riposte   a retort; a retaliatory verbal sally (French)

safari   a trip or journey (Swahili)

salaam   peace (as a salutation) (Arabic)

sanctum sanctorum   the holy of holies; the office of an awesome person (Latin)

sang froid   cold blood; self-possession, composure (French)

schadenfreude   pleasure at someone else's misfortunes (German)

sine qua non   indispensable (Latin)

soupçon   suspicion; a little bit or trace, as in a recipe (French)

sui genera   one of a kind (Latin)

tour de force   a feat of strength, skill, or ingenuity (French)

vendetta   a blood feud (Italian)

vis-à-vis   face to face with; in relation to; as compared with (French)

weltschmerz   sorrow over the evils of the world (German)

zeitgeist   the spirit of the times (German)

ALPHABETS AND THEIR CHARACTERISTICS

Alphabet	Characteristics/Comments
Cyrillic	Slavic and Russian languages
Cuneiform	Ancient Egyptian iconographic writing
Hieroglyphic	Ancient Egyptian ideographic writing
Devanagari	Indian writing with syllabic features
Greek	Ancient or modern; Greek alphabet
Hebrew	written right to left, no vowels
Arabic	written right to left, no vowels
Roman	used in Romance languages and English
ogham	Old Irish, 5th and 6th century, notches
rune	Germanic, from 3rd to 13th centuries

GEOGRAPHY

It is not possible to provide a review of basic geography here. Since questions involving name changes of countries and cities have appeared on some *MAT* exams, a table of such changes is given below.

Current Name	Previous Names
Angola	Portuguese West Africa
Bangladesh	East Pakistan
Belize	British Honduras
Cambodia	French Indo-China
Chad	French Equatorial Africa
Ethiopia	Abyssinia
Ghana	Gold Coast
Guyana	British Guiana
Ho Chi Minh City	Saigon
Indonesia	Netherlands East Indies
Iran	Persia
Iraq	Mesopotamia, Babylon, Assyria
Istanbul	Constantinople
Laos	French Indo-China
Madagascar	Malagasy
Namibia	South West Africa
Niger	French West Africa
Petrograd	Leningrad, Petrograd
Santo Domingo	Trujillo
Sri Lanka	Ceylon
Surinam	Dutch Guiana
Thailand	Siam
Volgograd	Stalingrad; Tsaritsyn
Zaire	Congo
Zambia	Northern Rhodesia
Zimbabwe	Rhodesia

HISTORY

MAT analogies may include the names of people, events, wars, treaties, conferences, and documents important in U.S. and world history. The following may serve as a quick review.

Explorers

Amundsen, Roald (1872–1928) (Norwegian) was first to reach South Pole and to fly over North Pole

Balboa, Vasco Núñez de (1475–1517) (Spanish) Pacific Ocean

Cabot, John (1450–1498) (English) explored North America

Cartier, Jacques (1491–1557) (French) St. Lawrence river region

Columbus, Christopher (1451–1506) (Italian/Spanish) discovery of the New World

Coronado, Francisco Vásquez de (1510–1554) (Spanish) mythical city of Cibola, SW region of the U.S.

Cortes, Hernando (1485–1547) (Spanish) Mexico, Aztec nation

de Soto, Hernando (1500–1542) (Spanish) Cuba, Florida, SE region of U.S.

Diaz, Bartolomeu (1450–1500) (Portuguese) Cape of Good Hope

Drake, Sir Francis (1540–1596) (British) circumnavigated the globe; helped defeat Spanish Armada

Hudson, Henry (d. 1611) (British) Hudson River, Hudson Bay area

Magellan, Ferdinand (1480–1521) (Portuguese) the first to sail around the world

Marquette, Jacques (1637–1675) (French) discovered the Mississippi

Peary, Robert E. (1856–1920) (American) North Pole (disputed claim; prior claim of Fred Cook)

Pizarro, Francisco (1470–1541) (Spanish) Peru, Inca empire

Polo, Marco (1254–1324) (Italian) explored China and Asia

Ponce de Leon, Juan (1460–1521) (Spanish) first European explorer in Florida

Raleigh, Sir Walter (1552–1618) (British) eastern coast of U.S.

Scott, Robert (1868–1912) (British) Antarctica, South Pole (prior claim of Amundsen)

Vasquez de Coronado, Francisco (1510–1554) (Spanish) first European to explore Arizona and New Mexico

Vespucci, Amerigo (1454–1521) (Italian) America was named after him; first to realize that the Americas were a different continent than Asia

Inventors

Beaufort, Francis (1774–1854) (French) Beaufort Scale: wind force scale named after him

Bell, Alexander Graham (1847–1922) (American) telephone

Benz, Karl (1844–1929) (German) the petrol-powered automobile

Berners-Lee, Tim (b. 1955) (English) with Robert Cailliau, the World Wide Web

Braille, Louis (1809–1852)   (French) the Braille writing system

Daimler, Gottlieb (1834–1900)   (German) first high-speed internal-combustion engine

Da Vinci, Leonardo (1452–1519)   (Italian) conceptualized a helicopter, painted the Mona Lisa, advanced anatomy, etc.

Diesel, Rudolf (1853–1913)   (German) first internal-combustion engine using fuel oil instead of gasoline

Drais, Karl (1785–1851)   (German) bicycle (Draisine)

Edison, Thomas Alva (1847–1931)   (American) lightbulb, phonograph

Einstein, Albert (1879–1955)   (German) theory of relativity

Engelbart, Douglas (b. 1925) (American) the computer mouse

Fermi, Enrico (1901–1954)   (Italian) one of the first developers of the nuclear reactor

Fleming, Alexander (1881–1955)   (English) penicillin

Ford, Henry (1863–1947)   (American) developed modern assembly lines for mass production

Franklin, Benjamin (1706–1790)   (American) lightning rod

Galilei, Galileo (1564–1642)   (Italian) improved the telescope, physicist

Gutenberg, Johannes (1400–1468)   (German) movable type, printing press

Marconi, Guglielmo (1874–1937)   (Italian) wireless radio

Montgolfier, Joseph-Michel (1740–1810)   (French) hot-air balloon

Newton, Isaac (1642–1727)   (English) reflecting telescope (reduces chromatic aberration)

Nobel, Alfred (1833–1896)   (Swedish) dynamite

Roentgen, Wilhelm Conrad (1845–1923)   (German) the X-ray machine

Stephenson, George (1781–1848)   (English) first steam locomotive

Whitney, Eli (1765–1825)   (American) interchangeable parts, cotton gin

Liberators or Unifiers

Bismarck, Otto von (1815–1898)   Germany

Bolívar, Simón (1783–1830)   Venezuela, Peru, Bolivia

Garibaldi, Giuseppe (1807–1882)   Italy

O'Higgins, Bernardo (1778–1842)   Chile

San Martin, José de (1778–1850)   Peru, Chile (march across the Andes)

Major Wars

Knowledge of the most important events and treaties associated with major wars will help in taking the *MAT*. Below is a list of some major items that may be found in analogies.

THE AMERICAN REVOLUTION

first battles—Lexington and Concord (1775)
major battles—Bunker Hill (1775), Fort Ticonderoga (1775), Saratoga (1777), Valley Forge (1777)

Declaration of Independence—declared that colonies were free from England, 1776

Continental Congress—federal legislature of the 13 colonies under the Articles of Confederation (1774, 1775)

Constitution—replaced Articles of Confederation in 1789

end of war—surrender of British General Cornwallis to George Washington at Yorktown (1781); treaty recognizing the United States as a separate nation signed in Paris (1782)

AMERICAN CIVIL WAR

start of war—Harper's Ferry (1859)

first battles—Fort Sumter (1861) and Bull Run (1861) (both Confederate victories)

major battles—Antietam (1862), Fredericksburg (1862), Gettysburg (1863), Shiloh (1862) (the Union named battles after towns; the Confederates named battles after streams), Sherman's March to the Sea (1864), Vicksburg (1863) (great victory for Grant)

end of war—surrender of General Lee to General Grant at Appomatox (1865)

FRENCH REVOLUTION

start of war—storming of the Bastille (1789)

important events/documents—Declaration of the Rights of Man and Citizen (Preamble to the Constitution), 1791; Reign of Terror, which ended 9 Thermidor (July 27, 1794) with the execution of Robespierre; coup d'etat of 18 Brumaire (November 9–10, 1799) whereby Napoleon I becomes consul

end of war—treaty of Amiens, France (1802)

RUSSIAN CIVIL WAR

conflicting sides—Bolsheviks (majority) vs. Mensheviks (minority)

leaders of opposing sides—Lenin and Trotsky (Reds) vs. Kerensky and Plekanov (Whites)

WORLD WAR I

start of war—assassination of Archduke Ferdinand (1914); sinking of *Lusitania* (British ship with American passengers) by the Germans led to U.S. entry into the war (1915)

major battles—Ypres (1917), Marne (1914), Verdun (1916), Somme (1916) offensive characteristics—trench warfare, use of poison gas

end of war—Treaty of Versailles (1918); attempt to divide nations on basis of national self-determination; establishment of the League of Nations

WORLD WAR II

major events—Munich Pact (1938), policy of appeasement, associated with British Prime Minister Chamberlain

start of war—blitzkrieg over Poland (1939); sinking of *Arizona* and other ships at Pearl Harbor attack in Honolulu led to U.S. declaration of war against Japan and Germany (1941)

major battles—Dunkirk (1940), Ardennes (1944), Alamein (North Africa 1942), Stalingrad (1942–1943)

characteristics—tank warfare, blitzkrieg, use of massive bombing by air force; development of atomic weapons

end of war—Japan surrenders unconditionally at Potsdam Conference (1945)

OTHER CONFERENCES AND PEACE TREATIES

Ghent, Belgium—end of War of 1812

Vienna, Congress of—end of Napoleonic Wars (1814–1815)

Yalta Conference—meeting of Roosevelt, Churchill, and Stalin during World War II (1945)

Potsdam (German) Conference—meeting of Truman, Churchill (replaced by Atlee), and Stalin during World War II (1945)

Panmunjon, Korea—end of Korean War (1953)

Reykjavik Conference—Reagan-Gorbachev summit meeting (1986)

SOCIAL SCIENCES

The following brief list of people and movements in the social sciences is intended as a quick review only.

Adler, Alfred (1870–1937)   Austrian psychiatrist; inferiority complex

Allison, Graham (b. 1940)   American political scientist, has worked in decision-making and is an important analyst of national security

Barzun, Jacques (b. 1907)   American historian specializing in expressions of culture like music, literature, and education

Behaviorism (Psychology)   School of thought in psychology since the early 1900s. Suggests that behavior can be explained by means of environmental causes. Proponents were John B. Watson, Ivan Pavlov, and B. F. Skinner, for example. Focus on classical and operant conditioning.

Benedict, Ruth (1887–1948)   American anthropologist; author of *Patterns of Culture*

Binet, Alfred (1851–1911) and **Simon, Théodore** (1873–1961)   French psychologists; development of IQ tests

Boas, Franz (1858–1942)   German American anthropologist; known for being the "father" of modern anthropology as he applied the scientific method to his anthropological studies

Cognitive Psychology   Focuses on mental processes including how people think, perceive, remember, and learn. One of the most influential theories was the stages of cognitive development theory proposed by Jean Piaget. Other cognitive psychologists include Albert Bandura, Daniel Kahneman, Steven Pinker, Daniel Schacter, and Robert Sternberg.

Coleman, James (1926–1995)   American sociologist; one of the early users of the term "social capital"

Cultural Materialism (Anthropology)   Attaches special importance to technology and economic factors in the development of a society.

Dewey, John (1859–1952)   American educator/philosopher; pragmatism

DuBois, W. E. B. (1868–1963)   American sociologist and historian; active in the area of racism

Durkheim, Emile (1859–1917)   French sociologist; considered one of the fathers of modern sociology

Erikson, Erik (1902–1994)   American psychologist; stage theory of development

Ferguson, Niall (b. 1964)   Scottish historian specializing in financial and economic history

Freud, Sigmund (1856–1939)   Austrian psychiatrist; sexual drive, Oedipus complex

Friedman, Milton (1912–2006)   American economist, recipient of the Nobel Prize in economics; opposed government regulation

Functionalism (Anthropology, Sociology)   Applies the scientific method to the examination of the social world (e.g., social surveys, interviews) and uses analogies between individual organisms and society. Emphasis is on use. Proponents include Emile Durkheim and Talcott Parsons.

Gall, Franz Joseph (1758–1828)   German anatomist/physiologist; study of nervous system and brain, founded pseudoscience of phrenology

Galton, Sir Francis (1822–1911)   English scientist; belief in heredity as predeterminant force, IQ tests

Geertz, Clifford (1926–2006)   American anthropologist; worked in the field of symbolic anthropology, which attributes special importance to thoughts (symbols)

Gestalt Psychology   Developed in Germany and Austria in the late 19th century. Gestalt psychologists believe that the conscious experience must be considered as a whole, rather than broken down into small elements. The whole is greater than just the sum of its parts. Prononents include Max Wertheimer, Kurt Koffka, Wolfgang Koehler, and Fritz Perls.

Gibbon, Edward (1737–1794)   English historian who wrote *The History of the Decline and Fall of the Roman Empire*

Goffman, Erving (1922–1982)   American sociologist who studied social interaction

Goodall, Jane (b. 1934)   American anthropologist and primatologist; known for her chimpanzee studies in Tanzania

Greenspan, Alan (b. 1926)   American economist; former chairman of the Federal Reserve

Harlow, Harry (1905–1981)   American psychologist; importance of attachment for baby monkeys

Heterodox economics   Economic schools of thought that are outside of mainstream economics. They include the Austrian School, ecological economics, and Post-Keynesian economics.

Horney, Karen (1885–1952)   American psychiatrist; importance of social and cultural influences on behavior

Huizinga, Johan (1872–1945)   Dutch historian, one of the founders of modern cultural history

Humanistic Psychology   Developed in the 1950s in response to both behaviorism and psychoanalysis. Focused on individual free will, personal growth, and self-actualization. Major proponents include Abraham Maslow and Carl Rogers.

Hume, David (1711–1776)   Scottish philosopher; use of induction

Huntington, Samuel (1927–2008)   American political scientist, famous for his theory of the "Clash of Civilizations"

James, William (1842–1910)   American philosopher; pragmatism, functionalism

Jung, Carl (1875–1961)   Swiss psychiatrist; self-realization

Kant, Immanuel (1724–1804)   German philosopher; proposed categorical imperative

Keynes, John Maynard (1883–1946)   British developer of Keynesian economics, founder of modern theoretical macroeconomics

Kohlberg, Lawrence (1927–1987)   American psychologist; moral stages of development

Köhler, Wolfgang (1887–1967)   German-American psychologist; Gestaltist, worked with chimps

Krugman, Paul (b. 1953)   American economist; won the Nobel Memorial Prize in Economic Sciences in 2008 for his work on New Trade Theory

Leibnitz, Gottfried (1646–1716)   German philosopher/mathematician; use of deduction

Malinowski, Bronislaw (1884–1942)   Polish anthropologist, pioneer in ethnographic fieldwork

Malthus, Thomas (1766–1834)   English demographer and political economist; noted the potential for populations to increase rapidly, and more rapidly than the food supply

Mansfield, Harvey (b. 1932)   American political scientist; conservative; author of *Manliness*

Marx, Karl (1818–1883)   German economist; founder of communism

Mill, John Stuart (1806–1873)   English philosopher; used principle of utility

Nye, Joseph (b. 1937)   American political scientist; developed the concepts of asymmetrical and complex interdependence with Robert Keohane

Parsons, Talcott (1902–1979)   American sociologist; developed structural functionalism as a means of analyzing society

Patterson, Orlando (b. 1940)   American sociologist known for his work on race

Pavlov, Ivan (1849–1936)   Russian physiologist/psychologist; conditioning of reflexes, worked with dogs

Peirce, Charles Sanders (1839–1914)   American philosopher; pragmatist

Piaget, Jean (1896–1980)   Swiss psychologist; stage theory of intellectual development

Psychoanalysis (Psychology)   Founded by Sigmund Freud. States that the human mind is composed of three elements: the id, the ego, and the superego. The unconscious plays an important role in the explanation of behavior. Other psychoanalysts include Anna Freud, Carl Jung, and Erik Erikson.

Sachs, Jeffrey (b. 1954)   American economist; author of *The End of Poverty*; Special Advisor to United Nations Secretary-General Ban Ki-Moon

Skinner, B[urrhus] F[rederic] (1904–1990)   American psychologist; behaviorist; studied effects of reinforcement on behavior; worked with rats, pigeons (Skinner box)

Smith, Adam (1723–1790)   English; one of the founders of modern economics, author of *The Wealth of Nations*

Strauss, Claude Levi (1908–2008)   French anthropologist; author of *Structural Anthropology*; viewed culture as a system of symbolic communication

Structuralism (Anthropology, Sociology)   Suggests that meaning is produced through practices and activities. The mind uses binary opposites (like day and night) that differ from culture to culture. Proponents include Claude Levi-Strauss.

Symbolic interactionism (Sociology)   People interact with each other by interpreting each other's actions. Their interactions are therefore based on the meaning they attach to the actions. Proponents include George H. Mead, Herbert Blumer, and Erving Goffman.

Thorndike, Edward (1874–1949)   American educator/psychologist; intelligence, IQ tests, worked with cats

Titchener, Edward (1867–1927)   American psychologist; structuralist

von Ranke, Leopold (1795–1886)   German historian considered one of the founders of modern source-based history

Walzer, Michael (b. 1935)   American political philosopher; known for his work on just and unjust wars, economic justice, and ethnicity

Watson, John (1878–1958)   American psychologist; behaviorist

Weber, Max (1864–1920)   German sociologist; argued in *The Protestant Ethic and the Spirit of Capitalism* that Protestantism influenced the development of capitalism

ART AND ARCHITECTURE

Use the following list of the most important artists and architects and schools and movements in art history as a quick review. The names of artists associated with the movement or school and the works of particular artists are given in parentheses.

Important Artists, Architects, and Schools/Movements

abstract art   art form that assumes that artistic values reside in form and color and are independent of the subject of the art or painting

abstract expressionism   1940s-to-1950s American art movement stressing spontaneous, nonrepresentational creation with emphasis on the paint itself; first truly American school of art (Pollock)

art deco   1920s-to-1930s art movement stressing highly decorative art, utilizing geometric, streamlined forms inspired by industrial design (Chrysler Building in New York City)

art nouveau   1895-to-1905 "new art" movement characterized by motifs of highly stylized flowing plants, curving lines, and fluent forms

ashcan school   early 20th century school of American realist painters who abandoned idealized subjects for more sordid aspects of urban life

Audubon, John James (1785–1851)   early 19th century American artist and illustrator known for his color engravings of birds (*Birds in America*)

Barbizon school   mid-19th century group of landscape artists who rejected the classical and romantic to portray nature as they perceived it; forerunner of impressionism (Rousseau)

baroque   late 16th-to-early 18th century movement, developed in Italy, that stressed grand theatrical effects and elaborate ornamentation (Palace of Versailles)

Bauhaus   most famous school of architecture and design of modern times; founded in Germany in 1919; austere, geometric style (founder: Gropius; teachers: Klee and Kandinsky)

beaux arts   architectural style, popular from 1890 to 1920, using formal and classical techniques

Bosch, Hieronymus (1450–1516)   early 16th century painter considered perhaps the greatest master of fantasy ever (*Garden of Earthly Delights*)

Botticelli, Sandro (1444–1510)   15th century Italian Renaissance artist (*The Birth of Venus, St. Sebastian*)

Brancusi, Constantin (1876–1957)   19th-to-20th century Romanian sculptor known for highly simplified archetypical human and animal forms (*The Kiss, Bird in Space*)

Brueghel, Pieter (the Elder) (1525–1569)   16th century Flemish painter known for peasant scenes and large landscapes; sometimes known as "Peasant Bruegel" (*Hunters in the Snow, The Harvesters*)

Byzantine art   Eastern (Greek) art of the 5th to 15th centuries, characterized by Oriental motifs, formal design, and free use of gilding

Caldecott, Randolph (1864–1886)   19th century English illustrator known for his illustrations of children's books; the prestigious Caldecott Award is given annually for excellence in children's book illustration

Calder, Alexander (1898–1976)   20th century American sculptor and abstract painter best known for mobiles and stabiles (nonmoving sculptures) (*Lobster Trap and Fish Tail, Spiral*)

Cellini, Benvenuto (1500–1571)   16th century Florentine sculptor, goldsmith, and designer of coins and medals (*Perseus* bronze, gold saltcellar)

Cézanne, Paul (1839–1906)   19th century French painter, often considered the forerunner of many 20th century art movements; romantic, impressionist, classical, and naturalistic influences are all condensed in his work (*Grande Baigneuses, Self Portrait, The Black Clock, Card Players*)

Chagall, Marc (1889–1985)   20th century French painter of Russian-Jewish origin, forerunner of surrealism (*The Juggler, The Green Violinist*)

chiaroscuro   the balance of light and shadow in a picture; used to describe works that are predominantly dark, like those of Rembrandt

classicism   art attributed to ancient Greece and Rome, characterized by discipline, harmony, objectivity, and reason

cloisonné   a process of enameling in which a design is displayed in strips of metal on a china or metal background, making channels, or cloisons, to hold the enamel colors

Cole, Thomas (1801–1848)   19th century American landscape painter; member of the Hudson River school of painting

collage   a picture built up wholly or partly from pieces of paper, cloth, or other material stuck on canvas or other surface (early cubists, dadaists, Matisse)

Constable, John (1776–1837)   19th century English landscape painter (*The Holy Wain*)

constructivism   movement, since the 1920s, principally in Russia, involving the creation of three-dimensional art, using iron, glass, plastic, and other materials to express technological society (Calder's mobiles)

Copley, John Singleton (1738–1815)   18th century American protrait painter

cubism   1907-to-1915 art movement, mainly French, characterized by fragmentation of reality; used geometric forms in nature as a departure from representational art; a reaction to impressionism (Picasso)

Currier, Nathaniel T. (1813–1888) and **Ives, James Merrit** (1824-1895)   19th century American lithographers known for prints depicting American life

dada   1915-to-1923 international anti-art movement reflecting cynicism by producing bizarre works that represented the absurd (*Mona Lisa with a Mustache*)

Dali, Salvador (1904–1989)   20th century Spanish painter, considered one of the foremost surrealists (*Premonition of the Civil War, Christ of St. John of the Cross, Persistence of Memory*)

Daumier, Honoré (1808–1879)   19th century French lithographer, cartoonist, and social satirist (*The Print Collector, The People of Justice*)

Degas, Edgar (1834–1917)   late 19th–early 20th century French painter (*Study of a Dancer, Woman on Horseback*)

de Kooning, Willem (1904–1997)   20th century Dutch abstract painter known for distorted shapes and tragic expressions (*Woman, I*)

Delacroix, Eugène (1798–1863)   19th century French painter of the Romantic period (*Liberty at the Barricades*)

Donatello (1386–1466)   15th century Florentine sculptor; one of the founders of Italian Renaissance sculpture (*David, St. George Slaying the Dragon*)

Dürer, Albrecht (1471–1528)   late 15th–early 16th century German artist known for his woodcuts and engravings (*His Mother*, a charcoal drawing; *Adam and Eve*, an engraving; and *The Apocalypse*, a series of woodcuts)

engraving   a method of multiplying prints. See also, **relief**, **intaglio**, and **lithography**

Ernst, Max (1891–1976)   20th century German-born French artist, a leading surrealist and one of the founders of dada; known for his "reveries" (*Europe After the Rain, Mundus est Fabula*)

expressionism   20th century art in which the expression of the artist takes precedence over rational and faithful rendering of the subject matter; stress on emotions and inner visions (van Gogh, El Greco)

fauvism   work of early 20th-century impressionists, characterized by strident color and distortion; first artistic revolution of the 20th century (Matisse, Roualt)

Fayum portrait   realistic form of portraiture found on shrouds and mummy cases from the 1st to 4th centuries

fresco   wall painting; painting on wet plaster

frieze   middle section of a building, where relief sculpture was often executed

Fuller, Buckminster (1895–1983)   20th century American avant-garde architect famous for his geodesic domes

futurism   1910 Italian art movement that stressed motion and sought to glorify the machine by painting and sculpting multitudes of moving parts

Gainsborough, Thomas (1727–1788)   18th century English painter of landscapes and portraits (*Blue Boy*)

gargoyle   in Gothic architecture, a bizarre creature whose open mouth was used as a gutter to carry water away from the walls

Gauguin, Paul (1848–1903)   19th century French painter best known for his depiction of simple life in Tahiti (*Indian Ocean Maiden*)

glazing   a process of applying a transparent layer of oil paint over a solid one so that the color of the first layer is greatly modified

Gothic   12th-to-16th century style of architecture typical of northern Europe (cathedrals with elaborate architecture and stained glass panels)

Goya, Francisco José de (1746–1828)   late 18th–early 19th century Spanish painter and printmaker (*Majas on a Balcony*)

Greco, El (1541–1614)   16th century Greek painter who lived and worked in Spain (*The Annunciation, The Burial of the Count of Orgaz*)

Hogarth, William (1697–1764)   18th century English artist (*Signing the Marriage Contract*)

Holbein, Hans (the Younger) (1497–1543)   16th century German Renaissance painter (*Dance of Death, Dead Christ*)

holograph   an image in three dimensions created by a laser passing through a photographic film or plate without a camera

Homer, Winslow (1836–1910)   late 19th century American painter and illustrator; Civil War illustrations

Hopper, Edward (1882–1967)   20th century American artist known for bleak, surreal scenes depicting city life and the ennui of workers

Hudson River school   mid-19th century American school of landscape painting known for its romantic scenes glorifying nature

impasto   thick application of pigment to canvas

impressionism   late 19th century French school that stressed visual impression; first of the modern art movements (Monet, Renoir, Degas)

intaglio   engraving on stone to achieve a concave effect; opposite of cameo

Johns, Jasper (b. 1930)   20th century American pop artist known for blown-up images (*Flags, Targets*)

Kandinsky, Wassily (1866–1944)   late 19th–early 20th century Russian-born German artist, one of the founders of the abstract movement; known for kinetic lines

Kinetic art   art that moves through magnets, motorized parts, etc.

Klee, Paul (1879–1940)   late 19th–early 20th century Swiss painter and etcher known for his whimsical works that sought to portray reality through its inner nature (*Inventions, Senecio*)

Leonardo da Vinci (1452–1519)   late 15th–early 16th century Italian artist and scientist; most versatile genius of the Renaissance (fresco: *The Last Supper*, painting: *Mona Lisa*; notebook drawings of human anatomy)

lithography   method of printing that uses wax and ink on hard plates

luminism   American art movement associated with impressionism, concerned with the effect of light

Maillol, Aristide (1861–1944)   late 19th–early 20th century French painter and sculptor (*The Three Graces, Seated Woman*)

Manet, Edouard (1832–1883)   19th century French painter who contributed much to the development of impressionism, although he himself was not a member of the group (*The Fifer, Guitarist*)

mannerism   1520s-to-1590s school of art and architecture characterized by the exotic and confusing and the distortion of the human form (El Greco, Vassari)

Matisse, Henri (1869–1954)   late 19th–early 20th century French artist known for his still-life subjects; a member of the fauve group and influenced by impressionism (*Jazz: Icarus, Fruits and Flowers*)

Michelangelo, Bounarotti (1475–1564)   late 15th–early 16th century Italian sculptor, painter, architect, and poet who embodied the Renaissance (*Pieta, David, Madonna and Child*, ceiling of the Sistine Chapel)

Mies van der Rohe, Ludwig (1886–1969)   20th century German-American architect known for clean-line skyscrapers of glass and metal and for steel-framed furniture (Barcelona chair)

minimal art   contemporary art movement that rejects emotional expression and stresses restraint, understatement, and precision

Miró, Joan (1893–1983)   20th century Spanish surrealist painter known for depicting fantasies (*Dutch Interior, Woman and Bird in the Moonlight*)

mobile   a kinetic sculpture consisting of shapes cut from different materials and hung at different levels (Calder)

modern art   art, since the 1850s, that has extricated itself from subject matter and stresses form

Modigliani, Amedeo (1884–1920)   late 19th–early 20th century Italian sculptor and painter known for his sad, elongated faces (*Seated Nude, The Brown Haired Girl*)

Mondrian, Piet (1872–1944)   late 19th–early 20th century Dutch abstract painter known for his geometric shapes (*Composition with Red, Yellow and Blue*)

Monet, Claude (1840–1926)   late 19th–early 20th century French painter, a leader of impressionism; known for seeing nature with an "objective eye" (*Water Lily* paintings)

montage   sticking one layer over another, especially photographs applied to an unusual background; associated with cubists

Moore, Henry (1898–1986)   20th century British sculptor known for large-scale abstract works and "truth to materials" doctrine (*Family Group*)

Moses, Anna Mary (Grandma) (1860–1961)   late 19th–early 20th century American painter known for her simple depictions of New England life and landscapes

Murillo, Bartolomé Estebon (1617–1682)   17th century Spanish painter (*Immaculate Conception, Beggar Boy*)

Nast, Thomas (1840–1902)   19th century American illustrator and cartoonist known for his depictions of Tweed ring and Tammany Hall

naturalism   late 19th century art movement that tried to depict humans and society true to life and in precise detail

neoclassicism   1790s-to-1830s rejection of rococo and a return to classical style; characterized by restraint and balance

O'Keeffe, Georgia (1887–1986)   20th century American painter known for her large New Mexican landscapes

op art   1960s American art movement derived from popular culture and commercial art, with art culled from everyday life (Warhol)

pastiche   piece of art created in the style of a particular artist or movement but not faked, as in forgery

Picasso, Pablo (1881–1973)   20th century Spanish painter, sculptor, and printmaker considered one of the foremost artists of the 20th century. After his "Blue period" paintings of despairing people and his "Rose period" circus paintings, he turned to cubism and still later to surrealism and collage (*Guernica, Three Musicians, Artists*)

pointillism   1880s art form in which tiny dots of paint, when viewed from a distance, take on the shape of objects (Seurat)

Pollock, Jackson (1912–1956)   20th century American painter of the abstract expressionist school known for his large canvases (later cut up) that aim to create subconscious reality

Raphael (1483–1520)   early 16th century Italian painter who, along with Leonardo da Vinci and Michelangelo, is considered a creator of the Renaissance (*Transfiguration, St. Michael, Saint George and the Dragon*)

realism   art form that attempts to search for the squalid and depressing with a style of strict attention to detail

relief   sculpture that is not free standing; in having a background, the sculpture resembles a painting

Rembrandt, Harmensz (1606–1669)   17th century Dutch painter who is best known for his portraits but who also did landscapes, Biblical subjects, and etchings (*Self Portrait with Sprouting Beard, Night Watch, The Anatomy Lesson of Dr. Nicolaes Tulp*)

Remington, Frederic (1861–1909)   19th century American painter, illustrator, and sculptor known for his romantic scenes of the American Old West

Renoir, Pierre-Auguste (1841–1919)   late 19th–early 20th century French painter; a founder of impressionism (*Moulin de la Galette, Les Grandes Baigneuses*)

Reynolds, Sir Joshua (1723–1792)   18th century British portrait painter

rococo   1730s-to-1780s style of European art that glorified asymmetrical ornamentation on paneling, porcelain, and jewelry to display a love of gaiety and elegance

Rodin, Auguste (1840–1917)   late 19th–early 20th century French sculptor, the most famous sculptor of the late 19th century (*The Thinker, The Kiss*)

romanticism   a current throughout art history that stresses the importance of fantasy and the imagination over reason and order

Rothko, Mark (1903–1970)   20th century Russian-born American abstract expressionist painter known for his canvases of irregular shapes and bands of color

Rouault, Georges (1871–1958)   late 19th–early 20th century French expressionist painter (*The Apprentice, Christian Nocturne, The Holy Face*)

Rousseau, Henri (1844–1910)   19th century French painter, one of the foremost primitive artists of the modern age (*The Sleeping Gypsy, The Dream*)

Rubens, Peter Paul (1577–1640)   late 16th–early 17th century Flemish baroque painter, the most famous artist of northern Europe in his day (*The Judgment of Paris, Portrait of Helene Fourment, The Descent from the Cross*)

Sargent, John Singer (1856–1925)   late 19th–early 20th century American portrait painter (*Lady Hamilton*)

serial art   the repetition, possibly with slight variation, of a particular image in a work of art (Warhol)

serigraphy   a type of silk screen painting

Seurat, Georges (1859–1891)   19th century French artist who introduced pointillism (*Sunday Afternoon on the Island of La Grande Jatte*)

sfumato   painting technique in which one tone is blended into another without an abrupt outline

still life   the depiction of inanimate objects

surrealism   art form, since 1924, that seeks to reveal psychological reality behind appearances; subject matter stresses dreams, fantasies, and the subconscious (Magritte, Dali, Miró)

symbolism   1885 movement in art that sought to depict the world through the visionary eye of dreams and illusions

Titian (1488–1576)   16th century Italian artist, one of the greatest masters of the Renaissance (*Assumption, Venus of Urbino, Venus and Adonis*)

Toulouse-Lautrec, Henri de (1864–1901)   19th century French artist influenced by the impressionists (*Jane Avril, The Moulin Rouge*)

triptych   three panels, usually arranged or joined by hinges so that the two wings can be folded over to cover the larger central panel

Turner, Joseph Mallord William (1775–1851)   late 18th–early 19th century British landscape artist (*Fighting Téméraire*)

Utrillo, Maurice (1883–1955)   late 19th–early 20th century French painter (*Sacré Coeur*)

van Dyck, Sir Anthony (1599–1641)   17th century Flemish painter (*Charles I of England in Hunting Dress, Portrait of Charles V*)

van Eyck, Jan (1390–1440)   15th century Flemish painter known for his perfection of the oil medium

van Gogh, Vincent (1853–1890)   19th century Dutch postimpressionist painter (*The Sunflowers, Starry Night, Self-Portrait*)

Velázquez, Diego (1599–1660)   17th century Spanish painter (*The Maids of Honor, Pope Innocent X*)

Vermeer, Jan (1632–1675)   17th century Dutch painter known for his domestic scenes (*Woman With a Water Jug, The Lacemaker*)

vignette   decoration, often of leaves, adorning the first letter of a chapter of book section

Vuillard, Edouard (1868–1940)   late 19th–early 20th century French post-impressionist painter (*Under the Trees*)

Warhol, Andy (1928–1987)   20th century American pop artist (*Ten-Foot Flowers*)

Whistler, James Abbott McNeill (1834–1903)   19th century American painter and etcher (*Whistler's Mother*)

Wood, Grant (1892–1942)   20th century American regionalist painter famous for midwestern American themes (*American Gothic*)

Wren, Sir Christopher (1632–1723)   late 17th–early 18th century English architect known for his reconstruction of St. Paul's Cathedral and other parts of London

Wright, Frank Lloyd (1867–1959)   20th century American architect known for "organic architecture" (Taliesin West, Guggenheim Museum in New York City)

Wyeth, Andrew (1917–2009)   20th century American painter known for his depictions of Chadds Ford, Pennsylvania, and Maine fishing village subjects (*Ground Hog Day*)

Famous Art Museums in the World

Guggenheim	New York
Hagia Sophia	Istanbul
Hermitage	Leningrad
Louvre	Paris
Metropolitan	New York
Pergamon	Berlin
Prado	Madrid
Rijks	Amsterdam
Tate	London
Tretyakov	Moscow
Uffizi	Florence

LITERARY FORMS AND FIGURES

The following is a list of many important writers and literary terms. The works of particular authors are given in parentheses.

Aeschylus (525–456 B.C.)   earliest Greek dramatist (*Prometheus Bound, The Oresteia*)

allegory   a narrative poem or prose work in which persons, events, and objects represent or stand for something else, frequently abstract ideas

alliteration   the repetition of consonant sounds in two or more neighboring words or syllables

assonance   the close repetition of similar vowel sounds

Aristophanes (445–380 B.C.)   Greek playwright, master of Old Comedy (*Lysistrata, The Frogs*)

Austen, Jane (1775–1817)   English novelist (*Pride and Prejudice, Emma*)

Baldwin, James (1924–1987)   American author (*Go Tell It on the Mountain*)

Balzac, Honoré de (1799–1850)   French novelist (*The Human Comedy, Cousin Bette, Pere Goriot*)

Baudelaire, Charles-Pierre (1821–1867)   French symbolist writer (*The Flowers of Evil*)

Beat Movement   American writers of the 1950s who expressed their feelings of alienation from society (Kerouac, Ginsberg, Ferlinghetti)

Beckett, Samuel (1906–1989)   Irish-born novelist, dramatist, and poet; lived in France (*Waiting for Godot, Molloy*)

Bellow, Saul (1915–2005)   American novelist (*Seize the Day, Herzog*)

Beyle, Marie-Henri (pseudonym **Stendhal**) (1783–1842)   one of the leading 19th century French novelists, famous for the psychological and political insight of his works (*The Red and the Black, The Charterhouse of Parma*)

bildungsroman   a novel, usually autobiographical, that covers the principal subject's life from adolescence to maturity

Blair, Eric (pseudonym **George Orwell**) (1903–1950)   British novelist (*Animal Farm, 1984*)

Blake, William (1757–1827)   visionary English poet, engraver, and artist; early Romantic (*Songs of Innocence, Songs of Experience, The Marriage of Heaven and Hell*)

blank verse   poetry in which each line must have 10 syllables and a specific rhythm (iambic pentameter); the lines are unrhymed

free verse   a verse form without regular meter (Whitman's *Leaves of Grass* is written in free verse)

Boswell, James (1740–1795)   wrote famous biography of Samuel Johnson

Brontë, Charlotte (1816–1855) and **Emily** (1818–1848)   English authors (Charlotte, *Jane Eyre*; Emily, *Wuthering Heights*)

Browning, Elizabeth Barrett (1806–1861)   English poet, married to Robert Browning (*Sonnets from the Portuguese*)

Browning, Robert (1812–1889)   English poet, married to Elizabeth Barrett Browning, known for dramatic monologues (*My Last Duchess*)

Bryant, William Cullen (1794–1878)   American nature poet ("Thanatopsis")

Bunyan, John (1628–1688) 17th century English writer of religious allegories (*Pilgrim's Progress*)

Byron, Lord George Gordon (1788–1824) English Romantic poet (*Childe Harold's Pilgrimage, Don Juan*)

Camus, Albert (1913–1960) French existentialist writer (*The Stranger*)

canto a major division of a long poem

Cather, Willa Sibert (1873–1947) American author, wrote about 1880s pioneering life in the Midwest (*O Pioneers!, My Antonia*)

Cervantes, Miguel de (1547–1616) Spanish writer (*Don Quixote de la Mancha*)

Chaucer, Geoffrey (1343–1400) 14th century English author, often called the Father of English Poetry (*The Canterbury Tales*)

Chekhov, Anton Pavlovich (1860–1904) Russian writer, best known for his plays (*The Cherry Orchard, The Three Sisters*)

Christie, Agatha (1890–1976) English mystery writer; created the famous detective Hercule Poirot

classicism literature characterized by balance, restraint, unity, and proportion; epitomized by Virgil, Pope, Homer

Clemens, Samuel (pseudonym **Mark Twain**) (1835–1910) American author (*Tom Sawyer, Huckleberry Finn, A Connecticut Yankee in King Arthur's Court*)

Coleridge, Samuel Taylor (1772–1834) English Romantic poet; with Wordsworth, published *Lyrical Ballads*, which inaugurated the romantic movement in England (*The Rime of the Ancient Mariner*, "Kubla Khan," "Christabel")

Conrad, Joseph (1857–1924) English novelist born in Poland (*Heart of Darkness, Lord Jim*)

Cooper, James Fenimore (1789–1851) 18th century American novelist who wrote about the American frontier (*Leather-Stocking Tales*, which includes *The Last of the Mohicans* and *The Deerslayer*)

couplet two successive rhyming lines of poetry, usually having the same meter

Dante (1265–1321) (13th–early 14th century) considered the greatest Italian poet (*The Divine Comedy*, an allegory in verse consisting of 100 cantos)

deconstructionism contemporary literary criticism

Defoe, Daniel (1660–1731) early English novelist (*Robinson Crusoe, Moll Flanders*)

Dickens, Charles (1812–1870) English novelist (*David Copperfield, A Tale of Two Cities, Oliver Twist, Nicholas Nickleby, A Christmas Carol*)

Dickinson, Emily (1830–1886) one of the great American poets of the 19th century ("Because I Could Not Stop for Death")

Donne, John (1572–1631) considered the greatest English metaphysical poet ("The Flea," "Death Be Not Proud")

Dos Passos, John (1896–1970) American author, best known for his trilogy *U.S.A.* about the first 30 years of 20th century America

Dostoyevsky, Fyodor Mikhaylovich (1821–1881) Russian novelist (*Crime and Punishment, The Brothers Karamazov, The Idiot*)

Doyle, Sir Arthur Conan (1859–1930)   English author, creator of Sherlock Holmes and his aide, Watson

Dreiser, Theodore (1871–1945)   American novelist associated with naturalist movement (*Sister Carrie, An American Tragedy*)

Dumas, Alexandre (1802–1870)   French novelist and dramatist (*The Three Musketeers, The Count of Monte Cristo*)

Eliot, T[homas] S[tearns] (1888–1965)   20th century English (American born) poet, dramatist, and critic (*Prufrock and Other Observations, The Waste Land, Murder in the Cathedral*)

Emerson, Ralph Waldo (1803–1882)   American poet and essayist; central figure in American transcendentalism

epistolary novel   a novel in which the story is carried forward entirely through letters from one or more persons (Richardson's *Pamela*)

epithalamion or **epithalamium**   a song or poem written to celebrate marriage

Euripides (480–406 B.C.)   Greek tragic dramatist (*Medea*)

Evans, Mary Anne (pseudonym **George Eliot**) (1819–1880)   English novelist (*Middlemarch, The Mill on the Floss, Silas Marner*)

existentialism   school of thought based on belief that people have free will and are therefore completely responsible for their actions (Sartre, Camus)

Faulkner, William (1897–1962)   20th century American novelist; wrote about the South; known for his use of stream of consciousness (*The Sound and the Fury, As I Lay Dying, Absalom, Absalom!*)

Fielding, Henry (1707–1754)   early English novelist (*Tom Jones, Joseph Andrews*)

Fitzgerald, F[rancis] Scott (1896–1940)   considered the literary spokesperson for America's "Jazz Age" [the "Lost Generation"] (*This Side of Paradise, The Great Gatsby*)

Flaubert, Gustave (1821–1880)   French novelist (*Madame Bovary*)

Frost, Robert (1874–1963)   most popular 20th century American poet ("Stopping by Woods on a Snowy Evening," "Mending Wall," "After Apple-Picking")

Gardner, Erle Stanley (1889–1970)   American writer, author of Perry Mason mysteries

genre   a type or classification of literary work (e.g., tragedy, comedy, epic, satire, lyric, novel, essay, biography)

Goethe, Johann Wolfgang von (1749–1832)   German poet, playwright, and novelist (*Faust*, a verse play in which the character Mephistopheles is the devil; *The Sorrows of Young Werther*, an epistolary novel)

Golding, William (1911–1993)   20th century English author (*Lord of the Flies*)

Gray, Thomas (1716–1771)   early English Romantic poet ("Elegy Written in a Country Churchyard")

haiku   form of verse or poetry made up of 3 unrhymed lines containing 5, 7, and 5 syllables, respectively

sonnet   14-line poem with rigidly prescribed rhyme scheme

Hardy, Thomas (1840–1928)   the last of England's great Victorian novelists (*Mayor of Casterbridge, Tess of the D'Urbervilles, Jude the Obscure, Far from the Madding Crowd, The Return of the Native*)

Hawthorne, Nathaniel (1804–1864)   19th century American author who set many of his stories against the somber background of Puritan New England (*The Scarlet Letter*, in which Hester Pryne is the adulteress, Arthur Dimmesdale the adulterer, and Roger Chillingworth the husband; *The House of the Seven Gables*)

Hemingway, Ernest (1899–1961)   American author, noted for his crisp, economical, highly charged prose style and his ideals of courage, endurance, and honor (*A Farewell to Arms, For Whom the Bell Tolls, The Old Man and the Sea*)

Hersey, John (1914–1993)   American novelist, known for his works about World War II (*A Bell for Adano*)

Hesse, Hermann (1877–1962)   German author (*Siddhartha, Steppenwolf, Narcissus and Goldmund, Magister Ludi*)

Homer (9th–8th century B.C.)   the earliest Greek writer whose works have survived; his two major epics, *The Iliad* and *The Odyssey*, are both about events connected with the Trojan War

hubris   excessive pride leading to the downfall of the hero in a tragic drama

Hugo, Victor (1802–1885)   French novelist (*The Hunchback of Notre Dame, Les Misérables*)

Huxley, Aldous (1894–1963)   English novelist and critic (*Brave New World*)

hyperbole   bold overstatement or extravagant exaggeration of fact, used for either serious or comic effect

Ibsen, Henrik (1828–1906)   Norwegian playwright; considered the father of modern realistic drama (*A Doll's House, Hedda Gabler*)

irony   a literary device in which the meaning stated is contrary to the one intended

James, Henry (1843–1916)   American author, known for his subtle psychological character studies (*The Turn of the Screw, The Ambassadors, Daisy Miller, Washington Square, The Portrait of a Lady*)

Johnson, Samuel (1709–1784)   18th century English writer, noted for Boswell's famous biography of him, as well as for his *Dictionary of the English Language, The Lives of the English Poets*, and *Rasselas*

Joyce, James (1882–1941)   Irish author, noted for use of interior monologue and stream of consciousness (*Ulysses, Portrait of the Artist as a Young Man, The Dubliners, Finnegan's Wake*)

Keats, John (1795–1821)   English Romantic poet ("Endymion," "Ode to a Nightingale," "Ode on a Grecian Urn," "La Belle Dame sans Merci")

kitsch   a German word that literally means "trash" and frequently is applied to a work of poor quality that appeals to low-brow tastes

Lamb, Charles (1775–1834)   English essayist

lampoon   in prose or poetry, a vicious character sketch or satire of a person

Lawrence, D[avid] H[erbert] (1885–1930)   English novelist, poet, and short-story writer (*Sons and Lovers, Lady Chatterley's Lover*)

Lewis, Sinclair (1885–1951)   early 20th century American novelist and social critic (*Main Street, Babbitt, Arrowsmith, Elmer Gantry*)

London, Jack (1876–1916)   American novelist and short-story writer, whose works deal romantically with elemental struggles for survival (*Call of the Wild*)

Longfellow, Henry Wadsworth (1807–1882)   most popular American poet of the 19th century (*Evangeline, Hiawatha*)

lost generation   term coined by Gertrude Stein, originally referring to the many young American writers who gathered in Paris after World War I (Hemingway, Fitzgerald)

Mailer, Norman (1923–2007)   contemporary American novelist, essayist, and journalist (*The Naked and the Dead*)

Mann, Thomas (1875–1955)   American (German-born) author (*Death in Venice, The Magic Mountain*)

Marlowe, Christopher (1564–1593)   16th century English poet and dramatist; he was the first to use blank verse on the stage, influenced Shakespeare (*Dr. Faustus, The Jew of Malta*)

Melville, Herman (1819–1891)   19th century American novelist (*Moby Dick*, in which Ismael narrates the story of Captain Ahab's search for a white whale; *Billy Budd; Typee*)

Mencken, H[enry] L[ouis] (1880–1956)   the most influential American critic of the 1920s and early '30s

Miller, Arthur (1915–2005)   contemporary American dramatist (*Death of a Salesman, The Crucible, The Misfits*)

Miller, Henry (1891–1980)   20th century American author (*Tropic of Cancer, Tropic of Capricorn*)

Milne, A[lan] A[lexander] (1882–1956)   English author, creator of *Winnie-the-Pooh*

Milton, John (1608–1674)   17th century English poet (*Paradise Lost, Paradise Regained, Samson Agonistes*, all three written when he was blind)

Molière (1622–1673)   (stage name of **Jean Baptiste Poquelin**) the greatest French writer of comedy (*Tartuffe, The Misanthrope*)

motif   the recurrence of a theme, word pattern, or character in a literary work

Nabokov, Vladimir (1899–1977)   American author (*Lolita, Invitation to a Beheading*)

naturalism   a type of realistic fiction that developed in France, America, and England in the late 19th and early 20th centuries. It presupposes that human beings are like puppets, controlled completely by external and internal forces

 realism   the idea that people have a measure of free will

octave   a poetic stanza with eight lines

 sestet   a poetic stanza with six lines

ode   a sustained lyric poem with a noble theme and intellectual tone

O'Neill, Eugene (1888–1953)   one of the greatest American playwrights (*The Emperor Jones, Desire Under the Elms, Ah! Wilderness, The Iceman Cometh, Long Day's Journey Into Night*)

onomatopoeia   a word whose sound is descriptive of its sense of meaning

Orwell   see **Eric Blair**

Ovid (43 B.C.–17 A.D.)   Roman poet (*Metamorphoses, The Art of Love*)

oxymoron   an expression that employs two opposing terms; for example, "benign neglect"

parable   a story told to illustrate a moral truth or lesson

parody   a humorous literary work that ridicules a serious work by imitating and exaggerating its style

personification   a figure of speech that gives human forms and characteristics to abstractions, objects, animals, etc.

Petrarch (1304–1374)   14th century Italian poet and scholar, known for his love poems and his discovery of classical authors (*Canzoniere* [*Book of Songs*], a collection of 400 of his poems, most of them about a woman named Laura)

Poe, Edgar Allan (1809–1849)   19th century American poet, critic, and short-story writer; the father of modern mystery and detective fiction ("The Murders in the Rue Morgue," "The Fall of the House of Usher," "The Raven")

Pope, Alexander (1688–1744)   the greatest English poet of the early 1700s, brilliant satirist (*The Rape of the Lock, An Essay on Criticism, An Essay on Man*)

potboiler   an inferior literary work written solely to provide the author with money

Pound, Ezra (1885–1972)   American poet and critic, one of the most influential poets and controversial figures of the 20th century (*Cantos*)

Proust, Marcel (1871–1922)   French author (*The Remembrance of Things Past*, the story of his life told as an allegorical search for truth)

Pushkin, Aleksandr Sergeyvich (1799–1837)   Russia's most celebrated poet; also wrote plays and other prose (*Eugene Onegin, The Bronze Horseman*)

Racine, Jean (1639–1699)   17th century French classicist writer of tragic drama (*Phaedra, Andromache*)

roman à clef   a novel based on real persons and events

romantic movement   19th century literary movement that began in England; contrasts with classicism; emphasizes passion rather than reason, and imagination and inspiration rather than logic (Blake, Wordsworth, Coleridge, Shelley, Keats, Byron)

Sandburg, Carl (1878–1967)   major 20th century American poet, also an historian and a biographer (*Abraham Lincoln*, "The Fog," "Chicago")

satire   a type of literary work that uses sarcasm, wit, and irony to ridicule and expose the follies of mankind (*The Rape of the Lock, Gulliver's Travels*)

Scott, Sir Walter (1771–1832)   later 18th–early 19th century Scottish novelist and poet; inventor of the historical novel (*The Lady of the Lake, Waverly, Ivanhoe*)

Shakespeare, William (1564–1616)   the towering figure in English literature, considered both the greatest dramatist and the greatest poet

Shaw, George Bernard (1856–1950)   English (Irish-born) author of satirical plays (*Pygmalion*, used as basis for *My Fair Lady; Man and Superman; Saint Joan*)

Shelley, Percy Bysshe (1792–1822)   early 19th century English Romantic poet (*Prometheus Unbound, Adonais, Ode to the West Wind*)

simile   figure of speech in which a comparison between two distinctly different things is indicated by the word *like* or *as* ("O my love is like a red, red rose")

metaphor   figure of speech in which a statement of identity instead of comparison is made ("O my love is a red, red rose")

sonnet   a poem of 14 iambic pentameter lines and a rigidly prescribed rhyme scheme; two types: Italian or Petrarchan, and English or Shakespearean

Sophocles (496–406 B.C.)   Greek dramatist (*Oedipus the King, Antigone*)

Spenser, Edmund (1552–1599)   great Elizabethan poet (*The Faerie Queene*)

Stein, Gertrude (1874–1946)   American author, central figure in a circle of outstanding artist and writer expatriates in Paris (*The Autobiography of Alice B. Toklas*)

Steinbeck, John (1902–1968)   20th century American author, known for his powerful novels about agricultural workers (*The Grapes of Wrath, Of Mice and Men, East of Eden*)

Stendhal   see **Beyle, Marie-Henri**

Stevenson, Robert Louis (1850–1894)   19th century Scottish novelist, essayist, and poet; known for his adventure stories (*Treasure Island, Kidnapped, A Child's Garden of Verses*)

stream of consciousness   literary style, employed especially by Joyce and Faulkner, that presents the inner thoughts of a character in an uneven, endless stream that simulates the character's consciousness

Swift, Jonathan (1667–1745)   late 17th–18th century English author, great satirist (*Gulliver's Travels*, "A Modest Proposal")

Thoreau, Henry David (1817–1862)   American philosopher and writer; renowned for having lived the doctrines of transcendentalism ("Civil Disobedience," *Walden*)

Tolkien, J. R. R. (1892–1973)   English author (*The Hobbit, The Lord of the Rings*)

Tolstoy, Count Leo (1828–1910)   19th century Russian author, one of the world's greatest novelists (*War and Peace, Anna Karenina*)

transcendentalism   school of thought based on belief in the essential unity of all creation, the innate goodness of human beings, and the supremacy of insight over logic and experience for the revelation of the deepest truths (Thoreau, Emerson)

Twain   see **Clemens, Samuel**

Updike, John (1932–2009)   contemporary American author (*Rabbit* series)

Vergil or **Virgil** (70–19 B.C.)   greatest Roman poet; wrote the *Aeneid*, the epic that tells of the founding of Rome and describes the adventures of Aeneas, the legendary Trojan hero who founded the city

Victorian Age   refers to 19th century England; typified by optimism and conservative ideals

Voltaire (1694–1778)   18th century French author (*Candide*)

Walker, Alice (b. 1944)   20th century American author (*The Color Purple*)

Whitman, Walt (1819–1892)   one of the great American poets; his poems sing the praise of America and democracy (*Leaves of Grass*, "O Captain! My Captain!" a poem on Lincoln's death)

Wilde, Oscar (1854–1900)   late 19th century Irish playwright, poet, and novelist; attacked Victorian narrow-mindedness and complacency (*The Picture of Dorian Gray, The Importance of Being Earnest*)

Wilder, Thornton (1897–1975)   American novelist and playwright (*The Bridge of San Luis Rey, Our Town, Matchmaker,* which was the basis for the Broadway musical *Hello, Dolly*)

Williams, Tennessee (1911–1983)   considered the greatest American playwright (*The Glass Menagerie, A Streetcar Named Desire, Cat on a Hot Tin Roof*)

Wolfe, Thomas (1900–1938)   American author, known for his autobiographical novels (*Look Homeward, Angel; You Can't Go Home Again*)

Woolf, Virginia (1882–1941)   English novelist and critic; with her husband Leonard, provided a center for the Bloomsbury Group, an informal group of famous intellectuals (*Mrs. Dalloway, To the Lighthouse*)

Wordsworth, William (1770–1850)   English romantic poet (*Lyrical Ballads, The Prelude*)

Wright, Richard (1908–1960)   20th century American author, known for his description of black life in America (*Native Son, Black Boy,* his autobiography)

Yeats, William Butler (1865–1939)   Irish poet and dramatist, considered by many the greatest poet of his time; led the Irish Literary Revival; his love for Maud Gonne, a beautiful Irish nationalist leader, influenced many of his plays and love lyrics

Zola, Émile (1840–1902)   leader of the French naturalistic school, which de-emphasized the role of free will in human life (*Nana; J'accuse,* which helped win a new trail for Alfred Dreyfus)

MUSIC

Use the following list of the most important composers and music terms as a quick review. The works of particular composers are given in parentheses.

adagio   slow; a slow movement; slower than andante, faster than largo

allegro   lively; rather fast, but not as fast as presto

alto   a high adult male voice, employing falsetto; a lower female voice

andante   at moderate speed, between allegro and adagio

Argerich, Martha (b. 1941)   Argentinean pianist

aria   air; song, especially a complex one in an opera or oratorio ("Batti, Batti" from Mozart's opera *Don Giovanni*)

arpeggio   chord (e.g., on a piano) performed spread out

Bach, Johann Sebastian (1685–1750)   late 17th–early 18th century German composer of baroque style; organ music and cantatas (*Brandenburg Concertos; St. Matthew Passion*)

bagatelle   short, light piece, often for piano (Beethoven)

ballad   old song, often a folk song, that tells a story, with the music repeated for each verse (Wagner's *The Flying Dutchman*)

ballet   form of dancing, of Italian origin, that usually uses orchestra music, full stage decoration (*The Sleeping Beauty, Giselle, The Nutcracker*)

Barenboim, Daniel (b. 1942)   Israeli conductor and pianist

baroque   1600-to-1750 style of music (Monteverdi, Bach)

Bartók, Béla (1881–1945)   20th century Hungarian composer who developed Hungarian national musical style; known for dissonant, atonal sounds (*Bluebeard's Castle*)

bass   lowest male voice; the lower regions of musical pitch

Beecham, Sir Thomas (1879–1961)   English conductor

Beethoven, Ludwig van (1770–1827)   late 18th–early 19th century German composer, considered one of the greatest composers of all time (9 symphonies, including *Eroica*, *Pastoral*, the *Ninth* or *Choral*; piano concerto *Emperor*; opera *Fidelio*)

Bell, Joshua (b. 1967)   American violinist

Berlioz, Hector (1803–1869)   19th century French composer (*Fantastic Symphony*)

Bernstein, Leonard (1918–1990)   20th century American conductor and composer (*The Age of Anxiety* symphony; *West Side Story* musical)

bolero   Spanish dance

Borodin, Aleksandr Porfiryevich (1833–1887)   19th century Russian composer (opera *Prince Igor*)

Brahms, Johannes (1833–1897)   19th century German composer and pianist known for his symphonies, piano concertos, and chamber music (*First, Second, Third, Fourth symphonies*; song *Lullaby*)

Brandenburg Concertos   six works by J. S. Bach for varying instrumental combinations

Britten, Benjamin (1913–1976)   English conductor and composer (*The Young Person's Guide to the Orchestra*)

Bruch, Max (1838–1920)   German composer and conductor (*Kol Nidrei*)

Bruckner, Anton (1824–1896)   19th century Austrian composer and organist known for his symphonies

buffo (buffa)   comic bass, as in an opera

cadence   a progression of chords giving an effect of closing a sentence

cantata   an extended choral work, with or without solo voices, and usually with orchestral accompaniment

Casals, Pablo (1876–1973)   20th century Spanish cellist

chamber music   music intended for a room as distinct from a large hall or theater

chanson   type of song popular in 14th-to-16th century France

Chopin, Frédéric (1810–1849)   19th century Polish composer known for his piano works

chorale   a type of traditional German hymn-tune for congregational use; an instrumental piece based on a chorale

chord   a blending of two or more notes

classicism   1770s-to-1830s period; opposed to romanticism and folk or popular music (Haydn, Mozart, and Beethoven)

coda   section of movement added as a rounding off rather than a structural necessity

coloratura   agile, florid style of vocal music

concerto   work making contrasted use of solo instruments and orchestra, generally in 3 movements (Beethoven, Mozart)

contralto   lowest female singing range

Copland, Aaron (1900–1990)   20th century American composer and pianist (opera *The Tender Land, Music for the Theater*, many film scores)

counterpart   simultaneous combination of 2 or more melodies to make musical sense

crescendo   music that gradually becomes louder

Debussy, Claude (1862–1918)   late 19th–early 20th century French impressionist-style composer (opera *Pelleas and Melisande, The Afternoon of a Faun, La Mer*)

diminuendo   music that slowly becomes softer

Du Pre, Jacqueline (1945–1987)   English cellist

Dvořák, Antonin (1841–1904)   19th century Czech (Bohemian) composer known for his symphonies (*From the New World*)

étude   an instrumental piece written to demonstrate the facility of the performer

fortissimo   music played very loudly

fugue   a musical composition in which one or two themes are repeated by different interweaving voices (Bach)

Gershwin, George (1898–1937)   20th century American pianist and composer of popular music (*Rhapsody in Blue, An American in Paris*)

Gould, Glenn (1932–1982)   Canadian pianist

Grieg, Edvard (1843–1907)   19th century Norwegian composer and pianist (music for *Peer Gynt*)

Hahn, Hilary (b. 1979)   American violinist

Handel, George Frideric (1685–1759)   late 17th–early 18th century German baroque composer (oratorio *Messiah*, opera *Rinaldo*)

Haydn, Franz Joseph (1732–1809)   18th century Austrian composer (symphonies *The Surprise* and *The Clock*, oratorios *The Creation* and *The Seasons*)

Heifetz, Jascha (1901–1967)   Lithuanian violinist

Horowitz, Vladimir (b. 1937) Russian pianist and conductor

interval   distance between 2 notes insofar as one is higher or lower than the other

Kodaly, Zoltán (1882–1967)   late 19th–20th century Hungarian composer; edited Hungarian folk songs (with Bartók) (*Psalmas Hungaricus*, opera *Háry Janos*)

largo   slow

lento   slow

libretto   text of an opera or oratorio

liederkranz   song-cycle (Schumann's *Liederkreis*)

Liszt, Franz (1811–1886)   19th century Hungarian romantic-style pianist and composer (*Dante Sonata, The Preludes*)

Ma, Yo-Yo (b. 1955) Chinese-American cellist

madrigal   16th–17th century composition for several voices

Mahler, Gustav (1860–1911)   late 19th–early 20th century Austrian composer and conductor (*Symphony of a Thousand*)

Mehta, Zubin (b. 1936)   Indian conductor

Mendelssohn, Felix (1809–1847)   19th century German composer and conductor (operetta *Son and Stranger, Scottish* symphony, *Elijah*, overture to *Midsummer Night's Dream*)

Menotti, Gian Carlo (1911–2007)   20th century Italian-American composer of opera (*Amahl and the Night Visitors*)

Menuhin, Yehudi (1916–1999)   American-born British violinist, violist, and conductor

Milhaud, Darius (1892–1974)   20th century French composer (operas *David* and *Christopher Columbus*, ballets *Jeux de printemps* and *Creation of the World*)

Monteverdi, Claudio (1567–1643)   late 16th–early 17th century Italian composer (opera *La favola d'Orfeo*)

Mozart, Wolfgang Amadeus (1756–1791)   18th century Austrian composer, mainly of operas and piano concertos (*Don Giovanni, The Marriage of Figaro, The Magic Flute, Cosi Fan Tutte*)

Mussorgsky, Modest Petrovich (1839–1881)   19th century Russian composer (operas *Boris Godunov, Pictures at an Exhibition, Night on Bald Mountain*)

Mutter, Anne-Sofie (b. 1963)   German violinist

nocturne   melancholy composition for one or more instruments

opera   drama in which all or most characters sing and music constitutes a principal element

opera buffa   comic opera

oratorio   religious compositions for orchestra, chorus, and soloists

Orff, Carl (1895–1982)   20th century German composer and conductor (operas: *Oedipus the Tyrant*, incidental music and choral works, *Songs of Catullus, Carmina Burana*)

Pachelbel, Johann (1653–1706)   17th century German organist and composer of keyboard music

Paganini, Nicolò (1782–1840)   late 18th–early 19th century Italian violinist and composer (*Bell Rondo, The Carnival of Venice*)

presto   fast

Prokofiev, Sergey Sergeyevich (1891–1953)   20th century Russian composer and pianist (*Peter and the Wolf*)

Puccini, Giacomo (1858–1924)   late 19th–early 20th century Italian composer (operas *Madame Butterfly, La Bohème, Tosca*)

quartet   four musical instruments played together

Rachmaninoff, Sergey Vasilyevich (1873–1943)   late 19th–early 20th century Russian composer and pianist (*Rhapsody on a Theme of Paganini, The Isle of the Dead*)

Rameau, Jean-Philippe (1683–1764)   18th century French composer and organist (*Castor et Pollux*)

Ravel, Maurice Joseph (1875–1937)   late 19th–early 20th century French composer (*Bolero, Gaspard de la Nuit, Spanish Rhapsody*)

Rodgers, Richard (1902–1979)   20th century American composer of light music; worked with writers Hart and Hammerstein (*The Sound of Music, A Connecticut Yankee, Oklahoma!*)

rondo   form of composition in which one section recurs intermittently

Rossini, Gioacchino Antonio (1792–1868)   19th century Italian composer (operas *The Barber of Seville, Othello, William Tell*)

Rubinstein, Anton (1829–1894)   20th century Polish-born American pianist

Scarlatti, Domenico (1685–1757)   late 17th–early 18th century Italian composer, chiefly of opera

Schoenberg, Arnold (1874–1951)   20th century Austrian-American composer (*Ode to Napoleon*, opera *Moses and Aaron*)

Schubert, Franz (1797–1828)   19th century Austrian composer (*Impromptus, Moments Musicaux*)

Schumann, Robert (1810–1856)   19th century German composer and pianist

Scriabin, Aleksandr Nikoloyevich (1872–1915)   late 19th–early 20th century Russian composer and pianist (*Divine Poem*)

Segovia, Andrés (1893–1987)   20th century Spanish classical guitarist

Shostakovich, Dmitry Dmitriyevich (1906–1975)   20th century Russian composer (*Leningrad* symphony, opera *The Golden Age*, ballet *Songs of the Forests*)

Sibelius, Jean (1865–1957)   late 19th–early 20th century Finnish composer (*Finlandia*)

Smetana, Bedřich (1824–1884)   19th century Czech composer and pianist (opera *The Bartered Bride*)

sonata   instrumental musical composition usually of 3 or 4 movements (sonatina–short sonata)

soprano   highest female voice

Sousa, John Philip (1854–1932)   late 19th–early 20th century American band conductor and composer of marches (*Stars and Stripes Forever*)

Stern, Isaac (1920–2001)   20th century Russian-born American violinist

Stradivari   family of renowned violin makers

Strauss, Johann (1825–1899)   19th century Austrian violinist, conductor, and composer of waltzes (*The Blue Danube, Tales from the Vienna Woods*)

Strauss, Richard (1864–1949)   late 19th–early 20th century German composer and conductor (*Symphonic Poem*, operas *Salome, Elektra*)

Stravinsky, Igor (1882–1971)   20th century Russian-born composer, pianist, and conductor (ballets *The Firebird, Petrushka*, and *The Rite of Spring*, opera *The Rake's Progress*)

symphony   grand orchestral work in 4 movements

Tchaikovsky, Pyotr Ilich (1840–1893)   19th century Russian composer (*Pathéthique* symphony, ballets *Swan Lake, The Sleeping Beauty, The Nutcracker*)

tenor   highest normal male voice (apart from alto, which uses falsetto)

Toscanini, Arturo (1867–1957)   Italian conductor

Verdi, Giuseppe (1813–1901)   19th century Italian composer (operas *Rigoletto, il Trovatore, Don Carlos, Falstaff, Aïda, Requiem*)

Vivaldi, Antonio (1678–1741)   late 17th–early 18th century Italian violinist and composer (*The Four Seasons*)

von Karajan, Herbert (1908–1989)   Austrian-born German conductor

Wagner, Richard (1813–1883)   19th century German composer and conductor known for cycles of opera and use of leitmotif (operas *The Flying Dutchman, Tristan and Isolde, Der Ring*)

Weber, Carl Maria von (1786–1826)   late 18th–early 19th century German composer, conductor, and pianist (operas *Der Freischütz, Oberon*)

Weil, Kurt (1900–1950)   20th century German-born American composer (opera *The Threepenny Opera*)

SCIENCE

Detailed knowledge of the sciences is not required for the *MAT*. What is necessary is a general familiarity with the major people, theories, and terms of science. It is impossible to review biology, physics, chemistry, geology and the other sciences here. Below are a list of major scientists, a table of animal names that include vocabulary that may appear in an analogy, a brief explanation of classification terms, and a geologic time scale chart.

Important Scientists

Becquerel, Antoine (1788–1878)   (French) discovered radioactivity

Copernicus, Nicolaus (1473–1543)   (Polish) founded modern astronomy, declared that sun is center of solar system

Curie, Marie (1867–1934) and **Pierre** (1859–1906)   (French) discovered radium, polonium

Darwin, Charles (1809–1882)   (English) natural selection, theory of evolution

Einstein, Albert (1879–1955)   (German) theory of relativity

Fermi, Enrico (1901–1954)   (Italian-American) radioactivity, chain reactions, H-bomb

Fleming, Sir Alexander (1881–1955)   (British) discovered penicillin

Galen (129–199 A.D.)   (ancient Greek) physician, studied personality

Galileo (1564–1642)   (Italian) astronomer and physicist, laws of gravity

Gauss, Carl Friedrich (1777–1855)   (German) mathematician and astronomer, invented electric telegraph

Herschel, Sir John Frederick William (1738–1822)   (British) astronomer

Hippocrates (460–377 B.C.)   (ancient Greek) physician, father of medicine (oath)

Jenner, Edward (1749–1823)   (British) physician, cowpox vaccine

Lamarck, Chevalier de (1744–1829)   (French) naturalist, theory of inheritance of acquired characteristics

Linnaeus, Carolus (1707–1778)   (Swedish) devised system of classifying living organisms

Lister, Joseph (1827–1912)   (British) surgeon, promoted antiseptic methods

Lysenko, Trofim Denisovich (1898–1976)   (Soviet) geneticist, follower of Lamarck, led to demise of Soviet biology

Mendel, Gregor (1822–1884)   (Austrian) botanist, transmission of characteristics in plants (genetics)

Pasteur, Louis (1822–1895) (French) chemist, germ theory, use of heat to destroy bacteria

Ptolemy (90–168 A.D.) (Egyptian) astronomer, geocentric theory of solar system

Rutherford, Ernest (1871–1937) (British) physicist, radioactivity

Sabin, Albert (1906–1993) (American) developed oral vaccine against polio

Salk, Jonas (1914–1995) (American) developed first vaccine against polio

Watson, James (b. 1928) (American) and **Crick, Francis** (b. 1916–2004) (British) biophysicists, discovered structure of DNA molecule (double helix)

Animal Names

Animal	Male	Female	Offspring	Adjective Form
bear	boar	sow	cub	ursine
cattle	bull steer (castrated)	cow	calf	bovine
chicken	rooster capon (castrated)	hen	chick	
deer	buck	doe	fawn	cervine
fox	fox	vixen	cub/kit	vulpine
goat	billy	nanny	kid	
hog	boar	sow	shoat	
horse	stallion gelding (castrated)	mare	foal, colt (m.) filly (f.)	equine
lion	lion	lioness	cub	leonine
pig	boar	sow	piglet	porcine
sheep	ram	ewe	lamb	ovine
swan	cob	pen	cygnet	

Taxonomy

Taxonomy is the science of classifying living organisms. Each living organism is given a scientific name—for example, *Homo sapiens* for human beings—that consists of a genus name—in our example, *Homo*—and a species name—*sapiens*. Organisms are also grouped into larger taxa (singular, taxon) based on similarities in structure and evolutionary relationships. The following table lists the major taxonomic groups, briefly describes each, and provides an example.

Classification Group	Definition	Example
kingdom	largest classification unit; most scientists agree on a basic 5-kingdom system	Animalia
phylum	major division of a kingdom	Chordata
class	division of a phylum	Vertebrata
order	division of a class; contains one or more related families	Primates
family	division of an order; contains one or more related genera; members often show obvious similarities	Hominidae
genus	division of a family; contains one or more closely related species; part of scientific name (written with initial capital letter and italicized)	*Homo*
species	basic unit of classification; a group of organisms that can mate and produce offspring; second word of scientific name; always lower case and italicized	*sapiens*

Geologic Time Scale

Era	Periods	Life Forms
Azoic era	(earliest period after formation of the earth)	
Precambrian time:		
Archeozoic era (3800–2500 mya)		
Proterozoic era (2500–543 mya)		spores, marine algae

Geologic Time Scale (continued)

Era	Periods	Life Forms
Paleozoic era (543–249 mya)	Cambrian period (543–490 mya)	
	Ordovician (490–443 mya)	fishes
	Silurian (443–417 mya)	
	Devonian (417–354 mya)	amphibians
	Carboniferous (354–290 mya)	insects, reptiles, gymnosperm
	Permian (290–248 mya)	ferns
Mesozoic (248–65 mya)	Triassic (248–206 mya)	first dinosaurs
	Jurassic (206–144 mya)	reptiles dominant, first birds, mammals
	Cretacious (144–65 mya)	dinosaurs climax, disappear; flowering plants
Cenozoic (65 mya–today)	Tertiary	
	Paleocene (65–54.8 mya)	earliest placental mammals
	Eocene (54.8–33.7 mya)	modern mammals
	Oligocene (33.7–23.8 mya)	
	Miocene (23.8–5.3 mya)	
	Pliocene Epochs (5.3–1.8 mya)	
	Quaternary	humankind (glacial)
	Pleistocene epoch (1.8 mya–10,000 years ago)	
	Holocene epoch (10,000 years–today)	

Note: mya is million years ago

MYTHOLOGY

Adonis   Greek god of male beauty

Aphrodite   Greek goddess of love, beauty, and fertility. Roman counterpart: Venus; Norse counterpart: Freya

Apollo   one of the twin children of Zeus (the other twin is Artemis); Greek god of prophecy, medicine, and music. Norse counterpart: Frey

Ares   Greek god of war; son of Zeus and Hera. Roman counterpart: Mars

Artemis   one of the twin children of Zeus (the other twin is Apollo); Greek goddess of the moon, woods, forest, animals, and the hunt. Roman counterpart: Diana

Asgard   home of the Norse gods

Athena   Greek goddess of wisdom, cities, and handicrafts; "sprung full-blown from the head of Zeus." Roman counterpart: Minerva

Balder   Norse god of the sun. Greek counterpart: Helios

Ceres   Roman god of grain. Greek counterpart: Demeter

Cronus and **Rhea**   Greek gods; parents of the gods. Roman counterparts: Saturn and Ops

Demeter   Greek goddess of harvest and fertility. Roman counterpart: Ceres

Diana   Roman goddess of the moon, forest, animals, and the hunt. Greek counterpart: Artemis

Dionysus   Greek god of wine and joy, son of Zeus. Roman counterpart: Bacchus

Frey   Norse god; twin brother of Freyja. Greek counterpart: Apollo

Freyja   Norse goddess; twin of Frey; goddess of love and fertility. Greek counterpart: Aphrodite

Frigga   Norse goddess of heavens, love, and household; wife of Odin

Hades   Greek ruler of the dead and god of the underworld. Roman counterpart: Pluto

Helios   Greek sun god. Roman counterpart: Sol; Norse counterpart: Balder

Hera   Greek goddess; sister and wife of Zeus and queen of the gods. Roman counterpart: Juno; Norse counterpart: Frigga

Hermes   Greek messenger of the gods; symbol is caduceus. Roman counterpart: Mercury

Ishtar   Babylonian goddess of love and war. Greek counterpart: Aphrodite

Juno   Roman goddess; wife and sister of Jupiter. Greek counterpart: Hera; Norse counterpart: Frigga

Jupiter   Roman king of the gods. Greek counterpart: Zeus; Norse counterpart: Odin

Mercury   Roman messenger and god of commerce. Greek counterpart: Hermes

Minerva   Roman goddess of wisdom, cities, and handicrafts; like Greek Athena, said to have sprung fullblown from king of the gods. Greek counterpart: Athena

Neptune   Roman sea god. Greek counterpart: Poseidon; Norse counterpart: Njord

Njord   Norse god of the sea. Greek counterpart: Poseidon; Roman counterpart: Neptune

Odin   Norse king of the gods. Greek counterpart: Zeus; Roman counterpart: Jupiter

Olympus   Home of the Greek gods

Pluto   Roman ruler of the underworld. Greek counterpart: Hades

Poseidon   Greek god of the sea; symbol is a trident. Roman counterpart: Neptune; Norse counterpart: Njord

Saturn and **Ops**   Roman gods; parents of the gods. Greek counterparts: Cronus and Rhea

Thor   Norse god of thunder

Valhalla   Norse hall of heroes

Venus   Roman goddess of love, good fortune, and vegetation. Greek counterpart: Aphrodite; Norse counterpart: Freyja

Zeus   Greek king of the gods. Roman counterpart: Jupiter; Norse counterpart: Odin

10 Complete Analogy Tests for *MAT* Practice

In the following you will find ten complete Practice Tests. They are preceded by an answer sheet that you can use to mark your responses. Each test consists of 120 items that need to be completed within 60 minutes. At the end of each test you will find an answer key for scoring as well as explanations of the answers. Good luck!

Answer Sheet

PRACTICE TEST 1

1 Ⓐ Ⓑ Ⓒ Ⓓ	31 Ⓐ Ⓑ Ⓒ Ⓓ	61 Ⓐ Ⓑ Ⓒ Ⓓ	91 Ⓐ Ⓑ Ⓒ Ⓓ
2 Ⓐ Ⓑ Ⓒ Ⓓ	32 Ⓐ Ⓑ Ⓒ Ⓓ	62 Ⓐ Ⓑ Ⓒ Ⓓ	92 Ⓐ Ⓑ Ⓒ Ⓓ
3 Ⓐ Ⓑ Ⓒ Ⓓ	33 Ⓐ Ⓑ Ⓒ Ⓓ	63 Ⓐ Ⓑ Ⓒ Ⓓ	93 Ⓐ Ⓑ Ⓒ Ⓓ
4 Ⓐ Ⓑ Ⓒ Ⓓ	34 Ⓐ Ⓑ Ⓒ Ⓓ	64 Ⓐ Ⓑ Ⓒ Ⓓ	94 Ⓐ Ⓑ Ⓒ Ⓓ
5 Ⓐ Ⓑ Ⓒ Ⓓ	35 Ⓐ Ⓑ Ⓒ Ⓓ	65 Ⓐ Ⓑ Ⓒ Ⓓ	95 Ⓐ Ⓑ Ⓒ Ⓓ
6 Ⓐ Ⓑ Ⓒ Ⓓ	36 Ⓐ Ⓑ Ⓒ Ⓓ	66 Ⓐ Ⓑ Ⓒ Ⓓ	96 Ⓐ Ⓑ Ⓒ Ⓓ
7 Ⓐ Ⓑ Ⓒ Ⓓ	37 Ⓐ Ⓑ Ⓒ Ⓓ	67 Ⓐ Ⓑ Ⓒ Ⓓ	97 Ⓐ Ⓑ Ⓒ Ⓓ
8 Ⓐ Ⓑ Ⓒ Ⓓ	38 Ⓐ Ⓑ Ⓒ Ⓓ	68 Ⓐ Ⓑ Ⓒ Ⓓ	98 Ⓐ Ⓑ Ⓒ Ⓓ
9 Ⓐ Ⓑ Ⓒ Ⓓ	39 Ⓐ Ⓑ Ⓒ Ⓓ	69 Ⓐ Ⓑ Ⓒ Ⓓ	99 Ⓐ Ⓑ Ⓒ Ⓓ
10 Ⓐ Ⓑ Ⓒ Ⓓ	40 Ⓐ Ⓑ Ⓒ Ⓓ	70 Ⓐ Ⓑ Ⓒ Ⓓ	100 Ⓐ Ⓑ Ⓒ Ⓓ
11 Ⓐ Ⓑ Ⓒ Ⓓ	41 Ⓐ Ⓑ Ⓒ Ⓓ	71 Ⓐ Ⓑ Ⓒ Ⓓ	101 Ⓐ Ⓑ Ⓒ Ⓓ
12 Ⓐ Ⓑ Ⓒ Ⓓ	42 Ⓐ Ⓑ Ⓒ Ⓓ	72 Ⓐ Ⓑ Ⓒ Ⓓ	102 Ⓐ Ⓑ Ⓒ Ⓓ
13 Ⓐ Ⓑ Ⓒ Ⓓ	43 Ⓐ Ⓑ Ⓒ Ⓓ	73 Ⓐ Ⓑ Ⓒ Ⓓ	103 Ⓐ Ⓑ Ⓒ Ⓓ
14 Ⓐ Ⓑ Ⓒ Ⓓ	44 Ⓐ Ⓑ Ⓒ Ⓓ	74 Ⓐ Ⓑ Ⓒ Ⓓ	104 Ⓐ Ⓑ Ⓒ Ⓓ
15 Ⓐ Ⓑ Ⓒ Ⓓ	45 Ⓐ Ⓑ Ⓒ Ⓓ	75 Ⓐ Ⓑ Ⓒ Ⓓ	105 Ⓐ Ⓑ Ⓒ Ⓓ
16 Ⓐ Ⓑ Ⓒ Ⓓ	46 Ⓐ Ⓑ Ⓒ Ⓓ	76 Ⓐ Ⓑ Ⓒ Ⓓ	106 Ⓐ Ⓑ Ⓒ Ⓓ
17 Ⓐ Ⓑ Ⓒ Ⓓ	47 Ⓐ Ⓑ Ⓒ Ⓓ	77 Ⓐ Ⓑ Ⓒ Ⓓ	107 Ⓐ Ⓑ Ⓒ Ⓓ
18 Ⓐ Ⓑ Ⓒ Ⓓ	48 Ⓐ Ⓑ Ⓒ Ⓓ	78 Ⓐ Ⓑ Ⓒ Ⓓ	108 Ⓐ Ⓑ Ⓒ Ⓓ
19 Ⓐ Ⓑ Ⓒ Ⓓ	49 Ⓐ Ⓑ Ⓒ Ⓓ	79 Ⓐ Ⓑ Ⓒ Ⓓ	109 Ⓐ Ⓑ Ⓒ Ⓓ
20 Ⓐ Ⓑ Ⓒ Ⓓ	50 Ⓐ Ⓑ Ⓒ Ⓓ	80 Ⓐ Ⓑ Ⓒ Ⓓ	110 Ⓐ Ⓑ Ⓒ Ⓓ
21 Ⓐ Ⓑ Ⓒ Ⓓ	51 Ⓐ Ⓑ Ⓒ Ⓓ	81 Ⓐ Ⓑ Ⓒ Ⓓ	111 Ⓐ Ⓑ Ⓒ Ⓓ
22 Ⓐ Ⓑ Ⓒ Ⓓ	52 Ⓐ Ⓑ Ⓒ Ⓓ	82 Ⓐ Ⓑ Ⓒ Ⓓ	112 Ⓐ Ⓑ Ⓒ Ⓓ
23 Ⓐ Ⓑ Ⓒ Ⓓ	53 Ⓐ Ⓑ Ⓒ Ⓓ	83 Ⓐ Ⓑ Ⓒ Ⓓ	113 Ⓐ Ⓑ Ⓒ Ⓓ
24 Ⓐ Ⓑ Ⓒ Ⓓ	54 Ⓐ Ⓑ Ⓒ Ⓓ	84 Ⓐ Ⓑ Ⓒ Ⓓ	114 Ⓐ Ⓑ Ⓒ Ⓓ
25 Ⓐ Ⓑ Ⓒ Ⓓ	55 Ⓐ Ⓑ Ⓒ Ⓓ	85 Ⓐ Ⓑ Ⓒ Ⓓ	115 Ⓐ Ⓑ Ⓒ Ⓓ
26 Ⓐ Ⓑ Ⓒ Ⓓ	56 Ⓐ Ⓑ Ⓒ Ⓓ	86 Ⓐ Ⓑ Ⓒ Ⓓ	116 Ⓐ Ⓑ Ⓒ Ⓓ
27 Ⓐ Ⓑ Ⓒ Ⓓ	57 Ⓐ Ⓑ Ⓒ Ⓓ	87 Ⓐ Ⓑ Ⓒ Ⓓ	117 Ⓐ Ⓑ Ⓒ Ⓓ
28 Ⓐ Ⓑ Ⓒ Ⓓ	58 Ⓐ Ⓑ Ⓒ Ⓓ	88 Ⓐ Ⓑ Ⓒ Ⓓ	118 Ⓐ Ⓑ Ⓒ Ⓓ
29 Ⓐ Ⓑ Ⓒ Ⓓ	59 Ⓐ Ⓑ Ⓒ Ⓓ	89 Ⓐ Ⓑ Ⓒ Ⓓ	119 Ⓐ Ⓑ Ⓒ Ⓓ
30 Ⓐ Ⓑ Ⓒ Ⓓ	60 Ⓐ Ⓑ Ⓒ Ⓓ	90 Ⓐ Ⓑ Ⓒ Ⓓ	120 Ⓐ Ⓑ Ⓒ Ⓓ

Practice Test 1

Directions: In each of the following questions, you will find three initial terms and, in parentheses, four answer options designated *a, b, c,* and *d.* You are to select from the four answer options the one that best completes the analogy with the three initial terms. To record your answers, use the answer sheet provided.

Time: 60 minutes

1. CANARY : (*a.* red, *b.* blue, *c.* brown, *d.* yellow) :: POLAR BEAR : WHITE

2. SHIRT : WEAR :: BLOODY MARY : (*a.* kill, *b.* eat, *c.* dress, *d.* drink)

3. DAY : NIGHT :: DIURNAL : (*a.* nocturnal, *b.* eternal, *c.* vernal, *d.* external)

4. (*a.* Howard, *b.* Phineas, *c.* Ernest, *d.* Millard) : FILLMORE :: THOMAS : JEFFERSON

5. APRIL : 2 × 15 :: FEBRUARY : (*a.* 2 × 14, *b.* 2 × 15, *c.* 2 × 16, *d.* 2 × 17)

6. COMPARATIVE : (*a.* good, *b.* better, *c.* best, *d.* great) :: SUPERLATIVE : BEST

7. WINE : FRUIT :: BEER : (*a.* grape, *b.* hay, *c.* grain, *d.* lemon)

8. OTHELLO : JEALOUS :: HAMLET : (*a.* greedy, *b.* reflective, *c.* unintelligent, *d.* joyous)

9. (*a.* skirmish, *b.* war, *c.* disaster, *d.* truce) : BATTLE :: DRIZZLE : RAINFALL

10. SHETLAND : (*a.* monkey, *b.* lion, *c.* chicken, *d.* pony) :: HOLSTEIN : COW

11. (*a.* donkey, *b.* horse, *c.* bulldog, *d.* cougar) : DEMOCRAT :: ELEPHANT : REPUBLICAN

12. (*a.* green, *b.* red, *c.* blue, *d.* yellow) : CARDINAL :: ORANGE : ORIOLE

13. GERIATRICS : (*a.* old age, *b.* childhood, *c.* adolescence, *d.* adulthood) :: PEDIATRICS : CHILDHOOD

14. DOVE : PEACE :: (*a.* falcon, *b.* hawk, *c.* bluejay, *d.* vulture) : WAR

15. CHECK : (*a.* account, *b.* finesse, *c.* no trump, *d.* checkmate) :: TENTATIVE : FINAL

16. PHENOMENOLOGIST : HUSSERL :: EXISTENTIALIST : (*a.* Camus, *b.* Russell, *c.* Ryle, *d.* Quine)

17. GONDOLA : (*a.* canal, *b.* air, *c.* ocean, *d.* hangar) :: TRAIN : TRACK

18. (*a.* Babylonia, *b.* Phoenecia, *c.* Egypt, *d.* India) : PHARAOH :: ROMAN EMPIRE : EMPEROR

19. ACHILLES : TROJANS :: SAMSON : (*a.* Egyptians, *b.* Canaanites, *c.* Philistines, *d.* Moabites)

20. SPUMONI : TORTONI :: PARMESAN : (*a.* amontillado, *b.* mozzarella, *c.* manzanilla, *d.* maraschino)

21. HYPERBOLE : (*a.* geometric object, *b.* exaggeration, *c.* understatement, *d.* metaphysical object) :: HYPOCRITE : PRETENDER

22. MOOT COURT : HYPOTHETICAL CASES :: (*a.* kangaroo court, *b.* monkey court, *c.* cabbage court, *d.* dandelion court) : IRREGULAR PROCEDURES

23. ETHYL : METHYL :: GRAIN : (*a.* petrol, *b.* alcohol, *c.* sulfur, *d.* wood)

24. NEAPOLITAN : ITALY :: MUSCOVITE : (*a.* U.S.A., *b.* Hungary, *c.* Russia, *d.* Turkey)

25. APEX : SUMMIT :: ZENITH : (*a.* nadir, *b.* end, *c.* top, *d.* beginning)

26. (*a.* temporary, *b.* porous, *c.* impenetrable, *d.* permanent) : IMPERMEABLE :: COMMENCE : COMPLETE

27. PHILE : (*a.* love, *b.* hate, *c.* trust, *d.* distrust) :: PHOBE : FEAR

28. SOCRATES : (*a.* dagger, *b.* suffocation, *c.* noose, *d.* hemlock) :: GARFIELD : BULLET

29. OCHLOCRACY : MOB :: AUTOCRACY : (*a.* intellectual elite, *b.* rich, *c.* dictator, *d.* senate)

30. MOOR : PIN :: ROOM : (*a.* cue, *b.* nip, *c.* swim, *d.* thread)

31. FIREWATER : (*a.* acid, *b.* fire, *c.* liquor, *d.* lye) :: POTLATCH : FESTIVAL

32. (*a.* voluble, *b.* mum, *c.* lively, *d.* deaf) : MUTE :: SILENT : TACITURN

33. ATOM : MOLECULE :: CELL : (*a.* DNA, *b.* cytoplasm, *c.* tissue,
    d. ectoplasm)

34. AZURE : (*a.* blue, *b.* red, *c.* yellow, *d.* brown) :: MAGENTA : PURPLE

35. (*a.* quail, *b.* turkey, *c.* duck, *d.* pheasant) : DRAKE :: CHICKEN :
    ROOSTER

36. CIRRHOSIS : LIVER :: NEPHROSIS : (*a.* gallbladder, *b.* lung,
    c. pancreas, *d.* kidneys)

37. IMPEACH : HOUSE :: (*a.* protect, *b.* convict, *c.* rebut, *d.* remand) :
    SENATE

38. (*a.* metabolism, *b.* anabolism, *c.* menabolism, *d.* atabolism) :
    CONSTRUCTION :: CATABOLISM : DESTRUCTION

39. GALAHAD : (*a.* size, *b.* cowardice, *c.* nobility, *d.* lechery) ::
    GRISELDA : PATIENCE

40. INDUCTION : DEDUCTION :: (*a.* synthetic, *b.* inferential, *c.* a priori,
    d. a fortiori) : ANALYTIC

41. FLOOZY : DISREPUTABLE :: FLIBBERTIGIBBET : (*a.* immoral,
    b. unintelligent, *c.* mentally unbalanced, *d.* flighty)

42. RED : LONGEST :: (*a.* blue, *b.* yellow, *c.* violet, *d.* green) : SHORTEST

43. STABLE : TABLE :: START : (*a.* motion, *b.* horse, *c.* stop, *d.* tart)

44. IN VIVO : (*a.* in vitro, *b.* in moribus, *c.* in extremis, *d.* in vacuo) ::
    LIVING ORGANISM : TEST TUBE

45. f″ : f′ :: (*a.* speed, *b.* distance, *c.* time, *d.* acceleration) : VELOCITY

46. UNICYCLE : BICYCLE :: BICYCLE : (*a.* locomotive, *b.* dirigible,
    c. motorcycle, *d.* automobile)

47. SPELUNKER : (*a.* deserts, *b.* caves, *c.* glaciers, *d.* forests) :: ALPINIST :
    MOUNTAINS

48. APOTHECARY : (*a.* doctor, *b.* pharmacist, *c.* drug addict, *d.* patient) ::
    LAWYER : ATTORNEY

49. (*a.* Daniel Boone, *b.* The Headless Horseman, *c.* Paul Bunyan, *d.* Tonto) :
    BABE :: LONE RANGER : SILVER

50. SCULPTOR : STATUE :: (*a.* composer, *b.* politician, *c.* psychiatrist, *d.* blacksmith) : FUGUE

51. JOURNEYMAN : APPRENTICE :: ASSOCIATE PROFESSOR : (*a.* professor, *b.* research associate, *c.* assistant professor, *d.* teacher)

52. HOLMES : (*a.* Baker, *b.* Bond, *c.* Watson, *d.* Moriarty) :: CRUSOE : FRIDAY

53. FILLY : MARE :: GIRL : (*a.* adult, *b.* human, *c.* mother, *d.* woman)

54. IMPECUNIOUS : (*a.* generous, *b.* poor, *c.* wealthy, *d.* greedy) :: OBESE : CORPULENT

55. WAR BETWEEN THE STATES : CIVIL WAR :: GREAT WAR : (*a.* American Revolution, *b.* Hundred Years War, *c.* World War I, *d.* World War II)

56. HISTOLOGIST : TISSUE :: GRAPHOLOGIST : (*a.* maps, *b.* weather, *c.* handwriting, *d.* earthquakes)

57. (*a.* to play, *b.* will have played, *c.* playing, *d.* having played) : INFINITIVE :: WAITING : PARTICIPLE

58. PEDOMETER : (*a.* breaths, *b.* steps, *c.* heart beats, *d.* salivations) :: PROTRACTOR : DEGREES

59. ANGLE OF INCIDENCE : 45° :: ANGLE OF REFLECTION : (*a.* 0°, *b.* 22.5°, *c.* 45°, *d.* 90°)

60. (*a.* professional, *b.* hireling, *c.* journeyman, *d.* tyro) : NOVICE :: AMATEUR : BEGINNER

61. (*a.* novella, *b.* trial, *c.* soliloquy, *d.* epic) : POETRY :: NOVEL : PROSE

62. CONGLOMERATION : AGGLOMERATION :: CLUSTER : (*a.* heap, *b.* dispersion, *c.* hierarchy, *d.* aggrandizement)

63. (*a.* Jackson, *b.* Jefferson, *c.* Howe, *d.* Taylor) : DAVIS :: SHERMAN : LINCOLN

64. UMBRAGE : (*a.* offense, *b.* defense, *c.* innocence, *d.* responsibility) :: GUILT : CULPABILITY

65. PERFECT : PREFECT :: FLAWLESS : (*a.* caretaker, *b.* government official, *c.* refectory, *d.* preface)

66. DOZEN : 12 :: BAKER'S DOZEN : (*a.* 8, *b.* 11, *c.* 13, *d.* 16)

67. (*a.* tawdry, *b.* dehiscent, *c.* seraphic, *d.* edacious) : GAUDY :: NADIR : BOTTOM

68. PLUTO : (*a.* Hades, *b.* Thanatos, *c.* heaven, *d.* purgatory) :: SATAN : HELL

69. DEMONSTRATE : SHOW :: FORSWEAR : (*a.* promise, *b.* curse, *c.* renounce, *d.* conceal)

70. SHEEP : SHEEP :: (*a.* rhinocerii, *b.* rhinoceres, *c.* rhinoceroses, *d.* rhinocerae) : RHINOCEROS

71. PRETEND : PORTEND :: FEIGN : (*a.* fain, *b.* act realistically, *c.* presage, *d.* look back on)

72. UNIVERSAL DONOR : (*a.* A, *b.* B, *c.* O, *d.* Rh⁻) :: UNIVERSAL RECIPIENT : AB

73. (*a.* landscape, *b.* portrait, *c.* madonna, *d.* still life) : CLAUDE LORRAIN :: CARICATURE : HONORÉ DAUMIER

74. BRUNET : DARK BROWN :: HOARY : (*a.* red, *b.* white, *c.* black, *d.* blonde)

75. POINT : LINE :: LINE : (*a.* solid, *b.* plane, *c.* hypersphere, *d.* polygon)

76. LA BOHEME : PUCCINI :: LA TRAVIATA : (*a.* Berlioz, *b.* Menotti, *c.* Verdi, *d.* Rossini)

77. PESETA : SPANIARDS :: SHEKEL : (*a.* Chinese, *b.* Israelis, *c.* French, *d.* Indians)

78. (*a.* Declaration of Independence, *b.* Articles of Confederation, *c.* Declaration of Rights and Grievances, *d.* Townshend Acts) : U.S. CONSTITUTION :: LEAGUE OF NATIONS : UNITED NATIONS

79. MILLIMETER : CENTIMETER :: CENTIMETER : (*a.* decimeter, *b.* meter, *c.* decameter, *d.* kilometer)

80. ENSIGN : NAVY :: (*a.* private, *b.* sergeant, *c.* second lieutenant, *d.* colonel) : ARMY

81. COLT : REVOLVER :: NOBEL : (*a.* A-bomb, *b.* tear gas, *c.* rifle, *d.* dynamite)

82. HYDRATED : WATER :: ORGANIC : (*a.* hydrogen, *b.* nitrogen, *c.* oxygen, *d.* carbon)

83. (*a.* doctors, *b.* officers, *c.* clergymen, *d.* saboteurs) : FIFTH COLUMN :: SPIES : INTELLIGENCE

84. PING-PONG : BADMINTON :: TENNIS : (*a.* lacrosse, *b.* football, *c.* handball, *d.* soccer)

85. (*a.* Aegisthus, *b.* Priam, *c.* Agamemnon, *d.* Theseus) : PARIS :: DAEDALUS : ICARUS

86. BLACKSTONE : (*a.* medicine, *b.* politics, *c.* law, *d.* teaching) :: ROBERTS : PARLIAMENTARY PROCEDURE

87. WIFE OF BATH : (*a.* Chaucer, *b.* Milton, *c.* Wordsworth, *d.* Spenser) :: BELINDA : POPE

88. CATTON : CIVIL WAR :: (*a.* Plutarch, *b.* Thucydides, *c.* Herodotus, *d.* Pliny the Elder) : PELOPONNESIAN WAR

89. JEHOVAH'S WITNESSES : RUSSELL :: MORMONS : (*a.* Wesley, *b.* Smith, *c.* Thomas, *d.* Kirby)

90. 10 : OCTAL :: (*a.* 1, *b.* 1000, *c.* 111, *d.* 101) : BINARY

91. NEW JERSEY : THIRD :: (*a.* Virginia, *b.* New York, *c.* Delaware, *d.* New Hampshire) : FIRST

92. URIAH HEEP : HYPOCRITICALLY HUMBLE : WILKINS MICAWBER : (*a.* poor but optimistic, *b.* poor and pessimistic, *c.* rich and optimistic, *d.* rich but pessimistic)

93. ABBOTT : FLATLAND :: DANTE : (*a.* China, *b.* Purgatory, *c.* Never-Never Land, *d.* Moonland)

94. (*a.* catharsis, *b.* tragedy, *c.* bathos, *d.* ethos) UNIVERSAL :: PATHOS : PERSONAL

95. CANTOR : RABBI :: MUEZZIN : (*a.* minaret, *b.* guru, *c.* Brahmin, *d.* imam)

96. ORPHEUS : RETURN OF EURYDICE TO HADES :: WIFE OF LOT : (*a.* transformation into a star, *b.* return to Sodom, *c.* transformation into a pillar of salt, *d.* return to Canaan)

97. CENTIGRADE : 100 :: KELVIN : (*a.* 132, *b.* 100, *c.* 0, *d.* 373)

98. LA GIACONDA : (*a.* Mona Lisa, *b.* Pieta, *c.* Madonna, *d.* Venus de Milo) :: ARRANGEMENT IN BLACK AND GRAY : WHISTLER'S MOTHER

99. EMPIRICIST : UTILITARIAN :: HUME : (*a.* Spinoza, *b.* Leibnitz, *c.* Kant, *d.* Mill)

100. BLOOMFIELD : SURFACE STRUCTURE :: (*a.* Whorf, *b.* Sapir, *c.* Skinner, *d.* Chomsky) : DEEP STRUCTURE

101. GERMANIC : EUROPE :: (*a.* Swahili, *b.* Bantu, *c.* Zulu, *d.* Nigerian) : AFRICA

102. EVAPORATE : (*a.* freeze, *b.* melt, *c.* dehydrate, *d.* condense) :: VAPOR : SOLID

103. POSITION : VELOCITY :: VELOCITY : (*a.* speed, *b.* acceleration, *c.* torque, *d.* jerk)

104. TESTOSTERONE : HORMONE :: NEURON : (*a.* brain, *b.* dendrite, *c.* tissue, *d.* cell)

105. 1066 : BATTLE OF HASTINGS :: 1588 : (*a.* defeat of Napoleon, *b.* King Philip's War, *c.* defeat of the Spanish Armada, *d.* establishment of Jamestown)

106. PSYCHOSOCIAL STAGES : (*a.* Erickson, *b.* Freud, *c.* Chomsky, *d.* Lewin) :: DEVELOPMENTAL STAGES : PIAGET

107. HIP : PELVIS:: (*a.* shoulder blade, *b.* kneecap, *c.* jaw, *d.* cranium) : MANDIBLE

108. TANTALUS : SUSTENANCE :: SISYPHUS : (*a.* food, *b.* mobility, *c.* oxygen, *d.* rest)

109. (*a.* tsetse fly, *b.* snail, *c.* roundworm, *d.* housefly) : SLEEPING SICKNESS :: MOSQUITO : MALARIA

110. RICE : CHRISTOPHER :: (*a.* Kissinger, *b.* Christopher, *c.* Shultz, *d.* Baker III) : EAGLEBURG

111. (*a.* Mussolini, *b.* Carbonari, *c.* Ciampi, *d.* Virgil) : ITALY :: HIROHITO : JAPAN

112. VIRILE : FERAL :: ENERGETIC : (*a.* potent, *b.* tame, *c.* angry, *d.* wild)

113. EVA PERON : ARGENTINA :: IMELDA MARCOS : (*a.* Indonesia, *b.* Portugal, *c.* The Philippines, *d.* Spain)

114. (*a.* Rudyard Kipling, *b.* Salman Rushdie, *c.* Chinua Achebe, *d.* Graham Greene) : INDIA :: JOSEPH CONRAD : THE CONGO

115. MARY ANN CROSS : (*a.* Jane Eyre, *b.* Sense and Sensibility, *c.* Virginia Woolf, *d.* Middlemarch) :: SAMUEL CLEMENS : TOM SAWYER

116. TITANIC : ATLANTIC OCEAN :: EDMUND FITZGERALD : (*a.* Pacific Ocean, *b.* Lake Superior, *c.* Lake Michigan, *d.* Indian Ocean)

117. MURINE : RODENT :: (*a.* ursine, *b.* lupine, *c.* equine, *d.* vulpine) : FOX

118. (*a.* Sancho Panza, *b.* Tuesday, *c.* Don Quixote, *d.* Candide) : CERVANTES :: FRIDAY : DEFOE

119. SAILING: (*a.* trim, *b.* batten, *c.* jibe, *d.* turnbuckle) :: SKIING : SLALOM

120. NaCl : SALT :: NH_3 : (*a.* bleach, *b.* pepper, *c.* baking soda, *d.* ammonia)

Answer Key
PRACTICE TEST 1

1. **D**	31. **C**	61. **D**	91. **C**
2. **D**	32. **B**	62. **A**	92. **A**
3. **A**	33. **C**	63. **A**	93. **B**
4. **D**	34. **A**	64. **A**	94. **D**
5. **A**	35. **C**	65. **B**	95. **D**
6. **B**	36. **D**	66. **C**	96. **C**
7. **C**	37. **B**	67. **A**	97. **D**
8. **B**	38. **B**	68. **A**	98. **A**
9. **A**	39. **C**	69. **C**	99. **D**
10. **D**	40. **A**	70. **C**	100. **D**
11. **A**	41. **D**	71. **C**	101. **B**
12. **B**	42. **C**	72. **C**	102. **A**
13. **A**	43. **D**	73. **A**	103. **B**
14. **B**	44. **A**	74. **B**	104. **D**
15. **D**	45. **D**	75. **B**	105. **C**
16. **A**	46. **D**	76. **C**	106. **A**
17. **A**	47. **B**	77. **B**	107. **C**
18. **C**	48. **B**	78. **B**	108. **D**
19. **C**	49. **C**	79. **A**	109. **A**
20. **B**	50. **A**	80. **C**	110. **A**
21. **B**	51. **C**	81. **D**	111. **A**
22. **A**	52. **C**	82. **D**	112. **D**
23. **D**	53. **D**	83. **D**	113. **C**
24. **C**	54. **B**	84. **A**	114. **A**
25. **C**	55. **C**	85. **B**	115. **D**
26. **B**	56. **C**	86. **C**	116. **B**
27. **A**	57. **A**	87. **A**	117. **D**
28. **D**	58. **B**	88. **B**	118. **A**
29. **C**	59. **C**	89. **B**	119. **C**
30. **B**	60. **D**	90. **B**	120. **D**

EXPLANATION OF ANSWERS FOR PRACTICE TEST 1

In the following explanations of answers, explanations concerning the correct response are in a large font. Explanations regarding distracters (incorrect responses) that are not self-explaining or could be misinterpreted are in a smaller font in order to highlight the explanations of the answers that are correct.

1. CANARY : (*a.* red, *b.* blue, *c.* brown, ***d.* yellow**) :: POLAR BEAR : WHITE

   (**d**) A canary is usually yellow; a polar bear is generally white.
   General Information—Description

2. SHIRT : WEAR :: BLOODY MARY : (*a.* kill, *b.* eat, *c.* dress, ***d.* drink**)

   (**d**) One wears a shirt; one drinks a Bloody Mary.
   General Information—Description

3. DAY : NIGHT :: DIURNAL : (***a.* nocturnal**, *b.* eternal, *c.* vernal, *d.* external)

   (**a**) *Diurnal* refers to the daytime, while *nocturnal* refers to the nighttime.
   Eternal means "endless"; *vernal* means "youthful"; *external* means "outward."
   Vocabulary—Similarity/Contrast

4. (*a.* Howard, *b.* Phineas, *c.* Ernest, ***d.* Millard**) : FILLMORE :: THOMAS : JEFFERSON

   (**d**) Millard Fillmore and Thomas Jefferson were both presidents of the United States.
   Humanities—Completion

5. APRIL : 2 × 15 :: FEBRUARY : (***a.* 2 × 14**, *b.* 2 × 15, *c.* 2 × 16, *d.* 2 × 17)

   (**a**) April has 2 × 15, or 30 days; February usually has 2 × 14, or 28 days.
   General Information—Description

6. COMPARATIVE : (*a.* good, ***b.* better**, *c.* best, *d.* great) :: SUPERLATIVE : BEST

   (**b**) *Better* is the comparative form and *best* the superlative form of the adjective *good.*
   General Information—Description

7. WINE : FRUIT :: BEER : (*a.* grape, *b.* hay, ***c.* grain**, *d.* lemon)

   (**c**) Wine is fermented fruit; beer is fermented grain.
   General Information—Description

8. OTHELLO : JEALOUS :: HAMLET : (*a.* greedy, ***b.* reflective**, *c.* unintelligent, *d.* joyous)

(**b**) In the respective Shakespearean plays in which they appear, Othello is a jealous character and Hamlet a reflective one.
Humanities—Description

9. (***a.* skirmish**, *b.* war, *c.* disaster, *d.* truce) : BATTLE :: DRIZZLE : RAINFALL

(**a**) A skirmish is a minor battle; a drizzle is a minor rainfall.
Vocabulary—Class

10. SHETLAND : (*a.* monkey, *b.* lion, *c.* chicken, ***d.* pony**) :: HOLSTEIN : COW

(**d**) A Shetland is a type of pony; a Holstein is a type of cow.
General Information—Class

11. (***a.* donkey**, *b.* horse, *c.* bulldog, *d.* cougar) : DEMOCRAT :: ELEPHANT : REPUBLICAN

(**a**) A donkey is the symbol of the Democratic Party, while an elephant is the symbol of the Republican Party.
General Information—Description

12. (*a.* green, ***b.* red**, *c.* blue, *d.* yellow) : CARDINAL :: ORANGE : ORIOLE

(**b**) A cardinal is red; an oriole is orange.
General Information—Description

13. GERIATRICS : (***a.* old age**, *b.* childhood, *c.* adolescence, *d.* adulthood) :: PEDIATRICS : CHILDHOOD

(**a**) Geriatrics is the branch of medicine dealing with old age; pediatrics is the branch of medicine dealing with childhood.
Natural Science—Description

14. DOVE : PEACE :: (*a.* falcon, ***b.* hawk**, *c.* bluejay, *d.* vulture) : WAR

(**b**) A dove is a symbol of peace; a hawk is a symbol of war.
General Information—Description

15. CHECK : (*a.* account, *b.* finesse, *c.* no trump. ***d.* checkmate**) :: TENTATIVE : FINAL

(**d**) In the game of chess, a king is in tentative danger when in check, and in final danger when in checkmate.
General Information—Description

16. PHENOMENOLOGIST : HUSSERL :: EXISTENTIALIST : (***a.* Camus**, *b.* Russell, *c.* Ryle, *d.* Quine)

(**a**) In modern philosophy, Husserl is identified with the phenomenologist movement, Camus with the existentialist movement. Gilbert Ryle is primarily known for his critique of Cartesian Dualism; Bertrand Russell was a founder of Analytic Philosophy; Willard Van Orman Quine was an analytic philosopher.
Humanities—Description

17. GONDOLA : (***a.* canal**, *b.* air, *c.* ocean, *d.* hangar) :: TRAIN : TRACK

(**a**) A gondola moves along a canal; a train moves along a track.
General Information—Description

18. (*a.* Babylonia, *b.* Phoenecia, ***c.* Egypt**, *d.* India) : PHARAOH :: ROMAN EMPIRE : EMPEROR

(**c**) In ancient times, Egypt was ruled by a pharaoh and the Roman Empire was ruled by an emperor.
Humanities—Description

19. ACHILLES : TROJANS :: SAMSON : (*a.* Egyptians, *b.* Canaanites, ***c.* Philistines**, *d.* Moabites)

(**c**) Achilles fought against the Trojans, Samson against the Philistines. Samson is a biblical figure; Achilles is a figure from Greek mythology.
Humanities—Description

20. SPUMONI : TORTONI :: PARMESAN : (*a.* amontillado, ***b.* mozzarella**, *c.* manzanilla, *d.* maraschino)

(**b**) Spumoni and tortoni are both Italian ice-cream desserts; Parmesan and mozzarella are both Italian cheeses.
General Information—Class

21. HYPERBOLE : (*a.* geometric object, ***b.* exaggeration**, *c.* understatement, *d.* metaphysical object) :: HYPOCRITE : PRETENDER

(**b**) A hyperbole is an exaggeration; a hypocrite is a pretender.
Vocabulary—Similarity/Contrast

22. MOOT COURT : HYPOTHETICAL CASES :: (***a.* kangaroo court**, *b.* monkey court, *c.* cabbage court, *d.* dandelion court) : IRREGULAR PROCEDURES

(**a**) A moot court tries hypothetical cases; a kangaroo court exhibits irregular procedures.
Social Science—Description

23. ETHYL : METHYL :: GRAIN : (*a.* petrol, *b.* alcohol, *c.* sulfur, *d.* **wood**)

    (**d**) Ethyl alcohol is grain alcohol; methyl alcohol is wood alcohol.
    Natural Science—Description

24. NEAPOLITAN : ITALY :: MUSCOVITE : (*a.* U.S.A., *b.* Hungary, *c.* **Russia**, *d.* Turkey)

    (**c**) A Neapolitan is a resident of Naples, and thus lives in Italy.
    A Muscovite is a resident of Moscow, and therefore lives in Russia.
    General Information—Description

25. APEX : SUMMIT :: ZENITH : (*a.* nadir, *b.* end, *c.* **top**, *d.* beginning)

    (**c**) *Apex, summit, zenith,* and *top* are all synonyms. The nadir is the point
    directly below the observer directly opposite the zenith.
    Vocabulary—Similarity/Contrast

26. (*a.* temporary, *b.* **porous**, *c.* impenetrable, *d.* permanent) :
    IMPERMEABLE :: COMMENCE : COMPLETE

    (**b**) *Porous* and *impermeable* are antonyms, as are *commence* and *complete.*
    Vocabulary—Similarity/Contrast

27. PHILE : (*a.* **love**, *b.* hate, *c.* trust, *d.* distrust) :: PHOBE : FEAR

    (**a**) *-phile* is a suffix denoting love for something, while *-phobe* is a suffix
    denoting fear of something. Both suffixes are derived from the Greek
    language.
    Vocabulary—Description

28. SOCRATES : (*a.* dagger, *b.* suffocation, *c.* noose, *d.* **hemlock**) ::
    GARFIELD : BULLET

    (**d**) Socrates died from drinking hemlock, Garfield from being shot with a
    bullet.
    Humanities—Description

29. OCHLOCRACY : MOB :: AUTOCRACY : (*a.* intellectual elite, *b.* rich, *c.* **dictator**, *d.* senate)

    (**c**) Ochlocracy is rule by a mob; autocracy is rule by a single dictator.
    Social Science—Description

30. MOOR : PIN :: ROOM : (*a.* cue, *b.* **nip**, *c.* swim, *d.* thread)

    (**b**) *Room* is *moor* spelled backwards; *nip* is *pin* spelled backwards.
    Nonsemantic

31. FIREWATER : (*a.* acid, *b.* fire, *c.* **liquor**, *d.* lye) :: POTLATCH : FESTIVAL

    (**c**) *Potlatch* was an Indian name for a winter festival; *firewater* was an Indian name for liquor.
    General Information—Similarity/Contrast

32. (*a.* voluble, *b.* **mum**, *c.* lively, *d.* deaf) : MUTE :: SILENT : TACITURN

    (**b**) *Mum* and *mute* are synonyms, as are *silent* and *tactiturn*.
    Vocabulary—Similarity/Contrast

33. ATOM : MOLECULE :: CELL : (*a.* DNA, *b.* cytoplasm, *c.* **tissue**, *d.* ectoplasm)

    (**c**) Atoms combine to form molecules. Cells combine to form tissue.
    Natural Science—Part/Whole

34. AZURE : (*a.* **blue**, *b.* red, *c.* yellow, *d.* brown) :: MAGENTA : PURPLE

    (**a**) Azure is a shade of blue; magenta is a shade of purple.
    General Information—Description

35. (*a.* quail, *b.* turkey, *c.* **duck**, *d.* pheasant) : DRAKE :: CHICKEN : ROOSTER

    (**c**) A drake is a male duck; a rooster is a male chicken.
    General Information—Description

36. CIRRHOSIS : LIVER :: NEPHROSIS : (*a.* gallbladder, *b.* lung, *c.* pancreas, *d.* **kidneys**)

    (**d**) Cirrhosis is a disease that usually strikes the liver; nephrosis is a disease of the kidneys. In cirrhosis, scar tissue replaces the healthy tissue in the liver impairing normal functioning of the liver. There are many causes, for example, alcoholism or hepatitis. Nephrosis is a non-inflammatory disease that may manifest itself, for example, in low albumin level and high cholesterol level in the blood. A disease of the gallbladder is gallstones; gallstones are crystalline bodies that form when the fluid in the gallbladder hardens. The pancreas stores digestive enzymes; therefore, it may be very difficult if it gets injured or punctured. A disease of the lung is asthma, whereby the airways constrict and become inflamed, leading to wheezing and troubled breathing.
    Natural Science—Description

37. IMPEACH : HOUSE :: (*a.* protect, *b.* **convict**, *c.* rebut, *d.* remand) : SENATE

    (**b**) The House has the power to impeach the President, while the Senate has the power to convict him or her. Impeachment is the first stage in the

process of removing a government official. It is a legal statement of charges. The second step is conviction, in which the Senate tries the accused. A two-third majority is required for conviction.
Social Science—Description

38. (*a*. metabolism, ***b*. anabolism**, *c*. menabolism, *d*. atabolism) : CONSTRUCTION :: CATABOLISM : DESTRUCTION

(**b**) Anabolism is constructive metabolism, while catabolism is destructive metabolism. Anabolism constructs molecules from smaller units and requires energy. Catabolism breaks down molecules into smaller units and releases energy. Metabolism is the process by which living cells absorb nutrients and convert them into living substance.
Natural Science—Description

39. GALAHAD : (*a*. size, *b*. cowardice, ***c*. nobility**, *d*. lechery) :: GRISELDA : PATIENCE

(**c**) Galahad was the most virtuous knight in the Arthurian legend and was distinguished for his nobility. Griselda is a character from folklore who stands for patience.
Humanities—Description

40. INDUCTION : DEDUCTION :: (***a*. synthetic**, *b*. inferential, *c*. a priori, *d*. a fortiori) : ANALYTIC

(**a**) Induction is a synthetic form of thinking, while deduction is an analytic form of thinking. Synthetic thinking involves the combination of several ideas into one whole. Analytic thinking involves the separation of a whole into its parts. Inferential thinking is reasoning that is based on circumstantial evidence (rather than observations) in order to make a logical judgment. *A priori* means that something is derived by logic without need of observed facts. *A fortiori* means "for a stronger reason."
Humanities—Class

41. FLOOZY : DISREPUTABLE :: FLIBBERTIGIBBET : (*a*. immoral, *b*. unintelligent, *c*. mentally unbalanced, ***d*. flighty**)

(**d**) A floozy is disreputable, while a flibbertigibbet is flighty.
Vocabulary—Description

42. RED : LONGEST :: (*a*. blue, *b*. yellow, ***c*. violet**, *d*. green) : SHORTEST

(**c**) Red light waves are the longest in the spectrum; violet waves, the shortest. The order from the shortest to the longest wavelength is violet, blue, green, yellow, orange, and red.
Natural Science—Description

43. STABLE : TABLE :: START : (*a.* motion, *b.* horse, *c.* stop, ***d.* tart**)

   (**d**) The word *table* is the same as the word *stable*, but without the initial *s*. Similarly, the word *tart* is the same as the word *start*, again without the initial *s*.
   Nonsemantic

44. IN VIVO : (***a.* in vitro**, *b.* in moribus, *c.* in extremis, *d.* in vacuo) :: LIVING ORGANISM : TEST TUBE

   (**a**) Something grown *in vivo* is grown inside a living organism. Something grown *in vitro* is grown inside a test tube. *In vacuo* means "in an empty space"; *in moribus* means "in a dead object"; *in extremis* means "to the furthest degree."
   Natural Science—Description

45. f'' : f' :: (*a.* speed, *b.* distance, *c.* time, ***d.* acceleration**) : VELOCITY

   (**d**) The second derivative of a function, f'', can be used to determine acceleration. The first derivative, f', can be used to determine velocity.
   Natural Science—Description

46. UNICYCLE : BICYCLE :: BICYCLE : (*a.* locomotive, *b.* dirigible, *c.* motorcycle, ***d.* automobile**)

   (**d**) A bicycle has twice as many wheels as a unicycle. An automobile has twice as many wheels as a bicycle.
   General Information—Equality/Negation

47. SPELUNKER : (*a.* deserts, ***b.* caves**, *c.* glaciers, *d.* forests) :: ALPINIST : MOUNTAINS

   (**b**) A spelunker explores caves; an alpinist climbs mountains.
   General Information—Description

48. APOTHECARY : (*a.* doctor, ***b.* pharmacist**, *c.* drug addict, *d.* patient) :: LAWYER : ATTORNEY

   (**b**) An apothecary is a pharmacist; a lawyer is an attorney.
   General Information—Similarity/Contrast

49. (*a.* Daniel Boone, *b.* The Headless Horseman, ***c.* Paul Bunyan**, *d.* Tonto) : BABE :: LONE RANGER : SILVER

   (**c**) Babe was an animal (ox) belonging to Paul Bunyan. Silver was an animal (horse) belonging to the Lone Ranger. Paul Bunyan was a legendary lumberjack who embodied frontier vitality in American folklore. Daniel Boone (1734–1820), a pioneer and hunter, was one of the first American folk heroes. The Headless Horseman is a character from Washington Irving's short story "The Legend of

Sleepy Hollow." Tonto was the Native American assistant of the Lone Ranger, both of whom are fictional characters who were created by George Trendle and Fran Striker.
Humanities—Description

50. SCULPTOR : STATUE :: (***a. composer***, *b.* politician, *c.* psychiatrist, *d.* blacksmith) : FUGUE

    (**a**) A statue is a work of art created by a sculptor; a fugue is a work of art created by a composer.
    Humanities—Description

51. JOURNEYMAN : APPRENTICE :: ASSOCIATE PROFESSOR : (*a.* professor, *b.* research associate, ***c. assistant professor***, *d.* teacher)

    (**c**) In craft guilds, a journeyman is one step above an apprentice. In colleges and universities, an associate professor is one step above an assistant professor.
    General Information—Description

52. HOLMES : (*a.* Baker, *b.* Bond, ***c. Watson***, *d.* Moriarty) :: CRUSOE : FRIDAY

    (**c**) In their respective exploits, Holmes was assisted by Watson, Crusoe by Friday. James Bond is a fictitious British agent in a series of novels (later made into films) by Ian Fleming. 221B Baker Street is the street address at which Holmes' office was located. Moriarty was his mortal enemy, a mathematics professor but also a villain.
    Humanities—Description

53. FILLY : MARE :: GIRL : (*a.* adult, *b.* human, *c.* mother, ***d. woman***)

    (**d**) A filly grows into a mare; a girl grows into a woman.
    General Information—Description

54. IMPECUNIOUS : (*a.* generous, ***b. poor***, *c.* wealthy, *d.* greedy) :: OBESE : CORPULENT

    (**b**) *Impecunious* and *poor* are synonyms, as are *obese* and *corpulent*.
    Vocabulary—Similarity/Contrast

55. WAR BETWEEN THE STATES : CIVIL WAR :: GREAT WAR : (*a.* American Revolution, *b.* Hundred Years War, ***c. World War I***, *d.* World War II)

    (**c**) The Civil War is often called the War Between the States. World War I is often called the Great War.
    Humanities—Similarity/Contrast

56. HISTOLOGIST : TISSUE :: GRAPHOLOGIST : (*a.* maps, *b.* weather, **c. handwriting**, *d.* earthquakes)

    (**c**) A histologist studies tissue; a graphologist studies handwriting.
    General Information—Description

57. (**a. to play**, *b.* will have played, *c.* playing, *d.* having played) :
    INFINITIVE :: WAITING : PARTICIPLE

    (**a**) *To play* is an infinitive; *waiting* is a participle.
    General Information—Description

58. PEDOMETER : (*a.* breaths, **b. steps**, *c.* heart beats, *d.* salivations) ::
    PROTRACTOR : DEGREES

    (**b**) A pedometer measures numbers of steps; a protractor measures numbers
    of degrees.
    General Information—Description

59. ANGLE OF INCIDENCE : 45° :: ANGLE OF REFLECTION : (*a.* 0°,
    b. 22.5°, **c. 45°**, *d.* 90°)

    (**c**) If the angle of incidence of a light ray is 45°, its angle of reflection is
    also 45°.
    Natural Science—Equality/Negation

60. (*a.* professional, *b.* hireling, *c.* journeyman, **d. tyro**) : NOVICE ::
    AMATEUR : BEGINNER

    (**d**) *Tyro, novice, amateur,* and *beginner* are all synonymous.
    Vocabulary—Similarity/Contrast

61. (*a.* novella, *b.* trial, *c.* soliloquy, **d. epic**) : POETRY :: NOVEL : PROSE

    (**d**) An epic is a form of poetry; a novel is a form of prose. A novella
    is a form of prose as well, being shorter than a novel but longer than a novelette.
    A soliloquy is a form of dramatic monologue where the speaker is addressing himself.
    The Trial is a novel by Franz Kafka.
    Humanities—Description

62. CONGLOMERATION : AGGLOMERATION :: CLUSTER : (**a. heap**,
    b. dispersion, *c.* hierarchy, *d.* aggrandizement)

    (**a**) A conglomeration is a cluster; an agglomeration, a heap.
    Vocabulary—Similarity/Contrast

63. (*a.* **Jackson**, *b.* Jefferson, *c.* Howe, *d.* Taylor) : DAVIS :: SHERMAN : LINCOLN

    (**a**) Stonewall Jackson was a Confederate general under Jefferson Davis, while William Sherman was a Union general under Abraham Lincoln. Thomas Jefferson (1743–1826) was the third president of the United States. Both Albion Howe (1818–1897) and George Taylor (1808–1862) were generals in the Union Army.
    Humanities—Description

64. UMBRAGE : (*a.* **offense**, *b.* defense, *c.* innocence, *d.* responsibility) :: GUILT : CULPABILITY

    (**a**) *Umbrage* and *offense* are synonymous, as are *guilt* and *culpability.*
    Vocabulary—Similarity/Contrast

65. PERFECT : PREFECT :: FLAWLESS : (*a.* caretaker, *b.* **government official**, *c.* refectory, *d.* preface)

    (**b**) Something that is perfect is flawless. A prefect is a government official.
    General Information—Similarity/Contrast

66. DOZEN : 12 :: BAKER'S DOZEN : (*a.* 8, *b.* 11, *c.* **13**, *d.* 16)

    (**c**) There are 12 objects in a dozen, and 13 objects in a baker's dozen. The expression of a baker's dozen comes from 13th century England, where bakers could be severely punished if they were found to gyp their customers. Therefore, they often preferred to bake more items to ensure they would not betray their customers.
    General Information—Equality/Negation

67. (*a.* **tawdry**, *b.* dehiscent, *c.* seraphic, *d.* edacious) : GAUDY :: NADIR : BOTTOM

    (**a**) *Tawdry* and *gaudy* are synonyms, as are *nadir* and *bottom.*
    Vocabulary—Similarity/Contrast

68. PLUTO : (*a.* **Hades**, *b.* Thanatos, *c.* heaven, *d.* purgatory) :: SATAN : HELL

    (**a**) According to Roman mythology, Pluto resided in Hades. According to certain Christian doctrine, Satan resides in hell. Thanatos was the Greek personification of death. Heaven is the abode of God, angels, and the souls who received salvation. Purgatory is a Roman Catholic concept of a place for those who are ultimately destined to go to heaven but who need to be purged of their imperfections.
    Humanities—Description

69. DEMONSTRATE : SHOW :: FORSWEAR : (*a.* promise, *b.* curse, *c.* **renounce**, *d.* conceal)

(**c**) *Demonstrate* and *show* are synonyms, as are *forswear* and *renounce*.
Vocabulary—Similarity/Contrast

70. SHEEP : SHEEP :: (*a.* rhinocerii, *b.* rhinoceres, *c.* **rhinoceroses**, *d.* rhinocerae) : RHINOCEROS

(**c**) *Sheep* is the plural form of *sheep*; *rhinoceroses* is the preferred plural form of *rhinoceros*.
Nonsemantic

71. PRETEND : PORTEND :: FEIGN : (*a.* fain, *b.* act realistically, *c.* **presage**, *d.* look back on)

(**c**) *Pretend* and *feign* are synonyms, as are *portend* and *presage*.
Vocabulary—Similarity/Contrast

72. UNIVERSAL DONOR : (*a.* A, *b.* B, *c.* **O**, *d.* Rh⁻) :: UNIVERSAL RECIPIENT : AB

(**c**) People with blood type O are called universal donors because people with all blood types can receive their blood; people with blood type AB are called universal recipients because they can receive every blood type.
Natural Science—Description

73. (*a.* **landscape**, *b.* portrait, *c.* madonna, *d.* still life) : CLAUDE LORRAIN :: CARICATURE : HONORÉ DAUMIER

(**a**) Claude Lorrain (ca. 1602–1682) is best known for his landscapes, Honoré Daumier (1808–1879) for his caricatures.
Humanities—Description

74. BRUNET : DARK BROWN :: HOARY : (*a.* red, *b.* **white**, *c.* black, *d.* blonde)

(**b**) Brunet coloring is dark brown, while hoary coloring is white.
General Information—Similarity/Contrast

75. POINT : LINE :: LINE : (*a.* solid, *b.* **plane**, *c.* hypersphere, *d.* polygon)

(**b**) An infinite collection of consecutive points forms a line. An infinite collection of consecutive lines forms a plane.
Mathematics—Part/Whole

76. LA BOHEME : PUCCINI :: LA TRAVIATA : (*a.* Berlioz, *b.* Menotti, *c.* **Verdi**, *d.* Rossini)

(**c**) *La Boheme* is an opera composed by Puccini (1858–1924); *La Traviata* is an opera composed by Verdi (1813–1901).
Humanities—Description

77. PESETA : SPANIARDS :: SHEKEL : (*a.* Chinese, *b.* **Israelis**, *c.* French, *d.* Indians)

(**b**) A peseta is a coin that was used by Spaniards; a shekel is a coin used by Israelis. The French used francs as currency; the Indians use rupees as a currency; the Chinese use yuans as a currency.
Humanities—Description

78. (*a.* Declaration of Independence, *b.* **Articles of Confederation**, *c.* Declaration of Rights and Grievances, *d.* Townshend Acts) : U.S. CONSTITUTION :: LEAGUE OF NATIONS : UNITED NATIONS

(**b**) The U.S. Constitution replaced the Articles of Confederation. The United Nations replaced the League of Nations. The Townshend Acts were passed by the British Parliament in 1767 to establish that Britain had the right to raise revenue and to tax the colonies. In 1774, the British Parliament passed the Coercive Acts in response to which the First Congress drafted the Declaration of Rights and Grievances, which declared that taxes imposed on British colonists were unconstitutional lest British colonists had consented. The Articles of Confederation (completed in 1781) was the first attempt at establishing a constitution of the alliance of the 13 independent states.
Humanities—Description

79. MILLIMETER : CENTIMETER :: CENTIMETER : (*a.* **decimeter**, *b.* meter, *c.* decameter, *d.* kilometer)

(**a**) There are 10 millimeters in a centimeter, and 10 centimeters in a decimeter.
Mathematics—Part/Whole

80. ENSIGN : NAVY :: (*a.* private, *b.* sergeant, *c.* **second lieutenant**, *d.* colonel) : ARMY

(**c**) An ensign is the lowest ranking commissioned officer in the Navy; a second lieutenant is the lowest ranking commissioned officer in the Army.
General Information—Description

81. COLT : REVOLVER :: NOBEL : (*a.* A-bomb, *b.* tear gas, *c.* rifle, ***d.* dynamite**)

(**d**) Colt invented a type of revolver; Nobel invented dynamite.
General Information—Description

82. HYDRATED : WATER :: ORGANIC : (*a.* hydrogen, *b.* nitrogen, *c.* oxygen, ***d.* carbon**)

(**d**) A hydrated substance contains water; an organic substance contains carbon.
Natural Science—Description

83. (*a.* doctors, *b.* officers, *c.* clergymen, ***d.* saboteurs**) : FIFTH COLUMN :: SPIES : INTELLIGENCE

(**d**) During a war, saboteurs comprise a network that is often called a fifth column. Spies work in an intelligence network.
General Information—Description

84. PING-PONG : BADMINTON :: TENNIS : (***a.* lacrosse**, *b.* football, *c.* handball, *d.* soccer)

(**a**) The games of Ping-Pong, badminton, tennis, and lacrosse are all played with rackets.
General Information—Class

85. (*a.* Aegisthus, ***b.* Priam**, *c.* Agamemnon, *d.* Theseus) : PARIS :: DAEDALUS : ICARUS

(**b**) Priam was the father of Paris; Daedalus was the father of Icarus and tried to escape to Crete by flight. Aegisthus was the son of Thyestes and of his daughter, Pelopia. Agamemnon was the the son of King Atreus of Mycenae and Queen Aerope. He was eventually murdered by his wife Clytemnestra. Theseus was a king of Athens.
Humanities—Description

86. BLACKSTONE : (*a.* medicine, *b.* politics, ***c.* law**, *d.* teaching) :: ROBERTS : PARLIAMENTARY PROCEDURE

(**c**) Blackstone is known for his work on law, Roberts for his work on parliamentary procedure.
Social Science—Description

87. WIFE OF BATH : (***a*. Chaucer**, *b*. Milton, *c*. Wordsworth, *d*. Spenser) :: BELINDA : POPE

(**a**) The Wife of Bath is a literary character created by Geoffrey Chaucer for *The Wife of Bath's Tale*. Belinda is the name of a fictional character in Alexander Pope's *The Rape of the Lock*.
Humanities—Description

88. CATTON : CIVIL WAR :: (*a*. Plutarch, ***b*. Thucydides**, *c*. Herodotus, *d*. Pliny the Elder) : PELOPONNESIAN WAR

(**b**) Catton is known for his historical writing on the Civil War (1861–1865), Thucydides for his historical work on the Peloponnesian War (431–404 B.C.) Plutarch was a Roman historian and wrote *Parallel Lives* and *Moralia*. Herodotus was a Greek historian who was the first to have a "scientific" approach to history. His most famous work is *The Histories*. Pliny the Elder was a Roman writer who wrote *Naturalis Historia*.
Humanities—Description

89. JEHOVAH'S WITNESSES : RUSSELL :: MORMONS : (*a*. Wesley, ***b*. Smith**, *c*. Thomas, *d*. Kirby)

(**b**) The Jehovah's Witnesses sect was founded by Charles Russell; the Mormons were founded by Joseph Smith.
Humanities—Description

90. 10 : OCTAL :: (*a*. 1, ***b*. 1000**, *c*. 111, *d*. 101) : BINARY

(**b**) 10 in octal is equal to 1000 in binary; both are equal to 8 in conventional decimal notation.
Mathematics—Equality/Negation

91. NEW JERSEY : THIRD :: (*a*. Virginia, *b*. New York, ***c*. Delaware**, *d*. New Hampshire) : FIRST

(**c**) New Jersey was the third state to join the Union; Delaware was the first. New Hampshire was the 9th state to join the Union, Virginia was 10th, and New York 11th.
Humanities—Description

92. URIAH HEEP : HYPOCRITICALLY HUMBLE : WILKINS MICAWBER :
(***a*. poor but optimistic**, *b*. poor and pessimistic, *c*. rich and optimistic, *d*. rich but pessimistic)

(**a**) In Charles Dickens' *David Copperfield*, Uriah Heep is a character who is hypocritically humble, while Wilkins Micawber is poor but optimistic.
Humanities—Description

93. ABBOTT : FLATLAND :: DANTE : (*a.* China, ***b.* Purgatory**, *c.* Never-Never Land, *d.* Moonland)

(**b**) Abbott wrote a narrative describing his travels in Flatland; Dante wrote *The Divine Comedy*, describing in the second part of the trilogy his travels in Purgatory.
Humanities—Description

94. (*a.* catharsis, *b.* tragedy, *c.* bathos, ***d.* ethos**) : UNIVERSAL :: PATHOS : PERSONAL

(**d**) Ethos describes universal elements in a work of art, while pathos describes personal ones.
Humanities—Description

95. CANTOR : RABBI :: MUEZZIN : (*a.* minaret, *b.* guru, *c.* Brahmin, ***d.* imam**)

(**d**) A cantor and a rabbi are both religious functionaries in the Jewish religion, while a muezzin and an imam are both functionaries in Islam. Gurus are commonly found in the religions of Hinduism, Buddhism, and Sikhism. A minaret is the spire of a mosque. Brahmin is the highest of the four traditional social castes in India. The term today is used more broadly to refer to a charismatic leader with many followers.
Humanities—Class

96. ORPHEUS : RETURN OF EURYDICE TO HADES :: WIFE OF LOT : (*a.* transformation into a star, *b.* return to Sodom, ***c.* transformation into a pillar of salt**, *d.* return to Canaan)

(**c**) As a result of Orpheus' looking back when he went to fetch her from the underworld, Eurydice was forced to return to Hades (Greek mythology). As a result of Lot's wife's looking back on Sodom, she was transformed into a pillar of salt (Book of Genesis in the Bible).
Humanities—Description

97. CENTIGRADE : 100 :: KELVIN : (*a.* 132, *b.* 100, *c.* 0, ***d.* 373**)

(**d**) The boiling point of water is 100° Centigrade, and (to the nearest unit) 373 Kelvin.
Natural Science—Description

98. LA GIACONDA : (***a.* Mona Lisa**, *b.* La Pieta, *c.* Madonna, *d.* Venus de Milo) :: ARRANGEMENT IN BLACK AND GRAY : WHISTLER'S MOTHER

(**a**) *La Giaconda* and *Mona Lisa* refer to the same painting by Leonardo da Vinci. *Arrangement in Black and Gray* and *Whistler's Mother* refer to the same painting by Whistler.
Humanities—Similarity/Contrast

99. EMPIRICIST : UTILITARIAN :: HUME : (*a.* Spinoza, *b.* Leibnitz, *c.* Kant, *d.* **Mill**)

(**d**) Hume was an empiricist philosopher; Mill, a utilitarian philosopher. Spinoza and Leibniz were rationalists. Kant tried with his work to build a bridge between empiricists and rationalists.
Humanities—Description

100. BLOOMFIELD : SURFACE STRUCTURE :: (*a.* Whorf, *b.* Sapir, *c.* Skinner, *d.* **Chomsky**) : DEEP STRUCTURE

(**d**) In their respective linguistic analyses, Bloomfield theorized on the basis of surface structure, while Chomsky has theorized primarily on the basis of deep structure. Benjamin Whorf was an American linguist who developed the theory of linguistic relativity. Together with Edward Sapir who was his teacher, he proposed that language affects thoughts (the Sapir-Whorf hypothesis). Burrhus F. Skinner was a psychologist who is known for his work on operant conditioning.
Social Science—Description

101. GERMANIC : EUROPE :: (*a.* Swahili, *b.* **Bantu**, *c.* Zulu, *d.* Nigerian) : AFRICA

(**b**) Germanic languages are found throughout Europe. Bantu languages are found throughout Africa.
General Information—Description

102. EVAPORATE : (*a.* **freeze**, *b.* melt, *c.* dehydrate, *d.* condense) :: VAPOR : SOLID

(**a**) To evaporate is to become vapor. To freeze is to become solid.
Natural Science—Description

103. POSITION : VELOCITY :: VELOCITY : (*a.* speed, *b.* **acceleration**, *c.* torque, *d.* jerk)

(**b**) The measure of the rate of change of position is velocity just as the measure of the rate of change of velocity is acceleration.
Natural Science—Description

104. TESTOSTERONE : HORMONE :: NEURON : (*a.* brain, *b.* dendrite, *c.* tissue, *d.* **cell**)

(**d**) Testosterone is one of many different types of hormones just as a neuron is one of many different types of cells.
Natural Science—Class

105. 1066 : BATTLE OF HASTINGS :: 1588 : (*a.* defeat of Napoleon, *b.* King Philip's War, *c.* **defeat of the Spanish Armada**, *d.* establishment of Jamestown)

(**c**) The year 1066 was when the Battle of Hastings was fought, and 1588 was the year of the defeat of the Spanish Armada. Napoleon's failed invasion of Russia took place in 1812. King Philip's War took place from 1675 to 1676. Jamestown, the first permanent English settlement in North America, was established in 1607.
General Information—Description

106. PSYCHOSOCIAL STAGES : (*a.* **Erickson**, *b.* Freud, *c.* Chomsky, *d.* Lewin) :: DEVELOPMENTAL STAGES : PIAGET

(**a**) This analogy is about theories of psychological stages. A series of psychosocial stages was proposed by Erickson. A series of developmental stages was proposed by Piaget. Freud is famous for the development of psychoanalysis. Chomsky developed a theory of generative grammar; Lewin is considered one of the founders of social psychology.
Social Science—Description

107. HIP : PELVIS:: (*a.* shoulder blade, *b.* kneecap, *c.* **jaw**, *d.* cranium) : MANDIBLE

(**c**) The name of the hipbone is the pelvis just as the name of the jawbone is the mandible.
Natural Science—Similarity/Contrast

108. TANTALUS : SUSTENANCE :: SISYPHUS : (*a.* food, *b.* mobility, *c.* oxygen, *d.* **rest**)

(**d**) In classical mythology, Hades denied Tantalus of sustenance and Sisyphus of rest.
Humanities—Description

109. (*a.* **tsetse fly**, *b.* snail, *c.* roundworm, *d.* housefly) : SLEEPING SICKNESS :: MOSQUITO : MALARIA

(**a**) The tsetse fly is known to spread sleeping sickness, while the mosquito passes malaria.
General Information—Description

110. RICE : CHRISTOPHER :: (*a.* **Kissinger**, *b.* Christopher, *c.* Shultz, *d.* Baker III) : EAGLEBURG

(**a**) Rice and Kissinger were both political scientists who became Secretaries of State. Christopher and Eagleburg were both diplomats who became Secretaries of State. Shultz was an economist, and Baker III was a lawyer.
General Information—Similarity/Contrast

111. (***a*. Mussolini**, *b*. Carbonari, *c*. Ciampi, *d*. Virgil) : ITALY :: HIROHITO : JAPAN

    (**a**) During World War II, Mussolini was the leader of Italy while Hirohito was the leader of Japan. The Carbonari were a secret brotherhood founded in the early 19th century in Italy to overthrow the government. Carlo Ciampi was President of Italy from 1999 to 2006. Virgil was a Roman poet (70 B.C.–19 B.C.).
    General Information—Description

112. VIRILE : FERAL :: ENERGETIC : (*a*. potent, *b*. tame, *c*. angry, ***d*. wild**)

    (**d**) Virile means energetic, while feral means wild and undomesticated.
    Vocabulary—Similarity/Contrast

113. EVA PERON : ARGENTINA :: IMELDA MARCOS : (*a*. Indonesia, *b*. Portugal, ***c*. The Philippines**, *d*. Spain)

    (**c**) Eva Peron was a world-famous first lady of Argentina, and Imelda Marcos was a world-famous first lady of The Philippines.
    General Information—Description

114. (***a*. Rudyard Kipling**, *b*. Salman Rushdie, *c*. Chinua Achebe, *d*. Graham Greene) : INDIA :: JOSEPH CONRAD : THE CONGO

    (**a**) Rudyard Kipling traveled to and wrote fictional literature set in India. Joseph Conrad traveled to and wrote fictional literature set in The Congo. Salman Rushdie is a British-Indian writer who faced death threats by Muslims after the publication of *The Satanic Verses*. Chinua Achebe is a Nigerian writer best known for *Things Fall Apart*. Graham Greene is an English writer whose works often revolved around Catholicism.
    Humanities—Description

115. MARY ANN CROSS : (*a*. Jane Eyre, *b*. Sense and Sensibility, *c*. Virginia Woolf, ***d*. Middlemarch**) :: SAMUEL CLEMENS : TOM SAWYER

    (**d**) Mary Ann Cross used a pen name (George Eliot) in writing her famous novel, *Middlemarch*. Samuel Clemens used a pen name (Mark Twain) in writing his famous novel, *Tom Sawyer*.
    Humanities—Similarity/Contrast

116. TITANIC : ATLANTIC OCEAN :: EDMUND FITZGERALD : (*a*. Pacific Ocean, ***b*. Lake Superior**, *c*. Lake Michigan, *d*. Indian Ocean)

    (**b**) The *Titanic* was a ship that sank in the Atlantic Ocean, and the *Edmund Fitzgerald* was a ship that sank in Lake Superior.
    General Information—Description

117. MURINE : RODENT :: (*a.* ursine, *b.* lupine, *c.* equine, ***d.* vulpine**) : FOX

(**d**) The word murine describes something that is in some way like or relating to a rodent and the word vulpine describes something that is in some way like or relating to a fox. *Ursine* describes something that is like a bear. *Lupine* describes something that is like a wolf, and *equine* describes something that is like a horse.
Vocabulary—Description

118. (***a.* Sancho Panza**, *b.* Tuesday, *c.* Don Quixote, *d.* Candide) : CERVANTES :: FRIDAY : DEFOE

(**a**) Sancho Panza was the loyal friend of the title character in Cervantes' novel *Don Quixote*. Friday was the loyal friend of the title character in Defoe's *Robinson Crusoe*.
Humanities—Description

119. SAILING: (*a.* trim, *b.* batten, ***c.* jibe**, *d.* turnbuckle) :: SKIING : SLALOM

(**c**) To turn back and forth in a zigzag through the water while sailing is called to jibe. To do the same motion while downhill skiing is called to slalom.
General Information—Description

120. NaCl : SALT :: NH_3 : (*a.* bleach, *b.* pepper, *c.* baking soda, ***d.* ammonia**)

(**d**) NaCl is the chemical formula for household salt, while NH_3 is the chemical formula for household ammonia.
Natural Science—Equality/Negation

PRACTICE TEST 1

Item Classification Chart

CONTENT \ RELATIONSHIP	Similarity/ Contrast	Description	Class	Completion	Part/ Whole	Equality/ Negation	Nonsemantic
Vocabulary	3, 21, 25, 26, 54, 67, 69, 60, 62, 64, 71, 112	27, 41, 117	9				
General Information	31, 32, 48, 65, 74, 107, 110	1, 2, 5, 6, 7, 11, 12, 14, 15, 17, 24, 34, 35, 38, 47, 51, 53, 56, 57, 58, 80, 81, 83, 101, 105, 109, 111, 113, 116, 119	10, 20, 84			46, 66	
Humanities	55, 98	8, 16, 18, 19, 28, 39, 49, 50, 52, 61, 63, 68, 73, 76, 77, 78, 85, 87, 88, 89, 91, 92, 93, 94, 96, 99, 108, 114, 115, 118	40, 95	4			
Social Science		22, 29, 37, 86, 100, 106					
Natural Science		13, 23, 36, 42, 44, 45, 72, 82, 97, 102, 103, 104, 120			33	59	
Mathematics					75, 79	90	
Nonsemantic							30, 43, 70

Answer Sheet
PRACTICE TEST 2

1 ⒶⒷⒸⒹ	31 ⒶⒷⒸⒹ	61 ⒶⒷⒸⒹ	91 ⒶⒷⒸⒹ	
2 ⒶⒷⒸⒹ	32 ⒶⒷⒸⒹ	62 ⒶⒷⒸⒹ	92 ⒶⒷⒸⒹ	
3 ⒶⒷⒸⒹ	33 ⒶⒷⒸⒹ	63 ⒶⒷⒸⒹ	93 ⒶⒷⒸⒹ	
4 ⒶⒷⒸⒹ	34 ⒶⒷⒸⒹ	64 ⒶⒷⒸⒹ	94 ⒶⒷⒸⒹ	
5 ⒶⒷⒸⒹ	35 ⒶⒷⒸⒹ	65 ⒶⒷⒸⒹ	95 ⒶⒷⒸⒹ	
6 ⒶⒷⒸⒹ	36 ⒶⒷⒸⒹ	66 ⒶⒷⒸⒹ	96 ⒶⒷⒸⒹ	
7 ⒶⒷⒸⒹ	37 ⒶⒷⒸⒹ	67 ⒶⒷⒸⒹ	97 ⒶⒷⒸⒹ	
8 ⒶⒷⒸⒹ	38 ⒶⒷⒸⒹ	68 ⒶⒷⒸⒹ	98 ⒶⒷⒸⒹ	
9 ⒶⒷⒸⒹ	39 ⒶⒷⒸⒹ	69 ⒶⒷⒸⒹ	99 ⒶⒷⒸⒹ	
10 ⒶⒷⒸⒹ	40 ⒶⒷⒸⒹ	70 ⒶⒷⒸⒹ	100 ⒶⒷⒸⒹ	
11 ⒶⒷⒸⒹ	41 ⒶⒷⒸⒹ	71 ⒶⒷⒸⒹ	101 ⒶⒷⒸⒹ	
12 ⒶⒷⒸⒹ	42 ⒶⒷⒸⒹ	72 ⒶⒷⒸⒹ	102 ⒶⒷⒸⒹ	
13 ⒶⒷⒸⒹ	43 ⒶⒷⒸⒹ	73 ⒶⒷⒸⒹ	103 ⒶⒷⒸⒹ	
14 ⒶⒷⒸⒹ	44 ⒶⒷⒸⒹ	74 ⒶⒷⒸⒹ	104 ⒶⒷⒸⒹ	
15 ⒶⒷⒸⒹ	45 ⒶⒷⒸⒹ	75 ⒶⒷⒸⒹ	105 ⒶⒷⒸⒹ	
16 ⒶⒷⒸⒹ	46 ⒶⒷⒸⒹ	76 ⒶⒷⒸⒹ	106 ⒶⒷⒸⒹ	
17 ⒶⒷⒸⒹ	47 ⒶⒷⒸⒹ	77 ⒶⒷⒸⒹ	107 ⒶⒷⒸⒹ	
18 ⒶⒷⒸⒹ	48 ⒶⒷⒸⒹ	78 ⒶⒷⒸⒹ	108 ⒶⒷⒸⒹ	
19 ⒶⒷⒸⒹ	49 ⒶⒷⒸⒹ	79 ⒶⒷⒸⒹ	109 ⒶⒷⒸⒹ	
20 ⒶⒷⒸⒹ	50 ⒶⒷⒸⒹ	80 ⒶⒷⒸⒹ	110 ⒶⒷⒸⒹ	
21 ⒶⒷⒸⒹ	51 ⒶⒷⒸⒹ	81 ⒶⒷⒸⒹ	111 ⒶⒷⒸⒹ	
22 ⒶⒷⒸⒹ	52 ⒶⒷⒸⒹ	82 ⒶⒷⒸⒹ	112 ⒶⒷⒸⒹ	
23 ⒶⒷⒸⒹ	53 ⒶⒷⒸⒹ	83 ⒶⒷⒸⒹ	113 ⒶⒷⒸⒹ	
24 ⒶⒷⒸⒹ	54 ⒶⒷⒸⒹ	84 ⒶⒷⒸⒹ	114 ⒶⒷⒸⒹ	
25 ⒶⒷⒸⒹ	55 ⒶⒷⒸⒹ	85 ⒶⒷⒸⒹ	115 ⒶⒷⒸⒹ	
26 ⒶⒷⒸⒹ	56 ⒶⒷⒸⒹ	86 ⒶⒷⒸⒹ	116 ⒶⒷⒸⒹ	
27 ⒶⒷⒸⒹ	57 ⒶⒷⒸⒹ	87 ⒶⒷⒸⒹ	117 ⒶⒷⒸⒹ	
28 ⒶⒷⒸⒹ	58 ⒶⒷⒸⒹ	88 ⒶⒷⒸⒹ	118 ⒶⒷⒸⒹ	
29 ⒶⒷⒸⒹ	59 ⒶⒷⒸⒹ	89 ⒶⒷⒸⒹ	119 ⒶⒷⒸⒹ	
30 ⒶⒷⒸⒹ	60 ⒶⒷⒸⒹ	90 ⒶⒷⒸⒹ	120 ⒶⒷⒸⒹ	

Answer Sheet

Practice Test 2

Directions: In each of the following questions, you will find three initial terms and, in parentheses, four answer options designated *a*, *b*, *c*, and *d*. You are to select from the four answer options the one that best completes the analogy with the three initial terms. To record your answers, use the answer sheet provided.

Time: 60 minutes

1. CANDLE : TALLOW :: TIRE : (*a.* automobile, *b.* round, *c.* rubber, *d.* hollow)

2. TERRESTRIAL : (*a.* palatial, *b.* partial, *c.* martial, *d.* celestial) :: EARTH : HEAVEN

3. (*a.* father, *b.* uncle, *c.* brother, *d.* son) : SIBLING :: HUSBAND : SPOUSE

4. 3.6% : (*a.* 0.0036, *b.* 0.036, *c.* 0.36, *d.* 3.6) :: 480% : 4.8

5. PERIODIC : INTERMITTENT :: CONSTANT : (*a.* incessant, *b.* occasional, *c.* infrequent, *d.* never)

6. DARWIN : (*a.* gravity, *b.* planetary orbits, *c.* evolution, *d.* magnetism) :: EINSTEIN : RELATIVITY

7. COMPOSER : SONATA :: (*a.* physicist, *b.* artist, *c.* sculptor, *d.* author) : LITHOGRAPH

8. HUNGRY : LION :: BUSY : (*a.* squirrel, *b.* beaver, *c.* hare, *d.* chipmunk)

9. MATRICIDE : MOTHER :: FRATRICIDE : (*a.* uncle, *b.* father, *c.* brother, *d.* son)

10. (*a.* United, *b.* League, *c.* National, *d.* NFL) : DODGERS :: AMERICAN : YANKEES

11. KNOCK : PIGEON :: KNEED : (*a.* toed, *b.* waisted, *c.* armed, *d.* headed)

12. (*a.* Memorial Day, *b.* Thanksgiving, *c.* Christmas, *d.* Labor Day) : DECORATION DAY :: VETERANS' DAY : ARMISTICE DAY

13. HANG : NOOSE :: BEHEAD : (*a.* guillotine, *b.* Savonarola, *c.* Robespierre, *d.* ablation)

14. APPROPRIATE : INAPPROPRIATE :: APROPOS : (*a.* inapropos, *b.* misapropos, *c.* anapropos, *d.* malapropos)

15. (*a.* gases, *b.* good eating, *c.* intestinal tract, *d.* gasoline) : GASTRONOMY :: HEAVENLY BODIES : ASTRONOMY

16. CONGRESS : UNITED STATES :: (*a.* UNICEF, *b.* Secretary-General, *c.* Security Council, *d.* General Assembly) : UNITED NATIONS

17. EXECUTOR : (*a.* executriss, *b.* executress, *c.* executrex, *d.* executrix) :: ACTOR : ACTRESS

18. CANCEROUS : NONCANCEROUS :: MALIGNANT : (*a.* benign, *b.* benevolent, *c.* beneficent, *d.* latent)

19. (*a.* syllogism, *b.* intellect, *c.* troop movements, *d.* weapons) : LOGISTICS :: LANGUAGE : LINGUISTICS

20. SUBWAY : NEW YORK :: (*a.* Metro, *b.* monorail, *c.* cable car, *d.* airplane) : PARIS

21. (*a.* velocity, *b.* humidity, *c.* pressure, *d.* THI) : BAROMETER :: MILEAGE : ODOMETER

22. KANSAS : WHEAT :: (*a.* Nebraska, *b.* Arkansas, *c.* Wisconsin, *d.* Idaho) : POTATO

23. HYPO : DERMIC :: UNDER : (*a.* skin, *b.* medicine, *c.* blood, *d.* syringe)

24. PECCADILLO : (*a.* stutter, *b.* pretense, *c.* amnesia, *d.* sin) :: MISDEMEANOR : CRIME

25. MISANTHROPE : (*a.* life, *b.* religion, *c.* women, *d.* people) :: MISOGAMIST : MARRIAGE

26. OSTENTATIOUS : (*a.* showy, *b.* proud, *c.* modest, *d.* fickle) :: ONEROUS : BURDENSOME

27. NATURE : NURTURE :: HEREDITY : (*a.* gene, *b.* progenitor, *c.* evolution, *d.* environment)

28. HURRY : SCURRY :: HURLY : (*a.* burly, *b.* curly, *c.* gurly, *d.* wurly)

29. STEM : METS :: (*a.* tab, *b.* ball, *c.* team, *d.* root) : BAT

30. SATAN : BEELZEBUB :: DEVIL : (*a.* Charon, *b.* Pandemonium, *c.* Lucifer, *d.* Hades)

31. FORT SUMTER : CIVIL WAR :: (*a.* Valley Forge, *b.* Princeton, *c.* Lexington, *d.* Trenton) : AMERICAN REVOLUTION

32. (*a.* chameleon, *b.* salamander, *c.* tadpole, *d.* chamois) : FICKLE :: MULE : STUBBORN

33. NEW AMSTERDAM : NEW YORK :: CONSTANTINOPLE : (*a.* Budapest, *b.* Istanbul, *c.* Cairo, *d.* Baghdad)

34. ANESTHESIA : FEEL :: (*a.* eyeball, *b.* eyes, *c.* glasses, *d.* blindness) : SEE

35. CORPORAL : BEAT :: CAPITAL : (*a.* stun, *b.* spend, *c.* kill, *d.* shock)

36. (*a.* neutron, *b.* electron, *c.* nucleon, *d.* positron) : PROTON :: NEGATIVE : POSITIVE

37. CARPE : DIEM :: CAVEAT : (*a.* corpus, *b.* emptor, *c.* deum, *d.* mandamus)

38. RAIN : (*a.* tempest, *b.* frost, *c.* hail, *d.* dry ice) :: WATER : ICE

39. FEINT : (*a.* fall, *b.* remove, *c.* pretend, *d.* authenticate) :: SEVER : SEPARATE

40. 10 : COMMANDMENTS :: (*a.* 5, *b.* 7, *c.* 10, *d.* 12) : DEADLY SINS

41. DOUBLE ENTENDRE : (*a.* ambiguity, *b.* treachery, *c.* meaninglessness, *d.* misperception) :: DOUBLE TAKE : DELAYED REACTION

42. (*a.* nominalism, *b.* phenomenalism, *c.* determinism, *d.* rationalism) : FATALISM :: EXISTENTIALISM : FREE WILL

43. (*a.* carmine, *b.* yellow, *c.* brown, *d.* orange) : RED :: AZURE : BLUE

44. FRAME : PICTURE :: (*a.* cell wall, *b.* endoplasmic reticulum, *c.* cytoplasm, *d.* nuclear envelope) : CELL

45. (*a.* keno, *b.* kalaha, *c.* wari, *d.* soma) : CRAPS :: ROULETTE : TWENTY-ONE

46. HECTOR : (*a.* Rome, *b.* Carthage, *c.* Sicily, *d.* Troy) :: ACHILLES : GREECE

47. KUNG FU : JUDO :: (*a.* Korean, *b.* Chinese, *c.* Vietnamese, *d.* Japanese) : JAPANESE

48. SWARM : BEES :: (*a.* colony, *b.* covey, *c.* pack, *d.* pride) : QUAIL

49. BITUMINOUS : ANTHRACITE :: (*a.* wood, *b.* lead, *c.* lignite, *d.* oil) : STEEL

50. CARRY NATION : (*a.* women's suffrage, *b.* low-income housing, *c.* temperance, *d.* abolition of child labor) :: MARTIN LUTHER KING, JR. : CIVIL RIGHTS

51. STENCIL : LETTERS :: COMPASS : (*a.* time, *b.* direction, *c.* northwest, *d.* circle)

52. (*a.* proposal, *b.* talk, *c.* dissertation, *d.* dialogue) : ORATION :: QUIZ : EXAMINATION

53. ANTERIOR : POSTERIOR :: (*a.* ventral, *b.* lateral, *c.* external, *d.* internal) : DORSAL

54. IMMIGRATION : EMIGRATION :: ENTRY : (*a.* expulsion, *b.* migration, *c.* egress, *d.* estuary)

55. SATRAP : (*a.* ruler, *b.* bush, *c.* miser, *d.* loner) :: TRAP : AMBUSH

56. ELEGY : LAMENTING :: EPIGRAM : (*a.* inane, *b.* abstruse, *c.* witty, *d.* obtuse)

57. REFORMATION : PROTESTANTS :: COUNTER-REFORMATION : (*a.* Catholics, *b.* Protestants, *c.* Anglicans, *d.* Jews)

58. (*a.* beriberi, *b.* rickets, *c.* anemia, *d.* pellagra) : D :: SCURVY : C

59. GO DUTCH : PAY YOUR OWN EXPENSES :: IN DUTCH : (*a.* in luck, *b.* in trouble, *c.* rich, *d.* poor)

60. FOOL'S GOLD : (*a.* ore, *b.* pyrite, *c.* bauxite, *d.* manganese) :: PENCIL LEAD : GRAPHITE

61. MILL : (*a.* franc, *b.* centime, *c.* shilling, *d.* cent) :: PENNY : DIME

62. (*a.* Spain, *b.* Italy, *c.* Israel, *d.* Lebanon) : RUSSIA :: EL AL : AEROFLOT

63. GAUGUIN : (*a.* England, *b.* U.S.A., *c.* Tahiti, *d.* Madagascar) :: GOYA : SPAIN

64. (*a.* bifteck, *b.* legume, *c.* glace, *d.* poulet) : STEAK :: ESCARGOTS : SNAILS

65. TEMERITY : AUDACITY :: (*a.* softness, *b.* boldness, *c.* shyness, *d.* depravity) : BRAVERY

66. CALORIE : (*a.* weight, *b.* basal metabolism, *c.* fat, *d.* energy) :: DECADE : TIME

67. PETROLOGY : (*a.* sandstone, *b.* brontosaurus, *c.* moth, *d.* nylon) :: BOTANY : ROSE

68. HANSEL : GRETEL :: ORESTES : (*a.* Jocasta, *b.* Electra, *c.* Ophelia, *d.* Alicia)

69. (*a.* rude, *b.* talkative, *c.* immodest, *d.* brash) : GARRULOUS :: PETULANT : PEEVISH

70. PONCE DE LEON : (*a.* Atlantic Ocean, *b.* Mexico, *c.* Georgia, *d.* Florida) :: BALBOA : PACIFIC OCEAN

71. ATTENUATE : (*a.* disprove, *b.* weaken, *c.* prove, *d.* strengthen) :: ATTRACT : REPEL

72. CEREBRUM : THINKING :: CEREBELLUM : (*a.* olfaction, *b.* muscular coordination, *c.* glandular secretion, *d.* audition)

73. BEHAVIORISM : U.S.A. :: GESTALT : (*a.* France, *b.* England, *c.* Switzerland, *d.* Germany)

74. MONROE : (*a.* Treatise, *b.* Edict, *c.* Decree, *d.* Code) :: DOCTRINE : NAPOLEON

75. LXII : CLXXXVI :: D : (*a.* M, *b.* MC, *c.* MD, *d.* MM)

76. (*a.* loudness, *b.* compression, *c.* brightness, *d.* hardness) : MOHS :: TEMPERATURE : KELVIN

77. FOX : OWL :: (*a.* Saul, *b.* David, *c.* Iago, *d.* Lear) : SOLOMON

78. 1 : LINE :: 2 : (*a.* length, *b.* ellipse, *c.* point, *d.* sphere)

79. EXOSKELETON : LOBSTER :: ENDOSKELETON : (*a.* oyster, *b.* tiger, *c.* barnacle, *d.* worm)

80. FEZ : SOMBRERO :: BERET : (*a.* phylactery, *b.* millinery, *c.* muffler, *d.* fedora)

81. (*a.* angry, *b.* sanguine, *c.* dejected, *d.* pale) : PESSIMISTIC :: HOPEFUL : DISPIRITED

82. $4^{1/2}$: $9^{1/2}$ :: $36^{1/2}$: (*a.* 6, *b.* 9, *c.* 12, *d.* 81)

83. INCUBUS : (*a.* faccubus, *b.* excubus, *c.* succubus, *d.* maccubus) :: WOMEN : MEN

84. HEAD MONEY : (*a.* warn, *b.* punish, *c.* capture, *d.* bribe) :: HUSH MONEY : SILENCE

85. SUSTAIN : OVERRULE :: IN CAMERA : (*a.* in trouble, *b.* in public, *c.* in court, *d.* out of court)

86. CRONUS : SATURN :: (*a.* Poseidon, *b.* Ares, *c.* Zeus, *d.* Hermes) : MARS

87. D MINOR : F MAJOR :: (*a.* E minor, *b.* F minor, *c.* F# minor, *d.* G# minor) : A MAJOR

88. TAME : MATE :: LAME : (*a.* female, *b.* injured, *c.* male, *d.* excuse)

89. (*a.* spinal, *b.* neutral, *c.* temporal, *d.* spatial) : PARIETAL :: OCCIPITAL : FRONTAL

90. PARADISE : LOST :: JERUSALEM : (*a.* Sanctified, *b.* Discovered, *c.* Delivered, *d.* Vanquished)

91. PENN : PENNSYLVANIA :: CALVERT : (*a.* South Carolina, *b.* Vermont, *c.* Maryland, *d.* Rhode Island)

92. ETEOCLES : (*a.* Theseus, *b.* Laius, *c.* Oedipus, *d.* Polynices) :: ANTIGONE : ISMENE

93. DECIMAL : 10 :: DUODECIMAL : (*a.* 2, *b.* 8, *c.* 12, *d.* 16)

94. RATIONALIST : EMPIRICIST :: (*a.* Berkeley, *b.* Hume, *c.* Mill, *d.* Leibniz) : LOCKE

95. (*a.* Ivan Karamazov, *b.* Anna Karenina, *c.* Nicolai Gogol, *d.* Grigory Smirnov) : DOSTOYEVSKY :: THÉRÈSE : MAURIAC

96. PALESTRINA : 16th :: (*a.* Beethoven, *b.* Bach, *c.* Tchaikovsky, *d.* Stravinsky) : 20th

97. NICHOLAS II : RUSSIAN REVOLUTION :: (*a.* Louis XIV, *b.* Louis XV, *c.* Louis XVI, *d.* Louis XVII) : FRENCH REVOLUTION

98. GLENN GOULD : PIANO :: YO-YO MA : (*a.* piano, *b.* violin, *c.* cello, *d.* clarinet)

99. (*a.* Versailles, *b.* Xanadu, *c.* St. Malo, *d.* Rouen) : LOUIS XIV :: AMBOISE : FRANCIS II

100. ISHMAEL : (*a.* Hagar, *b.* Rebeccah, *c.* Esther, *d.* Sophia) :: ISAAC : SARAH

101. COLITIS : COLON :: ENCEPHALITIS : (*a.* brain, *b.* duodenum, *c.* pancreas, *d.* liver)

102. GOLDA MEIR : (*a.* Poland, *b.* Israel, *c.* United States, *d.* Czech Republic) :: MARGARET THATCHER : GREAT BRITAIN

103. PICCOLO : FLUTE :: EUPHONIUM : (*a.* phonograph, *b.* tuba, *c.* organ, *d.* homonym)

104. FORCE : DISTANCE :: (*a.* mass × acceleration, *b.* friction × momentum, *c.* volume / temperature, *d.* mass / energy) : RATE × TIME

105. (*a.* spear, *b.* cupid, *c.* arrow, *d.* wing) : LOVE :: SCYTHE : DEATH

106. CEILING : GLASS :: (*a.* heart, *b.* wall, *c.* side, *d.* curtain) : IRON

107. LEGS : EGGS :: FROG : (*a.* chicken, *b.* dolphin, *c.* sturgeon, *d.* goose)

108. GOAT : (*a.* pan, *b.* faun, *c.* pegasus, *d.* minotaur) :: HORSE : CENTAUR

109. ORCZY : PIMPERNEL :: HAWTHORNE : (*a.* letter, *b.* rose, *c.* wind, *d.* tide)

110. GUSTAV : (*a.* Wolfgang, *b.* Friedrich, *c.* Johann, *d.* Ludwig) :: MAHLER : BEETHOVEN

111. RESTIVE : TRANQUIL :: VERBOSE : (*a.* loquacious, *b.* timorous, *c.* talkative, *d.* taciturn)

112. HOLY SEE : (*a.* Rome, *b.* Hungary, *c.* Italy, *d.* Chad) :: LESOTHO : SOUTH AFRICA

113. LEAGUE OF NATIONS : UNITED NATIONS :: THE ARTICLES OF CONFEDERATION : (*a.* U.S. Constitution, *b.* The Bill of Rights, *c.* Human Rights Treaty, *d.* The Constitution of the Confederate States)

114. AM : AMPLITUDE :: FM : (*a.* force, *b.* frequency, *c.* Fahrenheit, *d.* friction)

115. (*a.* England, *b.* Waterloo, *c.* Russia, *d.* Elba) : NAPOLEON :: LITTLE BIG HORN RIVER : CUSTER

116. ROMEO : JULIET :: PYRAMUS : (*a.* Thisbe, *b.* Titania, *c.* Helen, *d.* Athena)

117. GOAT : WORM :: (*a.* wool, *b.* felt, *c.* cashmere, *d.* chinchilla) : SILK

118. XXIX : 29 :: MDVI : (*a.* 1551, *b.* 1056, *c.* 1061, *d.* 1506)

119. GUANINE : (*a.* cytosine, *b.* purine, *c.* uracil, *d.* pyrimidine) :: ADENINE : THYMINE

120. ESOPHAGUS : SARCOPHAGUS :: GULLET : (*a.* trachea, *b.* monument, *c.* stone coffin, *d.* crystal chandelier)

Answer Key
PRACTICE TEST 2

1.	C	31.	C	61.	D	91.	C
2.	D	32.	A	62.	C	92.	D
3.	C	33.	B	63.	C	93.	C
4.	B	34.	D	64.	A	94.	D
5.	A	35.	C	65.	B	95.	A
6.	C	36.	B	66.	D	96.	D
7.	B	37.	B	67.	A	97.	C
8.	B	38.	C	68.	B	98.	C
9.	C	39.	C	69.	B	99.	A
10.	C	40.	B	70.	D	100.	A
11.	A	41.	A	71.	D	101.	A
12.	A	42.	C	72.	B	102.	B
13.	A	43.	A	73.	D	103.	B
14.	D	44.	A	74.	D	104.	A
15.	B	45.	A	75.	C	105.	C
16.	D	46.	D	76.	D	106.	D
17.	D	47.	B	77.	C	107.	C
18.	A	48.	B	78.	B	108.	B
19.	C	49.	B	79.	B	109.	A
20.	A	50.	C	80.	D	110.	D
21.	C	51.	D	81.	B	111.	D
22.	D	52.	B	82.	B	112.	C
23.	A	53.	A	83.	C	113.	A
24.	D	54.	C	84.	C	114.	B
25.	D	55.	A	85.	B	115.	B
26.	A	56.	C	86.	B	116.	A
27.	D	57.	A	87.	C	117.	C
28.	A	58.	B	88.	C	118.	D
29.	A	59.	B	89.	C	119.	A
30.	C	60.	B	90.	C	120.	C

Answer Key

EXPLANATION OF ANSWERS FOR PRACTICE TEST 2

In the following explanations of answers, explanations concerning the correct response are in a large font. Explanations regarding distracters (incorrect responses) that are not self-explaining or could be misinterpreted are in a smaller font in order to highlight the explanations of the answers that are correct.

1. CANDLE : TALLOW :: TIRE : (*a.* automobile, *b.* round, *c.* **rubber**, *d.* hollow)

   (**c**) A candle is frequently made of tallow. A tire is frequently made of rubber.
   General Information—Description

2. TERRESTRIAL : (*a.* palatial, *b.* partial, *c.* martial, *d.* **celestial**) :: EARTH : HEAVEN

   (**d**) Something that is terrestrial is of the earth. Something that is celestial is of heaven.
   Vocabulary—Description

3. (*a.* father, *b.* uncle, *c.* **brother**, *d.* son) : SIBLING :: HUSBAND : SPOUSE

   (**c**) A brother is a sibling. A husband is a spouse.
   Vocabulary—Description

4. 3.6% : (*a.* 0.0036, *b.* **0.036**, *c.* 0.36, *d.* 3.6) :: 480% : 4.8

   (**b**) 3.6% is equal to 0.036. 480% is equal to 4.8.
   Mathematics—Equality/Negation

5. PERIODIC : INTERMITTENT :: CONSTANT : (*a.* **incessant**, *b.* occasional, *c.* infrequent, *d.* never)

   (**a**) *Periodic* and *intermittent* are synonyms, as are *constant* and *incessant*.
   Vocabulary—Similarity/Contrast

6. DARWIN : (*a.* gravity, *b.* planetary orbits, *c.* **evolution**, *d.* magnetism) :: EINSTEIN : RELATIVITY

   (**c**) Charles Darwin is primarily responsible for the theory of evolution, while Albert Einstein is primarily responsible for relativity theory.
   Natural Scicence—Description

7. COMPOSER : SONATA :: (*a.* physicist, ***b.* artist**, *c.* sculptor, *d.* author) : LITHOGRAPH

(**b**) A sonata is the creation of a composer. A lithograph is the creation of an artist.
Humanities—Description

8. HUNGRY : LION :: BUSY : (*a.* squirrel, ***b.* beaver**, *c.* hare, *d.* chipmunk)

(**b**) "Hungry as a lion" and "busy as a beaver" are both common similes used in everyday speech.
General Information—Description

9. MATRICIDE : MOTHER :: FRATRICIDE : (*a.* uncle, *b.* father, ***c.* brother**, *d.* son)

(**c**) The act of killing one's mother is called matricide. The act of killing one's brother is called fratricide. The act of killing one's uncle is called avunculicide; the act of killing one's father is called patricide; the act of killing one's son is called filicide.
Vocabulary—Description

10. (*a.* United, *b.* League, ***c.* National**, *d.* NFL) : DODGERS :: AMERICAN : YANKEES

(**c**) The Dodgers are a National League baseball team, while the Yankees are an American League team. The American League is the more recent of the two leagues making up American Major League Baseball. The older is the National League.
General Information—Description

11. KNOCK : PIGEON :: KNEED : (***a.* toed**, *b.* waisted, *c.* armed, *d.* headed)

(**a**) A person may be referred to as knock-kneed or pigeon-toed. *Knock-kneed* means that a person's knees touch each other when he or she is standing straight. A pigeon-toed person's toes point inward when he or she walks.
General Information—Completion

12. (***a.* Memorial Day**, *b.* Thanksgiving, *c.* Christmas, *d.* Labor Day) : DECORATION DAY :: VETERANS' DAY : ARMISTICE DAY

(**a**) Memorial Day and Decoration Day are two names for the same holiday. Veterans' Day and Armistice Day are also two names for the same holiday.
General Information—Similarity/Contrast

13. HANG : NOOSE :: BEHEAD : (*a.* **guillotine**, *b.* Savonarola, *c.* Robespierre, *d.* ablation)

(**a**) A person is hanged with a noose, but beheaded with a guillotine. Girolamo Savonarola was a religious and political reformer, known for his book burnings and opposition to Pope Alexander VI. Maximilien Robespierre was one of the most famous personalities of the French Revolution and played an important role during what is known as the *Reign of Terror. Ablation* refers to the surgical removal of a body part or tissue.
General Information—Description

14. APPROPRIATE : INAPPROPRIATE :: APROPOS : (*a.* inapropos, *b.* misapropos, *c.* anapropos, *d.* **malapropos**)

(**d**) Something that is not appropriate is inappropriate. Something that is not apropos is malapropos.
Vocabulary—Similarity/Contrast

15. (*a.* gases, *b.* **good eating**, *c.* intestinal tract, *d.* gasoline) : GASTRONOMY :: HEAVENLY BODIES : ASTRONOMY

(**b**) Gastronomy is the study of good eating. Astronomy is the study of heavenly bodies.
General Information—Description

16. CONGRESS : UNITED STATES :: (*a.* UNICEF, *b.* Secretary-General, *c.* Security Council, *d.* **General Assembly**) : UNITED NATIONS

(**d**) The Congress is the main legislative body of the United States. The General Assembly is the main legislative body of the United Nations.
General Information—Description

17. EXECUTOR : (*a.* executriss, *b.* executress, *c.* executrex, *d.* **executrix**) :: ACTOR : ACTRESS

(**d**) The feminine form of *executor* is *executrix*. The feminine form of *actor* is *actress*.
General Information—Class

18. CANCEROUS : NONCANCEROUS :: MALIGNANT : (*a.* **benign**, *b.* benevolent, *c.* beneficent, *d.* latent)

(**a**) A cancerous tumor is called malignant. A noncancerous tumor is called benign.
General Information—Similarity/Contrast

19. (*a*. syllogism, *b*. intellect, **c. troop movements**, *d*. weapons) :
LOGISTICS :: LANGUAGE : LINGUISTICS

(**c**) Logistics is the study of troop movements. Linguistics is the study
of language.
General Information—Description

20. SUBWAY : NEW YORK :: (**a. Metro**, *b*. monorail, *c*. cable car, *d*. airplane) :
PARIS

(**a**) What is called a subway in New York is called the Metro in Paris.
General Information—Description

21. (*a*. velocity, *b*. humidity, **c. pressure**, *d*. THI) : BAROMETER :: MILEAGE
: ODOMETER

(**c**) A barometer measures pressure. An odometer measures mileage.
General Information—Description

22. KANSAS : WHEAT :: (*a*. Nebraska, *b*. Arkansas, *c*. Wisconsin, **d. Idaho**) :
POTATO

(**d**) Kansas is known for its wheat fields, Idaho for its potato fields.
General Information—Description

23. HYPO : DERMIC :: UNDER : (**a. skin**, *b*. medicine, *c*. blood, *d*. syringe)

(**a**) A hypodermic needle goes under (hypo) the skin (dermis).
Vocabulary—Similarity/Contrast

24. PECCADILLO : (*a*. stutter, *b*. pretense, *c*. amnesia, **d. sin**) ::
MISDEMEANOR : CRIME

(**d**) A peccadillo is a minor sin. A misdemeanor is a minor crime.
Vocabulary—Description

25. MISANTHROPE : (*a*. life, *b*. religion, *c*. women, **d. people**) ::
MISOGAMIST : MARRIAGE

(**d**) A misanthrope detests people. A misogamist detests marriage.
Vocabulary—Description

26. OSTENTATIOUS : (**a. showy**, *b*. proud, *c*. modest, *d*. fickle) ::
ONEROUS : BURDENSOME

(**a**) *Ostentatious* means showy. *Onerous* means burdensome.
Vocabulary—Similarity/Contrast

Explanation of Answers

27. NATURE : NURTURE :: HEREDITY : (*a.* gene, *b.* progenitor, *c.* evolution, ***d.* environment**)

(**d**) A "nature—nurture" controversy is one between the effects of heredity and environment.
General Information—Description

28. HURRY : SCURRY :: HURLY : (***a.* burly**, *b.* curly, *c.* gurly, *d.* wurly)

(**a**) *Hurry-scurry* and *hurly-burly* both refer to disorder and confusion.
Vocabulary—Completion

29. STEM : METS :: (***a.* tab**, *b.* ball, *c.* team, *d.* root) : BAT

(**a**) *Stem* spelled backwards is *mets*. *Tab* spelled backwards is *bat*.
Nonsemantic

30. SATAN : BEELZEBUB :: DEVIL : (*a.* Charon, *b.* Pandemonium, ***c.* Lucifer**, *d.* Hades)

(**c**) Satan, Beelzebub, the Devil, and Lucifer are all different names for the same entity. Charon is a figure from Greek mythology. He was a ferryman and carried the dead across the river Styx into the underworld, Hades. Pandemonium commonly refers to a state of wild confusion and is derived from its Greek mythological meaning of "the entirety of all Demons."
Humanities—Similarity/Contrast

31. FORT SUMTER : CIVIL WAR :: (*a.* Valley Forge, *b.* Princeton, ***c.* Lexington**, *d.* Trenton) : AMERICAN REVOLUTION

(**c**) Fort Sumter was the scene of the first battle of the Civil War. Lexington was the scene of the first battle of the American Revolution. The Continental Army had its campsite over the winter of 1777–1778 in Valley Forge during the American Revolutionary War. The forces of General Washington defeated the British in the Battle of Princeton in 1777. The Battle of Trenton took place in 1776 after General Washington's crossing of the Delaware.
Humanities—Description

32. (***a.* chameleon**, *b.* salamander, *c.* tadpole, *d.* chamois) : FICKLE :: MULE : STUBBORN

(**a**) A chameleon is fickle; a mule, stubborn.
General Information—Description

33. NEW AMSTERDAM : NEW YORK :: CONSTANTINOPLE : (*a.* Budapest, ***b.* Istanbul**, *c.* Cairo, *d.* Baghdad)

(**b**) New Amsterdam is a former name of New York City. Constantinople is a former name of Istanbul.
General Information—Similarity/Contrast

34. ANESTHESIA : FEEL :: (*a.* eyeball, *b.* eyes, *c.* glasses, ***d.* blindness**) : SEE

(**d**) Anesthesia is a state in which one does not feel. Blindness is a state in which one does not see.
General Information—Description

35. CORPORAL : BEAT :: CAPITAL : (*a.* stun, *b.* spend, ***c.* kill**, *d.* shock)

(**c**) In corporal punishment, a person is beaten. In capital punishment, a person is killed.
General Information—Description

36. (*a.* neutron, ***b.* electron**, *c.* nucleon, *d.* positron) : PROTON :: NEGATIVE : POSITIVE

(**b**) An electron has a negative electrical charge. A proton has a positive electrical charge.
Natural Science—Description

37. CARPE : DIEM :: CAVEAT : (*a.* corpus, ***b.* emptor**, *c.* deum, *d.* mandamus)

(**b**) *Carpe diem* (seize the opportunity—literally, the day) and *caveat emptor* (let the buyer beware) are both Latinisms used in English. *Corpus* means "body"; *deum* is the accusative of the Latin word *deus* (God); *mandamus* means "we command."
Vocabulary—Completion

38. RAIN : (*a.* tempest, *b.* frost, ***c.* hail**, *d.* dry ice) :: WATER : ICE

(**c**) Hail is frozen rain; ice is frozen water.
General Information—Class

39. FEINT : (*a.* fall, *b.* remove, ***c.* pretend**, *d.* authenticate) :: SEVER : SEPARATE

(**c**) To feint is to pretend. To sever is to separate.
Vocabulary—Similarity/Contrast

40. 10 : COMMANDMENTS :: (*a.* 5, ***b.* 7**, *c.* 10, *d.* 12) : DEADLY SINS

(**b**) There are 10 Commandments and 7 deadly sins. The 10 Commandments are found in the Old Testament of the Bible; the 7 deadly sins originated in early Christian doctrine.
General Information—Class

41. DOUBLE ENTENDRE : (***a.* ambiguity**, *b.* treachery, *c.* meaninglessness, *d.* misperception) :: DOUBLE TAKE : DELAYED REACTION

(**a**) A double entendre is characterized by ambiguity. A double take is characterized by a delayed reaction.
Vocabulary—Similarity/Contrast

42. (*a.* nominalism, *b.* phenomenalism, *c.* **determinism**, *d.* rationalism) : FATALISM :: EXISTENTIALISM : FREE WILL

(**c**) The philosophical doctrine of determinism argues for fatalism. The doctrine of existentialism argues for free will. Nominalism refers to a doctrine stating that various objects that have the same name have nothing in common but that name. Phenomenalism refers to a theory that limits knowledge to phenomena only. Rationalism is a theory stating that reason is a source of knowledge superior to the perceptions of senses.
Humanities—Description

43. (*a.* **carmine**, *b.* yellow, *c.* brown, *d.* orange) : RED :: AZURE : BLUE

(**a**) Carmine is a shade of red. Azure is a shade of blue.
General Information—Class

44. FRAME : PICTURE :: (*a.* **cell wall**, *b.* endoplasmic reticulum, *c.* cytoplasm, *d.* nuclear envelope) : CELL

(**a**) A frame surrounds a picture. A cell wall surrounds a cell. The endoplasmic reticulum is a system of interconnected cytoplasmic membranes that functions especially in the transport of materials within the cell. Cytoplasm is the organized complex of inorganic and organic substances external to the nuclear membrane of a cell. The nuclear envelope is a membrane system that surrounds the nucleus of eukaryotic cells.
Natural Science—Description

45. (*a.* **keno**, *b.* kalaha, *c.* wari, *d.* soma) : CRAPS :: ROULETTE : TWENTY-ONE

(**a**) Keno, craps, roulette, and twenty-one are all gambling games. Kalaha is a game in the mancala family (board games mainly played in Africa that have a role similar to chess in Western culture). Wari is the Malinese name of an adult game often called Oware, which is played in Africa and the Caribbean. Soma is an intoxicating, ritual drink used in Ancient India.
General Information—Class

46. HECTOR : (*a.* Rome, *b.* Carthage, *c.* Sicily, *d.* **Troy**) :: ACHILLES : GREECE

(**d**) In the Trojan War, Hector fought for Troy and Achilles fought for Greece.
Humanities—Description

47. KUNG FU : JUDO :: (*a.* Korean, *b.* **Chinese**, *c.* Vietnamese, *d.* Japanese) : JAPANESE

   (**b**) Kung Fu is a Chinese form of martial arts; Judo is a Japanese form of martial arts.
   General Information—Class

48. SWARM : BEES :: (*a.* colony, *b.* **covey**, *c.* pack, *d.* pride) : QUAIL

   (**b**) A group of bees is referred to as a swarm. A group of quail is referred to as a covey.
   General Information—Description

49. BITUMINOUS : ANTHRACITE :: (*a.* wood, *b.* **lead**, *c.* lignite, *d.* oil) : STEEL

   (**b**) Bituminous coal is soft, and anthracite coal is hard. Lead is a soft metal, and steel a hard metal.
   General Information—Class

50. CARRY NATION : (*a.* women's suffrage, *b.* low-income housing, *c.* **temperance**, *d.* abolition of child labor) :: MARTIN LUTHER KING, JR. : CIVIL RIGHTS

   (**c**) Carry Nation fought for temperance, while Martin Luther King, Jr. fought for civil rights.
   Humanities—Description

51. STENCIL : LETTERS :: COMPASS : (*a.* time, *b.* direction, *c.* northwest, *d.* **circle**)

   (**d**) A stencil is used to draw letters. A compass is used to draw a circle.
   Mathematics—Description

52. (*a.* proposal, *b.* **talk**, *c.* dissertation, *d.* dialogue) : ORATION :: QUIZ : EXAMINATION

   (**b**) An oration is a large-scale talk. An examination is a large-scale quiz.
   Vocabulary—Description

53. ANTERIOR : POSTERIOR :: (*a.* **ventral**, *b.* lateral, *c.* external, *d.* internal) : DORSAL

   (**a**) In humans, the anterior and ventral sides are the front. The posterior and dorsal sides are the rear.
   Natural Science—Similarity/Contrast

54. IMMIGRATION : EMIGRATION :: ENTRY : (*a.* expulsion, *b.* migration, ***c.* egress**, *d.* estuary)

    (**c**) Immigration is entry into a country, while emigration is egress from a country.
    Vocabulary—Similarity/Contrast

55. SATRAP : (***a.* ruler**, *b.* bush, *c.* miser, *d.* loner) :: TRAP : AMBUSH

    (**a**) A satrap is one kind of ruler (a governor of provinces in Ancient Persia). A trap is a kind of ambush.
    Vocabulary—Similarity/Contrast

56. ELEGY : LAMENTING :: EPIGRAM : (*a.* inane, *b.* abstruse, ***b.* witty**, *d.* obtuse)

    (**c**) An elegy is lamenting. An epigram is witty.
    Vocabulary—Description

57. REFORMATION : PROTESTANTS :: COUNTER-REFORMATION : (***a.* Catholics**, *b.* Protestants, *c.* Anglicans, *d.* Jews)

    (**a**) The Reformation was staged by Protestants, while the Counter-Reformation was staged by Catholics.
    Humanities—Description

58. (*a.* beriberi, ***b.* rickets**, *c.* anemia, *d.* pellagra) : D :: SCURVY : C

    (**b**) Rickets is caused by a deficiency of vitamin D. Scurvy is caused by a deficiency of vitamin C. Beriberi is caused by a lack of thiamine. Anemia can be caused through a decreased production of red blood cells in the bone marrow or heavy blood loss, among other causes. Pellagra is caused by lack of niacin.
    Natural Sciences—Description

59. GO DUTCH : PAY YOUR OWN EXPENSES :: IN DUTCH : (*a.* in luck, ***b.* in trouble**, *c.* rich, *d.* poor)

    (**b**) To go Dutch is to pay your own expenses. To be in Dutch is to be in trouble.
    Vocabulary—Similarity/Contrast

60. FOOL'S GOLD : (*a.* ore, ***b.* pyrite**, *c.* bauxite, *d.* manganese) :: PENCIL LEAD : GRAPHITE

    (**b**) Fool's gold is pyrite. Pencil lead is graphite.
    General Information—Similarity/Contrast

61. MILL : (*a.* franc, *b.* centime, *c.* shilling, ***d.* cent**) :: PENNY : DIME

(**d**) A mill is a tenth of a cent. A penny is a tenth of a dime.
General Information—Part/Whole

62. (*a.* Spain, *b.* Italy, ***c.* Israel**, *d.* Lebanon) : RUSSIA :: EL AL : AEROFLOT

(**c**) El Al is an Israeli airline, while Aeroflot is an airline of Russia.
An airline in Spain is Iberia, an airline in Italy is Alitalia, and an airline in Lebanon
is Airliban.
General Information—Description

63. GAUGUIN : (*a.* England, *b.* U.S.A., ***c.* Tahiti**, *d.* Madagascar) :: GOYA :
SPAIN

(**c**) Gauguin is famous for his paintings relating to Tahiti. Goya is famous
for his paintings relating to Spain.
Humanities—Description

64. (***a.* bifteck**, *b.* legume, *c.* glace, *d.* poulet) : STEAK :: ESCARGOTS :
SNAILS

(**a**) In France, steak is called bifteck, while snails are called escargots.
General Information—Similarity/Contrast

65. TEMERITY : AUDACITY :: (*a.* softness, ***b.* boldness**, *c.* shyness,
d. depravity) : BRAVERY

(**b**) *Temerity, audacity, boldness,* and *bravery* are synonyms.
Vocabulary—Similarity/Contrast

66. CALORIE : (*a.* weight, *b.* basal metabolism, *c.* fat, ***d.* energy**) :: DECADE :
TIME

(**d**) A calorie is a measure of energy. A decade is a measure of time.
Natural Science—Description

67. PETROLOGY : (***a.* sandstone**, *b.* Brontosaurus, *c.* moth, *d.* nylon) ::
BOTANY : ROSE

(**a**) Petrology is the study of rocks, among which is sandstone.
Botany is the study of plants, among which is a rose.
Natural Science—Description

Explanation of Answers

68. HANSEL : GRETEL :: ORESTES : (*a.* Jocasta, ***b.* Electra**, *c.* Ophelia, *d.* Alicia)

(**b**) Hansel and Gretel were brother and sister, as were Orestes and Electra. Hansel and Gretel are characters in one of the Brother Grimm's fairytales. Orestes and Electra were son and daughter of Agamemnon. Jocasta was the wife of Laius, mother and wife of Oedipus, and the mother of Antigone. Ophelia is Hamlet's love in Shakespeare's play *Hamlet*. Alicia is a distracter term that has no particular meaning in this context.
Humanities—Class

69. (*a.* rude, ***b.* talkative**, *c.* immodest, *d.* brash) : GARRULOUS ::
PETULANT : PEEVISH

(**b**) A garrulous person is talkative; a petulant person is peevish.
Vocabulary—Similarity/Contrast

70. PONCE DE LEON : (*a.* Atlantic Ocean, *b.* Mexico, *c.* Georgia, ***d.* Florida**) :: BALBOA : PACIFIC OCEAN

(**d**) Ponce de Leon discovered Florida; Balboa discovered the Pacific Ocean.
Humanities—Description

71. ATTENUATE : (*a.* disprove, *b.* weaken, *c.* prove, ***d.* strengthen**) ::
ATTRACT : REPEL

(**d**) *Attenuate* and *strengthen* are antonyms, as are *attract* and *repel*.
Vocabulary—Similarity/Contrast

72. CEREBRUM : THINKING :: CEREBELLUM : (*a.* olfaction, ***b.* muscular coordination**, *c.* glandular secretion, *d.* audition)

(**b**) In the brain, the cerebrum controls thinking, while the cerebellum controls muscular coordination.
Natural Sciences—Description

73. BEHAVIORISM : U.S.A. :: GESTALT : (*a.* France, *b.* England, *c.* Switzerland, ***d.* Germany**)

(**d**) In psychology, behaviorism originated in the United States, while the Gestalt movement originated in Germany.
Social Science—Description

74. MONROE : (*a.* Treatise, *b.* Edict, *c.* Decree, *d.* **Code**) :: DOCTRINE : NAPOLEON

(**d**) The Monroe Doctrine and the Code Napoleon were both policy statements. The Monroe Doctrine (1823) states that the European powers were no longer to regard the countries of the western hemisphere as "subjects for future colonization." The Code Napoleon is a set of civil laws that Napoleon instituted.
Humanities—Completion

75. LXII : CLXXXVI :: D : (*a.* M, *b.* MC, *b.* **MD**, *d.* MM)

(**c**) 62 is to 186 as 500 is to 1,500. In Roman numerals, I = 1, V = 5, X = 10, L = 50, C = 100, D = 500, M = 1,000.
Mathematics—Equality/Negation

76. (*a.* loudness, *b.* compression, *c.* brightness, *d.* **hardness**) : MOHS :: TEMPERATURE : KELVIN

(**d**) The Mohs scale measures hardness, while the Kelvin scale measures temperature.
Natural Science—Description

77. FOX : OWL :: (*a.* Saul, *b.* David, *c.* **Iago**, *d.* Lear) : SOLOMON

(**c**) Iago was cunning, as a fox is supposed to be. Solomon was wise, as an owl is supposed to be. Iago tricked Othello into murdering his wife in Shakespeare's tragedy *King Lear*. Solomon was the son of David and also became a king of the Israelites. Saul was the first king of the Israelites. David was the second king of the Israelites and fought the giant Goliath. Lear was betrayed by two of his daughters in Shakespeare's *King Lear*.
Humanities—Description

78. 1 : LINE :: 2 : (*a.* length, *b.* **ellipse**, *c.* point, *d.* sphere)

(**b**) A line is one-dimensional, while an ellipse is two-dimensional.
Mathematics—Description

79. EXOSKELETON : LOBSTER :: ENDOSKELETON : (*a.* oyster, *b.* **tiger**, *c.* barnacle, *d.* worm)

(**b**) A lobster has an exoskeleton; a tiger has an endoskeleton.
An exoskeleton is an external supportive covering of an animal.
An endoskeleton is an internal skeleton.
Natural Science—Description

Explanation of Answers

80. FEZ : SOMBRERO :: BERET : (*a.* phylactery, *b.* millinery, *c.* muffler, **d. fedora**)

(**d**) A fez, a sombrero, a beret, and a fedora are all forms of headgear. A phylactery is an amulet worn by observant Jewish men. Millinery refers to hats for women or the shop that sells them. A muffler is a noise-reducing device in the exhaust system of a car as well as a thick scarf.
General Information—Class

81. (*a.* angry, **b. sanguine**, *c.* dejected, *d.* pale) : PESSIMISTIC :: HOPEFUL : DISPIRITED

(**b**) *Sanguine* means *hopeful; pessimistic* means *dispirited.*
Vocabulary—Similarity/Contrast

82. $4^{1/2} : 9^{1/2} :: 36^{1/2}$: (*a.* 6, **b. 9**, *c.* 12, *d.* 81)

(**b**) 2 is to 3 as 6 is to 9.
Mathematics—Equality/Negation

83. INCUBUS : (*a.* faccubus, *b.* excubus, **c. succubus**, *d.* maccubus) :: WOMEN : MEN

(**c**) An incubus was once thought to be a demon that sought to have intercourse with sleeping women. A succubus sought to have intercourse with sleeping men.
General Information—Description

84. HEAD MONEY : (*a.* warn, *b.* punish, **c. capture**, *d.* bribe) :: HUSH MONEY : SILENCE

(**c**) Head money is used as payment for capture. Hush money is used as payment for silence.
General Information—Description

85. SUSTAIN : OVERRULE :: IN CAMERA : (*a.* in trouble, **b. in public**, *c.* in court, *d.* out of court)

(**b**) *Sustain* and *overrule* are opposites, as are *in camera* and *in public.*
Social Science—Similarity/Contrast

86. CRONUS : SATURN :: (*a.* Poseidon, **b. Ares**, *c.* Zeus, *d.* Hermes) : MARS

(**b**) Cronus was the Greek name, and Saturn the Roman name, of the Titan who overthrew his father to become ruler of the universe, only to be overthrown by his own son (named Zeus by the Greeks, Jupiter by the Romans). Ares is the Greek name and Mars is the Roman name for the god of war.
Humanities—Similarity/Contrast

87. D MINOR : F MAJOR :: (*a*. E minor, *b*. F minor, *c*. **F# minor**, *d*. G# minor) : A MAJOR

    (**c**) The musical keys of D minor and F major both have one flat, while the keys of F# minor and A major both have three sharps.
    Humanities—Description

88. TAME : MATE :: LAME : (*a*. female, *b*. injured, *c*. **male**, *d*. excuse)

    (**c**) *Mate* can be obtained from *tame* by reversing the initial three letters. *Male* can be obtained from *lame*, also by reversing the initial three letters.
    Nonsemantic

89. (*a*. spinal, *b*. neutral, *c*. **temporal**, *d*. spatial) : PARIETAL :: OCCIPITAL : FRONTAL

    (**c**) The four lobes of the brain are the temporal, parietal, occipital, and frontal.
    Natural Science—Class

90. PARADISE : LOST :: JERUSALEM : (*a*. Sanctified, *b*. Discovered, *c*. **Delivered**, *d*. Vanquished)

    (**c**) *Paradise Lost* and *Jerusalem Delivered* are both epics, the former by Milton and the latter by Tasso.
    Humanities—Completion

91. PENN : PENNSYLVANIA :: CALVERT : (*a*. South Carolina, *b*. Vermont, *c*. **Maryland**, *d*. Rhode Island)

    (**c**) Penn founded Pennsylvania, while Calvert founded Maryland. South Carolina was named by King Charles II of England. Vermont was created by Ethan Allen and his brothers as well as Seth Warner whom they recruited for an informal militia, the Green Mountain Boys. Roger Williams was the founder of Rhode Island.
    Humanities—Description

92. ETEOCLES : (*a*. Theseus, *b*. Laius, *c*. Oedipus, *d*. **Polynices**) :: ANTIGONE : ISMENE

    (**d**) Eteocles and Polynices were siblings, as were Antigone and Ismene. Theseus was a king of Athens and son of either Aegeus and Aethra or of Poseidon and Aethra. Laius was a king of Thebes who was killed by his son Oedipus.
    Humanities—Class

93. DECIMAL : 10 :: DUODECIMAL : (*a*. 2, *b*. 8, *c*.**12**, *d*. 16)

    (**c**) The decimal system has 10 as its base. The duodecimal system has 12 as its base.
    Mathematics—Description

94. RATIONALIST : EMPIRICIST :: (*a.* Berkeley, *b.* Hume, *c.* Mill, ***d.* Leibniz**) : LOCKE

    (**d**) Leibniz was a famous rationalist philosopher. Locke was a famous empiricist. Hume and Berkeley were empiricists. John Stuart Mill was a utilitarianist.
    Humanities—Description

95. (***a.* Ivan Karamazov**, *b.* Anna Karenina, *c.* Nicolai Gogol, *d.* Grigory Smirnov) : DOSTOYEVSKY :: THÉRÈSE : MAURIAC

    (**a**) Ivan Karamazov is a literary character created by Dostoyevsky. Thérèse is a literary character created by Mauriac. *Anna Karenina* is a novel by Leo Tolstoy. Nicolai Gogol was a Russian writer. Grigory Smirnov is a distracter term.
    Humanities—Description

96. PALESTRINA : 16th :: (*a.* Beethoven, *b.* Bach, *c.* Tchaikovsky, ***d.* Stravinsky**) : 20th

    (**d**) Palestrina (ca. 1525–1594) was a 16th century composer; Stravinsky (1882–1971) was a 20th century composer. Beethoven lived from 1770 to 1827. Johann Sebastian Bach lived from 1685 to 1750. Tchaikovsky lived from 1840 to 1893.
    Humanities—Description

97. NICHOLAS II : RUSSIAN REVOLUTION :: (*a.* Louis XIV, *b.* Louis XV, ***c.* Louis XVI**, *d.* Louis XVII) : FRENCH REVOLUTION

    (**c**) The Russian Revolution overthrew Nicholas II in 1905. The French Revolution (1789–1799) overthrew Louis XVI.
    Humanities—Description

98. GLENN GOULD : PIANO :: YO-YO MA : (*a.* piano, *b.* violin, ***c.* cello**, *d.* clarinet)

    (**c**) Glenn Gould was a famous pianist; Yo-Yo Ma is a famous cellist.
    Humanities—Description

99. (***a.* Versailles**, *b.* Xanadu, *c.* St. Malo, *d.* Rouen) : LOUIS XIV :: AMBOISE : FRANCIS II

    (**a**) Amboise is the location of the palace of Francis II. Versailles is the location of the palace of Louis XIV.
    Humanities—Description

100. ISHMAEL : (***a*. Hagar**, *b.* Rebeccah, *c.* Esther, *d.* Sophia) :: ISAAC : SARAH

   (**a**) According to the Bible, Ishmael was the son of Hagar and Abraham, while Isaac was the son of Sarah and Abraham. Rebeccah was the wife of Isaac. Esther was a queen of Persia; a book in the Old Testament is named after her. Sophia is a Greek name meaning "wisdom."
   Humanities—Description

101. COLITIS : COLON :: ENCEPHALITIS : (***a*. brain**, *b.* duodenum, *c.* pancreas, *d.* liver)

   (**a**) Colitis refers to a swelling of the colon and encephalitis describes a swelling of the brain.
   General Information—Description

102. GOLDA MEIR : (*a.* Poland, ***b*. Israel**, *c.* United States, *d.* Czech Republic) :: MARGARET THATCHER : GREAT BRITAIN

   (**b**) Golda Meir was the first female prime minister of Israel (1969–1973). Margaret Thatcher was the first female prime minister of Great Britain (1979–1990).
   General Information—Description

103. PICCOLO : FLUTE :: EUPHONIUM : (*a.* phonograph, ***b*. tuba**, *c.* organ, *d.* homonym)

   (**b**) A piccolo is an instrument much like a flute, but smaller. A euphonium is an instrument much like a tuba, but smaller.
   Humanities—Description

104. FORCE : DISTANCE :: (***a*. mass × acceleration**, *b.* friction × momentum, *c.* volume / temperature, *d.* mass / energy) : RATE × TIME

   (**a**) Force is equal to mass times acceleration just as distance is equal to rate times time.
   Natural Science—Equality/Negation

105. (*a.* spear, *b.* cupid, ***c*. arrow**, *d.* wing) : LOVE :: SCYTHE : DEATH

   (**c**) An arrow is the classical symbol of impending love, and the scythe is the classical symbol of impending death.
   Humanities—Description

106. CEILING : GLASS :: (*a.* heart, *b.* wall, *c.* side, ***d*. curtain**) : IRON

   (**d**) One metaphorical barrier is a glass ceiling. Another is the iron curtain.
   General Information—Completion

107. LEGS : EGGS :: FROG : (*a.* chicken, *b.* dolphin, ***c.* sturgeon**, *d.* goose)

(**c**) Frog legs are considered a delicacy, while eggs from a sturgeon, also known as caviar, are also a delicacy.
General Information—Description

108. GOAT : (*a.* pan, ***b.* faun**, *c.* pegasus, *d.* minotaur) :: HORSE : CENTAUR

(**b**) The mythical creature of a man combined with a goat is called a faun. A man combined with a horse is called a centaur. Minotaur is a creature with the head of a bull and the body of a man. Pegasus was a winged horse that sprang from Medusa's body when she was killed. Pan is the Greek god of sheperds, woods, and mountains.
Humanities—Description

109. ORCZY : PIMPERNEL :: HAWTHORNE : (***a.* letter**, *b.* rose, *c.* wind, *d.* tide)

(**a**) Orczy wrote the novel *The Scarlet Pimpernel*. Hawthorne wrote the novel *The Scarlet Letter*.
Humanities—Description

110. GUSTAV : (*a.* Wolfgang, *b.* Friedrich, *c.* Johann, ***d.* Ludwig**) :: MAHLER : BEETHOVEN

(**d**) Gustav is the first name of composer Mahler. Ludwig is the first name of composer Beethoven.
Humanities—Completion

111. RESTIVE : TRANQUIL :: VERBOSE : (*a.* loquacious, *b.* timorous, *c.* talkative, ***d.* taciturn**)

(**d**) Restive, which describes someone who is active or restless, means the opposite of tranquil. Verbose, which describes someone who is very talkative, means the opposite of taciturn.
Vocabulary—Similarity/Contrast

112. HOLY SEE : (*a.* Rome, *b.* Hungary, ***c.* Italy**, *d.* Chad) :: LESOTHO : SOUTH AFRICA

(**c**) Holy See is a country completely landlocked within Italy. Lesotho is a country completely landlocked within South Africa.
General Information—Description

113. LEAGUE OF NATIONS : UNITED NATIONS :: THE ARTICLES
OF CONFEDERATION : (*a.* **U.S. Constitution**, *b.* The Bill of Rights,
c. Human Rights Treaty, *d.* The Constitution of the Confederate States)

(**a**) The League of Nations was the failed predecessor of the United Nations,
just as The Articles of Confederation were the failed predecessor of the U.S.
Constitution.
General Information—Description

114. AM : AMPLITUDE :: FM : (*a.* force, ***b.* frequency**, *c.* Fahrenheit,
d. friction)

(**b**) The radio term AM stands for Amplitude Modulation just as the term
FM stands for Frequency Modulation.
Natural Science—Equality/Negation

115. (*a.* England, ***b.* Waterloo**, *c.* Russia, *d.* Elba) : NAPOLEON :: LITTLE
BIG HORN RIVER : CUSTER

(**b**) Waterloo was where Napoleon was defeated. The Little Big Horn River
was where Custer was defeated.
General Information—Description

116. ROMEO : JULIET :: PYRAMUS : (***a.*Thisbe**, *b.* Titania, *c.* Helen,
d. Athena)

(**a**) Romeo died while in love with Juliet just as Pyramus died while in love
with Thisbe. *Romeo and Juliet* was written by Shakespeare. The story of
Pyramus and Thisbe was told by Ovid. Titania is the name of a character in
Shakespeare's *A Midsummer Night's Dream*. Helen was the daughter of Zeus and Leda and
was abducted by Paris, which led to the Trojan War. Athena was the goddess of wisdom,
useful arts, and prudent warfare.
Humanities—Description

117. GOAT : WORM :: (*a.* wool, *b.* felt, ***c.* cashmere**, *d.* chinchilla) : SILK

(**c**) The goat produces the hair that is used to make the fabric cashmere.
A worm produces the thread used to make the fabric silk.
General Information—Description

118. XXIX : 29 :: MDVI : (*a.* 1551, *b.* 1056, *c.* 1061 ***d.* 1506**)

(**d**) XXIX is the Roman numeral expression of the value 29. MDVI
is the Roman numeral expression of the value 1,506. In Roman numerals,
I = 1, V = 5, X = 10, L = 50, C = 100, D = 500, M = 1,000.
Mathematics—Equality/Negation

119. GUANINE : (***a. cytosine***, *b.* purine, *c.* uracil, *d.* pyrimidine) ::
ADENINE : THYMINE

(**a**) In human DNA, guanine is the purine that pairs with the pyrimidine
cytosine. Likewise, adenine is the purine that pairs with the pyrimidine
thymine. Pyrimidine is a base that is a component of DNA.
Natural Science—Description

120. ESOPHAGUS : SARCOPHAGUS :: GULLET : (*a.* trachea, *b.* monument,
***c.* stone coffin**, *d.* crystal chandelier)

(**c**) Esophagus is another name for the gullet. Sarcophagus is the name for
a stone coffin.
Vocabulary—Similarity/Contrast

PRACTICE TEST 2

Item Classification Chart

		RELATIONSHIP						
		Similarity/ Contrast	Description	Class	Completion	Part/ Whole	Equality/ Negation	Nonsemantic
C O N T E N T	**Vocabulary**	5, 14, 23, 26, 39, 41, 54, 55, 59, 65, 69, 71, 81, 111, 120	2, 3, 9, 24, 25, 52, 56		28, 37			
	General Information	12, 18, 33, 60, 64	1, 8, 10, 13, 15, 16, 19, 20, 21, 22, 27, 32, 34, 35, 48, 62, 83, 84, 101, 102, 107, 112, 113, 115, 117	17, 38, 40, 43, 45, 48, 49	11, 106	61		
	Humanities	30, 86	7, 31, 42, 46, 50, 57, 63, 70, 77, 87, 91, 94, 95, 96, 97, 98, 99, 100, 103, 105, 108, 109, 116	68, 80, 92	74, 90, 110			
	Social Science	85	73					
	Natural Science	53	6, 36, 44, 58, 66, 67, 72, 76, 79, 119	89			104, 114	
	Mathematics		51, 78, 93				4, 75, 82, 118	
	Nonsemantic							29, 88

Answer Sheet
PRACTICE TEST 3

1	Ⓐ Ⓑ Ⓒ Ⓓ	31	Ⓐ Ⓑ Ⓒ Ⓓ	61	Ⓐ Ⓑ Ⓒ Ⓓ	91	Ⓐ Ⓑ Ⓒ Ⓓ
2	Ⓐ Ⓑ Ⓒ Ⓓ	32	Ⓐ Ⓑ Ⓒ Ⓓ	62	Ⓐ Ⓑ Ⓒ Ⓓ	92	Ⓐ Ⓑ Ⓒ Ⓓ
3	Ⓐ Ⓑ Ⓒ Ⓓ	33	Ⓐ Ⓑ Ⓒ Ⓓ	63	Ⓐ Ⓑ Ⓒ Ⓓ	93	Ⓐ Ⓑ Ⓒ Ⓓ
4	Ⓐ Ⓑ Ⓒ Ⓓ	34	Ⓐ Ⓑ Ⓒ Ⓓ	64	Ⓐ Ⓑ Ⓒ Ⓓ	94	Ⓐ Ⓑ Ⓒ Ⓓ
5	Ⓐ Ⓑ Ⓒ Ⓓ	35	Ⓐ Ⓑ Ⓒ Ⓓ	65	Ⓐ Ⓑ Ⓒ Ⓓ	95	Ⓐ Ⓑ Ⓒ Ⓓ
6	Ⓐ Ⓑ Ⓒ Ⓓ	36	Ⓐ Ⓑ Ⓒ Ⓓ	66	Ⓐ Ⓑ Ⓒ Ⓓ	96	Ⓐ Ⓑ Ⓒ Ⓓ
7	Ⓐ Ⓑ Ⓒ Ⓓ	37	Ⓐ Ⓑ Ⓒ Ⓓ	67	Ⓐ Ⓑ Ⓒ Ⓓ	97	Ⓐ Ⓑ Ⓒ Ⓓ
8	Ⓐ Ⓑ Ⓒ Ⓓ	38	Ⓐ Ⓑ Ⓒ Ⓓ	68	Ⓐ Ⓑ Ⓒ Ⓓ	98	Ⓐ Ⓑ Ⓒ Ⓓ
9	Ⓐ Ⓑ Ⓒ Ⓓ	39	Ⓐ Ⓑ Ⓒ Ⓓ	69	Ⓐ Ⓑ Ⓒ Ⓓ	99	Ⓐ Ⓑ Ⓒ Ⓓ
10	Ⓐ Ⓑ Ⓒ Ⓓ	40	Ⓐ Ⓑ Ⓒ Ⓓ	70	Ⓐ Ⓑ Ⓒ Ⓓ	100	Ⓐ Ⓑ Ⓒ Ⓓ
11	Ⓐ Ⓑ Ⓒ Ⓓ	41	Ⓐ Ⓑ Ⓒ Ⓓ	71	Ⓐ Ⓑ Ⓒ Ⓓ	101	Ⓐ Ⓑ Ⓒ Ⓓ
12	Ⓐ Ⓑ Ⓒ Ⓓ	42	Ⓐ Ⓑ Ⓒ Ⓓ	72	Ⓐ Ⓑ Ⓒ Ⓓ	102	Ⓐ Ⓑ Ⓒ Ⓓ
13	Ⓐ Ⓑ Ⓒ Ⓓ	43	Ⓐ Ⓑ Ⓒ Ⓓ	73	Ⓐ Ⓑ Ⓒ Ⓓ	103	Ⓐ Ⓑ Ⓒ Ⓓ
14	Ⓐ Ⓑ Ⓒ Ⓓ	44	Ⓐ Ⓑ Ⓒ Ⓓ	74	Ⓐ Ⓑ Ⓒ Ⓓ	104	Ⓐ Ⓑ Ⓒ Ⓓ
15	Ⓐ Ⓑ Ⓒ Ⓓ	45	Ⓐ Ⓑ Ⓒ Ⓓ	75	Ⓐ Ⓑ Ⓒ Ⓓ	105	Ⓐ Ⓑ Ⓒ Ⓓ
16	Ⓐ Ⓑ Ⓒ Ⓓ	46	Ⓐ Ⓑ Ⓒ Ⓓ	76	Ⓐ Ⓑ Ⓒ Ⓓ	106	Ⓐ Ⓑ Ⓒ Ⓓ
17	Ⓐ Ⓑ Ⓒ Ⓓ	47	Ⓐ Ⓑ Ⓒ Ⓓ	77	Ⓐ Ⓑ Ⓒ Ⓓ	107	Ⓐ Ⓑ Ⓒ Ⓓ
18	Ⓐ Ⓑ Ⓒ Ⓓ	48	Ⓐ Ⓑ Ⓒ Ⓓ	78	Ⓐ Ⓑ Ⓒ Ⓓ	108	Ⓐ Ⓑ Ⓒ Ⓓ
19	Ⓐ Ⓑ Ⓒ Ⓓ	49	Ⓐ Ⓑ Ⓒ Ⓓ	79	Ⓐ Ⓑ Ⓒ Ⓓ	109	Ⓐ Ⓑ Ⓒ Ⓓ
20	Ⓐ Ⓑ Ⓒ Ⓓ	50	Ⓐ Ⓑ Ⓒ Ⓓ	80	Ⓐ Ⓑ Ⓒ Ⓓ	110	Ⓐ Ⓑ Ⓒ Ⓓ
21	Ⓐ Ⓑ Ⓒ Ⓓ	51	Ⓐ Ⓑ Ⓒ Ⓓ	81	Ⓐ Ⓑ Ⓒ Ⓓ	111	Ⓐ Ⓑ Ⓒ Ⓓ
22	Ⓐ Ⓑ Ⓒ Ⓓ	52	Ⓐ Ⓑ Ⓒ Ⓓ	82	Ⓐ Ⓑ Ⓒ Ⓓ	112	Ⓐ Ⓑ Ⓒ Ⓓ
23	Ⓐ Ⓑ Ⓒ Ⓓ	53	Ⓐ Ⓑ Ⓒ Ⓓ	83	Ⓐ Ⓑ Ⓒ Ⓓ	113	Ⓐ Ⓑ Ⓒ Ⓓ
24	Ⓐ Ⓑ Ⓒ Ⓓ	54	Ⓐ Ⓑ Ⓒ Ⓓ	84	Ⓐ Ⓑ Ⓒ Ⓓ	114	Ⓐ Ⓑ Ⓒ Ⓓ
25	Ⓐ Ⓑ Ⓒ Ⓓ	55	Ⓐ Ⓑ Ⓒ Ⓓ	85	Ⓐ Ⓑ Ⓒ Ⓓ	115	Ⓐ Ⓑ Ⓒ Ⓓ
26	Ⓐ Ⓑ Ⓒ Ⓓ	56	Ⓐ Ⓑ Ⓒ Ⓓ	86	Ⓐ Ⓑ Ⓒ Ⓓ	116	Ⓐ Ⓑ Ⓒ Ⓓ
27	Ⓐ Ⓑ Ⓒ Ⓓ	57	Ⓐ Ⓑ Ⓒ Ⓓ	87	Ⓐ Ⓑ Ⓒ Ⓓ	117	Ⓐ Ⓑ Ⓒ Ⓓ
28	Ⓐ Ⓑ Ⓒ Ⓓ	58	Ⓐ Ⓑ Ⓒ Ⓓ	88	Ⓐ Ⓑ Ⓒ Ⓓ	118	Ⓐ Ⓑ Ⓒ Ⓓ
29	Ⓐ Ⓑ Ⓒ Ⓓ	59	Ⓐ Ⓑ Ⓒ Ⓓ	89	Ⓐ Ⓑ Ⓒ Ⓓ	119	Ⓐ Ⓑ Ⓒ Ⓓ
30	Ⓐ Ⓑ Ⓒ Ⓓ	60	Ⓐ Ⓑ Ⓒ Ⓓ	90	Ⓐ Ⓑ Ⓒ Ⓓ	120	Ⓐ Ⓑ Ⓒ Ⓓ

Answer Sheet

Practice Test 3

Directions: In each of the following questions, you will find three initial terms and, in parentheses, four answer options designated *a*, *b*, *c*, and *d*. You are to select from the four answer options the one that best completes the analogy with the three initial terms. To record your answers, use the answer sheet provided.

Time: 60 minutes

1. LAMB : (*a.* goat, *b.* sheep, *c.* mule, *d.* cow) :: COLT : HORSE

2. DOCTOR : ACCOUNTANT :: PATIENT : (*a.* judge, *b.* client, *c.* jury, *d.* district attorney)

3. IRELAND : EIRE :: (*a.* Holland, *b.* Switzerland, *c.* Denmark, *d.* Germany) : DEUTSCHLAND

4. DEFICIT : RED :: SURPLUS : (*a.* black, *b.* green, *c.* brown, *d.* white)

5. LEMON : SOUR :: TOBACCO : (*a.* tasty, *b.* sour, *c.* bitter, *d.* salty)

6. YELLOW : (*a.* blue, *b.* white, *c.* green, *d.* red) :: COWARDLY : GLOOMY

7. HOUDINI : (*a.* magician, *b.* surgeon, *c.* lawyer, *d.* detective) :: FRANKLIN : STATESMAN

8. CURRIER : (*a.* Loewe, *b.* Ives, *c.* Cowe, *d.* Best) :: GILBERT : SULLIVAN

9. DE FACTO : IN FACT :: (*a.* de jure, *b.* de legibus, *c.* ex facto, *d.* ex legato) : IN LAW

10. SQUARE : CUBE :: CIRCLE : (*a.* rectangle, *b.* solid, *c.* ellipse, *d.* sphere)

11. FIDDLER : PRAYING :: (*a.* bow, *b.* bear, *c.* violinist, *d.* crab) : MANTIS

12. WINCHESTER : SHOOT :: CAT-O'-NINE-TAILS : (*a.* stab, *b.* whip, *c.* poison, *d.* drown)

13. FULTON : (*a.* locomotive, *b.* steamboat, *c.* incandescent lamp, *d.* crystal radio) :: WHITNEY : COTTON GIN

14. (*a.* jugular, *b.* carotid, *c.* thorax, *d.* sclerotic) : VEIN :: AORTA : ARTERY

15. HISTRIONICS : (*a.* geriatrics, *b.* hysterics, *c.* theatrics, *d.* pediatrics) :: PATRONYMICS : SURNAMES

16. NUN : HABIT :: (*a.* postal carrier, *b.* surgeon, *c.* knight, *d.* solicitor) : COAT OF MAIL

17. (*a.* people, *b.* automobiles, *c.* horses, *d.* bicycles) : INDIANAPOLIS 500 :: HORSES : KENTUCKY DERBY

18. LOBBYIST : LEGISLATOR :: (*a.* lawyer, *b.* judge, *c.* court stenographer, *d.* foreman) : JURY

19. CONGRESSIONAL MEDAL OF HONOR : SOLDIER :: PULITZER PRIZE : (*a.* lawyer, *b.* journalist, *c.* chemist, *d.* doctor)

20. PART : TRAP :: (*a.* good-bye, *b.* whole, *c.* bait, *d.* tar) : RAT

21. BARTON : (*a.* Candy, *b.* Helen, *c.* Clara, *d.* Elsa) :: NIGHTINGALE : FLORENCE

22. EMERALD : MINE :: PEARL : (*a.* oyster, *b.* clam, *c.* mine, *d.* river)

23. BIOGRAPHY : AUTOBIOGRAPHY :: (*a.* first, *b.* third, *c.* fourth, *d.* fifth) : FIRST

24. DUET : PAIR :: DIALOGUE : (*a.* monologue, *b.* quandary, *c.* bipolar, *d.* quartet)

25. (*a.* foot, *b.* ball, *c.* skate, *d.* stick) : HOCKEY :: BAT : BASEBALL

26. (*a.* chroma, *b.* violet, *c.* rainbow, *d.* black) : COLOR :: VACUUM : AIR

27. FLORIDA : PENINSULA :: CUBA : (*a.* state, *b.* gulf, *c.* nation, *d.* island)

28. URBAN : RURAL :: URBANE : (*a.* lazy, *b.* suburban, *c.* boorish, *d.* effete)

29. (*a.* air, *b.* earth, *c.* fire, *d.* plastic) : PYRO :: WATER : HYDRO

30. (*a.* sailor, *b.* mountebank, *c.* salesman, *d.* villain) : CHARLATAN :: FRAUD : QUACK

31. RULER : LINE SEGMENT :: PROTRACTOR : (*a.* distance, *b.* angle, *c.* perimeter, *d.* velocity)

32. WILLIAMS : (*a.* Massachusetts, *b.* Vermont, *c.* New Hampshire, *d.* Rhode Island) :: PENN : PENNSYLVANIA

33. OLD : (*a.* Two, *b.* Twenty, *c.* Forty, *d.* Sixty) :: MAID : ONE

34. (*a.* princess, *b.* worker, *c.* drone, *d.* servant) : QUEEN :: GANDER : GOOSE

35. XL : LX :: CC : (*a.* CCC, *b.* CD, *c.* DC, *d.* CM)

36. CASTOR : (*a.* Pisces, *b.* Orion, *c.* Pollux, *d.* Andromeda) :: JACOB : ESAU

37. KEYNES : (*a.* psychology, *b.* economics, *c.* anthropology, *d.* ecology) :: EINSTEIN : PHYSICS

38. (*a.* New Jersey, *b.* Missouri, *c.* Indian, *d.* Byrd) : ANTARCTIC :: HUDSON : MISSISSIPPI

39. SPRINGS : PALM :: (*a.* Old, *b.* Mineral, *c.* York, *d.* Tree) : NEW

40. MEGAPHONE : CONE :: (*a.* funnel, *b.* cloud, *c.* hurricane, *d.* dictaphone) : TORNADO

41. HARVARD : CAMBRIDGE :: CAMBRIDGE : (*a.* Oxford, *b.* Yale, *c.* Cambridge, *d.* Gloucester)

42. ACTUAL : VIRTUAL :: IN FACT : (*a.* in cause, *b.* in time, *c.* in truth, *d.* in effect)

43. BRAVE NEW WORLD : (*a.* Winston, *b.* Huxley, *c.* O'Brian, *d.* Wells) :: 1984: ORWELL

44. CANINE : DOG :: EQUINE : (*a.* cow, *b.* goat, *c.* horse, *d.* pig)

45. CENSURE : (*a.* expurgate, *b.* condemn, *c.* praise, *d.* oppose) :: OBTUSE : DULL

46. USHER : POE :: (*a.* ill Repute, *b.* Seven Gables, *c.* Tara, *d.* No Return) : HAWTHORNE

47. NUMISMATIST : PHILATELIST :: (*a.* coins, *b.* numbers, *c.* rocks, *d.* trinkets) : STAMPS

48. CASTLE : BISHOP :: HORIZONTAL : (*a.* vertical, *b.* diagonal, *c.* cathedral, *d.* abbey)

49. (*a.* endemic, *b.* mercurial, *c.* unabating, *d.* retrogressive) : CONSTANT :: CHANGEABLE : IMMUTABLE

50. TRAGEDY : MELODRAMA :: PATHOS : (*a.* bathos, *b.* ethos, *c.* comedy, *d.* catharsis)

51. PERVADE : PERMEATE :: (*a.* trusting, *b.* mistrustful, *c.* favorable, *d.* unfavorable) : AUSPICIOUS

52. GOOSE : GEESE :: MOOSE : (*a.* moosen, *b.* meese, *c.* mooses, *d.* moose)

53. (*a.* passenger pigeon, *b.* sphinx, *c.* phoenix, *d.* hummingbird) : DODO :: RAVEN : SPARROW

54. EASTERN STANDARD : 8 A.M. :: PACIFIC STANDARD : (*a.* 5 A.M., *b.* 6 A.M., *c.* 10 A.M., *d.* 11 A.M.)

55. CENTIGRADE : 100 :: CELSIUS : (*a.* −173, *b.* 0, *c.* 100, *d.* 212)

56. SURFEIT : EXCESS :: EVANESCENT : (*a.* silent, *b.* eternal, *c.* ephemeral, *d.* celestial)

57. PLUTARCH : (*a.* drama, *b.* biography, *c.* epic, *d.* oration) :: AESOP : FABLE

58. HYDRO : AQUA :: (*a.* air, *b.* gas, *c.* liquid, *d.* water) : WATER

59. REMISS : (*a.* negligent, *b.* careful, *c.* auspicious, *d.* remote) :: DARK : LIGHT

60. FUSTIAN : GALATEA :: MUSLIN : (*a.* grandam, *b.* lydgate, *c.* gabardine, *d.* rhodium)

61. BLUE : STRAW :: RASP : (*a.* yellow, *b.* hay, *c.* black, *d.* shriek)

62. BUFFALO BILL : (*a.* Cody, *b.* James, *c.* Bowman, *d.* Broderick) :: WILD BILL : HICKOK

63. MOURNER : TEARS :: (*a.* hypochondriac, *b.* lover, *c.* troglodyte, *d.* hypocrite) : CROCODILE TEARS

64. CEDE : SEED :: (*a.* run, *b.* win, *c.* yield, *d.* go) : PLANT

65. INGENUOUS : (*a.* clever, *b.* innocent, *c.* pastoral, *d.* hopeful) :: INFRACTION : VIOLATION

66. SECULAR : (*a.* sacred, *b.* ecclesiastical, *c.* lay, *d.* regular) :: BISHOP : MONK

67. EXTIRPATE : (*a.* evade, *b.* examine, *c.* exude, *d.* eradicate) :: BUOY : ENCOURAGE

68. THREE : (*a.* Two, *b.* Five, *c.* Seven, *d.* Ten) :: MUSKETEERS : LITTLE PEPPERS

69. WEND : END :: (*a.* food, *b.* wait, *c.* tend, *d.* beginning) : ATE

70. VOLT : POTENTIAL DIFFERENCE :: WATT : (*a.* resistance, *b.* brightness, *c.* power, *d.* actual difference)

71. POINT : 0 :: HEXAGON : (*a.* 1, *b.* 2, *c.* 3, *d.* 4)

72. (*a.* Troy, *b.* Athens, *c.* Carthage, *d.* Milan) : PUNIC :: SPARTA : PELOPONNESIAN

73. WINDY CITY : CHICAGO :: GOTHAM : (*a.* San Francisco, *b.* Paris, *c.* New York City, *d.* London)

74. INCANDESCENT : FILAMENT :: FLUORESCENT : (*a.* air, *b.* vacuum, *c.* energy, *d.* phosphor)

75. CABAL : (*a.* trivia, *b.* plot, *c.* wire, *d.* quibble) :: CAPABLE : COMPETENT

76. ORDER : (*a.* human, *b.* primates, *c.* erectus, *d.* mammalia) :: SPECIES : SAPIENS

77. GRENDEL : BEOWULF :: HYDRA : (*a.* Achilles, *b.* Vulcan, *c.* Atlas, *d.* Hercules)

78. $2^{-2} : 2^{-1} :: 2^2 : ($*a.* $2^0,$ *b.* $2^1,$ *c.* $2^2,$ *d.* $2^3)$

79. DEARTH : SHORTAGE :: PLETHORA : (*a.* abundance, *b.* scarcity, *c.* excess, *d.* necessity)

80. WANDERING JEW : EARTH :: FLYING DUTCHMAN : (*a.* seas, *b.* stars, *c.* heaven, *d.* hell)

81. ASTROLABE : SEXTANT :: SUNDIAL : (*a.* time, *b.* electric clock, *c.* ruler, *d.* light rays)

82. VENAL : (*a.* rigid, *b.* cold, *c.* humorless, *d.* mercenary) :: VENIAL : EXCUSABLE

83. E# : Fb :: B : (*a.* Cb, *b.* Bb, *c.* C, *d.* B)

84. MELIORATE : AMELIORATE :: HASTEN : (*a.* speed up, *b.* slow down, *c.* better, *d.* worsen)

85. MACHIAVELLI : PRINCE :: CASTIGLIONE : (*a.* Knight, *b.* Courtier, *c.* King, *d.* Yeoman)

86. NOSTRUM : (*a.* pedestal, *b.* disease, *c.* panacea, *d.* pabulum) :: VERACIOUS : HONEST

87. DWARF : PITUITARY :: CRETIN : (*a.* endocrine, *b.* thyroid, *c.* thalamus, *d.* hypothalamus)

88. (*a.* barometer, *b.* tachometer, *c.* hydrometer, *d.* voltmeter) : THERMOMETER :: SPEED : TEMPERATURE

89. FROWARD : BACKWARD :: (*a.* dilatory, *b.* upside down, *c.* refractory, *d.* right side up) : REVERSED

90. LEWIN : (*a.* attribution theory, *b.* dissonance theory, *c.* field theory, *d.* psychoanalytic theory) :: JUNG : ANALYTIC THEORY

91. BUNSEN BURNER : GAS :: AUTOCLAVE : (*a.* oil, *b.* electricity, *c.* steam, *d.* solar energy)

92. BACH : (*a.* invention, *b.* symphony, *c.* waltz, *d.* polyphony) :: CHOPIN : MAZURKA

93. BANISHMENT : COUNTRY :: DEFENESTRATION : (*a.* ceiling, *b.* floor, *c.* city, *d.* window)

94. CADMEAN : (*a.* Caesarian, *b.* Augustan, *c.* Napoleonic, *d.* Pyrrhic) :: EXPENSIVE : COSTLY

95. MOSES : (*a.* Abraham, *b.* Joseph, *c.* Joshua, *d.* Gideon) :: ROOSEVELT : TRUMAN

96. PARASYMPATHETIC : (*a.* sympathetic, *b.* protosympathetic, *c.* asympathetic, *d.* prosympathetic) :: SLOW DOWN : SPEED UP

97. (*a.* Galileo, *b.* Newton, *c.* Galen, *d.* Ptolemy) : COPERNICUS :: GEOCENTRIC : HELIOCENTRIC

98. TOSCANINI : (*a.* Fournier, *b.* Ormandy, *c.* Goodman, *d.* Heifetz) :: VAN CLIBURN : RUBENSTEIN

99. RICHELIEU : CARDINAL :: (*a.* Henry IV, *b.* Louis XIII, *c.* Francis I, *d.* Napoleon III) : KING

100. JAMES : FUNCTIONALISM :: (*a.* Dewey, *b.* Levi-Strauss, *c.* Watson, *d.* Klineberg) : STRUCTURALISM

101. FAUST : DR. FAUSTUS :: (*a.* Goethe, *b.* Mr. Marlowe, *c.* Hyde, *d.* Kafka) : MARLOWE

102. RHODESIA : (*a.* Indonesia, *b.* Zimbabwe, *c.* Namibia, *d.* Israel) :: BURMA : MYANMAR

103. SALT : WATER :: (*a.* desalinate, *b.* desaltify, *c.* purify, *d.* reduce) : DEHYDRATE

104. HART : DEER :: COLT : (*a.* stallion, *b.* horse, *c.* filly, *d.* foal)

105. (*a.* liver, *b.* brain, *c.* ear, *d.* pancreas) : HEART :: LOBE : CHAMBER

106. NADIR : (*a.* penultimate, *b.* depth, *c.* zenith, *d.* low) :: STYGIAN : BRIGHT

107. 32 : FAHRENHEIT :: (*a.* −32, *b.* 100, *c.* 10, *d.* 0) : CELSIUS

108. GRAPE : RAISIN :: PLUM : (*a.* date, *b.* fig, *c.* prune, *d.* currant)

109. NORTH : CANCER :: SOUTH : (*a.* Virgo, *b.* Capricorn, *c.* Sagittarius, *d.* Equator)

110. EVELYN : DACTYL :: (*a.* Michelle, *b.* Holly, *c.* Erica, *d.* Emily) : IAMB

111. MOZART : (*a.* Violin, *b.* Flute, *c.* Viola, *d.* Cello) :: BACH : ORGAN

112. (*a.* pizzicato, *b.* staccato, *c.* diminuendo, *d.* piano) : FORTE :: SOFT : LOUD

113. INDIA : HINDUISM :: INDONESIA : (*a.* Buddhism, *b.* Confucianism, *c.* Christianity, *d.* Islam)

114. OBOE : REED :: (*a.* viola, *b.* bassoon, *c.* timpani, *d.* french horn) : STRING

115. MORE : (*a.* Utopia, *b.* Paradise Lost, *c.* 1984, *d.* On the Beach) :: HUXLEY : BRAVE NEW WORLD

116. BASEBALL : BAT :: TABLE TENNIS : (*a.* mallet, *b.* paddle, *c.* stick, *d.* racquet)

117. ETYMOLOGY : ENTOMOLOGY :: (*a.* letters, *b.* arachnids, *c.* disease, *d.* words) : INSECTS

118. ADAM : (*a.* Eden, *b.* Israel, *c.* heaven, *d.* hell) :: ROMEO : VERONA

119. $8^{1/3}$: $25^{1/2}$ :: (*a.* 25^2, *b.* $100^{1/3}$, *c.* $100^{1/2}$, *d.* $16^{1/2}$) : $625^{1/2}$

120. AUGMENTED THIRD : DIMINISHED THIRD :: FOUR : (*a.* two and a half, *b.* three, *c.* two, *d.* three and a half)

Answer Key
PRACTICE TEST 3

1. **B**	31. **B**	61. **C**	91. **C**
2. **B**	32. **D**	62. **A**	92. **A**
3. **D**	33. **B**	63. **D**	93. **D**
4. **A**	34. **C**	64. **C**	94. **D**
5. **C**	35. **A**	65. **B**	95. **C**
6. **A**	36. **C**	66. **D**	96. **A**
7. **A**	37. **B**	67. **D**	97. **D**
8. **B**	38. **C**	68. **B**	98. **B**
9. **A**	39. **C**	69. **B**	99. **B**
10. **D**	40. **A**	70. **C**	100. **B**
11. **D**	41. **C**	71. **B**	101. **A**
12. **B**	42. **D**	72. **C**	102. **B**
13. **B**	43. **B**	73. **A**	103. **A**
14. **A**	44. **C**	74. **D**	104. **D**
15. **C**	45. **B**	75. **B**	105. **B**
16. **C**	46. **B**	76. **B**	106. **C**
17. **B**	47. **A**	77. **D**	107. **D**
18. **A**	48. **B**	78. **D**	108. **C**
19. **B**	49. **B**	79. **C**	109. **B**
20. **D**	50. **A**	80. **A**	110. **A**
21. **C**	51. **C**	81. **B**	111. **A**
22. **A**	52. **D**	82. **D**	112. **D**
23. **B**	53. **A**	83. **B**	113. **D**
24. **C**	54. **A**	84. **A**	114. **A**
25. **D**	55. **C**	85. **B**	115. **A**
26. **D**	56. **C**	86. **C**	116. **B**
27. **D**	57. **B**	87. **B**	117. **D**
28. **C**	58. **D**	88. **B**	118. **A**
29. **C**	59. **B**	89. **C**	119. **C**
30. **B**	60. **C**	90. **C**	120. **A**

EXPLANATION OF ANSWERS FOR PRACTICE TEST 3

In the following explanations of answers, explanations concerning the correct response are in a large font. Explanations regarding distracters (incorrect responses) that are not self-explaining or could be misinterpreted are in a smaller font in order to highlight the explanations of the answers that are correct.

1. LAMB : (*a.* goat, ***b.* sheep**, *c.* mule, *d.* cow) :: COLT : HORSE
   (**b**) A lamb is a young sheep; a colt is a young horse.
   General Information—Description

2. DOCTOR : ACCOUNTANT :: PATIENT : (*a.* judge, ***b.* client**, *c.* jury, *d.* district attorney)

   (**b**) A doctor serves patients; an accountant serves clients.
   General Information—Description

3. IRELAND : EIRE :: (*a.* Holland, *b.* Switzerland, *c.* Denmark, ***d.* Germany**) : DEUTSCHLAND

   (**d**) Ireland and Eire are the same country, as are Germany and Deutschland.
   General Information—Similarity/Contrast

4. DEFICIT : RED :: SURPLUS : (***a.* black**, *b.* green, *c.* brown, *d.* white)

   (**a**) To be in the red is to show a deficit, while to be in the black is to show a surplus.
   General Information—Similarity/Contrast

5. LEMON : SOUR :: TOBACCO : (*a.* tasty, *b.* sour, ***c.* bitter**, *d.* salty)

   (**c**) A lemon is sour; tobacco is bitter.
   General Information—Description

6. YELLOW : (***a.* blue**, *b.* white, *c.* green, *d.* red) :: COWARDLY : GLOOMY

   (**a**) A cowardly person is sometimes referred to as "yellow." A gloomy person is sometimes referred to as feeling "blue."
   General Information—Similarity/Contrast

7. HOUDINI : (***a.* magician**, *b.* surgeon, *c.* lawyer, *d.* detective) :: FRANKLIN : STATESMAN

   (**a**) Harry Houdini was a magician; Benjamin Franklin, a statesman.
   General Information—Description

8. CURRIER : (*a.* Loewe, ***b.* Ives**, *c.* Cowe, *d.* Best) :: GILBERT : SULLIVAN

(**b**) Currier and Ives were a team of artists, while Gilbert and Sullivan were a team who wrote operettas, including "The Mikado." Currier and Ives had a printmaking firm that produced some of the most popular art of the 19th century.
Humanities—Class

9. DE FACTO : IN FACT :: (***a.* de jure**, *b.* de legibus, *c.* ex facto, *d.* ex legato) : IN LAW

(**a**) *De facto* means "in fact." *De jure* means "in law." *De legibus* is a dialogue written by Cicero. *Ex facto* means "after the fact."
Vocabulary—Similarity/Contrast

10. SQUARE : CUBE :: CIRCLE : (*a.* rectangle, *b.* solid, *c.* ellipse, ***d.* sphere**)

(**d**) A two-dimensional "slice" through a cube yields a square. A two-dimensional "slice" through a sphere yields a circle.
Mathematics—Description

11. FIDDLER : PRAYING :: (*a.* bow, *b.* bear, *c.* violinist, ***d.* crab**) : MANTIS

(**d**) The fiddler crab and praying mantis are both types of animal.
Natural Science—Completion

12. WINCHESTER : SHOOT :: CAT-O'-NINE-TAILS : (*a.* stab, ***b.* whip**, *c.* poison, *d.* drown)

(**b**) A Winchester can be used to shoot someone. A cat-o'-nine-tails can be used to whip someone. A Winchester is a shoulder rifle. A cat-o'-nine-tails is a whip with nine separate woven tails.
General Information—Description

13. FULTON : (*a.* locomotive, ***b.* steamboat**, *c.* incandescent lamp, *d.* crystal radio) :: WHITNEY : COTTON GIN

(**b**) Robert Fulton invented the steamboat. Eli Whitney invented the cotton gin.
Social Science—Description

14. (***a.* jugular**, *b.* carotid, *c.* thorax, *d.* sclerotic) : VEIN :: AORTA : ARTERY

(**a**) The jugular is a vein; the aorta is an artery. *Carotid* relates to the chief arteries that pass up the neck. The thorax is the part of the body between the neck and abdomen. *Sclerotic* relates to the dense fibrous outer coat of the eyeball.
Natural Science—Class

15. HISTRIONICS : (*a.* geriatrics, *b.* hysterics, **c. theatrics**, *d.* pediatrics) :: PATRONYMICS : SURNAMES

(**c**) Histrionics are theatrics; patronymics are surnames.
Vocabulary—Similarity/Contrast

16. NUN : HABIT :: (*a.* postal carrier, *b.* surgeon, **c. knight**, *d.* solicitor) : COAT OF MAIL

(**c**) A nun sometimes wears a habit. A knight wore a coat of mail.
General Information—Similarity/Contrast

17. (*a.* people, **b. automobiles**, *c.* horses, *d.* bicycles) : INDIANAPOLIS 500 :: HORSES : KENTUCKY DERBY

(**b**) The Indianapolis 500 is an automobile race. The Kentucky Derby is a horse race.
General Information—Description

18. LOBBYIST : LEGISLATOR :: (***a.* lawyer**, *b.* judge, *c.* court stenographer, *d.* foreman) : JURY

(**a**) The job of a lobbyist is to persuade a legislator. The job of a lawyer is to persuade a jury.
General Information—Description

19. CONGRESSIONAL MEDAL OF HONOR : SOLDIER :: PULITZER PRIZE : (*a.* lawyer, ***b.* journalist**, *c.* chemist, *d.* doctor)

(**b**) The Congressional Medal of Honor is given to outstanding soldiers. The Pulitzer Prize is given to outstanding journalists.
General Information—Description

20. PART : TRAP :: (*a.* good-bye, *b.* whole, *c.* bait, ***d.* tar**) : RAT

(**d**) *Part* is *trap* spelled backwards. *Tar* is *rat* spelled backwards.
Nonsemantic

21. BARTON : (*a.* Candy, *b.* Helen, **c. Clara**, *d.* Elsa) :: NIGHTINGALE : FLORENCE

(**c**) Clara Barton (1821–1912) and Florence Nightingale (1821–1910) are both famous for their work in nursing.
General Information—Completion

22. EMERALD : MINE :: PEARL : (***a.* oyster**, *b.* clam, *c.* mine, *d.* river)

(**a**) Emeralds are found in mines. Pearls are found in oysters.
Natural Science—Description

23. BIOGRAPHY : AUTOBIOGRAPHY :: (*a.* first, ***b.* third**, *c.* fourth, *d.* fifth) : FIRST

    (**b**) A biography is written in third person. An autobiography is written in first person.
    Humanities—Description

24. DUET : PAIR :: DIALOGUE : (*a.* monologue, *b.* quandary, ***c.* bipolar**, *d.* quartet)

    (**c**) *Duet, pair, dialogue,* and *bipolar* all refer to two of something. A *monologue* refers to one; a *quartet* to four; a *quandary* refers to a state of perplexity or doubt.
    General Information—Similarity/Contrast

25. (*a.* foot, *b.* ball, *c.* skate, ***d.* stick**) : HOCKEY :: BAT : BASEBALL

    (**d**) In hockey, players hit a puck with a stick. In baseball, players hit a ball with a bat.
    General Information—Description

26. (*a.* chroma, *b.* violet, *c.* rainbow, ***d.* black**) : COLOR :: VACUUM : AIR

    (**d**) Black is an absence of color. A vacuum is an absence of air.
    Natural Science—Description

27. FLORIDA : PENINSULA :: CUBA : (*a.* state, *b.* gulf, *c.* nation, ***d.* island**)

    (**d**) Florida is a peninsula. Cuba is an island.
    General Information—Description

28. URBAN : RURAL :: URBANE : (*a.* lazy, *b.* suburban, ***c.* boorish**, *d.* effete)

    (**c**) *Urban* and *rural* are antonyms, as are *urbane* and *boorish.*
    Vocabulary—Similarity/Contrast

29. (*a.* air, *b.* earth, ***c.* fire**, *d.* plastic) : PYRO :: WATER : HYDRO

    (**c**) *Pyro-* is a prefix meaning *fire*, while *hydro-* is a prefix meaning *water.*
    Vocabulary—Similarity/Contrast

30. (*a.* sailor, ***b.* mountebank**, *c.* salesman, *d.* villain) : CHARLATAN :: FRAUD : QUACK

    (**b**) A mountebank is a charlatan, and a fraud is a quack.
    Vocabulary—Similarity/Contrast

Explanation of Answers

31. RULER : LINE SEGMENT :: PROTRACTOR : (*a.* distance, ***b.* angle**, *c.* perimeter, *d.* velocity)

(**b**) A ruler is used to measure a line segment, while a protractor is used to measure an angle.
Mathematics—Description

32. WILLIAMS : (*a.* Massachusetts, *b.* Vermont, *c.* New Hampshire, ***d.* Rhode Island**) :: PENN : PENNSYLVANIA

(**d**) Roger Williams founded the state of Rhode Island; William Penn founded the state of Pennsylvania. The colony of Massachusetts Bay was founded by John Winthrop. Vermont was founded by Ethan Allen and his brothers as well as Seth Warner, whom they recruited for an informal militia, the Green Mountain Boys. John Mason was the founder of New Hampshire.
Humanities—Description

33. OLD : (*a.* Two, ***b.* Twenty**, *c.* Forty, *d.* Sixty) :: MAID : ONE

(**b**) Old Maid and Twenty-One are both card games.
General Information—Completion

34. (*a.* princess, *b.* worker, ***c.* drone**, *d.* servant) : QUEEN :: GANDER : GOOSE

(**c**) A drone bee is male, and a queen bee is female. A gander is a male, and a goose is a female.
Natural Science—Class

35. XL : LX :: CC : (***a.* CCC**, *b.* CD, *c.* DC, *d.* CM)

(**a**) 40 is to 60 as 200 is to 300. In Roman numerals, I = 1, V = 5, X = 10, L = 50, C = 100, D = 500, M = 1,000.
Mathematics—Equality/Negation

36. CASTOR : (*a.* Pisces, *b.* Orion, ***c.* Pollux**, *d.* Andromeda) :: JACOB : ESAU

(**c**) Castor and Pollux were twins, as were Jacob and Esau. Pisces, Orion, and Andromeda are all constellations. Orion was a hunter in Greek mythology. Andromeda was the wife of Perseus.
Humanities—Class

37. KEYNES : (*a.* psychology, ***b.* economics**, *c.* anthropology, *d.* ecology) :: EINSTEIN : PHYSICS

(**b**) John Maynard Keynes revolutionized economic theory, while Albert Einstein revolutionized theory in physics.
Social Science—Description

38. (*a.* New Jersey, *b.* Missouri, **c. Indian**, *d.* Byrd) : ANTARCTIC ::
HUDSON : MISSISSIPPI

(**c**) The Indian and the Antarctic are both oceans. The Hudson and the
Mississippi are both rivers.
General Information—Class

39. SPRINGS : PALM :: (*a.* Old, *b.* Mineral, **c. York**, *d.* Tree) : NEW

(**c**) Palm Springs and New York are both major cities.
General Information—Completion

40. MEGAPHONE : CONE :: (**a. funnel**, *b.* cloud, *c.* hurricane,
d. dictaphone) : TORNADO

(**a**) A megaphone, a funnel, a cone, and a tornado all have approximately
the same shape.
General Information—Class

41. HARVARD : CAMBRIDGE :: CAMBRIDGE : (*a.* Oxford, *b.* Yale,
c. Cambridge, *d.* Gloucester)

(**c**) Harvard University is in Cambridge, Massachusetts, and Cambridge
University is in Cambridge, England.
General Information—Description

42. ACTUAL : VIRTUAL :: IN FACT : (*a.* in cause, *b.* in time, *c.* in truth,
d. in effect)

(**d**) *Actual* means *in fact*. *Virtual* means *in effect*.
Vocabulary—Similarity/Contrast

43. BRAVE NEW WORLD : (*a.* Winston, **b. Huxley**, *c.* O'Brian, *d.* Wells) ::
1984 : ORWELL

(**b**) *Brave New World* is a novel by Huxley; *1984* is a novel by Orwell. (Both
describe nightmarish societies of the future.)
Humanities—Description

44. CANINE : DOG :: EQUINE : (*a.* cow, *b.* goat, **c. horse**, *d.* pig)

(**c**) *Canine* means *doglike*. *Equine* means *horselike*. Cowlike is *bovine*, goatlike is
hircine, and piglike is *porcine*.
General Information—Description

45. CENSURE : (*a.* expurgate, **b. condemn**, *c.* praise, *d.* oppose) :: OBTUSE :
DULL

(**b**) To censure is to condemn. To be obtuse is to be dull.
Vocabulary—Similarity/Contrast

46. USHER : POE :: (*a.* ill Repute, ***b.* Seven Gables**, *c.* Tara, *d.* No Return) : HAWTHORNE

(**b**) Poe wrote about the House of Usher; Hawthorne wrote about the House of the Seven Gables.
Humanities—Description

47. NUMISMATIST : PHILATELIST :: (***a.* coins**, *b.* numbers, *c.* rocks, *d.* trinkets) : STAMPS

(**a**) A numismatist collects coins; a philatelist collects stamps.
General Information—Description

48. CASTLE : BISHOP :: HORIZONTAL : (*a.* vertical, ***b.* diagonal**, *c.* cathedral, *d.* abbey)

(**b**) In the game of chess, a castle is capable of horizontal movement, while a bishop is capable of diagonal movement.
General Information—Description

49. (*a.* endemic, ***b.* mercurial**, *c.* unabating, *d.* retrogressive) : CONSTANT :: CHANGEABLE : IMMUTABLE

(**b**) *Mercurial* and *constant* are antonyms, as are *changeable* and *immutable*.
Vocabulary—Similarity/Contrast

50. TRAGEDY : MELODRAMA :: PATHOS : (***a.* bathos**, *b.* ethos, *c.* comedy, *d.* catharsis)

(**a**) Tragedy expresses pathos, while melodrama expresses bathos.
Humanities—Description

51. PERVADE : PERMEATE :: (*a.* trusting, *b.* mistrustful, ***c.* favorable**, *d.* unfavorable) : AUSPICIOUS

(**c**) *Pervade* and *permeate* are synonyms, as are *favorable* and *auspicious*.
Vocabulary—Similarity/Contrast

52. GOOSE : GEESE :: MOOSE : (*a.* moosen, *b.* meese, *c.* mooses, ***d.* moose**)

(**d**) The plural of *goose* is *geese*. The plural of *moose* is *moose*.
Nonsemantic

53. (**a. passenger pigeon**, *b.* sphinx, *c.* phoenix, *d.* hummingbird) : DODO ::
RAVEN : SPARROW

(**a**) The passenger pigeon and the dodo are both extinct species of birds.
The raven and the sparrow are not extinct. The hummingbird is also not extinct; a
phoenix is a mythical bird that burned itself and arose from the ashes to live again; the
sphinx is a mythical Egyptian creature that has the body of a lion and the head of a man.
Natural Science—Class

54. EASTERN STANDARD : 8 A.M. :: PACIFIC STANDARD : (**a. 5 A.M.**,
b. 6 A.M., *c.* 10 A.M., *d.* 11 A.M.)

(**a**) When it is 8 A.M. Eastern Standard Time, it is 5 A.M. Pacific Standard
Time.
General Information—Similarity/Contrast

55. CENTIGRADE : 100 :: CELSIUS : (*a.* −173, *b.* 0, **c. 100**, *d.* 212)

(**c**) The centigrade and Celsius temperature scales are identical, so 100
degrees centigrade equals 100 degrees Celsius.
Natural Science—Equality/Negation

56. SURFEIT : EXCESS :: EVANESCENT : (*a.* silent, *b.* eternal, **c. ephemeral**,
d. celestial)

(**c**) *Surfeit* and *excess* are synonyms, as are *evanescent* and *ephemeral*.
Vocabulary—Similarity/Contrast

57. PLUTARCH : (*a.* drama, **b. biography**, *c.* epic, *d.* oration) :: AESOP :
FABLE

(**b**) Plutarch is famous as a writer of biography. Aesop is famous as a writer
of fables. Plutarch wrote *Parallel Lives*; famous fables of Aesop are, for
example, *The Fox and the Grapes* and *The Tortoise and the Hare*.
Humanities—Description

58. HYDRO : AQUA :: (*a.* air, *b.* gas, *c.* liquid, **d. water**) : WATER

(**d**) *Hydro-* and *aqua-* are both prefixes meaning *water*.
Vocabulary—Similarity/Contrast

59. REMISS : (*a.* negligent, **b. careful**, *c.* auspicious, *d.* remote) :: DARK :
LIGHT

(**b**) *Remiss* is the opposite of *careful*; *dark* is the opposite of *light*.
Vocabulary—Similarity/Contrast

60. FUSTIAN : GALATEA :: MUSLIN : (*a.* grandam, *b.* lydgate, **c. gabardine**, *d.* rhodium)

(**c**) Fustian, galatea, muslin, and gabardine are all types of cloth.
Grandam refers to an old woman. John Lydgate was an English poet (ca. 1370–1450). Rhodium is a rare metallic element.
General Information—Class

61. BLUE : STRAW :: RASP : (*a.* yellow, *b.* hay, **c. black**, *d.* shriek)

(**c**) A blueberry, a strawberry, a raspberry, and a blackberry are all types of berries.
General Information—Class

62. BUFFALO BILL : (**a. Cody**, *b.* James, *c.* Bowman, *d.* Broderick) :: WILD BILL : HICKOK

(**a**) Buffalo Bill Cody and Wild Bill Hickok were both famous cowboys.
General Information—Completion

63. MOURNER : TEARS :: (*a.* hypochondriac, *b.* lover, *c.* troglodyte, **d. hypocrite**) : CROCODILE TEARS

(**d**) A mourner sheds tears. A hypocrite sheds crocodile tears.
Vocabulary—Description

64. CEDE : SEED :: (*a.* run, *b.* win, **c. yield**, *d.* go) : PLANT

(**c**) To cede is to yield. To seed is to plant.
Vocabulary—Similarity/Contrast

65. INGENUOUS : (*a.* clever, **b. innocent**, *c.* pastoral, *d.* hopeful) :: INFRACTION : VIOLATION

(**b**) *Ingenuous* and *innocent* are synonyms, as are *infraction* and *violation*.
Vocabulary—Similarity/Contrast

66. SECULAR : (*a.* sacred, *b.* ecclesiastical, *c.* lay, **d. regular**) :: BISHOP : MONK

(**d**) A bishop is a member of the secular clergy. A monk is a member of the regular clergy. Secular and regular clergy are terms from the Catholic Church. Secular clergy are priests and deacons, for example, who are not bound by the vows of a monastic order. Regular clergy, to the contrary, take vows of a monastic order, such as poverty and obedience.
Humanities—Class

67. EXTIRPATE : (*a.* evade, *b.* examine, *c.* exude, ***d.* eradicate**) :: BUOY : ENCOURAGE

    (**d**) To extirpate is to eradicate. To buoy is to encourage.
    Vocabulary—Similarity/Contrast

68. THREE : (*a.* Two, ***b.* Five**, *c.* Seven, *d.* Ten) :: MUSKETEERS : LITTLE PEPPERS

    (**b**) There were, so the stories go, Three Musketeers, but five little peppers.
    Humanities—Completion

69. WEND : END :: (*a.* food, ***b.* wait**, *c.* tend, *d.* beginning) : ATE

    (**b**) *Wend* is pronounced like end, except for the added initial *w* consonant sound. *Wait* is pronounced like *ate*, also except for the initial *w* consonant sound.
    Nonsemantic

70. VOLT : POTENTIAL DIFFERENCE :: WATT : (*a.* resistance, *b.* brightness, ***c.* power**, *d.* actual difference)

    (**c**) The volt is a measure of potential difference. The watt is a measure of power.
    Natural Science—Description

71. POINT : 0 :: HEXAGON : (*a.* 1, ***b.* 2**, *c.* 3, *d.* 4)

    (**b**) A point occupies 0 dimension, while a hexagon occupies 2 dimensions.
    Mathematics—Description

72. (*a.* Troy, *b.* Athens, ***c.* Carthage**, *d.* Milan) : PUNIC :: SPARTA : PELOPONNESIAN

    (**c**) Carthage was one of the opposing sides in the Punic Wars (264–241 B.C., 218–201 B.C., 149–146 B.C.); the other side was Rome. Sparta was one of the opposing sides in the Peloponnesian Wars (431–404 B.C.); the other side was Athens and its allies. Rome and Sparta eventually won their respective wars.
    Humanities—Description

73. WINDY CITY : CHICAGO :: GOTHAM : (*a.* San Francisco, *b.* Paris, ***a.* New York City**, *d.* London)

    (**c**) Windy City is another name for Chicago. Gotham is another name for New York City.
    General Information—Similarity/Contrast

74. INCANDESCENT : FILAMENT :: FLUORESCENT : (*a.* air, *b.* vacuum, *c.* energy, ***d.* phosphor**)

(**d**) The filament glows in an incandescent lamp. The phosphor glows in a fluorescent lamp.
Natural Science—Description

75. CABAL : (*a.* trivia, ***b.* plot**, *c.* wire, *d.* quibble) :: CAPABLE : COMPETENT

(**b**) *Cabal* and *plot* are synonyms, as are *capable* and *competent*.
Vocabulary—Similarity/Contrast

76. ORDER : (*a.* human, ***b.* primates**, *c.* erectus, *d.* mammalia) :: SPECIES : SAPIENS

(**b**) Human beings are of order Primates and species *sapiens*.
Natural Science—Class

77. GRENDEL : BEOWULF :: HYDRA : (*a.* Achilles, *b.* Vulcan, *c.* Atlas, ***d.* Hercules**)

(**d**) Beowulf slew Grendel; Hercules slew Hydra. Achilles was the greatest warrior of the Greeks in the Trojan War. Vulcan was the god of fire and metalworking in Roman mythology. Atlas was a titan who was forced by Zeus to carry the heavens on his shoulders.
Humanities—Description

78. $2^{-2} : 2^{-1} :: 2^2 : (a.\ 2^0, b.\ 2^1, c.\ 2^2, \textbf{\textit{d.}\ 2^3})$

(**d**) $\frac{1}{4}$ is to $\frac{1}{2}$ as 4 is to 8.
Mathematics—Class

79. DEARTH : SHORTAGE :: PLETHORA : (*a.* abundance, *b.* scarcity, ***c.* excess**, *d.* necessity)

(**c**) A dearth is a shortage. A plethora is an excess.
Vocabulary—Similarity/Contrast

80. WANDERING JEW : EARTH :: FLYING DUTCHMAN : (***a.* seas**, *b.* stars, *c.* heaven, *d.* hell)

(**a**) The Wandering Jew was doomed to wander the earth. The Flying Dutchman was doomed to wander the seas.
Humanities—Description

81. ASTROLABE : SEXTANT :: SUNDIAL : (*a.* time, ***b.* electric clock**, *c.* ruler, *d.* light rays)

   (**b**) The sextant replaced the astrolabe; the electric clock replaced the sundial.
   Natural Science—Description

82. VENAL : (*a.* rigid, *b.* cold, *c.* humorless, ***d.* mercenary**) :: VENIAL : EXCUSABLE

   (**d**) *Venal* and *mercenary* are synonyms, as are *venial* and *excusable*.
   Vocabulary—Similarity/Contrast

83. E# : Fb :: B : (*a.* Cb, ***b.* B**$_b$, *c.* C, *d.* B)

   (**b**) E# is a half-tone higher than F$_b$. B is a half-tone higher than B$_b$.
   Humanities—Description

84. MELIORATE : AMELIORATE :: HASTEN : (***a.* speed up**, *b.* slow down, *c.* better, *d.* worsen)

   (**a**) *Meliorate* and *ameliorate* mean the same thing, as do *hasten* and *speed up*.
   Vocabulary—Similarity/Contrast

85. MACHIAVELLI : PRINCE :: CASTIGLIONE : (*a.* Knight, ***b.* Courtier**, *c.* King, *d.* Yeoman)

   (**b**) Machiavelli is the author of *The Prince*. Castiglione is the author of *The Courtier*.
   Humanities—Description

86. NOSTRUM : (*a.* pedestal, *b.* disease, ***c.* panacea**, *d.* pabulum) :: VERACIOUS : HONEST

   (**c**) A nostrum is a panacea (remedy for all ills). A veracious person is an honest person.
   Vocabulary—Similarity/Contrast

87. DWARF : PITUITARY :: CRETIN : (*a.* endocrine, ***b.* thyroid**, *c.* thalamus, *d.* hypothalamus)

   (**b**) A dwarf has a malfunctioning pituitary gland. A cretin has a malfunctioning thyroid gland.
   Natural Science—Description

88. (*a.* barometer, ***b.* tachometer**, *c.* hydrometer, *d.* voltmeter) :: THERMOMETER :: SPEED : TEMPERATURE

   (**b**) A tachometer measures speed. A thermometer measures temperature.
   Natural Science—Description

Explanation of Answers

89. FROWARD : BACKWARD :: (*a.* dilatory, *b.* upside down, **c. refractory**, *d.* right side up) : REVERSED

(**c**) *Froward* means *refractory*. *Backward* means *reversed*.
Vocabulary—Similarity/Contrast

90. LEWIN : (*a.* attribution theory, *b.* dissonance theory, **c. field theory**, *d.* psychoanalytic theory) :: JUNG : ANALYTIC THEORY

(**c**) Lewin's theory of personality is classified as a field theory. Jung's theory of personality is called analytic theory.
Social Science—Description

91. BUNSEN BURNER : GAS :: AUTOCLAVE : (*a.* oil, *b.* electricity, **c. steam**, *d.* solar energy)

(**c**) A Bunsen burner produces heat through gas. An autoclave produces heat through steam.
Natural Science—Description

92. BACH : (**a. invention**, *b.* symphony, *c.* waltz, *d.* polyphony) :: CHOPIN : MAZURKA

(**a**) Bach was a composer of inventions. Chopin was a composer of mazurkas. Mazurkas are Polish folk dances; inventions are short pieces developing a single theme contrapuntally.
Humanities—Description

93. BANISHMENT : COUNTRY :: DEFENESTRATION : (*a.* ceiling, *b.* floor, *c.* city, ***d.* window**)

(**d**) Banishment occurs when someone is thrown out of a country. Defenestration occurs when someone is thrown out of a window.
Vocabulary—Description

94. CADMEAN : (*a.* Caesarian, *b.* Augustan, *c.* Napoleonic, ***d.* Pyrrhic**) :: EXPENSIVE : COSTLY

(**d**) Both a Cadmean and a Pyrrhic victory are excessively (costly) types of victory. The armed men who sprang from the teeth of the dragon sown by Cadmus killed each other. A Pyrrhic victory is so called because the army of King Pyrrhus of Epirus suffered enormous losses during the Pyrrhic War in which the Romans were eventually defeated at Heraclea (280 B.C.) and Asculum (279 B.C.).
Humanities—Similarity/Contrast

95. MOSES : (*a.* Abraham, *b.* Joseph, *c.* **Joshua**, *d.* Gideon) :: ROOSEVELT : TRUMAN

(**c**) Joshua succeeded Moses as leader of the Israelites. Truman succeeded Roosevelt as president of the United States. Abraham is regarded by Jews as the founder of the Hebrew people (via his son Isaac) and by Muslims as the founder of the Muslim people (via his son Ishmael). Joseph was one of Jacob's sons who was sold into slavery by his brothers; Joseph was also the name of Mary's husband. Gideon appears in the Book of Judges and defeated the Midianites.
Humanities—Description

96. PARASYMPATHETIC : (***a.* sympathetic**, *b.* protosympathetic, *c.* asympathetic, *d.* prosympathetic) :: SLOW DOWN : SPEED UP

(**a**) The parasympathetic nervous system slows down the heartbeat, while the sympathetic nervous system speeds it up.
Natural Science—Description

97. (*a.* Galileo, *b.* Newton, *c.* Galen, ***d.* Ptolemy**) : COPERNICUS :: GEOCENTRIC : HELIOCENTRIC

(**d**) Ptolemy is known for his geocentric theory of the solar system, while Copernicus is known for his heliocentric theory. Newton is known for describing universal gravitation; Galen was a Greek physician and one of the first experimental physiologists. Galileo was an Italian physicist and astronomer who improved the telescope and is called the "father of modern observational astronomy." He was a supporter of Copernicanism.
Natural Science—Description

98. TOSCANINI : (*a.* Fournier, ***b.* Ormandy**, *c.* Goodman, *d.* Heifetz) :: VAN CLIBURN : RUBENSTEIN

(**b**) Toscanini and Ormandy attained fame as conductors; Van Cliburn and Rubenstein became famous as pianists.
Humanities—Class

99. RICHELIEU : CARDINAL :: (*a.* Henry IV, ***b.* Louis XIII**, *c.* Francis I, *d.* Napoleon III) : KING

(**b**) Richelieu (1585–1642) was cardinal when Louis XIII (1601–1643) was king.
Humanities—Description

100. JAMES : FUNCTIONALISM :: (*a.* Dewey, *b.* **Levi-Strauss**, *c.* Watson, *d.* Klineberg) : STRUCTURALISM ·

(**b**) James was a functionalist; Levi-Strauss, a structuralist. Dewey was a pragmatist and functionalist. John B. Watson was a behaviorist. Klineberg was an anthropologist.
Social Science—Description

101. FAUST : DR. FAUSTUS :: (*a.* **Goethe**, *b.* Mr. Marlowe, *c.* Hyde, *d.* Kafka) : MARLOWE

(**a**) *Faust* was written by Goethe just as *Dr. Faustus* was written by Marlowe.
Humanities—Description

102. RHODESIA : (*a.* Indonesia, *b.* **Zimbabwe**, *c.* Namibia, *d.* Israel) :: BURMA : MYANMAR

(**b**) Rhodesia is the former name of the country today known as Zimbabwe. Burma is the former name of present-day Myanmar. Indonesia was previously known as Dutch East Indies. Namibia was formerly known as German Southwest Africa.
General Information—Similarity/Contrast

103. SALT : WATER :: (*a.* **desalinate**, *b.* desaltify, *c.* purify, *d.* reduce) : DEHYDRATE

(**a**) To reduce salt content is to desalinate. To reduce water content is to dehydrate.
Vocabulary—Description

104. HART : DEER :: COLT : (*a.* stallion, *b.* horse, *c.* filly, *d.* **foal**)

(**d**) A hart is a male deer, and a colt is a male foal.
Vocabulary—Class

105. (*a.* liver, *b.* **brain**, *c.* ear, *d.* pancreas) : HEART :: LOBE : CHAMBER

(**b**) The brain is made up of separate lobes, while the heart is made up of separate chambers.
General Information—Part/Whole

106. NADIR : (*a.* penultimate, *b.* depth, *c.* **zenith**, *d.* low) :: STYGIAN : BRIGHT

(**c**) The nadir, or lowest point, is the opposite of the zenith. Likewise, stygian, meaning dark and dismal, is the opposite of bright.
Vocabulary—Similarity/Contrast

107. 32 : FAHRENHEIT :: (*a.* –32, *b.* 100, *c.* 10, **_d._ 0**) : CELSIUS

(**d**) 32 degrees Fahrenheit is the point at which water freezes just as 0 degrees Celsius is the point at which water freezes.
Natural Science—Equality/Negation

108. GRAPE : RAISIN :: PLUM : (*a.* date, *b.* fig, **_c._ prune**, *d.* currant)

(**c**) A dried grape is called a raisin and a dried plum is called a prune.
General Information—Class

109. NORTH : CANCER :: SOUTH : (*a.* Virgo, **_b._ Capricorn**, *c.* Sagittarius, *d.* Equator)

(**b**) North of the equator lies the Tropic of Cancer and south of it lies the Tropic of Capricorn (lines of altitude about 23° north and south of the equator).
General Information—Description

110. EVELYN : DACTYL :: (**_a._ Michelle**, *b.* Holly, *c.* Erica, *d.* Emily) : IAMB

(**a**) Evelyn is a name whose metric foot is a dactyl. Michelle is a name whose metric foot is an iamb. A dactyl is a metrical foot consisting of one stressed and two unstressed syllables. An iamb is a metrical foot that consists of one unstressed and one stressed syllable.
Humanities—Description

111. MOZART : (**_a._ Violin**, *b.* Flute, *c.* Viola, *d.* Cello) :: BACH : ORGAN

(**a**) Mozart was most accomplished instrumentally on the violin. Bach was most accomplished on the organ.
Humanities—Description

112. (*a.* pizzicato, *b.* staccato, *c.* diminuendo, **_d._ piano**) : FORTE :: SOFT : LOUD

(**d**) The musical term *piano* indicates that one should play softly, whereas *forte* directs one to play loudly. A *pizzicato* is a passage played by plucking strings. *Staccato* means that notes are being played in a detached manner that separates them from each other. *Diminuendo* means decreasing the volume of a played passage.
Humanities—Similarity/Contrast

113. INDIA : HINDUISM :: INDONESIA : (*a.* Buddhism, *b.* Confucianism, *c.* Christianity, **_d._ Islam**)

(**d**) India is the country with the greatest population of people practicing Hinduism, whereas Indonesia is the country with the greatest population of people practicing Islam.
General Information—Description

114. OBOE : REED :: (*a.* **viola**, *b.* bassoon, *c.* timpani, *d.* french horn) :
STRING

(**a**) The vibration of a reed produces the sound of an oboe, just as the
vibration of a string produces the sound of a viola.
Humanities—Part/Whole

115. MORE : (*a.* **Utopia**, *b.* Paradise Lost, *c.* 1984, *d.* On the Beach) ::
HUXLEY : BRAVE NEW WORLD

(**a**) Aldous Huxley wrote a futuristic novel entitled *Brave New World*.
Thomas Moore wrote about a ficticious island in a book entitled *Utopia*.
Humanities—Description

116. BASEBALL : BAT :: TABLE TENNIS : (*a.* mallet, ***b.* paddle**, *c.* stick,
d. racquet)

(**b**) In baseball, the ball is hit with a bat. In table tennis, the ball is hit with
a paddle.
General Information—Description

117. ETYMOLOGY : ENTOMOLOGY :: (*a.* letters, *b.* arachnids, *c.* disease,
***d.* words**) : INSECTS

(**d**) Etymology is the study of words just as entomology is the study
of insects.
Vocabulary—Description

118. ADAM : (***a.* Eden**, *b.* Israel, *c.* heaven, *d.* hell) :: ROMEO : VERONA

(**a**) Adam was banished from Eden and Romeo was banished from Verona.
Humanities—Description

119. $8^{1/3}$: $25^{1/2}$ :: (*a.* 25^2, *b.* $100^{1/3}$, ***c.* $100^{1/2}$**, *d.* $16^{1/2}$) : $625^{1/2}$

(**c**) The cube root of eight is 2, and the square root of 25 is 5, creating a
ratio of 2 to 5. Similarly, the square root of 100 is 10 and the square root of
625 is 25, creating a ratio of 2 to 5.
Mathematics—Equality/Negation

120. AUGMENTED THIRD : DIMINISHED THIRD :: FOUR :
(***a.* two and a half**, *b.* three, *c.* two, *d.* three and a half)

(**a**) An augmented third is the equivalent of four steps in music.
A diminished third is the equivalent of two and a half steps in music.
Humanities—Equality/Negation

PRACTICE TEST 3

Item Classification Chart

		RELATIONSHIP						
		Similarity/ Contrast	Description	Class	Completion	Part/ Whole	Equality/ Negation	Nonsemantic
C O N T E N T	**Vocabulary**	9, 15, 28, 29, 30, 42, 45, 49, 51, 56, 58, 59, 64, 65, 67, 75, 79, 82, 84, 86, 89, 106	63, 93, 103, 117	104				
	General Information	3, 4, 6, 16, 24, 54, 73, 102	1, 2, 5, 7, 12, 17, 18, 19, 25, 27, 41, 44, 47, 48, 109, 113, 116	38, 40, 60, 61, 108	21, 33, 39, 62	105		
	Humanities	94, 112	23, 32, 43, 46, 50, 57, 72, 77, 80, 83, 85, 92, 95, 99, 101, 110, 111, 115, 118	8, 36, 66, 98	68	114	120	
	Social Science		13, 37, 90, 100					
	Natural Science		22, 26, 70, 74, 81, 87, 88, 91, 96, 97	14, 34, 53, 76	11		55, 107	
	Mathematics	10, 31, 71		78			35, 119	
	Nonsemantic							20, 52, 69

Answer Sheet
PRACTICE TEST 4

1 Ⓐ Ⓑ Ⓒ Ⓓ	31 Ⓐ Ⓑ Ⓒ Ⓓ	61 Ⓐ Ⓑ Ⓒ Ⓓ	91 Ⓐ Ⓑ Ⓒ Ⓓ
2 Ⓐ Ⓑ Ⓒ Ⓓ	32 Ⓐ Ⓑ Ⓒ Ⓓ	62 Ⓐ Ⓑ Ⓒ Ⓓ	92 Ⓐ Ⓑ Ⓒ Ⓓ
3 Ⓐ Ⓑ Ⓒ Ⓓ	33 Ⓐ Ⓑ Ⓒ Ⓓ	63 Ⓐ Ⓑ Ⓒ Ⓓ	93 Ⓐ Ⓑ Ⓒ Ⓓ
4 Ⓐ Ⓑ Ⓒ Ⓓ	34 Ⓐ Ⓑ Ⓒ Ⓓ	64 Ⓐ Ⓑ Ⓒ Ⓓ	94 Ⓐ Ⓑ Ⓒ Ⓓ
5 Ⓐ Ⓑ Ⓒ Ⓓ	35 Ⓐ Ⓑ Ⓒ Ⓓ	65 Ⓐ Ⓑ Ⓒ Ⓓ	95 Ⓐ Ⓑ Ⓒ Ⓓ
6 Ⓐ Ⓑ Ⓒ Ⓓ	36 Ⓐ Ⓑ Ⓒ Ⓓ	66 Ⓐ Ⓑ Ⓒ Ⓓ	96 Ⓐ Ⓑ Ⓒ Ⓓ
7 Ⓐ Ⓑ Ⓒ Ⓓ	37 Ⓐ Ⓑ Ⓒ Ⓓ	67 Ⓐ Ⓑ Ⓒ Ⓓ	97 Ⓐ Ⓑ Ⓒ Ⓓ
8 Ⓐ Ⓑ Ⓒ Ⓓ	38 Ⓐ Ⓑ Ⓒ Ⓓ	68 Ⓐ Ⓑ Ⓒ Ⓓ	98 Ⓐ Ⓑ Ⓒ Ⓓ
9 Ⓐ Ⓑ Ⓒ Ⓓ	39 Ⓐ Ⓑ Ⓒ Ⓓ	69 Ⓐ Ⓑ Ⓒ Ⓓ	99 Ⓐ Ⓑ Ⓒ Ⓓ
10 Ⓐ Ⓑ Ⓒ Ⓓ	40 Ⓐ Ⓑ Ⓒ Ⓓ	70 Ⓐ Ⓑ Ⓒ Ⓓ	100 Ⓐ Ⓑ Ⓒ Ⓓ
11 Ⓐ Ⓑ Ⓒ Ⓓ	41 Ⓐ Ⓑ Ⓒ Ⓓ	71 Ⓐ Ⓑ Ⓒ Ⓓ	101 Ⓐ Ⓑ Ⓒ Ⓓ
12 Ⓐ Ⓑ Ⓒ Ⓓ	42 Ⓐ Ⓑ Ⓒ Ⓓ	72 Ⓐ Ⓑ Ⓒ Ⓓ	102 Ⓐ Ⓑ Ⓒ Ⓓ
13 Ⓐ Ⓑ Ⓒ Ⓓ	43 Ⓐ Ⓑ Ⓒ Ⓓ	73 Ⓐ Ⓑ Ⓒ Ⓓ	103 Ⓐ Ⓑ Ⓒ Ⓓ
14 Ⓐ Ⓑ Ⓒ Ⓓ	44 Ⓐ Ⓑ Ⓒ Ⓓ	74 Ⓐ Ⓑ Ⓒ Ⓓ	104 Ⓐ Ⓑ Ⓒ Ⓓ
15 Ⓐ Ⓑ Ⓒ Ⓓ	45 Ⓐ Ⓑ Ⓒ Ⓓ	75 Ⓐ Ⓑ Ⓒ Ⓓ	105 Ⓐ Ⓑ Ⓒ Ⓓ
16 Ⓐ Ⓑ Ⓒ Ⓓ	46 Ⓐ Ⓑ Ⓒ Ⓓ	76 Ⓐ Ⓑ Ⓒ Ⓓ	106 Ⓐ Ⓑ Ⓒ Ⓓ
17 Ⓐ Ⓑ Ⓒ Ⓓ	47 Ⓐ Ⓑ Ⓒ Ⓓ	77 Ⓐ Ⓑ Ⓒ Ⓓ	107 Ⓐ Ⓑ Ⓒ Ⓓ
18 Ⓐ Ⓑ Ⓒ Ⓓ	48 Ⓐ Ⓑ Ⓒ Ⓓ	78 Ⓐ Ⓑ Ⓒ Ⓓ	108 Ⓐ Ⓑ Ⓒ Ⓓ
19 Ⓐ Ⓑ Ⓒ Ⓓ	49 Ⓐ Ⓑ Ⓒ Ⓓ	79 Ⓐ Ⓑ Ⓒ Ⓓ	109 Ⓐ Ⓑ Ⓒ Ⓓ
20 Ⓐ Ⓑ Ⓒ Ⓓ	50 Ⓐ Ⓑ Ⓒ Ⓓ	80 Ⓐ Ⓑ Ⓒ Ⓓ	110 Ⓐ Ⓑ Ⓒ Ⓓ
21 Ⓐ Ⓑ Ⓒ Ⓓ	51 Ⓐ Ⓑ Ⓒ Ⓓ	81 Ⓐ Ⓑ Ⓒ Ⓓ	111 Ⓐ Ⓑ Ⓒ Ⓓ
22 Ⓐ Ⓑ Ⓒ Ⓓ	52 Ⓐ Ⓑ Ⓒ Ⓓ	82 Ⓐ Ⓑ Ⓒ Ⓓ	112 Ⓐ Ⓑ Ⓒ Ⓓ
23 Ⓐ Ⓑ Ⓒ Ⓓ	53 Ⓐ Ⓑ Ⓒ Ⓓ	83 Ⓐ Ⓑ Ⓒ Ⓓ	113 Ⓐ Ⓑ Ⓒ Ⓓ
24 Ⓐ Ⓑ Ⓒ Ⓓ	54 Ⓐ Ⓑ Ⓒ Ⓓ	84 Ⓐ Ⓑ Ⓒ Ⓓ	114 Ⓐ Ⓑ Ⓒ Ⓓ
25 Ⓐ Ⓑ Ⓒ Ⓓ	55 Ⓐ Ⓑ Ⓒ Ⓓ	85 Ⓐ Ⓑ Ⓒ Ⓓ	115 Ⓐ Ⓑ Ⓒ Ⓓ
26 Ⓐ Ⓑ Ⓒ Ⓓ	56 Ⓐ Ⓑ Ⓒ Ⓓ	86 Ⓐ Ⓑ Ⓒ Ⓓ	116 Ⓐ Ⓑ Ⓒ Ⓓ
27 Ⓐ Ⓑ Ⓒ Ⓓ	57 Ⓐ Ⓑ Ⓒ Ⓓ	87 Ⓐ Ⓑ Ⓒ Ⓓ	117 Ⓐ Ⓑ Ⓒ Ⓓ
28 Ⓐ Ⓑ Ⓒ Ⓓ	58 Ⓐ Ⓑ Ⓒ Ⓓ	88 Ⓐ Ⓑ Ⓒ Ⓓ	118 Ⓐ Ⓑ Ⓒ Ⓓ
29 Ⓐ Ⓑ Ⓒ Ⓓ	59 Ⓐ Ⓑ Ⓒ Ⓓ	89 Ⓐ Ⓑ Ⓒ Ⓓ	119 Ⓐ Ⓑ Ⓒ Ⓓ
30 Ⓐ Ⓑ Ⓒ Ⓓ	60 Ⓐ Ⓑ Ⓒ Ⓓ	90 Ⓐ Ⓑ Ⓒ Ⓓ	120 Ⓐ Ⓑ Ⓒ Ⓓ

Practice Test 4

Directions: In each of the following questions, you will find three initial terms and, in parentheses, four answer options designated *a, b, c,* and *d.* You are to select from the four answer options the one that best completes the analogy with the three initial terms. To record your answers, use the answer sheet provided.

Time: 60 minutes

1. POLAND : POLISH :: (*a.* Holland, *b.* Dublin, *c.* Denmark, *d.* Dansk) : DANISH

2. UNION : (*a.* green, *b.* brown, *c.* blue, *d.* white) :: CONFEDERACY : GRAY

3. ARTICLE : (*a.* preposition, *b.* conjunction, *c.* adjective, *d.* verb) :: THE : AND

4. SAFETY : 2 :: TOUCHDOWN : (*a.* 2, *b.* 4, *c.* 6, *d.* 8)

5. CIRCLE : ELLIPSE :: SQUARE : (*a.* triangle, *b.* rectangle, *c.* pentagon, *d.* hexagon)

6. BIRD : (*a.* nest, *b.* worm, *c.* wings, *d.* fly) :: GENIE : MAGIC CARPET

7. FOXHOLE : (*a.* foxes, *b.* gunfire, *c.* discovery, *d.* earthquakes) :: RAINCOAT : RAIN

8. FOOLISH : OWL :: (*a.* timid, *b.* large, *c.* wise, *d.* temperamental) : LION

9. SINBAD : (*a.* sailor, *b.* squire, *c.* sinner, *d.* poet) :: ARTHUR : KING

10. SOLOMON : WISE :: NERO : (*a.* stupid, *b.* bold, *c.* just, *d.* cruel)

11. GRAPE : VINE :: RUBBER : (*a.* tree, *b.* conifer, *c.* root, *d.* leaf)

12. (*a.* Georgia, *b.* Massachusetts, *c.* New Jersey, *d.* Ohio) : MIDDLE ATLANTIC : VERMONT : NEW ENGLAND

13. BALD : HAIR :: ALBINO : (*a.* height, *b.* pain, *c.* sight, *d.* pigment)

14. BOW : (*a.* arrow, *b.* curtsey, *c.* stern, *d.* fore) :: FRONT : REAR

15. MONOGYNY : POLYGYNY :: ONE : (*a.* none, *b.* two, *c.* eight, *d.* many)

16. ATTA : AL-SHEHHI :: JARRAH : (*a.* Mohammed, *b.* bin Laden, *c.* Binalshibh, *d.* Atef)

17. (*a.* secret codes, *b.* inscriptions on church vaults, *c.* science fiction, *d.* religious rituals) : CRYPTOGRAPHY :: DICTIONARIES : LEXICOGRAPHY

18. E = mc^2 : EINSTEIN :: $C^2 = A^2 + B^2$: (*a.* Bernoulli, *b.* Cauchy, *c.* Descartes, *d.* Pythagoras)

19. GREEK : GREEK :: ROMAN : (*a.* Indo-European, *b.* Latin, *c.* Mediterranean, *d.* Romanish)

20. (*a.* Jesus, *b.* hell, *c.* heaven, *d.* Satan) : CHRISTIANITY :: NIRVANA : BUDDHISM

21. U.S. CALENDAR : U.S. FISCAL CALENDAR :: JANUARY : (*a.* December, *b.* March, *c.* July, *d.* September)

22. PHOTOMETER : (*a.* light, *b.* distance, *c.* magnetism, *d.* velocity) :: AUDIOMETER : SOUND

23. (*a.* believable, *b.* wrong, *c.* fanciful, *d.* humorous) : INCREDIBLE :: AUGMENT : DIMINISH

24. INFINITIVE : (*a.* having eaten, *b.* to sleep, *c.* has tried, *d.* to the store) :: PARTICIPLE : WALKING

25. MARX : COMMUNISM :: (*a.* Hamilton, *b.* Lenin, *c.* Smith, *d.* Davis) : CAPITALISM

26. (*a.* Iambic, *b.* Doric, *c.* Spartan, *d.* Grecian) : CORINTHIAN :: SONATA : CONCERTO

27. SOCCER : BALL :: (*a.* cricket, *b.* rugby, *c.* hockey, *d.* lacrosse) : PUCK

28. (*a.* sheep, *b.* plasma, *c.* vulture, *d.* harass) : BLOOD :: DOG : HOUND

29. (*a.* hawk, *b.* owl, *c.* bluejay, *d.* ostrich) : NOCTURNAL :: ROBIN : DIURNAL

30. PHLEGM : PHLEGMATIC :: BILE : (*a.* bilious, *b.* billiard, *c.* binding, *d.* bilabial)

31. HEAVY-HANDED : (*a.* uncoordinated, *b.* tactless, *c.* strong, *d.* coordinated) :: HEAVY-FOOTED : PLODDING

32. PALEFACE : WHITE :: BLUENOSE : (*a.* frigid, *b.* tough, *c.* unkind, *d.* puritanical)

33. PROTON : NEUTRON :: POSITIVE : (*a.* negative, *b.* uncharged, *c.* positive, *d.* nucleonic)

34. SPHINX : (*a.* pterodactyl, *b.* dodo, *c.* vulture, *d.* phoenix) :: LION : EAGLE

35. ANDAMAN : ACEH :: SRI LANKA : (*a.* Bali, *b.* Phuket, *c.* Fiji, *d.* Guam)

36. RADIUS : 4 :: DIAMETER : (*a.* 16, *b.* 8, *c.* 87π, *d.* 167π)

37. PIKE : (*a.* sturgeon, *b.* lion, *c.* whale, *d.* buffalo) :: COW : PIG

38. WASSERMANN : (*a.* heart disease, *b.* diabetes, *c.* syphilis, *d.* lung cancer) :: PAP : CERVICAL CANCER

39. COMPLEMENTARY : SUPPLEMENTARY :: (*a.* 0, *b.* 45, *c.* 90, *d.* 360) : 180

40. E.G. : FOR EXAMPLE :: VIZ. : (*a.* namely, *b.* except for, *c.* according to, *d.* generally)

41. GRAPE : WINE :: (*a.* apple, *b.* potato, *c.* pomegranate, *d.* malt) : VODKA

42. RISING : FALLING :: (*a.* bull, *b.* bird, *c.* sparrow, *d.* antelope) : BEAR

43. XX : FEMALE :: (*a.* XY, *b.* YY, *c.* XZ, *d.* ZZ) : MALE

44. RESPECT : (*a.* love, *b.* protect, *c.* revere, *d.* obey) :: DISLIKE : HATE

45. PARLIAMENT : LORDS :: (*a.* House of Representatives, *b.* Congress, *c.* White House, *d.* Supreme Court) : SENATE

46. (*a.* parsing, *b.* gender, *c.* case, *d.* declension) : NOUN :: CONJUGATION : VERB

47. MC : MD :: MMCC : (*a.* MCM, *b.* MGM, *c.* MDM, *d.* MMM)

48. (*a.* dour, *b.* caustic, *c.* sweet, *d.* mild) : ACRID :: BITTER : ACRIMONIOUS

49. PORCINE : (*a.* porcupine, *b.* goat, *c.* dog, *d.* pig) :: FELINE : CAT

50. TIPPECANOE : AND TYLER TOO :: FIFTY-FOUR FORTY : (*a.* forever, *b.* or fight, *c.* and forward, *d.* to fortune)

51. IMPEACH : (*a.* prove the guilt of, *b.* overturn, *c.* acquit, *d.* accuse) :: CONVICT : FIND GUILTY

52. CITY OF SEVEN HILLS : ROME :: CITY OF GOD : (*a.* heaven, *b.* Jerusalem, *c.* Bethlehem, *d.* Jericho)

53. WOOD : PAPER :: LATEX : (*a.* cotton, *b.* plastic, *c.* rayon, *d.* rubber)

54. TEXTILE : RAYON :: GEM : (*a.* sapphire, *b.* diamond, *c.* spinel, *d.* quartz)

55. SIAM : (*a.* Mongolia, *b.* China, *c.* Thailand, *d.* Nepal) :: PERSIA : IRAN

56. HABEAS CORPUS : LAW :: EXEUNT OMNES : (*a.* medicine, *b.* drama, *c.* law, *d.* political theory)

57. PENTHOUSE APARTMENT : TOP FLOOR :: DUPLEX APARTMENT : (*a.* two rooms, *b.* two floors, *c.* two bedrooms, *d.* two persons)

58. XENOPHOBIA : (*a.* foreigners, *b.* death, *c.* insanity, *d.* live burial) :: CLAUSTROPHOBIA : CONFINED PLACES

59. LOCKJAW : TETANUS :: HYDROPHOBIA : (*a.* encephalitis, *b.* malaria, *c.* syphilis, *d.* rabies)

60. ENGLISH : CANADA :: (*a.* Italian, *b.* Portuguese, *c.* Brazilian, *d.* French) : BRAZIL

61. MITIGATE : ASSUAGE :: MODERATE : (*a.* lessen, *b.* make worse, *c.* disprove, *d.* approve)

62. 1^0 : 1^{10} :: 10^0 : (*a.* 10^0, *b.* 10^1, *c.* 10^2, *d.* 10^{10})

63. PUSILLANIMOUS : AUDACIOUS :: (*a.* brave, *b.* purposive, *c.* cowardly, *d.* evanescent) : BOLD

64. HANNIBAL : (*a.* Theseus, *b.* Scipio, *c.* Cicero, *d.* Marcion) :: NAPOLEON : WELLINGTON

65. EPITOME : (*a.* monologue, *b.* prevarication, *c.* summary, *d.* diatribe) :: PREFACE : PROLOGUE

66. (*a.* wave, *b.* radian, *c.* alpha, *d.* roentgen) : RADIATION :: MINUTE : TIME

67. VERACIOUS : (*a.* repeated, *b.* horizontal, *c.* diagonal, *d.* truthful) :: CONTINUAL : INCESSANT

68. SOLAR : SUN :: (*a.* lunar, *b.* diurnal, *c.* stellar, *d.* nocturnal) : MOON

69. LINCOLN STEFFENS : POLITICAL MACHINES :: UPTON SINCLAIR :
    (*a.* meat-packing industry, *b.* financial speculators, *c.* railroad magnates, *d.* patent medicine quacks)

70. FAMILY : HOMINIDAE :: (*a.* sapiens, *b.* species, *c.* genus, *d.* class) : HOMO

71. OVERWEENING : (*a.* conceited, *b.* modest, *c.* spoiled, *d.* underprotected) :: BLUNT : SHARP

72. HEARSAY : GOSSIP :: GAINSAY : (*a.* oppose, *b.* protect, *c.* lose, *d.* take)

73. (*a.* thin, *b.* analogy, *c.* happy, *d.* fat) : FIAT :: SMILE : SIMILE

74. ROUNDHEAD : SHORT HAIR :: (*a.* Tory, *b.* Whig, *c.* Royalist, *d.* Cavalier) : LONG HAIR

75. EUGENICS : HEREDITY :: (*a.* euthanasia, *b.* euthenics, *c.* mnemonics, *d.* dialectics) : ENVIRONMENT

76. THERMO : (*a.* cryo, *b.* iso, *c.* crypto, *d.* paleo) :: HOT : COLD

77. (*a.* North Carolina, *b.* South Carolina, *c.* Georgia, *d.* Florida) : OGLETHORPE :: PENNSYLVANIA : PENN

78. BANEFUL : (*a.* baleful, *b.* salutary, *c.* promiscuous, *d.* remorseful) :: PERSONABLE : HANDSOME

79. WERTHEIMER : GESTALT :: (*a.* Watson, *b.* Köhler, *c.* Koffka, *d.* Piaget) : BEHAVIORIST

80. (*a.* depilate, *b.* dampen, *c.* derogate, *d.* desiccate) : DRY :: MOISTEN : WET

81. GLUCOSE : (*a.* comatose, *b.* malactose, *c.* lactose, *d.* adipose) :: SUCROSE : FRUCTOSE

82. ABLE : MELBA :: (*a.* colt, *b.* peach, *c.* era, *d.* willing) : MARE

83. (*a.* Mars, *b.* Jupiter, *c.* Venus, *d.* Pluto) : PROSERPINA :: ZEUS : HERA

84. FLEET STREET : (*a.* press, *b.* police, *c.* amusement, *d.* high fashion) :: DOWNING STREET : GOVERNMENT

85. ARTUR RUBINSTEIN : PIANO :: ISAAC STERN : (*a.* piano, *b.* violin, *c.* trumpet, *d.* oboe)

86. DURKHEIM : (*a.* Homocide, *b.* Matricide, *c.* Suicide, *d.* Genocide) :: BECKER : OUTSIDERS

87. JOHN WESLEY : METHODIST :: MARY BAKER EDDY : (*a.* Presbyterian, *b.* Baha'i, *c.* Jehovah's Witness, *d.* Christian Science)

88. BACH : BAROQUE :: GRIEG : (*a.* classical, *b.* modern, *c.* romantic, *d.* medieval)

89. (*a.* Husserl, *b.* Heidegger, *c.* Comte, *d.* Camus) : POSITIVISM :: SARTRE : EXISTENTIALISM

90. F# : Gb :: B : (*a.* C_b, *b.* A_b, *c.* G#, *d.* G_b)

91. SECOND : THIRD :: (*a.* clergy, *b.* king, *c.* commoners, *d.* nobility) : BOURGEOISIE

92. ALEXANDER : GREAT :: JULIAN : (*a.* Ingenious, *b.* Meek, *c.* Bold, *d.* Apostate)

93. (*a.* Helen, *b.* Jezebel, *c.* Una, *d.* Archimago) : DUESSA :: GOOD : EVIL

94. D : R × T :: (*a.* A, *b.* C, *c.* F, *d.* H) : M × A

95. PURLOINED : (*a.* Melville, *b.* Doyle, *c.* Poe, *d.* Conrad) :: SCARLET : HAWTHORNE

96. PROPHASE : METAPHASE :: ANAPHASE : (*a.* meiophase, *b.* telophase, *c.* mitophase, *d.* protophase)

97. NEWBERY : (*a.* Wohlenberg, *b.* Caldecott, *c.* Pulitzer, *d.* Thompsen) :: STORY : ARTWORK

98. COUNTESS AURELIA : THE MADWOMAN OF CHAILLOT :: (*a.* Lear, *b.* Othello, *c.* Antonio, *d.* Iago) : THE MERCHANT OF VENICE

99. PICASSO : GUERNICA :: (*a.* Manet, *b.* Raphael, *c.* David, *d.* Leger) : LUNCHEON ON THE GRASS

100. RACINE : MOLIÈRE :: SOPHOCLES : (*a.* Zeno, *b.* Aristophanes, *c.* Plato, *d.* Aristotle)

101. (*a.* Queen Victoria, *b.* Queen Virginia, *c.* Queen Elizabeth, *d.* Queen Mary) : VIRGINIA :: KING GEORGE : GEORGIA

102. MITOSIS : MEIOSIS :: (*a.* 1, *b.* 2, *c.* 4, *d.* 8) : 4

103. DAGGER : STAR :: (*a.* rune, *b.* allograph, *c.* knife, *d.* obelisk) : ASTERISK

104. MISER : (*a.* chary, *b.* mercurial, *c.* acquisitive, *d.* munificent) :: GLUTTON : ABSTEMIOUS

105. (*a.* pork, *b.* sweet, *c.* appetizer, *d.* vegetable) : SWEETMEAT :: FRUIT : BREADFRUIT

106. $2\pi r^2 : \pi(2r)^2$ :: LW : (*a.* (1/2)LW, *b.* LW, *c.* 2LW, *d.* 4LW)

107. (*a.* hatred, *b.* naiveté, *c.* envy, *d.* sickness) : SORROW :: GREEN : BLUE

108. MOHS : HARDNESS :: RICHTER : (*a.* magnitude, *b.* earthquake, *c.* quality, *d.* extremity)

109. FROGS : SEAGULL :: (*a.* Shakespeare, *b.* Marlowe, *c.* Wilde, *d.* Aristophanes) : CHEKHOV

110. INDIA : PAKISTAN :: PAKISTAN : (*a.* Kashmir, *b.* Bangladesh, *c.* Nepal, *d.* Sri Lanka)

111. ORGAN : ORGANELLE :: LIVER : (*a.* vacuole, *b.* pancreas, *c.* kidney, *d.* cell)

112. MASS AND ENERGY : (*a.* Bernoulli, *b.* Newton, *c.* Gauss, *d.* Einstein) :: VOLUME AND DISPLACEMENT : ARCHIMEDES

113. DOGS : PEAS :: PAVLOV : (*a.* Darwin, *b.* Gauss, *c.* Curie, *d.* Mendel)

114. (*a.* King, *b.* Martha, *c.* Reverend, *d.* Priest) : CARVER :: MARTIN LUTHER : GEORGE WASHINGTON

115. SESAME SEEDS : TAHINI :: PEANUTS : (*a.* roots, *b.* shell, *c.* peanut butter, *d.* oil)

116. BASS : (*a.* clarinet, *b.* viola, *c.* cello, *d.* trumpet) :: TREBLE : FLUTE

117. MAL : BEN :: ANTI : (*a.* un, *b.* inter, *c.* pro, *d.* pre)

118. (*a.* meat packing, *b.* clear cutting, *c.* poaching, *d.* iron mining) :
PESTICIDES :: THE JUNGLE : SILENT SPRING

119. HANUKKAH : DIVALI :: JUDAISM : (*a.* Buddhism, *b.* Hinduism,
c. Zoroastrianism, *d.* Islam)

120. SQUARE ROOT : SQUARE :: (*a.* dividend, *b.* root, *c.* log, *d.* integral) :
DERIVATIVE

Answer Key
PRACTICE TEST 4

1. C	31. B	61. A	91. D
2. C	32. D	62. A	92. D
3. B	33. B	63. C	93. C
4. C	34. D	64. B	94. C
5. B	35. B	65. C	95. C
6. C	36. B	66. D	96. B
7. B	37. A	67. D	97. B
8. A	38. C	68. A	98. C
9. A	39. C	69. A	99. A
10. D	40. A	70. C	100. B
11. A	41. B	71. B	101. C
12. C	42. A	72. A	102. B
13. D	43. A	73. D	103. D
14. C	44. C	74. D	104 D
15. D	45. B	75. B	105 B
16. C	46. D	76. A	106. C
17. A	47. D	77. C	107. C
18. D	48. B	78. A	108. A
19. B	49. D	79. A	109. D
20. C	50. B	80. D	110. B
21. C	51. D	81. C	111. A
22. A	52. A	82. C	112. D
23. A	53. D	83. D	113. D
24. B	54. C	84. A	114. A
25. C	55. C	85. B	115. C
26. B	56. B	86. C	116. C
27. C	57. B	87. D	117. C
28. A	58. A	88. C	118. A
29. B	59. D	89. C	119. B
30. A	60. B	90. A	120. D

EXPLANATION OF ANSWERS FOR PRACTICE TEST 4

In the following explanations of answers, explanations concerning the correct response are in a large font. Explanations regarding distracters (incorrect responses) that are not self-explaining or could be misinterpreted are in a smaller font in order to highlight the explanations of the answers that are correct.

1. POLAND : POLISH :: (*a.* Holland, *b.* Dublin, *c.* **Denmark**, *d.* Dansk) : DANISH
   (**c**) A Polish person is from Poland; a Danish person is from Denmark.
   General Information—Description

2. UNION : (*a.* green, *b.* brown, *c.* **blue**, *d.* white) :: CONFEDERACY : GRAY

   (**c**) During the Civil War, Union soldiers wore blue uniforms and soldiers of the Confederacy wore gray uniforms.
   Humanities—Description

3. ARTICLE : (*a.* preposition, ***b.* conjunction**, *c.* adjective, *d.* verb) :: THE : AND

   (**b**) *The* is an article; *and* is a conjunction. A conjunction is a linguistic form that connects two complete clauses.
   Humanities—Description

4. SAFETY : 2 :: TOUCHDOWN : (*a.* 2, *b.* 4, *c.* **6**, *d.* 8)

   (**c**) In football, a safety is worth 2 points and a touchdown is worth 6 points.
   General Information—Description

5. CIRCLE : ELLIPSE :: SQUARE : (*a.* triangle, ***b.* rectangle**, *c.* pentagon, *d.* hexagon)

   (**b**) Both a circle and an ellipse are closed curves. Both a square and a rectangle are polygons with four sides.
   Mathematics—Class

6. BIRD : (*a.* nest, *b.* worm, *c.* **wings**, *d.* fly) :: GENIE : MAGIC CARPET

   (**c**) A bird flies by means of its wings. A genie flies by means of a magic carpet.
   General Information—Description

7. FOXHOLE : (*a.* foxes, ***b.* gunfire**, *c.* discovery, *d.* earthquakes) ::
RAINCOAT : RAIN

(**b**) A foxhole provides protection from gunfire. A raincoat provides
protection from rain.
General Information—Description

8. FOOLISH : OWL :: (***a.* timid**, *b.* large, *c.* wise, *d.* temperamental) : LION

(**a**) An owl is reputed to be wise, which is the opposite of foolish.
A lion is reputed to be bold, which is the opposite of timid.
General Information—Description

9. SINBAD : (***a.* sailor**, *b.* squire, *c.* sinner, *d.* poet) :: ARTHUR : KING

(**a**) Sinbad was a sailor, Arthur a king. Sinbad was a sailor whose stories
are told in *The Book of One Thousand and One Nights*; King Arthur was
a legendary king of the Britons.
Humanities—Description

10. SOLOMON : WISE :: NERO : (*a.* stupid, *b.* bold, *c.* just, ***d.* cruel**)

(**d**) Solomon was wise; Nero was cruel.
Humanities—Description

11. GRAPE : VINE :: RUBBER : (***a.* tree**, *b.* conifer, *c.* root, *d.* leaf)
(**a**) Grapes come from a vine; rubber comes from a tree.
General Information—Description

12. (*a.* Georgia, *b.* Massachusetts, ***c.* New Jersey**, *d.* Ohio) : MIDDLE
ATLANTIC :: VERMONT : NEW ENGLAND

(**c**) New Jersey is a Middle Atlantic state. Vermont is a New England state.
Massachusetts is a New England state, Georgia a Southern state, and Ohio is a Midwestern
state.
General Information—Description

13. BALD : HAIR :: ALBINO : (*a.* height, *b.* pain, *c.* sight, ***d.* pigment**)

(**d**) A bald person lacks hair. An albino lacks pigment.
General Information—Description

14. BOW : (*a.* arrow, *b.* curtsey, ***c.* stern**, *d.* fore) :: FRONT : REAR

(**c**) The bow is the front of a ship; the stern is the rear.
General Information—Similarity/Contrast

15. MONOGYNY : POLYGYNY :: ONE : (*a.* none, *b.* two, *c.* eight, ***d.* many**)

    (**d**) Monogyny is marriage to one spouse. Polygyny is marriage to many spouses.
    Social Science—Description

16. ATTA : AL-SHEHHI :: JARRAH : (*a.* Mohammed, *b.* bin Laden, ***c.* Binalshibh**, *d.* Atef)

    (**c**) Mohamed Atta, Marwan al-Shehhi, Ziad Jarrah, and Ramzi Binalshibh were hijackers in the September 11 attacks. Osama bin Laden, Khalid Sheikh Mohammed, and Mohammed Atef were involved in the planning of the September 11 attacks.
    General Information—Description

17. (***a.* secret codes**, *b.* inscriptions on church vaults, *c.* science fiction, *d.* religious rituals) : CRYPTOGRAPHY :: DICTIONARIES : LEXICOGRAPHY

    (**a**) Cryptography is the art of writing secret codes. Lexicography is the art of writing dictionaries.
    General Information—Description

18. $E = mc^2$: EINSTEIN :: $C^2 = A^2 + B^2$: (*a.* Bernoulli, *b.* Cauchy, *c.* Descartes, ***d.* Pythagoras**)

    (**d**) The equation $E = mc^2$ is attributable to Einstein. The equation $C^2 = A^2 + B^2$ is attributable to Pythagoras. Bernoulli applied mathematics to mechanics and is especially known for the Bernoulli principle. Descartes introduced the use of coordinates to locate a point in one or two dimensions (Cartesian coordinate system). Cauchy (a French mathematician) was a pioneer in analysis and the theory of substitution of groups.
    Mathematics—Description

19. GREEK : GREEK :: ROMAN : (*a.* Indo-European, ***b.* Latin**, *c.* Mediterranean, *d.* Romansh)

    (**b**) The ancient Greeks spoke Greek. The ancient Romans spoke Latin.
    Humanities—Description

20. (*a.* Jesus, *b.* Hell, ***c.* Heaven**, *d.* Satan) : CHRISTIANITY :: NIRVANA : BUDDHISM

    (**c**) The concept of heaven in Christianity serves a function similar to that of nirvana in Buddhism.
    Humanities—Description

21. U.S. CALENDAR : U.S. FISCAL CALENDAR :: JANUARY :
(*a.* December, *b.* March, **c. July**, *d.* September)

(**c**) The first month of the U.S. calendar is January. The first month of the
U.S. fiscal calendar is July.
General Information—Description

22. PHOTOMETER : (**a. light**, *b.* distance, *c.* magnetism, *d.* velocity) ::
AUDIOMETER : SOUND

(**a**) A photometer is used to measure light; an audiometer is used to measure
sound.
Natural Science—Description

23. (**a. believable**, *b.* wrong, *c.* fanciful, *d.* humorous) : INCREDIBLE ::
AUGMENT : DIMINISH

(**a**) *Incredible* and *believable* are antonyms, as are *augment* and *diminish*.
Vocabulary—Similarity/Contrast

24. INFINITIVE : (*a.* having eaten, ***b.* to sleep**, *c.* has tried, *d.* to the store) ::
PARTICIPLE : WALKING

(**b**) *To sleep* is an infinitive. *Walking* is a participle.
Humanities—Class

25. MARX : COMMUNISM :: (*a.* Hamilton, *b.* Lenin, ***c.* Smith**, *d.* Davis) :
CAPITALISM

(**c**) Karl Marx is famous for his writing on communism. Adam Smith is
famous for his writing on capitalism. Hamilton was the first Secretary of Treasury in
the United States as well as an economist and philosopher. Lenin was the first head of the
Soviet Socialist Republic. Davis is a distracter term.
Social Science—Description

26. (*a.* Iambic, ***b.* Doric**, *c.* Spartan, *d.* Grecian) : CORINTHIAN :: SONATA :
CONCERTO

(**b**) Doric and Corinthian are both types of columns. A sonata and a
concerto are both types of musical compositions. Doric refers to the Ancient
Greeks of Doris or to a dialect of Ancient Greek that is spoken in the
Peloponnesus. Corinthian refers to somebody from the city of Corinth or
to somebody who likes to seek pleasure. A sonata is a composition for one
or two instruments that typically has three or four movements. A concerto
is a composition for an entire orchestra and one or more soloists. Iamb is
a metrical foot that consists of one unstressed and one stressed syllable. Grecian refers to
something from Greece. Spartan refers to something from the Greek city of Sparta.
Humanities—Class

27. SOCCER : BALL :: (*a.* cricket, *b.* rugby, ***c.* hockey**, *d.* lacrosse) : PUCK

    (**c**) Soccer is played with a ball, hockey with a puck.
    General Information—Description

28. (***a.* sheep**, *b.* plasma, *c.* vulture, *d.* harass) : BLOOD :: DOG : HOUND

    (**a**) A sheep dog and a bloodhound are both types of dogs.
    General Information—Completion

29. (*a.* hawk, ***b.* owl**, *c.* bluejay, *d.* ostrich) : NOCTURNAL :: ROBIN : DIURNAL

    (**b**) An owl is a nocturnal bird; a robin is a diurnal bird.
    Natural Science—Description

30. PHLEGM : PHLEGMATIC :: BILE : (***a.* bilious**, *b.* billiard, *c.* binding, *d.* bilabial)

    (**a**) The word *phlegmatic* derives from *phlegm*. The word *bilious* derives from *bile*.
    Vocabulary—Description

31. HEAVY-HANDED : (*a.* uncoordinated, ***b.* tactless**, *c.* strong, *d.* coordinated) :: HEAVY-FOOTED : PLODDING

    (**b**) Someone who is heavy-handed is tactless. Someone who is heavy-footed is plodding.
    Vocabulary—Similarity/Contrast

32. PALEFACE : WHITE :: BLUENOSE : (*a.* frigid, *b.* tough, *c.* unkind, ***d.* puritanical**)

    (**d**) A paleface is a white person. A bluenose is puritanical.
    General Information—Description

33. PROTON : NEUTRON :: POSITIVE : (*a.* negative, ***b.* uncharged**, *c.* positive, *d.* nucleonic)

    (**b**) A proton has a positive electrical charge. A neutron is uncharged.
    Natural Science—Description

34. SPHINX : (*a.* pterodactyl, *b.* dodo, *c.* vulture, ***d.* phoenix**) :: LION : EAGLE

    (**d**) A sphinx and a phoenix are both mythological animals. A lion and an eagle are both real animals. The sphinx is a mythical Egyptian creature that has a lion's body and a man's head. A phoenix is a mythical bird that burned itself and arose from the ashes to live again. A pterodactyl is a winged flying reptile that is extinct. A dodo is an extinct flightless bird from Mauritius.
    Humanities—Class

35. ANDAMAN : ACEH :: SRI LANKA : (*a.* Bali, ***b.* Phuket**, *c.* Fiji, *d.* Guam)

    (**b**) The Andaman Islands, Aceh, Sri Lanka, and Phuket were regions that were affected by the Indian Ocean Tsunami on December 26, 2004.
    General Information—Description

36. RADIUS : 4 :: DIAMETER : (*a.* 16, ***b.* 8**, *c.* 87π, *d.* 167π)

    (**b**) If the radius of a circle is 4, the circle's diameter is 8.
    Mathematics—Description

37. PIKE : (***a.* sturgeon**, *b.* lion, *c.* whale, *d.* buffalo) :: COW : PIG

    (**a**) A pike and a sturgeon are both fishes. A cow and a pig are both mammals.
    Natural Science—Class

38. WASSERMANN : (*a.* heart disease, *b.* diabetes, ***c.* syphilis**, *d.* lung cancer) :: PAP : CERVICAL CANCER

    (**c**) The Wassermann test is for syphilis. The Pap test is for cervical cancer.
    Natural Science—Description

39. COMPLEMENTARY : SUPPLEMENTARY :: (*a.* 0, *b.* 45, ***c.* 90**, *d.* 360) : 180

    (**c**) Complementary angles sum to 90 degrees. Supplementary angles sum to 180 degrees.
    Mathematics—Description

40. e.g. : FOR EXAMPLE :: viz. : (***a.* namely**, *b.* except for, *c.* according to, *d.* generally)

    (**a**) The abbreviation *e.g.* means "for example"; *viz.* means "namely." *e.g.* is the abbreviation for *exempli gratia* (for example); *viz.* is the abbreviation for *videlicet* (namely).
    General Information—Similarity/Contrast

41. GRAPE : WINE :: (*a.* apple, ***b.* potato**, *c.* pomegranate, *d.* malt) : VODKA

    (**b**) Grapes are used to make wine, potatoes to make vodka.
    General Information—Description

42. RISING : FALLING :: (***a.* bull**, *b.* bird, *c.* sparrow, *d.* antelope) : BEAR

    (**a**) A rising market is a bull market. A falling market is a bear market.
    Social Science—Similarity/Contrast

43. XX : FEMALE :: (***a.* XY**, *b.* YY, *c.* XZ, *d.* ZZ) : MALE

    (**a**) A female is distinguished by an XX chromosome. A male is
    distinguished by an XY chromosome.
    Natural Science—Description

44. RESPECT : (*a.* love, *b.* protect, ***c.* revere**, *d.* obey) :: DISLIKE : HATE

    (**c**) To revere is to respect a great deal. To hate is to dislike a great deal.
    Vocabulary—Description

45. PARLIAMENT : LORDS :: (*a.* House of Representatives, ***b.* Congress**,
    c. White House, *d.* Supreme Court) : SENATE

    (**b**) The House of Lords is the upper chamber of the British Parliament.
    The Senate is the upper chamber of the U.S. Congress.
    Social Science—Description

46. (*a.* parsing, *b.* gender, *c.* case, ***d.* declension**) : NOUN :: CONJUGATION :
    VERB

    (**d**) Nouns may belong to a declension, verbs to a conjugation.
    Humanities—Description

47. MC : MD :: MMCC : (*a.* MCM, *b.* MGM, *c.* MDM, ***d.* MMM**)

    (**d**) 1,100 is to 1,500 as 2,200 is to 3,000. In Roman numerals, I = 1, V = 5,
    X = 10, L = 50, C = 100, D = 500, M = 1,000.
    Mathematics—Equality/Negation

48. (*a.* dour, ***b.* caustic**, *c.* sweet, *d.* mild) : ACRID :: BITTER :
    ACRIMONIOUS

    (**b**) *Caustic, acrid, bitter,* and *acrimonious* all mean the same thing.
    Vocabulary—Similarity/Contrast

49. PORCINE : (*a.* porcupine, *b.* goat, *c.* dog, ***d.* pig**) :: FELINE : CAT

    (**d**) *Porcine* means *piglike. Feline* means *catlike.* Goatlike is hircine.
    Doglike is canine. A porcupine is a rodent.
    Vocabulary—Description

50. TIPPECANOE : AND TYLER TOO :: FIFTY-FOUR FORTY : (*a.* forever, ***b.* or fight**, *c.* and forward, *d.* to fortune)

(**b**) "Tippecanoe and Tyler too" and "Fifty-four forty or fight" were both slogans in the American past.
Humanities—Completion

51. IMPEACH : (*a.* prove the guilt of, *b.* overturn, *c.* acquit, ***d.* accuse**) :: CONVICT : FIND GUILTY

(**d**) To impeach is to accuse. To convict is to find guilty. In the United States, the House of Representatives can impeach a person; the Senate tries the accused.
Vocabulary—Similarity/Contrast

52. CITY OF SEVEN HILLS : ROME :: CITY OF GOD : (***a.* heaven**, *b.* Jerusalem, *c.* Bethlehem, *d.* Jericho)

(**a**) Rome is the City of Seven Hills. Heaven is the City of God. The seven hills of Rome are called Palatine, Capitoline, Quirinal, Viminal, Esquiline, Caelian, and Aventine.
Humanities—Similarity/Contrast

53. WOOD : PAPER :: LATEX : (*a.* cotton, *b.* plastic, *c.* rayon, ***d.* rubber**)

(**d**) Wood is used to make paper. Latex is used to make rubber.
Natural Science—Description

54. TEXTILE : RAYON :: GEM : (*a.* sapphire, *b.* diamond, ***c.* spinel**, *d.* quartz)

(**c**) Rayon is a synthetic textile. Spinel is a synthetic gem.
Natural Science—Class

55. SIAM : (*a.* Mongolia, *b.* China, ***c.* Thailand**, *d.* Nepal) :: PERSIA : IRAN

(**c**) Siam is the former name of Thailand. Persia is the former name of Iran.
Nepal was once the Kingdom of Mustang.
General Information—Similarity/Contrast

56. HABEAS CORPUS : LAW :: EXEUNT OMNES : (*a.* medicine, ***b.* drama**, *c.* law, *d.* political theory)

(**b**) *Habeas corpus* is an expression used in law. *Exeunt omnes* is an expression used in drama. *Habeas corpus* refers to a writ needed to bring a party before court. *Exeunt omnes* means that all characters exit the stage.
Humanities—Description

57. PENTHOUSE APARTMENT : TOP FLOOR :: DUPLEX APARTMENT : (*a.* two rooms, ***b.* two floors**, *c.* two bedrooms, *d.* two persons)

(**b**) A penthouse apartment is on the top floor. A duplex apartment has two floors.
General Information—Description

58. XENOPHOBIA : (***a.* foreigners**, *b.* death, *c.* insanity, *d.* live burial) :: CLAUSTROPHOBIA : CONFINED PLACES

(**a**) Xenophobia is a fear of foreigners. Claustrophobia is a fear of confined places.
Vocabulary—Description

59. LOCKJAW : TETANUS :: HYDROPHOBIA : (*a.* encephalitis, *b.* malaria, *c.* syphilis, ***d.* rabies**)

(**d**) Tetanus is sometimes called lockjaw. Rabies is sometimes called hydrophobia.
Natural Science—Similarity/Contrast

60. ENGLISH : CANADA :: (*a.* Italian, ***b.* Portuguese**, *c.* Brazilian, *d.* French) : BRAZIL

(**b**) English is the most widely spoken language in Canada. Portuguese is the most widely spoken language in Brazil.
General Information—Description

61. MITIGATE : ASSUAGE :: MODERATE : (***a.* lessen**, *b.* make worse, *c.* disprove, *d.* approve)

(**a**) *Mitigate, assuage, moderate,* and *lessen* can all be used interchangeably.
Vocabulary—Similarity/Contrast

62. 1^0 : 1^{10} :: 10^0 : (***a.* 10^0**, *b.* 10^1, *c.* 10^2, *d.* 10^{10})

(**a**) 1 is to 1 as 1 is to 1.
Mathematics—Equality/Negation

63. PUSILLANIMOUS : AUDACIOUS :: (*a.* brave, *b.* purposive, ***c.* cowardly**, *d.* evanescent) : BOLD

(**c**) *Pusillanimous* and *cowardly* are synonyms, as are *audacious* and *bold.*
Vocabulary—Similarity/Contrast

64. HANNIBAL : (*a.* Theseus, ***b.* Scipio**, *c.* Cicero, *d.* Marcion) ::
NAPOLEON : WELLINGTON

   (**b**) Hannibal was defeated by Scipio in the Punic Wars. Napoleon was
   defeated by Wellington at the Battle of Waterloo. Theseus was a king of Athens.
   Cicero was a Roman statesman and philosopher. Marcion was an early Christian theologian
   who was excommunicated by the Church at Rome.
   Humanities—Description

65. EPITOME : (*a.* monologue, *b.* prevarication, ***c.* summary**, *d.* diatribe) ::
PREFACE : PROLOGUE

   (**c**) An epitome is a summary. A preface is a prologue. To prevaricate means
   to deviate from the truth. A monologue is a long speech by one person. A diatribe is
   a sharp denunciation.
   Vocabulary—Similarity/Contrast

66. (*a.* wave, *b.* radian, *c.* alpha, ***d.* roentgen**) : RADIATION :: MINUTE :
TIME

   (**d**) A roentgen is a unit of radiation. A minute is a unit of time.
   Natural Science—Description

67. VERACIOUS : (*a.* repeated, *b.* horizontal, *c.* diagonal, ***d.* truthful**) ::
CONTINUAL : INCESSANT

   (**d**) *Veracious* means *truthful*. *Continual* means *incessant*.
   Vocabulary—Similarity/Contrast

68. SOLAR : SUN :: (***a.* lunar**, *b.* diurnal, *c.* stellar, *d.* nocturnal) : MOON

   (**a**) The word *solar* derives from Sol, the Roman god of the sun.
   The word *lunar* derives from Luna, the Roman goddess of the moon.
   Humanities—Description

69. LINCOLN STEFFENS : POLITICAL MACHINES :: UPTON
SINCLAIR :
(***a.* meat-packing industry**, *b.* financial speculators, *c.* railroad magnates,
d. patent medicine quacks)

   (**a**) Lincoln Steffens was a muckraker who exposed political machines.
   Upton Sinclair was a muckraker who exposed the sordid conditions in
   the meat-packing industry.
   Humanities—Description

70. FAMILY : HOMINIDAE :: (*a.* sapiens, *b.* species, *c.* **genus**, *d.* class) : HOMO

    (**c**) Human beings are of family Hominidae and genus *Homo*.
    Natural Science—Class

71. OVERWEENING : (*a.* conceited, *b.* **modest**, *c.* spoiled, *d.* underprotected) :: BLUNT : SHARP

    (**b**) *Overweening* is the opposite of *modest*. *Blunt* is the opposite of *sharp*.
    Vocabulary—Similarity/Contrast

72. HEARSAY : GOSSIP :: GAINSAY : (*a.* **oppose**, *b.* protect, *c.* lose, *d.* take)

    (**a**) Hearsay is gossip. To gainsay is to oppose.
    Vocabulary—Similarity/Contrast

73. (*a.* thin, *b.* analogy, *c.* happy, *d.* **fat**) : FIAT :: SMILE : SIMILE

    (**d**) *Simile* is *smile* with an *i* added to the interior of the word. *Fiat* is *fat* with an *i* added to the interior of the word.
    Nonsemantic

74. ROUNDHEAD : SHORT HAIR :: (*a.* Tory, *b.* Whig, *c.* Royalist, *d.* **Cavalier**) : LONG HAIR

    (**d**) The Roundheads were known for their short hair. The Cavaliers were known for their long hair. Roundheads was a nickname for the supporters of the English Parliament during the English Civil War. Cavaliers were Royalist supporters during that war.
    Humanities—Description

75. EUGENICS : HEREDITY :: (*a.* euthanasia, *b.* **euthenics**, *c.* mnemonics, *d.* dialectics) : ENVIRONMENT

    (**b**) Eugenics studies how to "improve" the human "race" through the manipulation of heredity. Euthenics studies how to do the same through the manipulation of the environment. *Euthanasia* means "to kill someone painlessly." *Mnemonics* are techniques to improve memory. *Dialectics* involve reasoning by dialogue.
    Vocabulary—Description

76. THERMO : (*a.* **cryo**, *b.* iso, *c.* crypto, *d.* paleo) :: HOT : COLD

    (**a**) *Thermo-* is a prefix meaning *heat*. *Cryo-* is a prefix meaning *cold*.
    Vocabulary—Similarity/Contrast

77. (*a.* North Carolina, *b.* South Carolina, **c. Georgia**, *d.* Florida) : OGLETHORPE :: PENNSYLVANIA : PENN

    (**c**) Oglethorpe founded Georgia. Penn founded Pennsylvania. Ponce de Leon discovered Florida and gave it its name. South Carolina was named by King Charles II of England. North Carolina is not associated with a single founder.
    Humanities—Description

78. BANEFUL : (**a. baleful**, *b.* salutary, *c.* promiscuous, *d.* remorseful) :: PERSONABLE : HANDSOME

    (**a**) *Baneful* means *baleful. Personable* means *handsome.*
    Vocabulary—Similarity/Contrast

79. WERTHEIMER : GESTALT :: (**a. Watson**, *b.* Köhler, *c.* Koffka, *d.* Piaget) : BEHAVIORIST

    (**a**) Wertheimer was a leading psychologist in the Gestalt movement. Watson was a leading psychologist in the behaviorist movement. Kurt Koffka was a Gestalt psychologist, as was Wolfgang Köhler. Jean Piaget was a famous developmental psychologist and genetic epistemologist.
    Social Science—Description

80. (*a.* depilate, *b.* dampen, *c.* derogate, **d. desiccate**) : DRY :: MOISTEN : WET

    (**d**) To desiccate is to dry. To moisten is to wet.
    Vocabulary—Similarity/Contrast

81. GLUCOSE : (*a.* comatose, *b.* malactose, **c. lactose**, *d.* adipose) :: SUCROSE : FRUCTOSE

    (**c**) Glucose, lactose, sucrose, and fructose are all sugars.
    Natural Science—Class

82. ABLE : MELBA :: (*a.* colt, *b.* peach, **c. era**, *d.* willing) : MARE

    (**c**) *Melba* is *able* spelled backwards, with an added initial *m. Mare* is *era* spelled backwards, with an added initial *m.*
    Nonsemantic

83. (*a.* Mars, *b.* Jupiter, *c.* Venus, **d. Pluto**) : PROSERPINA :: ZEUS : HERA

    (**d**) In Greek mythology, Proserpina was the wife of Pluto, Hera the wife of Zeus. Mars was the god of war in Roman mythology. Jupiter was the god of sky and thunder. Venus was the Roman goddess of love and beauty.
    Humanities—Class

84. FLEET STREET : (*a.* **press**, *b.* police, *c.* amusement, *d.* high fashion) ::
DOWNING STREET : GOVERNMENT

(**a**) In London, Fleet Street has many of the offices of the press, while
Downing Street has many of the offices of the government.
General Information—Description

85. ARTUR RUBINSTEIN : PIANO :: ISAAC STERN : (*a.* piano, *b.* **violin**,
c. trumpet, *d.* oboe)

(**b**) Artur Rubenstein was a pianist. Isaac Stern is a violinist.
Humanities—Description

86. DURKHEIM : (*a.* Homocide, *b.* Matricide, *c.* **Suicide**, *d.* Genocide) ::
BECKER : OUTSIDERS

(**c**) Durkheim is the author of the sociological work *Suicide*. Becker is the
author of the sociological study *Outsiders*.
Social Science—Description

87. JOHN WESLEY : METHODIST :: MARY BAKER EDDY :
(*a.* Presbyterian, *b.* Baha'i, *c.* Jehovah's Witness, *d.* **Christian Science**)

(**d**) John Wesley was the founder of the Methodist church. Mary Baker
Eddy was the founder of the Christian Science church. The founder of the
Presbyterian church was John Calvin; the founder of the Baha'i faith was the Baha'u'llah;
the founder of Jehovah's Witnesses was Charles Russell.
Humanities—Description

88. BACH : BAROQUE :: GRIEG : (*a.* classical, *b.* modern, *c.* **romantic**,
d. medieval)

(**c**) Bach was a composer in the baroque period of music. Grieg was a
romantic composer.
Humanities—Description

89. (*a.* Husserl, *b.* Heidegger, *c.* **Comte**, *d.* Camus) : POSITIVISM :: SARTRE :
EXISTENTIALISM

(**c**) Comte helped shape the movement in philosophy now known as
positivism. Sartre was a major shaper of existentialism. Edmund Husserl was the
founder of phenomenology. Martin Heidegger was a philosopher; his most popular book is
Being and Time. Albert Camus was a French writer who wrote *The Plague*.
Humanities—Description

90. F# : Gb :: B : (***a.*** **C**b, *b.* Ab, *c.* G#, *d.* Gb)

    (**a**) F# is the same as Gb. B is the same as Cb.
    Humanities—Similarity/Contrast

91. SECOND : THIRD :: (*a.* clergy, *b.* king, *c.* commoners, ***d.*** **nobility**) :
    BOURGEOISIE

    (**d**) The nobility comprised the Second Estate of the French Estates-General.
    The bourgeoisie comprised the Third Estate.
    Humanities—Description

92. ALEXANDER : GREAT :: JULIAN : (*a.* Ingenious, *b.* Meek, *c.* Bold,
    d. **Apostate**)

    (**d**) Alexander was called the Great and was an ancient Greek king of
    Macedon. Julian was called the Apostate and was a Roman Emperor.
    Humanities—Description

93. (*a.* Helen, *b.* Jezebel, ***c.*** **Una**, *d.* Archimago) : DUESSA :: GOOD : EVIL

    (**c**) In Spenser's poem, *The Faerie Queene*, Una represents the forces of good
    and Duessa the forces of evil. Archimago is a sorcerer in Spenser's *Faerie Queene*.
    Helen was the daughter of Zeus and Leda, and was abducted by Paris, which led to the
    Trojan War. Jezebel was a queen of Ancient Israel, married to King Ahab.
    Humanities—Description

94. D : R × T :: (*a.* A, *b.* C, ***c.*** **F**, *d.* H) : M × A

    (**c**) In physics, Distance = Rate × Time and Force = Mass × Acceleration.
    Natural Science—Equality/Negation

95. PURLOINED : (*a.* Melville, *b.* Doyle, ***c.*** **Poe**, *d.* Conrad) :: SCARLET :
    HAWTHORNE

    (**c**) *The Purloined Letter* is a story by Poe. *The Scarlet Letter* is a story by
    Hawthorne.
    Humanities—Description

96. PROPHASE : METAPHASE :: ANAPHASE : (*a.* meiophase, ***b.*** **telophase**,
    c. mitophase, *d.* protophase)

    (**b**) Prophase, metaphase, anaphase, and telophase are all stages in mitosis
    (a form of cell division).
    Natural Science—Class

97. NEWBERY : (*a.* Wohlenberg, ***b.* Caldecott**, *c.* Pulitzer, *d.* Thompsen) :: STORY : ARTWORK

(**b**) The Newbery Medal is awarded annually to a distinguished children's story book. The Caldecott Medal is also awarded annually for distinguished artwork in a children's book. The Wohlenberg Prize is a prize for seniors of the physical sciences or engineering at Berkeley College of Yale. The Pulitzer Prize is a prize in journalism and literature. Thompson is a distracter term.
General Information—Description

98. COUNTESS AURELIA : THE MADWOMAN OF CHAILLOT :: (*a.* Lear, *b.* Othello, ***c.* Antonio**, *d.* Iago) : THE MERCHANT OF VENICE

(**c**) Countess Aurelia is the Madwoman of Chaillot in the play by the same name. Antonio is the Merchant of Venice in the play by the same name. Iago tricked Othello into murdering his wife in Shakespeare's tragedy *Othello*. *King Lear* is another tragedy written by Shakespeare.
Humanities—Similarity/Contrast

99. PICASSO : GUERNICA :: (***a.* Manet**, *b.* Raphael, *c.* David, *d.* Leger) : LUNCHEON ON THE GRASS

(**a**) Picasso is the artist who painted *Guernica*. Manet is the artist who painted *Luncheon on the Grass*. A famous work of Raphael is the *Sistine Madonna*. A famous painting of Fernand Leger is *Nudes in the Forest*. A well-known painting of Jacques-Louis David is the *Oath of the Horatii*.
Humanities—Description

100. RACINE : MOLIÈRE :: SOPHOCLES : (*a.* Zeno, ***b.* Aristophanes**, *c.* Plato, *d.* Aristotle)

(**b**) Racine was a French playwright who wrote tragedies, while Molière was a French playwright who wrote comedies. Sophocles was a Greek playwright who wrote tragedies, while Aristophanes was a Greek playwright who wrote comedies. Zeno, Plato, and Aristotle were ancient Greek philosophers.
Humanities—Class

101. (*a.* Queen Victoria, *b.* Queen Virginia, ***c.* Queen Elizabeth**, *d.* Queen Mary) : VIRGINIA :: KING GEORGE : GEORGIA

(**c**) Queen Elizabeth, known as "the virgin queen," had the state of Virginia named for her. King George inspired the naming of the state of Georgia.
General Information—Description

102. MITOSIS : MEIOSIS :: (*a.* 1, *b.* **2**, *c.* 4, *d.* 8) : 4

(**b**) Mitosis is the process of cell division that results in two discrete cells. Meiosis results in four.
Natural Science—Description

103. DAGGER : STAR :: (*a.* rune, *b.* allograph, *c.* knife, *d.* **obelisk**) : ASTERISK

(**d**) The name of the written symbol that looks like a dagger is an obelisk just as the star-shaped symbol is called an asterisk. Rune is the name for any letter belonging to the ancient Germanic alphabet. An allograph is a signature that is made by one person for another.
General Information—Similarity/Contrast

104. MISER : (*a.* chary, *b.* mercurial, *c.* acquisitive, *d.* **munificent**) :: GLUTTON : ABSTEMIOUS

(**d**) A miser is the opposite of munificent, meaning giving, and a glutton is the opposite of abstemious, meaning abstaining from excess food and drink.
Vocabulary—Description

105. (*a.* pork, *b.* **sweet**, *c.* appetizer, *d.* vegetable) : SWEETMEAT :: FRUIT : BREADFRUIT

(**b**) A sweetmeat is a type of sweet food, and a breadfruit is a type of fruit.
General Information—Class

106. $2\pi r^2$: $\pi(2r)^2$ :: LW : (*a.* $(1/2)$LW, *b.* LW, *c.* **2LW**, *d.* 4LW)

(**c**) $2\pi r^2$ is half of $\pi(2r)^2$, which is to say the area of two circles of the same radius is half the size of the area of one circle with twice that radius. Similarly, LW, the area of a rectangle, is half of 2LW.
Mathematics—Equality/Negation

107. (*a.* hatred, *b.* naiveté, *c.* **envy**, *d.* sickness) : SORROW :: GREEN : BLUE

(**c**) Envy is the emotion that is evoked by the color green just as sorrow is the emotion evoked by the color blue.
General Information—Description

108. MOHS : HARDNESS :: RICHTER : (*a.* **magnitude**, *b.* earthquake, *c.* quality, *d.* extremity)

(**a**) The Mohs Scale measures hardness (of solid objects). The Richter Scale measures magnitude (of earthquakes).
Natural Science—Description

109. FROGS : SEAGULL :: (*a.* Shakespeare, *b.* Marlowe, *c.* Wilde, ***d.* Aristophanes**) : CHEKHOV

(**d**) *The Frogs* was a play written by Aristophanes, and *The Seagull* was a play written by Chekhov. Shakespeare is known, among others, for his tragedies *Hamlet*, *King Lear*, and *Macbeth*. Marlowe is known for his plays which include *Doctor Faustus* and *The Massacre at Paris*. Oscar Wilde is known, for example, for his play *The Importance of Being Earnest*.
Humanities—Description

110. INDIA : PAKISTAN :: PAKISTAN : (*a.* Kashmir, ***b.* Bangladesh**, *c.* Nepal, *d.* Sri Lanka)

(**b**) Pakistan was part of India until it seceded and became sovereign. Bangladesh was part of Pakistan until it seceded and became sovereign.
General Information—Description

111. ORGAN : ORGANELLE :: LIVER : (***a.* vacuole**, *b.* pancreas, *c.* kidney, *d.* cell)

(**a**) The liver is an example of an organ and a vacuole is an example of an organelle, or intracellular structure.
Natural Science—Class

112. MASS AND ENERGY : (*a.* Bernoulli, *b.* Newton, *c.* Gauss, ***d.* Einstein**) :: VOLUME AND DISPLACEMENT : ARCHIMEDES

(**d**) Einstein was the first to directly relate mass and energy and Archimedes was the first to relate volume and displacement. Bernoulli applied mathematics to mechanics and is especially known for the Bernoulli principle. Newton is known for describing universal gravitation. Gauss is associated with the normal distribution, also called Gaussian distribution.
Natural Science—Description

113. DOGS : PEAS :: PAVLOV : (*a.* Darwin, *b.* Gauss, *c.* Curie, ***d.* Mendel**)

(**d**) Pavlov is famous for his groundbreaking scientific work with dogs in classical conditioning. Mendel is famous for his scientific discoveries made with peas in the area of genetics and inheritance. Darwin developed the Theory of Evolution. Gauss is associated with the normal distribution, also called Gaussian distribution. Curie won the Nobel Prize in chemistry in 1911 for her discovery of the elements radium and polonium.
Social Science—Description

114. (***a.* King**, *b.* Martha, *c.* Reverend, *d.* Priest) : CARVER :: MARTIN LUTHER : GEORGE WASHINGTON

(**a**) Both Martin Luther King (Jr.) and George Washington Carver went on to become famous, as were those men for whom they were named at birth.
General Information—Description

115. SESAME SEEDS : TAHINI :: PEANUTS : (*a.* roots, *b.* shell, ***c.* peanut butter**, *d.* oil)

(**c**) Sesame seeds are ground to make the spread known as tahini just as peanuts are ground to make peanut butter.
General Information—Description

116. BASS : (*a.* clarinet, *b.* viola, ***c.* cello**, *d.* trumpet) :: TREBLE : FLUTE

(**c**) Most written music for the cello is presented in the bass cleft. Most flute music is written in the treble cleft.
Humanities—Description

117. MAL : BEN :: ANTI : (*a.* un, *b.* inter, ***c.* pro**, *d.* pre)

(**c**) Mal- and ben- are prefixes with opposite connotations (negative and positive, respectively). Likewise, anti- and pro- are prefixes with opposite meanings (negating and supporting, respectively). The prefix *un-* means "not, or lack of"; *inter-* means "in between"; *pre-* means "before."
Vocabulary—Similarity/Contrast

118. (***a.* meat packing**, *b.* clear cutting, *c.* poaching, *d.* iron mining) : PESTICIDES :: THE JUNGLE : SILENT SPRING

(**a**) Upton Sinclair's book *The Jungle* exposed abuses in the meat-packing industry just as Rachel Carson's *Silent Spring* exposed abuses of pesticides.
Humanities—Description

119. HANUKKAH : DIVALI :: JUDAISM : (*a.* Buddhism, ***b.* Hinduism**, *c.* Zoroastrianism, *d.* Islam)

(**b**) The holidays Hanukkah and Divali are also known in their respective religions, Judaism and Hinduism, as the Festival of Lights.
Humanities—Description

120. SQUARE ROOT : SQUARE :: (*a.* dividend, *b.* root, *c.* log, ***d.* integral**) : DERIVATIVE

(**d**) Finding the square root requires the opposite action as finding the square of a number. Likewise, finding the integral is the opposite of finding the derivative of a number.
Mathematics—Equality/Negation

Item Classification

PRACTICE TEST 4

Item Classification Chart

		RELATIONSHIP						
		Similarity/ Contrast	Description	Class	Completion	Part/ Whole	Equality/ Negation	Nonsemantic
C O N T E N T	**Vocabulary**	23, 31, 48, 51, 61, 63, 65, 67, 71, 72, 76, 78, 80, 117	30, 44, 49, 58, 75, 104					
	General Information	14, 40, 55, 103	1, 4, 6, 7, 8, 11, 12, 13, 16, 17, 21, 27, 32, 35, 41, 57, 60, 84, 97, 101, 107, 110, 114, 115	105	28			
	Humanities	52, 90, 98	2, 3, 9, 10, 19, 20, 46, 56, 64, 68, 69, 74, 77, 85, 87, 88, 89, 91, 92, 93, 95, 99, 109, 116, 118, 119	24, 26, 34, 83, 100	50			
	Social Science	42	15, 25, 45, 79, 86, 113					
	Natural Science	59	22, 29, 33, 38, 43, 53, 66, 102, 108, 112	37, 54, 70, 81, 96, 111			94	
	Mathematics		18, 36, 39	5			47, 62, 106, 120	
	Nonsemantic							73, 82

Answer Sheet
PRACTICE TEST 5

1 Ⓐ Ⓑ Ⓒ Ⓓ	31 Ⓐ Ⓑ Ⓒ Ⓓ	61 Ⓐ Ⓑ Ⓒ Ⓓ	91 Ⓐ Ⓑ Ⓒ Ⓓ
2 Ⓐ Ⓑ Ⓒ Ⓓ	32 Ⓐ Ⓑ Ⓒ Ⓓ	62 Ⓐ Ⓑ Ⓒ Ⓓ	92 Ⓐ Ⓑ Ⓒ Ⓓ
3 Ⓐ Ⓑ Ⓒ Ⓓ	33 Ⓐ Ⓑ Ⓒ Ⓓ	63 Ⓐ Ⓑ Ⓒ Ⓓ	93 Ⓐ Ⓑ Ⓒ Ⓓ
4 Ⓐ Ⓑ Ⓒ Ⓓ	34 Ⓐ Ⓑ Ⓒ Ⓓ	64 Ⓐ Ⓑ Ⓒ Ⓓ	94 Ⓐ Ⓑ Ⓒ Ⓓ
5 Ⓐ Ⓑ Ⓒ Ⓓ	35 Ⓐ Ⓑ Ⓒ Ⓓ	65 Ⓐ Ⓑ Ⓒ Ⓓ	95 Ⓐ Ⓑ Ⓒ Ⓓ
6 Ⓐ Ⓑ Ⓒ Ⓓ	36 Ⓐ Ⓑ Ⓒ Ⓓ	66 Ⓐ Ⓑ Ⓒ Ⓓ	96 Ⓐ Ⓑ Ⓒ Ⓓ
7 Ⓐ Ⓑ Ⓒ Ⓓ	37 Ⓐ Ⓑ Ⓒ Ⓓ	67 Ⓐ Ⓑ Ⓒ Ⓓ	97 Ⓐ Ⓑ Ⓒ Ⓓ
8 Ⓐ Ⓑ Ⓒ Ⓓ	38 Ⓐ Ⓑ Ⓒ Ⓓ	68 Ⓐ Ⓑ Ⓒ Ⓓ	98 Ⓐ Ⓑ Ⓒ Ⓓ
9 Ⓐ Ⓑ Ⓒ Ⓓ	39 Ⓐ Ⓑ Ⓒ Ⓓ	69 Ⓐ Ⓑ Ⓒ Ⓓ	99 Ⓐ Ⓑ Ⓒ Ⓓ
10 Ⓐ Ⓑ Ⓒ Ⓓ	40 Ⓐ Ⓑ Ⓒ Ⓓ	70 Ⓐ Ⓑ Ⓒ Ⓓ	100 Ⓐ Ⓑ Ⓒ Ⓓ
11 Ⓐ Ⓑ Ⓒ Ⓓ	41 Ⓐ Ⓑ Ⓒ Ⓓ	71 Ⓐ Ⓑ Ⓒ Ⓓ	101 Ⓐ Ⓑ Ⓒ Ⓓ
12 Ⓐ Ⓑ Ⓒ Ⓓ	42 Ⓐ Ⓑ Ⓒ Ⓓ	72 Ⓐ Ⓑ Ⓒ Ⓓ	102 Ⓐ Ⓑ Ⓒ Ⓓ
13 Ⓐ Ⓑ Ⓒ Ⓓ	43 Ⓐ Ⓑ Ⓒ Ⓓ	73 Ⓐ Ⓑ Ⓒ Ⓓ	103 Ⓐ Ⓑ Ⓒ Ⓓ
14 Ⓐ Ⓑ Ⓒ Ⓓ	44 Ⓐ Ⓑ Ⓒ Ⓓ	74 Ⓐ Ⓑ Ⓒ Ⓓ	104 Ⓐ Ⓑ Ⓒ Ⓓ
15 Ⓐ Ⓑ Ⓒ Ⓓ	45 Ⓐ Ⓑ Ⓒ Ⓓ	75 Ⓐ Ⓑ Ⓒ Ⓓ	105 Ⓐ Ⓑ Ⓒ Ⓓ
16 Ⓐ Ⓑ Ⓒ Ⓓ	46 Ⓐ Ⓑ Ⓒ Ⓓ	76 Ⓐ Ⓑ Ⓒ Ⓓ	106 Ⓐ Ⓑ Ⓒ Ⓓ
17 Ⓐ Ⓑ Ⓒ Ⓓ	47 Ⓐ Ⓑ Ⓒ Ⓓ	77 Ⓐ Ⓑ Ⓒ Ⓓ	107 Ⓐ Ⓑ Ⓒ Ⓓ
18 Ⓐ Ⓑ Ⓒ Ⓓ	48 Ⓐ Ⓑ Ⓒ Ⓓ	78 Ⓐ Ⓑ Ⓒ Ⓓ	108 Ⓐ Ⓑ Ⓒ Ⓓ
19 Ⓐ Ⓑ Ⓒ Ⓓ	49 Ⓐ Ⓑ Ⓒ Ⓓ	79 Ⓐ Ⓑ Ⓒ Ⓓ	109 Ⓐ Ⓑ Ⓒ Ⓓ
20 Ⓐ Ⓑ Ⓒ Ⓓ	50 Ⓐ Ⓑ Ⓒ Ⓓ	80 Ⓐ Ⓑ Ⓒ Ⓓ	110 Ⓐ Ⓑ Ⓒ Ⓓ
21 Ⓐ Ⓑ Ⓒ Ⓓ	51 Ⓐ Ⓑ Ⓒ Ⓓ	81 Ⓐ Ⓑ Ⓒ Ⓓ	111 Ⓐ Ⓑ Ⓒ Ⓓ
22 Ⓐ Ⓑ Ⓒ Ⓓ	52 Ⓐ Ⓑ Ⓒ Ⓓ	82 Ⓐ Ⓑ Ⓒ Ⓓ	112 Ⓐ Ⓑ Ⓒ Ⓓ
23 Ⓐ Ⓑ Ⓒ Ⓓ	53 Ⓐ Ⓑ Ⓒ Ⓓ	83 Ⓐ Ⓑ Ⓒ Ⓓ	113 Ⓐ Ⓑ Ⓒ Ⓓ
24 Ⓐ Ⓑ Ⓒ Ⓓ	54 Ⓐ Ⓑ Ⓒ Ⓓ	84 Ⓐ Ⓑ Ⓒ Ⓓ	114 Ⓐ Ⓑ Ⓒ Ⓓ
25 Ⓐ Ⓑ Ⓒ Ⓓ	55 Ⓐ Ⓑ Ⓒ Ⓓ	85 Ⓐ Ⓑ Ⓒ Ⓓ	115 Ⓐ Ⓑ Ⓒ Ⓓ
26 Ⓐ Ⓑ Ⓒ Ⓓ	56 Ⓐ Ⓑ Ⓒ Ⓓ	86 Ⓐ Ⓑ Ⓒ Ⓓ	116 Ⓐ Ⓑ Ⓒ Ⓓ
27 Ⓐ Ⓑ Ⓒ Ⓓ	57 Ⓐ Ⓑ Ⓒ Ⓓ	87 Ⓐ Ⓑ Ⓒ Ⓓ	117 Ⓐ Ⓑ Ⓒ Ⓓ
28 Ⓐ Ⓑ Ⓒ Ⓓ	58 Ⓐ Ⓑ Ⓒ Ⓓ	88 Ⓐ Ⓑ Ⓒ Ⓓ	118 Ⓐ Ⓑ Ⓒ Ⓓ
29 Ⓐ Ⓑ Ⓒ Ⓓ	59 Ⓐ Ⓑ Ⓒ Ⓓ	89 Ⓐ Ⓑ Ⓒ Ⓓ	119 Ⓐ Ⓑ Ⓒ Ⓓ
30 Ⓐ Ⓑ Ⓒ Ⓓ	60 Ⓐ Ⓑ Ⓒ Ⓓ	90 Ⓐ Ⓑ Ⓒ Ⓓ	120 Ⓐ Ⓑ Ⓒ Ⓓ

Answer Sheet

Practice Test 5

Directions: In each of the following questions, you will find three initial terms and, in parentheses, four answer options designated *a*, *b*, *c*, and *d*. You are to select from the four answer options the one that best completes the analogy with the three initial terms. To record your answers, use the answer sheet provided.

Time: 60 minutes

1. BOW : (*a.* arrow, *b.* grenade, *c.* quiver, *d.* target) :: RIFLE : BULLET

2. MARK TWAIN : HANNIBAL :: (*a.* Ernest Hemingway, *b.* Stephen Crane, *c.* William Shakespeare, *d.* Victor Hugo) : STRATFORD-UPON-AVON

3. UNITED : STAND :: DIVIDED : (*a.* fall, *b.* sit, *c.* lie, *d.* rise)

4. (*a.* Asia, *b.* South America, *c.* Africa, *d.* North America) : SAHARA :: NORTH AMERICA : PAINTED

5. TARANTULA : (*a.* spider, *b.* rabbit, *c.* cat, *d.* cockroach) :: COBRA : SNAKE

6. (*a.* 6, *b.* 9, *c.* 12, *d.* 15) : BASEBALL :: 5 : BASKETBALL

7. SEINE : (*a.* Canada, *b.* Holland, *c.* Germany, *d.* France) :: THAMES : ENGLAND

8. PLIABLE : BEND :: (*a.* brittle, *b.* transparent, *c.* opaque, *d.* flexible) : BREAK

9. ADVERB : HAPPILY :: PREPOSITION : (*a.* the, *b.* or, *c.* on, *d.* none)

10. RIGHT ANGLE : (*a.* 0, *b.* 45, *c.* 90, *d.* 360) :: STRAIGHT ANGLE : 180

11. AUTHOR : PEN :: PAINTER : (*a.* brush, *b.* paint, *c.* canvas, *d.* picture)

12. ASTRONAUT : ROCKET SHIP :: WITCH : (*a.* cauldron, *b.* vulture, *c.* black cat, *d.* broomstick)

13. (*a.* achievement, *b.* permission, *c.* month, *d.* desire) : ABILITY :: MAY : CAN

14. IBM : (*a.* Industrial Business Machines, *b.* Innovative Business Machines, *c.* International Business Machines, *d.* Intelligent Business Machines) :: GOP : REPUBLICAN PARTY

15. (*a.* earthling, *b.* earthian, *c.* earthing, *d.* earthan) : EARTH :: MARTIAN : MARS

16. ASBESTOS : FIRE :: (*a.* vinyl, *b.* air, *c.* cotton, *d.* faucet) : WATER

17. DAVY JONES : (*a.* Great Britain, *b.* Planet Earth, *c.* the sun, *d.* the sea) :: LAND OF THE RISING SUN : JAPAN

18. PAIR : PARE :: COUPLE : (*a.* several, *b.* one, *c.* pear, *d.* prune)

19. ASCETIC : (*a.* businessman, *b.* monk, *c.* carpenter, *d.* policeman) :: CRAFTY : CONFIDENCE MAN

20. GUILLOTINE : ROBESPIERRE :: (*a.* noose, *b.* poison, *c.* knife, *d.* illness) : SOCRATES

21. GIN : BLACK :: (*a.* apple, *b.* whiskey, *c.* cotton, *d.* rummy) : JACK

22. PESO : MEXICO :: (*a.* ounce, *b.* pound, *c.* ruble, *d.* mark) : ENGLAND

23. SILVER : GOLD :: (*a.* Si, *b.* Sl, *c.* Ag, *d.* Hg) : Au

24. VALEDICTORIAN : SALUTATORIAN :: PRIME : (*a.* excellent, *b.* good, *c.* choice, *d.* alternative)

25. CHEROKEE : (*a.* Indian, *b.* aborigine, *c.* Seminole, *d.* pariah) :: APACHE : NAVAHO

26. (*a.* musical instruments, *b.* books, *c.* weather systems, *d.* diseases) : DEWEY :: LIVING THINGS : LINNAEUS

27. IVAN : TERRIBLE :: PETER : (*a.* Hairy, *b.* Reformer, *c.* Great, *d.* Awful)

28. SQUARE : 360 :: RECTANGLE : (*a.* 90, *b.* 180, *c.* 270, *d.* 360)

29. WHALE : (*a.* mammal, *b.* reptile, *c.* amphibian, *d.* fish) :: LIZARD : REPTILE

30. LINCOLN : (*a.* 1, *b.* 5, *c.* 10, *d.* 16) :: JACKSON : 20

31. CONJUNCTION : DISJUNCTION :: AND : (*a.* but, *b.* if . . . then, *c.* or, *d.* because)

32. AENEAS : (*a.* Virgil, *b.* Plutarch, *c.* Caesar, *d.* Demosthenes) :: ODYSSEUS: HOMER

33. AGORAPHOBIA : ARACHNOPHOBIA :: OPEN SPACES : (*a.* lizards, *b.* snakes, *c.* spiders, *d.* dragons)

34. GRIMM : (*a.* Donne, *b.* Petrarch, *c.* Nash, *d.* Andersen) :: CHAUCER : BOCCACCIO

35. CYCLONE : TORNADO :: HURRICANE : (*a.* storm, *b.* typhoon, *c.* rain, *d.* miasma)

36. GREENHOUSE : PLANTS :: AVIARY : (*a.* birds, *b.* bees, *c.* rodents, *d.* fish)

37. (*a.* $A \cap B$, *b.* $B \cap A$, *c.* $A \cup B$, *d.* $B \cup A$) : $B \cup A$ :: $X \wedge Y$: $Y \vee X$

38. OFFER : JOB :: TENDER : (*a.* resignation, *b.* retirement, *c.* delicate, *d.* rough)

39. HICCUP : HICCOUGH :: EYE : (*a.* light, *b.* ice, *c.* I, *d.* iris)

40. (*a.* black, *b.* white, *c.* orange, *d.* brown) : BLUE :: RED : GREEN

41. ASPIRIN : (*a.* anaphoric, *b.* mycin, *c.* antibiotic, *d.* analgesic) :: PENICILLIN : ANTIBIOTIC

42. (*a.* Istanbul, *b.* Dar es Salaam, *c.* Jerusalem, *d.* Mecca) : MOHAMMED :: BETHLEHEM : JESUS

43. CETANE : DIESEL FUEL OIL :: (*a.* octane, *b.* heptane, *c.* methane, *d.* propane) : GASOLINE

44. DEAD DUCK : GONER :: LAME DUCK : (*a.* one who finishes a term after failing re-election, *b.* one who gives up easily, *c.* one who invests cautiously, *d.* one who complains incessantly)

45. ARGONAUTS : (*a.* Francis Marion, *b.* Jason, *c.* Achilles, *d.* George Washington) :: GREEN MOUNTAIN BOYS : ETHAN ALLEN

46. LYNX : CAT :: BOAR : (*a.* hog, *b.* dog, *c.* goat, *d.* ram)

47. LENIN : BOLSHEVIK :: (*a.* Stalin, *b.* Kerensky, *c.* Trotsky, *d.* Marx) : MENSHEVIK

48. (*a.* oak, *b.* walnut, *c.* balsa, *d.* corundum) : HICKORY :: TIN : STEEL

49. ROCK : ROCKET :: (*a.* coat, *b.* cloth, *c.* jack, *d.* wasp) : JACKET

50. MALARIA : CHILLS :: GOITER : (*a.* pockmarks, *b.* swelling, *c.* fever, *d.* hypertension)

51. PIZARRO : INCA :: (*a.* Ponce de Leon, *b.* Hudson, *c.* Velásquez, *d.* Cortez) : AZTEC

52. ASTROLOGY : (*a.* astronomy, *b.* physics, *c.* pharmacology, *d.* phrenology) :: ASTRONOMY : ANATOMY

53. DUET : SEXTET :: SOLO : (*a.* quartet, *b.* quintet, *c.* chorus, *d.* trio)

54. ANDES : (*a.* Asia, *b.* Africa, *c.* South America, *d.* Europe) :: ALPS : EUROPE

55. MYOPIA : (*a.* hyperopia, *b.* scotopia, *c.* photopia, *d.* metropia) :: NEARSIGHTED : FARSIGHTED

56. PASTORAL : (*a.* religious, *b.* rustic, *c.* metropolitan, *d.* worldly) :: URBAN : CITIFIED

57. SEA : TIGER :: LION : (*a.* land, *b.* fauna, *c.* lily, *d.* heart)

58. ASTRONAUT : SPACESUIT :: (*a.* judge, *b.* baker, *c.* ballerina, *d.* monk) : HABIT

59. MONOGAMY : BIGAMY :: BIPED : (*a.* unipod, *b.* pedate, *c.* millipede, *d.* quadruped)

60. POPE : ROMAN :: (*a.* Metropolitan, *b.* Patriarch, *c.* Cardinal, *d.* Bishop) : GREEK ORTHODOX

61. SEXTANT : (*a.* navigator, *b.* architect, *c.* archeologist, *d.* priest) :: SCALPEL : SURGEON

62. PRIDE : PREJUDICE :: SENSE : (*a.* Folly, *b.* Prentense, *c.* Sensibility, *d.* Sanity)

63. PACIFIST : PEACE :: (*a.* revolutionary, *b.* diplomat, *c.* charlatan, *d.* traitor) : WAR

64. (*a.* brown, *b.* gray, *c.* purple, *d.* blue) : UMBER :: GREEN : CHARTREUSE

65. INCREASE : LESSEN :: (*a.* fair, *b.* final, *c.* incipient, *d.* unfair) : INCHOATE

66. EXCALIBUR : (*a.* sword, *b.* pony, *c.* lioness, *d.* cannon) :: LASSIE : DOG

67. (*a.* Bern, *b.* Geneva, *c.* Zurich, *d.* Lucerne) : SWITZERLAND :: NEW DELHI : INDIA

68. SILVER-TONGUED : ELOQUENT :: JANUS-FACED : (*a.* duplicitous, *b.* versatile, *c.* incredibly ugly, *d.* honest)

69. PRESENT : FUTURE PERFECT :: GO : (*a.* would go, *b.* will go, *c.* will have gone, *d.* would have gone)

70. AMPLITUDE : FREQUENCY :: RATE : (*a.* distance, *b.* velocity, *c.* acceleration, *d.* time)

71. GREENHORN : NOVICE :: NEOPHYTE : (*a.* expert, *b.* priest, *c.* beginner, *d.* novelist)

72. PANEGYRIC : (*a.* prayer, *b.* joke, *c.* threat, *d.* eulogy) :: TEMPEST : STORM

73. CARMEN : (*a.* Verdi, *b.* Bizet, *c.* Gounod, *d.* Wagner) :: BARBER OF SEVILLE : ROSSINI

74. PALPITATE : QUIVER :: MASTICATE : (*a.* abuse, *b.* remove, *c.* stomp, *d.* chew)

75. BOLÍVAR : (*a.* Venezuela, *b.* Spain, *c.* United States, *d.* Mexico) :: WASHINGTON : ENGLAND

76. CORNUCOPIA : (*a.* horn of plenty, *b.* horn of Roland, *c.* hornpipe, *d.* hornstone) :: TENET : PRECEPT

77. SHRIMP : CRUSTACEAN :: (*a.* snail, *b.* lobster, *c.* goldfish, *d.* brine) : MOLLUSK

78. NEW AMSTERDAM : NEW YORK :: SIAM : (*a.* Thailand, *b.* Cambodia, *c.* Laos, *d.* China)

79. HIRSUTE : (*a.* pleasantly plump, *b.* well-dressed, *c.* handsome, *d.* hairy) :: EXTROVERTED : OUTGOING

80. EYE : LIP :: ELBOW : (*a.* forehead, *b.* nose, *c.* foot, *d.* chest)

81. (*a.* feldspar, *b.* talc, *c.* quartz, *d.* topaz) : 1 :: DIAMOND : 10

82. TORTUOUS : (*a.* painless, *b.* painful, *c.* straight, *d.* winding) :: SOBER : INEBRIATED

83. NONPLUS : (*a.* perplexity, *b.* disappointment, *c.* deletion, *d.* elation) ::
    NONPAREIL : UNEQUALED

84. CROCKETT : ALAMO :: BONAPARTE : (*a.* Madrid, *b.* St. Helena,
    c. Rome, *d.* London)

85. EL GRECO : (*a.* impressionist, *b.* mannerist, *c.* expressionist, *d.* realist) ::
    DAVID : NEOCLASSICIST

86. GRAY : COUNTRY CHURCHYARD :: (*a.* Keats, *b.* Poe, *c.* Byron,
    d. Longfellow) : GRECIAN URN

87. MITER : (*a.* dancer, *b.* cartoonist, *c.* queen, *d.* bishop) :: CROWN : KING

88. $2^0 : 2^{-2} :: 2^2 : $ (*a.* $2^{1/4}$, *b.* 2^0, *c.* 2^1, *d.* 2^{-1})

89. FLOWER : GARDEN :: (*a.* pinnacle, *b.* stalagmite, *c.* cavern, *d.* explorer) :
    CAVE

90. LEVITICUS : OLD :: (*a.* Deuteronomy, *b.* Isaiah, *c.* Numbers,
    d. Ephesians) : NEW

91. LOUVRE : PARIS :: PRADO : (*a.* Madrid, *b.* Seville, *c.* Florence,
    d. Chartres)

92. CUL-DE-SAC : BLIND ALLEY :: SANGFROID : (*a.* carelessness,
    b. timidity, *c.* courage, *d.* imperturbability)

93. ENCOMIUM : TRIBUTE :: (*a.* admonition, *b.* excoriation, *c.* benison,
    d. exegesis) : CRITICAL ANALYSIS

94. CARPETBAGGER : NORTH :: (*a.* Granger, *b.* Scalawag, *c.* Bull Moose,
    d. Tweedy Pie) : SOUTH

95. MERCURIAL : (*a.* pretty, *b.* plutonic, *c.* hateful, *d.* hermetic) :: MARTIAL :
    AREOLOGY

96. LEGATO : BOW :: PIZZICATO : (*a.* fingers, *b.* bow, *c.* reed, *d.* feet)

97. NICK ADAMS : (*a.* Fitzgerald, *b.* Faulkner, *c.* Hemingway, *d.* Joyce) ::
    ARROWSMITH : LEWIS

98. (*a.* Burgundian, *b.* Prussian, *c.* Turkish, *d.* Bulgarian) : OTTOMAN ::
    FRENCH : BOURBON

99. ORPHEUS : EURYDICE :: DAPHNIS : (*a.* Pyramus, *b.* Thisbe, *c.* Chloe,
    d. Helen)

100. (*a.* darling, *b.* wench, *c.* harridan, *d.* myrmidon) : SHREW :: MOLLYCODDLE : SISSY

101. PULLEY : (*a.* screw, *b.* saw, *c.* pliers, *d.* nail) :: WEDGE : INCLINED PLANE

102. LIVE WIRE : LOOSE CANNON :: ENERGETIC : (*a.* powerful, *b.* threatening, *c.* reckless, *d.* peaceable)

103. ARM : LEG :: (*a.* radius, *b.* ulna, *c.* humerus, *d.* scapula) : FEMUR

104. VENUSIAN : (*a.* Venus, *b.* Earth, *c.* Moon, *d.* Mercury) :: MARTIAN : JUPITER

105. (*a.* oil, *b.* air, *c.* nitrates, *d.* blood) : TOURNIQUET :: WATER : DAM

106. OBJURGATE : (*a.* vituperate, *b.* venerate, *c.* abrogate, *d.* enervate) :: RECANT : RETRACT

107. PERFIDIOUS : BENEFICENT :: (*a.* obvious, *b.* capricious, *c.* intractable, *d.* renitent) : STEADFAST

108. MAN : LAZARUS :: BIRD : (*a.* dragon, *b.* albatross, *c.* phoenix, *d.* dodo)

109. FIREWORKS : (*a.* Japan, *b.* Korea, *c.* Indonesia, *d.* China) :: LIGHTBULB : THE UNITED STATES

110. GI TRACT : GI JOE :: GASTROINTESTINAL : (*a.* General Infantry, *b.* Galvanized Iron, *c.* Government Issue, *d.* General Information)

111. WET SUIT : (*a.* spandex, *b.* neoprene, *c.* nylon, *d.* Lycra) :: BULLETPROOF VEST : KEVLAR

112. (*a.* yellow, *b.* pink, *c.* white, *d.* green) : BLUE :: JAUNDICED : CYANOTIC

113. MONET : WATER LILIES :: DEGAS : (*a.* windmills, *b.* sailboats, *c.* polo players, *d.* ballet dancers)

114. WAR : (*a.* birth, *b.* flood, *c.* death, *d.* fall) :: ANTEBELLUM : ANTEDILUVIAN

115. DILETTANTE : DEBUTANTE :: (*a.* amateur, *b.* professional, *c.* actor, *d.* student) : YOUNG WOMAN

116. DOG : CAT :: (*a.* loud, *b.* skinny, *c.* under, *d.* hound) : FAT

117. RIDE : (*a*. U.S. senator, *b*. doctor, *c*. pilot, *d*. astronaut) :: O'CONNOR : SUPREME COURT JUSTICE

118. (*a*. panda, *b*. opossum, *c*. mouse, *d*. anteater) : WALLABY :: KANGAROO : WOMBAT

119. ANDREW : ABRAHAM :: LYNDON : (*a*. John, *b*. Robert, *c*. Joseph, *d*. Edward)

120. MYOPIA: CONCAVE :: (*a*. mytopia, *b*. astigmatism, *c*. hyperopia, *d*. diopia) : CONVEX

Answer Key
PRACTICE TEST 5

1. **A**	31. **C**	61. **A**	91. **A**
2. **C**	32. **A**	62. **C**	92. **D**
3. **A**	33. **C**	63. **A**	93. **D**
4. **C**	34. **D**	64. **A**	94. **B**
5. **A**	35. **B**	65. **B**	95. **D**
6. **B**	36. **A**	66. **A**	96. **A**
7. **D**	37. **A**	67. **A**	97. **C**
8. **A**	38. **A**	68. **A**	98. **C**
9. **C**	39. **C**	69. **C**	99. **C**
10. **C**	40. **C**	70. **D**	100. **C**
11. **A**	41. **D**	71. **C**	101. **A**
12. **D**	42. **D**	72. **D**	102. **C**
13. **B**	43. **A**	73. **B**	103. **C**
14. **C**	44. **A**	74. **D**	104. **B**
15. **A**	45. **B**	75. **B**	105. **D**
16. **A**	46. **A**	76. **A**	106. **A**
17. **D**	47. **B**	77. **A**	107. **B**
18. **D**	48. **C**	78. **A**	108. **C**
19. **B**	49. **C**	79. **D**	109. **D**
20. **B**	50. **B**	80. **C**	110. **C**
21. **D**	51. **D**	81. **B**	111. **B**
22. **B**	52. **D**	82. **C**	112. **A**
23. **C**	53. **D**	83. **A**	113. **D**
24. **C**	54. **C**	84. **B**	114. **B**
25. **C**	55. **A**	85. **B**	115. **A**
26. **B**	56. **B**	86. **A**	116. **C**
27. **C**	57. **C**	87. **D**	117. **D**
28. **D**	58. **D**	88. **B**	118. **B**
29. **A**	59. **D**	89. **B**	119. **A**
30. **B**	60. **B**	90. **D**	120. **C**

Answer Key

EXPLANATION OF ANSWERS FOR PRACTICE TEST 5

In the following explanations of answers, explanations concerning the correct response are in a large font. Explanations regarding distracters (incorrect responses) that are not self-explaining or could be misinterpreted are in a smaller font in order to highlight the explanations of the answers that are correct.

1. BOW : (*a.* **arrow**, *b.* grenade, *c.* quiver, *d.* target) :: RIFLE : BULLET

    (**a**) An arrow is shot from a bow; a bullet is shot from a rifle.
    General Information—Description

2. MARK TWAIN : HANNIBAL :: (*a.* Ernest Hemingway, *b.* Stephen Crane, *c.* **William Shakespeare**, *d.* Victor Hugo) : STRATFORD-UPON-AVON

    (**c**) Mark Twain was born in Hannibal, Missouri. William Shakespeare was born in Stratford-upon-Avon, England. Ernest Hemingway was born in Oak Park, Illinois; Stephen Crane was born in Newark, New Jersey; Victor Hugo was born in Besancon, France.
    Humanities—Description

3. UNITED : STAND :: DIVIDED : (*a.* **fall**, *b.* sit, *c.* lie, *d.* rise)

    (**a**) "United we stand, divided we fall" is a familiar saying.
    General Information—Completion

4. (*a.* Asia, *b.* South America, *c.* **Africa**, *d.* North America) : SAHARA :: NORTH AMERICA : PAINTED

    (**c**) The Sahara Desert is in Africa. The Painted Desert is in North America.
    General Information—Description

5. TARANTULA : (*a.* **spider**, *b.* rabbit, *c.* cat, *d.* cockroach) :: COBRA : SNAKE

    (**a**) A tarantula is a type of spider; a cobra is a type of snake.
    Natural Science—Class

6. (*a.* 6, *b.* **9**, *c.* 12, *d.* 15) : BASEBALL :: 5 : BASKETBALL

    (**b**) There are 9 players on a baseball team, and 5 on a basketball team.
    General Information—Description

7. SEINE : (*a.* Canada, *b.* Holland, *c.* Germany, *d.* **France**) :: THAMES : ENGLAND

    (**d**) The Seine River is in France, while the Thames River is in England.
    General Information—Description

8. PLIABLE : BEND :: (***a.* brittle**, *b.* transparent, *c.* opaque, *d.* flexible) :
BREAK

(**a**) A pliable object will easily bend, while a brittle substance will easily
break.
General Information—Description

9. ADVERB : HAPPILY :: PREPOSITION : (*a.* the, *b.* or, ***c.* on**, *d.* none)

(**c**) *Happily* is an adverb. *On* is a preposition.
Humanities—Description

10. RIGHT ANGLE : (*a.* 0, *b.* 45, ***c.* 90**, *d.* 360) :: STRAIGHT ANGLE : 180

(**c**) A right angle is 90 degrees; a straight angle is 180 degrees.
Mathematics—Description

11. AUTHOR : PEN :: PAINTER : (***a.* brush**, *b.* paint, *c.* canvas, *d.* picture)

(**a**) An author does his or her writing with a pen; a painter does his or her
painting with a brush.
General Information—Description

12. ASTRONAUT : ROCKET SHIP :: WITCH : (*a.* cauldron, *b.* vulture,
c. black cat, ***d.* broomstick**)

(**d**) An astronaut flies by rocket ship. A witch "flies" by broomstick.
General Information—Description

13. (*a.* achievement, ***b.* permission**, *c.* month, *d.* desire) : ABILITY :: MAY :
CAN

(**b**) Someone who can do something is able to do it. Someone who may do
something has permission to do it.
General Information—Description

14. IBM : (*a.* Industrial Business Machines, *b.* Innovative Business Machines,
***c.* International Business Machines**, *d.* Intelligent Business Machines) ::
GOP : Republican Party

(**c**) IBM is a common abbreviation for International Business Machines.
GOP is an abbreviation for the Grand Old Party, which is the
Republican Party.
General Information—Similarity/Contrast

15. (***a.* earthling**, *b.* earthian, *c.* earthing, *d.* earthan) : EARTH :: MARTIAN :
MARS

(**a**) An earthling is an inhabitant of the Earth. A Martian is an inhabitant
of Mars.
General Information—Description

Explanation of Answers

16. ASBESTOS : FIRE :: (*a.* **vinyl**, *b.* air, *c.* cotton, *d.* faucet) : WATER

    (**a**) Asbestos is fireproof. Vinyl is waterproof.
    General Information—Description

17. DAVY JONES : (*a.* Great Britain, *b.* Planet Earth, *c.* the sun, *d.* **the sea**) :: LAND OF THE RISING SUN : JAPAN

    (**d**) Davy Jones refers to the bottom of the sea; the origins of this term are unclear. The Land of the Rising Sun is Japan.
    General Information—Similarity/Contrast

18. PAIR : PARE :: COUPLE : (*a.* several, *b.* one, *c.* pear, *d.* **prune**)

    (**d**) A pair is a couple. To pare is to prune.
    Vocabulary—Similarity/Contrast

19. ASCETIC : (*a.* businessman, *b.* **monk**, *c.* carpenter, *d.* policeman) :: CRAFTY : CONFIDENCE MAN

    (**b**) A monk is ascetic. A confidence man is crafty.
    General Information—Description

20. GUILLOTINE : ROBESPIERRE :: (*a.* noose, *b.* **poison**, *c.* knife, *d.* illness) : SOCRATES

    (**b**) Robespierre was killed by the guillotine. Socrates was killed by poison.
    Humanities—Description

21. GIN : BLACK :: (*a.* apple, *b.* whiskey, *c.* cotton, *d.* **rummy**) : JACK

    (**d**) Gin rummy and blackjack are both card games.
    General Information—Completion

22. PESO : MEXICO :: (*a.* ounce, *b.* **pound**, *c.* ruble, *d.* mark) : ENGLAND

    (**b**) The peso is the unit of currency in Mexico. The pound is the unit of currency in England. An ounce is a unit of weight. The ruble is the unit of currency in Russia. The mark was formerly the unit of currency in Germany.
    General Information—Description

23. SILVER : GOLD :: (*a.* Si, *b.* Sl, *c.* **Ag**, *d.* Hg) : Au

    (**c**) The chemical symbol for silver is Ag; that for gold is Au. Si stands for silicon; Hg stands for mercury.
    Natural Science—Similarity/Contrast

24. VALEDICTORIAN : SALUTATORIAN :: PRIME : (*a.* excellent, *b.* good, *c.* **choice**, *d.* alternative)

(**c**) A valedictorian is the highest-ranking student in a class, while a salutatorian is the second highest. Prime meat is the highest-ranked type of meat, while choice meat is the second highest-ranked.
General Information—Class

25. CHEROKEE : (*a.* Indian, *b.* aborigine, *c.* **Seminole**, *d.* pariah) :: APACHE : NAVAJO

(**c**) The Cherokee, Seminole, Apache, and Navajo are all tribes of American Indians. Aborigines are members of the original population of a place, as opposed to the colonizing people. Pariahs are members of a traditionally low caste in India.
Social Science—Class

26. (*a.* musical instruments, *b.* **books**, *c.* weather systems, *d.* diseases) : DEWEY :: LIVING THINGS : LINNAEUS

(**b**) Dewey devised a system for classifying books (Dewey Decimal Classification, DDC). Linnaeus devised a system for classifying living things (biological classification).
Humanities—Description

27. IVAN : TERRIBLE :: PETER : (*a.* Hairy, *b.* Reformer, *c.* **Great**, *d.* Awful)

(**c**) Ivan the Terrible (1530–1584) and Peter the Great (1672–1725) were both rulers of Russia.
Humanities—Completion

28. SQUARE : 360 :: RECTANGLE : (*a.* 90, *b.* 180, *c.* 270, *d.* **360**)

(**d**) Both a square and a rectangle have interior angles summing to 360 degrees.
Mathematics—Description

29. WHALE : (*a.* **mammal**, *b.* reptile, *c.* amphibian, *d.* fish) :: LIZARD : REPTILE

(**a**) A whale is a mammal; a lizard is a reptile.
Natural Science—Class

30. LINCOLN : (*a.* 1, *b.* **5**, *c.* 10, *d.* 16) :: JACKSON : 20

(**b**) President Lincoln's portrait appears on a $5 bill; President Jackson's portrait appears on a $20 bill. George Washington appears on the $1 bill. Alexander Hamilton appears on the $10 bill. Ulysses Grant appears on the $50 bill. Benjamin Franklin appears on the $100 bill.
General Information—Description

31. CONJUNCTION : DISJUNCTION :: AND : (*a.* but, *b.* if . . . then, *c.* **or**, *d.* because)

    (**c**) In logic, *and* expresses conjunction and *or* expresses disjunction.
    Mathematics—Class

32. AENEAS : (*a.* **Virgil**, *b.* Plutarch, *c.* Caesar, *d.* Demosthenes) :: ODYSSEUS : HOMER

    (**a**) Virgil wrote about the travels of Aeneas; Homer wrote about the travels of Odysseus. Plutarch wrote *Parallel Lives*; famous fables of Aesop are, for example, *The Fox and the Grapes* and *The Tortoise and the Hare*. Caesar was a dictator of the Roman Republic and wrote *Commentarii de Bello Gallico*, among other works. Demosthenes was a Greek orator who published many of his orations.
    Humanities—Description

33. AGORAPHOBIA : ARACHNOPHOBIA :: OPEN SPACES : (*a.* lizards, *b.* snakes, *c.* **spiders**, *d.* dragons)

    (**c**) Claustrophobia is a fear of confined places. Agoraphobia is a fear of open spaces.
    Vocabulary—Description

34. GRIMM : (*a.* Donne, *b.* Petrarch, *c.* Nash, *d.* **Andersen**) :: CHAUCER : BOCCACCIO

    (**d**) Grimm and Andersen both wrote fairy tales. Chaucer and Boccaccio both wrote collections of tales told by groups of people.
    Humanities—Class

35. CYCLONE : TORNADO :: HURRICANE : (*a.* storm, *b.* **typhoon**, *c.* rain, *d.* miasma)

    (**b**) Cyclone, tornado, hurricane, and typhoon are all types of major storms. Cyclones are storms that rotate around a center and often come with rain. Hurricanes are tropical cyclones that are faster than 73 miles per hour; they mostly appear in the western Atlantic. Typhoons are a kind of hurricane that mostly appears in the China Sea or the Philippines. Tornadoes occur over land.
    Natural Science—Class

36. GREENHOUSE : PLANTS :: AVIARY : (*a.* **birds**, *b.* bees, *c.* rodents, *d.* fish)

    (**a**) A greenhouse houses plants. An aviary houses birds.
    Natural Science—Description

37. (**a.** $A \cap B$, *b.* $B \cap A$, *c.* $A \cup B$, *d.* $B \cup A$) : $B \cup A$ :: $X \wedge Y$: $Y \vee X$

    (**a**) $A \cap B$ and $X \wedge Y$ are equivalent, as are $B \cup A$ and $Y \vee X$.
    Mathematics—Equality/Negation

38. OFFER : JOB :: TENDER : (**a. resignation**, *b.* retirement, *c.* delicate, *d.* rough)

    (**a**) One offers a job, but tenders a resignation.
    General Information—Description

39. HICCUP : HICCOUGH :: EYE : (*a.* light, *b.* ice, **c. I**, *d.* iris)

    (**c**) *Hiccup* and *hiccough* are pronounced identically, as are *eye* and *I*.
    Nonsemantic

40. (*a.* black, *b.* white, **c. orange**, *d.* brown) : BLUE :: RED : GREEN

    (**c**) Orange and blue are complementary colors, as are red and green. Complementary colors are colors that produce white light when combined.
    Natural Science—Similarity/Contrast

41. ASPIRIN : (*a.* anaphoric, *b.* mycin, *c.* antibiotic, **d. analgesic**) :: PENICILLIN : ANTIBIOTIC

    (**d**) Aspirin is an analgesic, while penicillin is an antibiotic. Analgesic medication alleviates pain. An antibiotic kills or inhibits the growth of microorganisms. Anaphoric refers to the repetition of a word or phrase at the beginning of a clause; mycin is a suffix that refers to a substance gained from a fungus-like bacterium.
    Natural Science—Class

42. (*a.* Istanbul, *b.* Dar es Salaam, *c.* Jerusalem, **d. Mecca**) : MOHAMMED :: BETHLEHEM : JESUS

    (**d**) Mecca was the birthplace of Mohammed, while Bethlehem was the birthplace of Jesus.
    Humanities—Description

43. CETANE : DIESEL FUEL OIL :: (**a. octane**, *b.* heptane, *c.* methane, *d.* propane) : GASOLINE

    (**a**) Diesel fuel oil is given a cetane rating as an index of quality, while gasoline is given an octane rating for the same purpose.
    Natural Science—Description

Explanation of Answers

44. DEAD DUCK : GONER :: LAME DUCK : (***a. one who finishes a term after failing re-election***, *b.* one who gives up easily, *c.* one who invests cautiously, *d.* one who complains incessantly)

    (**a**) A dead duck is a goner; a lame duck is an elected official who finishes his or her term after failing re-election.
    General Information—Similarity/Contrast

45. ARGONAUTS : (*a.* Francis Marion, ***b. Jason***, *c.* Achilles, *d.* George Washington) :: GREEN MOUNTAIN BOYS : ETHAN ALLEN

    (**b**) The Argonauts accompanied Jason in his exploits; the Green Mountain Boys accompanied Ethan Allen in his exploits. *Argonautica* is an Ancient Greek poem. The Green Mountain Boys were an informal militia of the Vermont Republic.
    Humanities—Description

46. LYNX : CAT :: BOAR : (***a. hog***, *b.* dog, *c.* goat, *d.* ram)

    (**a**) A lynx is a type of wild cat. A boar is a type of wild hog.
    Natural Science—Class

47. LENIN : BOLSHEVIK :: (*a.* Stalin, ***b. Kerensky***, *c.* Trotsky, *d.* Marx) : MENSHEVIK

    (**b**) After the Russian Revolution, Lenin led the Bolsheviks and Kerensky led the Mensheviks.
    Humanities—Description

48. (*a.* oak, *b.* walnut, ***c. balsa***, *d.* corundum) : HICKORY :: TIN : STEEL

    (**c**) Balsa is a soft wood; hickory a hard wood. Tin is a soft metal; steel a hard metal. Oak is a hard wood, as is walnut. Corundum is a very hard mineral.
    Natural Science—Class

49. ROCK : ROCKET :: (*a.* coat, *b.* cloth, ***c. jack***, *d.* wasp) : JACKET

    (**c**) Rocket is rock with *-et* at the end. *Jacket* is *jack* with *-et* at the end.
    Nonsemantic

50. MALARIA : CHILLS :: GOITER : (*a.* pockmarks, ***b. swelling***, *c.* fever, *d.* hypertension)

    (**b**) Malaria results in chills. Goiter results in swelling.
    Natural Science—Description

51. PIZARRO : INCA :: (*a.* Ponce de Leon, *b.* Hudson, *c.* Velásquez, *d.* **Cortez**) : AZTEC

   (**d**) Pizarro (ca. 1475–1541) conquered the Inca Indians. Cortez (1485–1547) conquered the Aztecs.
   Humanities—Description

52. ASTROLOGY : (*a.* astronomy, *b.* physics, *c.* pharmacology, *d.* **phrenology**) :: ASTRONOMY : ANATOMY

   (**d**) Astrology and phrenology (drawing conclusions from the shape of skull to character traits) are commonly considered pseudosciences, while astronomy and anatomy are accepted as natural sciences.
   Natural Science—Class

53. DUET : SEXTET :: SOLO : (*a.* quartet, *b.* quintet, *c.* chorus, *d.* **trio**)

   (**d**) Two is to six as one is to three.
   Mathematics—Equality/Negation

54. ANDES : (*a.* Asia, *b.* Africa, ***c.* South America**, *d.* Europe) :: ALPS : EUROPE

   (**c**) The Andes mountain range is in South America; the Alps are in Europe.
   General Information—Description

55. MYOPIA : (***a.* hyperopia**, *b.* scotopia, *c.* photopia, *d.* metropia) :: NEARSIGHTED : FARSIGHTED

   (**a**) A nearsighted person has myopia, while a farsighted person has hyperopia. Scotopia is the ability to see in darkness. Photopia is vision in bright light.
   Natural Science—Description

56. PASTORAL : (*a.* religious, ***b.* rustic**, *c.* metropolitan, *d.* worldly) :: URBAN : CITIFIED

   (**b**) *Pastoral* and *rustic* are synonyms, as are *urban* and *citified*.
   Vocabulary—Similarity/Contrast

57. SEA : TIGER :: LION : (*a.* land, *b.* fauna, ***c.* lily**, *d.* heart)

   (**c**) A sea lion and a tiger lily are both living things.
   General Information—Class

58. ASTRONAUT : SPACESUIT :: (*a.* judge, *b.* baker, *c.* ballerina, *d.* **monk**) : HABIT

   (**d**) An astronaut wears a spacesuit; a monk wears a habit.
   General Information—Description

59. MONOGAMY : BIGAMY :: BIPED : (*a.* unipod, *b.* pedate, *c.* millipede, *d.* **quadruped**)

    (**d**) One is to two as two is to four. A biped is a two-footed animal.
    A millipede is an invertebrate with many legs. *Pedate* means "having or resembling a foot."
    A unipod is a pole to support cameras (similar to a tripod).
    Mathematics—Class

60. POPE : ROMAN :: (*a.* Metropolitan, *b.* **Patriarch**, *c.* Cardinal, *d.* Bishop) :
    GREEK ORTHODOX

    (**b**) The Pope is the spiritual leader of the Roman Catholic Church, while
    the Patriarch is the spiritual leader of the Greek Orthodox Catholic Church.
    A cardinal is a member of the Sacred College in the Roman Catholic Church. Cardinals
    elect the Pope and serve as his advisors. A bishop is a clergyman overseeing a diocese.
    Humanities—Description

61. SEXTANT : (*a.* **navigator**, *b.* architect, *c.* archeologist, *d.* priest) ::
    SCALPEL : SURGEON

    (**a**) A sextant is used by a navigator, while a scalpel is used by a surgeon.
    Natural Science—Description

62. PRIDE : PREJUDICE :: SENSE : (*a.* Folly, *b.* Pretense, *c.* **Sensibility**,
    d. Sanity)

    (**c**) *Pride and Prejudice* and *Sense and Sensibility* are both novels by Jane
    Austen.
    Humanities—Completion

63. PACIFIST : PEACE :: (*a.* **revolutionary**, *b.* diplomat, *c.* charlatan,
    d. traitor) : WAR

    (**a**) A pacifist seeks peace; a revolutionary seeks war.
    Vocabulary—Description

64. (*a.* **brown**, *b.* gray, *c.* purple, *d.* blue) : UMBER :: GREEN :
    CHARTREUSE

    (**a**) Umber is a shade of brown; chartreuse is a shade of green.
    Vocabulary—Class

65. INCREASE : LESSEN :: (*a.* fair, *b.* **final**, *c.* incipient, *d.* unfair) :
    INCHOATE

    (**b**) *Increase* and *lessen* are antonyms, as are *final* and *inchoate*.
    Vocabulary—Similarity/Contrast

66. EXCALIBUR : (***a.* sword**, *b.* pony, *c.* lioness, *d.* cannon) :: LASSIE : DOG

   (**a**) Excalibur was the name of a sword (King Arthur's). Lassie was the name of a dog (Jeff Miller's).
   Humanities—Description

67. (***a.* Bern**, *b.* Geneva, *c.* Zurich, *d.* Lucerne) : SWITZERLAND :: NEW DELHI : INDIA

   (**a**) Bern is the capital of Switzerland; New Delhi is the capital of India.
   General Information—Description

68. SILVER-TONGUED : ELOQUENT :: JANUS-FACED : (***a.* duplicitous**, *b.* versatile, *c.* incredibly ugly, *d.* honest)

   (**a**) A silver-tongued person is eloquent. A Janus-faced person is duplicitous—literally, two-faced.
   Vocabulary—Similarity/Contrast

69. PRESENT : FUTURE PERFECT :: GO : (*a.* would go, *b.* will go, ***c.* will have gone**, *d.* would have gone)

   (**c**) *Go* is the present tense, and *will have gone* the future perfect tense, of the same verb.
   Humanities—Description

70. AMPLITUDE : FREQUENCY :: RATE : (*a.* distance, *b.* velocity, *c.* acceleration, ***d.* time**)

   (**d**) Amplitude and frequency of a wave are inversely related, as are rate and time traveled by an object.
   Natural Science—Equality/Negation

71. GREENHORN : NOVICE :: NEOPHYTE : (*a.* expert, *b.* priest, ***c.* beginner**, *d.* novelist)

   (**c**) *Greenhorn, novice, neophyte*, and *beginner* are all synonymous.
   Vocabulary—Similarity/Contrast

72. PANEGYRIC : (*a.* prayer, *b.* joke, *c.* threat, ***d.* eulogy**) :: TEMPEST : STORM

   (**d**) A panegyric is a eulogy. A tempest is a storm.
   Vocabulary—Similarity/Contrast

Explanation of Answers

73. CARMEN : (*a.* Verdi, ***b.* Bizet**, *c.* Gounod, *d.* Wagner) ::
BARBER OF SEVILLE : ROSSINI

   (**b**) *Carmen* is an opera by Bizet. *The Barber of Seville* is an opera by Rossini. *Rigoletto* and *Nabucco* were composed by Verdi. The opera *Faust* is by Gounod. Wagner wrote *The Ring of the Nibelung*.
   Humanities—Description

74. PALPITATE : QUIVER :: MASTICATE : (*a.* abuse, *b.* remove, *c.* stomp,
***d.* chew**)

   (**d**) To palpitate is to quiver. To masticate is to chew.
   Vocabulary—Similarity/Contrast

75. BOLÍVAR : (*a.* Venezuela, ***b.* Spain**, *c.* United States, *d.* Mexico) ::
WASHINGTON : ENGLAND

   (**b**) Simon Bolívar fought against Spain for the liberation of South American countries. George Washington fought against England for the liberation of the newly formed United States.
   Humanities—Description

76. CORNUCOPIA : (***a.* horn of plenty**, *b.* horn of Roland, *c.* hornpipe,
d. hornstone) :: TENET : PRECEPT

   (**a**) A cornucopia is a horn of plenty. A tenet is a precept.
   Vocabulary—Similarity/Contrast

77. SHRIMP : CRUSTACEAN :: (***a.* snail**, *b.* lobster, *c.* goldfish, *d.* brine) :
MOLLUSK

   (**a**) A shrimp is a form of crustacean. A snail is a form of mollusk. A lobster is a crustacean; a goldfish is a freshwater fish; brine is water containing salts.
   Natural Science—Class

78. NEW AMSTERDAM : NEW YORK :: SIAM : (***a.* Thailand**, *b.* Cambodia,
c. Laos, *d.* China)

   (**a**) New York was formerly called New Amsterdam. Thailand was formerly called Siam. Cambodia was formerly named the Khmer Republic and Kampuchea.
   General Information—Similarity/Contrast

79. HIRSUTE : (*a.* pleasantly plump, *b.* well-dressed, *c.* handsome, ***d.* hairy**) ::
EXTROVERTED : OUTGOING

   (**d**) A hirsute person is hairy. An extroverted person is outgoing.
   Vocabulary—Similarity/Contrast

80. EYE : LIP :: ELBOW : (*a.* forehead, *b.* nose, ***c.* foot**, *d.* chest)

   (**c**) A normal human being has two eyes, lips, elbows, and feet.
   General Information—Class

81. (*a.* feldspar, ***b.* talc**, *c.* quartz, *d.* topaz) : 1 :: DIAMOND : 10

   (**b**) On the Mohs scale of hardness, talc is rated 1 (softest) and diamond is rated 10 (hardest). Quartz is rated 7; feldspar is rated 6; topaz is rated 8.
   Natural Science—Description

82. TORTUOUS : (*a.* painless, *b.* painful, ***c.* straight**, *d.* winding) :: SOBER : INEBRIATED

   (**c**) *Tortuous* and *straight* are opposites, as are *sober* and *inebriated*.
   Vocabulary—Similarity/Contrast

83. NONPLUS : (***a.* perplexity**, *b.* disappointment, *c.* deletion, *d.* elation) :: NONPAREIL : UNEQUALED

   (**a**) Nonplus is perplexity. Something that is nonpareil is unequaled.
   Vocabulary—Similarity/Contrast

84. CROCKETT : ALAMO :: BONAPARTE : (*a.* Madrid, ***b.* St. Helena**, *c.* Rome, *d.* London)

   (**b**) Davy Crockett died at the Alamo. Napoleon Bonaparte died on St. Helena.
   Humanities—Description

85. EL GRECO : (*a.* impressionist, ***b.* mannerist**, *c.* expressionist, *d.* realist) :: DAVID : NEOCLASSICIST

   (**b**) El Greco was a mannerist painter. David was a neoclassicist painter.
   Humanities—Description

86. GRAY : COUNTRY CHURCHYARD :: (***a.* Keats**, *b.* Poe, *c.* Byron, *d.* Longfellow) : GRECIAN URN

   (**a**) Thomas Gray is famous for his "Elegy in a Country Churchyard," while John Keats is famous for his "Ode on a Grecian Urn." Edgar Allan Poe is famous as a mystery writer; one of his works is *The Pit and the Pendulum*. Henry Wadsworth Longfellow was an American poet whose works include *Paul Revere's Ride*. George Byron was a British poet and wrote *When We Two Parted*.
   Humanities—Description

87. MITER : (*a.* dancer, *b.* cartoonist, *c.* queen, ***d.* bishop**) :: CROWN : KING

   (**d**) A miter is a headpiece worn by a bishop. A crown is a headpiece worn by a king.
   General Information—Description

88. $2^0 : 2^{-2} :: 2^2 : ($*a.* $2^{1/4}$, ***b.*** 2^0, *c.* 2^1, *d.* $2^{-1})$

    (**b**) 1 is to $^1/_4$ as 4 is to 1.
    Mathematics—Equality/Negation

89. FLOWER : GARDEN :: (*a.* pinnacle, ***b.*** **stalagmite**, *c.* cavern, *d.* explorer) : CAVE

    (**b**) Flowers grow up from a garden; stalagmites "grow" up from the floor of a cave.
    Natural Science—Description

90. LEVITICUS : OLD :: (*a.* Deuteronomy, *b.* Isaiah, *c.* Numbers, ***d.*** **Ephesians**) : NEW

    (**d**) Leviticus is a book in the Old Testament, while Ephesians is a book in the New Testament. Deuteronomy, Numbers, and Isaiah are books in the Old Testament of the Bible.
    Humanities—Description

91. LOUVRE : PARIS :: PRADO : (***a.*** **Madrid**, *b.* Seville, *c.* Florence, *d.* Chartres)

    (**a**) The Louvre is an art museum in Paris; the Prado is an art museum in Madrid.
    Humanities—Description

92. CUL-DE-SAC : BLIND ALLEY :: SANGFROID : (*a.* carelessness, *b.* timidity, *c.* courage, ***d.*** **imperturbability**)

    (**d**) A cul-de-sac is a blind alley. Sangfroid is imperturbability.
    Vocabulary—Similarity/Contrast

93. ENCOMIUM : TRIBUTE :: (*a.* admonition, *b.* excoriation, *c.* benison, ***d.*** **exegesis**) : CRITICAL ANALYSIS

    (**d**) An encomium is a tribute. An exegesis is a critical analysis.
    Vocabulary—Similarity/Contrast

94. CARPETBAGGER : NORTH :: (*a.* Granger, ***b.*** **Scalawag**, *c.* Bull Moose, *d.* Tweedy Pie) : SOUTH

    (**b**) After the Civil War, intruders from the North were called carpetbaggers, and Northern sympathizers (usually Republicans) from the South were called scalawags. The Bull Moose Party is a former political party in the United States founded by Theodore Roosevelt. Tweedy Pie is a cartoon character. A granger is a farmer.
    Humanities—Description

95. MERCURIAL : (*a.* pretty, *b.* plutonic, *c.* hateful, ***d.* hermetic**) ::
MARTIAL : AREOLOGY

(**d**) The word *mercurial* is derived from the Roman name and the word
hermetic from the Greek name, for the messenger of the gods (Mercury or
Hermes, respectively). The word *martial* is derived from the Roman name,
and the word *areology* from the Greek name, for the god of war (Mars or
Ares, respectively).
Humanities—Description

96. LEGATO : BOW :: PIZZICATO : (***a.* fingers**, *b.* bow, *c.* reed, *d.* feet)

(**a**) On a string instrument, legato notes are played with a bow, while
pizzicato notes are played with the fingers.
Humanities—Description

97. NICK ADAMS : (*a.* Fitzgerald, *b.* Faulkner, ***c.* Hemingway**, *d.* Joyce) ::
ARROWSMITH : LEWIS

(**c**) Nick Adams was a character in stories by Ernest Hemingway.
Arrowsmith was a character in a novel (entitled *Arrowsmith*)
by Sinclair Lewis.
Humanities—Description

98. (*a.* Burgundian, *b.* Prussian, ***c.* Turkish**, *d.* Bulgarian) : OTTOMAN ::
FRENCH : BOURBON

(**c**) The Ottomans were Turkish; the Bourbons were French. The Burgundians
were French; the Prussians were German.
Humanities—Description

99. ORPHEUS : EURYDICE :: DAPHNIS : (*a.* Pyramus, *b.* Thisbe, ***c.* Chloe**,
d. Helen)

(**c**) Orpheus and Eurydice were lovers, as were Daphnis and Chloe. The story
of Pyramus and Thisbe was told by Ovid; they were lovers as well. Helen was the daughter
of Zeus and Leda and was abducted by Paris, which led to the Trojan War.
Humanities—Class

100. (*a.* darling, *b.* wench, ***c.* harridan**, *d.* myrmidon) : SHREW ::
MOLLYCODDLE : SISSY

(**c**) A harridan is a shrew. A mollycoddle is a sissy.
Vocabulary—Similarity/Contrast

101. PULLEY : (***a. screw***, *b.* saw, *c.* pliers, *d.* nail) :: WEDGE : INCLINED PLANE

    (**a**) Among the six basic simple machines are a pulley, screw, wedge, and inclined plane (as well as the lever and the wheel and axle).
    Natural Science—Class

102. LIVE WIRE : LOOSE CANNON :: ENERGETIC : (*a.* powerful, *b.* threatening, ***c. reckless***, *d.* peaceable)

    (**c**) A person who is very energetic can be described as a live wire, whereas a reckless person can be described as a loose cannon.
    General Information—Similarity/Contrast

103. ARM : LEG :: (*a.* radius, *b.* ulna, ***c. humerus***, *d.* scapula) : FEMUR

    (**c**) The humerus is the upper armbone just as the femur is the upper legbone. The ulna is the elbow bone. The radius is the bone on the side of the thumb of a forearm. The scapulae are a pair of large triangular bones that form the posterior part of the shoulder.
    Natural Science—Description

104. VENUSIAN : (*a.* Venus, ***b. Earth***, *c.* Moon, *d.* Mercury) :: MARTIAN : JUPITER

    (**b**) A Venusian is a hypothetical inhabitant of the planet whose orbit around the Sun is just inside that of the planet Earth. A Martian is a hypothetical inhabitant of the planet whose orbit is just inside that of Jupiter. The order of the planets orbiting the Sun is (in order from the Sun): Mercury, Venus, Earth, Mars, Jupiter, Saturn, Uranus, Neptune.
    General Information—Description

105. (*a.* oil, *b.* air, *c.* nitrates, ***d. blood***) : TOURNIQUET :: WATER : DAM

    (**d**) The function of a tourniquet is to stop the flow of blood beyond a certain point just as the function of a dam is to stop the flow of water beyond a certain point.
    Vocabulary—Description

106. OBJURGATE : (***a. vituperate***, *b.* venerate, *c.* abrogate, *d.* enervate) :: RECANT : RETRACT

    (**a**) To objurgate is to harshly criticize, as is to vituperate. Likewise, recant and retract share the same meaning, to withdraw in a way.
    Vocabulary—Similarity/Contrast

107. PERFIDIOUS : BENEFICENT :: (*a.* obvious, ***b.*** **capricious**, *c.* intractable, *d.* renitent) : STEADFAST

(**b**) Perfidious and beneficent are antonyms, as are capricious, meaning changing quickly, and steadfast, meaning dependable and constant.
Vocabulary—Similarity/Contrast

108. MAN : LAZARUS :: BIRD : (*a.* dragon, *b.* albatross, ***c.*** **phoenix**, *d.* dodo)

(**c**) Lazarus was a man said to rise from the dead. The phoenix was a bird said to rise from the dead.
Humanities—Description

109. FIREWORKS : (*a.* Japan, *b.* Korea, *c.* Indonesia, ***d.*** **China**) :: LIGHTBULB : THE UNITED STATES

(**d**) Fireworks were first invented in China just as the lightbulb was first known in the United States.
General Information—Description

110. GI TRACT : GI JOE :: GASTROINTESTINAL : (*a.* General Infantry, *b.* Galvanized Iron, ***c.*** **Government Issue**, *d.* General Information)

(**c**) GI Tract is short for Gastrointestinal Tract. GI Joe is short for Government Issue Joe (which is also an action figure).
General Information—Equality/Negation

111. WET SUIT : (*a.* spandex, ***b.*** **neoprene**, *c.* nylon, *d.* Lycra) :: BULLETPROOF VEST : KEVLAR

(**b**) The artificial material used to make wet suits is neoprene just as the artificial material used to make bulletproof vests is Kevlar. Spandex is an elastic synthetic fiber; the most famous brand name associated with Spandex is Lycra. Nylon is a strong elastic polyamide material.
General Information—Part/Whole

112. (***a.*** **yellow**, *b.* pink, *c.* white, *d.* green) : BLUE :: JAUNDICED : CYANOTIC

(**a**) Someone who is jaundiced has a skin color that is tinted yellow. Likewise, a cyanotic person has blue-tinted skin.
Natural Science—Description

113. MONET : WATER LILIES :: DEGAS : (*a.* windmills, *b.* sailboats, *c.* polo players, ***d.*** **ballet dancers**)

(**d**) Just as Monet had water lilies as a favorite subject for his art, so did Degas often feature ballet dancers in his paintings and sculptures.
Humanities—Description

114. WAR : (*a.* birth, ***b.* flood**, *c.* death, *d.* fall) :: ANTEBELLUM : ANTEDILUVIAN

(**b**) Antebellum refers to a time before a war and antediluvian refers to a time before the flood. *Prenatal* means "before birth"; *antemortem* refers to the time before death.
Vocabulary—Description

115. DILETTANTE : DEBUTANTE :: (***a.* amateur**, *b.* professional, *c.* actor, *d.* student) : YOUNG WOMAN

(**a**) Dilettantes are amateurs and debutantes are young women.
Vocabulary—Class

116. DOG : CAT :: (*a.* loud, *b.* skinny, ***c.* under**, *d.* hound) : FAT

(**c**) "Underdog" and "fat cat" are both terms used to describe types of people.
General Information—Completion

117. RIDE : (*a.* U.S. senator, *b.* doctor, *c.* pilot, ***d.* astronaut**) :: O'CONNOR : SUPREME COURT JUSTICE

(**d**) Sally Ride was the first female astronaut. Sandra Day O'Connor was the first female Supreme Court Justice.
General Information—Description

118. (*a.* panda, ***b.* opossum**, *c.* mouse, *d.* anteater) : WALLABY :: KANGAROO : WOMBAT

(**b**) Opossums, wallabies, kangaroos, and wombats are all marsupial mammals.
General Information—Class

119. ANDREW : ABRAHAM :: LYNDON : (***a.* John**, *b.* Robert, *c.* Joseph, *d.* Edward)

(**a**) Andrew Johnson succeeded Abraham Lincoln as president. Lyndon Johnson succeeded John Kennedy as president.
General Information—Description

120. MYOPIA: CONCAVE :: (*a.* mytopia, *b.* astigmatism, ***c.* hyperopia**, *d.* diopia) : CONVEX

(**c**) A concave lens is typically used to correct for myopia, or nearsightedness. A convex lens corrects for hyperopia (farsightedness).
Natural Science—Description

PRACTICE TEST 5

Item Classification Chart

		RELATIONSHIP						
		Similarity/ Contrast	Description	Class	Completion	Part/ Whole	Equality/ Negation	Nonsemantic
C O N T E N T	**Vocabulary**	18, 56, 65, 68, 71, 72, 74, 76, 79, 82, 83, 92, 93, 100, 106, 107	33, 63, 105, 114	64, 115				
	General Information	14, 17, 44, 78, 102	1, 4, 6, 7, 8, 11, 12, 13, 15, 16, 19, 22, 30, 38, 54, 58, 67, 87, 104, 109, 117, 119	24, 57, 80, 118	3, 21, 116	111	110	
	Humanities		2, 9, 20, 26, 32, 42, 45, 47, 51, 60, 66, 69, 73, 75, 84, 85, 86, 90, 91, 94, 95, 96, 97, 98, 108, 113	34, 99	27, 62			
	Social Science			25				
	Natural Science	23, 40	36, 43, 50, 55, 61, 81, 89, 103, 112, 120	5, 29, 35, 41, 46, 48, 52, 77,101			70	
	Mathematics		10, 28	31, 59			37, 53, 88	
	Nonsemantic							39, 49

Answer Sheet
PRACTICE TEST 6

1 Ⓐ Ⓑ Ⓒ Ⓓ	31 Ⓐ Ⓑ Ⓒ Ⓓ	61 Ⓐ Ⓑ Ⓒ Ⓓ	91 Ⓐ Ⓑ Ⓒ Ⓓ
2 Ⓐ Ⓑ Ⓒ Ⓓ	32 Ⓐ Ⓑ Ⓒ Ⓓ	62 Ⓐ Ⓑ Ⓒ Ⓓ	92 Ⓐ Ⓑ Ⓒ Ⓓ
3 Ⓐ Ⓑ Ⓒ Ⓓ	33 Ⓐ Ⓑ Ⓒ Ⓓ	63 Ⓐ Ⓑ Ⓒ Ⓓ	93 Ⓐ Ⓑ Ⓒ Ⓓ
4 Ⓐ Ⓑ Ⓒ Ⓓ	34 Ⓐ Ⓑ Ⓒ Ⓓ	64 Ⓐ Ⓑ Ⓒ Ⓓ	94 Ⓐ Ⓑ Ⓒ Ⓓ
5 Ⓐ Ⓑ Ⓒ Ⓓ	35 Ⓐ Ⓑ Ⓒ Ⓓ	65 Ⓐ Ⓑ Ⓒ Ⓓ	95 Ⓐ Ⓑ Ⓒ Ⓓ
6 Ⓐ Ⓑ Ⓒ Ⓓ	36 Ⓐ Ⓑ Ⓒ Ⓓ	66 Ⓐ Ⓑ Ⓒ Ⓓ	96 Ⓐ Ⓑ Ⓒ Ⓓ
7 Ⓐ Ⓑ Ⓒ Ⓓ	37 Ⓐ Ⓑ Ⓒ Ⓓ	67 Ⓐ Ⓑ Ⓒ Ⓓ	97 Ⓐ Ⓑ Ⓒ Ⓓ
8 Ⓐ Ⓑ Ⓒ Ⓓ	38 Ⓐ Ⓑ Ⓒ Ⓓ	68 Ⓐ Ⓑ Ⓒ Ⓓ	98 Ⓐ Ⓑ Ⓒ Ⓓ
9 Ⓐ Ⓑ Ⓒ Ⓓ	39 Ⓐ Ⓑ Ⓒ Ⓓ	69 Ⓐ Ⓑ Ⓒ Ⓓ	99 Ⓐ Ⓑ Ⓒ Ⓓ
10 Ⓐ Ⓑ Ⓒ Ⓓ	40 Ⓐ Ⓑ Ⓒ Ⓓ	70 Ⓐ Ⓑ Ⓒ Ⓓ	100 Ⓐ Ⓑ Ⓒ Ⓓ
11 Ⓐ Ⓑ Ⓒ Ⓓ	41 Ⓐ Ⓑ Ⓒ Ⓓ	71 Ⓐ Ⓑ Ⓒ Ⓓ	101 Ⓐ Ⓑ Ⓒ Ⓓ
12 Ⓐ Ⓑ Ⓒ Ⓓ	42 Ⓐ Ⓑ Ⓒ Ⓓ	72 Ⓐ Ⓑ Ⓒ Ⓓ	102 Ⓐ Ⓑ Ⓒ Ⓓ
13 Ⓐ Ⓑ Ⓒ Ⓓ	43 Ⓐ Ⓑ Ⓒ Ⓓ	73 Ⓐ Ⓑ Ⓒ Ⓓ	103 Ⓐ Ⓑ Ⓒ Ⓓ
14 Ⓐ Ⓑ Ⓒ Ⓓ	44 Ⓐ Ⓑ Ⓒ Ⓓ	74 Ⓐ Ⓑ Ⓒ Ⓓ	104 Ⓐ Ⓑ Ⓒ Ⓓ
15 Ⓐ Ⓑ Ⓒ Ⓓ	45 Ⓐ Ⓑ Ⓒ Ⓓ	75 Ⓐ Ⓑ Ⓒ Ⓓ	105 Ⓐ Ⓑ Ⓒ Ⓓ
16 Ⓐ Ⓑ Ⓒ Ⓓ	46 Ⓐ Ⓑ Ⓒ Ⓓ	76 Ⓐ Ⓑ Ⓒ Ⓓ	106 Ⓐ Ⓑ Ⓒ Ⓓ
17 Ⓐ Ⓑ Ⓒ Ⓓ	47 Ⓐ Ⓑ Ⓒ Ⓓ	77 Ⓐ Ⓑ Ⓒ Ⓓ	107 Ⓐ Ⓑ Ⓒ Ⓓ
18 Ⓐ Ⓑ Ⓒ Ⓓ	48 Ⓐ Ⓑ Ⓒ Ⓓ	78 Ⓐ Ⓑ Ⓒ Ⓓ	108 Ⓐ Ⓑ Ⓒ Ⓓ
19 Ⓐ Ⓑ Ⓒ Ⓓ	49 Ⓐ Ⓑ Ⓒ Ⓓ	79 Ⓐ Ⓑ Ⓒ Ⓓ	109 Ⓐ Ⓑ Ⓒ Ⓓ
20 Ⓐ Ⓑ Ⓒ Ⓓ	50 Ⓐ Ⓑ Ⓒ Ⓓ	80 Ⓐ Ⓑ Ⓒ Ⓓ	110 Ⓐ Ⓑ Ⓒ Ⓓ
21 Ⓐ Ⓑ Ⓒ Ⓓ	51 Ⓐ Ⓑ Ⓒ Ⓓ	81 Ⓐ Ⓑ Ⓒ Ⓓ	111 Ⓐ Ⓑ Ⓒ Ⓓ
22 Ⓐ Ⓑ Ⓒ Ⓓ	52 Ⓐ Ⓑ Ⓒ Ⓓ	82 Ⓐ Ⓑ Ⓒ Ⓓ	112 Ⓐ Ⓑ Ⓒ Ⓓ
23 Ⓐ Ⓑ Ⓒ Ⓓ	53 Ⓐ Ⓑ Ⓒ Ⓓ	83 Ⓐ Ⓑ Ⓒ Ⓓ	113 Ⓐ Ⓑ Ⓒ Ⓓ
24 Ⓐ Ⓑ Ⓒ Ⓓ	54 Ⓐ Ⓑ Ⓒ Ⓓ	84 Ⓐ Ⓑ Ⓒ Ⓓ	114 Ⓐ Ⓑ Ⓒ Ⓓ
25 Ⓐ Ⓑ Ⓒ Ⓓ	55 Ⓐ Ⓑ Ⓒ Ⓓ	85 Ⓐ Ⓑ Ⓒ Ⓓ	115 Ⓐ Ⓑ Ⓒ Ⓓ
26 Ⓐ Ⓑ Ⓒ Ⓓ	56 Ⓐ Ⓑ Ⓒ Ⓓ	86 Ⓐ Ⓑ Ⓒ Ⓓ	116 Ⓐ Ⓑ Ⓒ Ⓓ
27 Ⓐ Ⓑ Ⓒ Ⓓ	57 Ⓐ Ⓑ Ⓒ Ⓓ	87 Ⓐ Ⓑ Ⓒ Ⓓ	117 Ⓐ Ⓑ Ⓒ Ⓓ
28 Ⓐ Ⓑ Ⓒ Ⓓ	58 Ⓐ Ⓑ Ⓒ Ⓓ	88 Ⓐ Ⓑ Ⓒ Ⓓ	118 Ⓐ Ⓑ Ⓒ Ⓓ
29 Ⓐ Ⓑ Ⓒ Ⓓ	59 Ⓐ Ⓑ Ⓒ Ⓓ	89 Ⓐ Ⓑ Ⓒ Ⓓ	119 Ⓐ Ⓑ Ⓒ Ⓓ
30 Ⓐ Ⓑ Ⓒ Ⓓ	60 Ⓐ Ⓑ Ⓒ Ⓓ	90 Ⓐ Ⓑ Ⓒ Ⓓ	120 Ⓐ Ⓑ Ⓒ Ⓓ

Answer Sheet

Practice Test 6

Directions: In each of the following questions, you will find three initial terms and, in parentheses, four answer options designated *a*, *b*, *c*, and *d*. You are to select from the four answer options the one that best completes the analogy with the three initial terms. To record your answers, use the answer sheet provided.

Time: 60 minutes

1. LETTER : WORD :: (*a.* paragraph, *b.* word, *c.* period, *d.* meaning) : SENTENCE

2. GIVEN NAME : FIRST :: (*a.* Christian name, *b.* real name, *c.* nickname, *d.* surname) : LAST

3. JUDICIARY : (*a.* Circuit Court, *b.* Supreme Court, *c.* District Court, *d.* Court of Appeals) :: LEGISLATIVE : CONGRESS

4. (*a.* magna cum laude, *b.* optima cum laude, *c.* puella cum laude, *d.* summa cum laude) : HIGHEST HONOR :: CUM LAUDE : HONOR

5. WILLIAM JAMES : PHILOSOPHER :: HENRY JAMES : (*a.* chemist, *b.* novelist, *c.* lawyer, *d.* politician)

6. OUNCE : PREVENTION :: POUND : (*a.* remedy, *b.* prophylaxis, *c.* medicine, *d.* cure)

7. (*a.* decline, *b.* recline, *c.* acclaim, *d.* reclaim) : ASCEND :: INCLINE : DESCEND

8. CARNIVORE : ANIMALS :: (*a.* omnivore, *b.* herbivore, *c.* carnivore, *d.* vegetivore) : VEGETABLES

9. COLD : (*a.* caress, *b.* shiver, *c.* legs, *d.* shoulder) :: OPEN : ARMS

10. DROUGHT : (*a.* desert, *b.* thirst, *c.* rain, *d.* crops) :: FAMINE : FOOD

11. WESTMINSTER ABBEY : ENGLAND :: TAJ MAHAL : (*a.* Iran, *b.* India, *c.* Pakistan, *d.* China)

12. LEGISLATOR : MAKES :: POLICE OFFICER : (*a.* interprets, *b.* enforces, *c.* breaks, *d.* enacts)

13. DIRECT : INDIRECT :: HIM : (*a.* him, *b.* his, *c.* he, *d.* he'd)

14. ZIP : LETTER :: AREA : (*a.* volume, *b.* πr^2, *c.* post box, *d.* telephone call)

15. COURSE : COARSE :: (*a.* ruffle, *b.* direction, *c.* jagged, *d.* golf) : ROUGH

16. DIRIGIBLE : (*a.* air, *b.* sea, *c.* land, *d.* underground) :: AUTOMOBILE : LAND

17. MENDEL : (*a.* inequality, *b.* dominance, *c.* depression, *d.* orbits) :: MENDELEEV : PERIODICITY

18. LIVID : ASHEN :: JAUNDICED : (*a.* white, *b.* black, *c.* red, *d.* yellow)

19. AMIABLE : UNFRIENDLY :: AFFABLE : (*a.* unpleasant, *b.* ugly, *c.* beautiful, *d.* kindly)

20. JUNEAU : ALASKA :: (*a.* Waikiki, *b.* Honolulu, *c.* Oahu, *d.* Hawaii) : HAWAII

21. EAT : DRINK :: EDIBLE : (*a.* palpable, *b.* potable, *c.* lacteal, *d.* labile)

22. WHITE LIE : LIE :: (*a.* hurricane, *b.* drizzle, *c.* storm, *d.* humidity) : RAINFALL

23. (*a.* net, *b.* ten, *c.* met, *d.* end) : TEND :: MEN : MEND

24. FLAPJACK : (*a.* pumpkin pie, *b.* pancake, *c.* sponge cake, *d.* paddycake) :: GRIDDLECAKE : HOTCAKE

25. BINOMIAL : POLYNOMIAL :: TWO : (*a.* four, *b.* eight, *c.* all, *d.* many)

26. SAUDI ARABIA : OIL :: (*a.* Iran, *b.* Brazil, *c.* Hungary, *d.* Guatemala) : COFFEE

27. MONARCHY : ONE :: OLIGARCHY : (*a.* two, *b.* three, *c.* several, *d.* multitudes)

28. PASADENA : FOOTBALL :: WIMBLEDON : (*a.* tennis, *b.* boxing, *c.* golf, *d.* basketball)

29. MOLEHILL : EARTH :: DUNE : (*a.* rock, *b.* desert, *c.* mud, *d.* sand)

30. (*a.* plankton, *b.* gizzard, *c.* oyster, *d.* dinosaur) : REPTILE :: FROG : AMPHIBIAN

31. (*a.* Andersen, *b.* Grimm, *c.* Milne, *d.* Alcott) : WINNIE :: DISNEY : MICKEY

32. PATRICIAN : PLEBEIAN :: NOBILITY : (*a.* clergy, *b.* lordship, *c.* proletariat, *d.* bourgeoisie)

33. (*a.* fungi, *b.* water, *c.* gases, *d.* algae) : HYDROLOGY :: LIFE : BIOLOGY

34. GOTHIC : POINTED :: ROMANESQUE : (*a.* rounded, *b.* scalloped, *c.* squared, *d.* buttressed)

35. (*a.* 7, *b.* 9, *c.* 10, *d.* 12) : PLAGUES :: 7 : DEADLY SINS

36. STEP : PETS :: REEL : (*a.* fishes, *b.* rod, *c.* leer, *d.* real)

37. HAWK : PREY :: SWINDLER : (*a.* dupe, *b.* dodge, *c.* doll, *d.* dolt)

38. SOPORIFIC : (*a.* pain, *b.* sleepiness, *c.* hunger, *d.* thirst) :: APHRODISIAC : SEXUAL DESIRE

39. PASTEURIZE : (*a.* chemically treat, *b.* strain, *c.* chill, *d.* partially sterilize) :: HOMOGENIZE : MAKE UNIFORM

40. DECLARATIVE : . :: INTERROGATIVE : (*a.* !, *b.* :, *c.* –, *d.* ?)

41. ALLEGRO : (*a.* largo, *b.* presto, *c.* crescendo, *d.* cantabile) :: FAST : SLOW

42. PENCE : POUND :: CENTS : (*a.* nickel, *b.* dime, *c.* quarter, *d.* dollar)

43. CLANDESTINE : (*a.* surreptitious, *b.* tacit, *c.* sanguine, *d.* outgoing) :: SHY : DIFFIDENT

44. INCOGNITO : (*a.* ignorant, *b.* uninterested, *c.* unofficial, *d.* disguised) :: SATISFACTORY : ADEQUATE

45. ANTIDOTE : POISON :: (*a.* mycin, *b.* antibiotic, *c.* analgesic, *d.* antigen) : BACTERIA

46. DIRTY : LINEN :: FILTHY : (*a.* flax, *b.* burlap, *c.* lummox, *d.* lucre)

47. POLAR : (*a.* equatorial, *b.* mammoth, *c.* coordinate, *d.* grizzly) :: FORD : CHEVROLET

48. ONTOLOGY : BEING :: EPISTEMOLOGY : (*a.* spirit, *b.* knowledge, *c.* metaphysics, *d.* causality)

49. RECORDER : (*a.* flute, *b.* magnetic tape, *c.* player piano, *d.* trombone) :: LUTE : GUITAR

50. MILLIMETER : METER :: METER : (*a.* centimeter, *b.* decimeter, *c.* decameter, *d.* kilometer)

51. GENDARMES : FRANCE :: CARABINIERI : (*a.* Spain, *b.* Italy, *c.* Switzerland, *d.* Turkey)

52. RENOIR : IMPRESSIONIST :: (*a.* Braque, *b.* Matisse, *c.* Monet, *d.* Stella) : CUBIST

53. SCOTLAND YARD : CRIME :: EXCHEQUER : (*a.* agriculture, *b.* industry, *c.* defense, *d.* money)

54. (*a.* magician, *b.* tycoon, *c.* adventurer, *d.* usurer) : GENTLEMAN OF FORTUNE :: ATTENDANT : GENTLEMAN IN WAITING

55. HALCYON : (*a.* tranquil, *b.* agitated, *c.* bounteous, *d.* impoverished) :: FORTUITOUS : PLANNED

56. UTOPIA : (*a.* More, *b.* Plato, *c.* Becket, *d.* Aquinas) :: LILLIPUT : SWIFT

57. MERIDIAN : LONGITUDE :: (*a.* meridian, *b.* prime, *c.* parallel, *d.* perpendicular) : LATITUDE

58. CENTURY : HUNDRED :: MILLENNIUM : (*a.* A.D. 1, *b.* eternity, *c.* thousand, *d.* million)

59. COLD-BLOODED : HARD-HEARTED :: HOT-BLOODED : (*a.* cruel, *b.* listless, *c.* cold-hearted, *d.* excitable)

60. ASSIDUOUS : (*a.* ambitious, *b.* favorable, *c.* diligent, *d.* evergreen) :: ASSIMILATE : ABSORB

61. NETREBKO : SOPRANO :: DOMINGO : (*a.* soprano, *b.* contralto, *c.* tenor, *d.* bass)

62. CARDINAL : ORDINAL :: 8 : (*a.* −2, *b.* 60%, *c.* 5th, *d.* 9)

63. VALJEAN : (*a.* Mauriac, *b.* Balzac, *c.* Hugo, *d.* Molière) :: GORIOT : BALZAC

64. MAUVE : (*a.* brown, *b.* red, *c.* purple, *d.* green) :: TAN : BROWN

65. RANGERS : (*a.* basketball, *b.* polo, *c.* football, *d.* hockey) :: CARDINALS : BASEBALL

66. CARTIER : (*a.* Hudson, *b.* Missouri, *c.* St. Lawrence, *d.* Cartesian) :: MARQUETTE : MISSISSIPPI

67. BUCOLIC : (*a.* rural, *b.* urban, *c.* spicy, *d.* mild) :: TIMID : SHY

68. MERSEAULT : (*a.* Linda, *b.* Suzanne, *c.* Jacqueline, *d.* Marie) :: TOM : BECKY

69. (*a.* scrupulous, *b.* shrewd, *c.* ingenuous, *d.* indigenous) : WILY :: NAIVE : SOPHISTICATED

70. MAXIM : (*a.* chisel, *b.* saw, *c.* palindrome, *d.* deed) :: ADAGE : PROVERB

71. BUCKINGHAM PALACE : MONARCH OF ENGLAND :: PANDEMONIUM : (*a.* Neptune, *b.* Genghis Khan, *c.* Satan, *d.* Citizen Kane)

72. TAXONOMY : LIFE FORMS :: NOSOLOGY : (*a.* noses, *b.* laws, *c.* coins, *d.* diseases)

73. PENOLOGY : OENOLOGY :: PEAL : (*a.* wine, *b.* oil, *c.* poll, *d.* eel)

74. FATHERS : SONS :: SONS (*a.* Daughters, *b.* Lovers, *c.* Strangers, *d.* Mothers)

75. CATATONIC : HEBEPHRENIC :: ANAL : (*a.* genital, *b.* phallic, *c.* oral, *d.* Oedipal)

76. (*a.* Joyce, *b.* Wilde, *c.* James, *d.* O'Henry) : DORIAN GRAY :: JOYCE : ARTIST AS A YOUNG MAN

77. EISENHOWER : REPUBLICAN :: (*a.* T. Roosevelt, *b.* Harrison, *c.* Fillmore, *d.* Wilson) : BULL MOOSE

78. TANGENT X : COTANGENT X :: X : (*a.* X^2, *b.* $1/X$, *c.* $X - 1$, *d.* $\tan X - \sin X$)

79. (*a.* mammals, *b.* life, *c.* fish, *d.* humans) : PALEOZOIC :: DINOSAURS : MESOZOIC

80. CITY OF SEVEN HILLS : ROME :: CITY OF LIGHT : (*a.* New York, *b.* Paris, *c.* London, *d.* Venice)

81. SLEEP : SOMNAMBULIST :: (*a.* pimp, *b.* crime, *c.* street, *d.* bed) : PROSTITUTE

82. CELSIUS : 0 :: KELVIN : (*a.* 32, *b.* 0, *c.* −100, *d.* 273)

83. DIONYSUS : DAMOCLES :: (*a.* Zeus, *b.* Pandora, *c.* Ares, *d.* Cronus) : PROMETHEUS

84. PENCIL LEAD : GRAPHITE :: CHALK : (*a.* limestone, *b.* sandstone, *c.* talc, *d.* gypsum)

85. MAUDLIN : (*a.* immature, *b.* humorous, *c.* munificent, *d.* mawkish) :: MODERATE : TEMPERATE

86. RHEOSTAT : ELECTRICITY :: (*a.* automobile, *b.* traffic light, *c.* car-counter, *d.* bottleneck) : TRAFFIC

87. CHAUCER : SWEET SHOWERS :: ELIOT : (*a.* stinging rain, *b.* sweet breath, *c.* swich licour, *d.* cruellest month)

88. $8^{-1} : 8^1 :: -1 :$ (*a.* −64, *b.* −8, *c.* 8, *d.* 64)

89. BIGOT : ZEALOT :: TROGLODYTE : (*a.* cave dweller, *b.* hero, *c.* traitor, *d.* reformer)

90. TEMPER : (*a.* piano, *b.* moisture, *c.* docility, *d.* tape recorder) :: FOCUS : CAMERA

91. ZEUS : HERA :: (*a.* Ulysses, *b.* Orestes, *c.* Agamemnon, *d.* Paris) : CLYTEMNESTRA

92. TRITIUM : HYDROGEN :: OZONE : (*a.* oxygen, *b.* nitrogen, *c.* carbon dioxide, *d.* cesium)

93. METROPOLITAN MUSEUM : NEW YORK :: RIJKSMUSEUM : (*a.* Utrecht, *b.* Munich, *c.* Paris, *d.* Amsterdam)

94. POSEIDON : (*a.* Uranus, *b.* Mars, *c.* Saturn, *d.* Neptune) :: ZEUS : JUPITER

95. (*a.* zz, *b.* Zuider, *c.* zero, *d.* zee) : ZED :: BAR : PUB

96. (*a.* hot, *b.* bacterium, *c.* virus, *d.* lungs) : TUBERCULOSIS :: VIRUS : COLD

97. MOLLY : (*a.* Madison, *b.* Monroe, *c.* Maguire, *d.* Malone) :: KNOW : NOTHING

98. ANEMOMETER : WIND SPEED :: MANOMETER : (*a.* blood pressure, *b.* heart rate, *c.* visual acuity, *d.* auditory acuity)

99. HERODOTUS : (*a.* history, *b.* medicine, *c.* his city, *d.* Greece) ::
WASHINGTON : HIS COUNTRY

100. (*a.* Washington, *b.* Jackson, *c.* Eisenhower, *d.* Polk) : CORNWALLIS ::
GRANT : LEE

101. Y = X^2: PARABOLA :: Y = X + 1 : (*a.* cube, *b.* slope, *c.* circle, *d.* line)

102. NOM DE PLUME : (*a.* maiden name, *b.* middle name, *c.* pen name,
d. married name) :: JE NE SAIS QUOI : INDEFINABLE QUALITY

103. (*a.* sheep, *b.* mutton, *c.* offal, *d.* venison) : LAMB :: BEEF : VEAL

104. RADIOACTIVE FALLOUT : CHERNOBYL :: (*a.* oil, *b.* propane,
c. carbon monoxide, *d.* benzene) : VALDEZ

105. HELIUM : NEON :: ARGON : (*a.* cryon, *b.* iodine, *c.* xenon, *d.* hydrogen)

106. BATHYSPHERE : (*a.* rain forest, *b.* ice field, *c.* ocean, *d.* cave) ::
SHUTTLE : SPACE

107. DEBUT : GURU :: FRENCH : (*a.* Greek, *b.* Spanish, *c.* Zulu, *d.* Hindi)

108. SHEPHERD : (*a.* sheep, *b.* human, *c.* goat, *d.* dog) :: MAHOUT :
ELEPHANT

109. HMS : GREAT BRITAIN :: (*a.* SSS, *b.* SOS, *c.* USAS, *d.* USS) :
UNITED STATES

110. (*a.* Ethiopia, *b.* Somalia, *c.* Djibouti, *d.* Eritrea) : MOGADISHU ::
KENYA : NAIROBI

111. ALLUSION : ALLEGORY :: REFERENCE : (*a.* summary, *b.* parable,
c. idiom, *d.* anecdote)

112. HORUS : (*a.* horse, *b.* dog, *c.* hawk, *d.* hare) :: ANUBIS : JACKAL

113. GOERING : NUREMBERG :: (*a.* Hitler, *b.* Hussein, *c.* Mussolini,
d. Milosevic) : THE HAGUE

114. FOUR SCORE : (*a.* 40, *b.* 4, *c.* 28, *d.* 80) :: BAKER'S DOZEN : 13

115. KHOI SAN : SOUTH AFRICA :: MAORI : (*a.* New Zealand,
b. Papua New Guinea, *c.* Fiji, *d.* Australia)

116. BEMUSE : AMUSE :: (*a.* humor, *b.* confuse, *c.* irritate, *d.* inspire) :: ENTERTAIN

117. PLESSY : FERGUSON :: BROWN : (*a.* The State, *b.* Topeka, *c.* Board of Education, *d.* Wade)

118. HONG KONG : (*a.* Hang Seng, *b.* NASDAQ, *c.* HKSE, *d.* Nikkei) :: UNITED STATES : DOW JONES

119. LAKERS : DODGERS :: (*a.* Orlando, *b.* Minneapolis, *c.* Albany, *d.* New Orleans) : BROOKLYN

120. (*a.* juniper, *b.* hickory, *c.* aspen, *d.* beech) : CEDAR :: TAMARAC : PINE

Answer Key
PRACTICE TEST 6

1. B	31. C	61. C	91. C
2. D	32. C	62. C	92. A
3. B	33. B	63. C	93. D
4. D	34. A	64. C	94. D
5. B	35. C	65. D	95. D
6. D	36. C	66. C	96. B
7. A	37. A	67. A	97. C
8. B	38. B	68. D	98. A
9. D	39. D	69. C	99. A
10. C	40. D	70. B	100. A
11. B	41. A	71. C	101. D
12. B	42. D	72. D	102. C
13. A	43. A	73. D	103. B
14. D	44. D	74. B	104. A
15. B	45. B	75. C	105. C
16. A	46. D	76. B	106. C
17. B	47. D	77. A	107. D
18. D	48. B	78. B	108. A
19. A	49. A	79. C	109. D
20. B	50. D	80. B	110. B
21. B	51. B	81. C	111. B
22. B	52. A	82. D	112. C
23. B	53. C	83. A	113. D
24. B	54. C	84. A	114. D
25. D	55. B	85. D	115. A
26. B	56. A	86. B	116. B
27. C	57. C	87. D	117. C
28. A	58. C	88. A	118. A
29. D	59. D	89. A	119. B
30. D	60. C	90. A	120. A

EXPLANATION OF ANSWERS FOR PRACTICE TEST 6

In the following explanations of answers, explanations concerning the correct response are in a large font. Explanations regarding distracters (incorrect responses) that are not self-explaining or could be misinterpreted are in a smaller font in order to highlight the explanations of the answers that are correct.

1. LETTER : WORD :: (*a.* paragraph, *b.* **word**, *c.* period, *d.* meaning) : SENTENCE

   (**b**) A word is composed of letters. A sentence is composed of words.
   General Information—Part/Whole

2. GIVEN NAME : FIRST :: (*a.* Christian name, *b.* real name, *c.* nickname, *d.* **surname**) : LAST

   (**d**) A given name is a first name. A surname is a last name.
   Vocabulary—Similarity/Contrast

3. JUDICIARY : (*a.* Circuit Court, *b.* **Supreme Court**, *c.* District Court, *d.* Court of Appeals) :: LEGISLATIVE : CONGRESS

   (**b**) The Supreme Court is the highest judiciary body in the United States. The Congress is the highest legislative body in the United States.
   Social Science—Description

4. (*a.* magna cum laude, *b.* optima cum laude, *c.* puella cum laude, *d.* **summa cum laude**) :: HIGHEST HONOR :: CUM LAUDE : HONOR

   (**d**) *Summa cum laude* denotes highest honor; *cum laude*, honor. *Magna cum laude* means "with great honor."
   General Information—Similarity/Contrast

5. WILLIAM JAMES : PHILOSOPHER :: HENRY JAMES : (*a.* chemist, *b.* **novelist**, *c.* lawyer, *d.* politician)

   (**b**) William James was a philosopher; his brother Henry was a novelist.
   Humanities—Description

6. OUNCE : PREVENTION :: POUND : (*a.* remedy, *b.* prophylaxis, *c.* medicine, *d.* **cure**)

   (**d**) "An ounce of prevention is worth a pound of cure," or so the saying goes.
   General Information—Completion

7. (*a. decline*, *b.* recline, *c.* acclaim, *d.* reclaim) : ASCEND :: INCLINE : DESCEND

   (**a**) *Decline* and *incline* are antonyms, as are *ascend* and *descend*.
   Vocabulary—Similarity/Contrast

8. CARNIVORE : ANIMALS :: (*a.* omnivore, *b. herbivore*, *c.* carnivore, *d.* vegetivore) : VEGETABLES

   (**b**) A carnivore eats (the flesh of) animals; an herbivore eats vegetables.
   An omnivore eats both plants and animals.
   Vocabulary—Description

9. COLD : (*a.* caress, *b.* shiver, *c.* legs, *d. shoulder*) :: OPEN : ARMS

   (**d**) A person may be greeted either with a cold shoulder or with open arms.
   General Information—Completion

10. DROUGHT : (*a.* desert, *b.* thirst, *c. rain*, *d.* crops) :: FAMINE : FOOD

    (**c**) A drought is caused by lack of rain; a famine is caused by lack of food.
    Vocabulary—Description

11. WESTMINSTER ABBEY : ENGLAND :: TAJ MAHAL : (*a.* Iran, *b. India*, *c.* Pakistan, *d.* China)

    (**b**) Westminster Abbey is in England. The Taj Mahal is in India.
    General Information—Description

12. LEGISLATOR : MAKES :: POLICE OFFICER : (*a.* interprets, *b. enforces*, *c.* breaks, *d.* enacts)

    (**b**) A legislator makes laws; a police officer enforces them.
    General Information—Description

13. DIRECT : INDIRECT :: HIM : (*a. him*, *b.* his, *c.* he, *d.* he'd)

    (**a**) *Him* is the correct form of the personal pronoun for use as either a direct or an indirect object.
    Humanities—Description

14. ZIP : LETTER :: AREA : (*a.* volume, *b.* πr^2, *c.* post box, *d. telephone call*)

    (**d**) A zip code is used for a letter, while an area code is used for a telephone call.
    General Information—Description

15. COURSE : COARSE :: (*a.* ruffle, *b. direction*, *c.* jagged, *d.* golf) : ROUGH

    (**b**) *Course* and *direction* are synonyms, as are *coarse* and *rough*.
    Vocabulary—Similarity/Contrast

16. DIRIGIBLE : (*a.* **air**, *b.* sea, *c.* land, *d.* underground) :: AUTOMOBILE : LAND

    (**a**) A dirigible travels by air, while an automobile travels by land.
    General Information—Description

17. MENDEL : (*a.* inequality, *b.* **dominance**, *c.* depression, *d.* orbits) :: MENDELEEV : PERIODICITY

    (**b**) Mendel formulated the law of dominance (in the field of inheritance); Mendeleev formulated the law of periodicity (in the field of chemistry).
    Natural Science—Description

18. LIVID : ASHEN :: JAUNDICED : (*a.* white, *b.* black, *c.* red, *d.* **yellow**)

    (**d**) Something that is livid is ashen. Something that is jaundiced is yellow.
    Vocabulary—Similarity/Contrast

19. AMIABLE : UNFRIENDLY :: AFFABLE : (*a.* **unpleasant**, *b.* ugly, *c.* beautiful, *d.* kindly)

    (**a**) *Amiable* and *unfriendly* are opposites, as are *affable* and *unpleasant*.
    Vocabulary—Similarity/Contrast

20. JUNEAU : ALASKA :: (*a.* Waikiki, *b.* **Honolulu**, *c.* Oahu, *d.* Hawaii) : HAWAII

    (**b**) Juneau is the capital of Alaska; Honolulu is the capital of Hawaii. Hawaii and Oahu are islands that are part of Hawaii. Waikiki is a neighborhood of Honolulu.
    General Information—Description

21. EAT : DRINK :: EDIBLE : (*a.* palpable, *b.* **potable**, *c.* lacteal, *d.* labile)

    (**b**) One can eat what is edible and drink what is potable.
    Vocabulary—Description

22. WHITE LIE : LIE :: (*a.* hurricane, *b.* **drizzle**, *c.* storm, *d.* humidity) : RAINFALL

    (**b**) A white lie is a minor lie; a drizzle is a minor rainfall.
    Vocabulary—Description

23. (*a.* net, *b.* **ten**, *c.* met, *d.* end) : TEND :: MEN : MEND

    (**b**) *Tend* is pronounced as *ten*, but with an added *d* consonant sound at the end. *Mend* is pronounced as *men*, but again with an added *d* consonant sound at the end.
    Nonsemantic

24. FLAPJACK : (*a.* pumpkin pie, *b.* **pancake**, *c.* sponge cake, *d.* paddycake) :: GRIDDLECAKE : HOTCAKE

(**b**) Flapjack, pancake, griddlecake, and hotcake are all names for the same food.
General Information—Similarity/Contrast

25. BINOMIAL : POLYNOMIAL :: TWO : (*a.* four, *b.* eight, *c.* all, *d.* **many**)

(**d**) A binomial is an equation with two terms. A polynomial is an equation with many terms.
Mathematics—Description

26. SAUDI ARABIA : OIL :: (*a.* Iran, *b.* **Brazil**, *c.* Hungary, *d.* Guatemala) : COFFEE

(**b**) Saudi Arabia is a major source of oil. Brazil is a major source of coffee.
General Information—Description

27. MONARCHY : ONE :: OLIGARCHY : (*a.* two, *b.* three, *c.* **several**, *d.* multitudes)

(**c**) A monarchy is a government of one ruler; an oligarchy is a government several individuals rule jointly.
Social Science—Description

28. PASADENA : FOOTBALL :: WIMBLEDON : (*a.* **tennis**, *b.* boxing, *c.* golf, *d.* basketball)

(**a**) Pasadena is the location of a major football game (the Rose Bowl). Wimbledon is the location of a major tennis tournament.
General Information—Description

29. MOLEHILL : EARTH :: DUNE : (*a.* rock, *b.* desert, *c.* mud, *d.* **sand**)

(**d**) A molehill is composed of earth. A dune is composed of sand.
General Information—Description

30. (*a.* plankton, *b.* gizzard, *c.* oyster, *d.* **dinosaur**) : REPTILE :: FROG : AMPHIBIAN

(**d**) A dinosaur is a form of reptile. A frog is a form of amphibian. Amphibians are cold-blooded vertebrates that have gilled aquatic larvae and air-breathing adults. Reptiles are cold-blooded vertebrates that are different from amphibians in that they have scales and lay hard-shelled amniotic eggs.
Natural Science—Class

31. (*a.* Andersen, *b.* Grimm, ***c.* Milne**, *d.* Alcott) : WINNIE :: DISNEY : MICKEY

    (**c**) A. A. Milne created the character Winnie (the Pooh). Walt Disney created the character Mickey (Mouse). Anderson wrote *The Princess and the Pea.* The Brothers Grimm wrote *Hansel and Gretel*, among other fairy tales. Alcott wrote *Little Women.*
    Humanities—Description

32. PATRICIAN : PLEBEIAN :: NOBILITY : (*a.* clergy, *b.* lordship, ***c.* proletariat**, *d.* bourgeoisie)

    (**c**) In ancient Rome, the patricians were members of the nobility and the plebeians were members of the proletariat.
    Humanities—Similarity/Contrast

33. (*a.* fungi, ***b.* water**, *c.* gases, *d.* algae) : HYDROLOGY :: LIFE : BIOLOGY

    (**b**) Hydrology is the study of water; biology is the study of life.
    Natural Science—Description

34. GOTHIC : POINTED :: ROMANESQUE : (***a.* rounded**, *b.* scalloped, *c.* squared, *d.* buttressed)

    (**a**) Gothic arches are pointed, while Romanesque arches are rounded.
    Humanities—Description

35. (*a.* 7, *b.* 9, ***c.* 10**, *d.* 12) : PLAGUES :: 7 : DEADLY SINS

    (**c**) There were 10 plagues in Egypt, and there are 7 deadly sins.
    The 7 deadly sins are pride, avarice, envy, wrath, lust, gluttony, and sloth.
    The 10 plagues were water to blood, frogs, lice, flies, livestock disease, boils, thunder and hail, locusts, darkness, and the death of the firstborns.
    Humanities—Description

36. STEP : PETS :: REEL : (*a.* fishes, *b.* rod, ***c.* leer**, *d.* real)

    (**c**) *Pets* is *step* spelled backwards. *Leer* is *reel* spelled backwards.
    Nonsemantic

37. HAWK : PREY :: SWINDLER : (***a.* dupe**, *b.* dodge, *c.* doll, *d.* dolt)

    (**a**) A hawk victimizes prey. A swindler victimizes dupes.
    General Information—Description

38. SOPORIFIC : (*a.* pain, ***b.* sleepiness**, *c.* hunger, *d.* thirst) :: APHRODISIAC : SEXUAL DESIRE

    (**b**) A soporific induces sleepiness. An aphrodisiac induces sexual desire.
    Vocabulary—Description

39. PASTEURIZE : (*a.* chemically treat, *b.* strain, *c.* chill, **d. partially sterilize**) :: HOMOGENIZE : MAKE UNIFORM

   (**d**) To pasteurize milk is to partially sterilize it. To homogenize milk is to make it uniform.
   General Information—Similarity/Contrast

40. DECLARATIVE : . :: INTERROGATIVE : (*a.* !, *b.* :, *c.* –, **d. ?**)

   (**d**) A declarative sentence ends with a period (.). An interrogative sentence ends with a question mark (?).
   Humanities—Description

41. ALLEGRO : (**a. largo**, *b.* presto, *c.* crescendo, *d.* cantabile) :: FAST : SLOW

   (**a**) In music, an allegro tempo is a fast one, while a largo tempo is a slow one. *Presto* means "fast," *crescendo* means "increasing loudness," and *cantabile* means "singing."
   Humanities—Similarity/Contrast

42. PENCE : POUND :: CENTS : (*a.* nickel, *b.* dime, *c.* quarter, **d. dollar**)

   (**d**) There are 100 pence in a pound (in English currency) and 100 cents in a dollar (in American currency).
   General Information—Part/Whole

43. CLANDESTINE : (**a. surreptitious**, *b.* tacit, *c.* sanguine, *d.* outgoing) :: SHY : DIFFIDENT

   (**a**) *Clandestine* means *surreptitious*. *Shy* means *diffident*.
   Vocabulary—Similarity/Contrast

44. INCOGNITO : (*a.* ignorant, *b.* uninterested, *c.* unofficial, **d. disguised**) :: SATISFACTORY : ADEQUATE

   (**d**) *Incognito* means *disguised*. *Satisfactory* means *adequate*.
   Vocabulary—Similarity/Contrast

45. ANTIDOTE : POISON :: (*a.* mycin, **b. antibiotic**, *c.* analgesic, *d.* antigen) : BACTERIA

   (**b**) An antidote is a cure for the effects of poison; an antibiotic is a remedy for the effects of bacteria. Mycin is a suffix that refers to a substance gained from a fungus-like bacterium. Analgesic medication alleviates pain. An antigen is a substance capable of triggering a response from the immune system.
   Natural Science—Description

46. DIRTY : LINEN :: FILTHY : (*a.* flax, *b.* burlap, *c.* lummox, ***d.* lucre**)

    (**d**) *Dirty linen* and *filthy lucre* are two common English expressions.
    General Information—Completion

47. POLAR : (*a.* equatorial, *b.* mammoth, *c.* coordinate, ***d.* grizzly**) :: FORD : CHEVROLET

    (**d**) A polar bear and a grizzly bear are two types of bears. A Ford and a Chevrolet are two types of cars.
    General Information—Class

48. ONTOLOGY : BEING :: EPISTEMOLOGY : (*a.* spirit, ***b.* knowledge**, *c.* metaphysics, *d.* causality)

    (**b**) Ontology is the study of being; epistemology, the study of knowledge.
    Humanities—Description

49. RECORDER : (***a.* flute**, *b.* magnetic tape, *c.* player piano, *d.* trombone) :: LUTE : GUITAR

    (**a**) A recorder is an early form of flute; a lute is an early form of guitar.
    Humanities—Class

50. MILLIMETER : METER :: METER : (*a.* centimeter, *b.* decimeter, *c.* decameter, ***d.* kilometer**)

    (**d**) There are 1000 millimeters in a meter, and 1000 meters in a kilometer.
    Mathematics—Part/Whole

51. GENDARMES : FRANCE :: CARABINIERI : (*a.* Spain, ***b.* Italy**, *c.* Switzerland, *d.* Turkey)

    (**b**) Police officers in France are called gendarmes; in Italy, they are called carabinieri.
    General Information—Description

52. RENOIR : IMPRESSIONIST :: (***a.* Braque**, *b.* Matisse, *c.* Monet, *d.* Stella) : CUBIST

    (**a**) Renoir was an impressionist painter; Braque was a cubist. Matisse was a leading figure in modern art. Monet was an impressionist. Stella was a minimalist.
    Humanities—Description

53. SCOTLAND YARD : CRIME :: EXCHEQUER : (*a.* agriculture, *b.* industry, *c.* defense, ***d.* money**)

    (**d**) In England, Scotland Yard is charged with the control of crime, the Exchequer with the control of money.
    General Information—Description

54. (*a.* magician, *b.* tycoon, ***c.* adventurer**, *d.* usurer) : GENTLEMAN OF FORTUNE :: ATTENDANT : GENTLEMAN IN WAITING

   (**c**) A gentleman of fortune is an adventurer. A gentleman in waiting is an attendant.
   General Information—Similarity/Contrast

55. HALCYON : (*a.* tranquil, ***b.* agitated**, *c.* bounteous, *d.* impoverished) :: FORTUITOUS : PLANNED

   (**b**) *Halcyon* in an antonym of *agitated*. *Fortuitous* is an antonym of *planned*.
   Vocabulary—Similarity/Contrast

56. UTOPIA : (***a.* More**, *b.* Plato, *c.* Becket, *d.* Aquinas) :: LILLIPUT : SWIFT

   (**a**) Utopia is a land invented by More; Lilliput is a land invented by Swift. Plato wrote the *Socratic Dialogues*. Becket was Archbishop of Canterbury from 1162 to 1170. Aquinas wrote *Summa Theologica* and the *Summa Contra Gentiles*.
   Humanities—Description

57. MERIDIAN : LONGITUDE :: (*a.* meridian, *b.* prime, ***c.* parallel**, *d.* perpendicular) : LATITUDE

   (**c**) A meridian is a line of longitude; a parallel is a line of latitude.
   General Information—Description

58. CENTURY : HUNDRED :: MILLENNIUM : (*a.* A.D. 1, *b.* eternity, ***c.* thousand**, *d.* million)

   (**c**) A century is one hundred years; a millennium is one thousand years.
   General Information—Description

59. COLD-BLOODED : HARD-HEARTED :: HOT-BLOODED : (*a.* cruel, *b.* listless, *c.* cold-hearted, ***d.* excitable**)

   (**d**) *Cold-blooded* means *hard-hearted*. *Hot-blooded* means *excitable*.
   Vocabulary—Similarity/Contrast

60. ASSIDUOUS : (*a.* ambitious, *b.* favorable, ***c.* diligent**, *d.* evergreen) :: ASSIMILATE : ABSORB

   (**c**) *Assiduous* is a synonym of *diligent*. *Assimilate* is a synonym of *absorb*.
   Vocabulary—Similarity/Contrast

61. NETREBKO : SOPRANO :: DOMINGO : (*a.* soprano, *b.* contralto, ***c.* tenor**, *d.* bass)

   (**c**) Anna Netrebko is a renowned soprano; Placido Domingo is a renowned tenor.
   Humanities—Description

62. CARDINAL : ORDINAL :: 8 : (*a.* −2, *b.* 60%, *c.* **5th**, *d.* 9)

(**c**) 8 is a cardinal number, and 5th is an ordinal number.
Mathematics—Class

63. VALJEAN : (*a.* Mauriac, *b.* Balzac, *c.* **Hugo**, *d.* Molière) :: GORIOT : BALZAC

(**c**) Jean Valjean is a character created by the French novelist Victor Hugo. Père Goriot is a character created by the French novelist Honoré de Balzac. Francois Mauriac wrote *Le Desert de l'Amour*. Honore de Balzac wrote *La Comedie Humaine*, which contains about 100 novels and plays that describe French life after the fall of Napoleon. Moliere (Jean-Baptiste Poquelin) is known for the drama *Le Misanthrope*, among other plays.
Humanities—Description

64. MAUVE : (*a.* brown, *b.* red, *c.* **purple**, *d.* green) :: TAN : BROWN

(**c**) Mauve is a shade of purple; tan is a shade of brown.
General Information—Class

65. RANGERS : (*a.* basketball, *b.* polo, *c.* football, *d.* **hockey**) :: CARDINALS : BASEBALL

(**d**) The Rangers are a hockey team. The Cardinals are a baseball team.
General Information—Description

66. CARTIER : (*a.* Hudson, *b.* Missouri, *c.* **St. Lawrence**, *d.* Cartesian) :: MARQUETTE : MISSISSIPPI

(**c**) Cartier explored the St. Lawrence River; Marquette explored the Mississippi River. Henry Hudson was the first European who sailed up the Hudson River. The Missouri was first explored by the French: Louis Jolliet and Jacques Marquette. Cartesian means that something is related to the French philosopher Rene Descartes.
Humanities—Description

67. BUCOLIC : (*a.* **rural**, *b.* urban, *c.* spicy, *d.* mild) :: TIMID : SHY

(**a**) *Bucolic* means *rural*; *timid* means *shy*.
Vocabulary—Similarity/Contrast

68. MERSEAULT : (*a.* Linda, *b.* Suzanne, *c.* Jacqueline, *d.* **Marie**) :: TOM : BECKY

(**d**) In *The Stranger* (by Albert Camus), Marie is the girlfriend of Merseault. In *Tom Sawyer* (by Mark Twain), Becky is the girlfriend to Tom.
Humanities—Class

69. (*a.* scrupulous, *b.* shrewd, ***c.* ingenuous**, *d.* indigenous) : WILY :: NAIVE : SOPHISTICATED

    (**c**) *Ingenuous* and *wily* are opposites, as are *naive* and *sophisticated*.
    Vocabulary—Similarity/Contrast

70. MAXIM : (*a.* chisel, ***b.* saw**, *c.* palindrome, *d.* deed) :: ADAGE : PROVERB

    (**b**) *Maxim, saw, adage,* and *proverb* are all synonymous. A palindrome is a word or number that can be read the same way in any direction (e.g., "mom" or "101").
    Vocabulary—Similarity/Contrast

71. BUCKINGHAM PALACE : MONARCH OF ENGLAND :: PANDEMONIUM : (*a.* Neptune, *b.* Genghis Khan, ***c.* Satan**, *d.* Citizen Kane)

    (**c**) Buckingham Palace is the palace of the monarch of England. Pandemonium, in *Paradise Lost* (by John Milton), is the palace of Satan.
    Humanities—Description

72. TAXONOMY : LIFE FORMS :: NOSOLOGY : (*a.* noses, *b.* laws, *c.* coins, ***d.* diseases**)

    (**d**) Taxonomy is classification of life forms. Nosology is classification of diseases.
    Natural Science—Description

73. PENOLOGY : OENOLOGY :: PEAL : (*a.* wine, *b.* oil, *c.* poll, ***d.* eel**)

    (**d**) *Penology* and *oenology* have the same initial vowel sound, as do *peal* and *eel*.
    Nonsemantic

74. FATHERS : SONS :: SONS (*a.* Daughters, ***b.* Lovers**, *c.* Strangers, *d.* Mothers)

    (**b**) *Fathers and Sons* is a novel by Ivan Turgenev. *Sons and Lovers* is a novel by D. H. Lawrence.
    Humanities—Completion

75. CATATONIC : HEBEPHRENIC :: ANAL : (*a.* genital, *b.* phallic, ***c.* oral**, *d.* Oedipal)

    (**c**) A catatonic shows anal symptomatology. A hebephrenic shows oral symptomatology.
    Social Science—Description

Explanation of Answers

76. (*a.* Joyce, ***b.* Wilde**, *c.* James, *d.* O'Henry) : DORIAN GRAY :: JOYCE : ARTIST AS A YOUNG MAN

    (**b**) Oscar Wilde wrote *The Picture of Dorian Gray*. James Joyce wrote *A Portrait of the Artist as a Young Man*.
    Humanities—Description

77. EISENHOWER : REPUBLICAN :: (***a.* T. Roosevelt**, *b.* Harrison, *c.* Fillmore, *d.* Wilson) : BULL MOOSE

    (**a**) President Eisenhower was a member of the Republican Party. President T. (Theodore) Roosevelt was a member of the Bull Moose Party. Harrison was a Republican; Fillmore was a member of the Whig Party; Wilson was a Democrat.
    Social Science—Description

78. TANGENT X : COTANGENT X :: X : (*a.* X^2, ***b.* 1/X**, *c.* $X-1$, *d.* $\tan X - \sin X$)

    (**b**) The cotangent of X is equal to 1 divided by the tangent of X.
    Mathematics—Description

79. (*a.* mammals, *b.* life, ***c.* fish**, *d.* humans) : PALEOZOIC :: DINOSAURS : MESOZOIC

    (**c**) Fish first appeared in the Paleozoic Era (542–751 million years ago). Dinosaurs first appeared in the Mesozoic Era (251–65 million years ago).
    Natural Science—Description

80. CITY OF SEVEN HILLS : ROME :: CITY OF LIGHT : (*a.* New York, ***b.* Paris**, *c.* London, *d.* Venice)

    (**b**) Rome is the City of Seven Hills; Paris is the City of Light. The seven hills of Rome are called Palatine, Capitoline, Quirinal, Viminal, Esquiline, Caelian, and Aventine.
    Humanities—Similarity/Contrast

81. SLEEP : SOMNAMBULIST :: (*a.* pimp, *b.* crime, ***c.* street**, *d.* bed) : PROSTITUTE

    (**c**) A somnambulist walks in his or her sleep. A prostitute walks in the streets.
    General Information—Description

82. CELSIUS : 0 :: KELVIN : (*a.* 32, *b.* 0, *c.* −100, ***d.* 273**)

    (**d**) Zero degrees Celsius is equal to 273 Kelvin (to the nearest unit).
    Natural Science—Equality/Negation

83. DIONYSUS : DAMOCLES :: (*a.* **Zeus**, *b.* Pandora, *c.* Ares, *d.* Cronus) : PROMETHEUS

   (**a**) Dionysus punished Damocles (by hanging a sword over his head). Zeus punished Prometheus (by chaining him to a rock). Pandora was the first woman in Greek mythology. Ares was the Greek god of war. Cronus was the Greek god of agriculture and harvest.
   Humanities—Description

84. PENCIL LEAD : GRAPHITE :: CHALK : (*a.* **limestone**, *b.* sandstone, *c.* talc, *d.* gypsum)

   (**a**) Pencil lead is made of graphite. Chalk is made of limestone.
   General Information—Description

85. MAUDLIN : (*a.* immature, *b.* humorous, *c.* munificent, *d.* **mawkish**) :: MODERATE : TEMPERATE

   (**d**) *Maudlin* means *mawkish*. *Moderate* means *temperate*.
   Vocabulary—Similarity/Contrast

86. RHEOSTAT : ELECTRICITY :: (*a.* automobile, *b.* **traffic light**, *c.* car-counter, *d.* bottleneck) : TRAFFIC

   (**b**) A rheostat regulates the flow of electricity. A traffic light regulates the flow of traffic.
   Natural Science—Description

87. CHAUCER : SWEET SHOWERS :: ELIOT : (*a.* stinging rain, *b.* sweet breath, *c.* swich licour, *d.* **cruellest month**)

   (**d**) In the opening line of *The Canterbury Tales*, Chaucer mentions April in the context of its sweet showers. In the opening line of *The Wasteland*, Eliot alludes to Chaucer, but changes things by mentioning April as the cruellest month.
   Humanities—Description

88. $8^{-1} : 8^1 :: -1 :$ (*a.* **−64**, *b.* −8, *c.* 8, *d.* 64)

   (**a**) $^1/_8$ is to 8 as −1 is to −64.
   Mathematics—Equality/Negation

89. BIGOT : ZEALOT :: TROGLODYTE : (*a.* **cave dweller**, *b.* hero, *c.* traitor, *d.* reformer)

   (**a**) A bigot is a zealot; a troglodyte was a cave dweller.
   Vocabulary—Similarity/Contrast

90. TEMPER : (***a*. piano**, *b*. moisture, *c*. docility, *d*. tape recorder) :: FOCUS : CAMERA

    (**a**) One tempers a piano; one focuses a camera.
    General Information—Description

91. ZEUS : HERA :: (*a*. Ulysses, *b*. Orestes, **c. Agamemnon**, *d*. Paris) : CLYTEMNESTRA

    (**c**) In Greek mythology, Zeus was the husband of Hera. In Greek literature, Agamemnon was the husband of Clytemnestra. Ulysses is the Latin name for Odysseus. Orestes and Electra were the son and daughter of Agamemnon. Paris was the son of Priam, who in turn was the youngest son of Laomedon and king of Troy during the Trojan War.
    Humanities—Class

92. TRITIUM : HYDROGEN :: OZONE : (***a*. oxygen**, *b*. nitrogen, *c*. carbon dioxide, *d*. cesium)

    (**a**) Tritium is a form of hydrogen, H_3. Ozone is a form of oxygen, O_3. Nitrogen is a chemical element (N). Cesium is a chemical element as well (Cs). Carbon dioxide (CO_2) is a chemical compound comprising two atoms of oxygen and one atom of carbon.
    Natural Science—Class

93. METROPOLITAN MUSEUM : NEW YORK :: RIJKSMUSEUM : (*a*. Utrecht, *b*. Munich, *c*. Paris, ***d*. Amsterdam**)

    (**d**) The Metropolitan Museum is in New York. The Rijksmuseum is in Amsterdam.
    General Information—Description

94. POSEIDON : (*a*. Uranus, *b*. Mars, *c*. Saturn, ***d*. Neptune**) :: ZEUS : JUPITER

    (**d**) Poseidon was the Greek name, and Neptune the Roman name, for the god of the sea. Zeus was the Greek name, and Jupiter the Roman name, for the king of the gods. Uranus was the god of the sky and had the same name in Greek and Latin. Mars was the god of war, his Greek name was Ares. Saturn is the Latin name of the Greek god Cronus (god of agriculture and harvest).
    Humanities—Similarity/Contrast

95. (*a*. zz, *b*. Zuider, *c*. zero, ***d*. zee**) : ZED :: BAR : PUB

    (**d**) The British call zed what Americans call zee (the letter Z). The British call a pub what Americans call a bar.
    General Information—Similarity/Contrast

96. (*a.* hot, ***b.* bacterium**, *c.* virus, *d.* lungs) : TUBERCULOSIS :: VIRUS : COLD

    (**b**) Tuberculosis is caused by a bacterium; a cold is caused by a virus.
    Natural Science—Description

97. MOLLY : (*a.* Madison, *b.* Monroe, ***c.* Maguire**, *d.* Malone) :: KNOW : NOTHING

    (**c**) The Molly Maguires and the Know-Nothings were both secret political action groups. The Molly Maguires were an Irish rebel group who fought for better working conditions in the coal mines of Pennsylvania (ca. 1860s–1870s). The Know-Nothings were a nativistic movement to combat foreign influences in the United States (ca. 1850s).
    Social Science—Completion

98. ANEMOMETER : WIND SPEED :: MANOMETER : (***a.* blood pressure**, *b.* heart rate, *c.* visual acuity, *d.* auditory acuity)

    (**a**) An anemometer measures wind speed; a manometer measures blood pressure.
    Natural Science—Description

99. HERODOTUS : (***a.* history**, *b.* medicine, *c.* his city, *d.* Greece) :: WASHINGTON : HIS COUNTRY

    (**a**) Herodotus is sometimes called the Father of History (and was the first to have a scientific approach to history). George Washington is sometimes called the Father of His Country.
    Social Science—Description

100. (***a.* Washington**, *b.* Jackson, *c.* Eisenhower, *d.* Polk) : CORNWALLIS :: GRANT : LEE

    (**a**) General Cornwallis surrendered to George Washington. General Lee surrendered to Ulysses S. Grant.
    Humanities—Description

101. $Y = X^2$: PARABOLA :: $Y = X + 1$: (*a.* cube, *b.* slope, *c.* circle, ***d.* line**)

    (**d**) When graphed, the equation $y = x^2$ produces a parabola just as when graphed, the equation $y = x + 1$ produces a line.
    Mathematics—Description

102. NOM DE PLUME : (*a.* maiden name, *b.* middle name, ***c.* pen name**, *d.* married name) :: JE NE SAIS QUOI : INDEFINABLE QUALITY

    (**c**) A *nom de plume* is the commonly used French term for a pen name, just as *je ne sais quoi* is the commonly used French term for an indefinable quality.
    Vocabulary—Similarity/Contrast

103. (*a.* sheep, ***b.* mutton**, *c.* offal, *d.* venison) : LAMB :: BEEF : VEAL

(**b**) Meat eaten from a full-grown sheep is called mutton, whereas meat from a young sheep is called lamb. Likewise, meat from full-grown cattle is called beef and from young cattle is called veal.
General Information—Similarity/Contrast

104. RADIOACTIVE FALLOUT : CHERNOBYL :: (***a.* oil**, *b.* propane, *c.* carbon monoxide, *d.* benzene) : VALDEZ

(**a**) Just as the Ukrainian city of Chernobyl was poisoned by radioactive fallout from a nuclear plant (1986), so was Valdez, Alaska, polluted by a massive oil spill (1989).
General Information—Description

105. HELIUM : NEON :: ARGON : (*a.* cryon, *b.* iodine, ***c.* xenon**, *d.* hydrogen)

(**c**) Helium, neon, argon, and xenon are all noble gasses.
Natural Science—Class

106. BATHYSPHERE : (*a.* rain forest, *b.* ice field, ***c.* ocean**, *d.* cave) :: SHUTTLE : SPACE

(**c**) A bathysphere transports people into the ocean just as a shuttle transports people into space.
Vocabulary—Description

107. DEBUT : GURU :: FRENCH : (*a.* Greek, *b.* Spanish, *c.* Zulu, ***d.* Hindi**)

(**d**) Just as the English language has borrowed the word *debut* from French, so has it also borrowed the word *guru* from Hindi.
Nonsemantic—Nonsemantic

108. SHEPHERD : (***a.* sheep**, *b.* human, *c.* goat, *d.* dog) :: MAHOUT : ELEPHANT

(**a**) A mahout cares for and leads elephants just as a shepherd cares for and leads sheep.
Vocabulary—Description

109. HMS : GREAT BRITAIN :: (*a.* SSS, *b.* SOS, *c.* USAS, ***d.* USS**) : UNITED STATES

(**d**) In Great Britain, state ships are prefixed with "HMS," for "Her Majesty's ship" and in the United States, state ships are prefixed with "USS," for "United States ship." SSS may refer to Server Side Scripting, among other things; SOS stands for Save Our Ship/Souls; USAS stands for the United States Antarctic Service, among other things.
General Information—Description

110. (*a*. Ethiopia, ***b*. Somalia**, *c*. Djibouti, *d*. Eritrea) : MOGADISHU ::
KENYA : NAIROBI

   (**b**) Somalia's capital city is Mogadishu just as Kenya's is Nairobi. The capital
   of Ethiopia is Addis Ababa. The capital of Djibouti is Djibouti. The capital of Eritrea
   is Asmara.
   General Information—Description

111. ALLUSION : ALLEGORY :: REFERENCE : (*a*. summary, ***b*. parable**,
c. idiom, *d*. anecdote)

   (**b**) Allusion is reference (either direct or indirect) to something. Allegory is
   a sort of parable.
   Vocabulary—Similarity/Contrast

112. HORUS : (*a*. horse, *b*. dog, ***c*. hawk**, *d*. hare) :: ANUBIS : JACKAL

   (**c**) The sons of Egyptian god Osiris, Horus, and Anubis had the heads of a
   hawk and a jackal respectively.
   Humanities—Description

113. GOERING : NUREMBERG :: (*a*. Hitler, *b*. Hussein, *c*. Mussolini,
***d*. Milosevic**) : THE HAGUE

   (**d**) Goering was prosecuted at an international war crimes tribunal in
   Nuremberg, Germany. Milosevic was prosecuted in The Hague, Netherlands.
   General Information—Description

114. FOUR SCORE : (*a*. 40, *b*. 4, *c*. 28, ***d*. 80**) :: BAKER'S DOZEN : 13

   (**d**) Four score is the equivalent of 80 (a score is 20), just as a baker's dozen is
   13. The expression of a baker's dozen comes from 13th century England
   where bakers could be severely punished if found to cheat their customers.
   Therefore, they preferred to bake more items to make sure they would not
   betray their customers.
   General Information—Equality/Negation

115. KHOI SAN : SOUTH AFRICA :: MAORI : (***a*. New Zealand**, *b*. Papua
New Guinea, *c*. Fiji, *d*. Australia)

   (**a**) The Khoi San are native peoples of South Africa and the Maori are native
   peoples of New Zealand.
   General Information—Description

116. BEMUSE : AMUSE :: (*a*. humor, ***b*. confuse**, *c*. irritate, *d*. inspire) ::
ENTERTAIN

   (**b**) To bemuse is to confuse, whereas to amuse is to entertain.
   Vocabulary—Similarity/Contrast

117. PLESSY : FERGUSON :: BROWN : (*a.* The State, *b.* Topeka,
c. Board of Education, *d.* Wade)

(**c**) *Plessy vs. Ferguson* was a historic Supreme Court Case (1886; it upheld
the constitutionality of racial segregation) as was *Brown vs. Board of
Education* (1954; it overturned rulings from the *Plessy vs. Ferguson* case).
General Information—Completion

118. HONG KONG : (**a. Hang Seng**, *b.* NASDAQ, *c.* HKSE, *d.* Nikkei) ::
UNITED STATES : DOW JONES

(**a**) Hong Kong's primary stock index is the Hang Seng. The primary stock
index of the United States is the Dow Jones. The Nikkei is the primary stock
index of Japan. HKSE stands for Hong Kong Stock Exchange. NASDAQ (National
Association of Securities Dealers Automated Quotations) is an electronic securities market
in the United States.
General Information—Description

119. LAKERS : DODGERS :: (*a.* Orlando, **b. Minneapolis**, *c.* Albany,
d. New Orleans) : BROOKLYN

(**b**) The Los Angeles Lakers were originally called the Minneapolis Lakers
just as the Los Angeles Dodgers were originally called the Brooklyn Dodgers.
General Information—Description

120. (**a. juniper**, *b.* hickory, *c.* aspen, *d.* beech) : CEDAR :: TAMARAC : PINE

(**a**) Juniper, cedar, tamarac, and pine trees are all coniferous evergreen trees.
Natural Science—Class

PRACTICE TEST 6

Item Classification Chart

	RELATIONSHIP						
	Similarity/ Contrast	Description	Class	Completion	Part/ Whole	Equality/ Negation	Nonsemantic
Vocabulary	2, 7, 15, 18, 19, 43, 44, 55, 59, 60, 67, 69, 70, 85, 89, 102, 111, 116	8, 10, 21, 22, 38, 106, 108					
General Information	4, 24, 39, 54, 95, 103	11, 12, 14, 16, 20, 26, 28, 29, 37, 51, 53, 57, 58, 65, 81, 84, 90, 93, 104, 109, 110, 113, 115, 118, 119	47, 64	6, 9, 46, 117	1, 42	114	
Humanities	32, 41, 80, 94	5, 13, 31, 34, 35, 40, 48, 52, 56, 61, 63, 66, 71, 76, 83, 87, 100, 112	49, 68, 91	74			
Social Science		3, 27, 75, 77, 97, 99					
Natural Science		17, 33, 45, 72, 79, 86, 96, 98	30, 92, 105, 120			82	
Mathematics		25, 78, 101	62		50	88	
Nonsemantic							23, 36, 73, 107

(Left margin, vertical: CONTENT)

Answer Sheet
PRACTICE TEST 7

1 Ⓐ Ⓑ Ⓒ Ⓓ	31 Ⓐ Ⓑ Ⓒ Ⓓ	61 Ⓐ Ⓑ Ⓒ Ⓓ	91 Ⓐ Ⓑ Ⓒ Ⓓ
2 Ⓐ Ⓑ Ⓒ Ⓓ	32 Ⓐ Ⓑ Ⓒ Ⓓ	62 Ⓐ Ⓑ Ⓒ Ⓓ	92 Ⓐ Ⓑ Ⓒ Ⓓ
3 Ⓐ Ⓑ Ⓒ Ⓓ	33 Ⓐ Ⓑ Ⓒ Ⓓ	63 Ⓐ Ⓑ Ⓒ Ⓓ	93 Ⓐ Ⓑ Ⓒ Ⓓ
4 Ⓐ Ⓑ Ⓒ Ⓓ	34 Ⓐ Ⓑ Ⓒ Ⓓ	64 Ⓐ Ⓑ Ⓒ Ⓓ	94 Ⓐ Ⓑ Ⓒ Ⓓ
5 Ⓐ Ⓑ Ⓒ Ⓓ	35 Ⓐ Ⓑ Ⓒ Ⓓ	65 Ⓐ Ⓑ Ⓒ Ⓓ	95 Ⓐ Ⓑ Ⓒ Ⓓ
6 Ⓐ Ⓑ Ⓒ Ⓓ	36 Ⓐ Ⓑ Ⓒ Ⓓ	66 Ⓐ Ⓑ Ⓒ Ⓓ	96 Ⓐ Ⓑ Ⓒ Ⓓ
7 Ⓐ Ⓑ Ⓒ Ⓓ	37 Ⓐ Ⓑ Ⓒ Ⓓ	67 Ⓐ Ⓑ Ⓒ Ⓓ	97 Ⓐ Ⓑ Ⓒ Ⓓ
8 Ⓐ Ⓑ Ⓒ Ⓓ	38 Ⓐ Ⓑ Ⓒ Ⓓ	68 Ⓐ Ⓑ Ⓒ Ⓓ	98 Ⓐ Ⓑ Ⓒ Ⓓ
9 Ⓐ Ⓑ Ⓒ Ⓓ	39 Ⓐ Ⓑ Ⓒ Ⓓ	69 Ⓐ Ⓑ Ⓒ Ⓓ	99 Ⓐ Ⓑ Ⓒ Ⓓ
10 Ⓐ Ⓑ Ⓒ Ⓓ	40 Ⓐ Ⓑ Ⓒ Ⓓ	70 Ⓐ Ⓑ Ⓒ Ⓓ	100 Ⓐ Ⓑ Ⓒ Ⓓ
11 Ⓐ Ⓑ Ⓒ Ⓓ	41 Ⓐ Ⓑ Ⓒ Ⓓ	71 Ⓐ Ⓑ Ⓒ Ⓓ	101 Ⓐ Ⓑ Ⓒ Ⓓ
12 Ⓐ Ⓑ Ⓒ Ⓓ	42 Ⓐ Ⓑ Ⓒ Ⓓ	72 Ⓐ Ⓑ Ⓒ Ⓓ	102 Ⓐ Ⓑ Ⓒ Ⓓ
13 Ⓐ Ⓑ Ⓒ Ⓓ	43 Ⓐ Ⓑ Ⓒ Ⓓ	73 Ⓐ Ⓑ Ⓒ Ⓓ	103 Ⓐ Ⓑ Ⓒ Ⓓ
14 Ⓐ Ⓑ Ⓒ Ⓓ	44 Ⓐ Ⓑ Ⓒ Ⓓ	74 Ⓐ Ⓑ Ⓒ Ⓓ	104 Ⓐ Ⓑ Ⓒ Ⓓ
15 Ⓐ Ⓑ Ⓒ Ⓓ	45 Ⓐ Ⓑ Ⓒ Ⓓ	75 Ⓐ Ⓑ Ⓒ Ⓓ	105 Ⓐ Ⓑ Ⓒ Ⓓ
16 Ⓐ Ⓑ Ⓒ Ⓓ	46 Ⓐ Ⓑ Ⓒ Ⓓ	76 Ⓐ Ⓑ Ⓒ Ⓓ	106 Ⓐ Ⓑ Ⓒ Ⓓ
17 Ⓐ Ⓑ Ⓒ Ⓓ	47 Ⓐ Ⓑ Ⓒ Ⓓ	77 Ⓐ Ⓑ Ⓒ Ⓓ	107 Ⓐ Ⓑ Ⓒ Ⓓ
18 Ⓐ Ⓑ Ⓒ Ⓓ	48 Ⓐ Ⓑ Ⓒ Ⓓ	78 Ⓐ Ⓑ Ⓒ Ⓓ	108 Ⓐ Ⓑ Ⓒ Ⓓ
19 Ⓐ Ⓑ Ⓒ Ⓓ	49 Ⓐ Ⓑ Ⓒ Ⓓ	79 Ⓐ Ⓑ Ⓒ Ⓓ	109 Ⓐ Ⓑ Ⓒ Ⓓ
20 Ⓐ Ⓑ Ⓒ Ⓓ	50 Ⓐ Ⓑ Ⓒ Ⓓ	80 Ⓐ Ⓑ Ⓒ Ⓓ	110 Ⓐ Ⓑ Ⓒ Ⓓ
21 Ⓐ Ⓑ Ⓒ Ⓓ	51 Ⓐ Ⓑ Ⓒ Ⓓ	81 Ⓐ Ⓑ Ⓒ Ⓓ	111 Ⓐ Ⓑ Ⓒ Ⓓ
22 Ⓐ Ⓑ Ⓒ Ⓓ	52 Ⓐ Ⓑ Ⓒ Ⓓ	82 Ⓐ Ⓑ Ⓒ Ⓓ	112 Ⓐ Ⓑ Ⓒ Ⓓ
23 Ⓐ Ⓑ Ⓒ Ⓓ	53 Ⓐ Ⓑ Ⓒ Ⓓ	83 Ⓐ Ⓑ Ⓒ Ⓓ	113 Ⓐ Ⓑ Ⓒ Ⓓ
24 Ⓐ Ⓑ Ⓒ Ⓓ	54 Ⓐ Ⓑ Ⓒ Ⓓ	84 Ⓐ Ⓑ Ⓒ Ⓓ	114 Ⓐ Ⓑ Ⓒ Ⓓ
25 Ⓐ Ⓑ Ⓒ Ⓓ	55 Ⓐ Ⓑ Ⓒ Ⓓ	85 Ⓐ Ⓑ Ⓒ Ⓓ	115 Ⓐ Ⓑ Ⓒ Ⓓ
26 Ⓐ Ⓑ Ⓒ Ⓓ	56 Ⓐ Ⓑ Ⓒ Ⓓ	86 Ⓐ Ⓑ Ⓒ Ⓓ	116 Ⓐ Ⓑ Ⓒ Ⓓ
27 Ⓐ Ⓑ Ⓒ Ⓓ	57 Ⓐ Ⓑ Ⓒ Ⓓ	87 Ⓐ Ⓑ Ⓒ Ⓓ	117 Ⓐ Ⓑ Ⓒ Ⓓ
28 Ⓐ Ⓑ Ⓒ Ⓓ	58 Ⓐ Ⓑ Ⓒ Ⓓ	88 Ⓐ Ⓑ Ⓒ Ⓓ	118 Ⓐ Ⓑ Ⓒ Ⓓ
29 Ⓐ Ⓑ Ⓒ Ⓓ	59 Ⓐ Ⓑ Ⓒ Ⓓ	89 Ⓐ Ⓑ Ⓒ Ⓓ	119 Ⓐ Ⓑ Ⓒ Ⓓ
30 Ⓐ Ⓑ Ⓒ Ⓓ	60 Ⓐ Ⓑ Ⓒ Ⓓ	90 Ⓐ Ⓑ Ⓒ Ⓓ	120 Ⓐ Ⓑ Ⓒ Ⓓ

Practice Test 7

Directions: In each of the following questions, you will find three initial terms and, in parentheses, four answer options designated *a*, *b*, *c*, and *d*. You are to select from the four answer options the one that best completes the analogy with the three initial terms. To record your answers, use the answer sheet provided.

Time: 60 minutes

1. SUFFOCATION : AIR :: DEHYDRATION : (*a.* food, *b.* shelter, *c.* water, *d.* sunlight)

2. RISE : (*a.* set, *b.* raise, *c.* sit, *d.* decrease) :: EAST : WEST

3. (*a.* greedy, *b.* pleasure-seeking, *c.* lazy, *d.* warlike) : SPARTA :: CULTURED : ATHENS

4. CUBE : SQUARE :: (*a.* ellipsis, *b.* ellipsoid, *c.* oblong, *d.* tetrahedron) : ELLIPSE

5. INFRARED : BELOW :: (*a.* maroon, *b.* aquamarine, *c.* chartreuse, *d.* ultraviolet) : ABOVE

6. (*a.* NW, *b.* SW, *c.* NE, *d.* SE) : SE :: S : N

7. DIASTOLIC : DILATATION :: (*a.* anatolic, *b.* controlic, *c.* catatolic, *d.* systolic) : CONTRACTION

8. CAVALRY : HORSE :: INFANTRY : (*a.* platoon, *b.* stallion, *c.* tank, *d.* foot)

9. MADISON : (*a.* American Revolution, *b.* French-Indian War, *c.* War of 1812, *d.* Spanish-American War) :: LINCOLN : CIVIL WAR

10. SHEEP : (*a.* sheeps, *b.* sheep, *c.* sheepes, *d.* sheepses) :: LIFE : LIVES

11. MICKEY : MOUSE :: POLYPHEMOUS : (*a.* Scylla, *b.* Cyclops, *c.* daemon, *d.* satyr)

12. LABOUR : (*a.* Conservative, *b.* Federalist, *c.* Socialist, *d.* Progressive) :: DEMOCRAT : REPUBLICAN

13. A.M. : (*a.* ab, *b.* ante, *c.* amon, *d.* annuo) :: P.M. : post

14. JUDAISM : TORAH :: (*a.* Hinduism, *b.* Buddhism, *c.* Islam, *d.* Confucianism) : KORAN

15. (*a.* gin, *b.* rummy, *c.* check, *d.* mate) : GIN RUMMY :: CHECKMATE : CHESS

16. SAWYER : THATCHER :: TOM : (*a.* Susie, *b.* Becky, *c.* Janey, *d.* Judy)

17. PRAIRIE SCHOONER : (*a.* covered wagon, *b.* horse, *c.* mule, *d.* railroad train) :: PRAIRIE WOLF : COYOTE

18. YEN : JAPAN :: MARK : (*a.* Germany, *b.* Sweden, *c.* Holland, *d.* France)

19. GENOTYPE : PHENOTYPE :: (*a.* expected, *b.* ontogeny, *c.* philogeny, *d.* environmental) : OBSERVED

20. HOLLAND : NETHERLANDS :: FORMOSA : (*a.* Kemoy, *b.* Matsu, *c.* Taiwan, *d.* Oahu)

21. TABLE : ABLE :: TRACK : (*a.* field, *b.* willing, *c.* rack, *d.* truck)

22. MIDWIFE : (*a.* marriage, *b.* birth, *c.* disease, *d.* death) :: SHERIFF : LAW ENFORCEMENT

23. PRISONER : RELEASE :: SOLDIER : (*a.* draft, *b.* fight, *c.* enlist, *d.* discharge)

24. YELLOW : (*a.* coat, *b.* chicken, *c.* hornet, *d.* jacket) :: BUMBLE : BEE

25. AMERICAN : (*a.* British, *b.* Swiss, *c.* Colombian, *d.* Belgian) :: PARMESAN : CAMEMBERT

26. (*a.* hawk, *b.* dove, *c.* eagle, *d.* robin) : U.S.A. :: MAPLE LEAF : CANADA

27. CIRCE : SWINE :: MEDUSA : (*a.* jackal, *b.* stone, *c.* gold, *d.* snake)

28. (*a.* bones, *b.* skin, *c.* muscles, *d.* blood) : DERMATOLOGY :: IMMUNITY : IMMUNOLOGY

29. TWIDDLE : TWADDLE :: (*a.* jambo, *b.* jimbo, *c.* mumbo, *d.* rumbo) : JUMBO

30. OLFACTORY : (*a.* mouth, *b.* ears, *c.* nose, *d.* fingers) :: VISUAL : EYES

31. ECUADOR : SOUTH AMERICA :: EGYPT : (*a.* Africa, *b.* Asia, *c.* Europe, *d.* India)

32. RED CROSS : RELIEF FROM DISASTERS :: BLUE CROSS :
(*a.* health insurance, *b.* relief from tyranny, *c.* relief from mental illness,
d. medical supplies)

33. EEG : BRAIN :: EKG : (*a.* heart, *b.* brain, *c.* gall bladder, *d.* vagus nerve)

34. ABRAHAM : SARAH :: PUNCH : (*a.* Judy, *b.* Paula, *c.* Pat, *d.* Joanie)

35. MPH : RPM :: MILES : (*a.* rotations, *b.* revolutions, *c.* minutes, *d.* hours)

36. ORDAIN : MINISTER :: (*a.* approve, *b.* obey, *c.* admit, *d.* certify) :
TEACHER

37. WATER : HYDROGEN :: TABLE SALT : (*a.* chlorine, *b.* potassium,
c. nitrogen, *d.* oxygen)

38. ELBOW : ARM :: (*a.* shin, *b.* thigh, *c.* calf, *d.* knee) : LEG

39. NUMBER : GENDER :: SINGULAR : (*a.* plural, *b.* feminine,
c. nominative, *d.* present)

40. PATRICIDE : FATHER :: GENOCIDE : (*a.* enemy, *b.* group, *c.* mother,
d. brother)

41. INCA : (*a.* Mexico, *b.* Panama, *c.* Honduras, *d.* Peru) :: AZTEC : MEXICO

42. ODIOUS : (*a.* burdensome, *b.* easy, *c.* pleasing, *d.* disgusting) ::
HONORABLE : DISGRACEFUL

43. SITTING BULL : CUSTER :: (*a.* Eddington, *b.* Howe, *c.* Sheridan,
d. Wellington) : NAPOLEON BONAPARTE

44. LOG 10 : 1 :: LOG 100 : (*a.* 2, *b.* 5, *c.* 10, *d.* 90)

45. HOMING PIGEON : CARRIER PIGEON :: STOOL PIGEON :
(*a.* fool, *b.* informer, *c.* loser, *d.* passenger pigeon)

46. STOP : POTS :: NOON : (*a.* morning, *b.* noon, *c.* night, *d.* never)

47. EBENEEZER SCROOGE : MISERLY :: SIMON LEGREE :
(*a.* humane, *b.* generous, *c.* stingy, *d.* cruel)

48. PALEONTOLOGIST : (*a.* vertebrates, *b.* rocks, *c.* earthquakes, *d.* fossils) ::
ZOOLOGIST : ANIMALS

49. (*a.* emperor, *b.* pharaoh, *c.* shah, *d.* diet) : CONGRESS ::
PRIME MINISTER : PRESIDENT

50. B_1 : THIAMINE :: (*a.* B_2, *b.* B_6, *c.* C, *d.* D) : RIBOFLAVIN

51. GUERNSEY : (*a.* York, *b.* Jersey, *c.* British, *d.* French) :: CHESHIRE : SIAMESE

52. TOURNEY : TOURNAMENT :: TEMPORARY : (*a.* permanent, *b.* sudden, *c.* transitory, *d.* temptation)

53. STOMACH : DIGESTION :: ANATOMY : (*a.* cartography, *b.* biology, *c.* physiology, *d.* proctology)

54. PRE : PRIOR :: PRETER : (*a.* beyond, *b.* as if, *c.* therefore, *d.* only)

55. LINCOLN : KENNEDY :: (*a.* Tyler, *b.* Johnson, *c.* Eisenhower, *d.* Garfield) : McKINLEY

56. FORTE : LOUD :: (*a.* largo, *b.* rubato, *c.* violin, *d.* piano) : SOFT

57. LATIN ALPHABET : FRENCH :: CYRILLIC ALPHABET : (*a.* Russian, *b.* Sanskrit, *c.* Greek, *d.* Chinese)

58. CENTRIFUGAL : (*a.* centripetal, *b.* centrigonal, *c.* centrobaric, *d.* centrosomal) :: AWAY FROM : TOWARD

59. ICHTHYOLOGY : (*a.* insects, *b.* reptiles, *c.* arthropods, *d.* fish) :: ORNITHOLOGY : BIRDS

60. (*a.* wool, *b.* synthetic, *c.* dinosaur, *d.* gasoline) : PETROL :: U.S.A. : BRITAIN

61. (*a.* overindulge, *b.* persevere, *c.* quit, *d.* deprive) : SURFEIT :: CLOY : SATIATE

62. (*a.* Hesse, *b.* Joyce, *c.* Mann, *d.* Proust) : DEATH IN VENICE :: SHAKESPEARE : MERCHANT OF VENICE

63. ROOK : CASTLE :: HORSE : (*a.* knight, *b.* track, *c.* chess, *d.* winner)

64. (*a.* Greuze, *b.* Utrillo, *c.* Seurat, *d.* Manet) : POINTILLISM :: DAVID : NEOCLASSICISM

65. BILL : BEAK :: (*a.* finger, *b.* leg, *c.* hand, *d.* kneecap) : DIGIT

66. GEWGAW : (*a.* trinket, *b.* bottle, *c.* rhinestone, *d.* candy) :: TACITURN : QUIET

67. (*a.* fortunate, *b.* entreat, *c.* unfortunate, *d.* order) : IMPORTUNE :: IMPREGNABLE : UNSHAKABLE

68. CULPABLE : GUILTY :: (*a.* preculpable, *b.* exculpable, *c.* multiculpable, *d.* malculpable) : ACQUITTED

69. FOX : (*a.* bovine, *b.* vulpine, *c.* porcine, *d.* equine) :: CAT : FELINE

70. AGONY : ECSTASY :: SOUND : (*a.* Light, *b.* Trumpet, *c.* Signpost, *d.* Fury)

71. LANG SYNE : (*a.* bygone days, *b.* future days, *c.* here and now, *d.* nonexistent times) :: IMMEDIATELY : AT ONCE

72. (*a.* India, *b.* Brazil, *c.* Mexico, *d.* Spain) : GUANAJUATO :: CANADA : MANITOBA

73. VERDI : AIDA :: (*a.* Bach, *b.* Mozart, *c.* Beethoven, *d.* Brahms) : FIDELIO

74. TORTUOUS : (*a.* winding, *b.* barbaric, *c.* long, *d.* incomprehensible) :: HAPPY : FELICITOUS

75. (*a.* present, *b.* past, *c.* recent, *d.* never) : CURRENT :: ERSTWHILE : FORMER

76. DAVID : GOLIATH :: HOLMES : (*a.* Moriarty, *b.* Watson, *c.* Doyle, *d.* Devlin)

77. LUGUBRIOUS : (*a.* shallow, *b.* cheerful, *c.* expensive, *d.* fatuous) :: PONDEROUS : LIGHT

78. EXPLETIVE : (*a.* interrogative, *b.* factotum, *c.* oath, *d.* lie) :: EXPOSÉ : DISCLOSURE

79. 11 : BINARY :: (*a.* 2, *b.* 3, *c.* 4, *d.* 10) : DECIMAL

80. CHALICE : GOBLET :: LEAF : (*a.* plant, *b.* tree, *c.* sheet, *d.* gold)

81. (*a.* nut, *b.* fruit, *c.* root, *d.* berry) : TURNIP :: STEM : CELERY

82. ABRAM : ABRAHAM :: (*a.* Sarabelle, *b.* Sarai, *c.* Salome, *d.* Sharon) : SARAH

83. VELÁSQUEZ : MAIDS OF HONOR :: (*a.* Botticelli, *b.* Bellini, *c.* Bosch, *d.* Uccello) : THE BIRTH OF VENUS

84. CIVIL : (*a.* misdemeanor, *b.* larceny, *c.* tort, *d.* perjury) :: CRIMINAL : FELONY

85. GREGORIAN : NOVEMBER :: FRENCH REVOLUTIONARY : (*a.* Novembre, *b.* February, *c.* Julian, *d.* Thermidor)

86. GOLDEN RULE : LUKE :: CATEGORICAL IMPERATIVE : (*a.* Hegel, *b.* Kant, *c.* Ardrey, *d.* Lorenz)

87. EQUIVOCATION : (*a.* perversity, *b.* exultation, *c.* veracity, *d.* perjury) :: UNCERTAINTY : CERTAINTY

88. TIMBREL : (*a.* cymbals, *b.* zither, *c.* flute, *d.* tambourine) :: LUTE : GUITAR

89. (*a.* Apollo, *b.* Phaeton, *c.* Furies, *d.* Sirens) : EUMENIDES :: PLUTO : HADES

90. JOSEPH K. : TRIAL :: GREGOR SAMSA : (*a.* Hunger Artist, *b.* Death in Venice, *c.* The Flies, *d.* Metamorphosis)

91. $\sqrt{2} : \sqrt{18}$ :: 1 : (*a.* 2, *b.* 3, *c.* 6, *d.* 9)

92. TRANSUBSTANTIATION : ACTUAL :: (*a.* insubstantiation, *b.* absubstantiation, *c.* consubstantiation, *d.* desubstantiation) : SYMBOLIC

93. ABACUS : COMPUTER :: DAGUERROTYPE : (*a.* stereo, *b.* photograph, *c.* tape recorder, *d.* telephone)

94. DECLARATION OF INDEPENDENCE : PHILADELPHIA :: MAGNA CARTA : (*a.* Gloucester, *b.* Runnymede, *c.* Canterbury, *d.* Norwalk)

95. MINTON : ROYAL DOULTON :: MIKASA (*a.* Sony, *b.* Rosenthal, *c.* Lenox, *d.* Noritake)

96. SHYLOCK : SCROOGE :: DON JUAN : (*a.* Antonio, *b.* Don Giovanni, *c.* Lothario, *d.* Don Quixote)

97. SKINNER : EMPIRICIST :: (*a.* Watson, *b.* Aristotle, *c.* Chomsky, *d.* Locke) : RATIONALIST

98. MOHAWK : IROQUOIS :: (*a.* Apache, *b.* Zuni, *c.* Seminole, *d.* Creek) : PUEBLO

99. (*a.* half-life, *b.* radioactivity, *c.* atomic mass, *d.* atomic number) : ISOTOPE :: ATOMIC WEIGHT : ISOBAR

100. SARACEN : (*a.* Hindu, *b.* Muslim, *c.* Shintoist, *d.* Taoist) :: EPISCOPALIAN : ANGLICAN

101. WATERGATE : NIXON :: IRAN CONTRA : (*a.* Ford, *b.* Carter, *c.* Reagan, *d.* Bush)

102. GALAPAGOS : SAMOA :: (*a.* Linnaeus, *b.* Magellan, *c.* Rhodes, *d.* Darwin) : MEAD

103. BIGGER THOMAS : (*a.* New York, *b.* Chicago, *c.* St. Louis, *d.* Montgomery) :: RODION RASKOLNIKOV : ST. PETERSBURG

104. TAXONOMY : CLASSIFY :: NOMENCLATURE : (*a.* order, *b.* color, *c.* name, *d.* number)

105. PHYSIOGNOMY : (*a.* face, *b.* stature, *c.* physiology, *d.* gate) :: CHIROMANCY : PALM

106. MUTINY : SHIP CAPTAIN :: COUP D'ÉTAT : (*a.* college dean, *b.* military commander, *c.* government, *d.* CEO)

107. (*a.* exaggerated, *b.* understated, *c.* metaphorical, *d.* literal) : HYPERBOLIC :: DRAMATIC : HISTRIONIC

108. APPLE : EVE :: (*a.* pear, *b.* pomegranate, *c.* peach, *d.* papaya) : PERSEPHONE

109. CEMENTUM : ROOT :: (*a.* bone, *b.* fluoride, *c.* keratin, *d.* enamel) : CROWN

110. (*a.* acorn, *b.* cornmeal, *c.* millet, *d.* filbert) : BULGUR :: QUINOA : BARLEY

111. MOBY DICK : LEVIATHAN :: MELVILLE : (*a.* Rousseau, *b.* Hobbes, *c.* Kant, *d.* Smith)

112. (*a.* Locke, *b.* Galileo, *c.* Bacon, *d.* Calvin) : ENLIGHTENMENT :: DESCARTES : RENAISSANCE

113. STEINWAY : (*a.* piano, *b.* cello, *c.* flute, *d.* organ) :: STRADIVARIUS : VIOLIN

114. TERKEL : (*a.* manuscripts, *b.* photographs, *c.* oral histories, *d.* maps) :: LOMAX : FOLK MUSIC

115. 6×10^{23} : (*a.* e, *b.* Avogadro's number, *c.* i, *d.* Planck's constant) :: 3.14 : PI

116. CIRRUS : NIMBUS :: CUMULUS : (*a.* bilious, *b.* birrus, *c.* mobius, *d.* stratus)

117. SOCIALISM : (*a.* state, *b.* family, *c.* town, *d.* universal) :: CAPITALISM : PRIVATE

118. (*a.* Pikes Peak, *b.* Mt. Kilimanjaro, *c.* Mt. Vesuvius, *d.* K2) : MT. ST. HELENS :: EXTINCT : ACTIVE

119. IMPERIOUS : IMPERVIOUS :: (*a.* grandiose, *b.* disbelieving, *c.* judgmental, *d.* domineering) : IMMUNE

120. NEUTRAL : NEUTRON :: NEGATIVE : (*a.* atom, *b.* electron, *c.* positron, *d.* negatron)

Answer Key
PRACTICE TEST 7

1.	C	31.	A	61.	A	91.	B
2.	A	32.	A	62.	C	92.	C
3.	D	33.	A	63.	A	93.	B
4.	B	34.	A	64.	C	94.	B
5.	D	35.	B	65.	A	95.	D
6.	A	36.	D	66.	A	96.	C
7.	D	37.	A	67.	B	97.	C
8.	D	38.	D	68.	B	98.	B
9.	C	39.	B	69.	B	99.	D
10.	B	40.	B	70.	D	100.	B
11.	B	41.	D	71.	A	101.	C
12.	A	42.	C	72.	C	102.	D
13.	B	43.	D	73.	C	103.	B
14.	C	44.	A	74.	A	104	C
15.	A	45.	B	75.	A	105	A
16.	B	46.	B	76.	A	106.	C
17.	A	47.	D	77.	B	107.	A
18.	A	48.	D	78.	C	108.	B
19.	A	49.	D	79.	B	109.	D
20.	C	50.	A	80.	C	110.	C
21.	C	51.	B	81.	C	111.	B
22.	B	52.	C	82.	B	112.	A
23.	D	53.	C	83.	A	113.	A
24.	D	54.	A	84.	C	114.	C
25.	B	55.	D	85.	D	115.	B
26.	C	56.	D	86.	B	116.	D
27.	B	57.	A	87.	C	117.	A
28.	B	58.	A	88.	D	118.	C
29.	C	59.	D	89.	C	119.	D
30.	C	60.	D	90.	D	120.	B

EXPLANATION OF ANSWERS FOR PRACTICE TEST 7

In the following explanations of answers, explanations concerning the correct response are in a large font. Explanations regarding distracters (incorrect responses) that are not self-explaining or could be misinterpreted are in a smaller font in order to highlight the explanations of the answers that are correct.

1. SUFFOCATION : AIR :: DEHYDRATION : (*a.* food, *b.* shelter, *c.* **water**, *d.* sunlight)

   (**c**) Suffocation is caused by lack of air. Dehydration is caused by lack of water.
   Natural Science—Description

2. RISE : (*a.* **set**, *b.* raise, *c.* sit, *d.* decrease) :: EAST : WEST

   (**a**) The sun rises in the east and sets in the west.
   General Information—Description

3. (*a.* greedy, *b.* pleasure-seeking, *c.* lazy, *d.* **warlike**) : SPARTA :: CULTURED : ATHENS

   (**d**) In ancient Greece, the people of Sparta were known to be warlike, while the people of Athens were known to be cultured.
   Humanities—Description

4. CUBE : SQUARE :: (*a.* ellipsis, *b.* **ellipsoid**, *c.* oblong, *d.* tetrahedron) : ELLIPSE

   (**b**) When a plane is passed through a cube at a right angle, the intersection is a square. When a plane is passed through an ellipsoid at a right angle, the intersection is an ellipse.
   Mathematics—Part/Whole

5. INFRARED : BELOW :: (*a.* maroon, *b.* aquamarine, *c.* chartreuse, *d.* **ultraviolet**) : ABOVE

   (**d**) Infrared light is below the visible spectrum for human beings; ultraviolet light is above the visible spectrum. The human eye can perceive wavelengths between 380 and 750 nm.
   Natural Science—Description

6. (*a.* **NW**, *b.* SW, *c.* NE, *d.* SE) : SE :: S : N

   (**a**) NW (northwest) and SE (southeast) are opposing directions, as are S (south) and N (north).
   General Information—Similarity/Contrast

7. DIASTOLIC : DILATATION :: (*a.* anatolic, *b.* controlic, *c.* catatolic, *d.* **systolic**) : CONTRACTION

   (**d**) Diastolic blood pressure refers to the dilatation of the heart, while systolic blood pressure refers to the contraction of the heart.
   Natural Science—Description

8. CAVALRY : HORSE :: INFANTRY : (*a.* platoon, *b.* stallion, *c.* tank, *d.* **foot**)

   (**d**) In an army, the cavalry travels by horse, the infantry by foot.
   General Information—Description

9. MADISON : (*a.* American Revolution, *b.* French-Indian War, *c.* **War of 1812**, *d.* Spanish-American War) :: LINCOLN : CIVIL WAR

   (**c**) Madison (1751–1836) was president during the War of 1812; Lincoln (1809–1865) was president during the Civil War.
   Social Science—Description

10. SHEEP : (*a.* sheeps, *b.* **sheep**, *c.* sheepes, *d.* sheepses) :: LIFE : LIVES

    (**b**) The plural of *sheep* is *sheep*. The plural of *life* is *lives*.
    Nonsemantic

11. MICKEY : MOUSE :: POLYPHEMOUS : (*a.* Scylla, *b.* **Cyclops**, *c.* daemon, *d.* satyr)

    (**b**) Mickey is the name of a fictional mouse; Polyphemous is the name of a fictional Cyclops (in Homer's *Odyssey*). In Greek mythology, Scylla was one of two monsters that lived on either side of a very narrow river. Daemons are supernatural beings between humans and gods in ancient Greek religion. They could be bad or good. Satyrs are woodland deities.
    Humanities—Description

12. LABOUR : (*a.* **Conservative**, *b.* Federalist, *c.* Socialist, *d.* Progressive) :: DEMOCRAT : REPUBLICAN

    (**a**) In British politics, the Labour party has generally been a left of center political party opposing the right of center Conservative party. In U.S. politics, the more left-leaning Democrats have traditionally opposed the more right-leaning Republicans.
    Social Science—Class

13. A.M. : (*a.* ab, *b.* **ante**, *c.* amon, *d.* annuo) :: P.M. : post

    (**b**) the *A* in *A.M.* is an abbreviation for *ante*; the *P* in *P.M.* is an abbreviation for *post*. The *m* stands for *meridiem*.
    General Information—Description

14. JUDAISM : TORAH :: (*a.* Hinduism, *b.* Buddhism, *c.* **Islam**, *d.* Confucianism) : KORAN

    (**c**) The Torah is a holy book of Judaism, while the Koran is a holy book of Islam. The holy scriptures of Hinduism are the Vedas. A holy text in Confucianism is the Analects. A holy text in Buddhism is the Tipitaka.
    Humanities—Description

15. (*a.* **gin**, *b.* rummy, *c.* check, *d.* mate) : GIN RUMMY :: CHECKMATE : CHESS

    (**a**) The state of gin ends a gin rummy game, just as the state of checkmate ends a chess game.
    General Information—Description

16. SAWYER : THATCHER :: TOM : (*a.* Susie, *b.* **Becky**, *c.* Janey, *d.* Judy)

    (**b**) Tom Sawyer and Becky Thatcher are both characters in Mark Twain's novel *Tom Sawyer*.
    Humanities—Completion

17. PRAIRIE SCHOONER : (*a.* **covered wagon**, *b.* horse, *c.* mule, *d.* railroad train) :: PRAIRIE WOLF : COYOTE

    (**a**) A prairie schooner is a covered wagon; a prairie wolf is a coyote.
    General Information—Similarity/Contrast

18. YEN : JAPAN :: MARK : (*a.* **Germany**, *b.* Sweden, *c.* Holland, *d.* France)

    (**a**) The yen is the unit of currency in Japan, while the mark was the unit of currency in Germany. The crown is the unit of currency in Sweden; in Holland it was the guilder; and in France, the franc. It is now the euro in Holland, France, and Germany.
    General Information—Description

19. GENOTYPE : PHENOTYPE :: (*a.* **expected**, *b.* ontogeny, *c.* philogeny, *d.* environmental) : OBSERVED

    (**a**) A genotype is what is expected on the basis of heredity, while a phenotype is what is observed on the basis of heredity, environment, and the interaction between them. Ontogeny is the process of an organism growing organically.
    Natural Science—Description

20. HOLLAND : NETHERLANDS :: FORMOSA : (*a.* Kemoy, *b.* Matsu, *c.* **Taiwan**, *d.* Oahu)

    (**c**) Holland and Netherlands refer to the same country, as do Formosa and Taiwan.
    General Information—Similarity/Contrast

21. TABLE : ABLE :: TRACK : (*a.* field, *b.* willing, **c. rack**, *d.* truck)

    (**c**) *Able* is *table* without the initial *t*; *rack* is *track* without the initial *t*.
    Nonsemantic

22. MIDWIFE : (*a.* marriage, **b. birth**, *c.* disease, *d.* death) :: SHERIFF : LAW ENFORCEMENT

    (**b**) The job of a midwife is to help in birth; the job of a sheriff is to help in law enforcement.
    General Information—Description

23. PRISONER : RELEASE :: SOLDIER : (*a.* draft, *b.* fight, *c.* enlist, **d. discharge**)

    (**d**) A prisoner receives a release from prison; a soldier receives a discharge from the army.
    General Information—Description

24. YELLOW : (*a.* coat, *b.* chicken, *c.* hornet, **d. jacket**) :: BUMBLE : BEE

    (**d**) A yellow jacket and a bumblebee are both types of insect.
    General Information—Description

25. AMERICAN : (*a.* British, **b. Swiss**, *c.* Colombian, *d.* Belgian) :: PARMESAN : CAMEMBERT

    (**b**) American, Swiss, Parmesan, and Camembert are all types of cheese.
    General Information—Class

26. (*a.* hawk, *b.* dove, **c. eagle**, *d.* robin) : U.S.A. :: MAPLE LEAF : CANADA

    (**c**) The eagle is an emblem of the United States, while the maple leaf is an emblem of Canada.
    Social Science—Description

27. CIRCE : SWINE :: MEDUSA : (*a.* jackal, **b. stone**, *c.* gold, *d.* snake)

    (**b**) Circe transformed men into swine; Medusa transformed them into stone.
    Humanities—Description

28. (*a.* bones, **b. skin**, *c.* muscles, *d.* blood) : DERMATOLOGY :: IMMUNITY : IMMUNOLOGY

    (**b**) Dermatology is the branch of medicine dealing with the skin; immunology is the branch of medicine dealing with immunity.
    Natural Science—Description

29. TWIDDLE : TWADDLE :: (*a.* jambo, *b.* jimbo, *c.* **mumbo**, *d.* rumbo) : JUMBO

(**c**) Twiddle twaddle and mumbo jumbo both refer to gibberish.
Vocabulary—Completion

30. OLFACTORY : (*a.* mouth, *b.* ears, *c.* **nose**, *d.* fingers) :: VISUAL : EYES

(**c**) The olfactory sense (smell) receives sensation through the nose; the visual sense (seeing) receives sensation through the eyes.
Natural Science—Description

31. ECUADOR : SOUTH AMERICA :: EGYPT : (*a.* **Africa**, *b.* Asia, *c.* Europe, *d.* India)

(**a**) Ecuador is a country in South America. Egypt is a country in Africa.
General Information—Description

32. RED CROSS : RELIEF FROM DISASTERS :: BLUE CROSS : (*a.* **health insurance**, *b.* relief from tyranny, *c.* relief from mental illness, *d.* medical supplies)

(**a**) The Red Cross organization provides relief from disasters; the Blue Cross organization provides health insurance.
General Information—Description

33. EEG : BRAIN :: EKG : (*a.* **heart**, *b.* brain, *c.* gall bladder, *d.* vagus nerve)

(**a**) An EEG is a tracing of the changes in electric potential produced by the brain, while an EKG is a tracing of the changes in electric potential produced by the heart. EEG stands for "electroencephalogram." EKG stands for "electrocardiogram."
Natural Science—Description

34. ABRAHAM : SARAH :: PUNCH : (*a.* **Judy**, *b.* Paula, *c.* Pat, *d.* Joanie)

(**a**) In the Bible, Abraham was the husband of Sarah. In a Punch-and-Judy puppet show, Punch is the husband of Judy.
Humanities—Class

35. MPH : RPM :: MILES : (*a.* rotations, *b.* **revolutions**, *c.* minutes, *d.* hours)

(**b**) The *m* in *mph* is an abbreviation for *miles* (per hour). The *r* in *rpm* is an abbreviation for *revolutions* (per minute).
Natural Science—Description

36. ORDAIN : MINISTER :: (*a.* approve, *b.* obey, *c.* admit, *d.* **certify**) : TEACHER

    (**d**) A minister is ordained before beginning to preach. A teacher is certified before beginning to teach.
    General Information—Description

37. WATER : HYDROGEN :: TABLE SALT : (*a.* **chlorine**, *b.* potassium, *c.* nitrogen, *d.* oxygen)

    (**a**) Water is a chemical compound containing hydrogen, while table salt is a chemical compound containing chlorine. Potassium, nitrogen, and oxygen are chemical elements.
    Natural Science—Part/Whole

38. ELBOW : ARM :: (*a.* shin, *b.* thigh, *c.* calf, *d.* **knee**) : LEG

    (**d**) The elbow is the joint separating the upper and lower arms. The knee is the joint separating the upper and lower legs.
    Natural Science—Part/Whole

39. NUMBER : GENDER :: SINGULAR : (*a.* plural, *b.* **feminine**, *c.* nominative, *d.* present)

    (**b**) In grammar, singular is an example of number, and feminine is an example of gender.
    Humanities—Class

40. PATRICIDE : FATHER :: GENOCIDE : (*a.* enemy, *b.* **group**, *c.* mother, *d.* brother)

    (**b**) Patricide is the murder of a father; genocide is the murder of a group. Matricide is the murder of a mother; fratricide is the murder of a brother.
    Vocabulary—Description

41. INCA : (*a.* Mexico, *b.* Panama, *c.* Honduras, *d.* **Peru**) :: AZTEC : MEXICO

    (**d**) The Inca Indians resided in Peru; the Aztecs resided in Mexico.
    Social Science—Description

42. ODIOUS : (*a.* burdensome, *b.* easy, *c.* **pleasing**, *d.* disgusting) :: HONORABLE : DISGRACEFUL

    (**c**) *Odious* and *pleasing* are antonyms, as are *honorable* and *disgraceful.*
    Vocabulary—Similarity/Contrast

43. SITTING BULL : CUSTER :: (*a.* Eddington, *b.* Howe, *c.* Sheridan, *d.* **Wellington**) : NAPOLEON BONAPARTE

    (**d**) Sitting Bull defeated General Custer at Little Big Horn in 1876. Wellington defeated Napoleon Bonaparte at the Battle of Waterloo in 1815. *Humanities—Description*

44. LOG 10 : 1 :: LOG 100 : (*a.* **2**, *b.* 5, *c.* 10, *d.* 90)

    (**a**) Log 10 is equal to 1. Log 100 is equal to 2. *Mathematics—Equality/Negation*

45. HOMING PIGEON : CARRIER PIGEON :: STOOL PIGEON : (*a.* fool, *b.* **informer**, *c.* loser, *d.* passenger pigeon)

    (**b**) A homing pigeon is a carrier pigeon. A stool pigeon is an informer. *Vocabulary—Similarity/Contrast*

46. STOP : POTS :: NOON : (*a.* morning, *b.* **noon**, *c.* night, *d.* never)

    (**b**) *Stop* spelled backwards is *pots*. *Noon* spelled backwards is *noon*. *Nonsemantic*

47. EBENEEZER SCROOGE : MISERLY :: SIMON LEGREE : (*a.* humane, *b.* generous, *c.* stingy, *d.* **cruel**)

    (**d**) The literary character Ebeneezer Scrooge was miserly (*A Christmas Carol*), while the character Simon Legree was cruel in *Uncle Tom's Cabin*. *Humanities—Description*

48. PALEONTOLOGIST : (*a.* vertebrates, *b.* rocks, *c.* earthquakes, *d.* **fossils**) :: ZOOLOGIST : ANIMALS

    (**d**) A paleontologist studies fossils; a zoologist studies animals. *Natural Science—Description*

49. (*a.* emperor, *b.* pharaoh, *c.* shah, *d.* **diet**) : CONGRESS :: PRIME MINISTER : PRESIDENT

    (**d**) A diet and a congress are both legislative bodies of government. A prime minister and a president are both executive officers of government. *Social Science—Class*

50. B_1 : THIAMINE :: (*a.* **B_2**, *b.* B_6, *c.* C, *d.* D) : RIBOFLAVIN

    (**a**) Thiamine is vitamin B_1. Riboflavin is vitamin B_2. Vitamin C is also called L-ascorbate. Vitamin B_6 can consist of different compounds: pyridoxine, pyridoxal, and pyridoxamine. Vitamin D comes in several different forms like D_2 (or ergocalciferol) and vitamin D_3 (or cholecalciferol). *Natural Science—Similarity/Contrast*

51. GUERNSEY : (*a.* York, ***b.*** **Jersey**, *c.* British, *d.* French) :: CHESHIRE : SIAMESE

    (**b**) Guernsey and Jersey are both types of cow. Cheshire and Siamese are both types of cat.
    General Information—Class

52. TOURNEY : TOURNAMENT :: TEMPORARY : (*a.* permanent, *b.* sudden, ***c.*** **transitory**, *d.* temptation)

    (**c**) *Tourney* and *tournament* are synonyms, as are *temporary* and *transitory*.
    Vocabulary—Similarity/Contrast

53. STOMACH : DIGESTION :: ANATOMY : (*a.* cartography, *b.* biology, ***c.*** **physiology**, *d.* proctology)

    (**c**) Anatomy is the study of body structures, such as the stomach. Physiology is the study of body functions, such as digestion.
    Natural Science—Description

54. PRE : PRIOR :: PRETER : (***a.*** **beyond**, *b.* as if, *c.* therefore, *d.* only)

    (**a**) *Pre-* is a prefix meaning *prior*. *Preter-* is a prefix meaning *beyond*.
    Vocabulary—Similarity/Contrast

55. LINCOLN : KENNEDY :: (*a.* Tyler, *b.* Johnson, *c.* Eisenhower, ***d.*** **Garfield**) : McKINLEY

    (**d**) Presidents Lincoln (1865), Garfield (1881), McKinley (1901), and Kennedy (1963) were all assassinated while in office.
    Humanities—Class

56. FORTE : LOUD :: (*a.* largo, *b.* rubato, *c.* violin, ***d.*** **piano**) : SOFT

    (**d**) In musical contexts, *forte* means loud and *piano* means soft. *Largo* means "slow"; *rubato* means that the tempo can slightly be varied at the discretion of the player.
    Humanities—Similarity/Contrast

57. LATIN ALPHABET : FRENCH :: CYRILLIC ALPHABET : (***a.*** **Russian**, *b.* Sanskrit, *c.* Greek, *d.* Chinese)

    (**a**) The Latin alphabet is used for writing French, while the Cyrillic alphabet is used for writing Russian.
    Humanities—Description

58. CENTRIFUGAL : (*a.* **centripetal**, *b.* centrigonal, *c.* centrobaric, *d.* centrosomal) :: AWAY FROM : TOWARD

    (**a**) *Centrifugal* means "away from center," while *centripetal* means "toward center." *Centrobaric refers to a center of gravity.*
    Natural Science—Description

59. ICHTHYOLOGY : (*a.* insects, *b.* reptiles, *c.* arthropods, *d.* **fish**) :: ORNITHOLOGY : BIRDS

    (**d**) Ichthyology is the study of fish; ornithology is the study of birds.
    Natural Science—Description

60. (*a.* wool, *b.* synthetic, *c.* dinosaur, *d.* **gasoline**) : PETROL :: U.S.A. : BRITAIN

    (**d**) The fuel called gasoline in the United States is called petrol in Britain.
    General Information—Similarity/Contrast

61. (*a.* **overindulge**, *b.* persevere, *c.* quit, *d.* deprive) : SURFEIT :: CLOY : SATIATE

    (**a**) *Overindulge, surfeit, cloy,* and *satiate* are synonyms.
    Vocabulary—Similarity/Contrast

62. (*a.* Hesse, *b.* Joyce, *c.* **Mann**, *d.* Proust) : DEATH IN VENICE :: SHAKESPEARE : MERCHANT OF VENICE

    (**c**) Mann is the author of *Death in Venice*; Shakespeare is the author of *The Merchant of Venice. Hesse is the author of Steppenwolf. Joyce is the author of Ulysses. Proust is the author of Remembrances of Times Past.*
    Humanities—Description

63. ROOK : CASTLE :: HORSE : (*a.* **knight**, *b.* track, *c.* chess, *d.* winner)

    (**a**) In the game of chess, *rook* and *castle* refer to the same piece, as do *knight* and *horse.*
    General Information—Similarity/Contrast

64. (*a.* Greuze, *b.* Utrillo, *c.* **Seurat**, *d.* Manet) : POINTILLISM :: DAVID : NEOCLASSICISM

    (**c**) Seurat was a leading member in the French school of pointillism. David was a leading member in the French school of neoclassicism. *Greuze was a Rococo era painter. Utrillo specialized in painting cityscapes. Manet was a realist/ impressionist painter.*
    Humanities—Description

65. BILL : BEAK :: (*a.* **finger**, *b.* leg, *c.* hand, *d.* kneecap) : DIGIT

    (**a**) A bill is a beak. A finger is a digit.
    Vocabulary—Similarity/Contrast

66. GEWGAW : (*a.* **trinket**, *b.* bottle, *c.* rhinestone, *d.* candy) ::
    TACITURN : QUIET

    (**a**) A gewgaw is a trinket. A taciturn person is quiet.
    Vocabulary—Similarity/Contrast

67. (*a.* fortunate, *b.* **entreat**, *c.* unfortunate, *d.* order) : IMPORTUNE ::
    IMPREGNABLE : UNSHAKABLE

    (**b**) *Entreat* and *importune* are synonyms, as are *impregnable* and *unshakable*.
    Vocabulary—Similarity/Contrast

68. CULPABLE : GUILTY :: (*a.* preculpable, *b.* **exculpable**, *c.* multiculpable,
    d. malculpable) : ACQUITTED

    (**b**) Someone who is culpable is guilty; someone who is exculpable
    is acquitted.
    Vocabulary—Similarity/Contrast

69. FOX : (*a.* bovine, *b.* **vulpine**, *c.* porcine, *d.* equine) :: CAT : FELINE

    (**b**) *Vulpine* means foxlike, while *feline* means catlike. *Bovine* means cowlike;
    porcine means piglike; *equine* means horselike.
    Vocabulary—Description

70. AGONY : ECSTASY :: SOUND : (*a.* Light, *b.* Trumpet, *c.* Signpost,
    d. **Fury**)

    (**d**) *The Agony and the Ecstasy* (by Irving Stone) and *The Sound and the Fury*
    (by William Faulkner) are both book titles.
    Humanities—Completion

71. LANG SYNE : (*a.* **bygone days**, *b.* future days, *c.* here and now,
    d. nonexistent times) :: IMMEDIATELY : AT ONCE

    (**a**) *Lang syne* means *bygone days*; *immediately* means *at once*.
    Vocabulary—Similarity/Contrast

72. (*a.* India, *b.* Brazil, *c.* **Mexico**, *d.* Spain) : GUANAJUATO :: CANADA :
    MANITOBA

    (**c**) Guanajuato is a political subdivision of Mexico. Manitoba is a political
    subdivision of Canada.
    Social Science—Part/Whole

73. VERDI : AIDA :: (*a.* Bach, *b.* Mozart, **c. Beethoven**, *d.* Brahms) : FIDELIO

    (**c**) Verdi composed the opera *Aida*. Beethoven composed the opera *Fidelio*. Bach composed *The Well-Tempered Clavier*; Mozart composed *The Magic Flute*; Brahms composed *A German Requiem*.
    Humanities—Description

74. TORTUOUS : (**a. winding**, *b.* barbaric, *c.* long, *d.* incomprehensible) :: HAPPY : FELICITOUS

    (**a**) *Tortuous* and *winding* are synonyms, as are *happy* and *felicitous*.
    Vocabulary—Similarity/Contrast

75. (**a. present**, *b.* past, *c.* recent, *d.* never) : CURRENT :: ERSTWHILE : FORMER

    (**a**) A present event is current; a former event is erstwhile.
    Vocabulary—Similarity/Contrast

76. DAVID : GOLIATH :: HOLMES : (**a. Moriarty**, *b.* Watson, *c.* Doyle, *d.* Devlin)

    (**a**) Goliath was the mortal enemy of David; Moriarty was the mortal enemy of Holmes. Arthur Conan Doyle was the author of Sherlock Holmes. Watson was Sherlock Holmes's assistant. Devlin is a distracter term.
    Humanities—Description

77. LUGUBRIOUS : (*a.* shallow, **b. cheerful**, *c.* expensive, *d.* fatuous) :: PONDEROUS : LIGHT

    (**b**) *Lugubrious* and *cheerful* are antonyms, as are *ponderous* and *light*.
    Vocabulary—Similarity/Contrast

78. EXPLETIVE : (*a.* interrogative, *b.* factotum, **c. oath**, *d.* lie) :: EXPOSÉ : DISCLOSURE

    (**c**) An expletive is an oath. An exposé is a disclosure.
    Vocabulary—Similarity/Contrast

79. 11 : BINARY :: (*a.* 2, **b. 3**, *c.* 4, *d.* 10) : DECIMAL

    (**b**) The number 11 in binary notation is equal to the number 3 in decimal notation.
    Mathematics—Equality/Negation

80. CHALICE : GOBLET :: LEAF : (*a.* plant, *b.* tree, **c. sheet**, *d.* gold)

    (**c**) A chalice is a goblet. A leaf is a sheet (of paper).
    Vocabulary—Similarity/Contrast

81. (*a.* nut, *b.* fruit, *c.* **root**, *d.* berry) : TURNIP :: STEM : CELERY

   (**c**) The stem of celery is edible, as is the root of turnip.
   General Information—Class

82. ABRAM : ABRAHAM :: (*a.* Sarabelle, *b.* **Sarai**, *c.* Salome, *d.* Sharon) :
   SARAH

   (**b**) After the Covenant with God, Abram's name was changed to Abraham,
   and Sarai's name was changed to Sarah.
   Humanities—Description

83. VELÁSQUEZ : MAIDS OF HONOR :: (*a.* **Botticelli**, *b.* Bellini, *c.* Bosch,
   d. Uccello) : THE BIRTH OF VENUS

   (**a**) *Maids of Honor* is a famous painting by Velásquez; *The Birth of Venus*
   is a famous painting by Botticelli. Bellini painted many Christian scenes, like
   St. Francis in Ecstasy. The Garden of Earthly Delights is one of Bosch's famous paintings.
   Uccello painted the *Battle of San Romano* in a series of three paintings.
   Humanities—Description

84. CIVIL : (*a.* misdemeanor, *b.* larceny, *c.* **tort**, *d.* perjury) :: CRIMINAL :
   FELONY

   (**c**) A tort is a civil offense, while a felony is a criminal offense.
   Social Science—Class

85. GREGORIAN : NOVEMBER :: FRENCH REVOLUTIONARY :
   (*a.* Novembre, *b.* February, *c.* Julian, *d.* **Thermidor**)

   (**d**) Thermidor in the French Revolutionary calendar corresponded to
   November in the conventional Gregorian calendar in their both being the
   11th month. The months of the French Revolutionary calendar (starting
   in September) were Vendémiaire, Brumaire, Frimaire, Nivôse, Pluviôse,
   Ventôse, Germinal, Floréal, Prairial, Messidor, Thermidor, Fructidor.
   Humanities—Similarity/Contrast

86. GOLDEN RULE : LUKE :: CATEGORICAL IMPERATIVE : (*a.* Hegel,
   b. **Kant**, *c.* Ardrey, *d.* Lorenz)

   (**b**) The golden rule—"Do unto others as you would have them do unto
   you"—is found in the Gospel of Luke. The categorical imperative—"One's
   behavior should be governed by the same principles that one would have
   govern other people's behavior"—is found in the philosophy of Kant.
   Humanities—Description

87. EQUIVOCATION : (*a.* perversity, *b.* exultation, **c. veracity**, *d.* perjury) :: UNCERTAINTY : CERTAINTY

(**c**) *Equivocation* is the opposite of *veracity. Uncertainty* is the opposite of *certainty.*
Vocabulary—Similarity/Contrast

88. TIMBREL : (*a.* cymbals, *b.* zither, *c.* flute, **d. tambourine**) :: LUTE : GUITAR

(**d**) A timbrel is an early form of tambourine; a lute is an early form of guitar.
Humanities—Class

89. (*a.* Apollo, *b.* Phaeton, **c. Furies**, *d.* Sirens) : EUMENIDES :: PLUTO : HADES

(**c**) The Furies and the Eumenides were one and the same; similarly, Pluto and Hades were one and the same. Apollo was the legendary son of Zeus and Leto; he is the Greek and Roman god of light, prophesy, poetry, and music. Phaeton was the son of Helios; he tried to drive his father's chariot and was killed when he came too close to Earth. A siren is a sea nymph that lures sailors into their demise.
Humanities—Similarity/Contrast

90. JOSEPH K. : TRIAL :: GREGOR SAMSA : (*a.* Hunger Artist, *b.* Death in Venice, *c.* The Flies, **d. Metamorphosis**)

(**d**) Joseph K. is the main character in Kafka's *The Trial.* Gregor Samsa is the main character in Kafka's *The Metamorphosis. Death in Venice* is by Thomas Mann; *The Flies* is by Jean-Paul Sartre; *A Hunger Artist* is by Franz Kafka.
Humanities—Description

91. $\sqrt{2} : \sqrt{18} :: 1 : $ (*a.* 2, ***b.* 3**, *c.* 6, *d.* 9)

(**b**) The ratio of $\sqrt{2}$ to $\sqrt{18}$ is equal to the ratio of 1 to 3.
Mathematics—Equality/Negation

92. TRANSUBSTANTIATION : ACTUAL :: (*a.* insubstantiation, *b.* absubstantiation, **c. consubstantiation**, *d.* desubstantiation) : SYMBOLIC

(**c**) According to the doctrine of transubstantiation, the actual substances of the bread and of the wine in the Eucharist are changed into the body and blood of Christ; according to the doctrine of consubstantiation, the bread and wine are merely symbolic.
Humanities—Description

93. ABACUS : COMPUTER :: DAGUERROTYPE : (*a.* stereo, ***b.* photograph**, *c.* tape recorder, *d.* telephone)

(**b**) The abacus is a primitive computer; the daguerrotype is a primitive photograph.
Humanities—Description

94. DECLARATION OF INDEPENDENCE : PHILADELPHIA :: MAGNA CARTA : (*a.* Gloucester, ***b.* Runnymede**, *c.* Canterbury, *d.* Norwalk)

(**b**) The Declaration of Independence (1776) was signed in Philadelphia; the Magna Carta was signed at Runnymede (1215). The Magna Carta was a charter given to the English barons by King John to recognize their rights and privileges.
Humanities—Description

95. MINTON : ROYAL DOULTON :: MIKASA (*a.* Sony, *b.* Rosenthal, *c.* Lenox, ***d.* Noritake**)

(**d**) Minton and Royal Doulton are both English makers of fine china, while Mikasa and Noritake are both Japanese makers of fine china. Rosenthal is a German brand of china. Lenox is an American brand of china.
General Information—Class

96. SHYLOCK : SCROOGE :: DON JUAN : (*a.* Antonio, *b.* Don Giovanni, ***c.* Lothario**, *d.* Don Quixote)

(**c**) In literature, Shylock (of *The Merchant of Venice by Shakespeare*) and Scrooge (of *A Christmas Carol* by Charles Dickens) are both miserly characters, while Don Juan (many authors, e.g. Moliere and Byron) and Lothario (of *The Fair Penitent* by Nicholas Rowe) are both great lovers.
Humanities—Class

97. SKINNER : EMPIRICIST :: (*a.* Watson, *b.* Aristotle, ***c.* Chomsky**, *d.* Locke) : RATIONALIST

(**c**) Skinner was a philosophical empiricist, while Chomsky is a philosophical rationalist. Watson was a behaviorist; Locke was an empiricist; Aristotle was a Greek empiricist philosopher.
Social Science—Description

98. MOHAWK : IROQUOIS :: (*a.* Apache, ***b.* Zuni**, *c.* Seminole, *d.* Creek) : PUEBLO

(**b**) The Mohawks were one of the Iroquois Indian tribes; the Zuni were one of the Pueblo Indian tribes. The Seminoles are a Native American people from the American southeast who now reside primarily in Florida. The Creek are closely related to the Seminoles and call themselves Muscogee today. Apache is a term that refers to several groups of Native Americans who lived in the Great Plains and the southwest of the United States.
Social Science—Class

99. (*a.* half-life, *b.* radioactivity, *c.* atomic mass, ***d.* atomic number**) : ISOTOPE :: ATOMIC WEIGHT : ISOBAR

(**d**) Chemical isotopes have the same atomic number; chemical isobars have the same atomic weight.
Natural Science—Description

100. SARACEN : (*a.* Hindu, ***b.* Muslim**, *c.* Shintoist, *d.* Taoist) :: EPISCOPALIAN : ANGLICAN

(**b**) A Saracen is a Muslim. An Episcopalian is an Anglican.
Humanities—Similarity/Contrast

101. WATERGATE : NIXON :: IRAN CONTRA : (*a.* Ford, *b.* Carter, ***c.* Reagan**, *d.* Bush)

(**c**) The Watergate and Iran Contra scandals respectively marred the presidential administrations of Nixon and Reagan. Watergate is a term for a series of scandals that resulted in President Nixon's resignation in 1974. The Iran Contra affair was a series of scandals under Ronald Reagan that involved arms sales to Iran and funding of Contra militants in Nicaragua.
General Information—Description

102. GALAPAGOS : SAMOA :: (*a.* Linnaeus, *b.* Magellan, *c.* Rhodes, ***d.* Darwin**) : MEAD

(**d**) Charles Darwin began some of his most prominent scientific work in the South Pacific Galapagos Islands. Likewise, Margaret Mead began some of her most prominent scientific work in the South Pacific, in Samoa.
Natural Science—Description

103. BIGGER THOMAS : (*a.* New York, ***b.* Chicago**, *c.* St. Louis, *d.* Montgomery) :: RODION RASKOLNIKOV : ST. PETERSBURG

(**b**) Fictional characters Bigger Thomas (in *Native Son* by Richard Wright) and Rodion Raskolnikov (in *Crime and Punishment* by Fyodor Dostoyevsky) despair after committing murders in their respective homes of Chicago and St. Petersburg.
Humanities—Description

104. TAXONOMY : CLASSIFY :: NOMENCLATURE : (*a.* order, *b.* color, ***c.* name**, *d.* number)

(**c**) A taxonomy is the principled system by which things are classified. Nomenclature is the principled system by which things are named.
Vocabulary—Description

105. PHYSIOGNOMY : (***a. face***, *b.* stature, *c.* physiology, *d.* gate) ::
CHIROMANCY : PALM

(**a**) Physiognomy is the art of determining something about a person from
his/her face. Chiromancy is the art of determining something about a person
from his/her palm.
General Information—Description

106. MUTINY : SHIP CAPTAIN :: COUP D'ÉTAT : (*a.* college dean,
b. military commander, ***c. government***, *d.* CEO)

(**c**) Just as a mutiny typically refers to the overthrow of a ship's captain,
so a *coup d'état* traditionally refers to the overthrow of a government.
Vocabulary—Description

107. (***a. exaggerated***, *b.* understated, *c.* metaphorical, *d.* literal) :
HYPERBOLIC :: DRAMATIC : HISTRIONIC

(**a**) An exaggerated statement may be described as hyperbolic just as
a dramatic display may be described as histrionic.
Vocabulary—Similarity/Contrast

108. APPLE : EVE :: (*a.* pear, ***b. pomegranate***, *c.* peach, *d.* papaya) :
PERSEPHONE

(**b**) Eve was punished for eating the forbidden fruit that tradition in the
Bible holds was an apple, and Persephone was punished in Greek mythology
for eating the forbidden fruit pomegranate.
Humanities—Description

109. CEMENTUM : ROOT :: (*a.* bone, *b.* fluoride, *c.* keratin, ***d. enamel***) :
CROWN

(**d**) Cementum makes up the outer surface of a tooth's root just as enamel
makes up the outer surface of a tooth's crown.
Natural Science—Part/Whole

110. (*a.* acorn, *b.* cornmeal, ***c. millet***, *d.* filbert) : BULGUR :: QUINOA :
BARLEY

(**c**) Millet, bulgur, quinoa, and barley are all whole grains.
General Information—Class

111. MOBY DICK : LEVIATHAN :: MELVILLE : (*a.* Rousseau, *b.* **Hobbes**, *c.* Kant, *d.* Smith)

(**b**) Melville is famous for his book *Moby Dick*, and Hobbes is famous for his book *Leviathan*. Rousseau is known for *Pygmalion* and the *Confessions of a Solitary Walker*. Kant is famous for his *Critique of Pure Reason*. Smith the author of *The Theory of Moral Sentiments*.
Humanities—Description

112. (*a.* **Locke**, *b.* Galileo, *c.* Bacon, *d.* Calvin) : ENLIGHTENMENT :: DESCARTES : RENAISSANCE

(**a**) Locke was a philosopher of the Enlightenment, as Descartes was a philosopher of the Renaissance. Galileo was an Italian physicist and astronomer who improved the telescope and is called the "father of modern observational astronomy." He was a supporter of Copernicanism. Bacon was an English philosopher and statesman. Calvin was the founder of the Presbyterian church.
Social Science—Description

113. STEINWAY : (*a.* **piano**, *b.* cello, *c.* flute, *d.* organ) :: STRADIVARIUS : VIOLIN

(**a**) Steinway is a maker of highly prized pianos, as Stradivarius is a maker of highly prized violins.
Humanities—Description

114. TERKEL : (*a.* manuscripts, *b.* photographs, *c.* **oral histories**, *d.* maps) :: LOMAX : FOLK MUSIC

(**c**) Terkel was a pioneering anthologist of oral histories and Lomax was a pioneering anthologist of folk music.
Humanities—Description

115. 6×10^{23} : (*a.* e, *b.* **Avogadro's number**, *c.* i, *d.* Planck's constant) :: 3.14 : PI

(**b**) 6×10^{23} (rounded) is also known as Avogadro's number. Likewise, 3.14 (rounded) is known as pi, or the symbol π.
Natural Science—Equality/Negation

116. CIRRUS : NIMBUS :: CUMULUS : (*a.* bilious, *b.* birrus, *c.* mobius, *d.* **stratus**)

(**d**) Cirrus, nimbus, cumulus, and stratus are all types of clouds. Bilious refers to the bile; a birrus is a coarse kind of cloth worn by poor people in the Middle Ages. Mobius was a German mathematician who developed the Mobius strip.
Natural Science—Class

117. SOCIALISM : (***a.* state**, *b.* family, *c.* town, *d.* universal) :: CAPITALISM : PRIVATE

(**a**) Socialism is an economic system based on state ownership of capital. Capitalism is an economic system based on private ownership of capital.
Social Science—Description

118. (*a.* Pikes Peak, *b.* Mt. Kilimanjaro, ***c.* Mt. Vesuvius**, *d.* K2) : MT. ST. HELENS :: EXTINCT : ACTIVE

(**c**) Mt. Vesuvius is an extinct volcano whereas Mt. St. Helens is an active volcano.
Natural Science—Description

119. IMPERIOUS : IMPERVIOUS :: (*a.* grandiose, *b.* disbelieving, *c.* judgmental, ***d.* domineering**) : IMMUNE

(**d**) Imperious means domineering just as impervious means immune.
Vocabulary—Similarity/Contrast

120. NEUTRAL : NEUTRON :: NEGATIVE : (*a.* atom, ***b.* electron**, *c.* positron, *d.* negatron)

(**b**) Neutrons are subatomic particles with a neutral charge. Electrons are subatomic particles with a negative charge.
Natural Science—Description

PRACTICE TEST 7

Item Classification Chart

		RELATIONSHIP					
CONTENT		Similarity/ Contrast	Description	Class	Completion	Part/ Whole	Equality/ Negation	Nonsemantic
	Vocabulary	42, 45, 52, 54, 61, 65, 66, 67, 68, 71, 74, 75, 77, 78, 80, 87, 107, 119	40, 69, 104, 106		29			
	General Information	6, 17, 20, 60, 63	2, 8, 13, 15, 18, 22, 23, 31, 32, 36, 101, 105	25, 51, 81, 95, 110	24			
	Humanities	56, 85, 89, 100	3, 11, 14, 27, 43, 47, 57, 62, 64, 73, 76, 82, 83, 86, 90, 92, 93, 94, 103, 108, 111, 113, 114	34, 39, 55, 88, 96	16, 70			
	Social Science		9, 26, 41, 97, 112, 117	12, 49, 84, 98		72		
	Natural Science	50	1, 5, 7, 19, 28, 30, 33, 35, 48, 53, 58, 59, 99, 102, 118, 120	116		37, 38, 109	115	
	Mathematics					4	44, 79, 91	
	Nonsemantic							10, 21, 46

Answer Sheet
PRACTICE TEST 8

1 Ⓐ Ⓑ Ⓒ Ⓓ	31 Ⓐ Ⓑ Ⓒ Ⓓ	61 Ⓐ Ⓑ Ⓒ Ⓓ	91 Ⓐ Ⓑ Ⓒ Ⓓ
2 Ⓐ Ⓑ Ⓒ Ⓓ	32 Ⓐ Ⓑ Ⓒ Ⓓ	62 Ⓐ Ⓑ Ⓒ Ⓓ	92 Ⓐ Ⓑ Ⓒ Ⓓ
3 Ⓐ Ⓑ Ⓒ Ⓓ	33 Ⓐ Ⓑ Ⓒ Ⓓ	63 Ⓐ Ⓑ Ⓒ Ⓓ	93 Ⓐ Ⓑ Ⓒ Ⓓ
4 Ⓐ Ⓑ Ⓒ Ⓓ	34 Ⓐ Ⓑ Ⓒ Ⓓ	64 Ⓐ Ⓑ Ⓒ Ⓓ	94 Ⓐ Ⓑ Ⓒ Ⓓ
5 Ⓐ Ⓑ Ⓒ Ⓓ	35 Ⓐ Ⓑ Ⓒ Ⓓ	65 Ⓐ Ⓑ Ⓒ Ⓓ	95 Ⓐ Ⓑ Ⓒ Ⓓ
6 Ⓐ Ⓑ Ⓒ Ⓓ	36 Ⓐ Ⓑ Ⓒ Ⓓ	66 Ⓐ Ⓑ Ⓒ Ⓓ	96 Ⓐ Ⓑ Ⓒ Ⓓ
7 Ⓐ Ⓑ Ⓒ Ⓓ	37 Ⓐ Ⓑ Ⓒ Ⓓ	67 Ⓐ Ⓑ Ⓒ Ⓓ	97 Ⓐ Ⓑ Ⓒ Ⓓ
8 Ⓐ Ⓑ Ⓒ Ⓓ	38 Ⓐ Ⓑ Ⓒ Ⓓ	68 Ⓐ Ⓑ Ⓒ Ⓓ	98 Ⓐ Ⓑ Ⓒ Ⓓ
9 Ⓐ Ⓑ Ⓒ Ⓓ	39 Ⓐ Ⓑ Ⓒ Ⓓ	69 Ⓐ Ⓑ Ⓒ Ⓓ	99 Ⓐ Ⓑ Ⓒ Ⓓ
10 Ⓐ Ⓑ Ⓒ Ⓓ	40 Ⓐ Ⓑ Ⓒ Ⓓ	70 Ⓐ Ⓑ Ⓒ Ⓓ	100 Ⓐ Ⓑ Ⓒ Ⓓ
11 Ⓐ Ⓑ Ⓒ Ⓓ	41 Ⓐ Ⓑ Ⓒ Ⓓ	71 Ⓐ Ⓑ Ⓒ Ⓓ	101 Ⓐ Ⓑ Ⓒ Ⓓ
12 Ⓐ Ⓑ Ⓒ Ⓓ	42 Ⓐ Ⓑ Ⓒ Ⓓ	72 Ⓐ Ⓑ Ⓒ Ⓓ	102 Ⓐ Ⓑ Ⓒ Ⓓ
13 Ⓐ Ⓑ Ⓒ Ⓓ	43 Ⓐ Ⓑ Ⓒ Ⓓ	73 Ⓐ Ⓑ Ⓒ Ⓓ	103 Ⓐ Ⓑ Ⓒ Ⓓ
14 Ⓐ Ⓑ Ⓒ Ⓓ	44 Ⓐ Ⓑ Ⓒ Ⓓ	74 Ⓐ Ⓑ Ⓒ Ⓓ	104 Ⓐ Ⓑ Ⓒ Ⓓ
15 Ⓐ Ⓑ Ⓒ Ⓓ	45 Ⓐ Ⓑ Ⓒ Ⓓ	75 Ⓐ Ⓑ Ⓒ Ⓓ	105 Ⓐ Ⓑ Ⓒ Ⓓ
16 Ⓐ Ⓑ Ⓒ Ⓓ	46 Ⓐ Ⓑ Ⓒ Ⓓ	76 Ⓐ Ⓑ Ⓒ Ⓓ	106 Ⓐ Ⓑ Ⓒ Ⓓ
17 Ⓐ Ⓑ Ⓒ Ⓓ	47 Ⓐ Ⓑ Ⓒ Ⓓ	77 Ⓐ Ⓑ Ⓒ Ⓓ	107 Ⓐ Ⓑ Ⓒ Ⓓ
18 Ⓐ Ⓑ Ⓒ Ⓓ	48 Ⓐ Ⓑ Ⓒ Ⓓ	78 Ⓐ Ⓑ Ⓒ Ⓓ	108 Ⓐ Ⓑ Ⓒ Ⓓ
19 Ⓐ Ⓑ Ⓒ Ⓓ	49 Ⓐ Ⓑ Ⓒ Ⓓ	79 Ⓐ Ⓑ Ⓒ Ⓓ	109 Ⓐ Ⓑ Ⓒ Ⓓ
20 Ⓐ Ⓑ Ⓒ Ⓓ	50 Ⓐ Ⓑ Ⓒ Ⓓ	80 Ⓐ Ⓑ Ⓒ Ⓓ	110 Ⓐ Ⓑ Ⓒ Ⓓ
21 Ⓐ Ⓑ Ⓒ Ⓓ	51 Ⓐ Ⓑ Ⓒ Ⓓ	81 Ⓐ Ⓑ Ⓒ Ⓓ	111 Ⓐ Ⓑ Ⓒ Ⓓ
22 Ⓐ Ⓑ Ⓒ Ⓓ	52 Ⓐ Ⓑ Ⓒ Ⓓ	82 Ⓐ Ⓑ Ⓒ Ⓓ	112 Ⓐ Ⓑ Ⓒ Ⓓ
23 Ⓐ Ⓑ Ⓒ Ⓓ	53 Ⓐ Ⓑ Ⓒ Ⓓ	83 Ⓐ Ⓑ Ⓒ Ⓓ	113 Ⓐ Ⓑ Ⓒ Ⓓ
24 Ⓐ Ⓑ Ⓒ Ⓓ	54 Ⓐ Ⓑ Ⓒ Ⓓ	84 Ⓐ Ⓑ Ⓒ Ⓓ	114 Ⓐ Ⓑ Ⓒ Ⓓ
25 Ⓐ Ⓑ Ⓒ Ⓓ	55 Ⓐ Ⓑ Ⓒ Ⓓ	85 Ⓐ Ⓑ Ⓒ Ⓓ	115 Ⓐ Ⓑ Ⓒ Ⓓ
26 Ⓐ Ⓑ Ⓒ Ⓓ	56 Ⓐ Ⓑ Ⓒ Ⓓ	86 Ⓐ Ⓑ Ⓒ Ⓓ	116 Ⓐ Ⓑ Ⓒ Ⓓ
27 Ⓐ Ⓑ Ⓒ Ⓓ	57 Ⓐ Ⓑ Ⓒ Ⓓ	87 Ⓐ Ⓑ Ⓒ Ⓓ	117 Ⓐ Ⓑ Ⓒ Ⓓ
28 Ⓐ Ⓑ Ⓒ Ⓓ	58 Ⓐ Ⓑ Ⓒ Ⓓ	88 Ⓐ Ⓑ Ⓒ Ⓓ	118 Ⓐ Ⓑ Ⓒ Ⓓ
29 Ⓐ Ⓑ Ⓒ Ⓓ	59 Ⓐ Ⓑ Ⓒ Ⓓ	89 Ⓐ Ⓑ Ⓒ Ⓓ	119 Ⓐ Ⓑ Ⓒ Ⓓ
30 Ⓐ Ⓑ Ⓒ Ⓓ	60 Ⓐ Ⓑ Ⓒ Ⓓ	90 Ⓐ Ⓑ Ⓒ Ⓓ	120 Ⓐ Ⓑ Ⓒ Ⓓ

Answer Sheet

Practice Test 8

Directions: In each of the following questions, you will find three initial terms and, in parentheses, four answer options designated *a*, *b*, *c*, and *d*. You are to select from the four answer options the one that best completes the analogy with the three initial terms. To record your answers, use the answer sheet provided.

Time: 60 minutes

1. STOCKHOLM : (*a*. Switzerland, *b*. Austria, *c*. Finland, *d*. Sweden) :: PARIS : FRANCE

2. ESCARGOTS : FRENCH :: SUKIYAKI : (*a*. Japanese, *b*. German, *c*. Hungarian, *d*. Mexican)

3. COBBLER : SHOES :: TAILOR : (*a*. needles, *b*. clothes, *c*. threads, *d*. thimbles)

4. (*a*. black, *b*. yellow, *c*. red, *d*. blue) : SULFUR :: WHITE : GYPSUM

5. TRANSITIVE : HIT :: (*a*. expletive, *b*. intransitive, *c*. nominative, *d*. subjunctive) : IS

6. COMPOSITE : 8 :: PRIME : (*a*. 4, *b*. 6, *c*. 7, *d*. 9)

7. FRESCO : PLASTER :: TAPESTRY : (*a*. stone, *b*. metal, *c*. cloth, *d*. wood)

8. VEGETARIAN : MEAT :: TEETOTALER : (*a*. fruit, *b*. alcoholic beverages, *c*. cooked food, *d*. tobacco)

9. TRAFALGAR SQUARE : (*a*. London, *b*. Florence, *c*. Moscow, *d*. Paris) :: TIMES SQUARE : NEW YORK

10. (*a*. appliance, *b*. food, *c*. explosive, *d*. automobile) :: TNT :: COUNTRY : U.S.A.

11. YELLOW : COWARDLY :: (*a*. blue, *b*. black, *c*. red, *d*. green) : INEXPERIENCED

12. 2 : QUART :: (*a*. 1, *b*. 4, *c*. 8, *d*. 16) : GALLON

13. RED FLAG : REVOLUTION :: WHITE FLAG : (*a*. victory, *b*. surrender, *c*. established order, *d*. purity)

14. ZEBRA : STRIPES :: LEOPARD : (*a.* spots, *b.* stripes, *c.* diagonals, *d.* zigzags)

15. (*a.* tyrant, *b.* wealthy merchant, *c.* explorer, *d.* pirate) : BUCCANEER :: SETTLER : PIONEER

16. CENTIGRADE : 100 :: FAHRENHEIT : (*a.* 0, *b.* 32, *c.* 100, *d.* 212)

17. (*a.* 1, *b.* 5, *c.* 20, *d.* 25) : SILVER :: 50 : GOLD

18. BEEF : STEER :: MUTTON : (*a.* ox, *b.* sheep, *c.* deer, *d.* goat)

19. ATOM : (*a.* molecule, *b.* electron, *c.* nucleus, *d.* gamma ray) :: TREE : FOREST

20. IGNORANCE : (*a.* intelligence, *b.* knowledge, *c.* foresight, *d.* attention) :: STUPIDITY : INTELLIGENCE

21. NONAGENARIAN : 90 :: OCTOGENARIAN : (*a.* 60, *b.* 70, *c.* 80, *d.* 100)

22. LISBON : (*a.* Spain, *b.* Portugal, *c.* Hungary, *d.* Denmark) :: THE HAGUE : NETHERLANDS

23. WAMPUM : (*a.* Dutchman, *b.* Portuguese, *c.* Pakistani, *d.* American Indian) :: DOUBLOON : SPANIARD

24. GREEK ALPHABET : GREEK :: LATIN ALPHABET : (*a.* Russian, *b.* Cyrillic, *c.* Sanskrit, *d.* English)

25. (*a.* 90, *b.* 180, *c.* 270, *d.* 360) : TRIANGLE :: 360 : SQUARE

26. COLUMBIA : (*a.* South America, *b.* North America, *c.* United States, *d.* Brazil) :: BRITANNIA : BRITAIN

27. FINALE : MUSICAL COMPOSITION :: (*a.* check, *b.* checkmate, *c.* rook, *d.* jeopardy) : CHESS

28. YAHWEH : JUDAISM :: ALLAH : (*a.* Islam, *b.* Judaism, *c.* Taoism, *d.* Confucianism)

29. (*a.* nominative, *b.* dative, *c.* accusative, *d.* ablative) : OBJECTIVE :: SHE : HIM

30. RECTANGLE : OCTAGON :: (*a.* triangle, *b.* square, *c.* pentagon, *d.* rhombus) : HEXAGON

31. (*a.* prize, *b.* damn, *c.* reflect, *d.* complete) : PRAISE :: COMPLEMENT : COMPLIMENT

32. SUB : BUS :: TAR : (*a.* car, *b.* road, *c.* vehicle, *d.* rat)

33. MANDATORY : (*a.* laudatory, *b.* damning, *c.* optional, *d.* compulsory) :: DEFINITE : UNCERTAIN

34. ONE : LAND :: TWO : (*a.* air, *b.* sea, *c.* ground, *d.* island)

35. (*a.* eat, *b.* drink, *c.* sever, *d.* mend) : CHALICE :: DIG : SHOVEL

36. CONSONANT : (*a.* syncopated, *b.* rhythmic, *c.* euphemistic, *d.* euphonious) :: DISSONANT : DISCORDANT

37. (*a.* Montague, *b.* Scali, *c.* Dunlop, *d.* Mineo) : ROMEO :: CAPULET : JULIET

38. EMANCIPATE : (*a.* emaciate, *b.* free, *c.* enslave, *d.* deliver) :: EMPTY : FULL

39. PALMISTRY : PALM :: PHRENOLOGY : (*a.* handwriting, *b.* EEG, *c.* eyes, *d.* skull)

40. (*a.* Columbia Gem, *b.* Union Jack, *c.* Royal Ensign, *d.* Fleur-de-Lis) : GREAT BRITAIN :: STARS AND STRIPES : U.S.A.

41. COMMON LOG : 10 :: NATURAL LOG : (*a.* π, *b.* e, *c.* i, *d.* 1)

42. MAE WEST : LIFE JACKET :: MICKEY FINN : (*a.* blackjack, *b.* Molotov cocktail, *c.* drugged liquor, *d.* time bomb)

43. EARTH : AIR :: (*a.* bile, *b.* carbon, *c.* phlogiston, *d.* fire) : WATER

44. CAMUS : STRANGER :: (*a.* Sartre, *b.* Camus, *c.* Mauriac, *d.* Ionesco) : PLAGUE

45. DOG : PIE :: HOT : (*a.* cold, *b.* cat, *c.* pizza, *d.* cake)

46. PIETÀ : MICHELANGELO :: THE KISS : (*a.* Rodin, *b.* Pisano, *c.* Ghiberti, *d.* da Vinci)

47. (*a.* Congress of Vienna, *b.* League of Nations, *c.* Warsaw Pact, *d.* NATO) : UNITED NATIONS :: GASLIGHT : ELECTRIC LIGHT

48. CARAT : (*a.* size, *b.* weight, *c.* brilliance, *d.* value) :: ACRE : AREA

49. $a + b : b + a :: a(b + a)b :$ (*a.* $2a^2b^2$, *b.* $(a + b)^2$, *c.* $a^2b + ab^2$, *d.* $a^2b^2 + ab$)

50. FRANCIS CRICK : STRUCTURE OF DNA MOLECULE :: MARIE CURIE : (*a.* nobelium, *b.* uranium, *c.* radium, *d.* plutonium)

51. ANALOG : SLIDE RULE :: DIGITAL : (*a.* odometer, *b.* ruler, *c.* compass, *d.* protractor)

52. CHARLOTTE'S : PILGRIM'S :: WEB : (*a.* Follies, *b.* Progress, *c.* Pretense, *d.* Journey)

53. VOID : VACUUM :: FULL : (*a.* replete, *b.* deplete, *c.* compact, *d.* empty)

54. HIGH : DIE :: (*a.* gregarious, *b.* reticent, *c.* low, *d.* buy) : SHY

55. (*a.* retina, *b.* iris, *c.* lens, *d.* cone) : ROD :: CHROMATIC : ACHROMATIC

56. BOVINE : (*a.* jackal, *b.* monkey, *c.* ox, *d.* rabbit) :: URSINE : BEAR

57. (*a.* Plato, *b.* Aristotle, *c.* Leibniz, *d.* Locke) : REPUBLIC :: DESCARTES : MEDITATIONS

58. DEER : DEER :: CORPUS : (*a.* corpi, *b.* corpuses, *c.* corpora, *d.* corpes)

59. BUDAPEST : HANOI :: HUNGARY : (*a.* Cambodia, *b.* Laos, *c.* Thailand, *d.* Vietnam)

60. PROMISED LAND : CANAAN :: LAND OF NOD : (*a.* wakefulness, *b.* hell, *c.* sleep, *d.* heaven)

61. MISOGYNIST : WOMEN :: MISOGAMIST : (*a.* men, *b.* people, *c.* marriage, *d.* religion)

62. (*a.* Achilles, *b.* Hector, *c.* Paris, *d.* Troilus) : HELEN :: PLUTO : PROSERPINA

63. BENIGN : BENEVOLENT :: (*a.* beneficent, *b.* nefarious, *c.* tortuous, *d.* voracious) : MALEVOLENT

64. BLOCKHEAD : LUNKHEAD :: MUTTONHEAD : (*a.* fathead, *b.* sleepyhead, *c.* bighead, *d.* egghead)

65. UNCLE TOM : SERVILE :: DUTCH UNCLE : (*a.* hoary, *b.* kind, *c.* stern, *d.* stingy)

66. ALPHA : (*a.* gamma, *b.* zed, *c.* epsilon, *d.* omega) :: A : Z

67. THIAMINE : ASCORBIC ACID :: B_1 : (*a.* B_6, *b.* B_{12}, *c.* C, *d.* E)

68. BRAZIL : (*a.* Portuguese, *b.* Spanish, *c.* French, *d.* Brazilian) :: AUSTRIA : GERMAN

69. CENTURY : EON :: DOZEN : (*a.* one hundred, *b.* gross, *c.* zero, *d.* myriad)

70. SITTING BULL : SIOUX :: GERONIMO : (*a.* Apache, *b.* Pueblo, *c.* Mohawk, *d.* Seminole)

71. AUTOCRACY : AUTARCHY :: MONARCHY : (*a.* democracy, *b.* anarchy, *c.* oligarchy, *d.* kingdom)

72. GOGGLE-EYED : BULGING :: HOOK-NOSED : (*a.* opercular, *b.* oviparous, *c.* ovine, *d.* aquiline)

73. NEPTUNE : DIANA :: SEA : (*a.* hearth, *b.* sun, *c.* moon, *d.* home)

74. EXPEL : DRIVE AWAY :: EXPIATE : (*a.* atone for, *b.* talk at length, *c.* forgive, *d.* speak briefly)

75. LARGO : SLOW :: (*a.* moderato, *b.* allegro, *c.* piano, *d.* fortissimo) : FAST

76. (*a.* with faith, *b.* with truth, *c.* with passion, *d.* with authority) : EX CATHEDRA :: ON THE FACE : EX FACIE

77. FIFE : CLARINET :: TROMBONE : (*a.* lute, *b.* bagpipe, *c.* piano, *d.* violin)

78. PARASITE : LIVING :: (*a.* saprophyte, *b.* neophyte, *c.* pteridophyte, *d.* bryophyte) : DEAD

79. PRINCE : MACHIAVELLI :: PETIT PRINCE : (*a.* Saint-Exupéry, *b.* Mauriac, *c.* Camus, *d.* Lescaut)

80. ITALY : LIRA :: (*a.* Switzerland, *b.* Netherlands, *c.* Portugal, *d.* Sweden) : GUILDER

81. DEMOSTHENES : (*a.* Cicero, *b.* Socrates, *c.* Pericles, *d.* Ovid) :: HOMER : VIRGIL

82. (*a.* mg, *b.* gg, *c.* kg, *d.* cg) : g :: m : mm

83. CIPANGO : JAPAN :: CATHAY : (*a.* China, *b.* Tibet, *c.* Polynesia, *d.* Mongolia)

84. IMPROMPTU : EXTEMPORE :: PROBITY : (*a.* open-mindedness, *b.* dishonesty, *c.* narrow-mindedness, *d.* honesty)

85. FERMI : NUCLEAR PHYSICS :: JANE ADDAMS : (*a.* nursing, *b.* physics, *c.* social work, *d.* drama)

86. (*a.* Inferno, *b.* Decameron, *c.* The Wasteland, *d.* No Exit) : CANTERBURY TALES :: ANTHOLOGY : COLLECTION

87. RICHELIEU : (*a.* Cushing, *b.* Mazarin, *c.* Metternich, *d.* Marat) :: KENNEDY : JOHNSON

88. (*a.* uncertainty, *b.* luck, *c.* sample, *d.* variance) : POPULATION :: STATISTIC : PARAMETER

89. REGAN : GONERIL :: LEAH : (*a.* Jacob, *b.* Rebeccah, *c.* Isaac, *d.* Rachel)

90. TEMPUS : CARPE :: FUGIT : (*a.* cibus, *b.* mater, *c.* diem, *d.* tempum)

91. ERSATZ : (*a.* genuine, *b.* superior, *c.* inferior, *d.* fake) :: FRESH : RANCID

92. EVE : DEED :: MADAM : (*a.* cuckoo, *b.* swoon, *c.* noon, *d.* pool)

93. SLEEPY : SOMNOLENT :: GROGGY : (*a.* asleep, *b.* unsteady, *c.* awake, *d.* dead)

94. AXON : DEPART :: (*a.* neuron, *b.* ganglion, *c.* dendrites, *d.* plasma) : APPROACH

95. BUDGE : TENNIS :: LOUIS : (*a.* hockey, *b.* football, *c.* baseball, *d.* boxing)

96. BLOOD : MELANCHOLY :: CHOLER : (*a.* plasma, *b.* lymph, *c.* phlegm, *d.* saliva)

97. MEXICO : YORK :: CAROLINA : (*a.* Virginia, *b.* Oregon, *c.* Washington, *d.* Dakota)

98. ARGON : NEON :: XENON : (*a.* helium, *b.* oxygen, *c.* mercury, *d.* carbon)

99. HORN : ROLAND :: HARP : (*a.* Gideon, *b.* David, *c.* Moses, *d.* Samuel)

100. GLUTTON : FOOD :: SATYR : (*a.* punishment, *b.* glory, *c.* alcoholic beverages, *d.* sex)

101. ACUTE : (*a.* small, *b.* obtuse, *c.* intense, *d.* right) :: APOGEE : PERIGEE

102. (*a.* berate, *b.* refine, *c.* attenuate, *d.* foreshadow) : ADUMBRATE :: INTIMATE : HINT

103. PNEUMONECTOMY : LUNG :: (*a.* tonsillectomy, *b.* meningectomy, *c.* lobotomy, *d.* encephalotomy) : BRAIN

104. EMPATHY : (*a.* lungs, *b.* soul, *c.* pancreas, *d.* heart) :: BRAVERY : LIVER

105. CIRCUMSPECT : CIRCUMSCRIBE :: (*a.* prudent, *b.* navigate, *c.* rounded, *d.* investigate) : ENCIRCLE

106. DEARTH : (*a.* poverty, *b.* abundance, *c.* warmth, *d.* nothing) :: PAUCITY : PLENTY

107. CAP : LID :: KNEE : (*a.* leg, *b.* patella, *c.* heel, *d.* eye)

108. (*a.* bitterness, *b.* wittiness, *c.* frivolity, *d.* accusation) : ACRIMONIOUS :: FRUGALITY : PARSIMONIOUS

109. CAESAR : DELIVERY :: ACHILLES : (*a.* surgery, *b.* ligament, *c.* tendon, *d.* bone)

110. PROMETHEUS : BOUND :: ATLAS : (*a.* carried, *b.* tied, *c.* shrugged, *d.* grew)

111. GENGHIS KHAN : (*a.* China, *b.* Mongolia, *c.* Persia, *d.* Prussia) :: SHAKA : SOUTH AFRICA

112. (*a.* right to bear arms, *b.* prohibition of alcohol, *c.* right to remain silent, *d.* freedom of religion) : 18th AMENDMENT :: WOMEN'S SUFFRAGE : 19th AMENDMENT

113. KID : (*a.* wolf, *b.* goat, *c.* moose, *d.* kangaroo) :: CALF : WHALE

114. HOPI : (*a.* southwest, *b.* southeast, *c.* northwest, *d.* great plains) :: TLINGIT : NORTHWEST

115. PTOLEMY : EARTH :: COPERNICUS : (*a.* Mars, *b.* Venus, *c.* Moon, *d.* Sun)

116. ADAM SMITH : 18th CENTURY :: JOHN MAYNARD KEYNES : (*a.* 20th century, *b.* 19th century, *c.* 17th century, *d.* 16th century)

117. (*a.* Laos, *b.* Japan, *c.* Taiwan, *d.* China) : JUDO :: KOREA :
TAE KWON DO

118. KHMER ROUGE : POL POT :: COMMUNIST PARTY OF CHINA :
(*a.* Kuomintang, *b.* Confucius, *c.* Mao Zedong, *d.* Chiang Kai-shek)

119. SUEZ CANAL : (*a.* Turkey, *b.* Morocco, *c.* Egypt, *d.* Israel) :: PANAMA
CANAL : PANAMA

120. SOVIET UNION : (*a.* Portugal, *b.* Brazil, *c.* Cuba, *d.* Spain) ::
CHAGALL : DALI

Answer Key
PRACTICE TEST 8

1. **D**	31. **D**	61. **C**	91. **A**
2. **A**	32. **D**	62. **C**	92. **C**
3. **B**	33. **C**	63. **B**	93. **B**
4. **B**	34. **B**	64. **A**	94. **C**
5. **B**	35. **B**	65. **C**	95. **D**
6. **C**	36. **D**	66. **D**	96. **C**
7. **C**	37. **A**	67. **C**	97. **D**
8. **B**	38. **C**	68. **A**	98. **A**
9. **A**	39. **D**	69. **D**	99. **B**
10. **C**	40. **B**	70. **A**	100. **D**
11. **D**	41. **B**	71. **D**	101. **B**
12. **C**	42. **C**	72. **D**	102. **D**
13. **B**	43. **D**	73. **C**	103. **C**
14. **A**	44. **B**	74. **A**	104. **D**
15. **D**	45. **C**	75. **B**	105. **A**
16. **D**	46. **A**	76. **D**	106. **B**
17. **D**	47. **B**	77. **B**	107. **D**
18. **B**	48. **B**	78. **A**	108. **A**
19. **A**	49. **C**	79. **A**	109. **C**
20. **B**	50. **C**	80. **B**	110. **C**
21. **C**	51. **A**	81. **A**	111. **B**
22. **B**	52. **B**	82. **C**	112. **B**
23. **D**	53. **A**	83. **A**	113. **B**
24. **D**	54. **D**	84. **D**	114. **A**
25. **B**	55. **D**	85. **C**	115. **D**
26. **C**	56. **C**	86. **B**	116. **A**
27. **B**	57. **A**	87. **B**	117. **B**
28. **A**	58. **C**	88. **C**	118. **C**
29. **A**	59. **D**	89. **D**	119. **C**
30. **A**	60. **C**	90. **C**	120. **D**

EXPLANATION OF ANSWERS FOR PRACTICE TEST 8

In the following explanations of answers, explanations concerning the correct response are in a large font. Explanations regarding distracters (incorrect responses) that are not self-explaining or could be misinterpreted are in a smaller font in order to highlight the explanations of the answers that are correct.

1. STOCKHOLM : (*a.* Switzerland, *b.* Austria, *c.* Finland, *d.* **Sweden**) :: PARIS : FRANCE

   (**d**) Stockholm is the capital of Sweden. Paris is the capital of France. The capital of Switzerland is Bern, the capital of Austria is Vienna, and the capital of Finland is Helsinki.
   General Information—Description

2. ESCARGOTS : FRENCH :: SUKIYAKI : (*a.* **Japanese**, *b.* German, *c.* Hungarian, *d.* Mexican)

   (**a**) Escargots are a French food (snails). Sukiyaki is a Japanese food dish (beef hot pot).
   General Information—Description

3. COBBLER : SHOES :: TAILOR : (*a.* needles, *b.* **clothes**, *c.* threads, *d.* thimbles)

   (**b**) A cobbler mends shoes; a tailor mends clothes.
   General Information—Description

4. (*a.* black, *b.* **yellow**, *c.* red, *d.* blue) : SULFUR :: WHITE : GYPSUM

   (**b**) Sulfur is usually yellow; gypsum is usually white.
   Natural Science—Description

5. TRANSITIVE : HIT :: (*a.* expletive, *b.* **intransitive**, *c.* nominative, *d.* subjunctive) : IS

   (**b**) *Hit* is a transitive verb. *Is* is an intransitive verb.
   Humanities—Description

6. COMPOSITE : 8 :: PRIME : (*a.* 4, *b.* 6, *c.* **7**, *d.* 9)

   (**c**) 8 is a composite number. 7 is a prime number. A composite number can be divided into two or more integers (whole numbers). A prime number is a number that is evenly divisible only by itself and 1.
   Mathematics—Description

7. FRESCO : PLASTER :: TAPESTRY : (*a.* stone, *b.* metal, **c. cloth**, *d.* wood)

   (**c**) A fresco is made of plaster. A tapestry is made of cloth.
   Humanities—Description

8. VEGETARIAN : MEAT :: TEETOTALER : (*a.* fruit,
   b. alcoholic beverages, *c.* cooked food, *d.* tobacco)

   (**b**) A vegetarian will not eat meat. A teetotaler will not drink alcoholic beverages.
   General Information—Description

9. TRAFALGAR SQUARE : (**a. London**, *b.* Florence, *c.* Moscow, *d.* Paris) ::
   TIMES SQUARE : NEW YORK

   (**a**) Trafalgar Square is in London. Times Square is in New York.
   General Information—Description

10. (*a.* appliance, *b.* food, **c. explosive**, *d.* automobile) :: TNT :: COUNTRY :
    U.S.A.

    (**c**) TNT is an explosive. The United States is a country.
    General Information—Class

11. YELLOW : COWARDLY :: (*a.* blue, *b.* black, *c.* red, **d. green**) :
    INEXPERIENCED

    (**d**) A cowardly person is sometimes referred to as yellow. An inexperienced person is sometimes referred to as green. The color blue stands for sadness. The color black stands for death. The color red stands for heat.
    General Information—Similarity/Contrast

12. 2 : QUART :: (*a.* 1, *b.* 4, **c. 8**, *d.* 16) : GALLON

    (**c**) There are 2 pints in a quart, and 8 pints in a gallon.
    Mathematics—Class

13. RED FLAG : REVOLUTION :: WHITE FLAG : (*a.* victory, **b. surrender**,
    c. established order, *d.* purity)

    (**b**) A red flag is often used to signify revolution, while a white flag is often used to signify surrender.
    General Information—Description

14. ZEBRA : STRIPES :: LEOPARD : (**a. spots**, *b.* stripes, *c.* diagonals,
    d. zigzags)

    (**a**) A zebra has stripes; a leopard spots.
    General Information—Description

15. (*a.* tyrant, *b.* wealthy merchant, *c.* explorer, ***d.* pirate**) : BUCCANEER ::
SETTLER : PIONEER

    (**d**) A buccaneer is a pirate; a pioneer is a settler.
    General Information—Similarity/Contrast

16. CENTIGRADE : 100 :: FAHRENHEIT : (*a.* 0, *b.* 32, *c.* 100, ***d.* 212**)

    (**d**) One hundred degrees centigrade (the boiling point of water) is equal to
    212 degrees Fahrenheit. Zero degree centigrade (the freezing point of water) is equal
    to 32 degrees Fahrenheit.
    Natural Science—Equality/Negation

17. (*a.* 1, *b.* 5, *c.* 20, ***d.* 25**) : SILVER :: 50 : GOLD

    (**d**) A 25th anniversary is often referred to as a silver anniversary, while a
    50th anniversary is gold. The 1st anniversary is often referred to as a paper anniversary;
    the 5th anniversary as a wood anniversary, and the 20th anniversary as a china anniversary.
    General Information—Description

18. BEEF : STEER :: MUTTON : (*a.* ox, ***b.* sheep**, *c.* deer, *d.* goat)

    (**b**) Beef comes from a steer; mutton comes from a sheep.
    General Information—Description

19. ATOM : (***a.* molecule**, *b.* electron, *c.* nucleus, *d.* gamma ray) :: TREE :
FOREST

    (**a**) Atoms combine to form a molecule; trees combine to form a forest.
    Natural Science—Part/Whole

20. IGNORANCE : (*a.* intelligence, ***b.* knowledge**, *c.* foresight, *d.* attention) ::
STUPIDITY : INTELLIGENCE

    (**b**) Ignorance is the absence of knowledge. Stupidity is the absence of
    intelligence.
    Vocabulary—Similarity/Contrast

21. NONAGENARIAN : 90 :: OCTOGENARIAN : (*a.* 60, *b.* 70, ***c.* 80**,
d. 100)

    (**c**) A nonagenarian has lived to the age of 90; an octogenarian has lived to
    the age of 80. Somebody who has lived to the age of 70 is a septuagenarian.
    Vocabulary—Description

22. LISBON : (*a.* Spain, ***b.* Portugal**, *c.* Hungary, *d.* Denmark) ::
THE HAGUE : NETHERLANDS

(**b**) Lisbon is the capital of Portugal; The Hague is the capital of the
Netherlands. Madrid is the capital of Spain; Budapest is the capital of Hungary;
Copenhagen is the capital of Denmark.
General Information—Description

23. WAMPUM : (*a.* Dutchman, *b.* Portuguese, *c.* Pakistani,
***d.* American Indian**) :: DOUBLOON : SPANIARD

(**d**) Wampum was used as a coin by certain American Indian tribes;
the doubloon was formerly a Spanish coin.
Humanities—Description

24. GREEK ALPHABET : GREEK :: LATIN ALPHABET : (*a.* Russian,
b. Cyrillic, *c.* Sanskrit, ***d.* English**)

(**d**) The Greek language uses the Greek alphabet. The English language uses
the Latin alphabet.
Humanities—Description

25. (*a.* 90, ***b.* 180**, *c.* 270, *d.* 360) : TRIANGLE :: 360 : SQUARE

(**b**) A triangle has 180 degrees; a square has 360 degrees.
Mathematics—Description

26. COLUMBIA : (*a.* South America, *b.* North America, ***c.* U.S.A.**, *d.* Brazil) ::
BRITANNIA : BRITAIN

(**c**) Columbia is a poetic name for the United States (from Columbus);
Britannia is a poetic name for Britain.
General Information—Similarity/Contrast

27. FINALE : MUSICAL COMPOSITION :: (*a.* check, ***b.* checkmate**, *c.* rook,
d. jeopardy) : CHESS

(**b**) A finale ends a musical composition. Checkmate ends a game of chess.
General Information—Description

28. YAHWEH : JUDAISM :: ALLAH : (***a.* Islam**, *b.* Judaism, *c.* Taoism,
d. Confucianism)

(**a**) The concept of Yahweh in Judaism is analogous to the concept of
Allah in Islam.
Humanities—Description

Explanation of Answers

29. (*a.* **nominative**, *b.* dative, *c.* accusative, *d.* ablative) : OBJECTIVE :: SHE : HIM

    (**a**) The word *she* is in the nominative case; the word *him* is in the objective case.
    General Information—Description

30. RECTANGLE : OCTAGON :: (*a.* **triangle**, *b.* square, *c.* pentagon, *d.* rhombus) : HEXAGON

    (**a**) An octagon has twice as many sides as a rectangle; a hexagon has twice as many sides as a triangle.
    Mathematics—Equality/Negation

31. (*a.* prize, *b.* damn, *c.* reflect, *d.* **complete**) : PRAISE :: COMPLEMENT : COMPLIMENT

    (**d**) A complement completes something; a compliment praises something.
    Vocabulary—Similarity/Contrast

32. SUB : BUS :: TAR : (*a.* car, *b.* road, *c.* vehicle, *d.* **rat**)

    (**d**) *Bus* is *sub* spelled backwards; *rat* is *tar* spelled backwards.
    Nonsemantic

33. MANDATORY : (*a.* laudatory, *b.* damning, *c.* **optional**, *d.* compulsory) :: DEFINITE : UNCERTAIN

    (**c**) *Mandatory* and *optional* are antonyms; *definite* and *uncertain* are antonyms.
    Vocabulary—Similarity/Contrast

34. ONE : LAND :: TWO : (*a.* air, *b.* **sea**, *c.* ground, *d.* island)

    (**b**) Paul Revere was to be informed of the means by which British troops were coming through a system of shining lanterns. One lantern meant the British were coming by land; two meant they were coming by sea.
    Humanities—Description

35. (*a.* eat, *b.* **drink**, *c.* sever, *d.* mend) : CHALICE :: DIG : SHOVEL

    (**b**) One uses a chalice to drink from, and a shovel to dig with.
    Vocabulary—Description

36. CONSONANT : (*a.* syncopated, *b.* rhythmic, *c.* euphemistic, **d. euphonious**) :: DISSONANT : DISCORDANT

    (**d**) Consonant sounds are euphonious; dissonant sounds are discordant. *Euphonious* means "pleasing to the ear." *Discordant* means "not harmonious, displeasing." *Syncopated* means that a usually weak beat is stressed. *Rhythmic* means that something occurs with regularity. *Euphemistic* means that something is softened in expression.
    Vocabulary—Similarity/Contrast

37. (**a. Montague**, *b.* Scali, *c.* Dunlop, *d.* Mineo) : ROMEO :: CAPULET : JULIET

    (**a**) In Shakespeare's play, Montague is the surname of Romeo, Capulet the surname of Juliet.
    Humanities—Description

38. EMANCIPATE : (*a.* emaciate, *b.* free, **c. enslave**, *d.* deliver) :: EMPTY : FULL

    (**c**) *Emancipate* and *enslave* are antonyms, as are *empty* and *full.*
    Vocabulary—Similarity/Contrast

39. PALMISTRY : PALM :: PHRENOLOGY : (*a.* handwriting, *b.* EEG, *c.* eyes, **d. skull**)

    (**d**) Palmistry makes use of the palm in telling about a person; phrenology makes use of the skull.
    General Information—Description

40. (*a.* Columbia Gem, **b. Union Jack**, *c.* Royal Ensign, *d.* Fleur-de-Lis) : GREAT BRITAIN :: STARS AND STRIPES : U.S.A.

    (**b**) The Union Jack is the flag of Great Britain; the Stars and Stripes is the flag of the United States. The fleur-de-lis is associated with the Spanish monarchy and the Grand Duchy of Luxembourg. "Columbia, Gem of the Ocean" is a song.
    Social Science—Description

41. COMMON LOG : 10 :: NATURAL LOG : (*a.* π, **b. e**, *c.* i, *d.* 1)

    (**b**) Common logs are to base 10. Natural logs are to base *e.*
    Mathematics—Description

42. MAE WEST : LIFE JACKET :: MICKEY FINN : (*a.* blackjack, *b.* Molotov cocktail, *c.* **drugged liquor**, *d.* time bomb)

(**c**) A Mae West is a type of life jacket. A Mickey Finn is a form of drugged liquor. Blackjack is a popular Casino game, and a Molotov cocktail is a name for a variety of incendiary weapons.
General Information—Similarity/Contrast

43. EARTH : AIR :: (*a.* bile, *b.* carbon, *c.* phlogiston, *d.* **fire**) : WATER

(**d**) Earth, air, fire, and water were once believed to be the four basic elements from which every other substance is composed.
Humanities—Class

44. CAMUS : STRANGER :: (*a.* Sartre, *b.* **Camus**, *c.* Mauriac, *d.* Ionesco) : PLAGUE

(**b**) Camus is the author of both *The Stranger* and *The Plague*. Sartre wrote *No Exit* and *The Flies*, among other plays. Mauriac wrote *Le Desert de l'Amour*. Ionesco wrote the play *Rhinoceros*.
Humanities—Description

45. DOG : PIE :: HOT : (*a.* cold, *b.* cat, *c.* **pizza**, *d.* cake)

(**c**) A hotdog and a pizza pie are both forms of food.
General Information—Completion

46. PIETÀ : MICHELANGELO :: THE KISS : (*a.* **Rodin**, *b.* Pisano, *c.* Ghiberti, *d.* da Vinci)

(**a**) *The Pietà* is a sculpture by Michelangelo. *The Kiss* is a sculpture by Rodin. Pisano was an Italian artist who was wrongly credited for the creation of the *Leaning Tower of Pisa*. Ghiberti is known for a set of metal panels called *Gates of Paradise*. Da Vinci painted the *Mona Lisa* and *The Last Supper*, among others.
Humanities—Description

47. (*a.* Congress of Vienna, *b.* **League of Nations**, *c.* Warsaw Pact, *d.* NATO) : UNITED NATIONS :: GASLIGHT : ELECTRIC LIGHT

(**b**) The United Nations replaced the League of Nations. The electric light replaced the gaslight. The League of Nations was a supranational organization that was created in the aftermath of World War I; its goals were the prevention of war, settlement of disputes, etc. The Congress of Vienna was a conference to reorganize Europe after the downfall of Napoleon I (1814–1815). The Warsaw Pact (1955) was an organization of Eastern European Communist states that was created in response to the creation of NATO.
General Information—Description

48. CARAT : (*a.* size, ***b.* weight**, *c.* brilliance, *d.* value) :: ACRE : AREA

    (**b**) A carat is a measure of weight. An acre is a measure of area.
    Natural Science—Description

49. $a + b : b + a :: a(b + a)b : ($*a.* $2a^2b^2$, *b.* $(a + b)^2$, ***c.* $a^2b + ab^2$**, *d.* $a^2b^2 + ab)$

    (**c**) $a + b$ is equal to $b + a$. $a(b + a)b$ is equal to $a^2b + ab^2$.
    Mathematics—Equality/Negation

50. FRANCIS CRICK : STRUCTURE OF DNA MOLECULE :: MARIE CURIE : (*a.* nobelium, *b.* uranium, ***c.* radium**, *d.* plutonium)

    (**c**) Francis Crick was a codiscoverer of the structure of the DNA molecule. Marie Curie was a codiscoverer of the element radium.
    Natural Science—Description

51. ANALOG : SLIDE RULE :: DIGITAL : (***a.* odometer**, *b.* ruler, *c.* compass, *d.* protractor)

    (**a**) A slide rule is an analog device. An odometer is a digital device.
    Natural Science—Description

52. CHARLOTTE'S : PILGRIM'S :: WEB : (*a.* Follies, ***b.* Progress**, *c.* Pretense, *d.* Journey)

    (**b**) *Charlotte's Web* (by E. B. White) and *Pilgrim's Progress* (by John Bunyan) are both titles of books.
    Humanities—Description

53. VOID : VACUUM :: FULL : (***a.* replete**, *b.* deplete, *c.* compact, *d.* empty)

    (**a**) *Void* and *vacuum* are synonyms, as are *full* and *replete*.
    Vocabulary—Similarity/Contrast

54. HIGH : DIE :: (*a.* gregarious, *b.* reticent, *c.* low, ***d.* buy**) : SHY

    (**d**) *High*, *die*, *buy*, and *shy* all rhyme.
    Nonsemantic

55. (*a.* retina, *b.* iris, *c.* lens, ***d.* cone**) : ROD :: CHROMATIC : ACHROMATIC

    (**d**) In the visual system, the cones are responsible for chromatic vision, and the rods for achromatic vision.
    Natural Science—Description

56. BOVINE : (*a.* jackal, *b.* monkey, ***c.* ox**, *d.* rabbit) :: URSINE : BEAR

    (**c**) A bovine creature is oxlike. An ursine creature is bearlike.
    General Information—Similarity/Contrast

57. (***a*. Plato**, *b*. Aristotle, *c*. Leibniz, *d*. Locke) : REPUBLIC :: DESCARTES : MEDITATIONS

    (**a**) Plato is the author of the *Republic*. Descartes is the author of *Meditations*. Aristotle's works are collected in the *Corpus Aristotelicum*. Leibniz wrote the *Theodicee*. Locke is the author of *An Essay Concerning Human Understanding* and *Some Thoughts Concerning Education*, among others.
    Humanities—Description

58. DEER : DEER :: CORPUS : (*a*. corpi, *b*. corpuses, ***c*. corpora**, *d*. corpes)

    (**c**) *Deer* is the plural form of *deer*. *Corpora* is the plural form of *corpus*.
    Nonsemantic

59. BUDAPEST : HANOI :: HUNGARY : (*a*. Cambodia, *b*. Laos, *c*. Thailand, ***d*. Vietnam**)

    (**d**) Budapest is the capital of Hungary. Hanoi is the capital of Vietnam. The capital of Thailand is Bangkok. The capital of Cambodia is Phnom Penh. The capital of Laos is Vientiane.
    General Information—Description

60. PROMISED LAND : CANAAN :: LAND OF NOD : (*a*. wakefulness, *b*. hell, ***c*. sleep**, *d*. heaven)

    (**c**) Canaan was the Promised Land for the Israelites. The Land of Nod is sleep. The Land of Nod has been mentioned in the Bible but has more recently been associated with sleep, as in Stevenson's poem "The Land of Nod."
    Humanities—Similarity/Contrast

61. MISOGYNIST : WOMEN :: MISOGAMIST : (*a*. men, *b*. people, ***c*. marriage**, *d*. religion)

    (**c**) A misogynist detests women. A misogamist detests marriage.
    Vocabulary—Description

62. (*a*. Achilles, *b*. Hector, ***c*. Paris**, *d*. Troilus) : HELEN :: PLUTO : PROSERPINA

    (**c**) Paris abducted Helen. Pluto abducted Proserpina. Achilles was the greatest warrior of the Greeks in the Trojan War. Hector was a Trojan prince and warrior in the Trojan War. Troilus was a Trojan prince murdered by Achilles.
    Humanities—Description

63. BENIGN : BENEVOLENT :: (*a*. beneficent, ***b*. nefarious**, *c*. tortuous, *d*. voracious) : MALEVOLENT

    (**b**) *Benign* and *benevolent* are synonyms, as are *nefarious* and *malevolent*.
    Vocabulary—Similarity/Contrast

64. BLOCKHEAD : LUNKHEAD :: MUTTONHEAD : (*a.* **fathead**, *b.* sleepyhead, *c.* bighead, *d.* egghead)

(**a**) A blockhead is a lunkhead is a muttonhead is a fathead.
Vocabulary—Similarity/Contrast

65. UNCLE TOM : SERVILE :: DUTCH UNCLE : (*a.* hoary, *b.* kind, *c.* **stern**, *d.* stingy)

(**c**) An Uncle Tom is servile. A Dutch uncle is stern.
Vocabulary—Description

66. ALPHA : (*a.* gamma, *b.* zed, *c.* epsilon, *d.* **omega**) :: A : Z

(**d**) *Alpha* is the first letter of the Greek alphabet, and *omega* is the last. *A* is the first letter of the English alphabet, and *Z* is the last.
Humanities—Similarity/Contrast

67. THIAMINE : ASCORBIC ACID :: B$_1$: (*a.* B$_6$, *b.* B$_{12}$, *c.* **C**, *d.* E)

(**c**) Thiamine is vitamin B$_1$. Ascorbic acid is vitamin C. Vitamin B$_6$ can consist of different compounds: pyridoxine, pyridoxal, and pyridoxamine. B$_{12}$ can be commonly found as cyanocobalamin. E refers to a group of tocopherols and tocotrienols.
Natural Science—Similarity/Contrast

68. BRAZIL : (*a.* **Portuguese**, *b.* Spanish, *c.* French, *d.* Brazilian) :: AUSTRIA : GERMAN

(**a**) Portuguese is the principal language spoken in Brazil. German is the principal language spoken in Austria.
Social Science—Description

69. CENTURY : EON :: DOZEN : (*a.* one hundred, *b.* gross, *c.* zero, *d.* **myriad**)

(**d**) A century is a specified period of time, and an eon is a long, unspecified period of time. A dozen is a specified amount, and a myriad is a large, unspecified amount.
Vocabulary—Description

70. SITTING BULL : SIOUX :: GERONIMO : (*a.* **Apache**, *b.* Pueblo, *c.* Mohawk, *d.* Seminole)

(**a**) Sitting Bull was a Sioux Indian chief; Geronimo was an Apache Indian chief.
Social Science—Description

Explanation of Answers

71. AUTOCRACY : AUTARCHY :: MONARCHY : (*a.* democracy, *b.* anarchy, *c.* oligarchy, ***d.* kingdom**)

    (**d**) An autocracy is an autarchy. A monarchy is a kingdom. Anarchy is the absence of government. Oligarchy is a form of government where power is placed in the hands of a small group of people.
    Social Science—Similarity/Contrast

72. GOGGLE-EYED : BULGING :: HOOK-NOSED : (*a.* opercular, *b.* oviparous, *c.* ovine, ***d.* aquiline**)

    (**d**) Someone who is goggle-eyed has bulging eyes. Someone who is hook-nosed has an aquiline nose.
    Vocabulary—Similarity/Contrast

73. NEPTUNE : DIANA :: SEA : (*a.* hearth, *b.* sun, ***c.* moon**, *d.* home)

    (**c**) In Roman mythology, Neptune was the god of the sea and Diana the goddess of the moon.
    Humanities—Description

74. EXPEL : DRIVE AWAY :: EXPIATE : (***a.* atone for**, *b.* talk at length, *c.* forgive, *d.* speak briefly)

    (**a**) To expel is to drive away. To expiate is to atone for.
    Vocabulary—Similarity/Contrast

75. LARGO : SLOW :: (*a.* moderato, ***b.* allegro**, *c.* piano, *d.* fortissimo) : FAST

    (**b**) In music, largo signifies a slow tempo; allegro, a fast tempo. *Moderato* means "moderately fast." *Piano* means "soft." *Fortissimo* means "very loud."
    Humanities—Similarity/Contrast

76. (*a.* with faith, *b.* with truth, *c.* with passion, ***d.* with authority**) : EX CATHEDRA :: ON THE FACE : EX FACIE

    (**d**) *Ex cathedra* means *with authority. Ex facie* means *on the face.*
    Vocabulary—Similarity/Contrast

77. FIFE : CLARINET :: TROMBONE : (*a.* lute, ***b.* bagpipe**, *c.* piano, *d.* violin)

    (**b**) A fife, a clarinet, a trombone, and a bagpipe are all wind instruments.
    Humanities—Class

78. PARASITE : LIVING :: (***a.* saprophyte**, *b.* neophyte, *c.* pteridophyte, *d.* bryophyte) : DEAD

    (**a**) A parasite lives off a living organism. A saprophyte lives off a dead organism.
    Natural Science—Description

79. PRINCE : MACHIAVELLI :: PETIT PRINCE : (*a.* **Saint-Exupéry**, *b.* Mauriac, *c.* Camus, *d.* Lescaut)

(**a**) *The Prince* was written by Machiavelli. *Le Petit Prince* was written by Saint-Exupéry. Francois Mauriac wrote *Le Desert de l'Amour*, for example. Albert Camus was a French writer who wrote *The Plague*. *Manon Lescaut* is an opera by Puccini. *Humanities—Description*

80. ITALY : LIRA :: (*a.* Switzerland, **b. Netherlands**, *c.* Portugal, *d.* Sweden) : GUILDER

(**b**) The lira is the unit of currency in Italy. The guilder is the unit of currency in the Netherlands. The currency of Switzerland is the franc. The currency of Portugal was the escudo but is now the euro. The currency of Sweden is the crown. *General Information—Description*

81. DEMOSTHENES : (*a.* **Cicero**, *b.* Socrates, *c.* Pericles, *d.* Ovid) :: HOMER : VIRGIL

(**a**) Demosthenes was a Greek orator, and Cicero a Roman orator. Homer was a Greek poet, and Virgil a Roman poet. Socrates was a Greek philosopher. Ovid was a Roman poet. Pericles was a Greek statesman and orator. *Humanities—Class*

82. (*a.* mg, *b.* gg, **c. kg**, *d.* cg) : g :: m : mm

(**c**) There are 1,000 grams (g) in a kilogram (kg). There are 1,000 millimeters (mm) in a meter (m). There are 1,000 milligrams (mg) in a gram (g). *Mathematics—Part/Whole*

83. CIPANGO : JAPAN :: CATHAY : (*a.* **China**, *b.* Tibet, *c.* Polynesia, *d.* Mongolia)

(**a**) Cipango is a poetic name for Japan. Cathay is a poetic name for China. *Humanities—Similarity/Contrast*

84. IMPROMPTU : EXTEMPORE :: PROBITY : (*a.* open-mindedness, *b.* dishonesty, *c.* narrow-mindedness, *d.* **honesty**)

(**d**) *Impromptu* and *extempore* are synonyms, as are *probity* and *honesty*. *Vocabulary—Similarity/Contrast*

Explanation of Answers

85. FERMI : NUCLEAR PHYSICS :: JANE ADDAMS : (*a.* nursing, *b.* physics, ***c.* social work**, *d.* drama)

    (**c**) Fermi is famous for his work in nuclear physics. Jane Addams is famous for her social work.
    Humanities—Description

86. (*a.* Inferno, ***b.* Decameron**, *c.* The Wasteland, *d.* No Exit) : CANTERBURY TALES :: ANTHOLOGY : COLLECTION

    (**b**) *The Decameron* (by Giovanni Boccacio) and *The Canterbury Tales* (by Geoffrey Chaucer) are both anthologies (collections) of stories. *Inferno* is the first canticle of Dante's *Divine Comedy*. *The Wasteland* is a poem by Eliot. *No Exit* is a play by Sartre.
    Humanities—Class

87. RICHELIEU : (*a.* Cushing, ***b.* Mazarin**, *c.* Metternich, *d.* Marat) :: KENNEDY : JOHNSON

    (**b**) Cardinal Mazarin succeeded Cardinal Richelieu in his French diplomatic role. Johnson succeeded Kennedy as president of the United States.
    Social Science—Description

88. (*a.* uncertainty, *b.* luck, ***c.* sample**, *d.* variance) : POPULATION :: STATISTIC : PARAMETER

    (**c**) A statistic is a sample value, while a parameter is a population value.
    Mathematics—Description

89. REGAN : GONERIL :: LEAH : (*a.* Jacob, *b.* Rebeccah, *c.* Isaac, ***d.* Rachel**)

    (**d**) Regan and Goneril were sisters (in *King Lear*), as were Leah and Rachel (in the Bible). Rebeccah was the wife of Isaac. Jacob was their son.
    Humanities—Class

90. TEMPUS : CARPE :: FUGIT : (*a.* cibus, *b.* mater, ***c.* diem**, *d.* tempum)

    (**c**) *Tempus fugit* and *carpe diem* are both Latinisms used in English. *Tempus fugit* means *time flies*, while *carpe diem* means *seize the opportunity*—literally, *the day*.
    Vocabulary—Completion

91. ERSATZ : (***a.* genuine**, *b.* superior, *c.* inferior, *d.* fake) :: FRESH : RANCID

    (**a**) *Ersatz* and *genuine* are antonyms, as are *fresh* and *rancid*.
    Vocabulary—Similarity/Contrast

92. EVE : DEED :: MADAM : (*a.* cuckoo, *b.* swoon, *c.* **noon**, *d.* pool)

    (**c**) *Eve, deed, madam,* and *noon* are all palindromes—they read the same whether spelled forward or backward.
    Nonsemantic

93. SLEEPY : SOMNOLENT :: GROGGY : (*a.* asleep, *b.* **unsteady**, *c.* awake, *d.* dead)

    (**b**) A sleepy person is somnolent; a groggy person is unsteady.
    Vocabulary—Similarity/Contrast

94. AXON : DEPART :: (*a.* neuron, *b.* ganglion, *c.* **dendrites**, *d.* plasma) : APPROACH

    (**c**) Nerve impulses depart from a cell body via the axon; they approach the cell body via the dendrites.
    Natural Science—Description

95. BUDGE : TENNIS :: LOUIS : (*a.* hockey, *b.* football, *c.* baseball, *d.* **boxing**)

    (**d**) Joe Louis was a famous boxer. Don Budge was a famous tennis player.
    General Information—Description

96. BLOOD : MELANCHOLY :: CHOLER : (*a.* plasma, *b.* lymph, *c.* **phlegm**, *d.* saliva)

    (**c**) Blood, phlegm, choler, and melancholy were once believed to be the four body humors (fluids). The idea of body humors is an old one dating back to ancient Egypt, but Hippocrates was the one who applied the concept to medicine.
    Humanities—Class

97. MEXICO : YORK :: CAROLINA : (*a.* Virginia, *b.* Oregon, *c.* Washington, *d.* **Dakota**)

    (**d**) Both (New) Mexico and (New) York are states. Both (North or South) Carolina and (North or South) Dakota are states.
    General Information—Description

98. ARGON : NEON :: XENON : (*a.* **helium**, *b.* oxygen, *c.* mercury, *d.* carbon)

    (**a**) Argon, neon, xenon, and helium are all inert (noble) gases.
    The six noble gases are helium, neon, argon, xenon, krypton, and radon.
    Natural Science—Class

Explanation of Answers

99. HORN : ROLAND :: HARP : (*a.* Gideon, *b.* **David**, *c.* Moses, *d.* Samuel)

    (**b**) Roland was famous for his horn, David for his harp.
    Humanities—Description

100. GLUTTON : FOOD :: SATYR : (*a.* punishment, *b.* glory,
    c. alcoholic beverages, *d.* **sex**)

    (**d**) A glutton overindulges in food, a satyr in sex.
    General Information—Description

101. ACUTE : (*a.* small, *b.* **obtuse**, *c.* intense, *d.* right) :: APOGEE : PERIGEE

    (**b**) When speaking either of angles or the ability to comprehend something,
    acute means the opposite of obtuse, just as the apogee is the opposite of
    the perigee.
    Vocabulary—Similarity/Contrast

102. (*a.* berate, *b.* refine, *c.* attenuate, *d.* **foreshadow**) : ADUMBRATE ::
    INTIMATE : HINT

    (**d**) To adumbrate is to foreshadow just as to intimate is to hint.
    Vocabulary—Similarity/Contrast

103. PNEUMONECTOMY : LUNG :: (*a.* tonsillectomy, *b.* meningectomy,
    c. **lobotomy**, *d.* encephalotomy) : BRAIN

    (**c**) Pneumonectomy is the removal of part of the lung and lobotomy is the
    removal of part of the brain.
    Natural Science—Description

104. EMPATHY : (*a.* lungs, *b.* soul, *c.* pancreas, *d.* **heart**) :: BRAVERY : LIVER

    (**d**) Tradition ascribes empathy and bravery to be seated in the organs of the
    heart and liver respectively.
    General Information—Description

105. CIRCUMSPECT : CIRCUMSCRIBE :: (*a.* **prudent**, *b.* navigate,
    c. rounded, *d.* investigate) : ENCIRCLE

    (**a**) To be circumspect is to be prudent, and to circumscribe is to encircle.
    Vocabulary—Similarity/Contrast

106. DEARTH : (*a.* poverty, *b.* **abundance**, *c.* warmth, *d.* nothing) :: PAUCITY :
    PLENTY

    (**b**) Dearth and paucity both describe an insufficiency, whereas abundance
    and plenty describe something bountiful.
    Vocabulary—Similarity/Contrast

107. CAP : LID :: KNEE : (*a.* leg, *b.* patella, *c.* heel, ***d.* eye**)

(**d**) The kneecap and eyelid are both parts of the body.
General Information—Completion

108. (***a.* bitterness**, *b.* wittiness, *c.* frivolity, *d.* accusation) : ACRIMONIOUS :: FRUGALITY : PARSIMONIOUS

(**a**) "Acrimonious" describes someone who acts with bitterness just as "parsimonious" describes someone who acts with frugality.
Vocabulary—Description

109. CAESAR : DELIVERY :: ACHILLES : (*a.* surgery, *b.* ligament, ***c.* tendon**, *d.* bone)

(**c**) The cesarean section, the name of a delivery, is named for Caesar. The Achilles tendon, the name of a tendon, is named for Achilles.
General Information—Description

110. PROMETHEUS : BOUND :: ATLAS : (*a.* carried, *b.* tied, ***c.* shrugged**, *d.* grew)

(**c**) *Prometheus Bound* (by Aeschylus) and *Atlas Shrugged* (by Ayn Rand) are both prominent works of literature.
Humanities—Completion

111. GENGHIS KHAN : (*a.* China, ***b.* Mongolia**, *c.* Persia, *d.* Prussia) :: SHAKA : SOUTH AFRICA

(**b**) Genghis Khan was a great conqueror born in present-day Mongolia. Shaka was a great conqueror born in present-day South Africa.
General Information—Description

112. (*a.* right to bear arms, ***b.* prohibition of alcohol**, *c.* right to remain silent, *d.* freedom of religion) : 18th AMENDMENT :: WOMEN'S SUFFRAGE : 19th AMENDMENT

(**b**) The 18th Amendment prohibited the consumption of alcohol. The 19th Amendment granted women's suffrage.
General Information—Similarity/Contrast

113. KID : (*a.* wolf, ***b.* goat**, *c.* moose, *d.* kangaroo) :: CALF : WHALE

(**b**) A young goat is called a kid just as a young whale is called a calf.
General Information—Class

114. HOPI : (*a.* **Southwest**, *b.* Southeast, *c.* Northwest, *d.* Great Plains) :: TLINGIT : NORTHWEST

    (**a**) The Hopi tribe is native to the Southwest of what is now the United States. The Tlingit tribe is native to the Northwest of what is now the United States.
    General Information—Description

115. PTOLEMY : EARTH :: COPERNICUS : (*a.* Mars, *b.* Venus, *c.* Moon, *d.* **Sun**)

    (**d**) Ptolemy proposed a geocentric system in which the Earth was the center of the solar system. Copernicus proposed a heliocentric system, in which the sun was the center.
    Natural Science—Description

116. ADAM SMITH : 18th CENTURY :: JOHN MAYNARD KEYNES : (*a.* **20th century**, *b.* 19th century, *c.* 17th century, *d.* 16th century)

    (**a**) Smith and Keynes were famous economists of the 18th and 20th centuries, respectively. Smith is well-known as the author of *The Wealth of Nations.* Keynes is the founder of Keynesian economics, which deals with total spending in the economy and its effects on output and inflation.
    Social Science—Description

117. (*a.* Laos, *b.* **Japan**, *c.* Taiwan, *d.* China) : JUDO :: KOREA : TAE KWON DO

    (**b**) The martial art of Judo originated in Japan just as the martial art Tae Kwon Do originated in Korea.
    General Information—Description

118. KHMER ROUGE : POL POT :: COMMUNIST PARTY OF CHINA : (*a.* Kuomintang, *b.* Confucius *c.* **Mao Zedong**, *d.* Chiang Kai-shek)

    (**c**) Pol Pot was a leader of the Cambodian Communist Party, commonly known as the Khmer Rouge. Mao Zedong was a leader of the Communist Party of China. Kuomintang is the founding party of Taiwan. Confucius was a Chinese thinker and philosopher in the 5th century B.C. Chiang Kai-shek was a Chinese political leader who served as head of state of the National Government of the Republic of China from 1928 to 1949.
    General Information—Description

119. SUEZ CANAL : (*a.* Turkey, *b.* Morocco, *c.* **Egypt**, *d.* Israel) :: PANAMA CANAL : PANAMA

    (**c**) The Suez Canal cuts through Egypt just as the Panama Canal cuts through Panama.
    General Information—Description

120. SOVIET UNION : (*a.* Portugal, *b.* Brazil, *c.* Cuba, *d.* Spain) :: CHAGALL
: DALI

(**d**) Chagall and Dali were artists known for their surrealistic paintings;
they were from the Soviet Union and Spain respectively.
Humanities—Description

PRACTICE TEST 8

Item Classification Chart

		RELATIONSHIP						
		Similarity/ Contrast	Description	Class	Completion	Part/ Whole	Equality/ Negation	Nonsemantic
C O N T E N T	**Vocabulary**	20, 31, 33, 36, 38, 53, 63, 64, 72, 74, 76, 84, 91, 93, 101, 102, 105, 106	21, 35, 61, 65, 69, 108		90			
	General Information	11, 15, 26, 42, 56, 112	1, 2, 3, 8, 9, 13, 14, 17, 18, 22, 27, 29, 39, 47, 59, 80, 95, 97, 100, 104, 109, 111, 114, 117, 118, 119	10, 113	45, 107			
	Humanities	60, 66, 75, 83	5, 7, 23, 24, 28, 34, 37, 44, 46, 52, 57, 62, 73, 79, 85, 99, 110, 120	43, 77, 81, 86, 89, 96				
	Social Science	71	40, 68, 70, 87, 116					
	Natural Science	67	4, 48, 50, 51, 55, 78, 94, 103, 115	98		19	16	
	Mathematics		6, 25, 41, 88	12		82	30, 49	
	Nonsemantic							32, 54, 58, 92

Answer Sheet
PRACTICE TEST 9

1 Ⓐ Ⓑ Ⓒ Ⓓ	31 Ⓐ Ⓑ Ⓒ Ⓓ	61 Ⓐ Ⓑ Ⓒ Ⓓ	91 Ⓐ Ⓑ Ⓒ Ⓓ
2 Ⓐ Ⓑ Ⓒ Ⓓ	32 Ⓐ Ⓑ Ⓒ Ⓓ	62 Ⓐ Ⓑ Ⓒ Ⓓ	92 Ⓐ Ⓑ Ⓒ Ⓓ
3 Ⓐ Ⓑ Ⓒ Ⓓ	33 Ⓐ Ⓑ Ⓒ Ⓓ	63 Ⓐ Ⓑ Ⓒ Ⓓ	93 Ⓐ Ⓑ Ⓒ Ⓓ
4 Ⓐ Ⓑ Ⓒ Ⓓ	34 Ⓐ Ⓑ Ⓒ Ⓓ	64 Ⓐ Ⓑ Ⓒ Ⓓ	94 Ⓐ Ⓑ Ⓒ Ⓓ
5 Ⓐ Ⓑ Ⓒ Ⓓ	35 Ⓐ Ⓑ Ⓒ Ⓓ	65 Ⓐ Ⓑ Ⓒ Ⓓ	95 Ⓐ Ⓑ Ⓒ Ⓓ
6 Ⓐ Ⓑ Ⓒ Ⓓ	36 Ⓐ Ⓑ Ⓒ Ⓓ	66 Ⓐ Ⓑ Ⓒ Ⓓ	96 Ⓐ Ⓑ Ⓒ Ⓓ
7 Ⓐ Ⓑ Ⓒ Ⓓ	37 Ⓐ Ⓑ Ⓒ Ⓓ	67 Ⓐ Ⓑ Ⓒ Ⓓ	97 Ⓐ Ⓑ Ⓒ Ⓓ
8 Ⓐ Ⓑ Ⓒ Ⓓ	38 Ⓐ Ⓑ Ⓒ Ⓓ	68 Ⓐ Ⓑ Ⓒ Ⓓ	98 Ⓐ Ⓑ Ⓒ Ⓓ
9 Ⓐ Ⓑ Ⓒ Ⓓ	39 Ⓐ Ⓑ Ⓒ Ⓓ	69 Ⓐ Ⓑ Ⓒ Ⓓ	99 Ⓐ Ⓑ Ⓒ Ⓓ
10 Ⓐ Ⓑ Ⓒ Ⓓ	40 Ⓐ Ⓑ Ⓒ Ⓓ	70 Ⓐ Ⓑ Ⓒ Ⓓ	100 Ⓐ Ⓑ Ⓒ Ⓓ
11 Ⓐ Ⓑ Ⓒ Ⓓ	41 Ⓐ Ⓑ Ⓒ Ⓓ	71 Ⓐ Ⓑ Ⓒ Ⓓ	101 Ⓐ Ⓑ Ⓒ Ⓓ
12 Ⓐ Ⓑ Ⓒ Ⓓ	42 Ⓐ Ⓑ Ⓒ Ⓓ	72 Ⓐ Ⓑ Ⓒ Ⓓ	102 Ⓐ Ⓑ Ⓒ Ⓓ
13 Ⓐ Ⓑ Ⓒ Ⓓ	43 Ⓐ Ⓑ Ⓒ Ⓓ	73 Ⓐ Ⓑ Ⓒ Ⓓ	103 Ⓐ Ⓑ Ⓒ Ⓓ
14 Ⓐ Ⓑ Ⓒ Ⓓ	44 Ⓐ Ⓑ Ⓒ Ⓓ	74 Ⓐ Ⓑ Ⓒ Ⓓ	104 Ⓐ Ⓑ Ⓒ Ⓓ
15 Ⓐ Ⓑ Ⓒ Ⓓ	45 Ⓐ Ⓑ Ⓒ Ⓓ	75 Ⓐ Ⓑ Ⓒ Ⓓ	105 Ⓐ Ⓑ Ⓒ Ⓓ
16 Ⓐ Ⓑ Ⓒ Ⓓ	46 Ⓐ Ⓑ Ⓒ Ⓓ	76 Ⓐ Ⓑ Ⓒ Ⓓ	106 Ⓐ Ⓑ Ⓒ Ⓓ
17 Ⓐ Ⓑ Ⓒ Ⓓ	47 Ⓐ Ⓑ Ⓒ Ⓓ	77 Ⓐ Ⓑ Ⓒ Ⓓ	107 Ⓐ Ⓑ Ⓒ Ⓓ
18 Ⓐ Ⓑ Ⓒ Ⓓ	48 Ⓐ Ⓑ Ⓒ Ⓓ	78 Ⓐ Ⓑ Ⓒ Ⓓ	108 Ⓐ Ⓑ Ⓒ Ⓓ
19 Ⓐ Ⓑ Ⓒ Ⓓ	49 Ⓐ Ⓑ Ⓒ Ⓓ	79 Ⓐ Ⓑ Ⓒ Ⓓ	109 Ⓐ Ⓑ Ⓒ Ⓓ
20 Ⓐ Ⓑ Ⓒ Ⓓ	50 Ⓐ Ⓑ Ⓒ Ⓓ	80 Ⓐ Ⓑ Ⓒ Ⓓ	110 Ⓐ Ⓑ Ⓒ Ⓓ
21 Ⓐ Ⓑ Ⓒ Ⓓ	51 Ⓐ Ⓑ Ⓒ Ⓓ	81 Ⓐ Ⓑ Ⓒ Ⓓ	111 Ⓐ Ⓑ Ⓒ Ⓓ
22 Ⓐ Ⓑ Ⓒ Ⓓ	52 Ⓐ Ⓑ Ⓒ Ⓓ	82 Ⓐ Ⓑ Ⓒ Ⓓ	112 Ⓐ Ⓑ Ⓒ Ⓓ
23 Ⓐ Ⓑ Ⓒ Ⓓ	53 Ⓐ Ⓑ Ⓒ Ⓓ	83 Ⓐ Ⓑ Ⓒ Ⓓ	113 Ⓐ Ⓑ Ⓒ Ⓓ
24 Ⓐ Ⓑ Ⓒ Ⓓ	54 Ⓐ Ⓑ Ⓒ Ⓓ	84 Ⓐ Ⓑ Ⓒ Ⓓ	114 Ⓐ Ⓑ Ⓒ Ⓓ
25 Ⓐ Ⓑ Ⓒ Ⓓ	55 Ⓐ Ⓑ Ⓒ Ⓓ	85 Ⓐ Ⓑ Ⓒ Ⓓ	115 Ⓐ Ⓑ Ⓒ Ⓓ
26 Ⓐ Ⓑ Ⓒ Ⓓ	56 Ⓐ Ⓑ Ⓒ Ⓓ	86 Ⓐ Ⓑ Ⓒ Ⓓ	116 Ⓐ Ⓑ Ⓒ Ⓓ
27 Ⓐ Ⓑ Ⓒ Ⓓ	57 Ⓐ Ⓑ Ⓒ Ⓓ	87 Ⓐ Ⓑ Ⓒ Ⓓ	117 Ⓐ Ⓑ Ⓒ Ⓓ
28 Ⓐ Ⓑ Ⓒ Ⓓ	58 Ⓐ Ⓑ Ⓒ Ⓓ	88 Ⓐ Ⓑ Ⓒ Ⓓ	118 Ⓐ Ⓑ Ⓒ Ⓓ
29 Ⓐ Ⓑ Ⓒ Ⓓ	59 Ⓐ Ⓑ Ⓒ Ⓓ	89 Ⓐ Ⓑ Ⓒ Ⓓ	119 Ⓐ Ⓑ Ⓒ Ⓓ
30 Ⓐ Ⓑ Ⓒ Ⓓ	60 Ⓐ Ⓑ Ⓒ Ⓓ	90 Ⓐ Ⓑ Ⓒ Ⓓ	120 Ⓐ Ⓑ Ⓒ Ⓓ

Answer Sheet

Practice Test 9

Directions: In each of the following questions, you will find three initial terms and, in parentheses, four answer options designated *a*, *b*, *c*, and *d*. You are to select from the four answer options the one that best completes the analogy with the three initial terms. To record your answers, use the answer sheet provided.

Time: 60 minutes

1. POSTMAN : LETTER :: (*a.* surgeon, *b.* orthopedist, *c.* obstetrician, *d.* podiatrist) : BABY

2. CHLOROPHYLL : GREEN :: HEMOGLOBIN : (*a.* red, *b.* black, *c.* green, *d.* blue)

3. HAPPY : (*a.* sad, *b.* gay, *c.* indifferent, *d.* ecstatic) :: BRIGHT : BRILLIANT

4. PENCIL : PEN :: (*a.* wood, *b.* ballpoint, *c.* graphite, *d.* boron) : INK

5. ONE BIRD : HAND :: TWO BIRDS : (*a.* bush, *b.* foot, *c.* nest, *d.* head)

6. SILVER : TARNISH :: IRON : (*a.* oxidation, *b.* rust, *c.* magnet, *d.* tin)

7. BUTTERFLY : CATERPILLAR :: (*a.* amphibian, *b.* frog, *c.* salamander, *d.* larva) : TADPOLE

8. GREEN : (*a.* cowardice, *b.* viciousness, *c.* envy, *d.* delight) :: PURPLE : RAGE

9. JUDAS : JESUS :: (*a.* Augustus, *b.* Brutus, *c.* Lucius, *d.* Antony) : JULIUS CAESAR

10. JOLLY ROGER : (*a.* communists, *b.* fascists, *c.* pirates, *d.* anarchists) :: UNION JACK : UNITED KINGDOM

11. DIALECTIC : HEGEL :: DIALECTICAL MATERIALISM : (*a.* Marx, *b.* Fichte, *c.* Schelling, *d.* Kant)

12. (*a.* screen, *b.* camera, *c.* projector, *d.* frame) : MOVIE FILM :: LINK : CHAIN

13. PROLOGUE : (*a.* decalogue, *b.* epilogue, *c.* preface, *d.* forward) :: APPETIZER : DESSERT

14. HAMMERSTEIN : (*a.* Sondheim, *b.* Rodgers, *c.* Gilbert, *d.* Herman) :: LERNER : LOEWE

15. (*a.* dumb, *b.* stupid, *c.* loquacious, *d.* brilliant) : MUTE :: SMART : INTELLIGENT

16. ARCHIVES : (*a.* munitions, *b.* tombs, *c.* documents, *d.* animals) :: PANTRY : KITCHEN UTENSILS

17. DUNCAN : MACBETH :: MACBETH : (*a.* Lady Macbeth, *b.* Macduff, *c.* Polonius, *d.* Claudius)

18. V : X :: D : (*a.* I, *b.* M, *c.* D, *d.* C)

19. JACK SPRAT'S WIFE : LEAN :: VEGETARIAN : (*a.* meat, *b.* fat, *c.* vegetables, *d.* roots)

20. (*a.* politics, *b.* law, *c.* music, *d.* medicine) : HIPPOCRATES :: HISTORY : HERODOTUS

21. (*a.* Russia, *b.* China, *c.* Japan, *d.* Hungary) : BALALAIKA :: SCOTLAND : BAGPIPES

22. TAILPIPE : EXHAUST :: RADIUM : (*a.* beta rays, *b.* strontium, *c.* cosmic rays, *d.* lead)

23. ARGUS : 100 :: CYCLOPS : (*a.* 1000, *b.* 10, *c.* 5, *d.* 1)

24. CANNON : BIG BERTHA :: (*a.* battleship, *b.* bazooka, *c.* bell, *d.* church steeple) : BIG BEN

25. (*a.* pretty, *b.* pretentious, *c.* proud, *d.* portly) : PEACOCK :: SILLY : GOOSE

26. HYPOCRITICAL : INSINCERE :: HYPERCRITICAL : (*a.* overcritical, *b.* sincere, *c.* oversincere, *d.* critical)

27. (*a.* cross, *b.* aisle, *c.* refectory, *d.* nave) : TRANSEPT :: VERTICAL : HORIZONTAL

28. MNEMONIC : (*a.* nymph, *b.* elf, *c.* anger, *d.* knock) :: PNEUMATIC : GNOME

29. FAITH : JOB :: (*a.* wisdom, *b.* age, *c.* wickedness, *d.* courage) : METHUSELAH

30. MRS. GRUNDY : NARROW-MINDED :: POLLYANNA : (*a.* witty, *b.* dull, *c.* pessimistic, *d.* optimistic)

31. MIDNIGHT SUN : (*a.* Russia, *b.* Norway, *c.* China, *d.* South Pole) :: RISING SUN : JAPAN

32. RED-BLOODED : VIGOROUS :: BLUE-BLOODED : (*a.* cowardly, *b.* sickly, *c.* prudish, *d.* aristocratic)

33. (*a.* battle, *b.* artillery, *c.* ammunition, *d.* armory) : WEAPONS :: CLOSET : CLOTHING

34. CHARACTERISTIC : DEFINING :: USUALLY : (*a.* never, *b.* sometimes, *c.* rarely, *d.* always)

35. OBVIATE : (*a.* make unnecessary, *b.* make necessary, *c.* make obvious, *d.* make obscure) :: EXPUNGE : DELETE

36. BROBDINGNAGIAN : GIGANTIC :: (*a.* Lilliputian, *b.* Houyhnhnm, *c.* Vespasian, *d.* Yahoo) :: TINY

37. RUSSIA : (*a.* tsar, *b.* king, *c.* emperor, *d.* autarch) :: FRANCE : KING

38. MINOTAUR : BULL :: CENTAUR : (*a.* cow, *b.* horse, *c.* pig, *d.* goat)

39. INTEGRAL : (*a.* acceleration, *b.* length, *c.* area, *d.* velocity) :: DERIVATIVE : SLOPE

40. GUSTATORY : (*a.* taste, *b.* touch, *c.* sight, *d.* smell) :: AUDITORY : HEARING

41. OCTOPI : OCTOPUSES :: (*a.* cannona, *b.* cannon, *c.* cannones, *d.* cannonade) : CANNONS

42. CRIME : WAR :: PUNISHMENT : (*a.* Destruction, *b.* Treaty, *c.* Peace, *d.* Retribution)

43. SUPPLY : DEMAND :: RATE : (*a.* distance, *b.* time, *c.* velocity, *d.* price)

44. ICONOCLAST : (*a.* religious images, *b.* autocracy, *c.* democratic ideals, *d.* anarchy) :: NIHILIST : SOCIAL ORDER

45. QUIXOTIC : CERVANTES :: FAUSTIAN : (*a.* Hegel, *b.* Faust, *c.* Schiller, *d.* Goethe)

46. EXPEL : STUDENT :: (*a.* expire, *b.* expunge, *c.* expropriate, *d.* exorcise) : SPIRIT

47. (*a.* Julian, *b.* Augustan, *c.* Caesarian, *d.* Publican) : GREGORIAN :: NEWTONIAN : EINSTEINIAN

48. (*a.* Koch, *b.* Pasteur, *c.* Lister, *d.* Sabin) : RABIES :: SALK : POLIO

49. MINNEAPOLIS : ST. PAUL :: (*a.* Uncle, *b.* Rabbit, *c.* Abelard, *d.* Romulus) : REMUS

50. POSSE : SHERIFF :: SQUIRE : (*a.* queen, *b.* bourgeoisie, *c.* knight, *d.* vassal)

51. UNTOUCHABLE : (*a.* Hindu, *b.* Vishnu, *c.* Brahman, *d.* Krishna) :: FLOOR : CEILING

52. PENTAGON : DECAGON :: RECTANGLE : (*a.* square, *b.* pentagon, *c.* heptagon, *d.* octagon)

53. TOWARD : IN THE DIRECTION OF :: UNTOWARD : (*a.* at the location of, *b.* away from, *c.* unseemly, *d.* unsafe)

54. EXOGAMY : OUTBREEDING :: (*a.* endogamy, *b.* inogamy, *c.* anogamy, *d.* onogamy) : INBREEDING

55. GRAND : (*a.* pauvre, *b.* petit, *c.* standard, *d.* legal) :: INDICT : CONVICT

56. CHROMATIC : PASTEL :: ACHROMATIC : (*a.* oil, *b.* tempera, *c.* chiasma, *d.* chiaroscuro)

57. EQUATOR : LATITUDE :: (*a.* North Pole, *b.* apogee, *c.* Greenwich, *d.* meridian) : LONGITUDE

58. ROMEO : JULIET :: PYRAMUS : (*a.* Chloe, *b.* Thisbe, *c.* Helen, *d.* Daphne)

59. PETROLEUM : GASOLINE :: BAUXITE : (*a.* aluminum, *b.* tin, *c.* lead, *d.* fool's gold)

60. 0 : ADDITION :: (*a.* 0, *b.* 1, *c.* −1, *d.* ∞) : MULTIPLICATION

61. GALAHAD : (*a.* Beatrice, *b.* Round Table, *c.* Holy Grail, *d.* True Cross) :: JASON : GOLDEN FLEECE

62. RED HERRING : (*a.* lie, *b.* peccadillo, *c.* diversion, *d.* secret plot) :: BLUE RIBBON : FIRST PRIZE

63. WATERMARK : EARMARK :: (*a.* crops, *b.* tide, *c.* silver, *d.* paper) : ANIMAL

64. ETHER : STARS :: PHLOGISTON : (*a.* earth, *b.* metal, *c.* fire, *d.* water)

65. PARTY : (*a.* revel, *b.* fight, *c.* meeting, *d.* dance) :: SWINE : BOAR

66. RHODE ISLAND : ALASKA :: MERCURY : (*a.* Earth, *b.* Jupiter, *c.* Saturn, *d.* Uranus)

67. MERETRICIOUS : (*a.* egregious, *b.* excellent, *c.* gaudy, *d.* plain) :: APEX : SUMMIT

68. ANTONY : CLEOPATRA :: (*a.* Lancelot, *b.* Arthur, *c.* Merlin, *d.* Gawain) : GUINEVERE

69. MERITOCRACY : MERIT :: PLUTOCRACY : (*a.* wisdom, *b.* money, *c.* power, *d.* physical prowess)

70. INTREPID : (*a.* cowardly, *b.* bold, *c.* voluble, *d.* taciturn) :: AGILE : CLUMSY

71. (*a.* Mars, *b.* Saturn, *c.* Jupiter, *d.* Mercury) : HERMES :: VENUS : APHRODITE

72. COMPLEMENTARY ANGLES : 90° :: COMPLEMENTARY COLORS : (*a.* white, *b.* black, *c.* violet, *d.* red)

73. (*a.* Jefferson, *b.* Adams, *c.* Hamilton, *d.* Madison) : BURR :: LINCOLN : BOOTH

74. PUFFIN : (*a.* bird, *b.* reptile, *c.* mammal, *d.* amphibian) :: STURGEON : FISH

75. BRONZE : (*a.* aluminum, *b.* tin, *c.* gold, *d.* silver) :: BRASS : ZINC

76. G MAJOR : (*a.* B minor, *b.* C minor, *c.* D minor, *d.* E minor) :: C MAJOR : A MINOR

77. (*a.* cow, *b.* jackal, *c.* wolf, *d.* rabbit) : LUPINE :: DOG : CANINE

78. (*a.* one, *b.* few, *c.* ten, *d.* all) : ISOCRACY :: ONE : AUTOCRACY

79. LOG 10 : LOG 100 :: LOG 100 : (*a.* log 1,000, *b.* log 10,000, *c.* log 100,000, *d.* log 1,000,000)

80. HAPPINESS : SHANGRI-LA :: (*a.* wealth, *b.* happiness, *c.* gods, *d.* freedom) : EL DORADO

81. DRACONIAN : (*a.* cowardly, *b.* bold, *c.* cruel, *d.* kindly) :: STENTORIAN : LOUD

82. MANSION : HOUSE :: TOME : (*a.* boat, *b.* book, *c.* desk, *d.* church)

83. NEUTRAL : 7 :: (*a.* alkaline, *b.* acidic, *c.* hydrated, *d.* oxidized) : 1

84. PERUSE : SKIM :: REPEL : (*a.* gloss, *b.* bowdlerize, *c.* drive back, *d.* attract)

85. NUCLEOLUS : NUCLEUS :: SET : (*a.* superset, *b.* set, *c.* subset, *d.* disjoint set)

86. HORSEBACK RIDING : EQUITATION :: (*a.* giving birth, *b.* skydiving, *c.* swimming, *d.* dancing) : NATATION

87. WHIGS : TORIES :: JACOBINS : (*a.* Fascists, *b.* Laborites, *c.* Roundheads, *d.* Girondists)

88. PRIME : (*a.* God, *b.* destiny, *c.* factum, *d.* mover) :: FIRST : CAUSE

89. FRANC : FRANCE :: (*a.* lira, *b.* mark, *c.* guilder, *d.* franc) : SWITZERLAND

90. (*a.* Jungfrau, *b.* Blanc, *c.* Matterhorn, *d.* Olympus) : ALPS :: EVEREST : HIMALAYAS

91. MELANCHOLY : (*a.* blue bile, *b.* green bile, *c.* red bile, *d.* black bile) :: CHOLER : YELLOW BILE

92. ORAL : ANAL :: DEPENDENCY : (*a.* lazy, *b.* thermometer, *c.* stinginess, *d.* independent)

93. (*a.* hit, *b.* die, *c.* invest, *d.* sprout) : BURGEON :: ENTREAT : IMPLORE

94. DEARTH : PAUCITY :: SCARCITY : (*a.* plethora, *b.* shortage, *c.* necessity, *d.* commodity)

95. DELFT : (*a.* glass, *b.* pottery, *c.* stoneware, *d.* silver) :: LIMOGES : CHINA

96. IAMB : RETURN :: TROCHEE : (*a.* stable, *b.* arrive, *c.* defend, *d.* eternal)

97. AUTOCHTHONOUS : (*a.* foreign, *b.* native, *c.* self-governing, *d.* dependent) :: LETTER : EPISTLE

98. (*a.* bells, *b.* horn, *c.* magpies, *d.* toads) : TINTINNABULATION :: GEESE : HONK

99. ELF : FLEE :: TON : (*a.* note, *b.* pound, *c.* dwarf, *d.* find)

100. CODA : (*a.* novel, *b.* musical composition, *c.* sculpture, *d.* ceramic jar) :: LANDING : FLIGHT

101. (*a.* months, *b.* tides, *c.* days, *d.* climates) : SEASONS :: MOON : SUN

102. TARANTELLA : ITALY :: CANCAN : (*a.* Argentina, *b.* Spain, *c.* Colombia, *d.* France)

103. AUDITORY : (*a.* olfactory, *b.* sensory, *c.* occipital, *d.* nasal) :: EAR : NOSE

104. TAILFEATHERS : PEACOCK :: (*a.* coat, *b.* tail, *c.* face, *d.* feet) : MANDRILL

105. BUFFALO : WHEAT :: NICKEL : (*a.* dollar, *b.* quarter, *c.* dime, *d.* penny)

106. ACIDIC : (*a.* 3, *b.* 7, *c.* 10, *d.* 14) :: ALKALINE : 12

107. (*a.* Romania, *b.* Croatia, *c.* Greece, *d.* Hungary) : YUGOSLAVIA :: CZECH REPUBLIC : CZECHOSLOVAKIA

108. ROCKY : SMOKY :: COLORADO : (*a.* West Virginia, *b.* New York, *c.* New Hampshire, *d.* Tennessee)

109. BADGER : DOG :: PESTER : (*a.* track, *b.* avoid, *c.* exhaust, *d.* behave)

110. ACCORDION : (*a.* bagpipe, *b.* flute, *c.* organ, *d.* clarinet) :: HARMONIUM : PIANO

111. RACECAR : RADAR :: (*a.* abbreviation, *b.* homonym, *c.* palindrome, *d.* gerund) : ACRONYM

112. (*a.* 82, *b.* 99, *c.* 22, *d.* 15) : 451 :: CATCH : FAHRENHEIT

113. A : Z :: Alpha : (*a.* Omega, *b.* Beta, *c.* Zed, *d.* Phi)

114. AMETHYST : (*a.* amber, *b.* purple, *c.* crimson, *d.* yellow) :: SAPPHIRE : BLUE

115. SYCOPHANT : TOADY :: MISCREANT : (*a.* artist, *b.* recluse, *c.* follower, *d.* criminal)

116. EKG : (*a.* heart, *b.* pancreas, *c.* bladder, *d.* lungs) :: EEG : brain

117. TONY : OSCAR :: (*a.* music, *b.* theater, *c.* literature, *d.* television) : FILM

118. (*a.* Colorado, *b.* Wyoming, *c.* Idaho, *d.* Alaska) : MCKINLEY :: NEPAL : EVEREST

119. I, CLAUDIUS : GRAVES :: (*a.* I, Julius, *b.* I, Criminal, *c.* I, Nixon, *d.* I, Robot) : ASIMOV

120. VIRGINIA : TENNESEE :: WOOLF : (*a.* Faulkner, *b.* Percy, *c.* Williams, *d.* O'Connor)

Answer Key

PRACTICE TEST 9

1. C	31. B	61. C	91. D
2. A	32. D	62. C	92. C
3. D	33. D	63. D	93. D
4. C	34. D	64. C	94. B
5. A	35. A	65. A	95. B
6. B	36. A	66. B	96. A
7. B	37. A	67. C	97. B
8. C	38. B	68. A	98. A
9. B	39. C	69. B	99. A
10. C	40. A	70. A	100. B
11. A	41. B	71. D	101. B
12. D	42. C	72. A	102. D
13. B	43. B	73. C	103. A
14. B	44. A	74. A	104. C
15. A	45. D	75. B	105. D
16. C	46. D	76. D	106. A
17. B	47. A	77. C	107. B
18. B	48. B	78. D	108. D
19. A	49. D	79. B	109. A
20. D	50. C	80. A	110. C
21. A	51. C	81. C	111. C
22. A	52. D	82. B	112. C
23. D	53. C	83. B	113. A
24. C	54. A	84. D	114. B
25. C	55. B	85. A	115. D
26. A	56. D	86. C	116. A
27. D	57. C	87. D	117. B
28. D	58. B	88. D	118. D
29. B	59. A	89. D	119. D
30. D	60. B	90. B	120. C

EXPLANATION OF ANSWERS FOR PRACTICE TEST 9

In the following explanations of answers, explanations concerning the correct response are in a large font. Explanations regarding distracters (incorrect responses) that are not self-explaining or could be misinterpreted are in a smaller font in order to highlight the explanations of the answers that are correct.

1. POSTMAN : LETTER :: (*a.* surgeon, *b.* orthopedist, ***c.* obstetrician**, *d.* podiatrist) : BABY

   (**c**) A postman delivers a letter; an obstetrician delivers a baby.
   General Information—Description

2. CHLOROPHYLL : GREEN :: HEMOGLOBIN : (***a.* red**, *b.* black, *c.* green, *d.* blue)

   (**a**) Chlorophyll is a green substance that gives leaves their green color; hemoglobin is a red substance that gives blood its red color.
   Natural Science—Description

3. HAPPY : (*a.* sad, *b.* gay, *c.* indifferent, ***d.* ecstatic**) :: BRIGHT : BRILLIANT

   (**d**) A person who is extremely happy is ecstatic; a person who is extremely bright is brilliant.
   Vocabulary—Description

4. PENCIL : PEN :: (*a.* wood, *b.* ballpoint, ***c.* graphite**, *d.* boron) : INK

   (**c**) The writing substance in a pencil is usually graphite; the writing substance in a pen is usually ink.
   General Information—Description

5. ONE BIRD : HAND :: TWO BIRDS : (***a.* bush**, *b.* foot, *c.* nest, *d.* head)

   (**a**) A familiar proverb states, "A bird in the hand is worth two in the bush."
   General Information—Completion

6. SILVER : TARNISH :: IRON : (*a.* oxidation, ***b.* rust**, *c.* magnet, *d.* tin)

   (**b**) When silver oxidizes, the result is called tarnish; when iron oxidizes, the result is called rust.
   General Information—Description

7. BUTTERFLY : CATERPILLAR :: (*a.* amphibian, ***b.* frog**, *c.* salamander, *d.* larva) : TADPOLE

   (**b**) A caterpillar is the larval form of a butterfly; a tadpole is the larval form of a frog.
   Natural Science—Description

8. GREEN : (*a.* cowardice, *b.* viciousness, ***c.* envy**, *d.* delight) :: PURPLE : RAGE

   (**c**) Green and purple are colors commonly used to denote emotional states. A person is said to be green with envy or purple with rage.
   General Information—Completion

9. JUDAS : JESUS :: (*a.* Augustus, ***b.* Brutus**, *c.* Lucius, *d.* Antony) : JULIUS CAESAR

   (**b**) Judas betrayed Jesus; Brutus betrayed Julius Caesar.
   Humanities—Description

10. JOLLY ROGER : (*a.* communists, *b.* fascists, ***c.* pirates**, *d.* anarchists) :: UNION JACK : UNITED KINGDOM

    (**c**) The Jolly Roger was the emblem of pirates, while the Union Jack is the emblem of the United Kingdom.
    General Information—Description

11. DIALECTIC : HEGEL :: DIALECTICAL MATERIALISM : (***a.* Marx**, *b.* Fichte, *c.* Schelling, *d.* Kant)

    (**a**) Hegel developed the philosophical notion of the dialectic, while Marx developed the philosophical notion of dialectical materialism. Fichte was one of the founders of German Idealism, which developed on the basis of Kant's thoughts. He investigated self-consciousness. Schelling was involved in German Idealism and investigated conceptions of nature in his *Naturphilosophie*. Kant is famous for his *Critique of Pure Reason*, which investigates reason itself.
    Humanities—Description

12. (*a.* screen, *b.* camera, *c.* projector, ***d.* frame**) : MOVIE FILM :: LINK : CHAIN

    (**d**) A movie film is composed of successive frames, while a chain is composed of successive links.
    General Information—Part/Whole

13. PROLOGUE : (*a.* decalogue, ***b.* epilogue**, *c.* preface, *d.* forward) :: APPETIZER : DESSERT

(**b**) A prologue introduces a book, and an epilogue closes it; an appetizer introduces a meal, and a dessert closes it.
Humanities—Class

14. HAMMERSTEIN : (*a.* Sondheim, ***b.* Rodgers**, *c.* Gilbert, *d.* Herman) :: LERNER : LOEWE

(**b**) Hammerstein and Rodgers created Broadway musicals, with Hammerstein writing the lyrics and Rodgers composing the music; Lerner and Loewe also created Broadway musicals, with Lerner writing the lyrics and Loewe composing the music.
Humanities—Class

15. (***a.* dumb**, *b.* stupid, *c.* loquacious, *d.* brilliant) : MUTE :: SMART : INTELLIGENT

(**a**) *Dumb* and *mute* are synonyms, as are *smart* and *intelligent*.
Vocabulary—Similarity/Contrast

16. ARCHIVES : (*a.* munitions, *b.* tombs, ***c.* documents**, *d.* animals) :: PANTRY : KITCHEN UTENSILS

(**c**) Documents are stored in archives, while kitchen utensils are stored in a pantry.
General Information—Description

17. DUNCAN : MACBETH :: MACBETH : (*a.* Lady Macbeth, ***b.* Macduff**, *c.* Polonius, *d.* Claudius)

(**b**) In Shakespeare's play *Macbeth*, Macbeth kills Duncan and Macduff kills Macbeth. Polonius was Chamberlain to King Claudius in Shakespeare's *Hamlet*. Lady Macbeth is the wife of Macbeth in Shakespeare's *Macbeth*.
Humanities—Description

18. V : X :: D : (*a.* I, ***b.* M**, *c.* D, *d.* C)

(**b**) The terms of the analogy are Roman numerals; 10 is equal to twice 5, and 1,000 is equal to twice 500. In Roman numerals, I = 1, V = 5, X = 10, L = 50, C = 100, D = 500, M = 1,000.
Mathematics—Equality/Negation

19. JACK SPRAT'S WIFE : LEAN :: VEGETARIAN : (***a.* meat**, *b.* fat, *c.* vegetables, *d.* roots)

(**a**) Jack Sprat's wife would eat no lean, according to the nursery rhyme; a vegetarian will eat no meat.
General Information—Description

20. (*a.* politics, *b.* law, *c.* music, ***d.* medicine**) : HIPPOCRATES :: HISTORY : HERODOTUS

    (**d**) Hippocrates is often referred to as the Father of Medicine, while Herodotus is known as the Father of History.
    Humanities—Description

21. (***a.* Russia**, *b.* China, *c.* Japan, *d.* Hungary) : BALALAIKA :: SCOTLAND : BAGPIPES

    (**a**) The balalaika is a Russian musical instrument; the bagpipes are a Scottish musical instrument.
    Humanities—Description

22. TAILPIPE : EXHAUST :: RADIUM : (***a.* beta rays**, *b.* strontium, *c.* cosmic rays, *d.* lead)

    (**a**) A tailpipe emits exhaust; radium emits beta rays.
    Natural Science—Description

23. ARGUS : 100 :: CYCLOPS : (*a.* 1000, *b.* 10, *c.* 5, ***d.* 1**)

    (**d**) According to legend, Argus had 100 eyes, while Cyclops had just 1.
    Humanities—Description

24. CANNON : BIG BERTHA :: (*a.* battleship, *b.* bazooka, ***c.* bell**, *d.* church steeple) : BIG BEN

    (**c**) Big Bertha is the name of a cannon; Big Ben is the name of a bell.
    General Information—Class

25. (*a.* pretty, *b.* pretentious, ***c.* proud**, *d.* portly) : PEACOCK :: SILLY : GOOSE

    (**c**) People are often likened either to a peacock or to a goose. One may be proud as a peacock, or silly as a goose.
    General Information—Completion

26. HYPOCRITICAL : INSINCERE :: HYPERCRITICAL : (***a.* overcritical**, *b.* sincere, *c.* oversincere, *d.* critical)

    (**a**) *Hypocritical* and *insincere* are synonyms, as are *hypercritical* and *overcritical*.
    Vocabulary—Similarity/Contrast

27. (*a.* cross, *b.* aisle, *c.* refectory, ***d.* nave**) : TRANSEPT :: VERTICAL : HORIZONTAL

(**d**) In a cross-shaped church, the nave and the transept are perpendicular to each other, as are any objects that are vertical and horizontal with respect to each other.
Humanities—Similarity/Contrast

28. MNEMONIC : (*a.* nymph, *b.* elf, *c.* anger, ***d.* knock**) :: PNEUMATIC : GNOME

(**d**) *Mnemonic, pneumatic, gnome,* and *knock* each has a silent consonant preceding the initial voiced consonant, *n.*
Nonsemantic

29. FAITH : JOB :: (*a.* wisdom, ***b.* age**, *c.* wickedness, *d.* courage) : METHUSELAH

(**b**) In the Bible, Job distinguished himself by his great faith in God, while Methuselah distinguished himself by the great age to which he lived (969 years).
Humanities—Description

30. MRS. GRUNDY : NARROW-MINDED :: POLLYANNA : (*a.* witty, *b.* dull, *c.* pessimistic, ***d.* optimistic**)

(**d**) Mrs. Grundy is a literary character in Thomas Morton's play *Speed the Plow,* known for her narrow-mindedness. Pollyanna is a literary character in *Pollyanna* by Eleanor Porter, known for her optimism.
Humanities—Description

31. MIDNIGHT SUN : (*a.* Russia, ***b.* Norway**, *c.* China, *d.* South Pole) :: RISING SUN : JAPAN

(**b**) Norway is the Land of the Midnight Sun, while Japan is the Land of the Rising Sun.
General Information—Description

32. RED-BLOODED : VIGOROUS :: BLUE-BLOODED : (*a.* cowardly, *b.* sickly, *c.* prudish, ***d.* aristocratic**)

(**d**) A vigorous person is sometimes referred to as red-blooded, while an aristocratic person is sometimes referred to as blue-blooded.
Vocabulary—Similarity/Contrast

33. (*a.* battle, *b.* artillery, *c.* ammunition, ***d.* armory**) : WEAPONS :: CLOSET : CLOTHING

(**d**) An armory is used to store weapons; a closet is used to store clothing.
General Information—Description

34. CHARACTERISTIC : DEFINING :: USUALLY : (*a.* never, *b.* sometimes, *c.* rarely, ***d.* always**)

(**d**) A characteristic feature is one usually possessed by an object, while a defining feature is one always possessed by an object.
General Information—Description

35. OBVIATE : (***a.* make unnecessary**, *b.* make necessary, *c.* make obvious, *d.* make obscure) :: EXPUNGE : DELETE

(**a**) To obviate is to make unnecessary; to expunge is to delete.
Vocabulary—Similarity/Contrast

36. BROBDINGNAGIAN : GIGANTIC :: (***a.* Lilliputian**, *b.* Houyhnhnm, *c.* Vespasian, *d.* Yahoo) :: TINY

(**a**) In the novel *Gulliver's Travels* (by Jonathan Swift), the Brobdingnagians are gigantic people, while the Lilliputians are tiny ones.
Humanities—Description

37. RUSSIA : (***a.* tsar**, *b.* king, *c.* emperor, *d.* autarch) :: FRANCE : KING

(**a**) Russia was formerly ruled by a tsar, France by a king.
Social Science—Description

38. MINOTAUR : BULL :: CENTAUR : (*a.* cow, ***b.* horse**, *c.* pig, *d.* goat)

(**b**) The minotaur, according to mythology, was part bull and part man; the centaur was part horse and part man.
Humanities—Description

39. INTEGRAL : (*a.* acceleration, *b.* length, ***c.* area**, *d.* velocity) :: DERIVATIVE : SLOPE

(**c**) In calculus, an integral can be computed to determine area, while a derivative can be calculated to determine slope.
Mathematics—Description

40. GUSTATORY : (***a.* taste**, *b.* touch, *c.* sight, *d.* smell) :: AUDITORY : HEARING

(**a**) *Gustatory* refers to taste; *auditory*, to hearing. *Kinesthetic* refers to touch, visual refers to sight, and olfactory refers to smell.
Natural Science—Description

41. OCTOPI : OCTOPUSES :: (*a.* cannona, ***b.* cannon**, *c.* cannones, *d.* cannonade) : CANNONS

(**b**) *Octopi* and *octopuses* are both plural forms of the word *octopus*; *cannon* and *cannons* are both plural forms of the word *cannon*.
Humanities—Similarity/Contrast

42. CRIME : WAR :: PUNISHMENT : (*a.* Destruction, *b.* Treaty, **c. Peace**, *d.* Retribution)

    (**c**) *Crime and Punishment* is a novel by the Russian author Dostoevski. *War and Peace* is a novel by the Russian author Tolstoy.
    Humanities—Completion

43. SUPPLY : DEMAND :: RATE : (*a.* distance, ***b.* time**, *c.* velocity, *d.* price)

    (**b**) Supply and demand are inversely related, as are rate and time.
    Mathematics—Equality/Negation

44. ICONOCLAST : (***a.* religious images**, *b.* autocracy, *c.* democratic ideals, *d.* anarchy) :: NIHILIST : SOCIAL ORDER

    (**a**) The goal of an iconoclast is to destroy religious images; the goal of a nihilist is to destroy social order.
    Vocabulary—Description

45. QUIXOTIC : CERVANTES :: FAUSTIAN : (*a.* Hegel, *b.* Faust, *c.* Schiller, ***d.* Goethe**)

    (**d**) The word *quixotic* is derived from the name of a literary character, Don Quixote, who is the subject of a work by Cervantes; the word *faustian* is derived from the name of a character, Faust, who is the subject of a work by Goethe.
    Humanities—Description

46. EXPEL : STUDENT :: (*a.* expire, *b.* expunge, *c.* expropriate, ***d.* exorcise**) : SPIRIT

    (**d**) A student is expelled from school; a spirit is exorcised from the body.
    Vocabulary—Description

47. (***a.* Julian**, *b.* Augustan, *c.* Caesarian, *d.* Publican) : GREGORIAN :: NEWTONIAN : EINSTEINIAN

    (**a**) The Julian calendar was replaced by the Gregorian calendar; Newtonian physics was replaced by Einsteinian physics.
    Humanities—Description

48. (*a.* Koch, ***b.* Pasteur**, *c.* Lister, *d.* Sabin) : RABIES :: SALK : POLIO

    (**b**) Pasteur developed an antirabies vaccine; Salk developed an antipolio vaccine. Lister promoted the idea of sterile surgery. Sabin developed the oral vaccine for polio. Koch is well known for isolating the tuberculosis bacillus, *Bacillus anthracis*.
    Natural Science—Description

49. MINNEAPOLIS : ST. PAUL :: (*a.* Uncle, *b.* Rabbit, *c.* Abelard, ***d.* Romulus**) : REMUS

    (**d**) Minneapolis and St. Paul are twin cities. Romulus and Remus, according to legend, were twin brothers.
    Humanities—Class

50. POSSE : SHERIFF :: SQUIRE : (*a.* queen, *b.* bourgeoisie, ***c.* knight**, *d.* vassal)

    (**c**) A posse assists a sheriff; a squire assisted a knight.
    General Information—Description

51. UNTOUCHABLE : (*a.* Hindu, *b.* Vishnu, ***c.* Brahman**, *d.* Krishna) :: FLOOR : CEILING

    (**c**) In former times, an untouchable was a member of the lowest Indian caste, while a Brahman was a member of the highest one. A floor is the lowest part of a room, while a ceiling is the highest part.
    General Information—Similarity/Contrast

52. PENTAGON : DECAGON :: RECTANGLE : (*a.* square, *b.* pentagon, *c.* heptagon, ***d.* octagon**)

    (**d**) A decagon has twice as many sides as a pentagon; an octagon has twice as many sides as a rectangle.
    Mathematics—Equality/Negation

53. TOWARD : IN THE DIRECTION OF :: UNTOWARD : (*a.* at the location of, *b.* away from, ***c.* unseemly**, *d.* unsafe)

    (**c**) *Toward* means in the direction of. *Untoward* means unseemly.
    Vocabulary Similarity/Contrast

54. EXOGAMY : OUTBREEDING :: (***a.* endogamy**, *b.* inogamy, *c.* anogamy, *d.* onogamy) : INBREEDING

    (**a**) *Exogamy* refers to outbreeding, while *endogamy* refers to inbreeding.
    Natural Science—Description

55. GRAND : (*a.* pauvre, ***b.* petit**, *c.* standard, *d.* legal) :: INDICT : CONVICT

    (**b**) A grand jury has the power to indict an individual for a crime, while a petit jury has the power to convict him or her of it.
    Social Science—Description

56. CHROMATIC : PASTEL :: ACHROMATIC : (*a.* oil, *b.* tempera, *c.* chiasma, ***d.* chiaroscuro**)

(**d**) Pastel is a chromatic form of artwork (with colors), while chiaroscuro is an achromatic form (black and white).
Humanities—Description

57. EQUATOR : LATITUDE :: (*a.* North Pole, *b.* apogee, ***c.* Greenwich**, *d.* meridian) : LONGITUDE

(**c**) The equator is at 0° latitude; Greenwich is at 0° longitude.
General Information—Description

58. ROMEO : JULIET :: PYRAMUS : (*a.* Chloe, ***b.* Thisbe**, *c.* Helen, *d.* Daphne)

(**b**) Romeo and Juliet were lovers, as were Pyramus and Thisbe. Chloe is another name for Demeter, who was the goddess of harvest and fertility in Greek mythology. Helen was the daughter of Zeus and Leda, wife of King Menelaus of Sparta, and was abducted by Paris, which led to the Trojan War. Daphne was a nymph in Greek mythology.
Humanities—Class

59. PETROLEUM : GASOLINE :: BAUXITE : (***a.* aluminum**, *b.* tin, *c.* lead, *d.* fool's gold)

(**a**) Petroleum is the raw material used to make gasoline, while bauxite is the raw material from which aluminum is obtained. Pewter is an alloy that contains tin. Lead is a heavy metal that may be added in smaller amounts to pewter as well.
Natural Science—Description

60. 0 : ADDITION :: (*a.* 0, ***b.* 1**, *c.* −1, *d.* ∞) : MULTIPLICATION

(**b**) Zero is the identity element for addition—any number plus 0 equals that number. One is the identity element for multiplication—any number times 1 equals that number.
Mathematics—Description

61. GALAHAD : (*a.* Beatrice, *b.* Round Table, ***c.* Holy Grail**, *d.* True Cross) :: JASON : GOLDEN FLEECE

(**c**) According to legend, Galahad succeeded in his quest for the Holy Grail, while Jason succeeded in his quest for the Golden Fleece.
Humanities—Description

62. RED HERRING : (*a.* lie, *b.* peccadillo, ***c.* diversion**, *d.* secret plot) ::
BLUE RIBBON : FIRST PRIZE

(**c**) A red herring is a diversion. A blue ribbon is a first prize.
Vocabulary—Description

63. WATERMARK : EARMARK :: (*a.* crops, *b.* tide, *c.* silver, ***d.* paper**) :
ANIMAL

(**d**) Paper is sometimes identified by a watermark; an animal is sometimes
identified by an earmark.
General Information—Description

64. ETHER : STARS :: PHLOGISTON : (*a.* earth, *b.* metal, ***c.* fire**, *d.* water)

(**c**) In medieval times, it was believed that the stars were composed of a
substance called ether, and that fire was composed of a substance called
phlogiston.
Natural Science—Description

65. PARTY : (***a.* revel**, *b.* fight, *c.* meeting, *d.* dance) :: SWINE : BOAR

(**a**) A revel is a wild party. A boar is a form of wild swine.
General Information—Description

66. RHODE ISLAND : ALASKA :: MERCURY : (*a.* Earth, ***b.* Jupiter**,
c. Saturn, *d.* Uranus)

(**b**) Rhode Island is the smallest state; Alaska, the largest. Mercury is the
smallest planet (in our solar system); Jupiter, the largest. The size of the
planets (starting with the smallest): Mercury, Mars, Venus, Earth, Neptune,
Uranus, Saturn, Jupiter.
Natural Science—Class

67. MERETRICIOUS : (*a.* egregious, *b.* excellent, ***c.* gaudy**, *d.* plain) :: APEX :
SUMMIT

(**c**) *Meretricious* and *gaudy* are synonyms, as are *apex* and *summit*.
Vocabulary—Similarity/Contrast

68. ANTONY : CLEOPATRA :: (***a.* Lancelot**, *b.* Arthur, *c.* Merlin, *d.* Gawain) :
GUINEVERE

(**a**) Cleopatra was the mistress of Antony; Guinevere was the mistress of
Lancelot. King Arthur was a British king in the 6th century who defended Britain against
invaders from Saxony. Merlin was a wizard from the Arthurian legend. Gawain was King
Arthur's nephew and a member of the Round Table.
Humanities—Class

69. MERITOCRACY : MERIT :: PLUTOCRACY : (*a.* wisdom, **b. money**, *c.* power, *d.* physical prowess)

(**b**) A meritocracy is rule by those demonstrating merit; a plutocracy is rule by the wealthy.
Social Science—Description

70. INTREPID : (**a. cowardly**, *b.* bold, *c.* voluble, *d.* taciturn) :: AGILE : CLUMSY

(**a**) *Intrepid* and *cowardly* are antonyms, as are *agile* and *clumsy*.
Vocabulary—Similarity/Contrast

71. (*a.* Mars, *b.* Saturn, *c.* Jupiter, **d. Mercury**) : HERMES :: VENUS : APHRODITE

(**d**) Mercury is the Roman name, and Hermes the Greek name, for the messenger of the gods. Venus is the Roman name, and Aphrodite the Greek name, for the goddess of beauty. Mars was the god of war in Roman mythology. Jupiter was the god of sky and thunder. Saturn was the god of agriculture and harvest.
Humanities—Similarity/Contrast

72. COMPLEMENTARY ANGLES : 90° :: COMPLEMENTARY COLORS : (**a. white**, *b.* black, *c.* violet, *d.* red)

(**a**) Complementary angles sum to 90°; complementary colors sum to white.
Natural Science—Description

73. (*a.* Jefferson, *b.* Adams, **c. Hamilton**, *d.* Madison) : BURR :: LINCOLN : BOOTH

(**c**) Aaron Burr killed Alexander Hamilton, while John Wilkes Booth killed Abraham Lincoln.
Humanities—Description

74. PUFFIN : (**a. bird**, *b.* reptile, *c.* mammal, *d.* amphibian) :: STURGEON : FISH

(**a**) A puffin is a kind of bird; a sturgeon is a kind of fish.
General Information—Description

75. BRONZE : (*a.* aluminum, **b. tin**, *c.* gold, *d.* silver) :: BRASS : ZINC

(**b**) Bronze is a combination of copper and tin, while brass is a combination of copper and zinc.
Natural Science—Description

76. G MAJOR : (*a.* B minor, *b.* C minor, *c.* D minor, *d.* **E minor**) ::
C MAJOR : A MINOR

(**d**) The keys of G major and E minor both have one sharp, while the keys of C major and A minor have none.
Humanities—Description

77. (*a.* cow, *b.* jackal, *c.* **wolf**, *d.* rabbit) : LUPINE :: DOG : CANINE

(**c**) To be lupine is to be wolflike; to be canine is to be doglike.
Vocabulary—Description

78. (*a.* one, *b.* few, *c.* ten, *d.* **all**) : ISOCRACY :: ONE : AUTOCRACY

(**d**) An isocracy is rule by all; an autocracy is rule by one.
Social Science—Description

79. LOG 10 : LOG 100 :: LOG 100 : (*a.* log 1,000, *b.* **log 10,000**, *c.* log 100,000, *d.* log 1,000,000)

(**b**) Log 100 is twice as great as log 10 (2 : 1). Log 10,000 is twice as great as log 100 (4 : 2).
Mathematics—Class

80. HAPPINESS : SHANGRI-LA :: (*a.* **wealth**, *b.* happiness, *c.* gods, *d.* freedom) : EL DORADO

(**a**) Shangri-La is an imaginary land of great happiness; El Dorado is an imaginary land of great wealth.
General Information—Description

81. DRACONIAN : (*a.* cowardly, *b.* bold, *c.* **cruel**, *d.* kindly) ::
STENTORIAN : LOUD

(**c**) A draconian person is cruel; a stentorian person is loud.
Vocabulary—Description

82. MANSION : HOUSE :: TOME : (*a.* boat, *b.* **book**, *c.* desk, *d.* church)

(**b**) A mansion is a large house. A tome is a large book.
Vocabulary—Description

83. NEUTRAL : 7 :: (*a.* alkaline, *b.* **acidic**, *c.* hydrated, *d.* oxidized) : 1

(**b**) On the pH scale, 7 is neutral and 1 is acidic. Numbers greater than 7 indicate alkalinity.
Natural Science—Description

84. PERUSE : SKIM :: REPEL : (*a.* gloss, *b.* bowdlerize, *c.* drive back, ***d.* attract**)

(**d**) *Peruse* and *skim* are antonyms, as are *repel* and *attract*.
Vocabulary—Similarity/Contrast

85. NUCLEOLUS : NUCLEUS :: SET : (***a.* superset**, *b.* set, *c.* subset, *d.* disjoint set)

(**a**) In a cell, the nucleolus is contained in the nucleus. Similarly, a set is contained in a superset.
Natural Science—Part/Whole

86. HORSEBACK RIDING : EQUITATION :: (*a.* giving birth, *b.* skydiving, ***c.* swimming**, *d.* dancing) : NATATION

(**c**) Equitation is the art of horseback riding; natation is the art of swimming.
General Information—Description

87. WHIGS : TORIES :: JACOBINS : (*a.* Fascists, *b.* Laborites, *c.* Roundheads, ***d.* Girondists**)

(**d**) During the American Revolution, the Whigs represented a radical faction and the Tories a more conservative one. During the French Revolution, the Jacobins represented a radical faction and the Girondists a more conservative one.
Humanities—Class

88. PRIME : (*a.* God, *b.* destiny, *c.* factum, ***d.* mover**) :: FIRST : CAUSE

(**d**) In Aristotelian philosophy, the prime mover was a first cause (of all movement).
Humanities—Completion

89. FRANC : FRANCE :: (*a.* lira, *b.* mark, *c.* guilder, ***d.* franc**) : SWITZERLAND

(**d**) The franc was the unit of currency in both France and Switzerland (although the two francs are not equivalent). The lira was the currency of Italy, the mark was the currency of Germany, and the guilder was the currency of the Netherlands (before the euro).
General Information—Description

90. (*a.* Jungfrau, ***b.* Blanc**, *c.* Matterhorn, *d.* Olympus) : ALPS :: EVEREST : HIMALAYAS

(**b**) Mont Blanc is the highest peak in the Alps; Mount Everest is the highest peak in the Himalayas. Jungfrau and Matterhorn are mountains of the Swiss Alps; Mount Olympus is the highest mountain of Greece.
General Information—Description

91. MELANCHOLY : (*a.* blue bile, *b.* green bile, *c.* red bile, *d.* **black bile**) ::
CHOLER : YELLOW BILE

(**d**) According to the physiology of days gone by, melancholy is black bile,
while choler is yellow bile.
Natural Science—Similarity/Contrast

92. ORAL : ANAL :: DEPENDENCY : (*a.* lazinesss, *b.* thermometer,
***c.* stinginess**, *d.* independence)

(**c**) In psychodynamic theory, dependency is an oral trait and stinginess an
anal trait.
Social Science—Description

93. (*a.* hit, *b.* die, *c.* invest, ***d.* sprout**) : BURGEON :: ENTREAT : IMPLORE

(**d**) *Sprout* and *burgeon* are synonyms, as are *entreat* and *implore*.
Vocabulary—Similarity/Contrast

94. DEARTH : PAUCITY :: SCARCITY : (*a.* plethora, ***b.* shortage**, *c.* necessity,
d. commodity)

(**b**) *Dearth* and *paucity* are synonyms, as are *scarcity* and *shortage*.
(All four words are synonymous.)
Vocabulary—Similarity/Contrast

95. DELFT : (*a.* glass, ***b.* pottery**, *c.* stoneware, *d.* silver) :: LIMOGES : CHINA

(**b**) Delft is known for its beautiful painted pottery; Limoges is known for
its beautiful painted china.
General Information—Description

96. IAMB : RETURN :: TROCHEE : (***a.* stable**, *b.* arrive, *c.* defend, *d.* eternal)

(**a**) *Return* is pronounced as an iamb; *stable* is pronounced as a trochee.
An iamb is a metrical foot that consists of one unstressed and one stressed
syllable; a trochee consists of one long (stressed) syllable that is followed
by a short (unstressed) one.
Humanities—Class

97. AUTOCHTHONOUS : (*a.* foreign, ***b.* native**, *c.* self-governing,
d. dependent) :: LETTER : EPISTLE

(**b**) *Autochthonous* and *native* are synonyms, as are *letter* and *epistle*.
Vocabulary—Similarity/Contrast

98. (***a.* bells**, *b.* horn, *c.* magpies, *d.* toads) : TINTINNABULATION ::
GEESE : HONK

(**a**) Tintinnabulation is a sound made by bells; honk is a sound made
by geese.
Vocabulary—Description

99. ELF : FLEE :: TON : (***a. note***, *b.* pound, *c.* dwarf, *d.* find)

(**a**) *Flee* is *elf* spelled backwards, but with an added *e* at the end.
Note is *ton* spelled backwards, also with an added *e* at the end.
Nonsemantic

100. CODA : (*a.* novel, ***b. musical composition***, *c.* sculpture, *d.* ceramic jar) ::
LANDING : FLIGHT

(**b**) A coda concludes a musical composition; a landing concludes a flight.
Humanities—Description

101. (*a.* months, ***b. tides***, *c.* days, *d.* climates) : SEASONS :: MOON : SUN

(**b**) The tides change as the Earth's positional relationship to the Moon
changes. The seasons change as the Earth's positional relationship to the
Sun changes.
Natural Science—Description

102. TARANTELLA : ITALY :: CANCAN : (*a.* Argentina, *b.* Spain,
c. Colombia, ***d. France***)

(**d**) The tarantella and cancan are dances that originated in Italy and France,
respectively. Flamenco is a dance from Spain, tango is from Argentina, and bambuco
is from Colombia.
Humanities—Description

103. AUDITORY : (***a. olfactory***, *b.* sensory, *c.* occipital, *d.* nasal) :: EAR :
NOSE

(**a**) The ear is responsible for auditory sensation, or hearing. The nose
is responsible for olfactory sensation, or smelling.
Vocabulary—Description

104. TAILFEATHERS : PEACOCK :: (*a.* coat, *b.* tail, ***c. face***, *d.* feet) :
MANDRILL

(**c**) A peacock is known for its brightly colored tailfeathers just as a mandrill
is known for its brightly colored face.
General Information—Description

105. BUFFALO : WHEAT :: NICKEL : (*a.* dollar, *b.* quarter, *c.* dime, ***d. penny***)

(**d**) A buffalo was formerly placed on one side of the nickel, and these coins
were known as buffalo nickels. A shaft of wheat was formerly placed on one
side of the penny, and these coins were known as wheat pennies.
General Information—Completion

106. ACIDIC : (**a. 3**, *b.* 7, *c.* 10, *d.* 14) :: ALKALINE : 12

> (**a**) A solution with a pH level of 3 is acidic, just as a solution with a pH level of 12 is alkaline.
> *Natural Science—Description*

107. (*a.* Romania, **b. Croatia**, *c.* Greece, *d.* Hungary) : YUGOSLAVIA :: CZECH REPUBLIC : CZECHOSLOVAKIA

> (**b**) Croatia is part of the country once known as Yugoslavia. The Czech Republic is part of the country once known as Czechoslovakia.
> *General Information—Description*

108. ROCKY : SMOKY :: COLORADO : (*a.* West Virginia, *b.* New York, *c.* New Hampshire, **d. Tennessee**)

> (**d**) The Rocky Mountains can be found in the state of Colorado just as the Smoky Mountains can be found in Tennessee.
> *General Information—Description*

109. BADGER : DOG :: PESTER : (**a. track**, *b.* avoid, *c.* exhaust, *d.* behave)

> (**a**) To badger is to pester someone persistently. To dog is to track someone or something persistently.
> *General Information—Similarity/Contrast*

110. ACCORDION : (*a.* bagpipe, *b.* flute, **c. organ**, *d.* clarinet) :: HARMONIUM : PIANO

> (**c**) The accordion, organ, harmonium, and piano are all instruments with black and white keyboards.
> *Humanities—Class*

111. RACECAR : RADAR :: (*a.* abbreviation, *b.* homonym, **c. palindrome**, *d.* gerund) : ACRONYM

> (**c**) The word racecar is a palindrome: it reads the same forward and backward. The word radar is an acronym: it stands for RAdio Detection And Ranging.
> *Nonsemantic—Nonsemantic*

112. (*a.* 82, *b.* 99, **c. 22**, *d.* 15) : 451 :: CATCH : FAHRENHEIT

> (**c**) *Catch 22* and *Fahrenheit 451* are both popular novels, by Joseph Heller and Ray Bradbury respectively.
> *Humanities—Description*

113. A : Z :: Alpha : (***a.* Omega**, *b.* Beta, *c.* Zed, *d.* Phi)

    (**a**) A is the first and Z (Zed) the last letter of the English alphabet.
    Alpha is the first and Omega the last letter of the Greek alphabet.
    General Information—Description

114. AMETHYST : (*a.* amber, ***b.* purple**, *c.* crimson, *d.* yellow) :: SAPPHIRE :
    BLUE

    (**b**) Amethyst is a gemstone that is typically purple in color. Sapphire is a
    gemstone that is typically blue in color.
    Natural Science—Description

115. SYCOPHANT : TOADY :: MISCREANT : (*a.* artist, *b.* recluse, *c.* follower,
    ***d.* criminal**)

    (**d**) A sycophant is a toady, just as a miscreant is a criminal.
    Vocabulary—Similarity/Contrast

116. EKG : (***a.* heart**, *b.* pancreas, *c.* bladder, *d.* lungs) :: EEG : brain

    (**a**) An EKG machine measures activity in the heart just as an EEG machine
    measures activity in the brain. EEG stands for electroencephalogram.
    EKG stands for electrocardiogram.
    Natural Science—Description

117. TONY : OSCAR :: (*a.* music, ***b.* theater**, *c.* literature, *d.* television) : FILM

    (**b**) The Tony Award is given for accomplishments in theater just as the
    Oscar is given for accomplishments in film.
    General Information—Description

118. (*a.* Colorado, *b.* Wyoming, *c.* Idaho, ***d.* Alaska**) : MCKINLEY :: NEPAL :
    EVEREST

    (**d**) Mount McKinley is in Alaska and Mount Everest is in Nepal.
    General Information—Description

119. I, CLAUDIUS : GRAVES :: (*a.* I, Julius, *b.* I, Criminal, *c.* I, Nixon,
    ***d.* I, Robot**) : ASIMOV

    (**d**) Graves wrote the novel *I, Claudius* and Asimov wrote the novel
    I, Robot.
    Humanities—Description

120. VIRGINIA : TENNESSEE :: WOOLF : (*a.* Faulkner, *b.* Percy, ***c.* Williams**,
    d. O'Connor)

    (**c**) Virginia Woolf and Tennessee Williams were both writers. Woolf wrote
    Mrs. Dalloway and *Orlando*, for example. Williams's works include *Cat on
    a Hot Tin Roof* and *A Streetcar Named Desire*.
    Humanities—Description

PRACTICE TEST 9

Item Classification Chart

		RELATIONSHIP						
		Similarity/ Contrast	Description	Class	Completion	Part/ Whole	Equality/ Negation	Nonsemantic
C O N T E N T	**Vocabulary**	15, 26, 32, 35, 53, 67, 70, 84, 93, 94, 97, 115	3, 44, 46, 62, 77, 81, 82, 98, 103					
	General Information	51, 109	1, 4, 6, 10, 16, 19, 31, 33, 34, 50, 57, 63, 65, 74, 80, 86, 89, 90, 95, 104, 107, 108, 113, 117, 118	24	5, 8, 25, 105	12		
	Humanities	27, 41, 71	9, 11, 17, 20, 21, 23, 29, 30, 36, 38, 45, 47, 56, 61, 73, 76, 100, 102, 112, 119, 120	13, 14, 49, 58, 68, 87, 96, 110	42, 88			
	Social Science		37, 55, 69, 78, 92					
	Natural Science	91	2, 7, 22, 40, 48, 54, 59, 64, 72, 75, 83, 101, 106, 114, 116	66		85		
	Mathematics		39, 60	79			18, 43, 52	
	Nonsemantic							28, 99, 111

Answer Sheet
PRACTICE TEST 10

1 Ⓐ Ⓑ Ⓒ Ⓓ	31 Ⓐ Ⓑ Ⓒ Ⓓ	61 Ⓐ Ⓑ Ⓒ Ⓓ	91 Ⓐ Ⓑ Ⓒ Ⓓ
2 Ⓐ Ⓑ Ⓒ Ⓓ	32 Ⓐ Ⓑ Ⓒ Ⓓ	62 Ⓐ Ⓑ Ⓒ Ⓓ	92 Ⓐ Ⓑ Ⓒ Ⓓ
3 Ⓐ Ⓑ Ⓒ Ⓓ	33 Ⓐ Ⓑ Ⓒ Ⓓ	63 Ⓐ Ⓑ Ⓒ Ⓓ	93 Ⓐ Ⓑ Ⓒ Ⓓ
4 Ⓐ Ⓑ Ⓒ Ⓓ	34 Ⓐ Ⓑ Ⓒ Ⓓ	64 Ⓐ Ⓑ Ⓒ Ⓓ	94 Ⓐ Ⓑ Ⓒ Ⓓ
5 Ⓐ Ⓑ Ⓒ Ⓓ	35 Ⓐ Ⓑ Ⓒ Ⓓ	65 Ⓐ Ⓑ Ⓒ Ⓓ	95 Ⓐ Ⓑ Ⓒ Ⓓ
6 Ⓐ Ⓑ Ⓒ Ⓓ	36 Ⓐ Ⓑ Ⓒ Ⓓ	66 Ⓐ Ⓑ Ⓒ Ⓓ	96 Ⓐ Ⓑ Ⓒ Ⓓ
7 Ⓐ Ⓑ Ⓒ Ⓓ	37 Ⓐ Ⓑ Ⓒ Ⓓ	67 Ⓐ Ⓑ Ⓒ Ⓓ	97 Ⓐ Ⓑ Ⓒ Ⓓ
8 Ⓐ Ⓑ Ⓒ Ⓓ	38 Ⓐ Ⓑ Ⓒ Ⓓ	68 Ⓐ Ⓑ Ⓒ Ⓓ	98 Ⓐ Ⓑ Ⓒ Ⓓ
9 Ⓐ Ⓑ Ⓒ Ⓓ	39 Ⓐ Ⓑ Ⓒ Ⓓ	69 Ⓐ Ⓑ Ⓒ Ⓓ	99 Ⓐ Ⓑ Ⓒ Ⓓ
10 Ⓐ Ⓑ Ⓒ Ⓓ	40 Ⓐ Ⓑ Ⓒ Ⓓ	70 Ⓐ Ⓑ Ⓒ Ⓓ	100 Ⓐ Ⓑ Ⓒ Ⓓ
11 Ⓐ Ⓑ Ⓒ Ⓓ	41 Ⓐ Ⓑ Ⓒ Ⓓ	71 Ⓐ Ⓑ Ⓒ Ⓓ	101 Ⓐ Ⓑ Ⓒ Ⓓ
12 Ⓐ Ⓑ Ⓒ Ⓓ	42 Ⓐ Ⓑ Ⓒ Ⓓ	72 Ⓐ Ⓑ Ⓒ Ⓓ	102 Ⓐ Ⓑ Ⓒ Ⓓ
13 Ⓐ Ⓑ Ⓒ Ⓓ	43 Ⓐ Ⓑ Ⓒ Ⓓ	73 Ⓐ Ⓑ Ⓒ Ⓓ	103 Ⓐ Ⓑ Ⓒ Ⓓ
14 Ⓐ Ⓑ Ⓒ Ⓓ	44 Ⓐ Ⓑ Ⓒ Ⓓ	74 Ⓐ Ⓑ Ⓒ Ⓓ	104 Ⓐ Ⓑ Ⓒ Ⓓ
15 Ⓐ Ⓑ Ⓒ Ⓓ	45 Ⓐ Ⓑ Ⓒ Ⓓ	75 Ⓐ Ⓑ Ⓒ Ⓓ	105 Ⓐ Ⓑ Ⓒ Ⓓ
16 Ⓐ Ⓑ Ⓒ Ⓓ	46 Ⓐ Ⓑ Ⓒ Ⓓ	76 Ⓐ Ⓑ Ⓒ Ⓓ	106 Ⓐ Ⓑ Ⓒ Ⓓ
17 Ⓐ Ⓑ Ⓒ Ⓓ	47 Ⓐ Ⓑ Ⓒ Ⓓ	77 Ⓐ Ⓑ Ⓒ Ⓓ	107 Ⓐ Ⓑ Ⓒ Ⓓ
18 Ⓐ Ⓑ Ⓒ Ⓓ	48 Ⓐ Ⓑ Ⓒ Ⓓ	78 Ⓐ Ⓑ Ⓒ Ⓓ	108 Ⓐ Ⓑ Ⓒ Ⓓ
19 Ⓐ Ⓑ Ⓒ Ⓓ	49 Ⓐ Ⓑ Ⓒ Ⓓ	79 Ⓐ Ⓑ Ⓒ Ⓓ	109 Ⓐ Ⓑ Ⓒ Ⓓ
20 Ⓐ Ⓑ Ⓒ Ⓓ	50 Ⓐ Ⓑ Ⓒ Ⓓ	80 Ⓐ Ⓑ Ⓒ Ⓓ	110 Ⓐ Ⓑ Ⓒ Ⓓ
21 Ⓐ Ⓑ Ⓒ Ⓓ	51 Ⓐ Ⓑ Ⓒ Ⓓ	81 Ⓐ Ⓑ Ⓒ Ⓓ	111 Ⓐ Ⓑ Ⓒ Ⓓ
22 Ⓐ Ⓑ Ⓒ Ⓓ	52 Ⓐ Ⓑ Ⓒ Ⓓ	82 Ⓐ Ⓑ Ⓒ Ⓓ	112 Ⓐ Ⓑ Ⓒ Ⓓ
23 Ⓐ Ⓑ Ⓒ Ⓓ	53 Ⓐ Ⓑ Ⓒ Ⓓ	83 Ⓐ Ⓑ Ⓒ Ⓓ	113 Ⓐ Ⓑ Ⓒ Ⓓ
24 Ⓐ Ⓑ Ⓒ Ⓓ	54 Ⓐ Ⓑ Ⓒ Ⓓ	84 Ⓐ Ⓑ Ⓒ Ⓓ	114 Ⓐ Ⓑ Ⓒ Ⓓ
25 Ⓐ Ⓑ Ⓒ Ⓓ	55 Ⓐ Ⓑ Ⓒ Ⓓ	85 Ⓐ Ⓑ Ⓒ Ⓓ	115 Ⓐ Ⓑ Ⓒ Ⓓ
26 Ⓐ Ⓑ Ⓒ Ⓓ	56 Ⓐ Ⓑ Ⓒ Ⓓ	86 Ⓐ Ⓑ Ⓒ Ⓓ	116 Ⓐ Ⓑ Ⓒ Ⓓ
27 Ⓐ Ⓑ Ⓒ Ⓓ	57 Ⓐ Ⓑ Ⓒ Ⓓ	87 Ⓐ Ⓑ Ⓒ Ⓓ	117 Ⓐ Ⓑ Ⓒ Ⓓ
28 Ⓐ Ⓑ Ⓒ Ⓓ	58 Ⓐ Ⓑ Ⓒ Ⓓ	88 Ⓐ Ⓑ Ⓒ Ⓓ	118 Ⓐ Ⓑ Ⓒ Ⓓ
29 Ⓐ Ⓑ Ⓒ Ⓓ	59 Ⓐ Ⓑ Ⓒ Ⓓ	89 Ⓐ Ⓑ Ⓒ Ⓓ	119 Ⓐ Ⓑ Ⓒ Ⓓ
30 Ⓐ Ⓑ Ⓒ Ⓓ	60 Ⓐ Ⓑ Ⓒ Ⓓ	90 Ⓐ Ⓑ Ⓒ Ⓓ	120 Ⓐ Ⓑ Ⓒ Ⓓ

Practice Test 10

Directions: In each of the following questions, you will find three initial terms and, in parentheses, four answer options designated *a*, *b*, *c*, and *d*. You are to select from the four answer options the one that best completes the analogy with the three initial terms. To record your answers, use the answer sheet provided.

Time: 60 minutes

1. PEN : INK :: PENCIL : (*a*. limestone, *b*. graphite, *c*. talc, *d*. gypsum)

2. (*a*. probably, *b*. possibly, *c*. virtually, *d*. certainly) : 1 :: MAYBE : .5

3. HORRIFIC : HORROR :: SOPORIFIC : (*a*. joy, *b*. boredom, *c*. sleep, *d*. stupidity)

4. A/B : B/A :: (*a*. 1/15, *b*. 1/3, *c*. 2/3, *d*. 3/2) : 1.5

5. UNINTERRUPTED : (*a*. discrete, *b*. repeated, *c*. endless, *d*. likely) :: CONTINUOUS : CONTINUAL

6. PTOLEMY : EARTH :: COPERNICUS : (*a*. moon, *b*. sun, *c*. Jupiter, *d*. universe)

7. (*a*. sculptor, *b*. painter, *c*. poet, *d*. architect) : VENUS DE MILO :: AUTHOR : THE SCARLET LETTER

8. QUICK : RABBIT :: (*a*. sleepy, *b*. wise, *c*. hungry, *d*. angry) : OWL

9. PATRICIDE : (*a*. brother, *b*. sister, *c*. king, *d*. father) :: MATRICIDE : MOTHER

10. AMA : DOCTORS :: ABA : (*a*. athletes, *b*. miners, *c*. lawyers, *d*. historians)

11. WOODHULL : PELOSI :: ALBRIGHT : (*a*. Day O'Connor, *b*. Bush, *c*. Sebelius, *d*. Ginsburg)

12. MADISON : WAR OF 1812 :: (*a*. Reagan, *b*. G. H. Bush, *c*. Clinton, *d*. G. W. Bush) : GULF WAR

13. BULLET : (*a*. noose, *b*. head, *c*. force, *d*. blade) :: GUN : GUILLOTINE

14. (*a*. ·, *b*. ÷, *c*. **, *d*. undefined) : MULTIPLICATION :: + : ADDITION

15. PSYCHOLOGY : MIND :: PHYCOLOGY : (*a.* herbivores, *b.* carnivores, *c.* algae, *d.* cacti)

16. (*a.* Third Estate, *b.* House, *c.* Parliament, *d.* Commons) : LOWER :: LORDS : UPPER

17. BACTERIA : (*a.* bacteria, *b.* bacterium, *c.* bacterius, *d.* bacterion) :: MANY : ONE

18. SCURVY : VITAMIN C :: KWASHIORKOR : (*a.* vitamin A, *b.* vitamin B$_{12}$, *c.* protein, *d.* niacin)

19. CONVERSE : CONTRAPOSITIVE :: (*a.* B → A, *b.* A → B, *c.* not B → A, *d.* not A → B) : NOT B → NOT A

20. (*a.* New York, *b.* New Mexico, *c.* Missouri, *d.* Michigan) : LAKE :: MISSISSIPPI : RIVER

21. 0 PERCENT : (*a.* pressure, *b.* wind chill, *c.* THI, *d.* humidity) :: ABSOLUTE 0 : TEMPERATURE

22. OBTUSE : ACUTE :: (*a.* 0, *b.* 100, *c.* 180, *d.* 270) : 45

23. AB : AWAY :: (*a.* a, *b.* contra, *c.* ex, *d.* ad) : WITHOUT

24. UNCLE : (*a.* paternal, *b.* avuncular, *c.* uncial, *d.* uncinate) :: BROTHER : FRATERNAL

25. (*a.* women, *b.* marriage, *c.* falsehood, *d.* enlightenment) : MISOLOGY :: NOVELTY : MISONEISM

26. LIE : (*a.* lie, *b.* lay, *c.* laid, *d.* lain) :: LAY : LAID

27. HELTER : SKELTER :: HIGGLEDY : (*a.* niggledy, *b.* piggledy, *c.* spiggledy, *d.* wiggledy)

28. SPOOL : LOOPS :: (*a.* water, *b.* pools, *c.* dinghy, *d.* tools) : SLOOP

29. RILL : (*a.* stream, *b.* lake, *c.* ocean, *d.* lagoon) : NOVELLA : NOVEL

30. SONATA : SONATINA :: CONCERTO : (*a.* concertino, *b.* concertina, *c.* concert, *d.* concerto grosso)

31. NEW JERSEY : 8:00 :: OREGON : (*a.* 5:00, *b.* 6:00, *c.* 9:00, *d.* 10:00)

32. LINCOLN : 1 :: JEFFERSON : (*a.* 3, *b.* 5, *c.* 10, *d.* 25)

33. PLINY THE ELDER : (*a.* Carthaginian, *b.* Athenian, *c.* Milanese, *d.* Roman) :: THUCYDIDES : GREEK

34. (*a.* Uruguay, *b.* Argentina, *c.* Paraguay, *d.* Guatemala) : CENTRAL :: BRAZIL : SOUTH

35. ETHER : GENERAL :: NOVOCAINE : (*a.* specific, *b.* particulate, *c.* local, *d.* toxic)

36. D'ARTAGNAN : (*a.* Hugo, *b.* Mauriac, *c.* Dumas, *d.* Balzac) :: GATSBY : FITZGERALD

37. ARMY : LAND :: (*a.* Marines, *b.* Navy, *c.* CIA, *d.* Secret Service) : AMPHIBIOUS

38. TWO : (*a.* hydrogen, *b.* uranium, *c.* americium, *d.* deuterium) :: THREE : TRITIUM

39. YORK : N.Y. :: ORLEANS : (*a.* N.O., *b.* La., *c.* Fr., *d.* Miss.)

40. (*a.* Copland, *b.* Mendelssohn, *c.* Shostakovich, *d.* Bach) : 19th :: MOZART : 18th

41. MENELAUS : (*a.* Agamemnon, *b.* Priam, *c.* Achilles, *d.* Spartacus) :: HECTOR : PARIS

42. MAJORITY : MINORITY :: (*a.* Bolshevik, *b.* Maoist, *c.* Marxist, *d.* Trotskyite) : MENSHEVIK

43. FEIGN : FINE :: (*a.* right, *b.* writ, *c.* rate, *d.* rat) : WRITE

44. FATUOUS : (*a.* bright, *b.* prodigal, *c.* contemptuous, *d.* foolish) :: FASTIDIOUS : HARD TO PLEASE

45. (*a.* Ayer, *b.* Peirce, *c.* Santayana, *d.* Russell) : PRAGMATIST :: SARTRE : EXISTENTIALIST

46. ADDITIVE : (*a.* blue, *b.* red, *c.* green, *d.* white) :: SUBTRACTIVE : YELLOW

47. PROTON : NUCLEON :: MUON : (*a.* meson, *b.* electron, *c.* pion, *d.* positron)

48. BOARD : (*a.* fifteen, *b.* checkers, *c.* bridge, *d.* thirty-six) :: DECK : TWENTY-ONE

49. C# : Db :: B# : (*a.* Cb, *b.* Bb, *c.* C, *d.* Db)

50. SEVER : PERSEVERANCE :: CUT : (*a.* perseveration, *b.* perspective, *c.* pertinence, *d.* persistence)

51. FREUD : (*a.* Skinner, *b.* Allport, *c.* Murray, *d.* Erikson) :: KOHLBERG : PIAGET

52. (*a.* ellipsoid, *b.* semicircle, *c.* rhombus, *d.* angle) : PROTRACTOR :: RECTANGLE : RULER

53. BIPOLARITY : MONOLOGUE :: (*a.* dicotyledon, *b.* stamen, *c.* deciduous, *d.* pistil) : UNION

54. (*a.* patent medicine, *b.* adage, *c.* theory, *d.* heretic) : APOTHEGM :: DEXTERITY : ADROITNESS

55. FROM : TO :: (*a.* artery, *b.* ventricle, *c.* atrium, *d.* carotid) : JUGULAR

56. SOUSA : (*a.* waltzes, *b.* symphonies, *c.* marches, *d.* hymns) :: VERDI : OPERAS

57. INVOCATION : (*a.* benediction, *b.* recessional, *c.* prayer, *d.* vesper) :: START : FINISH

58. SASKATCHEWAN : REGINA :: (*a.* Quebec, *b.* Alberta, *c.* Ontario, *d.* Manitoba) : TORONTO

59. (*a.* obvious, *b.* latent, *c.* proximate, *d.* apposite) : MANIFEST :: COVERT : OVERT

60. DIRGE : REQUIEM :: GRIEF : (*a.* thanksgiving, *b.* mourning, *c.* penitence, *d.* joy)

61. (*a.* metropolitan, *b.* synod, *c.* district, *d.* diocese) : BISHOP :: PARISH : PRIEST

62. CONSONANT : VOWEL :: COMPOSITE : (*a.* prime, *b.* irrational, *c.* integer, *d.* zero)

63. IMPLODE : (*a.* explode, *b.* beseech, *c.* implicate, *d.* burst inward) :: IMPLY : HINT AT

64. EARTH : SUN :: PLANET : (*a.* heavenly body, *b.* sol, *c.* star, *d.* nova)

65. OCTOPUS : (*a.* six, *b.* eight, *c.* ten, *d.* twelve) :: PERSON : TWO

66. QUARTER : DOLLAR :: (*a.* season, *b.* day, *c.* month, *d.* decade) : YEAR

67. CAPTAIN : (*a.* admiral, *b.* ensign, *c.* commodore, *d.* midshipman) ::
CORPORAL : SERGEANT

68. DAVID : VAN DYCK :: FRENCH : (*a.* Italian, *b.* German, *c.* Flemish,
d. British)

69. (*a.* poulet, *b.* glacé, *c.* citron, *d.* entrecote) : SWEET :: CAFÉ : BITTER

70. WAIVE : WAVE :: (*a.* relinquish, *b.* relegate, *c.* remand, *d.* redress) :
UNDULATE

71. WORK : (*a.* joule, *b.* ohm, *c.* ampere, *d.* coulomb) :: POTENTIAL
DIFFERENCE : VOLT

72. PHILOLOGY : LANGUAGES :: MYCOLOGY : (*a.* flowering plants,
b. ferns, *c.* weeds, *d.* fungi)

73. DEPENDENT : INDEPENDENT :: (*a.* autochthonous, *b.* canonical,
c. anaclitic, *d.* irrecusable) : SELF-RELIANT

74. CX : (*a.* CXV, *b.* CL, *c.* CLX, *d.* CC) :: LV : LXXV

75. CAMEL : RHINOCEROS :: HUMP : (*a.* armor, *b.* snout, *c.* horn, *d.* hide)

76. ONTOLOGY : (*a.* being, *b.* metaphysics, *c.* growth, *d.* knowledge) ::
DEONTOLOGY : ETHICS

77. (*a.* leukocytes, *b.* platelets, *c.* hormones, *d.* erythrocytes) : ANEMIA ::
INSULIN : DIABETES

78. CALVIN : COOLIDGE :: (*a.* Alexander, *b.* Franklin, *c.* William, *d.* Robert) :
PIERCE

79. PONTIUS PILATE : JESUS :: CREON : (*a.* Orestes, *b.* Oedipus,
c. Antigone, *d.* Electra)

80. (*a.* bellicose, *b.* periphrastic, *c.* altruistic, *d.* nihilistic) : AGGRESSION ::
IRENIC : PEACE

81. FIRST : LAST :: GENESIS : (*a.* Exodus, *b.* Deuteronomy, *c.* Leviticus,
d. Numbers)

82. πr^2 : $2\pi r$ :: AREA : (*a.* diameter, *b.* circumference, *c.* perimeter, *d.* volume)

83. BUCKINGHAM PALACE : XANADU :: ELIZABETH II :
(*a.* Genghis Khan, *b.* Charles V, *c.* Citizen Kane, *d.* Donald Trump)

84. MONOGYNY : (*a.* life, *b.* religion, *c.* child, *d.* wife) :: MONOTHEISM : GOD

85. ESPRESSO : BLACK :: ORANGE PEKOE : (*a.* green, *b.* white, *c.* black, *d.* red)

86. DIANA : (*a.* Artemis, *b.* Minerva, *c.* Aphrodite, *d.* Hera) :: JUPITER : ZEUS

87. (*a.* B$_b$ major, *b.* E$_b$ major, *c.* F major, *d.* A major) : C MINOR :: G MAJOR : E MINOR

88. MAN : NAME :: (*a.* rig, *b.* appellation, *c.* maiden, *d.* woman) : GIRL

89. MANON LESCAUT : (*a.* wise, *b.* arrogant, *c.* promiscuous, *d.* wicked) :: TOM SAWYER : ADVENTUROUS

90. (*a.* Bull Moose, *b.* Whig, *c.* Socialist, *d.* Know-Nothing) : DEBS :: DEMOCRAT : STEVENSON

91. FIRST : CLERGY :: FOURTH : (*a.* nobles, *b.* commoners, *c.* children, *d.* journalists)

92. AMETHYST : GARNET :: PURPLE : (*a.* red, *b.* green, *c.* transparent, *d.* blue)

93. (*a.* loquacious, *b.* refractory, *c.* ostentatious, *d.* timid) : GARRULOUS :: AUDACIOUS : BOLD

94. FOUR : APRIL FOOL'S DAY :: (*a.* one, *b.* two, *c.* five, *d.* ten) : MAY DAY

95. STEEPLE : CHURCH :: (*a.* minaret, *b.* muezzin, *c.* imam, *d.* arch) : MOSQUE

96. VANILLA : (*a.* bean, *b.* Sussex, *c.* hasty, *d.* Brazil) :: RICE : YORKSHIRE

97. (*a.* Saint-Saëns, *b.* Strindberg, *c.* Bernstein, *d.* Rubinstein) : PLAYS :: FROST : POEMS

98. THERMO : HEAT :: ISO : (*a.* cold, *b.* pressure, *c.* humidity, *d.* same)

99. (*a.* Scotch, *b.* vermouth, *c.* gin, *d.* bourbon) : TOM COLLINS :: VODKA : BLOODY MARY

100. BELLEEK : (*a.* Scotland, *b.* Ireland, *c.* Holland, *d.* Belgium) :: LIMOGES : FRANCE

101. AMPERE : (*a.* current, *b.* magnetism, *c.* speed, *d.* gravity) :: WATT : POWER

102. BAIKAL : RUSSIA :: (*a.* Michigan, *b.* Superior, *c.* Ontario, *d.* Placid) : UNITED STATES

103. (*a.* Lady's Man, *b.* Black Beauty, *c.* Secretariat, *d.* Fortune's Fool) : MAN O' WAR :: SEABISCUIT : WAR ADMIRAL

104. GAVRILO PRINCIP : ARCHDUKE FERDINAND :: (*a.* Robert E. Lee, *b.* Lee Harvey Oswald, *c.* John Hinckley, *d.* John Wilkes Booth) : PRESIDENT LINCOLN

105. KILOGRAM : POUND :: 1 : (*a.* 2.2, *b.* 5, *c.* 0.2, *d.* 7.3)

106. ROSEMARY : (*a.* oregano, *b.* cumin, *c.* nutmeg, *d.* cinnamon) :: BASIL : SAGE

107. COBBLER : SHOES :: (*a.* tanner, *b.* smith, *c.* cooper, *d.* miller) : BARRELS

108. EXPECTORATE : (*a.* bite, *b.* spit, *c.* deliver, *d.* swallow) :: MASTICATE : CHEW

109. (*a.* net, *b.* hat trick, *c.* goalie, *d.* puck) : ICE HOCKEY :: SHUTTLECOCK : BADMINTON

110. ARMSTRONG : TRUMPET :: COLTRANE : (*a.* piano, *b.* saxophone, *c.* clarinet, *d.* trombone)

111. MOHAMMED : JESUS :: (*a.* Judea, *b.* Constantinople, *c.* Mecca, *d.* Jerusalem) : BETHLEHEM

112. RHOMBUS : HEXAGON :: 4 : (*a.* 8, *b.* 7, *c.* 6, *d.* 5)

113. RECORD PLAYER : (*a.* loudest, *b.* loud, *c.* quiet, *d.* quieter) :: SUPERANNUATED : SUPERLATIVE

114. (*a.* feet, *b.* obedience, *c.* thought, *d.* memory) : ELEPHANT :: STRENGTH : ANT

115. DIAMOND : SAPPHIRE :: (*a.* Hope, *b.* Diana's, *c.* Indian, *d.* Pharoah's) : LOGAN

116. HEAVEN : ST. PETER :: HADES : (*a.* Lucifer, *b.* Scylla, *c.* Charybdis, *d.* Cerberus)

117. r-p-o-p-h-e-s-s-a-g-r : JABBERWOCKY :: CUMMINGS : (*a.* Milne, *b.* Cleary, *c.* Carroll, *d.* Eliot)

118. X : (*a.* w, *b.* y, *c.* u, *d.* a) :: VERTICAL : HORIZONTAL

119. (*a.* nostalgia, *b.* kindness, *c.* loyalty, *d.* naiveté) :: POLLYANNA :: DOUBT : THOMAS

120. MAASAI : EAST AFRICA :: LAPP : (*a.* Australia, *b.* Middle East, *c.* South Asia, *d.* Scandinavia)

Answer Key
PRACTICE TEST 10

1.	**B**	31.	**A**	61.	**D**	91.	**D**
2.	**D**	32.	**B**	62.	**D**	92.	**A**
3.	**C**	33.	**D**	63.	**D**	93.	**A**
4.	**C**	34.	**D**	64.	**C**	94.	**C**
5.	**B**	35.	**C**	65.	**B**	95.	**A**
6.	**B**	36.	**C**	66.	**A**	96.	**C**
7.	**A**	37.	**A**	67.	**C**	97.	**B**
8.	**B**	38.	**D**	68.	**C**	98.	**D**
9.	**D**	39.	**B**	69.	**B**	99.	**C**
10.	**C**	40.	**B**	70.	**A**	100.	**B**
11.	**A**	41.	**A**	71.	**A**	101.	**A**
12.	**B**	42.	**A**	72.	**D**	102.	**B**
13.	**D**	43.	**C**	73.	**C**	103.	**C**
14.	**A**	44.	**D**	74.	**B**	104.	**D**
15.	**C**	45.	**B**	75.	**C**	105.	**A**
16.	**D**	46.	**C**	76.	**A**	106.	**A**
17.	**B**	47.	**A**	77.	**D**	107.	**C**
18.	**C**	48.	**B**	78.	**B**	108.	**B**
19.	**A**	49.	**C**	79.	**C**	109.	**D**
20.	**D**	50.	**D**	80.	**A**	110.	**B**
21.	**D**	51.	**D**	81.	**B**	111.	**C**
22.	**B**	52.	**B**	82.	**B**	112.	**C**
23.	**A**	53.	**A**	83.	**C**	113.	**A**
24.	**B**	54.	**A**	84.	**D**	114.	**D**
25.	**D**	55.	**D**	85.	**C**	115.	**A**
26.	**B**	56.	**C**	86.	**A**	116.	**D**
27.	**B**	57.	**A**	87.	**B**	117.	**C**
28.	**B**	58.	**C**	88.	**A**	118.	**B**
29.	**A**	59.	**B**	89.	**C**	119.	**D**
30.	**A**	60.	**B**	90.	**C**	120.	**D**

EXPLANATION OF ANSWERS FOR PRACTICE TEST 10

In the following explanations of answers, explanations concerning the correct response are in a large font. Explanations regarding distracters (incorrect responses) that are not self-explaining or could be misinterpreted are in a smaller font in order to highlight the explanations of the answers that are correct.

1. PEN : INK :: PENCIL : (*a.* limestone, *b.* **graphite**, *c.* talc, *d.* gypsum)

   (**b**) A pen writes with ink; a pencil writes with graphite.
   General Information—Description

2. (*a.* probably, *b.* possibly, *c.* virtually, *d.* **certainly**) : 1 :: MAYBE : .5

   (**d**) Something that is certainly true has probability 1 of occurrence; something that is maybe true can have probability .5 of occurrence.
   General Information—Description

3. HORRIFIC : HORROR :: SOPORIFIC : (*a.* joy, *b.* boredom, *c.* **sleep**, *d.* stupidity)

   (**c**) Something horrific causes horror; something soporific causes sleep.
   Vocabulary—Description

4. A/B : B/A :: (*a.* 1/15, *b.* 1/3, *c.* **2/3**, *d.* 3/2) : 1.5

   (**c**) $B/A = 1/(A/B)$; $1.5 = 1/(2/3)$.
   Mathematics—Equality/Negation

5. UNINTERRUPTED : (*a.* discrete, *b.* **repeated**, *c.* endless, *d.* likely) :: CONTINUOUS : CONTINUAL

   (**b**) Something that is uninterrupted is continuous; something that is repeated is continual.
   Vocabulary—Similarity/Contrast

6. PTOLEMY : EARTH :: COPERNICUS : (*a.* moon, *b.* **sun**, *c.* Jupiter, *d.* universe)

   (**b**) Ptolemy believed that the earth is at the center of the planetary system; Copernicus believed that the sun is at the center.
   Natural Science—Description

7. (*a.* **sculptor**, *b.* painter, *c.* poet, *d.* architect) : VENUS DE MILO :: AUTHOR : THE SCARLET LETTER

   (**a**) Venus de Milo was created by a sculptor (unknown), *The Scarlet Letter* by an author (Nathaniel Hawthorne).
   Humanities—Description

8. QUICK : RABBIT :: (*a.* sleepy, *b.* **wise**, *c.* hungry, *d.* angry) : OWL

   (**b**) A rabbit is reputed to be quick; an owl is reputed to be wise.
   General Information—Description

9. PATRICIDE : (*a.* brother, *b.* sister, *c.* king, *d.* **father**) :: MATRICIDE : MOTHER

   (**d**) Patricide is the murder of one's father; matricide is the murder of one's mother. Fratricide stands for the murder of a brother; regicide refers to the murder of a monarch; sororicide stands for the murder of a sister.
   Vocabulary—Description

10. AMA : DOCTORS :: ABA : (*a.* athletes, *b.* miners, *c.* **lawyers**, *d.* historians)

    (**c**) The AMA (American Medical Association) is an association of doctors; the ABA (American Bar Association) is an association of lawyers.
    General Information—Description

11. WOODHULL : PELOSI :: ALBRIGHT : (*a.* **Day O'Connor**, *b.* Bush, *c.* Sebelius, *d.* Ginsburg)

    (**a**) Victoria Claflin Woodhull was the first woman to run for President; Nancy Pelosi was the first female Speaker of the U.S. House of Representatives; Madeleine Albright was the first woman to become U.S. Secretary of State; Sandra Day O'Connor was the first woman justice of the Supreme Court.
    General Information—Description

12. MADISON : WAR OF 1812 :: (*a.* Reagan, *b.* **G. H. Bush**, *c.* Clinton, *d.* G. W. Bush) : GULF WAR

    (**b**) Madison was president during the War of 1812. G. H. Bush was president during the Gulf War.
    Humanities—Description

13. BULLET : (*a.* noose, *b.* head, *c.* force, *d.* **blade**) : GUN : GUILLOTINE

    (**d**) A gun kills by a bullet; a guillotine kills by a blade.
    General Information—Description

14. (*a.* **·**, *b.* ÷, *c.* **, *d.* undefined) : MULTIPLICATION :: + : ADDITION

    (**a**) A raised dot (·) can be used to signify multiplication; a plus sign (+) can be used to signify addition.
    Mathematics—Description

15. PSYCHOLOGY : MIND :: PHYCOLOGY : (*a.* herbivores, *b.* carnivores, *c.* **algae**, *d.* cacti)

(**c**) Psychology is the science of the mind; phycology is the science of algae.
Natural Science—Description

16. (*a.* Third Estate, *b.* House, *c.* Parliament, *d.* **Commons**) : LOWER :: LORDS : UPPER

(**d**) The House of Commons is the lower house, and the House of Lords the upper house, of the British Parliament.
General Information—Description

17. BACTERIA : (*a.* bacteria, *b.* **bacterium**, *c.* bacterius, *d.* bacterion) :: MANY : ONE

(**b**) One refers to many bacteria (plural) or one bacterium (singular).
Vocabulary—Description

18. SCURVY : VITAMIN C :: KWASHIORKOR : (*a.* vitamin A, *b.* vitamin B_{12}, *c.* **protein**, *d.* niacin)

(**c**) Scurvy is caused by a deficiency of vitamin C; kwashiorkor is caused by a deficiency of protein. Pellagra is caused by lack of niacin. One of the results of vitamin A deficiency is impaired vision. A lack of vitamin B_{12} causes macrocytic anemia and cognitive deficits like memory loss.
Natural Science—Description

19. CONVERSE : CONTRAPOSITIVE :: (*a.* **B → A**, *b.* A → B, *c.* not B → A, *d.* not A → B) : (NOT B → NOT A)

(**a**) The converse of $A \rightarrow B$ is $B \rightarrow A$; the contrapositive of $A \rightarrow B$ is (not $B \rightarrow$ not A).
Humanities—Description

20. (*a.* New York, *b.* New Mexico, *c.* Missouri, *d.* **Michigan**) : LAKE :: MISSISSIPPI : RIVER

(**d**) Lake Michigan and the Mississippi River are bodies of water.
General Information—Completion

21. 0 PERCENT : (*a.* pressure, *b.* wind chill, *c.* THI, *d.* **humidity**) :: ABSOLUTE 0 : TEMPERATURE

(**d**) 0 percent is the minimum possible humidity; absolute 0 is the minimum possible temperature.
General Information—Description

22. OBTUSE : ACUTE :: (*a.* 0, ***b.* 100**, *c.* 180, *d.* 270) : 45

    (**b**) A 100° angle is obtuse; a 45° angle is acute.
    Mathematics—Description

23. AB : AWAY :: (***a.* a**, *b.* contra, *c.* ex, *d.* ad) : WITHOUT

    (**a**) The prefix *ab-* means "away"; the prefix *a-* means "without." The prefix *contra-* means "against." The prefix *ex-* means "excluding/without." The prefix *ad* means "to/towards."
    Vocabulary—Similarity/Contrast

24. UNCLE : (*a.* paternal, ***b.* avuncular**, *c.* uncial, *d.* uncinate) :: BROTHER : FRATERNAL

    (**b**) Someone who is avuncular is like an uncle; someone who is fraternal is like a brother. Someone who is paternal is like a father; uncial means written in capital letters; uncinate means that a tip is bent like a hook.
    Vocabulary—Description

25. (*a.* women, *b.* marriage, *c.* falsehood, ***d.* enlightenment**) : MISOLOGY :: NOVELTY : MISONEISM

    (**d**) Misology is hatred of enlightenment; misoneism is hatred of novelty.
    Vocabulary—Description

26. LIE : (*a.* lie, ***b.* lay**, *c.* laid, *d.* lain) :: LAY : LAID

    (**b**) The past tense of *lie* is *lay* (or, in another meaning of *lie*, *lied*, but this is not an option); the past tense of *lay* is *laid*.
    General Information—Class

27. HELTER : SKELTER :: HIGGLEDY : (*a.* niggledy, ***b.* piggledy**, *c.* spiggledy, *d.* wiggledy)

    (**b**) *Helter-skelter* and *higgledy-piggledy* are synonyms.
    Vocabulary—Completion

28. SPOOL : LOOPS :: (*a.* water, ***b.* pools**, *c.* dinghy, *d.* tools) : SLOOP

    (**b**) *Spool* spelled backward is *loops*; *pools* spelled backward is *sloop*.
    Nonsemantic

29. RILL : (***a.* stream**, *b.* lake, *c.* ocean, *d.* lagoon) : NOVELLA : NOVEL

    (**a**) A rill is a small stream; a novella is a small novel.
    Vocabulary—Description

30. SONATA : SONATINA :: CONCERTO : (*a.* **concertino**, *b.* concertina, *c.* concert, *d.* concerto grosso)

(**a**) A sonatina is a small sonata; a concertino is a small concerto. A concerto grosso is a baroque composition in which a small group of solo instruments play with an orchestra.
Humanities—Description

31. NEW JERSEY : 8:00 :: OREGON : (*a.* **5:00**, *b.* 6:00, *c.* 9:00, *d.* 10:00)

(**a**) When it is 8:00 in New Jersey, it is 5:00 in Oregon.
General Information—Description

32. LINCOLN : 1 :: JEFFERSON : (*a.* 3, *b.* **5**, *c.* 10, *d.* 25)

(**b**) The head of Lincoln appears on a 1-cent piece; the head of Jefferson appears on a 5-cent piece. Franklin Roosevelt is featured on a 10-cent piece. The regular 25-cent coin features George Washington.
General Information—Description

33. PLINY THE ELDER : (*a.* Carthaginian, *b.* Athenian, *c.* Milanese, *d.* **Roman**) :: THUCYDIDES : GREEK

(**d**) Pliny the Elder was a Roman writer who wrote *Naturalis Historia*. Thucydides was a Greek historian who wrote *History of the Peloponnesian War*.
Humanities—Description

34. (*a.* Uruguay, *b.* Argentina, *c.* Paraguay, *d.* **Guatemala**) : CENTRAL :: BRAZIL : SOUTH

(**d**) Guatemala is in Central America, Brazil in South America. Argentina, Uruguay, and Paraguay are in South America.
General Information—Part/Whole

35. ETHER : GENERAL :: NOVOCAINE : (*a.* specific, *b.* particulate, *c.* **local**, *d.* toxic

(**c**) Ether is a general anesthetic, novocaine a local anesthetic.
General Information—Description

36. D'ARTAGNAN : (*a.* Hugo, *b.* Mauriac, *c.* **Dumas**, *d.* Balzac) :: GATSBY : FITZGERALD

(**c**) D'Artagnan was a character created by Dumas in *The Three Musketeers*; Gatsby was a character created by Fitzgerald in *The Great Gatsby*. Francois Mauriac wrote *Le Desert de l'Amour*. Honore Balzac wrote *La Comedie Humaine*, which contains about 100 novels and plays that describe French life after the fall of Napoleon. Victor Hugo wrote *Les Miserables*.
Humanities—Description

37. ARMY : LAND :: (***a.* Marines**, *b.* Navy, *c.* CIA, *d.* Secret Service) : AMPHIBIOUS

    (**a**) The Army is intended to engage primarily in land warfare; the Marines are intended to engage primarily in amphibious warfare. The Navy is intended to engage primarily in sea warfare. The CIA is the intelligence agency of the United States that collects information about foreign governments and persons. The Secret Service protects leaders of the United States and visiting leaders from other countries. It also safeguards the payment and financial systems of the United States.
    General Information—Description

38. TWO : (*a.* hydrogen, *b.* uranium, *c.* americium, ***d.* deuterium**) :: THREE : TRITIUM

    (**d**) Deuterium is an isotope of hydrogen with an atomic weight of 2; tritium is an isotope of hydrogen with an atomic weight of 3.
    Natural Science—Description

39. YORK : N.Y. :: ORLEANS : (*a.* N.O., ***b.* La.**, *c.* Fr., *d.* Miss.)

    (**b**) (New) York (the city) is in the state of New York (N.Y.): (New) Orleans is in the state of Louisiana (La.).
    General Information—Part/Whole

40. (*a.* Copland, ***b.* Mendelssohn**, *c.* Shostakovich, *d.* Bach) : 19th :: MOZART : 18th

    (**b**) Mendelssohn was a 19th century composer (1809–1847), Mozart, an 18th century composer (1756–1791). Copland (1900–1990) was a 20th century composer. Shostakovich (1906–1975) was a 20th century composer. J. S. Bach (1685–1750) is an 18th century composer.
    Humanities—Completion

41. MENELAUS : (***a.* Agamemnon**, *b.* Priam, *c.* Achilles, *d.* Spartacus) :: HECTOR : PARIS

    (**a**) Menelaus and Agamemnon were brothers, as were Hector and Paris. Priam was the youngest son of Laomedon and king of Troy during the Trojan War. Achilles was the greatest warrior of the Greeks in the Trojan War. Spartacus was a Roman slave who led an unsuccessful slave uprising (the Third Servile War).
    Humanities—Class

42. MAJORITY : MINORITY :: (*a.* **Bolshevik**, *b.* Maoist, *c.* Marxist, *d.* Trotskyite) : MENSHEVIK

    (**a**) In Revolutionary Russia, the Bolsheviks were the majority, or greater (*bolshe*), party, and the Mensheviks were the minority, or smaller, (*mensche*) party.
    Humanities—Description

43. FEIGN : FINE :: (*a.* right, *b.* writ, *c.* **rate**, *d.* rat) : WRITE

    (**c**) The pronounced vowel sounds are the same in *feign* and *rate*, and in *fine* and *write*.
    Nonsemantic

44. FATUOUS : (*a.* bright, *b.* prodigal, *c.* contemptuous, *d.* **foolish**) :: FASTIDIOUS : HARD TO PLEASE

    (**d**) *Fatuous* and *foolish* are synonyms, as are *fastidious* and *hard to please*.
    Vocabulary—Similarity/Contrast

45. (*a.* Ayer, *b.* **Peirce**, *c.* Santayana, *d.* Russell) : PRAGMATIST :: SARTRE : EXISTENTIALIST

    (**b**) Peirce was a major philosopher in the pragmatist movement; Sartre was a major philosopher in the existentialist movement. Ayer was a logical positivist; Santayana was an aphorist; Russell was one of the founders of analytic philosophy.
    Humanities—Description

46. ADDITIVE : (*a.* blue, *b.* red, *c.* **green**, *d.* white) :: SUBTRACTIVE : YELLOW

    (**c**) Green is an additive (but not a subtractive) primary color in light; yellow is a subtractive (but not an additive) primary color. The subtractive color model involves pigments with colors that add up to black. The additive color model involves light with colors that add up to white.
    General Information—Description

47. PROTON : NUCLEON :: MUON : (*a.* **meson**, *b.* electron, *c.* pion, *d.* positron)

    (**a**) A proton is a nucleon; a muon is a meson (a fundamental particle responsible for the forces in the atomic nucleus).
    Natural Science—Class

48. BOARD : (*a.* fifteen, *b.* **checkers**, *c.* bridge, *d.* thirty-six) :: DECK : TWENTY-ONE

    (**b**) Checkers is played with a board, twenty-one with a deck.
    General Information—Description

49. C# : Db :: B# : (*a.* Cb, *b.* Bb, **c. C**, *d.* Db)

    (**c**) C# and D**b** are played instrumentally as the same note, as are B# and C.
    Humanities—Similarity/Contrast

50. SEVER : PERSEVERANCE :: CUT : (*a.* perseveration, *b.* perspective, *c.* pertinence, ***d.* persistence**)

    (**d**) *Sever* and *cut* are synonyms, as are *perseverance* and *persistence*.
    Vocabulary—Similarity/Contrast

51. FREUD : (*a.* Skinner, *b.* Allport, *c.* Murray, ***d.* Erikson**) :: KOHLBERG : PIAGET

    (**d**) Freud, Erikson, Kohlberg, and Piaget were all prominent psychological theorists postulating stages of development. Burrhus F. Skinner was a psychologist who is known for his work on operant conditioning. Gordon Allport is considered one of the founding fathers of personality psychology. Charles Murray is a political scientist and well known for writing *The Bell Curve* (with Richard Herrnstein) about the role of IQ in American society.
    Social Science—Class

52. (*a.* ellipsoid, ***b.* semicircle**, *c.* rhombus, *d.* angle) : PROTRACTOR :: RECTANGLE : RULER

    (**b**) A protractor is usually in the shape of a semicircle. A ruler is usually in the shape of a rectangle.
    Mathematics—Description

53. BIPOLARITY : MONOLOGUE :: (***a.* dicotyledon**, *b.* stamen, *c.* deciduous, *d.* pistil) : UNION

    (**a**) *Bipolarity* and *dicotyledon* refer to two of something; *monologue* and *union* refer to one of something.
    Vocabulary—Equality/Negation

54. (*a.* patent medicine, ***b.* adage**, *c.* theory, *d.* heretic) : APOTHEGM :: DEXTERITY : ADROITNESS

    (**b**) *Adage* and *apothegm* are synonyms, as are *dexterity* and *adroitness*.
    Vocabulary—Similarity/Contrast

55. FROM : TO :: (*a.* artery, *b.* ventricle, *c.* atrium, ***d.* carotid**) : JUGULAR

    (**d**) The carotid is an artery carrying blood away from the heart; the jugular is a vein carrying blood to the heart.
    Natural Science—Description

56. SOUSA : (*a.* waltzes, *b.* symphonies, ***c.* marches**, *d.* hymns) :: VERDI : OPERAS

   (**c**) Sousa (1854–1932) composed primarily marches; Verdi (1813–1901) composed primarily operas.
   Humanities—Description

57. INVOCATION : (***a.* benediction**, *b.* recessional, *c.* prayer, *d.* vesper) :: START : FINISH

   (**a**) An invocation starts a religious service; a benediction finishes it.
   General Information—Description

58. SASKATCHEWAN : REGINA :: (*a.* Quebec, *b.* Alberta, ***c.* Ontario**, *d.* Manitoba) :: TORONTO

   (**c**) The capital of the Canadian province of Saskatchewan is Regina; the capital of Ontario is Toronto. Quebec City is the capital of Quebec. Edmonton is the capital of Alberta. Winnipeg is the capital of Manitoba.
   General Information—Description

59. (*a.* obvious, ***b.* latent**, *c.* proximate, *d.* apposite) : MANIFEST :: COVERT : OVERT

   (**b**) *Latent* and *manifest* are antonyms, as are *covert* and *overt*.
   Vocabulary—Similarity/Contrast

60. DIRGE : REQUIEM :: GRIEF : (*a.* thanksgiving, ***b.* mourning**, *c.* penitence, *d.* joy)

   (**b**) A dirge and a requiem both express grief and mourning.
   Vocabulary—Description

61. (*a.* metropolitan, *b.* synod, *c.* district, ***d.* diocese**) : BISHOP :: PARISH : PRIEST

   (**d**) A diocese is under the jurisdiction of a bishop; a parish is under the jurisdiction of a priest.
   General Information—Description

62. CONSONANT : VOWEL :: COMPOSITE : (*a.* prime, *b.* irrational, *c.* integer, ***d.* zero**)

   (**d**) All letters are either consonants or vowels; all numbers are either composite or prime.
   Mathematics—Class

63. IMPLODE : (*a.* explode, *b.* beseech, *c.* implicate, ***d.* burst inward**) :: IMPLY : HINT AT

    (**d**) To implode is to burst inward; to imply is to hint at.
    Vocabulary—Similarity/Contrast

64. EARTH : SUN :: PLANET : (*a.* heavenly body, *b.* sol, ***c.* star**, *d.* nova)

    (**c**) The Earth is a planet; the Sun is a star. A nova is a star that abruptly increases its light output and later on fades back to its normal state.
    General Information—Class

65. OCTOPUS : (*a.* six, ***b.* eight**, *c.* ten, *d.* twelve) :: PERSON : TWO

    (**b**) An octopus has eight arms; a person has two arms.
    General Information—Description

66. QUARTER : DOLLAR :: (***a.* season**, *b.* day, *c.* month, *d.* decade) : YEAR

    (**a**) There are four quarters in a dollar, and four seasons in a year.
    General Information—Equality/Negation

67. CAPTAIN : (*a.* admiral, *b.* ensign, ***c.* commodore**, *d.* midshipman) :: CORPORAL : SERGEANT

    (**c**) In the Navy, a captain is immediately below a commodore in rank; in the Army, a corporal is immediately below a sergeant in rank.
    General Information—Description

68. DAVID : VAN DYCK :: FRENCH : (*a.* Italian, *b.* German, ***c.* Flemish**, *d.* British)

    (**c**) David was a French painter; Van Dyck was a Flemish painter (Flanders is part of Belgium).
    Humanities—Description

69. (*a.* poulet, ***b.* glacé**, *c.* citron, *d.* entrecote) : SWEET :: CAFÉ : BITTER

    (**b**) Glacé (ice cream) is sweet; café (coffee) is bitter.
    General Information—Description

70. WAIVE : WAVE :: (***a.* relinquish**, *b.* relegate, *c.* remand, *d.* redress) : UNDULATE

    (**a**) To waive is to relinquish; to wave is to undulate.
    Vocabulary—Similarity/Contrast

71. WORK : (*a.* **joule**, *b.* ohm, *c.* ampere, *d.* coulomb) :: POTENTIAL DIFFERENCE : VOLT

    (**a**) A joule is a unit of work; a volt is a measure of potential difference. Ohm is the unit of electrical resistance. Ampere is a unit of electric current. Coulomb is the unit of electric charge.
    Natural Science—Description

72. PHILOLOGY : LANGUAGES :: MYCOLOGY : (*a.* flowering plants, *b.* ferns, *c.* weeds, *d.* **fungi**)

    (**d**) Philology is the study of languages; mycology is the study of fungi.
    Natural Science—Description

73. DEPENDENT : INDEPENDENT :: (*a.* autochthonous, *b.* canonical, *c.* **anaclitic**, *d.* irrecusable) : SELF-RELIANT

    (**c**) *Dependent* and *anaclitic* are synonyms, as are *independent* and *self-reliant*.
    Vocabulary—Similarity/Contrast

74. CX : (*a.* CXV, *b.* **CL**, *c.* CLX, *d.* CC) :: LV : LXXV

    (**b**) The terms of the analogy are Roman numerals expressing the ratio 110 : 150 :: 55 : 75. In Roman numerals, I = 1, V = 5, X = 10, L = 50, C = 100, D = 500, M = 1,000.
    Mathematics—Equality/Negation

75. CAMEL : RHINOCEROS :: HUMP : (*a.* armor, *b.* snout, *c.* **horn**, *d.* hide)

    (**c**) A camel may have one hump or two; a rhinoceros may have one horn or two.
    General Information—Description

76. ONTOLOGY : (*a.* **being**, *b.* metaphysics, *c.* growth, *d.* knowledge) :: DEONTOLOGY : ETHICS

    (**a**) Ontology is the study of being; deontology is the study of ethics.
    Humanities—Description

77. (*a.* leukocytes, *b.* platelets, *c.* hormones, *d.* **erythrocytes**) : ANEMIA :: INSULIN : DIABETES

    (**d**) Anemia is characterized by a shortage of erythrocytes (red blood cells), diabetes by a shortage of insulin.
    Natural Science—Description

78. CALVIN : COOLIDGE :: (*a.* Alexander, *b.* **Franklin**, *c.* William, *d.* Robert) : PIERCE

(**b**) Calvin Coolidge and Franklin Pierce were both presidents of the United States.
General Information—Completion

79. PONTIUS PILATE : JESUS :: CREON : (*a.* Orestes, *b.* Oedipus, *c.* **Antigone**, *d.* Electra)

(**c**) Pontius Pilate sentenced Jesus to death; Creon sentenced Antigone to death. Orestes and Electra were the son and daughter, respectively, of Agamemnon. Oedipus was a king of Thebes in Greek mythology who killed his father and married his mother.
Humanities—Description

80. (*a.* **bellicose**, *b.* periphrastic, *c.* altruistic, *d.* nihilistic) : AGGRESSION :: IRENIC : PEACE

(**a**) Someone who is bellicose fosters aggression; someone who is irenic fosters peace.
Vocabulary—Description

81. FIRST : LAST :: GENESIS : (*a.* Exodus, *b.* **Deuteronomy**, *c.* Leviticus, *d.* Numbers)

(**b**) Genesis is the first book of the Torah; Deuteronomy, the last book.
Humanities—Description

82. πr^2 : $2\pi r$ :: AREA : (*a.* diameter, *b.* **circumference**, *c.* perimeter, *d.* volume)

(**b**) πr^2 is the formula for the area of a circle; $2\pi r$ is the formula for the circumference of a circle.
Mathematics—Equality/Negation

83. BUCKINGHAM PALACE : XANADU :: ELIZABETH II : (*a.* Genghis Khan, *b.* Charles V, *c.* **Citizen Kane**, *d.* Donald Trump)

(**c**) Buckingham Palace is the abode of Elizabeth II; Xanadu was the abode of Citizen Kane (a fictitious character fashioned after William Randolph Hearst).
General Information—Description

84. MONOGYNY : (*a.* life, *b.* religion, *c.* child, *d.* **wife**) :: MONOTHEISM : GOD

(**d**) Monogyny is belief in one wife; monotheism is belief in one God.
Vocabulary—Description

85. ESPRESSO : BLACK :: ORANGE PEKOE : (*a.* green, *b.* white, **c. black**, *d.* red)

(**c**) Espresso (coffee) is black in color; orange pekoe (tea) is also black in color.
General Information—Description

86. DIANA : (**a. Artemis**, *b.* Minerva, *c.* Aphrodite, *d.* Hera) :: JUPITER : ZEUS

(**a**) Diana and Artemis are the Roman and Greek names, respectively, for the goddess of the moon and of hunting; Jupiter and Zeus are the Roman and Greek names, respectively, for the king of the gods. Minerva was the Roman goddess of warriors, poetry, and medicine. Her Greek name was Athena. Aphrodite was the Greek goddess of love and beauty. Hera was the Greek goddess of women and marriage.
Humanities—Similarity/Contrast

87. (*a.* B♭ major, **b. E♭ major**, *c.* F major, *d.* A major) : C MINOR :: G MAJOR : E MINOR

(**b**) The keys of E♭ major and C minor both have three flats; the keys of G major and E minor both have one sharp.
Humanities—Similarity/Contrast

88. MAN : NAME :: (**a. rig**, *b.* appellation, *c.* maiden, *d.* woman) : GIRL

(**a**) The letters in *man* form the first three letters in *name* reversed; the letters in *rig* form the first three letters in *girl* reversed.
Nonsemantic

89. MANON LESCAUT : (*a.* wise, *b.* arrogant, **c. promiscuous**, *d.* wicked) :: TOM SAWYER : ADVENTUROUS

(**c**) Manon Lescaut is a promiscuous literary character (by Francois Prévost); Tom Sawyer is an adventurous one (by Mark Twain).
Humanities—Description

90. (*a.* Bull Moose, *b.* Whig, **c. Socialist**, *d.* Know-Nothing) : DEBS :: DEMOCRAT : STEVENSON

(**c**) Eugene Debs was an unsuccessful Socialist candidate for president; Adlai Stevenson was an unsuccessful Democratic candidate for president.
Humanities—Description

91. FIRST : CLERGY :: FOURTH : (*a.* nobles, *b.* commoners, *c.* children, ***d.* journalists**)

(**d**) The clergy formed the First Estate; journalists form what is sometimes called the Fourth Estate.
Vocabulary—Description

92. AMETHYST : GARNET :: PURPLE : (***a.* red**, *b.* green, *c.* transparent, *d.* blue)

(**a**) An amethyst is purple; a garnet is red.
General Information—Description

93. (***a.* loquacious**, *b.* refractory, *c.* ostentatious, *d.* timid) : GARRULOUS :: AUDACIOUS : BOLD

(**a**) *Loquacious* and *garrulous* have similar meanings, as do *audacious* and *bold*.
Vocabulary—Similarity/Contrast

94. FOUR : APRIL FOOL'S DAY :: (*a.* one, *b.* two, ***c.* five**, *d.* ten) : MAY DAY

(**c**) April Fool's Day is the first day of the fourth month; May Day is the first day of the fifth month.
General Information—Description

95. STEEPLE : CHURCH :: (***a.* minaret**, *b.* muezzin, *c.* imam, *d.* arch) : MOSQUE

(**a**) A steeple protrudes from the top of a church; a minaret protrudes from the top of a mosque.
General Information—Description

96. VANILLA : (*a.* bean, *b.* Sussex, ***c.* hasty**, *d.* Brazil) :: RICE : YORKSHIRE

(**c**) Four types of pudding are vanilla pudding, hasty pudding, rice pudding, and Yorkshire pudding.
General Information—Class

97. (*a.* Saint-Saëns, ***b.* Strindberg**, *c.* Bernstein, *d.* Rubinstein) : PLAYS :: FROST : POEMS

(**b**) Strindberg wrote plays; Frost wrote poems. Leonard Bernstein was a conductor. Arthur Rubinstein was a pianist.
Humanities—Description

98. THERMO : HEAT :: ISO : (*a.* cold, *b.* pressure, *c.* humidity, ***d.* same**)

(**d**) *Thermo-* is a prefix meaning *heat*; *iso-* is a prefix meaning *same*.
Vocabulary—Similarity/Contrast

99. (*a.* Scotch, *b.* vermouth, **c. gin**, *d.* bourbon) : TOM COLLINS :: VODKA : BLOODY MARY

(**d**) A Tom Collins is a mixed drink containing gin; a Bloody Mary is a mixed drink containing vodka.
General Information—Description

100. BELLEEK : (*a.* Scotland, **b. Ireland**, *c.* Holland, *d.* Belgium) :: LIMOGES : FRANCE

(**b**) Belleek is a town in Ireland (and also a generic name for a type of porcelain). Limoges is a town in France (and also a generic name for a type of china).
General Information—Description

101. AMPERE : (**a. current,** *b.* magnetism, *c.* speed, *d.* gravity) :: WATT : POWER

(**a**) An ampere is a unit used to measure current just as a watt is a unit used to measure power.
Natural Science—Description

102. BAIKAL : RUSSIA :: (*a.* Michigan, **b. Superior**, *c.* Ontario, *d.* Placid) : UNITED STATES

(**b**) Lake Baikal is the largest lake in Russia just as Lake Superior is the largest lake in the United States.
General Information—Description

103. (*a.* Lady's Man, *b.* Black Beauty, **c. Secretariat**, *d.* Fortune's Fool) : MAN O' WAR :: SEABISCUIT : WAR ADMIRAL

(**c**) Secretariat, Man o' War, Seabiscuit, and War Admiral are all famous race horses.
General Information—Class

104. GAVRILO PRINCIP : ARCHDUKE FERDINAND :: (*a.* Robert E. Lee, *b.* Lee Harvey Oswald, *c.* John Hinckley, **d. John Wilkes Booth**) : PRESIDENT LINCOLN

(**d**) Gavrilo Princip assassinated Archduke Ferdinand in 1914 just as John Wilkes Booth assassinated President Lincoln (1865).
General Information—Description

105. KILOGRAM : POUND :: 1 : (**a. 2.2**, *b.* 5, *c.* 0.2, *d.* 7.3)

(**a**) There are 2.2 pounds in 1 kilogram.
General Information—Equality/Negation

106. ROSEMARY : (***a. oregano***, *b.* cumin, *c.* nutmeg, *d.* cinnamon) :: BASIL : SAGE

(**a**) Rosemary, oregano, basil, and sage are all leafy herbs used to season food.
General Information—Class

107. COBBLER : SHOES :: (*a.* tanner, *b.* smith, ***c. cooper***, *d.* miller) : BARRELS

(**c**) The 18th century occupations cobbler and cooper worked on shoes and barrels respectively.
General Information—Description

108. EXPECTORATE : (*a.* bite, ***b. spit***, *c.* deliver, *d.* swallow) :: MASTICATE : CHEW

(**b**) To expectorate is to spit just as to masticate is to chew.
Vocabulary—Similarity/Contrast

109. (*a.* net, *b.* hat trick, *c.* goalie, ***d. puck***) : ICE HOCKEY :: SHUTTLECOCK : BADMINTON

(**d**) In the sports of ice hockey and badminton, the objects whose possession is passed between players and teams are the puck and shuttlecock respectively.
General Information—Description

110. ARMSTRONG : TRUMPET :: COLTRANE : (*a.* piano, ***b. saxophone***, *c.* clarinet, *d.* trombone)

(**b**) Louis Armstrong and John Coltrane are jazz musicians who played the trumpet and saxophone respectively.
Humanities—Description

111. MOHAMMED : JESUS :: (*a.* Judea, *b.* Constantinople, ***c. Mecca***, *d.* Jerusalem) : BETHLEHEM

(**c**) Religious tradition holds that Mohammed was born in Mecca and that Jesus was born in Bethlehem.
Humanities—Description

112. RHOMBUS : HEXAGON :: 4 : (*a.* 8, *b.* 7, ***c. 6***, *d.* 5)

(**c**) A rhombus has four sides just as a hexagon has six sides.
Mathematics—Description

113. RECORD PLAYER : (*a.* **loudest**, *b.* loud, *c.* quiet, *d.* quieter) :: SUPERANNUATED : SUPERLATIVE

(**a**) The record player, used for playing music, is superannuated, or obsolete. The word "loudest" is superlative, the most extreme degree of the adjective.
Vocabulary—Class

114. (*a.* feet, *b.* obedience, *c.* thought, ***d.* memory**) : ELEPHANT :: STRENGTH : ANT

(**d**) Elephants are known for their powers of memory just as ants are known for their feats of strength.
General Information—Description

115. DIAMOND : SAPPHIRE :: (*a.* **Hope**, *b.* Diana's, *c.* Indian, *d.* Pharoah's) : LOGAN

(**a**) The Hope Diamond and Logan Sapphire are famous examples of these gemstones.
General Information—Description

116. HEAVEN : ST. PETER :: HADES : (*a.* Lucifer, *b.* Scylla, *c.* Charybdis, ***d.* Cerberus**)

(**d**) Various traditions hold that St. Peter guards the gates to heaven just as Cerberus, the three-headed dog, guards the gates to Hades. Lucifer is the devil. In Greek mythology, Scylla and Charybdis were two monsters that lived on either side of a very narrow river. When sailors wanted to pass by, they got into reach of one monster when trying to avoid the other.
Humanities—Description

117. r-p-o-p-h-e-s-s-a-g-r : JABBERWOCKY :: CUMMINGS : (*a.* Milne, *b.* Cleary, ***c.* Carroll**, *d.* Eliot)

(**c**) e. e. cummings and Lewis Carroll wrote the somewhat nonsensical poems *r-p-o-p-h-e-s-s-a-g-r* and *Jabberwocky* respectively.
Humanities—Description

118. X : (*a.* w, ***b.* y**, *c.* u, *d.* a) :: VERTICAL : HORIZONTAL

(**b**) On two-dimensional graphs, the x-axis is vertical and the y-axis is horizontal.
Mathematics—Description